CMU Computer Science
A 25th Anniversary Commemorative

# ACM PRESS

**Editor-in-Chief:**

Peter Wegner, *Brown University*

ACM Press books represent a collaboration between the Association for Computing Machinery (ACM) and Addison-Wesley Publishing Company to develop and publish a broad range of new works. These works generally fall into one of four series.

*Frontier Series*. Books focused on novel and exploratory material at the leading edge of computer science and practice.

*Anthology Series*. Collected works of general interest to computer professionals and / or society at large.

*Tutorial Series*. Introductory books to help nonspecialists quickly grasp either the general concepts or the needed details of some specific topic.

*History Series*. Books documenting past developments in the field and linking them to the present.

In addition, ACM Press books include selected conference and workshop proceedings.

# CMU Computer Science

## A 25th Anniversary Commemorative

Edited by

## Richard F. Rashid
Carnegie Mellon University

ACM PRESS
New York, New York

ADDISON-WESLEY PUBLISHING COMPANY
Reading, Massachusetts □ Menlo Park, California □ New York
Don Mills, Ontario □ Wokingham, England □ Amsterdam □ Bonn
Sydney □ Singapore □ Tokyo □ Madrid □ San Juan □ Milan □ Paris

ACM Press Anthology Series

**Library of Congress Cataloging-in-Publication Data**

CMU computer science : a 25th anniversary commemorative / edited by
   Richard F. Rashid.
      p. cm. — (ACM Press anthology series)
   Includes bibliographical references and index.
   ISBN 0-201-52899-1
   1. Computer Science–Congresses. 2. Carnegie-Mellon University.
Computer Science Dept.–Congresses. I. Rashid, Richard F., 1951–
. II. Series.
QA75.5.C548 1991                                                    90-45503
004—dc20                                                            CIP

1 2 3 4 5 6 7 8 9 10–MA–9594939291

*This book is dedicated to the memory of Alan Perlis.*

# Preface

In the Fall of 1965, Allen Newell, Alan Perlis, and Herb Simon founded the Carnegie Institute of Technology Graduate Department of Computer Science. The Department evolved out of an earlier interdisciplinary program called Systems and Communications Sciences and in the beginning had only a couple of dozen faculty and graduate students.

Over the years much changed. Carnegie Institute of Technology became Carnegie Mellon University (CMU). The fledgling Graduate Department of Computer Science evolved into what is today a School of Computer Science with over 700 full time faculty, Ph.D. students, research staff, technical support, and administrative personel. The intervening 25 years saw the establishment of the CMU Robotics Institute, the Information Technology Center, and the Center for Machine Translation — all of which have become part of the School of Computer Science. Over 100 faculty participated in the growth of the Department over those years and more than 250 Ph.D. students completed their degrees.

The essays in this book were written by prominent computer scientists who, over the years, helped to create, build, and strengthen Computer Science at CMU. They range from thoughtful retrospectives to careful examinations of the state of the art in such areas as parallel systems, programming languages, artificial intelligence, theory, and hardware. They represent the accomplishments of CMU's past and the promise for its future

## Acknowledgments

I would like to thank Mary Shaw and Catherine Copetas for their help in interacting with the authors and Sid Chatterjee for his invaluable expertise in LaTeX. I would also like to thank Marian Sodini and Hide Tokuda for their help in scanning and processing some of the figures used in this volume.

*Pittsburgh, Pennsylvania*                                                      R. F. R

# About the Authors

### Erik Altmann

Erik Altmann is a doctoral candidate in the School of Computer Science at Carnegie Mellon University. He received his B.S. from the University of Alberta in 1987. His primary research interest is in task acquisition for knowledge-based systems. The vehicle for his research is Soar, an architecture for intelligent systems, whose computational model is being investigated and evaluated as a means for expressing problem solving in a wide spectrum of task domains. Joint work with Gregg Yost and Allen Newell has led to a language, TAQL, that abstracts from Soar and expresses problem-space computations directly.

### C. Gordon Bell

Gordon Bell is Chief Scientist at Stardent Computer, Sunnyvale, California, of which he was a founder, and former Vice-President of Research and Development. He spent 23 years at Digital Equipment Corporation as Vice-President of Research and Development, where he managed the engineering of Digital's products. He was the architect of various mini-computers and time-sharing computers and led the development of VAX and the VAX Computing Environment. Subsequently, he was a founder and Vice-Chairman of Encore Computer Company.

From 1966 to 1972, he was a Professor of Computer Science and Electrical Engineering at Carnegie Mellon University. During 1986 to 1987, he was the first Assistant Director of the National Science Foundation's (NSF's) Computing Directorate and was also responsible for NSF's national supercomputing centers.

Mr. Bell has authored numerous books and papers on computers and technology. He is a member of various professional organizations, including the American Academy for the Advancement of Science (AAAS)(Fellow), Association for Computing Machinery (ACM), Institute of Electrical and Electronics Engineers (IEEE), (Fellow), and the National Academy of Engineering. He is on the board of Cirrus Logic, Visix Software, and Velox and is an advisor to several computer companies including Kendall Square Research. He is also a founder and director of The Computer Museum in Boston.

Mr. Bell resides in Los Altos, California and Boston.

### Jon L. Bentley

Jon L. Bentley is a Member of Technical Staff in the Computing Sciences Research Center at AT&T Bell Laboratories. His research interests include programming methodology and algorithm design. Prior to joining Bell Labs in 1982, he was an Associate Professor of Computer Science and Mathematics at Carnegie Mellon University, where he is still an Adjunct Associate Professor. During Fall 1985, he was a Visiting Professor of Computer Science at the United States Military Academy at West Point.

Mr. Bentley received a B.S. degree in Mathematical Sciences from Stanford University in 1974, and M.S. and Ph.D. degrees in Computer Science from the University of North Carolina in 1976. He is a member of AAAS, ACM, IEEE, and Sigma Xi.

### Hans J. Berliner

Hans Berliner has been a researcher at Carnegie Mellon University since 1974, and is currently a Principal Research Computer Scientist. He received his B.A. in Psychology from George Washington University in 1954 and his Ph.D. in Computer Science from Carnegie Mellon in 1975.

Dr. Berliner is interested in problems of directing search and of knowledge organization and representation as they occur in relatively finite domains, as occur in game playing and puzzle solving. He is also concerned with problems of machine learning and the organization of memories to facilitate learning that is more animal-like. He likes to build systems the performance of which can be measured against the same criteria that are applied to humans doing the same task.

Dr. Berliner's current projects include the Hitech Chess Machine, a machine composed of special purpose hardware and a host computer for playing chess by generating and evaluating chess positions at an extremely high rate of speed. Hitech is rated among the top 0.5% of all registered chess players in the United States. There is also a project on the computational utility of chunking in which large performance gains are being achieved by recognizing chunks within a whole configuration, and allowing knowledge associated with differing types of chunks to drive the behavior of the system. Another project is the CONSENSUS system, attempting to do computation in the style and organization of animal brains using neuron-like computing elements in a network. There is also a project on a solitaire card game called SUPERPUZZ. The problem solver in this case is able to regularly discover solutions that are over 100 ply deep, and are so complex that it is nearly impossible for a human to understand them, not to speak of producing them in the first place.

Dr. Berliner has been ranked among the top U.S. chess players since 1950 and has attained the title of National Master in over-the-board chess play, and International Grandmaster in correspondence play. His backgammon program, BKG 9.8, defeated the then World Backgammon Champion, in a seven point match in 1979. He is the author of numerous articles for journals and conferences and is a member of the ACM, International Joint Conference on Artificial Intelligence, the American Association for Artificial Intelligence (AAAI), and the International Computer Chess Association. He is also a member of the editorial boards for the *Artificial Intelligence Journal*, the *Pitman Series on Artificial Intelligence*, and *International Journal of Intelligent Systems* published by John Wiley and Sons.

### Douglas W. Clark

Douglas W. Clark is a Senior Consulting Engineer at the Digital Equipment Corporation. He received his B.S. degree in Engineering and Applied Science from Yale in 1972 and his Ph.D. in Computer Science from Carnegie Mellon in 1976. He was a Member of the Research Staff at the Xerox Palo Alto Research Center (PARC) from 1976 to 1980, and has spent the last 10 years at Digital. For the academic year 1990–91 he is a Visiting Lecturer on Computer Science in the Aiken Computation Laboratory at Harvard.

Dr. Clark's work and interests are in the areas of computer architecture and design, performance measurement and evaluation, and hardware simulation. At Xerox PARC he was involved in the design and construction of the Dorado high-performance personal computer. After joining Digital, Dr. Clark (with several colleagues) first did a series of performance measurements of the VAX 11/780, using hardware monitors to observe this timesharing system in vivo. He then became one of the technical leaders of a midrange VAX system development, contributing to the architecture, design, simulation, and measurement of the Nautilus family of machines (VAX models 85xx, 8700, and 88xx), which were announced in 1986. Recently he was Central Processing Unit (CPU) Architect and then System Architect for two VAX projects that were cancelled.

Dr. Clark frequently serves on the program committees of several conferences in his fields of interest, and was program co-chairman of the 13th International Symposium on Computer Architecture. He is a member of the Advisory Committee for the Division of Microelectronic Information Processing Systems of the National Science Foundation. Since 1983 he has been an associate editor of the ACM *Transactions on Computer Systems*.

### Roger B. Dannenberg

Roger Dannenberg is a Senior Research Computer Scientist on the faculty of the School of Computer Science. He received a Ph.D. from Carnegie Mellon in 1982 after receiving a B.A. from Rice University (1977) and a M.S. from Case-Western Reserve University (1979), with fellowships from the National Science Foundation and the Hertz Foundation.

His research interests include human/computer interaction, programming language design and implementation, digital audio processing, and, in particular, the application of computer science techniques to the generation, control, and composition of computer music.

Dr. Dannenberg's current work includes research on music understanding, the automated accompaniment of live musicians, and the design and implementation of Arctic, a very high-level, functional language for real-time control. In addition, he is codirecting the Piano Tutor Project with the goal of applying music understanding and expert system technology to music education. His current artistic direction is toward real-time integrated computer music and computer graphics performance systems, for which he has developed tools for rapid software prototyping. Occasionally, he teaches computer and electronic music.

Dr. Dannenberg's publications include work on program verification, programming language design, computer architecture, computer music, and networks of personal computers. He is also a musician and composer. He performs frequently on trumpet in classical, jazz, and contemporary ensembles, and writes works for electronic and conventional media. He is currently performing with the free improvisation group Morphic Resonance. Dr. Dannenberg is a member of Phi Beta Kappa, Sigma Xi, Tau Beta Pi, Phi Mu Alpha, and the American Federation of Musicians.

## Samuel H. Fuller

Samuel H. Fuller, Vice-President, Research and Architecture, Digital Equipment Corporation, is responsible for the company's corporate research programs. These include Digital's research groups in Maynard, Massachusetts, Cambridge, Massachusetts, Palo Alto, California, and Paris, joint research with universities, and Digital participation in MCC.

Fuller joined Digital in 1978 as Engineering Manager for the VAX Architecture group. After holding a variety of engineering positions, he was appointed Group Manager, Corporate Research and Architecture, 1981. In 1983 he was appointed Vice-President, Research and Architecture. Fuller has been instrumental in initiating work in local area networks, high-performance workstations, applications of expert systems, and new computer architectures.

Prior to coming to Digital in 1978, Dr. Fuller was an Associate Professor of Computer Science and Electrical Engineering at Carnegie Mellon University. While at CMU he was involved in the performance evaluation and design of several experimental, multiprocessor computer systems.

He holds a B.S. degree in Electrical Engineering from the University of Michigan, as well as an M.S. and Ph.D from Stanford University.

## David Garlan

David Garlan is an Assistant Professor of Computer Science in the School of Computer Science at Carnegie Mellon University. Before joining the CMU faculty in September 1990, he was a Senior Computer Scientist in the Computer Research Labs of Tektronix, Inc. His research interests include the application of formal methods to the construction of reusable software architectures, programming environments, and tool integration. In recent years, he has been active in developing formal models of embedded instrumentation software and in building environments to support the development of these models. He received his Ph.D. in Computer Science from Carnegie Mellon University in 1987.

## A. Nico Habermann

Nico Habermann received his M.S. degree in Mathematics from the Free University in Amsterdam and his Ph.D. degree in Applied Mathematics from the Technological University at Eindhoven in 1967. He worked with Dr. E. W. Dijkstra on the THE system for which he wrote the Algol60 interface. After visiting CMU, Massachusetts Institute of Technology (MIT), Digital Equipment Corporation (DEC), and International Business Machines Corp. (IBM), he came to CMU as an Associate Professor in 1969. He was promoted to Full Professor in 1974 and became Department Head of Computer Science in 1979. In December 1988, he was appointed Dean of the School of Computer Science. He was instrumental in establishing the Software Engineering Institute at CMU and was the Acting Director of the Institute in 1985.

His main interests are in programming languages, operating systems, software engineering, and programming environments. He has worked on language design and implementation for Algol60, Bliss, Pascal, Ada, and various special purpose languages. He has worked on several practical and experimental operating systems such as the THE System, the Family of Operating Systems (FAMOS), the Dynamically Adaptable System (DAS), and UNIX. He has written two books: one on operating system design and one on the Ada language (with Dr. Perry). Some of his best known contributions to the field are a critique on the Pascal language, work on deadlock prevention, path expressions (with Dr. Campbell), an efficient implementation of Ada tasking (with Dr. Nassi), and the integrated approach to software development which is demonstrated in the Gandalf project. Professor Habermann has served on numerous program committees and consults for several computer firms. He spent a year at the University of Newcastle-upon-Tyne, England (1973), at the Technological University of Berlin, Germany (1976), and at Siemens Corporation in Munich, Germany (1983). He was a member of NSF's Advisory Committee for Computer Science and he serves as a member of IBM's Scientific Advisory Committee. He is an editor for *ACTA INFORMATICA, Transactions of Programming Languages and Systems* (TOPLAS), and *IEEE Transactions on Software Engineering*.

### Jessica Hodgins

Jessica Hodgins received a B.A. degree in Mathematics from Yale University in 1981 and a Ph.D. from Carnegie Mellon University in 1989. Her Ph.D. thesis, "Legged Robots on Rough Terrain: Experiments in Adjusting Step Length," explored algorithms, which allowed an actively balanced two-legged running machine to place its feet on chosen footholds while maintaining balanced running.

During 1989 and 1990, Hodgins was a postdoctoral researcher at the MIT Artificial Intelligence Laboratory. She studied the control of biped and quadruped galloping and reflexive responses to unpredictable terrain.

In the fall of 1990, Hodgins will join the Computer Animation Systems-Group at the IBM Thomas J. Watson Research Center. She will focus on applying control algorithms to physically accurate models in order to produce realistic animations of dynamic motor tasks.

### Takeo Kanade

Takeo Kanade is Professor of Computer Science and Co-Director of the Robotics Institute at Carnegie Mellon University. He is also Chairman of the newly established Robotics Ph.D. Program. He received his Ph.D. in Information Science from Kyoto University, Japan, in 1974. After having taught at Kyoto University as Associate Professor of Information Science, he joined Carnegie Mellon in 1980.

Dr. Kanade has worked on various problems in vision, sensors, manipulators, and mobile robots. His past accomplishments include a theory of the Origami World for shape recovery from line drawings, development of new direct-drive arm technologies (DD Arm I and DD Arm II), which were first conceived and prototyped at CMU, and development of a vision navigation system for the Navlab (a van with onboard sensors and computers). He has authored and edited three books, and authored over 80 papers and technical reports, and is the holder of five United States patents.

Currently Dr. Kanade is engaged in three major robotics research programs at CMU as the Principal Investigator: the Defense Advanced Projects Research Agency (DARPA) Image Understanding Project, the DARPA Natural Outdoor Navigation (NAVLAB) Vision System, and the National Aeronautics and Space Administration (NASA) Planetary Exploration Robot.

He has received an American Telephone and Telegraph (AT&T) Foundation

Special Award and the Japan Audio Visual Information Research Group Award. Dr. Kanade's current professional activities include acting as a consultant for NASA Advanced Technology Advisory Committee (congressionally mandated committee). He is also the founding editor of *International Journal of Computer Vision* and an Administrative Committee member of IEEE Robotics and Automation Society.

### Jeff Koechling

Jeff Koechling received a B.S. degree in Mechanical Engineering from Rose-Hulman Institute of Technology in 1980, an M.S.M.E. Degree from Carnegie Mellon University in 1984, and a Ph.D from Carnegie Mellon University in 1989. His Ph.D thesis, entitled "The Limits of Running Speed: Experiments with a legged robot," was done in the Department of Mechanical Engineering, the CMU Robotics Institute and The MIT Artificial Intelligence Laboratory.

From 1980 to 1982, Koechling was an engineer at the RCA Consumer Electronics Division in Indianapolis, Indiana. His work there focused on the computer aided manufacture of stamped sheet metal parts and injection molded plastic parts.

From 1982 to 1989, Koechling was a graduate student in Mechanical Engineering at Carnegie Mellon University. He worked with Marc Raibert on the experimental study of legged machines with active dynamic balance. From 1987 to 1989, Koechling visited the Artificial Intelligence laboratory at MIT.

Koechling is currently assistant professor in the Sibley School of Mechanical and Aerospace Engineering at Cornell University.

### H. T. Kung

H. T. Kung, a Professor since 1982, joined the faculty of Carnegie Mellon University in 1974 after receiving his Ph.D. degree here. During the period 1985 to 1990, he held the Shell Distinguished Chair in Computer Science, established by Shell Oil Company. He was an Architecture Consultant to TRW in 1981 while taking a leave of absence from Carnegie Mellon. He was also a Guggenheim Fellow in 1983–84, and during this period he visited General Electric Company to work on a computer tomography machine.

Dr. Kung's research interests lie in parallel computing, parallel computer architectures, and high-speed computer networks. He has published over 100 technical papers in these and other areas. Together with his students, he pioneered the concept of systolic array processing. For the past several years, he has lead a research team at CMU working on very high performance parallel computers and networks. During the period 1984 to 1987 this team developed a

100 million floating point operations per second (100 megaflops) systolic array machine, Warp. This experimental machine, manufactured by General Electric, has been used in a variety of applications in signal and image processing.

At present, Dr. Kung's team is working with Intel in developing a Very Large Scale Integration (VLSI) version of the Warp machine. The goal is to develop a single-chip processor, iWarp, capable of performing high-speed computation and interprocessor communication. The initial iWarp demonstration system in 1990 consisted of an $8 \times 8$ torus of iWarp processors, delivering a total of 1.28 gigaflops. The same system design is readily extendible to a 20.48 gigaflops, using a $32 \times 32$ torus.

In the area of high-speed networks, Dr. Kung works on the Nectar system using fiber-optic links, large crossbar switches, and dedicated network coprocessors. A prototype system employing 100 megabits/second links has been operational since early 1989. Currently the system has 26 hosts, and is readily extendible to 32 hosts. In addition, a 30 km Nectar connection to the CRAY Y-MP of the Pittsburgh Supercomputing Center is operational. With Network Systems Corporation his team is currently designing the next-generation system that will use fibers driven at the gigabits/second rate. The Nectar system is one of the five testbeds in a national effort to develop gigabits/second wide-area networks.

### John Laird

John Laird is Assistant Professor of Electrical Engineering and Computer Science at the University of Michigan. He received his B.S. from the University of Michigan in 1975 and his Ph.D. in Computer Science from Carnegie Mellon University in 1983. Before joining the faculty at the University of Michigan, Dr. Laird was a member of research staff at Xerox Palo Alto Research Center from 1984 to 1986. His primary research interests are in the nature of the architecture underlying artificial and natural intelligence. His work is centered on the development and use of Soar, a general cognitive architecture. His current interests revolve around building intelligent systems in Soar that interact with an external environment. This work has led to the creation of two experimental systems implemented in Soar, one for controlling a small mobile robot and one for controlling a Puma robot arm. Using these systems he is studying learning and problem solving in real-time reactive environments.

### Charles E. Leiserson

Charles E. Leiserson received the B.S. degree in computer science and mathematics from Yale University, New Haven, Connecticut, in 1975 and the Ph.D.

degree in computer science from Carnegie Mellon University, Pittsburgh, Pennsylvania, in 1981.

As a graduate student at CMU, he wrote the first paper on systolic architectures with his advisor H. T. Kung. His Ph.D. dissertation, "Area-Efficient VLSI Computation," which deals with the design of systolic systems and with the problem of determining the VLSI area of a graph, won the first ACM Doctoral Dissertation Award. In 1981, he joined the faculty of the Theory of Computation group in the Laboratory for Computer Science, Massachusetts Institute of Technology, Cambridge, Massachusetts. He is currently Associate Professor of Computer Science and Engineering in the Department of Electrical Engineering and Computer Science and leader of the VLSI and Parallel Systems group.

Prof. Leiserson pioneered the development of VLSI theory and has written over 25 papers on analysis of algorithms, layout theory, computer-aided design, and parallel algorithms and architectures. Among his contributions are systolic computation, the retiming method for optimizing digital circuitry, and the "fat-tree" interconnection network. His principal research interest is in the theoretical foundations of parallel computation, especially as they relate to engineering reality.

Prof. Leiserson is a member of ACM, IEEE, and SIAM. In 1985 he received a Presidential Young Investigator Award from the National Science Foundation. Recently, with Ronald L. Rivest and Thomas H. Cormen, he coauthored the textbook *Introduction to Algorithms*, published by the MIT Press and McGraw-Hill.

### Zohar Manna

Zohar Manna is a Professor of Computer Science both at Stanford University and the Weizmann Institute in Israel. He received his B.S. and M.S. degrees in Mathematics from The Technion in Israel and the Ph.D. degree in Computer Science from Carnegie Mellon University in 1968.

Dr. Manna's research interests include automated deduction, logic of programs, concurrent and real-time systems, and the verification and synthesis of programs. He has done pioneering work in program verification, program synthesis, and the mathematical theory of computation. He is the author of the classic text, *Mathematical Theory of Computation* (McGraw-Hill, 1974). He has supervised a long list of Ph.D. students.

In collaboration with Richard Waldinger, he has published a series of papers on the application of deductive methods to program synthesis. They formulated the deductive-tableau framework for proving theorems and extracting programs from proofs. They coauthored the two-volume textbook, *The Logical Basis for Computer Programming* (Addison-Wesley, 1985, 1989). In collaboration with Amir Pnueli, Dr. Manna has developed the theory of specification and verification of concurrent programs by temporal logic, laying the basis for a well-established proof methodology. They coauthored the forthcoming textbook, *The Temporal Logic of Reactive Systems* (Springer-Verlag, 1991).

## Allen Newell

Allen Newell joined Carnegie Mellon University in 1961 and is currently the U. A. and Helen Whitaker University Professor of Computer Science. He received his B.S. in Physics from Stanford University in 1949, completed 1 year of graduate work in mathematics at Princeton University in 1950, and received his Ph.D. in Industrial Administration from the Carnegie Institute of Technology (now Carnegie Mellon) in 1957. He was a member of the scientific staff at Rand Corporation from 1950 to 1961.

At Rand he was involved in the development of system training for the Air Force Air Defense system, which led to the formation of the System Development Corporation. He has worked in both artificial intelligence and cognitive psychology since their emergence in the mid-fifties, mostly on problem solving and the cognitive architecture that supports intelligent action. He has also worked throughout the field of computer science: list processing, computer description languages, hypertext systems, and psychologically based models of human/computer interaction.

Dr. Newell's current research is centered on Soar, an architecture for intelligent problem solving and learning (with John Laird and Paul Rosenbloom). Soar also provides a basis for continued research on knowledge acquisition systems, a unified theory of human cognition, human-computer interaction, and the efficiency of production systems.

He received the 1971 Harry Goode award of AFIPS; the 1975 A.M. Turing Award of the ACM (jointly with H. A. Simon); he was a 1976 to 1977 Guggenheim Fellow; he received the 1979 Alexander C. Williams Jr. Award of the Human Factors Society (jointly with W. Biel, R. Chapman, and J. Kennedy); the 1985 Distinguished Research Contribution Award of the American Psychological Association; he delivered the 1987 William James Lectures at Harvard University; he received the 1989 Research Excellence Award of the International Joint Conference on Artificial Intelligence and the 1990 Emanuel R. Piore Award of the IEEE. He is a member of the National Academy of Sciences, the National Academy of Engineering, and the American Academy of Arts and Sciences and was first president of the American Association for Artificial Intelligence. Dr. Newell is the author or coauthor of over 250 publications.

## David Notkin

David Notkin is currently in Japan at Tokyo Institute of Technology and Osaka University, on leave from his position as an Associate Professor in the Department of Computer Science and Engineering at the University of Washington. He started as an Assistant Professor at UW in 1984, after completing his Ph.D. at Carnegie Mellon University (under the supervision of Nico Habermann) in 1984. He received his Sc.B. from Brown University in 1977. He received an IBM Faculty Development Award in 1985 and an NSF Presidential Young Investigator Award in 1988.

## John K. Ousterhout

John K. Ousterhout is a Professor in the Department of Electrical Engineering and Computer Sciences at the University of California, Berkeley. His interests include operating systems, distributed systems, user interfaces, and computer-aided design. He is currently leading the development of Sprite, a network operating system for high-performance workstations. In the past, he and his students developed several widely used programs for computer-aided design, including Magic, Caesar, and Crystal. Ousterhout is a recipient of the ACM Grace Murray Hopper Award, the NSF Presidential Young Investigator Award, the National Academy of Sciences Award for Initiatives in Research, the IEEE Browder J. Thompson Award, and the University of California at Berkeley Distinguished Teaching Award. He received a B.S. degree in Physics from Yale University in 1975 and a Ph.D. in Computer Science from Carnegie Mellon University in 1980.

## Amir Pnueli

Amir Pnueli is a Professor of Computer Science at the Weizmann Institute of Science in Israel. He received his B.Sc. degree in Mathematics from The Technion in Israel and his Ph.D. in Applied Mathematics from the Weizmann Institute in 1967.

Dr. Pnueli's research interests include formal approaches to the specification, verification, and rigorous development of reactive systems, using tools of temporal logic and automata theory. He has done work in verification of concurrent and reactive programs and introduced temporal logic into computer science.

## Marc H. Raibert

Marc H. Raibert received a B.S. degree in Electrical Engineering from Northeastern University in 1973, and a Ph.D from MIT in 1977. His Ph.D thesis, entitled "Motor control and learning by the state space model," was done in the MIT Artifical Intelligence Laboratory and the Department of Psychology.

From 1977 through 1980, Raibert was an engineer at the Jet Propulsion Laboratory, and a Visiting Associate in Computer Science at the California Institute of Technology in Pasadena. His research focused on sensing for robots, including study of hybrid position/force control of manipulators and development of a VLSI tactile sensor.

From 1981 through 1986, Raibert was on Computer Science faculty and a member of the Robotics Institute at Carnegie Mellon University in Pittsburgh. He studied legged machines that are dynamic and actively balance themselves as they run.

Raibert is currently Professor of Electrical Engineering and Computer Science at the Massachusetts Institute of Technology. He is a member of the Artificial Intelligence Laboratory and has a joint appointment in the Department of Brain and Cognitive Sciences. Raibert's main research interest is in the interaction between computers and physical systems. He is studying the principles of legged locomotion as they apply to robots and animals, the theory of passive dynamic systems, biological motor control, and new actuator technology.

Marc Raibert is author of *Legged Robots That Balance*, published by MIT Press, and is on the Editorial Board of the *International Journal of Robotics Research*.

## Richard F. Rashid

Richard Rashid is an Associate Professor of Computer Science and has been on the faculty of Carnegie Mellon University since 1979. He received his M.S. (1977) and Ph.D. (1980) degrees in Computer Science from the University of Rochester. He had previously graduated with Honors in Mathematics from Stanford University (1974).

While at the University of Rochester, Dr. Rashid participated in the design and implementation of the RIG operating system and Rochester Virtual Terminal Management System. Since joining Carnegie Mellon, Dr. Rashid's responsibilities have included the direction of the CMU Distributed Sensor Testbed project, CMU's distributed personal computing project (SPICE), and the Mach multiprocessor operating system project. He is responsible for the design and implementation of a network interprocess communication facility for UNIX, the Accent network operating system kernel, and the Mach multiprocessor operating system. He has also participated in the design of the CMU Andrew file system.

Dr. Rashid is a past member of the DARPA UNIX Steering Committee and CSNet Executive Committee. He is also a former chairman of the ACM System Awards Committee.

### Raj Reddy

Raj Reddy is a University Professor of Computer Science and Robotics, and Director of the Robotics Institute at Carnegie Mellon University. He received his B.S. from the University of Madras, India in 1958; his M.S. from the University of New South Wales, Australia in 1961; and his Ph.D. from Stanford University in 1961.

His current research activities involve the study of artificial intelligence, including speech, vision, and robotics; man/machine communication; application-specific computer architectures; and rapid prototyping. Prior to joining Carnegie Mellon's Department of Computer Science in 1969, Dr. Reddy was an Assistant Professor of Computer Science at Stanford University. He also served as an Applied Science Representative for IBM in Sydney, Australia from 1960 to 1963.

His professional honors include: Fellow of the Institute of Electrical and Electronics Engineers (IEEE); Fellow of the Acoustical Society of America; Member of the National Academy of Engineering; and President of the American Association for Artificial Intelligence (1987 to 1989). Dr. Reddy was presented the Legion of Honor by President Mitterrand of France in 1984.

### Paul Rosenbloom

Paul Rosenbloom is Associate Professor of Computer Science at the University of Southern California, and a member of the Information Sciences Institute, where he has been since 1987. He received his B.S. degree in Mathematical Sciences from Stanford University in 1976 and his M.S. and Ph.D. degrees in Computer Science from Carnegie Mellon University in 1978 and 1983, respectively. He came to the University of Southern California in 1987, following several years as an Assistant Professor in the Computer Science and Psychology Departments at Stanford University. His primary research interests center around the nature of the cognitive architecture underlying artificial and natural intelligence. The current focus is on Soar, a multi-disciplinary, multi-site attempt at developing and applying such an architecture. This work extends into multiple subdisciplines of Artificial Intelligence and Cognitive Psychology, including especially learning, memory, problem solving and planning, and expert systems. He is Past Chair of SIGART (Special Interest Group on Artificial Intelligence of the Association for Computing Machinery) and an editor of the journal *Machine Learning*.

## Dana S. Scott

Dana S. Scott is the Hillman University Professor of Computer Science, Mathematical Logic, and Philosophy at Carnegie Mellon University, where he has been since 1981. He is a faculty member of the School of Computer Science and the Mathematics and Philosophy Departments. He received his B.A. in Mathematics from the University of California, Berkeley, in 1954 and his Ph.D. in Mathematics from Princeton University in 1958. Between 1972 and 1981 he was Professor of Mathematical Logic, Oxford University, and he previously held appointments at Chicago, Berkeley, Stanford, Amsterdam, and Princeton. He was recently awarded an honorary doctorate from the University of Utrecht in the Netherlands in Philosophy.

Dr. Scott is a member of many professional organizations and a Fellow of the American Academy of Arts and Sciences, the American Association for the Advancement of Science, the New York Academy of Sciences, the British Academy, and the Finnish Academy of Sciences and Letters. He was elected to the National Academy of Sciences in 1988. He received the LeRoy P. Steele Prize of the American Mathematical Society, and, jointly with Michael Rabin, he was the recipient of the Turing Award of the Association for Computing Machinery in 1976. He has been a Bell Telephone Fellow (Princeton), a Miller Institute Fellow (Berkeley), a Sloan Research Fellow, a Guggenheim Foundation Fellow, and was granted a Senior U.S. Scientist Award by the Humboldt Foundation in Germany. He is on the editorial boards of several technical journals and is also a series editor for the Springer-Verlag and for the Oxford University Press.

Dr. Scott's past work in logic has concerned mainly model theory, automata, set theory, modal and intuitionistic logic, constructive mathematics, and connections between category theory and logic. His interests in philosophy concern the foundations of logic, the philosophy of mathematics, and the semantical analysis of natural language. His work in computer science has been principally directed toward the development of denotational semantics of programming languages and the mathematical foundations of a suitable theory of computability. His current projects aim at unifying the semantical approach with constructive logical formalisms to be able to give rigorous and machine-implementable proof methods and development tools for the RinferentialS construction of correct programs. Part of the technique is based on modeling computational structures as partially ordered sets in special categories enjoying extensive closure conditions. Other current projects involve work in information retrieval, electronic publishing (and generally studies on the structure of electronic text), computational linguistics, and computer algebra. He has supervised 35 Ph.D. theses within this range of subjects.

### Joseph F. Traub

Joseph F. Traub is the Edwin Howard Armstrong Professor of Computer Science at Columbia University. He was founding Chairman of the Department at Columbia. From 1971 to 1979 he was head of the Computer Science Department at Carnegie Mellon University.

Starting in 1959, Traub did pioneering research on what is now called computational complexity. With his colleagues, he is developing information-based complexity which studies the intrinsic difficulty of the problems which occur in science, engineering, and economics. A topic of current interest is whether intractable problems can be broken by randomization; another is what intractability results of theoretical computer science imply for the foundations of physics and for supercomputing. He has authored or edited eight books and written about 100 papers.

He is chairman of the Computer Science and Technology Board of the National Academy of Sciences. The board produces studies on matters of national concern related to computing, such as a national research and education network, export control, computer security, software, and elementary education. A major current study is on scope and directions for computer science and technology.

He has received numerous honors including election to the National Academy of Engineering and fellow of the American Association for the Advancement of Science.

Traub is a member of the board of trustees of the Babbage Institute and has served on the executive committee of the Board of Governors of the New York Academy of Sciences. He has served as advisor or consultant to the senior management of numerous organizations, including IBM, Hewlett-Packard, Schlumberger, Stanford University, INRIA (Paris), DARPA, the Federal Judiciary Center, and the National Science Foundation.

### J. Douglas Tygar

J. Douglas Tygar has been an Assistant Professor of Computer Science at Carnegie Mellon University since 1986. He received his A.B. from the University of California, Berkeley, in 1982 and a Ph.D. from Harvard University in 1986. In 1988, he was named a National Science Foundation Presidential Young Investigator.

His research interests center on practical applications of algorithmic techniques, and currently include the development of secure operating systems. He concentrates on building a set of novel interlocking tools that can be configured to reflect the security needs demanded by the organizational structures at given sites. He is actively concerned with the design and implementation of algorithmic fences which prohibit security violations, improved human interfaces for specifying security requirements, extended tools for providing security to distributed operating systems, and parallel acceleration of basic security functions.

Dr. Tygar is currently directing the Strongbox project to generate self-securing programs, i.e., programs that run securely when the underlying operating system provides only minimal security support, and visual specification techniques for file system security. He is codirecting (with Jeannette Wing) the Miro project, a visual specification tool for operating system secruity. His current interests focus on building systems that work well in physically unsecure environments using new secure coprocessor technology.

Dr. Tygar was the implementor and codesigner of ITOSS, a version of UNIX with substantially enhanced security. He has also written a number of commercially available VLSI and logic design tools.

### Steven A. Shafer

Steven A. Shafer received his Ph.D. in Computer Science at Carnegie Mellon University in 1983, and is now a Senior Research Scientist studying machine vision and robotics at CMU. Dr. Shafer studies how images can be analyzed by the computer using optical models of illumination, reflection, and the imaging process. Analyzing such visual phenomena as color, gloss, texture, and shadows, he is developing methods to base computer vision on an understanding of physics rather than the current ad hoc statistical and pattern classification techniques. In 1984, Dr. Shafer developed the first physics-based theory of color and highlights for computer vision, called the Dichromatic Reflection Model. He subsequently designed and built the Calibrated Imaging Laboratory at CMU, which has become one of the world's centers of controlled experimentation for machine vision research. Using this laboratory, he and his students have achieved automated image segmentation without heuristic signal processing, and are now developing methods for texture analysis, three-dimensional (3D) shape inference, and active camera control using optics-based imaging models. The Calibrated Imaging Laboratory has also been active in exporting data and imaging methodology to other vision researchers around the nation. In addition to studying machine vision applications of optical physics, Dr. Shafer is active in the Optical Society of America and the Inter-Society Color Council, and is pursuing research in the description and measurement of basic appearance properties of materials.

Dr. Shafer is also studying architectures for mobile robot perception, planning, and control. He is one of the authors of CODGER, the distributed blackboard system used by the NAVLAB autonomous robot van at Carnegie Mellon, and has been active in designing the software for control of the NAVLAB. Dr. Shafer is also coauthor of the PHAROS "microscopic" traffic simulator, which is being used to study how to control a robot vehicle driving through traffic. In addition to his research work, Dr. Shafer is the Associate Director for the pioneering Robotics Ph.D. Program at Carnegie Mellon. He has taught several courses in robotics and computer science, including computer vision and computer graphics, and has had a leading role in developing the curriculum for the Robotics Ph.D. Program.

## Herbert A. Simon

Herbert A. Simon is Richard King Mellon University Professor of Computer Science and Psychology at Carnegie Mellon University, where he has taught since 1949. During the past 30 years he has been studying decision-making and problem-solving processes, using computers to simulate human thinking. He has published over 700 papers and 20 books and monographs.

Educated at the University of Chicago (B.A., 1936, Ph.D., 1943), his work has been recognized by honorary degrees from a number of universities.

Dr. Simon was elected to the National Academy of Sciences in 1967. He has received awards for his research from the American Psychological Association, the Association for Computing Machinery, the American Political Science Association, the American Economic Association, and the Institute of Electrical and Electronic Engineers. He received the Alfred Nobel Memorial Prize in Economics in 1978, and the National Medal of Science in 1986.

He has been Chairman of the Board of Directors of the Social Science Research Council, and of the Behavioral Science Division of the National Research Council, and was a member of the President's Science Advisory Committee.

## Ivan E. Sutherland

Since 1980, Ivan E. Sutherland has been a vice-president of the consulting firm, Sutherland, Sproull and Associates, Inc., and a founding partner of Advanced Technology Ventures, a Boston and California based venture capital partnership. He also serves as a director of several companies. Dr. Sutherland divides his time between consulting activities, venture capital, and his own creative technical work.

From 1976 to 1980, Dr. Sutherland was the Fletcher Jones Professor of Computer Science at Caltech and served as head of the Computer Science Department. During this period he and Professor Carver Mead initiated the Silicon Structures Project, a major research program staffed and funded cooperatively with industry. The pioneering work of the Caltech group gave many U.S. academic institutions the confidence to teach integrated circuit design and thus increased manyfold the number of engineers familiar with integrated circuits.

Prioring to joining the Caltech faculty, Dr. Sutherland and Dr. David Evans founded the Evans and Sutherland Computer Corporation (E&S), a $150 million per year firm manufacturing high-performance computer graphics equipment and supercomputers. He served as Vice-President and Chief Scientist for E&S and remains a major shareholder and active member of its Board of Directors. During this period, Drs. Sutherland and Evans also taught at the University of Utah, and between the company and the university made Salt Lake City the premier center for computer graphics.

Dr. Sutherland was an Associate Professor of Computer Science on the Gordon McKay endowment at Harvard University prior to founding E&S. His research on a head mounted display led to early use of dynamic three-dimensional computer graphics and provided the key ideas around which E&S was founded. Bob Sproull, cofounder of Sutherland, Sproull and Associates, participated in the Harvard work as an undergraduate. Both men formed a friendship and association during that period which carries on today in the consulting firm.

Prior to Harvard, Dr. Sutherland spent 2 years at the Defense Advanced Research Projects Agency, where he was Director of the Information Processing Techniques office. In that capacity, he was responsible for funding most of the academic research in advanced computer science in the country. His contracts included Project MAC at MIT, and the Illiac 4 project at the University of Illinois, as well as major programs led by Alan Perlis at Carnegie Mellon University and David Evans at the University of California at Berkeley. His contact with the U.S. Department of Defense continued after leaving DARPA, first as a member of the Naval Research Advisory Committee, and later as a member of the Defense Science Board, and as Chairman of the Technical Advisory Committee for the Defense Mapping Agency.

Since founding Sutherland, Sproull and Associates, Dr. Sutherland has maintained an active research program of his own. In the early eighties, the work centered on robots that walk; he built a six-legged hydraulic walking machine featured on the cover of *Scientific American* in January 1983. More recently, the research program has involved new designs and design techniques for asynchronous digital systems. Six companies have jointly sponsored this research activity in which Drs. Sutherland and Sproull have worked together. A Theory of Logical Effort resulted from this work which, together with other teaching materials fathered during the course of the work, should soon appear in book form. The asynchronous design style was the subject of Dr. Sutherland's 1988 ACM Turing Award Lecture, "Micropipelines."

Dr. Sutherland received a Ph.D. degree from the Massachusetts Institute of Technology (1963), an M.S. from Caltech (1960), and a B.S. degree from the Carnegie Institute of Technology (1959), all in Electrical Engineering. He holds honorary degrees from Harvard, Caltech, and the University of North Carolina.

In addition to the A.M. Turing Award, he is also a recipient of the Emanuel R. Piore Award for Pioneering Work in Computer Graphics (1986), a Distinguished Alumni Award from Caltech (1985), and the First Steven Anson Coons Award for Achievements in Computer Graphics (1983).

He is a member of both the National Academy of Science and the National Academy of Engineering, as well as IEEE and ACM. Dr. Sutherland is the author of eight patents as well as numerous publications and lectures.

### Gregg Yost

Gregg Yost is a doctoral candidate in the School of Computer Science at Carnegie Mellon University. He received his B.S. in Applied Math/Computer Science from Carnegie Mellon in 1985. His primary research interest is in knowledge acquisition for knowledge-based systems. His current research centers on developing TAQT, an integrated collection of problem-space oriented system development tools. These tools are based on a language, TAQL, that expresses tasks directly in terms of the problem space computational model.

# CONTENTS

CMU Computer Science
A 25th Anniversary Commemorative

# PART ONE

# Looking Back

# 1

# Three Decades of Multiprocessors

Gordon Bell

## 1.1 Introduction

During the last 25 years, the author has never really considered any alternative to the multiprocessor (mP) for general-purpose, cost-effective, nonminimal computers. This involvement with mPs at Digital Equipment Corporation (DEC), Carnegie Mellon University (CMU), Encore, Stardent, and Kendall Square Research (KSR) included 16 computers. Fourteen were built, including 7 for research or advanced development, and 6 were built for the marketplace. The reasons for designing mPs have been quite compelling.

The only alternatives for general-purpose use that the computing community support are the uniprocessor and evolving networks of computers (e.g., local area network (LAN) connected workstations). A uniprocessor with tens to hundreds of thousands of processing elements controlled by a single instruction stream is relatively easy to build and to learn to program. When considering efficiency, such a vector processor is limited to solving very large, simple problems because each processing element performs the same operation. This is equivalent to directing a very large chorus with only one type of voice. Connecting an arbitrary number of computers as a networked multicomputer in order to get higher performance or higher availability requires that computers have to communicate by passing messages in a fashion akin to problem solving in a human

3

organization. Programs have to be organized and written for message passing use in the same way one structures a human organization.

In 1990, all of the general-purpose computer classes are implemented as mPs: supers for the highest performance; mainframes for historic reasons; minis in order to become mainframes and to have higher performance than is available from micros; "multis" (for multiple microprocessor) as the mini replacement; and PC-based and workstation-based micros because it is nearly impossible to build a uniprocessor using modern microprocessors that are not multiprocessor capable.

Given that mPs are now standard computer structures, it is important to understand how they got that way, why build them versus other kinds of computers, why the author bet on them for supercomputing in the mid-1990s, what the impediments to their use have been, why they are built now, and the challenge to their evolution.

## 1.2   The Evolution of Multiprocessors

Each of the computer classes have evolved mPs at different rates depending on the technology and market need. Mainframe mPs have remained almost unchanged for nearly 30 years except to adapt to the cache (c. 1968) in their second generation, thereby allowing them to evolve beyond four processors. Supercomputers have evolved quite rapidly to more than a few processors with the adoption of the mP by Cray Research and the constant need for greater performance. With powerful, low-cost and very small microprocessors, and a "standard" operating system, UNIX, as a base, the multi was born circa 1983. These structures, which have several dozen processors, have evolved rapidly to support parallelism and to provide mainframe performance at relatively low cost. The hierarchical multi with several thousand processors is in the early formation process as it now appears possible to build a very large computer with a shared address space that all processors use. The slow adoption of mPs to date has come from the market and technology cycle operating in reverse: the lack of computers has inhibited the lack of progress and understanding about parallelism and this in turn has inhibited the lack of a market.

### 1.2.1   Mainframes

Exhibits 1.1, 1.2, and 1.3 show the evolution of a number of mPs beginning in 1962 with the Burroughs military (D825) and mainframe (B5000) computers.

| Type | 1962-63 | 1964 | 1965 | 1966 | 1967-69 |
|------|---------|------|------|------|---------|
| *Unique* | | | | | |
| | 2:G21 | | | | 10xSafeguard |
| | (Bendix/CMU) | | | | (BTL) |
| *Mainframes* | | | | | |
| Bourroughs | 2xB5000 | 2xB5500 | | | 4xB6500 |
| | 4xD825 | | | | |
| CDC | | 4x3600 | | 2x6500 | 2x6700 |
| Digital | | | | 2xPDP-6 | |
| Honeywell/Bull | | | 4x635,645 | | |
| IBM | | | | 2x/67 | 2x/65 |
| Univac/Unisys | | | 3x1108 | | |
| Type | 1970 | 1971 | 1974 | 1976 | 1979 |
| *Unique* | | | | | |
| | | | 16xC.mmp | 50!Cm*(CMU) | 4x11/784 |
| | | | (CMU) | 16xHydra(DEC) | (DEC) |
| *Mainframes* | | | | | |
| Bourroughs | 2xB5700 | | | | |
| CDC | | | | | |
| Digital | 2xPDP-10 | | | | |
| Honeywell/Bull | | 4x60XX | | | |
| IBM | | | | 2x158,168 | |
| Univac/Unisys | | 4x1110 | | | |

**EXHIBIT 1.1**
The evolution of mP computer families with time: 1962-1979. During the first
two decades, mPs were only used to build mainframes. Notation: x =
crosspoint using central switch or multiported memory, xx = multistage
crosspoint, : = bus connected, ! = hierarchical switch, # = dance hall,
multistage switch, v = vector processors.

The exhibits show how the mainframe companies adopted the mP as a means
of supplying greater throughput and access to a common database to a large,
user group. Mainframes are implemented with a cross-point switch (either located centrally or built as a multiported memory) to connect the processors and
input/output (i/o) to the memory. In 1968, the introduction of the cache caused
increased the complexity of mP designs in order to maintain memory coherence
in a distributed memory. On the other hand, the cache reduced memory access
latency, thereby enabling the design of mPs with greater than two processors

| Type | 1981 | 1982 | 1983 | 1984 | 1985 |
|------|------|------|------|------|------|
| *Unique* | | | | | |
| | 4xIntel432 | 28:Synapse | | | |
| | | 6:Elexsi | 4x784 | 12?:Firefly | |
| | | 20?HEP | (DEC) | (DEC) | |
| *Mainframes* | | | | | |
| Univac/Unisys | | | | 4x1194 | |
| *Supers/mainframes* | | | | | |
| Cray | 2xxXMP | | 4xxXMP | 4xxCray2 | |
| *Multis* | | | | | |
| Arix | | 4:Arete? | | | |
| Encore | | | | 20:Multimax | |
| Sequent | | | 12:Balance | | |

**EXHIBIT 1.2**

The evolution of mP computer families with time: 1981-1985. Beginning in 1982, mPs began to be used for supercomputers. Notation: x = crosspoint using central switch or multiported memory, xx = multistage crosspoint, : = bus connected, ! = hierarchical switch, # = dance hall, multistage switch, v = vector processors.

by reducing the demand to have very high-bandwidth, low-latency memory systems. The result has been a slow, but steady increase in the number of processors with time from 2 to 4 in 1962 to over 10 in 1990 (see Exhibits 1.1, 1.2, and 1.3). Only now are such systems being supplied with software to increase both throughput and single job performance through parallelism.

## 1.2.2  Supers

Cray Research introduced their first mP in 1982 and has moved aggressively to design mPs for both throughput and high performance using parallel processing. Exhibit 1.4 shows the reasons why Cray has adopted the larger mP:

1. The clock has improved only 14% per year on the entire line of Seymour Cray designs. The performance for the Cray 1-based technology (X, Y, C90) has improved less rapidly.

2. The main uniprocessor advances occurred over a decade ago going from simple overlap of instructions and data in the Control Data Corporation CDC 1604 (c. 1960, not shown), to multiple functions units in the 6600, to pipelining in the 7600, and to vector processing in the Cray 1.

| Type | 1986 | 1987 | 1988 | 1989 | 1990 |
|------|------|------|------|------|------|
| *Unique* | | | | | |
| | | 64:M31? | 8xBiin | 4x(8!Cedar) | |
| | | (DEC) | 8!(64!)RP3 | 8x(16x)ES1 | |
| | | | (IBM) | | |
| *Mainframes* | | | | | |
| Digital | | | | | 4vX9000 |
| IBM | | 3x2x3090 | | | 12v? |
| *Supers/mainframes* | | | | | |
| CDC/ETA | | | 8xxETA10 | | |
| Cray | | | 8xxYMP | | 16xxC90 |
| NEC | | | | | 4xxSX3 |
| *Large Multis* | | | | | |
| BBN | #Butterfly | | | #TC2000 | |
| Intergraph/EDS | | | | | 500? |
| KSR | | | | | 2000? |
| *Minisupers* | | | | | |
| Alliant | 8vFX8 | | | | |
| Convex | | | 4vxC240 | | |
| *Minis/superminis* | | | | | |
| Digital | | 4:8800 | 6:6206 | | |
| *Multis* | | | | | |
| Digital | | | 4:6000 | 6:6000 | |
| Sequent | 24?:? | | | | |
| *Workstations* | | | | | |
| Apollo | | | | 4:DN10K | |
| Digital | | | | 2:Firefly | |
| Solborne | | | | 4:? | |
| Silicon Graphics | | | 4:240 | 8:Power Series | |
| Stardent | | | 4v:Titan | | |
| *Personal* | | | | | |
| *computers* | | | | | |
| Compaq | | | | 2:8XX86 | |

**EXHIBIT 1.3**
The evolution of mP computer families with time: 1986-1990. By 1990, the
mP was used to build general-purpose computers of all types. Notation: x =
crosspoint using central switch or multiported memory, xx = multistage
crosspoint, : = bus connected, ! = hierarchical switch, # = dance hall,
multistage switch, v = vector processors.

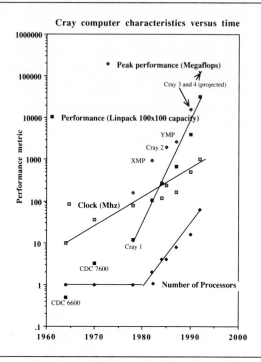

**EXHIBIT 1.4**
Cray research computer performance characteristics is plotted versus
introduction date. Characteristics include the clock, number of processors,
peak floating point operations per second, and throughput as measured by
Linpack 100 × 100 capacity (i.e., unit processor performance multiplied by
number of processors).

3.  Increases through the addition of more processors is the fastest way to
    increase overall performance.

It is important to note that the Cray architecture does not use a cache, and
hence building very high-performance computers is mainly a matter of designing
very high-bandwidth switches to couple the vector processors to memory. As
Exhibit 1.3 shows, all the supercomputer companies have adopted the mP model
in order to claim to have the highest peak performance.
    Supercomputers are leading the advance to both explicit and implicit (trans-
parent) parallel processing simply because, unlike mainframes, which have
evolved very slowly, the existence of supercomputers depends on building machines that have the highest computational performance.

### 1.2.3   Multis for Minicomputers, Workstations, and Personal Computers

In contrast to large machines, the "multi" is derived from technology. Single-bus, multiple microprocessors, called multis [2] began to be introduced in 1983 by Synapse (now defunct). Almost all computers outside of the largest, traditional supercomputers and mainframes are built using this model because microprocessors provide higher performance processing than multiple chip, gate array implementations of minis and mainframes (e.g., the VAX and the IBM 360). Because the structure of the multi, using a single bus, is the simplest computer that can be built, it is virtually impossible to avoid building a mP when connecting a microprocessor to primary memory. Exhibit 1.3 shows the large number of computers built in this fashion today. For the next decade, the author would expect the majority of nonworkstation, general-purpose, high-performance computers to be of this form.

### 1.2.4   Large (100) Multiprocessors

Several companies have worked on large mPs. IBM Research was the first to declare a 512-processor mP arranged in 8 clusters and called the RP3; only a 64-processor version was built. Evans and Sutherland, Inc., announced and withdrew their 256-node multi arranged in 16 processor clusters, although it built several four processor clusters. Bolt, Bernack, and Newman, Inc. has introduced its TC2000, a 64-processor computer based on its Butterfly switch that can be configured with 512 computer modules (each a Motorola 88K with built-in cache and local 4 to 32 megabytes of memory). The TC2000 is clearly a multicomputer since the latency to access memory on another computer is comparatively long. Intergraph has announced a plan for a 500-node mP development with Electronic Data Systems, Inc.

Kendall Square Research is introducing a hierarchical multi with 1024 processors, each delivering a peak of 40 Mflops. The hierarchical multi provides almost two orders of magnitude more aggregate processing power (10 to 20 billion instructions per second in 1024 10 to 20 mips processors) than any alternative general-purpose computer structure.

## 1.3   Why Build Multiprocessors Versus Other Types of Parallel Computers?

Many approaches are possible to increase performance and/or provide higher reliability. Although the numbers of computers have increased and become real and deployed, the kinds of computers have not changed significantly since the taxonomy posited by Bell and Newell [1].[1] The suitability of a given machine for an application depends on a number of factors beyond simple performance and price metrics, including the difficulty of adapting existing programs and algorithms, the range of problems a structure can solve, and even the novelty of the structure and supplier. Three kinds of usage are occurring in order of generality: (1) applications-specific hardware/software that is designed to solve one problem within a limited class of problems (e.g., image processing); (2) run-time-defined, application-specific, and monoprogrammed (reprogrammed) to be used on one problem at a time within limited classes of problems; (3) general-purpose computers that are configured with many resources and are used in a multiprogrammed fashion to solve a wide range of applications at a given time.

The uniprocessors and mPs are used in a general-purpose fashion. Multicomputers, such as the transputer or hypercube, can be made at almost any scale but are most often used in a monoprogrammed fashion since problems must be rewritten to exploit them. The single-instruction single-data (SIMD) structure can also be implemented to have an arbitrarily large amount of parallelism, but must be reprogrammed. Finally, machines with fixed function units or a fixed array of processing elements (e.g., systolic arrays) are highly problem specific.

The suitability of a structure to a problem or job mix also depends on the amount and granularity of parallelism inherent in the application. Even the most parallel application is likely to have significant sequential code which limits its overall performance. Thus a SIMD or multicomputer must be built to operate at the highest speed for sequential programs, not from slow components. For example, about half of the 24 Livermore Fortran Kernels are serial. Running just one of the kernels infinitely fast only increases the overall operation rate of the set by 4% whereas running one of the programs 1/25th the speed, lowers the operation rate a factor of two.

Not being multiprogrammed to a significant degree limits the utility of a computer, and hence drives up the cost per application. A uniprocessor, such as the Connection Machine, can be multiprogrammed to make more efficient use of its resources thereby improving the throughput. Multicomputers, on the other hand, are more difficult to multiprogram because each program from a set must be allocated to a particular set of machines. The operating system first has to statically allocate the programs to the computer and then to allocate dynamically the computers to the processing work (unknown a priori) on an efficient basis.

---

[1]The new introductions since 1971 include array and systolic processors.

## 1.4 The Bet: Multiprocessors Will Form the Fifth Generation

Given the bias toward general-purpose mP computers, the author bet Danny Hillis that in the last quarter of 1995 more supercomputer power, measured in sustained megaflops, will be shipped by evolving multiple processor supercomputers than by distributed memory computers such as today's SIMD or multicomputer. The bet centers on Hillis's plot (the number of processors versus the per processor power) of the supercomputer race as being run by a few, very fast processors (today's supers) versus a few million, slow processors.[2] mPs are evolving to have more processors and the SIMD is evolving to have higher-speed, more independent instruction streams and more processing elements per instruction stream.

By 1995, if supercomputers continue to exist as very large computers, they will most likely be constructed with a hierarchical memory (i.e., a distributed memory) and hence the bet may be difficult to interpret. For example, the Supercomputer Systems, Inc. computer is built as 4 clusters of 16 processors. A shared memory means a single, common address space and a model of implicit communication of data whereby any processor can access any data item. The opposite would imply multiple, private address spaces for each of the processors and require explicit messages in order to pass data among the processing elements.

## 1.5 Have the Impediments to Multiprocessors Been Removed?

It is essential to understand why a technology as compelling as mPs has been so slow to be adopted and whether all of the issues inhibiting their adoption in mainframes have been addressed as they relate to supercomputer and multi evolution. In this way, we may have some understanding about their future.

CMU's C.mmp. [7] enumerated many of the reasons why mPs were not part of mainstream computer design to rationalize the research for CMU's C.mmp mP. The report conjectured (and countered):

1. High total cost. The high cost of processors and memories limited the

---

[2]The author also takes issue with the plot because he still considers a SIMD computer such as the Connection Machine to be a vector uniprocessor with a very large number of processing elements connected to a widely dispersed memory inter-connected in a hypercube.

market to high-performance systems. Using the best price performance minicomputer components would allow the construction of a lower-cost mainframe.

2. High processor cost. Relative cost of processors such that the incremental processor failed to increase performance/price. With minis, the processor price is a small part of the system.

3. Unreliable, base software. Unreliability and performance degradation of operating systems in 1972. Constructing a more complex system would be futile. Software reliability is improving, and operating systems can be built in an engineered fashion.

4. High switch cost. Inability to construct switches cheaply. Medium Scale Integration (MSI) has enabled the design of low-cost, reliable switches.

5. Memory conflict. Performance loss through memory conflicts and access delays. Strecker's work [6] enabled this to be computed versus having to be simulated.

6. Parallel programming design and algorithms. Dividing a task to operate in parallel is unknown. Work has been started in several places. Indeed, this is one key area of research.

7. Parallel program construction. Difficulty and complexity of constructing programs to operate in a parallel environment. Mechanisms for synchronization exist including fork-join and P and V. Methods for constructing large complex programs are emerging. The experiment will focus on this.

The kinds of results the C.mmp research would address included

1. Processor Memory System (PMS) design to understand the hardware and system design issues

2. Hardware implementation to understand engineering aspects, especially reliability

3. Models of parallel computation, including parallel processing, network and pipelined processing of tasks, functional specialization, multiprogramming, partitioned operation

4. Decomposition of complex programs such as speech processing was somewhat understood and could serve as a user model

5. Operating system design and performance

6. Measurement and analysis of performance

7. Using mPs for reliable computation through higher level redundancy

Wulf et al [7] described the results of the research, which mainly included the design of a capabilities-based operating system (list item 5) Hydra. The

central cross-point switch design (items 1 and 2) drew concern from an unin-
formed academic community, but it proved to be straight-forward and reliable.
The principal advantage of a low cost, 16 × 16 cross-point built from a few
hundred MSI chips was that only 32 cables were needed to interconnect the
16 processors and 16 memory modules. A multiported memory design would,
by comparison, require 256 cables. Only a modest amount was learned about
performance because the PDP-11's limited floating-point arithmetic limited its
computational power and was of limited use to attract real users. The limited,
16-bit address not only exacerbated operating system and applications design,
but it lowered performance. Parallel programming (items 3, 4, 6, and 7) issues
were only addressed tangentially. It is important to observe that

> *any computer predicated on using many low power processors
> to provide very high performance will fail to be used unless the
> ultimate power is at least one to two orders of magnitude greater
> than is obtainable on any other computer.*

### 1.5.1  Does Computer Science Research Help?

In retrospect, one wonders how the line of research computers have helped mul-
tiprocessing outside of providing some design principles and training computer
scientists and engineers who can build computers. In reviewing research results,
it has become clear to the author that the "university" mPs could have had
a greater impact by simply expressing the understanding about parallelism in
units of work performed per unit of time in a comparative fashion, instead of
in units of speedup and time (universally poor for experimental machines). In
effect, good university research builds "toy" computers because of their scale
and speed.

Research computers must express performance metrics in terms of work
per clock unit. This allows experimental computers using slow components to
be built as "scale models" and "simulators" for "what could be a real computer"
so that it can be compared with a "real computer." The experimental researcher
is first obliged to understand what a "real computer" does. Thus any newfound
knowledge about architecture or parallelism can be compared with reality. That
is, does a new structure show promise against what already exists?

One of the flaws in research is the plethora of graphs of speedup versus
number of processors with no comparative metrics for real computers and with
no corresponding insight or theory. The common fatal flaws in most all research
showing speedup are

1. choosing an algorithm that can be sped up over a faster, but serial algorithm.

2. achieving speedup by having a very slow part of the program that would not exist in a "real" system. By having slow, floating point arithmetic the granularity of a problem can be increased, making more parallelism possible. This can only be solved by building a true, scale model of the entire computation and then normalizing the results to a clock. In this way "what could be a real computer" can be accurately simulated.

3. making a computer from mixed technologies (e.g., CMOS and ECL) to demonstrate scaling that could not exist in a real computer built from the fastest components.

4. holding one part of the computation constant while scaling other parts to test different communication paradigms and faster circuitry.

### 1.5.2    The Mainframe and Minicomputer Industries

Enslow [5] chronicled the early evolution of mPs and enumerated their disadvantages, including

- □ the complexity, expense, and difficulty of system software

- □ the hardware-software interaction

- □ the small and decreasing incremental gain in performance with each processor, hardware limitations for building extensive ($¿$ four) processor configurations

- □ the inability of software to exploit the hardware

Organizational inertia of large, old-line companies was a large factor in the poor adoption of mPs even though such companies were the first to introduce the mP. The inertia comes from having well established, unimaginative large groups and charters within engineering, fear of parallelism (including misunderstanding about memory conflict) and a quarter-century old operating system structure, including its maintainers, that defies change. With a growing market and a large engineering budget, it was always easier to start a new uniprocessor project with another technology (e.g., CMOS, TTL, ECL, GaAs) than to base one on using an existing processor to build a more complex mP. With physically large processors, the problem and cost of switching also made the mP more difficult to build and the gain harder to achieve.

With the introduction of the cache memory, the problem of memory coherence became large and further inhibited development for some time. Finally, in looking back, the myths about mPs (the second one increases performance 60 to 80%, the third 30 to 50% and there is no increase in performance by the fourth processor) failed to understand and segment the various effects, e.g., memory conflict, resource management, locks. Most systems were memory bandwidth-limited because of relatively large and expensive memory modules. More memory bandwidth (i.e., more modules) added significant access delays that a single stream processor was unable to overcome. Strecker's thesis [6] showed that such a system could be built provided enough memory bandwidth was available. Given the increased latency, a way to compensate for the delays would have been to build multistream processors (like the 6600 PPUs or Dennelcor HEP), but these structures would have appeared too radical and risky to mainframe engineers.

## 1.6 Why Build Multiprocessors Now?

Two basic market forces "pull" the introduction of mPs: performance and higher availability. Two technology forces "push" their inevitable adoption: the inherently lower cost of designing and building mPs that yield better performance/price and technology. Exhibit 1.5 shows these forces and factors.

### 1.6.1 Higher Performance and Greater Workload Throughput

Workload. The evolution of the Cray supercomputers[3] (Exhibit 1.4) illustrates the inevitability of mPs. Improvements in clock performance are relatively small and the basic forms of parallelism (pipelining and vector processing) have been extracted for a single job instruction stream. Therefore to increase performance mPs have to be adopted. Since supercomputers are time-shared and serve a large number of users in a multiprogrammed fashion, any increase in computing resources directly improves system effectiveness. Thus a mP provides more power through multiprocessed multiprogramming since each processor works independently on the workload stored in common memory. As previously suggested, unless structures such as the multicomputer can be used efficiently for multiprogramming, the economics will continue to relegate them to specialized tasks.

Although the "Cray" is used in both batch and time-shared modes, a mP is even more applicable for transaction processing because all the users are independent of one another and there is a high likelihood that all the users, such as those in a reservations system, will share common programs and data, i.e., the file system.

Peak Power. Peak power can be made available to a single user through both explicit and implicit forms of parallel processing. In 1987 and 1988, the ap-

---

[3] The highest performance computer(s) used for scientific and engineering computation.

❑ *Higher performance and greater workload throughput*
  - A large workload can be processed via multiprogrammed operation of a common job queue and common file system. Greater processing is available through
    - batch processing
    - time-shared, multiprogrammed server to LAN-based, X-windows clients and
    - arbitrarily large transaction-processing capacity with lower overhead (i.e., less context switching) than with a uniprocessor or multicomputer approach.
  - Peak performance is available to a single user through transparent parallel processing of
    - multiple jobs
    - multiple, pipelined processes
    - automatic (i.e., compiled) microtasking of blocks
  - Peak performance is available via explicit parallel processing for multiple processes.
  - Scalability. Incremental growth in performance with incremental growth in price is maintained. Computing power is provided in an incremental and scalable fashion as one computer.
  - A common pool of computational resources (processing, primary and secondary memory, networking) is available to trade-off among a large job mix.

❑ *Lower costs, providing improved performance/price*
  - A small set of PMS-level components forms a complete product line of a range of products in a scalable fashion.
  - Fewer component types imply
    - lower production cost and higher quality
    - better service through better spares availability and training
    - lower engineering costs and higher quality

❑ *Evolvability with time*
  - A well-designed system is evolvable with technology in an asynchronous fashion over several technology generations of processing, primary and secondary memory, and network.

❑ *Fault-tolerance and high availability*
  - Inherent redundancy using few component types provides higher system availability.
  - Nonstop hardware can be built (e.g., Stratus) in an incremental fashion.

❑ *Technology forces*
  - The mP is an evolutionary form of the computer, generalizing the processing resource in the same fashion as memory and input-output (e.g., terminals).
  - Properly designed operating systems provide mP parallelism as a by-product.
  - With a somewhat standard operating system, UNIX, the design of operating systems was taken away from engineers. Engineers have to create something, thus they are able to focus on mP versions of UNIX versus building another operating system.
  - Parallel processing has evolved to keep up with the evolution of hardware (e.g., processors).
  - Modern microprocessors (e.g., MIPS, Motorola) are designed to support multis, and as such it is becoming increasingly difficult to build uniprocessors.
  - For the largest machines, fast uniprocessors are technology-limited by scalar performance. mPs are the only way to provide higher throughput and peak power for general-purpose (i.e. "dusty deck") use.

**EXHIBIT 1.5**
Market and Technology Forces for Multiprocessors

plications that operated at the highest rates and greatest parallelism used the Cray XMP/416 and YMP8/32 supercomputers[4] operating at over 50% efficiency. Given that most computers use UNIX, the pipes mechanism provides the most basic form of parallelism, which though explicitly specified by a user, is identical to the uniprocessor case and is therefore used implicitly. With implicit parallelism, the compiler and operating system are responsible for detecting and exploiting the parallelism. The three forms of parallelism are shown in Exhibit 1.8. By explicitly segmenting a program into processes for parallel execution using primitives such as fork and join, a user can further exploit multiple processes.

The proof of the concept is in the machines that form the leading edge of technical computing. Exhibits 1.6, 1.7, and 1.8 compare various performance metrics and performance/price metrics versus the price of six leading edge technical computers.

Several observations can be made from these exhibits:

□ Large-scale, highly parallel applications (parallel Linpack) can exploit the peak performance of vector mPs.

□ Even for vectorizable applications, having a larger-scale problem (i.e., 1000 × 1000) is essential for high performance. Only on this problem do the multiple, vector processors attain their peak.

□ Vector processing, which is a basic parallel construct allowing parallelism to be exploited, doesn't help all applications. A totally scalar application characterized by Whetstones puts a large computer at a significant disadvantage.

□ A workload mix of scalar and vector characterized by the Livermore Kernels runs best on the fastest scalar machine. The MIPS R6000 performs half as well as the Cray YMP, which corresponds directly to the clock difference.

□ A vector processor improves the operation rate of a workload by only 50% since the amount of code that can be vectorized is limited.

□ Fast, Reduced-Instruction Set microprocessors (RISCs) are the basis of the most cost-effective computers. The first four systems are based on the MIPS, Inc. RISC chip. The MIPS 6000 is an ECL microprocessor.

□ No economy of scale exists across the range and lower-priced machines are more cost-effective. This reflects using CMOS micros versus ECL technology.

---

[4] Each year the Bell Prize is for parallelism in supercomputers, mPs, multicomputers, and compilers. In 1987, a 1024-node Ncube multicomputer won, operating at almost 100% efficiency.

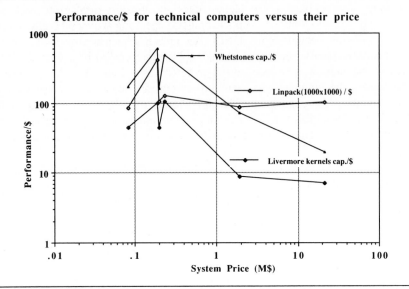

**Performance/$ for technical computers versus their price**

**EXHIBIT 1.6**
Performance characteristics measured by several common benchmarks are plotted against the price of various uni-, multi-, and vector multi-processor computers. The benchmarks are: Linpack running fully parallel, characterizing the best case for a vector mP, Whetstones as the worst case scalar application, and Livermore Kernels which typify a workload of technical computing.

- For all but two of the benchmarks, the MIPS 6000 is not as cost-effective as the other MIPS chip-based mP computers. In other words, going faster costs more per operation.

- Several scalar processors (e.g., the Silicon Graphics SGI 280) can be used in parallel for vector processing tasks. Roughly four processors are needed to equal one vector processor for highly vectorized applications.

- The SGI 280 is a classic, eight-processor multi and is most cost-effective for a scalar workload provided the workload does not saturate its low speed bus.

- The most cost-effective use of a mP is usually to run N programs on N processors.

Incremental Growth in Performance with Price.   The main advantage of mPs can be seen in how the Cray YMP is constructed to cover a range of price and performance (Exhibit 1.9) in a scalable fashion.

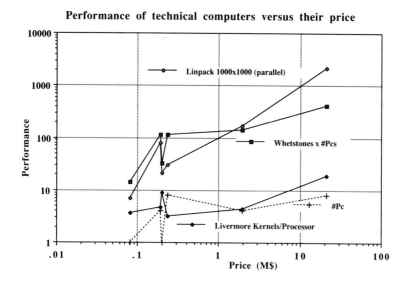

Performance of technical computers versus their price

**EXHIBIT 1.7**
Performance per price characteristics measured by several common benchmarks are plotted against the price of various uni-, multi-, and vector multi-processor computers.

## 1.6.2 Lower Costs, Providing Improved Performance/Price

The Cray YMP line of up to eight processors is constructed in three models: one to two, two to four, and five to eight processors. All use the same basic packaging and power scheme, and common processor and memory modules.

| Computer | Mhz | CPUs | Year | Peak Perf. | Memory | Price(M$) |
|---|---|---|---|---|---|---|
| MIPS 3000 | 25 | 1 | 1988 | 12 | 4 Mw | 0.082 |
| MIPS 6000 | 75 | 1 | 1990 | 38 | 8 Mw | 0.200 |
| SGI 280 | 25 | 8 | 1989 | 100 | 8 Mw | 0.230 |
| Stardent 3000 | 32 | 4v | 1989 | 128 | 8 Mw | 0.190 |
| Convex C240 | 25 | 4v | 1988 | 200 | 16 Mw | 1.900 |
| Cray YMP | 167 | 8v | 1987 | 2667 | 64 Mw | 21.000 |

**EXHIBIT 1.8**
Price and performance metrics for six leading edge technical computers.

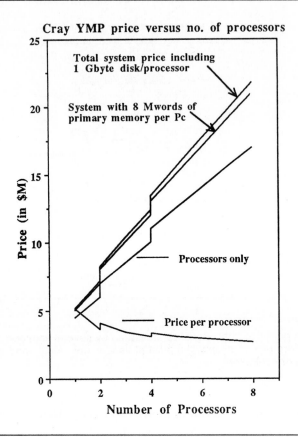

**EXHIBIT 1.9**
Cray YMP price is plotted for one to eight processors.

The difference in the system comes from building three basic packages that provide various amounts of memory bandwidth depending on the number of processors.

While the pricing is on the basis of processors, the individual processors each have a very small cost. Thus a disproportionate amount of the cost is in the basic package to house and interconnect (i.e., switch) the processors and memory. Nevertheless, Cray is able to use only a few basic components to provide a range of computing power over a range of price and cost.

| Model | Date | Cache | Performance range (vs. VAX 11/780) |
|-------|------|-------|-----------------------------------|
| 120 | 1985 | 32K | 1.5 to 15 |
| 320 | 1987 | 64K | 4.0 to 40 |
| 500 | 1989 | 256K | 17.0 to 170 |

**EXHIBIT 1.10**
Evolution of Multimax product line.

Fewer Components Reduces Costs.   The main benefit to such a scheme comes directly from the learning curve concept. With a learning curve, the cost of a product declines in relationship to the cumulative number of units produced. The amount of learning amounts to a 10 to 20% cost reduction for each doubling of produced units. This would amount to cost differentials of 50% versus comparable uniprocessor families. The author would expect the reliability of units to increase in a similar fashion.

Engineering.   Finally, having a few components requires a smaller engineering effort and this alone should produce a higher quality product. While the author believes that the product quality is inversely proportion to the number of people on a project, having a smaller number of systems to engineer will increase the quality provided that all the people who would have been working on alternative systems are not used on the design part.

### 1.6.3   Evolvability with Time

Exhibit 1.10 shows how the Encore Multimax product line evolved with time by just replacing the processor module with the next-generation microprocessor.[5]
    Thus, a principle benefit of the multi approach is evolvability. The key to evolution has been the evolution in cache size with time as provided by improved semiconductor density. Models 120 and 320 used a write-through protocol to maintain cache coherence. In Model 500, the cache protocol was changed to write-back on reference so as not to require a bus transaction each time a word needed to be written in memory. Note that only a few mainframe and supercomputers could deliver comparable performance, and none could equal the performance/price.

---

[5]The processing module has two processors. Up to 20 processors can exist in one system. The bus that interconnects processors and memory transfers 64-bit words at a 12.5 Mhz rate (100 Mbytes/sec).

### 1.6.4  Fault-Tolerance and High Availability

The basic mP provides inherent higher availability than its uniprocessor coun-
terpart by the redundancy of components (i.e., processors, memory, and i/o). In
all mPs, system operation is possible with any number of the components being
unavailable.

Stratus used the multi structure to provide fault-tolerant computing by constructing a computer with two pair of redundant elements. Each pair votes on a
memory by memory reference, and if an error occurs, the other redundant pair
is used for the result. Two copies of memory with appropriate error detection
and correction are maintained. By having nonfaulting hardware, the software
operating system task is significantly simplified.

### 1.6.5  Technology Forces

The mP is merely a generalization of the uniprocessor, providing incremental
processing resources in the same way that a computer can have more memory
or more terminals. By proper design, the mP introduces no significant design
problems to an operating system that are not inherent in a general-purpose,
multiprogrammed system, such as UNIX. The standardization of UNIX enabled
software engineers to extend an existing system rather than building one from
the scratch and thus to avoid the possibility of never getting around to support
mPs.

Today, it is virtually impossible to avoid building multis simply because,
after a decade of harassing microprocessor suppliers, the support for mPs exist
in nearly every micro. Furthermore, a large number of system engineers have
mP experience and simply apply market pressure. Finally, as a uniprocessor hits
a performance limit, the mP is the only way to provide more performance in an
evolutionary fashion.

## 1.7    What Are the Design and Use Issues?

Multiprocessors face various design and use issues in the next decade at all
the levels of integration, many of which may be common to other structures
(hardware, language, algorithm) employing increasing parallelism.

How are mPs with increasingly large amounts of parallelism measured,
and how efficient are they? Before one can embark on design, it is necessary
to have a way of measuring the system being designed because metrics should
have the greatest effect on the design. Benchmarks and kemels have historically
been used to characterize how a computer will perform on a particular user's

workload. As machines with more parallelism are constructed, older, small-scale benchmarks fail because a very large, parallel processor is unlikely to run them efficiently and hence is rejected a priori. Thus problem scale is a new parameter in understanding performance. Having a range of benchmarks that correspond to the range of algorithms a machine is likely to encounter is equally important because parallel machines have many new opportunities to stumble, and understanding potential bottlenecks is equally important. If a good way to characterize performance could be found, it would both improve computer designs and at the same time save customers and vendors great expense over the benchmarking that every user and vendor goes through today. SPEC, Illinois (the Perfect Club), the Lawrence Laboratories (Livermore and Los Alamos), the National Aeronautics and Space Administration (NASA), and even the newspaper *Digital Review* are all attempting to improve this critical situation.

What is the design goal of the system in terms of its size and the range of scalability and evolvability with technology and time? The right metrics for all the system design parameters must be specified from the start [4]. Today's systems have to be more effective in all forms of serial and parallel integer and floating point computation, memory management, and all forms of i/o for file management, interactive graphics, and all forms of visualization.

For example, the author posited 11 rules for supercomputer design [4] to reflect the complexity of design today.

1. Performance, performance, and performance are the three objective criteria for a supercomputer design. Rules 2 to 6 relate to performance.

2. Amdahl's law generalized implies that everything matters, a variant of "no chain is stronger than its weakest link," especially when measuring links by harmonic mean.

3. The scalar speed matters most and a super must be the fastest of comparable computers in its class, otherwise the harmonic mean measurement kills it as a super.

4. The vector speed can be arbitrarily high as costs allow. This is the advertised speed of the computer. The vector speed (peak) or advertised speed is the speed that the manufacturer guarantees the computer will not exceed on any application. The past rule of thumb is to have a vector unit that will produce two results per clock tick. IBM's mainframes have vector speeds about four times their scalar speeds. Large increases over the scalar speed beyond a hundred-fold provide a small benefit except for selected, very large scale applications, making the computer special-purpose (e.g., a Connection Machine). The recent NEC SX-3 announcement for a super has a peak speed of 16 times the clock.

5. Allow no holes in the performance space (e.g., arithmetic function, i/o,

mass storage) into which a benchmark can step, resulting in large performance losses.

6. Provide peaks in the performance space in order that extraordinary performance for a benchmark will result. Use this single number to advertize (characterize) the machine and to challenge other machines.

7. Obey computer design law no. 1: Provide enough address bits for a decade of constant architecture implementation.

8. Build at least two generations of the architecture. No first design supercomputer has ever been perfect. Do it again after the first one.

9. Build on the work of others. Designing a super is hard. Understand exactly why and how every machine works and move forward using this knowledge and any residual software.

10. Make it easy to use. Have a great compiler and diagnostic tools to aid users in vectorization and parallelization.[6]

11. Have slack resources when embarking on a supercomputer design. The fatality rate for companies making machines is at least 50%, and even though a design may be good, it has to be reiterated. Building a new super costs a minimum of $50 million to get a breadboard.

How scalable can a computer be? Scalability is a term that has been introduced into computer architecture in the last decade to connote building a range of computers from a common set of components. While scalability has increased, it is unclear that any computer that will scale effectively over an order of magnitude is possible. We have three scalable computer structures: mPs, microcomputers, and SIMDs (with many processing elements). The mPs are interesting over a range of 1 to 8 today (i.e., the largest machines are from 1 to 8 times the size of the smallest). Multicomputers built from weak, i.e., low performance components start performing competitively at 64 to 128 processors and a few have been built with 1024 elements for a range of 8 to 16. The Connection Machine is offered over a range of only 8 (8K to 64K processing elements). Will subsequent, hierarchical mPs be useful, i.e., operate economically over a wider range and hence be more scalable? More than likely the company supplying a computer limits scalability more than the computer might because each class of computer operates with different cost margins. It is unlikely that any company could be organized to sell a range of products that include low priced minis to large supers covering a $50K to $20M range (or 400:1).

---

[6]Training for supers is missing in academe since computer science departments are not oriented to training people to use computers or deal with computers that produce numbers. No texts exist on programming a parallel, vector processor (i.e., supercomputers), for example, and only few texts address parallelism in general. Only a few universities offer courses to teach supercomputer use and architecture.

In addition, one must ask, what are the parts and how many are there, how are they interconnected, how do they perform, and how reliable is the resulting structure? This is the PMS level design problem. Small-scale designs are bus-based and supers and mainframes use several levels of switching to supply high memory bandwidth to the processors. For the hundreds of processors that by their nature are advanced machines and that have the potential to advance the state of the art, the alteratives are: the big switch which for the "dance hall" model (processors, usually with both cache and significant local memory, on one side of the switch and memories on the other); or a hierarchy of clusters of computers such as Cm*, Cedar, E&S 1, KSR, and Ultramax.

How is memory kept coherent? Closely associated with PMS design is the problem of maintaining memory coherence when caches are used. For bus based multi design, the problem is simplest because all parts of the system can easily communicate with one another. The single bus and the cache of the multi serves three functions: caches provide the processors with fast access memory, caches avoid using precious system bandwidth, and the bus allows caches to "snoop" automatically as memory data are written so as to maintain overall memory coherence. As more complex switches are used, the caches become less accessible to one another and hence harder to keep in synchronization with one another except by explicit software control. Supercomputers do not use caches, but they should in order to build systems that are not limited by the "dance hall" switch capacity. A by-product is lower cost.

What are the Instruction Set Processor (ISP) architectural issues for mPs? The ISP design aspects of mPs have been fairly simple in the past with little support outside of basic memory locking primitives and facilities to aide processes to share common parts of memory. With large mPs, reducing the overhead for parallel processing requires operations on shared memory variables such as arithmetic on memory. For example, the Stardent computer has "do loop" variables in memory, which each processor accesses for its indices. Alliant goes further by locking variables that could depend on one another in a loop. The most interesting ISP is the Kendall Square Research computer that segments instructions into memory (including access, locking, data movement) and computation for separate parallel execution. Whether scalars, superscalars, or vector processors are used is a relatively small detail in the design of a large mP, because the overall ISP choice is so highly dependent on the overall design goals and especially the nature of the workload of the computer.

How do you build the hardware? Implementation follows from the previous PMS level decisions and the technology. The challenges today are having the right components (e.g., processors and switch and memory controllers) such that the implementation exploits them without undue overhead. For example, the Stardent processor and 32 or 128 Mbyte memory occupy board area of 2 x 19 inches by 22 inches using off the shelf components, whereas a KSR processor/memory module with the same amount of memory occupies roughly

150 square inches; the KSR processor/memory delivers roughly one half of the work load capacity of a Cray=1. Customization of silicon or GaAs beyond gate arrays is the key to building very large mPs.

How do you build computers that don't fail? The implementation of highly reliable computers continues to be an art unto itself. With more recent microprocessors the hardware design of multis for high availability is straightforward and commonplace even for ordinary computers. Operating systems can then evolve accordingly.

What does the software look like to manage mPs? Operating systems have evolved to support parallelism in the language operating environments for small-scale mPs. For mPs with several hundred processors, a different approach may be needed. Today, the leading candidate for such systems is CMU's MACH. Standard extensions such as the Argonne library are needed in all operating systems to provide a common set of primitives for all parallel programming environments to aid portability and simplify training (and texts). To exploit mPs effectively all forms of control for implicit and explicit parallelism are needed, including message passing.

What is the programming environment, including languages, debugging, and profiling tools, that encourage the exploitation of parallelism? Fortran is the language for technical computing but C is becoming common and standard extensions for vectorization and parallelization are needed. For commercial and transaction systems, database systems and C are an alternative to traditional Cobol. Whether traditional languages provide the right paradigm for parallelism is a moot question. Today's environments are all we have, and a research and development community that could develop alternatives is nonexistent.

How do users exploit mPs? By far the most significant limit to mP development is training. Training cannot occur on a wide scale basis until computer science and engineering get involved in parallelism to use, learn, teach, and write texts. Also, until this happens, no alternative to parallelism outside the evolutionary stream will occur.

## 1.8  Conclusions

mPs have been slow to evolve and become a staple of computer engineering. More progress has been made in the last 5 years than ever before because all classes of computers are built in this fashion. The next decade should be the most exciting in terms of challenges for builders and users alike. It is clear that we will be able to build mPs with thousands of processors, but the progress will be difficult because of the complexity of these designs and the difficulty users have in exploiting them for all but transaction processing and embarrassingly parallel programs.

## References

[1] C. G. Bell and A. Newell. *Computers Structures: Readings and Examples.* New York: McGraw-Hill, 1971.

[2] C. G. Bell. Multis: A new class of multiprocessor computers. *Science, 228*, 462-467, 1985.

[3] C. G. Bell. The 11 rules of supercomputer design. Videotape, University Video Communications, Los Gatos, CA, 1989.

[4] C. G. Bell, C. Mudge, and J. McNamara. *Computer Engineering.* Digital Press, 1978.

[5] P. H. Enslow, ed. *Multiprocessors and Parallel Processing.* John Wiley & Sons, 1974.

[6] W. D. Strecker. An analysis of the instruction execution rate in certain computing structures. Ph.D. dissertation, Carnegie Mellon University, 1971.

[7] W. A. Wulf and C. G. Bell. C.mmp—a multi-mini-processor. *Proceedings of the Fall Joint Computer Conference*, 1972.

# 2

---

# VLSI Theory and Parallel Supercomputing

Charles E. Leiserson

Since its inception, Very Large Scale Integration (VLSI) theory has expanded in many fruitful and interesting directions. One major branch is layout theory that studies the efficiency with which graphs can be embedded in the plane according to VLSI design rules. In this survey chapter, I review some of the major accomplishments of VLSI layout theory and discuss how layout theory engendered the notion of area and volume-universal networks, such as fat-trees. These scalable networks offer a flexible alternative to the more common hypercube-based networks for interconnecting the processors of large parallel supercomputers.

In 1978, H. T. Kung led a group of Carnegie Mellon University (CMU) graduate students, which included myself, to investigate the power of VLSI circuitry. At the time, we were amazed by this computational medium. Every one to two years, the number of devices that fit on a VLSI chip doubled. Remarkably, this exponential growth in device density showed no sign of subtantially slackening (and indeed, 12 years later it has not), and thus, our group looked forward to computation at an unprecedented scale.

Although it was apparent that semiconductor manufacturers were investing heavily to ensure that the fabrication technology would continue to scale, the paper-and-pencil methods by which these chips were being designed stood no chance of coping with the projected growth of circuit complexity. Many com-

puter scientists who became involved in VLSI naturally focused on the problems
of computer-aided design.

H. T. Kung and his students took a different path, however. Rather than con-
centrating on design issues, we investigated computational issues: algorithms,
architectures, and intrinsic capabilities of the medium. At the time, parallel
machine architectures, such as C.mmp and Cm*, were proliferating at CMU.
Despite our attempts to predict the behavior of algorithms running on these machines from the abstract machine models they implement, we discovered that
actual running times differed considerably. The abstract machine model covers
overhead costs, such as communication, which must be considered explicitly
to estimate running times. In VLSI technology, however, we found that communication costs are explicit: the capital cost of communicating between two
processors is the area of the wire connecting them. Thus, we embraced the
VLSI revolution, because it could provide a model in which the abstract costs
of algorithms and architectures correspond closely to real implementation costs.

Kung and I developed an accurate, yet abstract, model of VLSI computation, called *systolic* computation [9]. In a systolic algorithm, data values pulse
in a regular fashion through the processors of the system. Exhibit 2.1 shows
one such algorithm that we discovered for multiplying band matrices. (A band
matrix is a matrix whose only nonzero elements lie near the main diagonal.)
On each step of the algorithm shown in the exhibit, the nonzero entries of the
$A$ and $B$ matrices move down to the right and left, respectively, across the
hex-connected array of processors, and the result matrix $C = AB$ moves upward. Each processor in the systolic array performs the simple comptutation
$d \leftarrow c + a \cdot b$.

We argued that this systolic algorithm would have a good hardware implementation, since the two-dimensional array structure maps efficiently into the
planar VLSI medium. All communication between processors occurs between
nearest neighbors. There are no hidden communication costs. Although some
processors are idle at some steps, when the pipeline becomes full, a constant
fraction $(1/3)$ of the processors are busy at every step, which yields an asymp-
totically efficient parallel algorithm for multiplying band matrices. (With minor
changes, every processor can be kept busy at every step.)

While Kung and many of his students were busy inventing new systolic
algorithms, another of Kung's graduate students, Clark Thompson (now, Thom-
borson), formalized the problem of laying out a VLSI circuit [24]. Thompson
introduced a simple, graph-theoretic model for VLSI circuitry in which a circuit
is modeled as a graph whose vertices correspond to active circuit elements and
whose edges correspond to wires. A VLSI layout is a mapping of the graph to a
two-dimensional grid such that each vertex is mapped to a square region of the
grid and each edge is mapped to a path in the grid. Unlike the classical notions
of a graph embedding from mathematics, Thompson's model allows one edge
of a graph to cross over another, like wires on an integrated circuit.

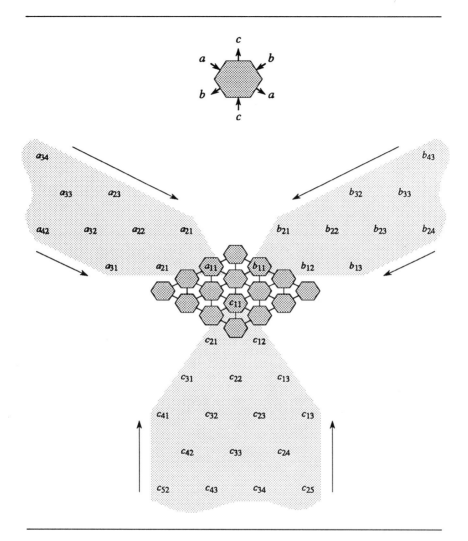

**EXHIBIT 2.1**
A systolic array for multiplying band matrices.

The interesting cost measure in VLSI is *area*. In Thompson's model, area can be measure as the number of grid points occupied by edges or vertices of the graph. For example, Exhibit 2.2 shows a layout of the complete bipartite graph $K_{3,3}$, which contains 6 vertices and 9 edges. A simpler measure for our purposes is the *bounding-box area*, which is simply the product of the number of occupied

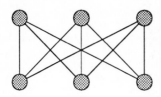 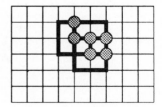

**EXHIBIT 2.2**
A layout of the complete bipartite graph $K_{3,3}$ with area $13$ and bounding-box area $15$.

rows in the layout times the number of occupied columns. In Exhibit 2.2, the area is $13$, and the bounding-box area is $15$. For simplicity in this discussion, we'll focus on bounding-box area.

Quickly, the minimum-area layouts for familiar graphs were catalogued. As shown in Exhibit 2.3, a mesh (two-dimensional array) with $n$ vertices ($\sqrt{n}$ by $\sqrt{n}$) has $\Theta(n)$ area.[1] The normal way of drawing a complete binary tree (Exhibit 2.4a) has $\Theta(n \lg n)$ area, but the "H-tree" layout (Exhibit 2.4b) is much better: it has $\Theta(n)$ area. A hypercube, which is a popular interconnection network for parallel computers, requires considerably more area—$\Theta(n^2)$.

What causes a hypercube to occupy so much area? Although the size of a vertex grows slowly with the number of vertices in a hypercube, most of the area of a hypercube layout is devoted to *wires*. Exhibit 2.5 shows how the problem of wiring a hypercube grows with the size of the hypercube. Wires are expensive, and wire area represents the capital cost of communication on a VLSI chip. By measuring communication costs in terms of the geometric concept of area, Thompson's model enabled a mathematical theory of communication in VLSI systems to develop.

From its origin, VLSI theory has expanded in many fruitful and interesting directions. Rather than attempting to describe the breadth of research in VLSI theory, however, I would like to revisit the accomplishments along one narrow path, layout theory, which I believe will have a fundamental impact on the architecture of large parallel supercomputers.

In his early work, Thompson discovered an important lower bound. The area of an $n$-vertex graph is related to its *bisection width*: the minimum number

---

[1]The notation $\Theta(f(n))$ means a function that grows at the same rate as $f(n)$ to within a constant factor as $n$ becomes large. The notation $O(f(n))$ means a function that grows no more quickly, and $\Omega(f(n))$ means a function that grows no more slowly. Formal definitions for these terms can be found in [4].

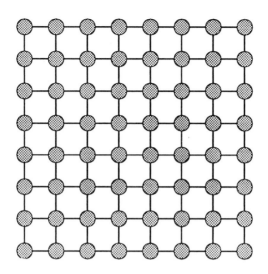

**EXHIBIT 2.3**
A mesh (two-dimensional array) on $n$ vertices has a VLSI layout with $\Theta(n)$ area.

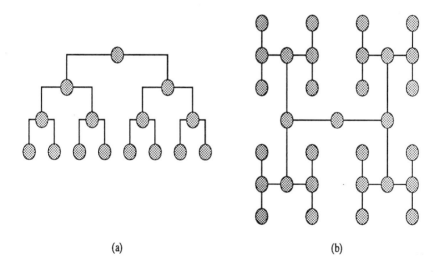

(a)                                                        (b)

**EXHIBIT 2.4**
A complete binary tree on $n$ vertices laid out in the standard way (a) takes $\Theta(n \lg n)$ area, but an H-tree layout (b) requires only $\Theta(n)$ area.

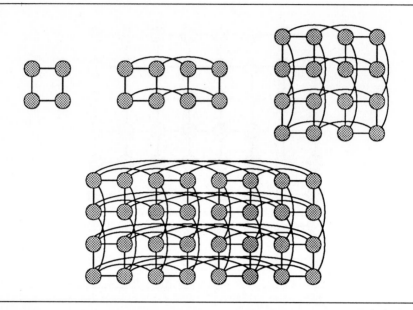

**EXHIBIT 2.5**
Illustrations (not layouts) of hypercubes on 4, 8, 16, and 32 vertices. Any
layout of an $n$-vertex hypercube requries $\Omega(n^2)$ area.

of edges that must be removed to partition the graph into two subgraphs of $n/2$
vertices (to within 1, if the number of vertices is odd). For example, an $n$-vertex
mesh has a bisection width of $\sqrt{n}$. A complete binary tree has a bisection width
of 1. A hypercube has a bisection width of $n/2$. Thompson proved that any
layout of a graph with bisection width $w$ requires $\Omega(w^2)$ area.

A simplified version of Thompson's lower-bound theorem is illustrated in
Exhibit 2.6. Let $G$ be a graph with bisection width $w$, and consider a VLSI
layout of the graph with area $A$. We'll show that the area of the bounding box
of the layout must be at least $w^2$. (Thompson actually showed the stronger result
that the area occupied by graph edges is at least $\Omega(w^2)$.)

Assume that the bounding box has dimensions $x \times y$, where $x \le y$. Move a
line parallel to the short side of the box from left to right until half the vertices
of the graph fall on each side. Such a line bisects the graph, and thus the number
of edges of $G$ cut by the line must be at least $w$ by definition of bisection width.
The number of edges that can cross from one side of the layout to the other is
at most $x$, however, since that is the length of the short dimension of the layout.
Thus, $w \le x$, from which it follows that $w^2 \le x^2 \le xy = A$.

It turns out that a small bisection width does not lead immediately to a

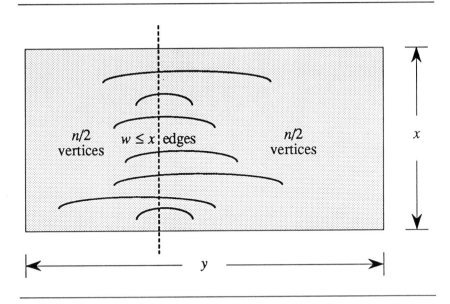

**EXHIBIT 2.6**
Any graph with bisection width $w$ requires $\Omega(w^2)$ area.

small-area layout. After all, if we take two $n/2$-vertex subgraphs, each with $\Theta(n^2)$ area, and connect them by a single edge, the resulting graph has a bisection width of 1 but still requires $\Theta(n^2)$ area. Under the tutelage of Jon Bentley, I was able to show [15,16], however, that if there is a good *recursive decomposition* of a graph—one where we can keep subdividing the subgraphs without cutting many edges—then the graph has a small layout. For example, not only complete binary trees, but *any* binary tree, no matter how badly balanced, can be laid out in $O(n)$ area by a divide-and-conquer method. This result was discovered independently by Leslie Valiant [25]. Valiant and I were also able to show that this method lays out any $n$-vertex planar graph in $O(n \lg^2 n)$ area. Later, Tom Leighton was able to show that a variant of our method was optimal on any graph to within a $O(\lg^2 n)$ factor in area [10].

Leighton also introduced an interesting graph, which he called the *tree-of-meshes* graph, shown in Exhibit 2.7. He was able to prove that this graph requires $\Omega(n \lg n)$ area, thereby refuting a conjecture of mine that all planar graphs could be laid out in $O(n)$ area. It remains an open question in VLSI theory as to whether there exists a planar graph that requires $\Omega(n \lg^2 n)$ area, or if all planar graphs can be laid out in $O(n \lg n)$ area.

Numerous other results in layout theory have been obtained—too many to

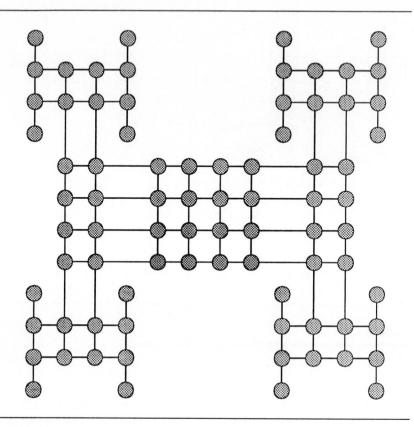

**EXHIBIT 2.7**
The tree-of-meshes graph.

mention them all. Paterson, Ruzzo, and Snyder [20] and Bhatt and Leiserson [2] studied how to keep wires short while preserving small area. Valiant [25], Ruzzo and Snyder [23], and Dolev, Leighton, and Trickey [5] studied VLSI layouts in which wires are not allowed to cross. Three-dimensional integration was studied by Rosenberg [21], Leighton and Rosenberg [14], and Greenberg and Leiserson [7]. Fault tolerance in wafer-scale circuits was studied by Rosenberg [22], Leighton and Leiserson [11,12], and Greene and El Gamal [8]. The packaging of graphs into chips was studied by Leiserson [16] and Bhatt and Leiserson [3].

In fact, packaging constraints are analogous to the constraints in Thompson's model. At any level of packaging—chips, boards, backplanes, racks, or cabinets—manufacturing technology constrains the number of external connections from a package to be much smaller than the number of components within

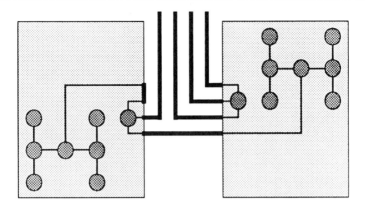

**EXHIBIT 2.8**
Packaging a complete binary tree.

the package. In Thompson's model, a square region with side $s$ can support $4s$ external connections, but it can contain $s^2$ vertices, which is considerably larger than $4s$ as $s$ becomes large.

As an example of a result [16] in packaging, Exhibit 2.8 shows a novel way to package a complete binary tree using 4-pin packages of a single type. Each chip contains one internal node of the tree, with three external connections, and the remainder of the chip is packed as full as possible with a complete binary tree, with one external connection. To assemble a tree with twice as many leaves, we use two chips. We wire up one of the unconnected internal nodes on one of the chips as the parent of the two complete binary trees. We are left with a complete binary tree with twice as many leaves, plus one unconnected internal node. Thus, considering the two chips as a single unit, the structure is the same as the one with which we began. By repeating the process, we can recursively assemble a complete binary tree of arbitrarily large size.

The work in layout theory culminated with the development by Bhatt and Leighton [1] of a general framework for VLSI layout. They proposed a layout method with which they were able to obtain optimal or near-optimal layouts for many graph-embedding problems. Their method has three steps. First, recursively bisect the graph, forming a decomposition tree of the graph. Second, embed the graph in the tree-of-meshes graph (Exhibit 2.7), typically with the vertices of the graph at the leaves of the tree-of-meshes graph. The meshes in the tree-of-meshes are used as crossbar switches for routing the edges of the graph. The layout of the graph is then obtained by looking at where the vertices and edges are mapped when the tree-of-meshes graph is laid out according to known good layouts.

It seemed to me at the time that Bhatt and Leighton had solved nearly all the interesting open problems in VLSI layout theory. I turned my attention toward parallel computation, in which I had continued to be involved since my work with H. T. Kung on systolic arrays [9].

In fact, I was very much a proponent of special-purpose parallel computation over general-purpose parallel computation, largely as a result of my work on VLSI layout theory. After all, as Kung and I had shown, and as Kung has continued to forcefully demonstrate, many computations can be performed efficiently on simple linear-area structures, such as one-dimensional and two-dimensional arrays. These special-purpose networks have the nice property that they can be laid out so that processors are dense and packaging costs are minimized. Moreover, for many problems, they offer speedup, which is linear in the number of processors in the systolic array.

General-purpose parallel computers, on the other hand, are typically based on interconnection networks, such as hypercubes, that are very costly for the computation they provide. For example, any hypercube network embedded in area $A$ has at most $O(\sqrt{A})$ processors. The processors are therefore sparse in the embedding, and interconnections dominate the cost. Similar results can be shown for three-dimensional VLSI models. Only $O(V^{2/3})$ processors of a hypercube network can fit in a volume $V$.

Hypercube networks do have a major advantage over many other networks for parallel computing, however. They are *universal*: a hypercube on $n$ processors can simulate any $n$-processor bounded-degree network in $O(\lg n)$ time. The simulation overhead is polylogarithmic (a polynomial of $\lg n$), an indication that the simulation is a parallel simulation. A polynomial overhead in simulation is less interesting, since $\Theta(n)$ overhead is easily obtained by a serial processor simulating each of the $n$ processors in turn.

The proof that an $n$-processor hypercube is universal goes roughly as follows. Suppose we have a bounded-degree network $R$ with $n$ processors. Each processor can communicate with all its neighbors in unit time. The hypercube can simulate the network, therefore, by sending at most a constant number of messages from each processor, where each message contains the information that travels on one of the interconnections in $R$. As it turns out, all messages can be routed on the hypercube to their destinations in $O(\lg n)$ time [26].

The notion of universality—the ability of one machine to efficiently simulate every machine in a class—is central to the origins of computer science. A universal machine is the computer theorist's idea of a general-purpose, as opposed to multipurpose, machine. A universal machine can do the function of any machine, just by programming it, or, in the case of parallel-processing networks, just by routing messages. A universal machine may not be the best machine for any given job, but it is never much worse than the best. The universality theorem for hypercubes does not say that a hypercube is the fastest network to build on $n$ processors. What it says is that the fastest special-purpose network for any given problem can't be much faster.

From a VLSI theory standpoint, however, a special-purpose parallel machine has a clear advantage over a universal parallel machine. Packaging its network can cost much less. And although universality is a selling point, our economy favors machines that are cheap and efficient, even if they are not universal. (How many combination telephone-lawnmower-toothbrushes have been sold recently?) Special-purpose networks for parallel computation are much cheaper than hypercube networks. Thus, for a long time, I was skeptical about the cost-effectiveness of general-purpose parallel computing.

I changed my mind, however, and became an advocate general-purpose parallel computing when I started to look more closely at the traditional assumptions concerning universal networks. In fact, from a VLSI theory perspective, I discovered that hypercubes are not really "universal" at all! An $n$-processor hypercube may be able to efficiently simulate any $n$-processor bounded-degree network, but if we normalize by area instead of by number of processors, we discover that an area-$A$ hypercube cannot simulate all area-$A$ networks efficiently. For example, since an area-$A$ hypercube has only $\Theta(\sqrt{A})$ processors, it can't simulate an area-$A$ mesh, which has $\Theta(A)$ processors, in polylogarithmic time. A network that is universal from a VLSI point of view should be a network that for a given area can efficiently simulate any other network of comparable area.

One such *area-universal* network is a *fat-tree* [6,17], which is based on Leighton's tree-of-meshes graph. As shown in Exhibit 2.9, processors occupy the leaves of the tree, and the meshes are replaced with switches. Unlike a computer scientist's traditional notion of a tree, a fat-tree is more like a real tree in that it gets thicker further from the leaves. Local messages can be routed within subtrees, like phone calls in a telephone exchange, thereby requiring no bandwidth higher in the tree. The number of external connections from a subtree with $m$ processors is proportional to $\sqrt{m}$, which is the perimeter of a region of area $m$. The area of the network is $O(n \lg^2 n)$, which is nearly linear in the number $n$ of processors. Thus, the processors are packed densely in the layout.

Any network $R$ that fits in a square of area $n$ can be efficiently simulated by an area-universal fat-tree on $n$ processors. To perform the simulation, we ignore the wires in $R$ and map the processors of $R$ to the processors of the fat-tree in the natural geometric way, as shown in Exhibit 2.10. As in the hypercube simulation, each wire of $R$ is replaced by a message in the fat-tree. If we look at any $m$-processor subtree of the fat-tree, it simulates at most a region of area $m$ in the layout of $R$. The number of wires that can leave this area-$m$ region in $R$'s layout is $O(\sqrt{m})$, and the fat-tree channel connecting to the root of the subtree has $\Theta(\sqrt{m})$ wires. Thus the *load factor* of the channel, the ratio of the number of messages to channel bandwidth, is $O(1)$. It turns out that there are routing algorithms [6,13,17] that effectively guarantee that all messages are

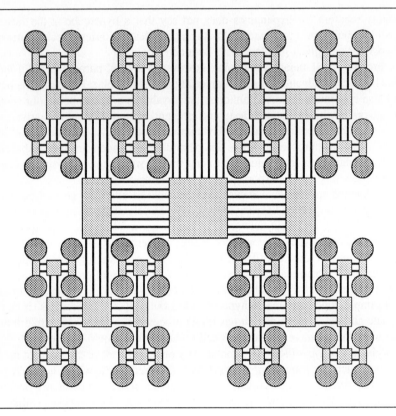

**EXHIBIT 2.9**
An area-universal fat-tree.

delivered in polylogarithmic time. (In fact, the algorithms can deliver messages near optimally even if the load factor is quite large.)

Similar universality theorems can be proved for three-dimensional VLSI models using *volume-universal* fat-trees. For a fat-tree to be universal for volume, however, the channel capacities must be selected differently from those in an area-universal network. Whereas the average growth rate of channels in an area-universal fat-tree is $\sqrt{2}$, the average growth rate in a volume-universal fat-tree is $\sqrt[3]{4}$.

In practice, of course, no mathematical rule governs interconnect technology. Most networks that have been proposed for parallel processing, such as meshes and hypercubes, are inflexible when it comes to adapting their topologies to the arbitrary bandwidths provided by packaging technology. The growth in channel bandwidth of a fat-tree, however, is not constrained to follow a

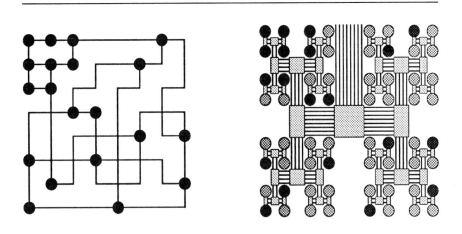

**EXHIBIT 2.10**
Any area-$n$ network $R$ can be efficiently simulated by an $n$-processor
area-universal fat-tree.

prescribed mathematical formula. The channels of a fat-tree can be adapted to
effectively utilize whatever bandwidths the technology can provide and which
make engineering sense in terms of cost and performance. Exhibit 2.11 shows
one variant of a fat-tree composed of two kinds of small switches: a three-
connection switch and a four-connection switch. By choosing one of these two
kinds of switches at each level of the fat-tree, the bandwidths of channels can be
adjusted. If the three-connection switch is always selected, an ordinary complete
binary tree results. If the four-connection switch is always selected, a butterfly
network, which is a relative of a hypercube, results. By suitably mixing these
two kinds of switches, a fat-tree that falls between these two extremes can be
constructed that closely matches the bandwidths provided by the interconnect
technology.

The notion of locality exploited by fat-trees is but one of three such notions
that arise in the engineering of a parallel computer. The most basic notion of
locality is exemplified by wire delay and measured in distance. Communication
is limited by the speed-of-light. If this notion of locality dominates, the nearest-
neighbor communication provided by a three-dimensional mesh is the best one
can hope. For many systems, however, wire delay is dominated by the time
it takes for logic circuits to compute their functions. The second notion of
locality is exemplified by levels of logic circuits and measured in gate delays.
Communication time is essentially limited by the number of switches a message
passes through. From this point of view, structures with small diameters, such

**EXHIBIT 2.11**
A scalable fat-tree.

as hypercubes, seem ideal. In a routing network, however, a heavy load of messages can cause congestion, and the time it takes to resolve this congestion can dominate both wire and gate delays. Congestion is especially likely to occur in networks that make efficient use of packaging technology. The last notion of locality is exemplified by the congestion of messages leaving a subsystem and measured by load factor. From this standpoint, fat-trees offer provably good performance by a general-purpose network that can be packaged efficiently. Recent work [19] has shown that efficient parallel algorithms can be designed for this kind of network as well.

Whatever the point of view, however, all three notions of locality must guide the engineering and programming of very large machines. There are problems in the sciences that cry out for massive amounts of computation, most of which exhibit locality naturally: problems in astronomy, such as galaxy simulation; problems in biology, such as the combinatorics of deoxyribonucleic acid (DNA) sequencing; problems in economics, such as market prediction; problems in aerospace, such as fluid-flow simulation; and problems in earth, atmospheric, and ocean sciences, such as earthquake and weather prediction. To address these problems effectively, very large parallel computers must be constructed. Some of these computers may even be "building size." To construct and program such large machines, however, locality must be exploited, and computer engineers must come to grips with the lessons of VLSI theory.

## 2..1    Acknowledgments

My research is supported in part by the Defense Advanced Research Projects Agency under Contract N00014-87-K-825 and in part by a National Science Foundation Presidential Young Investigator Award with matching funds provided by the IBM Corporation, AT&T Bell Laboratories, and Xerox Corporation. I am grateful to these institutions for their continuing support. An early version of this chapter appeared in the *Decennial Caltech Conference* on VLSI [18].

# References

[1] S. N. Bhatt and F. T. Leighton. A framework for solving VLSI graph layout problems. *Journal of Computer and System Sciences*, 28(2):300-343, 1984.

[2] S. N. Bhatt and C. E. Leiserson. Minimizing the longest edge in a VLSI layout. Unpublished memorandum, MIT Laboratory for Computer Science, 1981.

[3] S. N. Bhatt and C. E. Leiserson. How to assemble tree machines. *Advances in Computing Research*, 2:95-114, 1984.

[4] T. H. Cormen, C. E. Leiserson, and R. L. Rivest. *Introduction to Algorithms*. MIT Press and McGraw-Hill, 1990.

[5] D. Dolev, F. T. Leighton, and H. Trickey. Planar embedding of planar graphs. *Advances in Computing Research*, 2:147-161, 1984.

[6] R. I. Greenberg and C. E. Leiserson. Randomized routing on fat-trees. In *26th Annual IEEE Symposium on Foundations of Computer Science*, 241-249, 1985.

[7] R. I. Greenberg and C. E. Leiserson. A compact layout for the three-dimensional tree of meshes. *Applied Mathematics Letters*, 1(2):171-176, 1988.

[8] J. W. Greene and A. El Gamal. Configuration of VLSI arrays in the presence of defects. *Journal of the ACM*, 31(4):694-717, 1984.

[9] H. T. Kung and C. E. Leiserson. Systolic arrays (for VLSI). In I. S. Duff and G. W. Stewart (eds.), *Sparse Matrix Proceedings 1978*, 256-282. SIAM, 1979.

[10] F. T. Leighton. A layout strategy for VLSI which is provably good. In *14th Annual ACM Symposium on Theory of Computing*, 85-98, 1982.

[11] F. T. Leighton and C. E. Leiserson. Wafer-scale integration of systolic arrays. *IEEE Transactions on Computers*, C-34(5):448-461, 1985.

[12] F. T. Leighton and C. E. Leiserson. A survey of algorithms for integrating wafer-scale systolic arrays. In *IFIP Conference on Wafer-Scale Integration*, 177-195, 1986.

[13] F. T. Leighton, B. Maggs, and S. Rao. Universal packet routing algorithms. In *29th Annual IEEE Symposium on Foundations of Computer Science*, 256-271, 1988.

[14] F. T. Leighton and A. L. Rosenberg. Three-dimensional circuit layouts. *SIAM Journal on Computing*, 15(3):793-813, 1986.

[15] C. E. Leiserson. Area-efficient graph layouts for VLSI. In *21st Annual IEEE Symposium on Foundations of Computer Science*, 199-214, 1980.

[16] C. E. Leiserson. *Area-Efficient VLSI Computation*. ACM doctoral dissertation award series. MIT Press, Cambridge, MA, 1983.

[17] C. E. Leiserson. Fat-trees: universal networks for hardware-efficient super-computing. *IEEE Transactions on Computers*, C-34(10):892-901, 1985.

[18] C. E. Leiserson. VLSI theory and parallel supercomputing. In *Decennial Caltech Conference on VLSI*, 5-16. MIT Press, Cambridge, MA, 1989.

[19] C. E. Leiserson and B. M. Maggs. Communication-efficient parallel algorithms for distributed random-access machines. *Algorithmica*, 3:53-77, 1988.

[20] M. S. Paterson, W. L. Ruzzo, and L. Snyder. Bounds on minimax edge length for complete binary trees. In *13th Annual ACM Symposium on Theory of Computing*, 293-299, 1981.

[21] A. L. Rosenberg. Three-dimensional integrated circuitry. In H. T. Kung, R. Sproull, and G. L. Steele Jr. (eds.), *VLSI Systems and Computations*, 69-79. Computer Science Press, 1981.

[22] A. L. Rosenberg. The Diogenes approach to testable fault-tolerant networks of processors. Technical memorandum CS-1982-6.1, Department of Computer Science, Duke University, 1982.

[23] W. L. Ruzzo and L. Snyder. Minimum edge length planar embeddings of trees. In H. T. Kung, R. Sproull, and G. L. Steele Jr. (eds.), *VLSI Systems and Computations*, 119-123. Computer Science Press, 1981.

[24] C. D. Thompson. Area-time complexity for VLSI. In *Caltech Conference on Very Large Scale Integreation*, 495-508, 1979.

[25] L. G. Valiant. Universality considerations in VLSI circuits. *IEEE Transactions on Computers*, C-30(2):135-140, 1981.

[26] L. G. Valiant. A scheme for fast parallel computation. *SIAM Journal on Computing*, 11(2):350-361, 1982.

# PART TWO

# Languages and Tools

# 3

---

# Expressing Temporal Behavior Declaratively

Roger B. Dannenberg

The programming language Arctic specifies real-time behavior declaratively by using temporal control constructs and by indicating starting times and durations explicitly, much the way timing is specified in a cue sheet or a musical score. Values in Arctic are functions of time, which may be combined with various arithmetic and logical operators. Since Arctic is a single assignment language, the execution order is implied by data dependencies, simplifying synchronization problems for the programmer. Arctic supports behavioral abstraction, in which a single program module gives rise, through various transformations, to a class of behaviors. An implementation of Arctic is described, and experience with the declarative approach to real-time control is discussed.

---

## 3.1   Introduction

For the most part, traditional programming languages have been designed for applications where control over the timing of execution is not a primary concern. Users usually want their programs to run as fast as possible, but program correctness is not affected by program speed. In contrast, for some applications it is necessary to specify not only output values, but the times at which output values are to be produced. A "correct" value that is early or late is not acceptable.

The most common examples of applications where timing is central are real-time programs that control physical devices. Real-time systems are commonly used for controlling appliances, robots, vehicles, power plants, and manufacturing processes. Time is also important in non-real-time applications such as some computer animation and computer music systems. In these applications, images or sounds are computed and stored for real-time playback at a later time. Even though this computation is not in real-time, temporal behavior in the "virtual time" of the output medium (frames of film or samples of audio) is still of the utmost importance. Simulation is another example of a non-real-time application area in which (virtual) time is still important.

Research in computer music has resulted in a number of innovative languages [2,4,6,8,19] and systems [7,12,13,18] for dealing with virtual and real time. This is not too surprising given that music can be defined as sound organized in time. Long before electronic computers, traditional music notation allowed composers to create temporal specifications which include loops, counters, conditionals, and other constructs familiar to modern-day programmers [11].

In the following sections, I will describe the language Arctic [17], for expressing temporal behavior. Two variants of Arctic, called Canon [9] and Fugue [10], have similar semantics but deal with different domains. A real-time implementation of Arctic is in progress and will also be described.

## 3.2   Related Work

Arctic is based on earlier work in the computer music field including the Music V language [14] by Max Mathews and 4CED [1] by Curtis Abbot. Music V was designed to synthesize music in non-real-time and consists of two parts called the score language and the orchestra language. Music V was innovative in several ways:

□ First, the Music V score language allows users to specify a list of notes and when they should occur. The idea of associating an explicit time with program statements is quite different from the use of clocks and synchronization primitives in more traditional languages.

□ Second, statements in the Music V score language serve as "triggers" that start instances of instruments described in the orchestra language. This provides a natural form of parallelism and also serves to link discrete events to continuous-time[1] signals. (We will use the term signal throughout to mean a real-valued function of time. Do not confuse signals in Arctic with synchronization mechanisms of other languages by the same name.)

□ Third, the orchestra language is essentially a data-flow language in which operators are connected by data streams. (Music V predated data-flow architectures and streams by several years.) This turns out to be a natural way to describe operations on continuous-time signals.

The 4CED language was influenced by Music V but is more dynamic. 4CED is a real-time language for controlling a digital audio signal processor, hence external sensors can trigger timed sequences similar to Music V scores.

Assuming that these continuous-time signals in Arctic are actually implemented as sequences of discrete values, Arctic bears a similarity to the languages Lucid [3] and Val [16], which are also functional or data-flow languages for manipulating sequences. One major difference, however, is that in Arctic, variables are functions of a single global time, while in Lucid and Val, sequences can be computed and indexed without any connection to time. Another related language is L.0 [5], which treats time as a sequence of discrete steps and uses a very general naming and scoping mechanism but is otherwise much like Arctic.

## 3.3  The Programming Language Arctic

Arctic has two primary ingredients that distinguish it from other functional languages. First, there is a mechanism for specifying *when* things are to be computed. A variety of control constructs and operators make it possible to give explicit specifications of temporal behavior. Second, expressions manipulate functions of time. For example, writing

$a := b + c$

defines the signal $a(t)$ to be the sum of two signals $b(t) + c(t)$.

The primary abstraction mechanism in Arctic is the *prototype*, a named behavior that can be instantiated any number of times. A prototype in Arctic is analogous to a function or procedure in other languages, but it is important to note that prototypes specify behaviors that exist over time. Let us illustrate some simple Arctic expressions using prototypes. The expression

*ramp*

---

[1] Here, continuous-time refers to functions of time in which time is thought of as continuous (real). In contrast, discrete events occur at some countable set of time points. In practice, even continuous-time signals require a finite (and therefore discrete) representation such as samples or piecewise linear representations.

denotes an instance of *ramp*, a built-in prototype representing a linear interpolation from 0 to 1, nominally over the time interval (0, 1). (Signals are
always computed over some interval that is open on the left and closed on
the right.)

The ability to give explicit timing specifications is illustrated by the following expression:

> *ramp* @ 3

that denotes an instance of *ramp* that begins at time 3 and ends at time 4.

Notice in these examples how expressions for discrete-time events (e.g.,
"start the ramp at time 3") can give rise to continuous-time signals (e.g., in-
terpolate from 0 to 1 on the interval 3 to 4). This mechanism is an important
bridge between the worlds of discrete time and continuous time, both of which
are important in real-time systems.

---

## 3.4   Temporal Specification

This section expands upon the facilities in Arctic for specifying temporal behavior of discrete-time computation. Control constructs are provided to support
parallelism, sequential execution, shifting, and stretching, as well as temporal
versions of conditional and iterative expressions.

### 3.4.1   Parallel Collections

Arctic has constructs for parallel and sequential collections of behaviors. The
parallel collection is a list of expressions enclosed in brackets and separated by
semicolons: the expression

> [ *A*; *B*; *C* ]

denotes the simultaneous instantiation of prototypes *A*, *B*, and *C*.

### 3.4.2   Sequential Collections

The sequential collection uses the vertical bar as a separator: the expression

> [ *A* | *B* | *C* ]

denotes the sequence *A* followed by *B* followed by *C*. In Arctic, all instances of
prototypes have durations in addition to starting times so that sequential behavior
is well defined.

### 3.4.3  Transformations

When a prototype is instantiated, it is passed two implicit parameters, called the *start time* and *duration factor*. These tell the prototype instance when to start and by how much to stretch the nominal duration. These implicit parameters can be altered by various operators including @, @@, ˜, and ˜˜. To explain these operators, it is best to show the start time and duration factor explicitly within braces:

$$(A @ t)\{s, d\} \ \& = \& \ A\{s + td, d\}$$
$$(A \ ˜ \ x)\{s, d\} \ \& = \& \ A\{x, dx\}$$
$$(A @@ t)\{s, d\} \ \& = \& \ A\{t, d\}$$
$$(A \ ˜˜ \ x)\{s, d\} \ \& = \& \ A\{s, x\}$$

Thus @ (called *shift*) provides relative time-shift and @@ provides absolute time-shifting. Similarly, ˜ (called *stretch*) provides relative duration scaling and ˜˜ provides absolute duration scaling. As an example, consider the expression *A @ 5 ˜ 2* evaluated at the top-level, where the default starting time is 0 and duration factor is 1:

$$(A @ 5 \ ˜ \ 2)\{0, 1\} \ @!= (A @ 5)\{0, 2\}$$
$$@/= A\{10, 2\}$$

So *A @ 5 ˜ 2* starting at time 0 with duration factor 1 is equivalent to *A* starting at time 10 with duration factor 2.

Most Arctic expressions return two values: a signal and a stop time. Signals will be discussed in the next section. The stop time conveys the duration of the behavior, which is needed in sequential collections. The programmer can override the stop time by providing an explicit one: $A \ \$ \ x\{s, d\}$ has a stop time of $s + dx$ and $A \ \$\$ \ x\{s, d\}$ has a stop time of $x$.

### 3.4.4  Defining Prototypes

Transformations are dynamically scoped. If there is a definition

   *Name* **is** *Body*;

then *Name*$\{s, d\}$ denotes *Body*$\{s, d\}$. For example, a new prototype can be defined as follows:

   *MyProto* **is** [ *A*; *B* @ 1; *C* @ 2];

We can then write an expression such as *MyProto ˜ 2*, which means:

   [ *A*; *B* @ 1; *C* @ 2] ˜ 2

### 3.4.5  Conditionals and Iteration

Conditional execution can be obtained with a conventional-looking **if** construct:

**if** $C$ **then** $A$ **else** $B$;

where $C$ is a conditional expression and $A$ and $B$ are prototype expressions. The condition $C$ is tested at the start time of the **if** and then either $A$ or $B$ are instantiated.

Iteration can be accomplished using the **while** construct:

**while** $C$ **do** $A$

which is equivalent to an infinitely nested **if**:

**if** $C$ **then** [ @!$A$ |
@/**if** $C$ **then** @![ $A$ |
@/...
@/]];

The result is a sequence of $As$, which is terminated when $C$ becomes false. The condition $C$ is only tested before each instantiation of $A$.

## 3.5  Signals

The most interesting data type in Arctic is the signal, which represents a real-valued function of time over some interval. Signals are returned from instances of prototypes, including many built-in prototypes, signals may be assigned to variables, and signals may be combined using various arithmetic and logical operators.

### 3.5.1  Prototypes

The *ramp* prototype seen earlier is a good example of a built-in prototype that returns a signal and stop time. We can now give a more formal description of *ramp*. Just as we introduced the extended notation "$\{s, d\}$" to make start times and duration factors explicit, we will now introduce the notation "$(t)$" so that we can talk about signals as a function of time. If $s$ is a signal, then $s(t)$ is the value of the signal at time $t$. The stop time is indicated by the extended notation ".stop"; for example, if $I$ is an instance of a prototype, then $I$.stop denotes the stop time of the instance.

$ramp\{s, d\}(t) =$
& 0 for $t <= s$ or $t > s + d$

& $(t - s) / d$ for $s < t <= s + d$
$ramp\{s, d\}$.stop = $s + d$

We can now give a more formal description of parallel collections:

$[ A; B; ... ]\{s, d\} =$
& $[ A\{s, d\}; B\{s, d\}; ... ]$
$[A; B; ... ]\{s, d\}(t) =$
& $A\{s, d\}(t)$
$[A; B; ... ]\{s, d\}$.stop =
& $max(@!A\{s, d\}$.stop,
$@/B\{s, d\}$.stop,
$@/...)$

This description is in three parts. The first part indicates that an instance of a collection is simply a collection of instances with the same start time and duration factor. The second part indicates that the signal returned by the collection is the signal returned by the first instance of the collection. The third part indicates that the stop time of the collection is the maximum of the stop times of the instances of the collection. This description is still not complete because it omits any specification of naming, parameter passing, and effects on global variables. More detail will be presented in Section 3.5.2, and a complete description can be found in the Arctic reference manual [17].

We can also describe sequential collections in terms of the parallel collection:

$[ A \mid B \mid C \mid ... ]\{s, d\} =$
& $[ @!A\{s, d\};$
$@/B\{A\{s, d\}$.stop, $d\};$
$@/C\{B\{A\{s, d\}$.stop, $d\}$.stop, $d\};$
$@/... ]$
$[ A \mid B \mid C \mid ... ]\{s, d\}(t) =$
& $A\{s, d\}(t) +$
& $B\{A\{s, d\}$.stop), $d\} +$
& $C\{B\{A\{s, d\}$.stop), $d\}$.stop), $d\} +$
& ...
$[ A \mid B \mid C \mid ... \mid Y \mid Z ]\{s, d\}$.stop =
& $Z\{Y\{ ..., d\}$.stop, $d\}$.stop

This collection indicates that $B$ is instantiated at the stop time of $B$, and $C$ is instantiated at the stop time of $C$, etc. The definition is not quite correct because it calls for more than one instance of each prototype except the last one; however, the implementation must ensure that there is only one instance of each prototype in the sequence. The second part indicates that the signal returned is the sum of the signals returned by the elements of the sequence, and the third part indicates that the stop time of the sequence is the stop time of the last element of the sequence.

### 3.5.2  Values, Variables, and Assignment

Values in Arctic may be either real or boolean and may be scalars or signals, giving a cross-product of four types. In mixed expressions, scalars are coerced to constant signals; for example, in the expression $1 - ramp$, the scalar 1 is coerced to $step(1)$, which is defined as follows:

$step(c)\{s, d\}(t) =$
& 0 for $t <= s$
& c for $t > s$

In this definition, constants are coerced to signals that are zero previous to the start time. This definition is a desirable because we do not want the creation of an instance to affect history, making programs noncausal.

Variables may be declared in Arctic and used in expressions. Arctic is a single assignment language, so an instance of a variable may only be assigned once; however, the signal being assigned to a variable may be a function of time. For example, we can write

$output := x * input$;
$x := 1 - ramp$;

Here, $x$, $input$, and $output$ are variables. Assignments in Arctic establish one-way constraints:

$var := expr\{s, d\}$ implies
& $var(t) = expr(t)$ for $t > s$

This in turn imposes a partial ordering on the evaluation order of Arctic assignments and expressions. In the preceding example, it is necessary to evaluate the second assignment to obtain $x$ before evaluating the first assignment that uses $x$. (A real-time implementation would evaluate both assignments at every time-step in the implied partial order.)

## 3.6   Termination of Expressions

So far, we have seen how discrete events can give rise to continuous signals. In Arctic, events can also terminate computations and replace them with new ones. The **do-until** control construct is used for this purpose. For example,

**do** $A := ramp$ **until** $A >= input$ **then** $input$

means to compute a linear ramp and assign it to *A* as long as *A* is less than *input*. At that point, stop computing the ramp (*A* will subsequently be zero) and return the value of *input*. Assuming *input* is between 0 and 1, the value of the **do-until** expression makes a smooth transition from 0 to *input*.

If the **do** part of the **do-until** expression finishes before (or even when) the condition becomes true, then the entire expression finishes immediately. Otherwise, the expression finishes when the **then** part finishes.

It is possible to wait for the instantiation of a prototype using an **event** expression:

**do** *P* **until** (**event** *ButtonPress*(*b*) **where** *b* = 1)

which means to terminate *P* if *ButtonPress(1)* is instantiated. Whenever *ButtonPress* is instantiated, **event** *ButtonPress*(*x*) becomes true and *x* is bound to the current value of the parameter passed to the *ButtonPress* prototype. The scope of *x* is the expression following the keyword **where**.

Note the similarity between **event** expressions and the rendezvous in Ada. Both are a means of momentarily synchronizing the execution of two independent but communicating threads of control. In Arctic the joining is "instantaneous" and does not cause blocking or queueing.

## 3.7  Application in Various Domains

Variants of Arctic have been constructed for three different domains. All of the variants are interpreters that operate out of real time on data describing temporal behavior.

### 3.7.1  Interpreted Arctic

The first variant computes piecewise linear functions, which are typically used to control synthesis processes. For example, control functions might specify the pitch, amplitude, and harmonic content of an audio oscillator. This version of Arctic [17] has been used to compose music, to synthesize warning tones for nuclear reactors, and to generate test signals for laboratory instrumentation.

This is a "variant" of Arctic in the sense that functions are not computed in real time or even in time order. For example, the expression *(a + b) \* c* would be interpreted by constructing the sum of signals *a* and *b* and then multiplying[2]

---

[2] Since piecewise linear functions are not closed under multiplication, we conveniently define multiplication in the Arctic interpreter to yield correct breakpoints wherever breakpoints occur in the factors. All other points in the result are defined by the linear interpolation of these breakpoints.

by $c$. Because signals are piecewise linear, they can be stored compactly as a list of breakpoints. The interpreter uses static analysis of the parse tree to determine the order of expression evaluation.

### 3.7.2  Canon

Unlike the first variant, which implements Arctic syntax, the second variant, named Canon [9], is embedded in Lisp. Canon operates on sequences of musical notes that have several properties, including pitch, loudness, starting time, and duration. These properties can be altered using transformations analogous to the shift and stretch transformations already discussed. For example,

```
(defun triad ()
(seq (note C4) (note E4) (note G4)))
(play (transpose 3 (loud -20 (triad))))
```

defines `triad` to be a sequence of three notes with pitches C4, E4, and G4. (This sequence is called a major triad). The `triad` behavior is transposed by three semitones and softened through the use of a negative loudness offset.

Canon does not include signals as an ordinary data type as does Arctic. However, Canon does allow transformations to be time-varying. For example, it is often useful to gradually increase the loudness of a phrase of music. This can be accomplished in Canon by specifying a loudness contour to the `loud` transformation:

```
(loud (env (0 0) (1000 30) (2000 10))
(myscore))
```

In this example, the `env` function constructs a piecewise linear contour that increases from 0 to 30 over the first 10 seconds and then decreases to 10 after a total elapsed time of 20 seconds. The contour is evaluated at the note starting-times to determine the loudness offset for each note in `myscore`.

As with ordinary transformations, time-varying transformations can be nested. The most interesting time-varying transformation is **warp**, which implements time mapping. The time map transforms "program time" or "virtual time" into real time according to an arbitrary (but monotonically increasing) function, allowing easy specification of music that accelerates or slows down. Unfortunately, the contours used to specify time-varying transformation are not supported by a rich set of operations as are signals in Arctic. This is a limitation of the implementation but not of the general approach.

The Lisp environment used by Canon allows composers to take advantage of a rich language for expressions and data structures; it also minimizes the implementation effort. In fact, Canon control constructs are implemented as macros. The implementation is simplified by the fact that there are no signals or (single) assignments supported by Canon. Canon illustrates that the timing and transformation semantics of Arctic can be put to good use in other language contexts.

### 3.7.3  Fugue

The third variant, called Fugue, is also embedded in Lisp. Fugue is much like Canon, but rather than computing note-level information, Fugue is intended to compute sampled audio and control signals. Fugue expressions return values of type Sound. The implementation uses a modified Lisp where Sounds and various operations on Sounds are primitives. Operations include reading and writing Sounds from files and adding, scaling, multiplying, shifting, filtering, and stretching Sounds. Various Sound synthesis operations such as software oscillators are also present.

Although our modified Lisp could be used directly for sound synthesis by writing programs that call upon the primitive Sound operations, Fugue provides a higher-level language in which time and other transformations can be used to modify behaviors. For example, a programmer could develop a way of combining oscillators and filters to obtain an interesting sound. This technique could be encapsulated in a function called mysound. Then, using the Arctic-like semantics of Fugue, mysound could be instantiated with different transformations to construct a musical phrase:

```
(defun phrase ()
(sim (at 0.0 (mysound))
(at 1.0 (stretch 0.5 (transpose 3 (mysound))))
(at 1.5 (stretch 0.5 (transpose 2 (mysound))))
(at 2.0 (transpose 10 (mysound)))
(at 2.5 (transpose 9 (mysound)))))
```

In practice, mysound would probably take a pitch parameter to eliminate the need for the wordier transpose operations. Notice how easily (and declaratively) the sim (for "simultaneous") construct combined with the at (shift) operation allows the programmer to arrange instances of mysound in time. The sim construct sums (mixes) the resulting sounds so that phrase returns a single composite sound.

To illustrate how mysound might be written, here is a simple function that uses an oscillator scaled by an envelope to generate a sound:

```
(defun mysound ()
(s-mult (osc) (env (0 0) (0.1 1) (0.7 1) (1 0))))
```

Both the osc and env primitives respond appropriately to various transformations so transpose, at, and stretch transformations will have the desired effect.

An interesting aspect of the Fugue implementation is that many operations on sounds are implemented using lazy evaluation. This is possible because, in keeping with the functional style of Arctic, sounds are immutable values. When two sounds are added together, the sum is represented by a small node containing pointers to the two sounds. This reduces storage requirements (digital audio requires up to 200 KBytes/second) and allows multiple operations, such as shifting, scaling, and adding to be performed in a single pass over the data.

## 3.8    A Real-Time Implementation

One of the great challenges of Arctic has been to devise a reasonable real-time implementation. A real-time implementation must solve two problems: how to manage instantiation and timing of Arctic prototypes (discrete-time computation) and how to compute time-varying signals (continuous-time computation).

### 3.8.1    Data Dependencies

For the time being, assume that real-time Arctic signals will be represented as a stream of samples. For example, the signal denoted by the variable $A$ will be represented by a single memory location that is updated regularly at an interval called the time step. At any given instant during the execution of an Arctic program, there are a number of active primitives that generate signals as well as operators that combine signals, creating a data-flow graph. For example, the following expressions:

[ @!A := B + 5;
@/B := (ramp * 3);
@/C := B * input ]

would give rise to the graph in Exhibit 3.1.

If this graph were in effect for the duration of the program execution, it would be a simple matter to perform a topological sort on the data dependencies to derive an order of evaluation. This could then be used to produce a sequential program to be executed every sample time.

Unfortunately, this approach will not work because instantiation of prototypes and termination of instances modify the flow graph dynamically. The sequential collection and **do-until** constructs are language mechanisms that can give rise to dynamically changing graphs. Furthermore, instantiation can be driven by input data that is unknown at compile-time, and parameter-passing allows essentially arbitrary (and nonhierarchical) flow graphs to be realized.

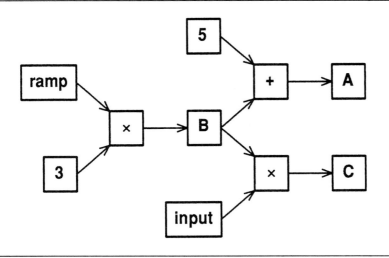

**EXHIBIT 3.1**
Data flow graph for an Arctic program.

Because of these complications, the current implementation approach uses "lazy" or demand-driven evaluation to compute signals. Instances of expressions have at least three components: a method called "update" for computing the current value, a storage location for holding a value, and a time-stamp denoting when the value was computed. The algorithm for computing the current value of an expression is the following:

```
access(exp)
     begin
          if exp.timestamp < globaltime
          then
               begin
                    exp.timestamp := globaltime;
                    exp.value := (exp.update)(exp);
               end
          return exp.value;
     end
```

To get the value of an expression, the time-stamp is compared to the global time. If less, the update method is called to produce a new value. Typically, the update method will recursively *access* subexpressions and variables. The effect is to bring values up-to-date in an order that is consistent with data dependencies.

The order is computed dynamically. Values are cached so that expressions are recomputed at most once per time step.

As in other lazy evaluation systems, computation is driven by the demand for output values. Arctic variables can be designated as output signals. The declaration "**out** *X*;" indicates that one of the system outputs is the value of the variable *X*. The main program calls *access* to get the value of each output variable on each time step. This serves to drive all necessary signal computation.

Lazy evaluation is not appropriate in prototypes that compute their signals incrementally. For example, the *ramp* prototype adds a slope to an accumulator on every time step to avoid a more expensive interpolation operation. The update method of *ramp* must be called on every sample to ensure correctness. For this reason, a list of active expressions is kept at run-time, and expressions on the list are updated on every time step along with output variables.

### 3.8.2  Instantiation

One of the features of Arctic is that prototypes can be instantiated dynamically and in parallel. Instances exist over time, and computation is interleaved among active instances. The current implementation solves this problem using object-oriented programming techniques. Prototypes are compiled into classes, and the run-time instantiation of an Arctic prototype is implemented by creating a new instance of the class at run time.

When an Arctic prototype is specified in terms of a collection of other prototypes, the implementation will be a collection of corresponding objects. What should be the granularity of objects? Should each arithmetic operator be handled by a separate object? Alternatively, can several assignments be grouped into a single object? In general, since the overhead of the *access* procedure is fairly high, objects should encompass as many operations as possible for efficiency. On the other hand, it is not always possible to determine whether two assignments are dependent, so in the current implementation, a class is generated for each assignment in the Arctic source program. Also, whenever the right-hand side of an assignment includes a prototype, the prototype is implemented by a separate object rather than being expanded in-line.

One of the greatest difficulties in the implementation has been getting correct behavior at the start and stop times of instances. The first approach attempted to use a signaling mechanism, whereby a child object (subexpression) would notify its parent at the stop time by invoking a prespecified method. One of the problems with this approach is the race condition where the parent's value for a particular time step might depend upon whether the value was updated before or after notification from a child.

The solution came with the realization that stop times can be treated as values rather than events and that data dependencies can be used to eliminate race conditions. This approach is supported by the existing lazy evaluation scheme. The view that stop time is a computed value is reflected in the descriptions of control constructs in Section 3.5.1.

### 3.8.3  Performance

The real-time Arctic implementation is still in progress, so only preliminary performance measurements are available. In order to develop and test implementation techniques, programs are hand-compiled into an object-oriented dialect of the C programming language. Arctic primitives are provided by a run-time system, and much of the behavior of collections, sequences, and assignments can be inherited from generic classes, so the translation effort is tedious but not exhausting.

A 16 MHz Motorola 68020 with a 68881 floating point coprocessor is used for real-time execution, and Arctic program outputs are used to control the pitch and amplitude of a bank of eight music synthesizers. Real-time input can be generated from a music keyboard, as well as from buttons and knobs.

A single program was used to measure performance. The program responds to input from a music keyboard and a knob. When a key is pressed, the Arctic program generates time-varying pitch and amplitude contours for one of the eight synthesizers until the key is released.

The real-time requirements of Arctic are application dependent, but for music it is desirable to process input and compute several interesting control functions at rates of 100 to 200 samples per second [15]. This data rate represents approximately the bandwidth of a human interacting with a musical instrument. The determination of what is an "interesting" control function is very subjective. With the expressive power of Arctic, the computation per sample can become substantial with only a modest programming effort.

Rather than measure samples computed per second, it is perhaps more informative to measure evaluations per second. By running as fast as possible and eliminating calls that actually output data, the current implementation performs 12,800 value accesses per second. Of these evaluations, 6,100 invoke an object's update method, and the other 6,700 find the object up-to-date and simply use the current value. Evaluations include not only expressions that do the real work but also expressions such as sequential collections that merely channel signals from subexpressions. About 2,800 "useful" expressions involving arithmetic operations are evaluated per second.

Another measure of performance is the latency from input to output. For signal input, input changes are received asynchronously and are read into Arctic variables at the beginning of every time step. This means that data arriving just after the beginning of a time step will not be seen until the next step. If the Arctic program takes an entire time step to compute outputs, then the latency from signal input to output is always less than two time steps. The variance of this latency could be made essentially zero by waiting for the full worst case delay before performing any output operations.

An alternative implementation approach would be to dispense with dependency checking and simply reevaluate all active objects as fast as possible. This makes sense if the speedup due to lower overhead compensates for the additional latency introduced by a less-than-optimal evaluation order. In the program studied, the maximum depth of recursion of the update algorithm was measured as 5, indicating that signals propagate through 5 levels of expressions even in fairly simple programs. The dependency checking and dynamic ordering of expressions is cost-effective because the overhead does not approach the delay that would result from the worst-case evaluation order.

Discrete event input is queued by the system, and the queue is checked at the beginning of each time step. Discrete outputs will be generated in response during the time step, so the latency is again less than two time steps. When would an output signal be affected by a discrete input? Intervals in Arctic are closed on the right, so a signal that is terminated in time step $T$ is not seen to change behavior until time $T + 1$. Similarly, if an instance is created at time $T$, it does not affect signals until time $T + 1$. Thus the latency from discrete input to an output signal is at most three time steps.

The current implementation is a "soft" real-time system; that is, it tries to deliver results as close to the specified output time as possible. When a deadline is not met, results are delivered late and in time order. Since Arctic programs respond to events by instantiating or terminating instances, it is important to know how long these operations take. A frequent cause of missing deadlines will be the extra load created by many simultaneous events. In the current system, the key-down event immediately instantiates 12 prototypes. By simulating simultaneous key-down events, an average prototype instantiation time of 660 $\mu$s (microseconds) was obtained.

All of these numbers reflect an implementation in C with a minimal amount of optimization. (One exception is that the already up-to-date case of *access* is compiled in-line.) In addition, the implementation includes extra code for instrumentation. Performance could probably be improved by a factor of 2 or 3, and a faster processor could be used for additional speedup.

## 3.9  Behavioral Abstraction

It is often easier to describe a class of similar behaviors than it is to describe each individual behavior separately. For example, if similar control sequences and signals of different durations are required, it is probably easier to parameterize one program than to write separate programs for each desired duration. A program or prototype that implements a class of similar behaviors is called a *behavioral abstraction*. Arctic, Fugue, and Canon all support the definition and use of behavioral abstractions.

A key idea behind behavioral abstraction is that behaviors do not always transform in a straightforward linear manner. For example, if a violinist were asked to play a note longer than its normal duration, what would be the expected result? Would the pitch be lowered so that the same number of oscillations would fill the allotted time? Would the violinist move the bow more slowly and thus play softer? Would the vibrato be slowed down as well? All of these suggestions are absurd, because we understand "playing a note" to be a particular abstract behavior, and we know (or at least a violinist knows) what it means to apply various transformations to "playing a note," such as stretching and transposing.

It is important that Arctic and its cousins be able to express behavioral abstractions of this sort. As the musical example illustrates, it is generally not sufficient simply to shift and stretch all subexpressions in order to "shift" or "stretch" a behavioral abstraction. Arctic allows the programmer to override the default behavior of transformations in order to achieve the desired behavior. The transformation details are a part of the prototype specification. Abstraction is achieved because the implementation details are separated (and hidden) from the rest of the program.

To illustrate with a concrete example, suppose we have a large program for controlling a household robot, a part of which is used for opening doors:

*openDoor(D)* **is**
    [ @!*moveToDoor(D)* | *turnDoorKnob(D)* |
@/*swingOpen(D)* | *releaseDoorKnob(D)* ];

so that instantiating *openDoor(D)* will cause the robot to open door *D*. Now suppose we want to instruct the robot to open a door slowly. Instantiating *open-Door(D)* ˜ 2 will do the job, but we notice that the robot approaches the door and turns the door knob slowly as well. This is not what we want, so the *openDoor* prototype is redefined as follows:

*openDoor(D)* **is**
    [ @![ *moveToDoor(D)* | *turnDoorKnob(D)* ] ˜˜ 1 |
@/*swingOpen(D)* | *releaseDoorKnob(D)* ˜˜ 1 ];

Here, the "absolute stretch" operator (˜˜) has been used to override the duration factor to all components of *openDoor* except for *swingOpen*. Thus the duration factor supplied to *openDoor* is only passed on to *swingOpen*, and the robot will now approach the door and turn the knob at normal speed.

Prototype specifications can access their own start time and duration factor using the symbols *time* and *dur*. Prototypes can also refer to global variables (signals). These mechanisms give the programmer complete access to the transformation environment and the ability to override the default transformation semantics with another behavior.

## 3.10    Discussion

After five years and four implementation efforts, much has been learned about Arctic, but there are still many open issues and problems to be solved. We will discuss the strengths and weaknesses of Arctic and suggest directions for future research.

### 3.10.1    Strengths of Arctic

Probably the most interesting feature of Arctic is its explicit and declarative approach to timing specification. Timing in procedural languages is implicit and arises as a consequence of sequential execution, while timing in Arctic is explicitly specified through the use of the *shift* transformation and various temporal control constructs. On the other hand, procedural languages use explicit syntax to indicate synchronization, while Arctic synchronization is implicit due to the single assignment rule and data dependencies.

A consequence of explicit timing in Arctic is that Arctic programs provide a very high-level declarative specification of temporal behavior that is similar in many ways to musical scores, scripts, and cue sheets used in the arts. The implicit synchronization provided by the single assignment rule has been the basis for a number of other languages and machines supporting parallelism, and it seems particularly appropriate for computing streams and signals.

### 3.10.2    Weaknesses of Arctic

Real-time systems have traditionally been programmed in fairly low-level procedural languages. Procedural languages provide a close match to the underlying hardware in terms of modifiable storage and sequential execution. When the synchronization support provided by Arctic is not needed and when discrete algorithms involving data structures are required, the synchronization and temporal specification features of Arctic are of little if any help.

Although techniques such as lazy evaluation, caching the results of functions, and various program transformations, can often evaluate declarative programs as efficiently as their imperative counterparts, the complexity of the implementation techniques can be high. The Arctic run-time system is an example of the relative complexity required for a declarative approach to real-time control. It is also telling that the Arctic run-time system is implemented using an imperative object-oriented technique.

Arctic is not really a complete language in that it lacks data structures and data abstraction mechanisms. Arctic is also lacking any mechanism for mutual exclusion. These are not so much problems with the approach as a result of focusing research on the interesting aspects of Arctic.

### 3.10.3   Directions for Future Research

There are a number of open issues related to the design and implementation of Arctic. One of the major sources of inefficiency in the current language and implementation is the fact that the execution order of expressions must be determined at run-time. One could argue that the execution order should be computed only after the data-flow graph is modified by an instantiation. This would reduce the total computation but would probably increase the worst-case latency.

At least four approaches might be taken to reduce the overhead of determining execution order. First, static analysis might be able to determine that fairly large subgraphs can be compiled as in-line code. Second, language restrictions might make it possible to determine execution order without lazy evaluation. For example, if variables and parameters were eliminated, the resulting dependency graph would be a tree, and a depth-first traversal of the tree would generate a legal execution order. Perhaps there are less restrictive alternatives. Third, special hardware support for checking time stamps might provide substantial speedup. Finally, in some situations, it makes sense to cache the execution order and reuse it until the graph changes. In general, this saves total execution time but increases the worst-case latency.

The present implementation spends a fair amount of time testing whether instances have stopped. Unlike signals, which tend to change at every time step, the boolean flag indicating that an instance has stopped only changes once. An implementation that propagates this change to dependents could eliminate the need to test for a change on every time step.

The current implementation does not perform storage reclamation. Both reference counting and parallel garbage collection are viable strategies. An interesting problem is how to stop the computation of "orphan" signals that can never affect any output variables. A related problem is the dynamic optimization of Arctic signal computations. For example, if two signals are being multiplied and one of them permanently goes to zero, then the multiplication can be replaced by the constant zero. The present system can successfully perform dynamic optimization, but good strategies for directing optimization effort have not been studied.

Another area for exploration is the use of multiple clocks and multiple time steps. In many real-time systems, periodic computations (corresponding to Arctic signals) are performed at different frequencies depending upon the latency requirements of each computation. Arctic has no mechanisms for specifying the sample rate of signals, and it is not clear how signals computed at different sample rates would be combined. A related area is the specification of time mapping or time deformation, essentially allowing the rate of passage of time to be virtualized and controlled by the program. This is of particular interest in musical applications, but might also be relevant to testing and debugging in other applications.

A "pure" approach is useful for exploring the implications of declarative-style programming for language design and implementation, but this may not be the most effective way to put the resulting techniques into practice. Just as "pure" Lisp is rarely if ever used for serious applications, it may be too much to expect that "pure" Arctic will be used for the serious implementation of real-time systems.

An alternative might be to look for ways that the declarative programming style and behavioral abstraction mechanisms of Arctic can be supported by more conventional imperative languages, run-time systems, and real-time operating systems. One idea is to implement a set of parameterized behaviors that can be instantiated from within an imperative language as in the existing object-oriented implementation. One might then supply an expression and let the run-time system keep the value of the expression up-to-date. Another idea is to extend an imperative language with some degree of lazy evaluation or other mechanism for maintaining one-way constraints.

## 3.11  Conclusions

Arctic has introduced a new declarative approach to the specification of temporal behavior. In contrast to imperative languages, Arctic allows timing to be specified explicitly and synchronization to be specified implicitly. One of the interesting aspects of Arctic is its support of behavioral abstraction in which real-time behavior classes called prototypes can be created and instantiated under different transformations. The standard transformations are stretching and shifting in time.

Four implementations and variations of Arctic have now been developed. These are an interpreter that operates on piecewise linear representations of signals, a language for describing and manipulating musical note sequences, a language for digital signal processing, and a real-time Arctic for processing data at moderate sample rates.

The Arctic approach seems particularly well suited to systems that synthesize rather complex output. These are applications where there is a need to assemble and schedule complex behaviors. In contrast, systems that test for conditions and respond immediately or that perform fixed arithmetic operations on a stream of samples are easily implemented in almost any language. An application area that has not been explored yet is computer animation. It seems reasonable that a language based on Arctic could provide temporal control over object positions and viewing parameters. In addition, the concept of behavioral abstraction could be applied with additional transformations to alter an object's size and position as well as the start time and duration of animated behaviors.

Future work on Arctic will include further development of the real time implementation and a continued effort to bring Arctic concepts into the realm of practical software engineering.

## 3.12  Acknowledgments

I am grateful to the School of Computer Science for making it possible to develop Arctic and for soliciting this report. Many people have played an important role in encouraging and supporting my work on computer music at Carnegie Mellon, and Arctic could not have developed without their enthusiasm. These include Nico Habermann, Phil Miller, Dana Scott, Raj Reddy, and Marilyn Taft Thomas. Others have worked more directly on Arctic. Paul McAvinney and I spent innumerable hours talking about and designing the first version of Arctic. Dean Rubine implemented the Arctic interpreter, which forced us to nail down a number of fuzzy design details. Chris Fraley implemented the bulk of Fugue, and George Polly provided additional development effort. Hal Mukaino helped design and begin the implementation of real-time Arctic. Frances Dannenberg provided helpful comments on this article.

Support for Arctic has come from the Defense Advanced Research Projects Agency and the Hughes Aircraft Corporation. The real-time Arctic effort and this chapter have been supported by a grant from Yamaha Music Technologies, Inc. Their support is greatly appreciated.

## References

[1] C. Abbot. The 4ced program. *Computer Music Journal*, 5(1):13-33, 1981.

[2] D. P. Anderson and R. Kuivila. Accurately timed generation of discrete musical events. *Computer Music Journal*, 10(3):48-56, 1986.

[3] E. A. Ashcroft and W. W. Wadge. Lucid, a nonprocedural language with iteration. *Communications of the ACM*, 20(7):519-526, 1977.

[4] M. Balaban.  Music structures: A temporal-hierarchical representation for music. Technical Report FC-TR-021 MCS-313, Ben Gurion University Department of Mathematics and Computer Science, 1989.

[5] D. M. Cohen, B. Gopinath, W. M. Keese II, L. Ness, P. Uppaluru, E. J. Cameron, and J. R. Vollaro. The ic* model of parallel computation and programming environment. *IEEE Transactions on Software Engineering*, 317-326, March 1988.

[6] P. Cointe and X. Rodet. Formes: an object and time oriented system for music composition and synthesis. In *ACM Symposium on LISP and Functional Programming*, 85-95. ACM, 1984.

[7] D. J. Collinge. Moxie: A language for computer music performance. In *Proceedings of the 1984 International Computer Music Conference*, 217-220, Computer Music Association, 1984.

[8] R. B. Dannenberg. Arctic: A functional language for real-time control. In *ACM Symposium on LISP and Functional Programming*, 96-103, ACM, 1984.

[9] Roger B. Dannenberg. The canon score language. *Computer Music Journal*, 13(1):47-56, 1989.

[10] R. B. Dannenberg and C. L. Fraley. Fugue: Composition and sound synthesis with lazy evaluation and behavioral abstraction. In *Proceedings of the 1989 International Computer Music Conference*, 76-79, Computer Music Association, San Francisco, CA, 1989.

[11] R. B. Dannenberg, F. K. Dannenberg and P. Miller. Teaching programming to musicians. In *1984 Proceedings of the Fourth Annual Symposium on Small Computers in the Arts*, 114-122, IEEE, October 1984.

[12] G. Greenberg. Procedural composition. In *Proceedings of the 1987 International Computer Music Conference*, 25-32, Computer Music Association, 1987.

[13] G. Greenberg. Composing with performer objects. In *Proceedings of the 1988 International Computer Music Conference*, 142-149, Computer Music Association, 1988.

[14] M. V. Mathews. *The Technology of Computer Music*. MIT Press, Boston, 1969.

[15] M. V. Mathews and F. R. Moore. A program to compose, store, and edit functions of time. *Communications of the ACM*, 13(12):715-721, 1970.

[16] J. R. McGraw. The val language: Description and analysis. *ACM Transactions on Programming Languages and Systems*, 4(1):44-82, 1982.

[17] D. Rubine and R. B. Dannenberg. Arctic programmer's manual and tutorial. Technical Report CMU-CS-87-110, Carnegie Mellon University, Pittsburgh, PA, 1987.

[18] C. Scaletti and E. Johnson. An interactive graphic environment for object-oriented music composition and sound synthesis. In *Proceedings of the 1988 Conference on Object-Oriented Languages and Systems*, 18-26, ACM, 1988.

[19] B. Schottstaedt. Pla: A composer's idea of a language. *Computer Music Journal*, 7(1):11-20, 1983.

# 4

# Generation of Integrated Task-Specific Software Environments

Nico Habermann, David Garlan, and David Notkin

Over the past 10 years (1980–1990) the Gandalf Project has investigated software environments that are interactive, integrated, task-specific, and have direct manipulation user interfaces. In this chapter we describe two major components of the research: tool integration and the generation of environments.

Tool integration is based on the sharing of structured collections of typed objects. Data sharing allows tools to communicate. Changes to data automatically trigger tool invocation. Using views, tools can define their own interface to shared objects.

Environment generation allows the practical development of a variety of task-specific environments. Each environment is generated by combining a formal description of its task-specific properties with a common environment kernel. A special environment has been constructed to ease the development of such a formal description and to generate the associated environment.

Using this special environment, numerous integrated, task-specific environments have been constructed. Our experience with generating these environments allows us to evaluate our overall approach and to identify fruitful ideas for improvements and for future work.

## 4.1   Introduction

A software environment provides software tools to help users perform a task. Examples include a programming language environment, which provides tools for editing, compiling, linking, and debugging computer programs, an electronic mail system, which provides tools for creating, viewing, and posting messages, an airline reservation system, which provides tools for booking flights, and a banking system, which provides tools to update and query customer accounts. Although each of these environments performs a vastly different function, each environment has the common objective of providing software tools to assist a user in accomplishing a task.

For more than a decade, research in software environments has been the primary objective of the Gandalf Project. Although the project designed and implemented many specific tools, it has primarily investigated the relationship among tools, the run-time support needed for operating a collection of tools, and the interfaces among users, tools, and the underlying operating system.

Naturally, the results of 10 years of research cannot be fully described in a single chapter. Consequently, this chapter focuses on two major research issues and provides pointers to documents covering other technical aspects of the project. The first issue is tool integration, which deals with the way tools work together and invoke each other without user intervention. The second issue is environment generation, which deals with the support provided to the designers of software environments for designing an environment and for generating the corresponding implementation.

Section 4.2 of the chapter discusses our basic assumptions about desirable properties of software environments. It then examines the consequences of incorporating these properties in all environments. Section 4.3 presents our specific approach to tool integration through the use of an active database and a view mechanism that allows objects to be handled in a tool-specific way. Section 4.4 describes the support facilities that the environment designer finds in the Gandalf System for defining tools and objects for the target environment. Section 4.5 appraises the main results of the project, discussing the original ideas and shortcomings of the project and comparing the project with others that adopted similar goals.

## 4.2   Desirable Characteristics

Numerous environments have been built to support software development. Some environments are constructed around a specific programming language; tools are then added for constructing systems out of program modules. Other environments are built as an extension of an operating system interface; they typically enhance a file system or a database with tools for system composition and version control. Yet others support a particular programming methodology that guides its users through the software development process.

The Gandalf approach to building environments (which it shares with other projects, as mentioned in Section 4.5) does not favor a particular programming language, nor does it promote a particular programming methodology. Instead, it emphasizes four basic characteristics, desirable in all environments, that determine the way tools work together and the way users interact with the environment. These four characteristics are the basic premises of our work: environments should be *interactive*, should be *task-specific*, should be based on *direct manipulation*, and should provide an *integrated* set of tools. Systems with one or more of these characteristics were available over ten years ago (in environments such as Interlisp [32] and Smalltalk [13]); further, they are commonplace today, as seen in systems like the Macintosh and Microsoft Windows. Gandalf is unique, however, in pioneering the combination of these four characteristics.

## 4.2.1  Interactive Environments

The popularity of interactive systems is evident from the ubiquitous use of personal workstations. The major advantage of interactive systems is the dialogue form of user-system interaction, which gives a user immediate feedback on whether a command has had the desired effect. This makes it easier for the user to find and fix simple errors. It also allows the user to try something and undo it if the result is not satisfactory. Such desirable properties are lacking in batch systems where input consists of long strings of instructions. (Even a source program can be viewed as an instruction sequence. This sequence is processed in batch-mode by a compiler.)

A potential drawback of interactive systems is the application of operations of long duration. Examples of such operations are compilers and linkers in program development, making up the inventory of a bank, and collecting flight route or mail traffic statistics. The general solution is to perform these actions incrementally. Whenever new data relevant to the desired information becomes available, it is immediately used for updating the information state. For example, in a compile-based system, source code is compiled incrementally, and system components are linked incrementally (see Section 4.3). For gathering statistics, as in banking systems and others, when accounts are modified or flights are booked, the changes are immediately propagated.

This approach has a profound impact on the design of software environments. The reason is that for incremental updates to be feasible, tools must be able to invoke other tools without explicit user intervention. Incremental processing would be virtually impossible if the user had to explicitly invoke tools to update all the places in a system that might be affected by each action. The design of a smooth interactive environment therefore must include facilities for implicit tool invocation.

One might argue that one can do without having tools invoke tools, because tools could be combined into a single system that performs more than one action. (This is basically the approach of traditional database management systems.) However, such a design makes adding new tools difficult and error-prone. Hence, it is generally better to provide a collection of separate, interacting tools that can be extended with new tools when additional functions are required.

However, even if tools can invoke other tools without user intervention, tools must know which other tools to activate. That is, a tool must contain at least a call to the tools it is supposed to invoke. As we discuss in Section 4.3, the Gandalf Project solves this problem through an event-driven, active database, which was designed to handle both tool invocation and data sharing among tools.

## 4.2.2 Task-Specific Environments

The term "software environment" can be applied to a wide variety of systems, ranging from general support systems to highly specialized programs. Operating system interfaces are at one end of this spectrum, providing general support for input/output and storage of objects. Application programs, such as spreadsheets, are at the other end of this spectrum, supporting only one particular activity very well.

The kind of environment we are interested in balances these extremes. What is good about an operating system interface is that it provides a collection of tools that support a number of related tasks. What is good about an application program is that it is specially tuned to the task.

Gandalf environments provide a framework for integrating a collection of related tools (as do operating systems), and yet each environment is an expert in accomplishing a given task (as are application programs). Instead of providing a single, general-purpose text editor for all editing tasks, a Gandalf environment provides a collection of specialized editors for individual tasks.

Adopting a task-specific approach implies the need to design a potentially large number of specialized environments. These environments must not be designed and implemented each time independently and from scratch. Rather, these environments must share both design and also common facilities. The issue of sharing and reuse across designs and the automation of the generation process have been central themes in the Gandalf Project. The result of this work consists of three parts: reusable design models, shared and reused code, and powerful support tools for generating environments. The structure and implementation of these design and generation facilities are the central topics of Section 4.4.

### 4.2.3  Direct Manipulation of Objects

Direct manipulation means that a user has direct access to the objects and can manipulate these with operations specific to each type of object. The essence of this style of interaction, which is also the basis of object-oriented systems, is that a user performs operations (essentially) directly on objects themselves rather than indirectly on significantly different representations of those objects.

To clarify this, consider the difference between a general text editor and a spreadsheet. A user writes a program with a text editor by generating a representation of the artifact the user is interested in. For modifications in the text to have an effect, another tool (the compiler) must translate the text into a new version of the target object (the executable object code). A spreadsheet program works quite differently. It gives the user more direct access to the target object so that changes the user makes are instantaneous and are immediately reflected in the target object itself and in its visualized form. A comparable editing tool that allows direct manipulation of a program object interacts with the user in terms of program constructs, instead of lines and characters, and it propagates user commands immediately to the object code.

Direct manipulation requires an interface that is different from a traditional database interface. The latter provides a procedural interface that hides the internal structure of the database. Hiding the internal structure is inappropriate for direct manipulation interfaces. What is needed instead of a procedural interface is a structured data interface that presents the objects to the user for creation and modification.

The designer of direct manipulation environments must consider two important issues regarding data presentation. The first issue is data collection traversal, which is needed for the user to access the objects he or she wants to manipulate. That is, the system must provide rich mechanisms allowing manipulation or gathering operations to be applied to related collections of user-level data. The second issue is multiple visualization, which is needed since the data that are relevant at a particular moment depend on the nature of the operation the user applies. For instance, if a user wants to see what kind of electronic mail messages he or she received, he or she typically wants to see the message header and not the full text. However, when the user focuses on a particular message, he or she wants to see the text and is no longer interested in the message header. A smooth environment will make it easy for the users to navigate through the collection of mailboxes, messages, and bulletin boards, while the environment will automatically display the data in a form most suitable for the user's current interest. The Gandalf Project has paid detailed attention to the visualization of data objects and has introduced a flexible facility for multiple visualization. Although multiple visualization is not addressed as one of the main topics in this chapter, the tools available to the designer for this purpose are discussed in Section 4.4.

### 4.2.4   Tool Integration

The term "tool integration" is not always used with the same meaning. We prefer a definition based on information sharing among tools and for tool communication, as these are the critical factors needed for tools to collaborate in supporting a task. (We also provide a consistent user interface to tools, which satisfies other definitions of "integration.")

Traditional environments, such as Unix, provide files for sharing and provide strings for representing data in these files. This very general approach has serious drawbacks. One problem is that logically related pieces of information may be stored in different files. Another is that tools can perform arbitrary operations on data, because the content of a files is not typed. Under these circumstances it is difficult to maintain data consistency. In addition, each tool must parse its data, since no tool can be sure that the data have the correct syntax. Parsing may also be needed to translate among different internal representations.

An object-oriented approach facilitates tool integration far better than the traditional untyped file approach. Basic consistency can easily be maintained, because each object type implicitly defines its own consistent states. And parsing is no longer needed, because the abstract object interface is known to all tools.

Of course, integration is not a binary property, but instead spans a spectrum. For example, a traditional compile-execute environment has a fairly low degree of integration, because the only way tools share and communicate is through input/output. A high degree of integration can be obtained if tools have concurrent access to information stored in a common database and if tools notify each other of their actions. This is discussed in Section 4.3.

All Gandalf environments are based on the combination of these four general characteristics. In the following sections we show that these ideas form a solid basis for designing software environments. In particular, we show how they lead to tightly integrated tools and to an approach to environment building that is substantially facilitated by reusable models, reusable code, and task-specific support tools.

## 4.3   Tool Integration

Gandalf's approach to tool integration is founded on three basic ideas: a common database through which tools share information, a tool invocation mechanism based on active data, and the use of views to define the relationship between tools and the shared database. In this section we examine each of these in turn, concluding with an example of their application to a specific Gandalf environment for interactive program development based on incremental compilation.

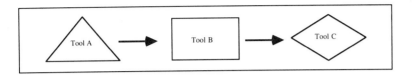

**EXHIBIT 4.1**
Traditional environments.


## 4.3.1  Shared Database

Traditionally, environments have consisted of loose collections of tools together with a host operating system. In these environments tools live more or less in isolation and typically communicate with each other in stages through input/output streams and files (see Exhibit 4.1). Examples of such systems are those based on Unix pipes, the common edit-compile-debug cycle, and tool box approaches (such as the Programmer's Workbench [4] and DSEE [20]). While these environments have several desirable properties—most notably the ability to change or add a tool independently of the other tools in the environment—they also have many serious shortcomings. In particular, it is difficult to achieve close integration among tools. Tools must (typically) be invoked explicitly and sequentially. Each tool requires a separate command language. The complete output of one tool must be generated before another tool can proceed. Further, new tools must understand the underlying data formats defined by existing tools.

In contrast, a Gandalf environment consists of a collection of cooperating tools that operate on a shared database of objects (Exhibit 4.2).[1] In this model the database becomes the primary communication medium for the tools. Such an architecture lends itself to much tighter integration, since the effects of one tool can be immediately seen and acted on by other tools. When tools can respond to changes in individual data objects, tools can be more interactive, and they can work together to achieve a user's goals. For example, in a software development environment, as a user modifies the list of module names on the import list of some module, an interface checker might validate that the imported modules are well defined, while another tool might select appropriate versions of these imported modules. As another example, in an environment that supports the creation of mail messages, as a user enters names of recipients for some message, one tool can check whether those names correspond to valid mail addresses while another tool can expand mail aliases.

---

[1]Other environments, including several of those listed in Section 4.5, take this approach as well.

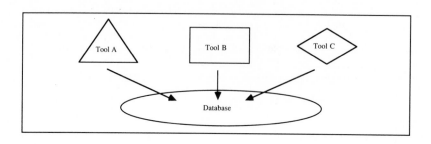

**EXHIBIT 4.2**
Integrated environments.

The shared database in a Gandalf environment is represented as a structured collection of typed objects. The objects represent the task-specific entities manipulated by tools in the environment. For instance, in a software development environment the database might contain source code objects (statements, modules, variables, etc.), symbol tables, and object code, while a mail environment would contain mail boxes, messages, routing tables, etc.

The database is structured as an attributed tree. Interior nodes in the tree represent composite objects (such as "IF" statements or mail messages), while leaf nodes represent atomic entities (such as integers, strings, and boolean values). Attributes are references to other objects that are typically not directly manipulated by a user. Exhibit 4.3 illustrates a portion of a database representing a mail message. As shown there, a mail message is an interior tree node with components representing the message header and body. The body is a leaf node containing the text of the message. The header is represented by another composite node containing a sender, a sending date, and a list of recipient addresses. An attribute of this node (not shown) might be an object representing routing information.

This design allows the shared database to perform a dual function. On the one hand, it serves as a general object-oriented database insofar as it supports persistent objects, versions, transactions, queries, object-oriented traversals, distribution, multiuser accessing, etc.[2] On the other hand, since the objects are structured as an attributed tree (as opposed to a graph, as found in most object-oriented databases), the database can also support numerous specialized func-

---

[2] Many of these are important research topics in the field object-oriented databases. While the Gandalf Project has not dealt with them in full generality, each issue has been handled with respect to the specific problems that arise in generating task-specific, direct-manipulation environments.

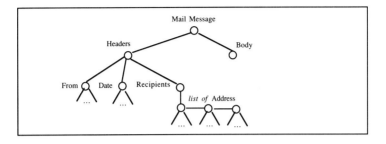

**EXHIBIT 4.3**
A mail message.

tions that take advantage of this structure. These functions include various forms of tree traversal, tree-oriented pattern matching, and structural transformations, such as grafting, pruning, and global replacement. Further, when the database is used to represent programs, there is a natural mapping between the abstract syntax trees of those programs and the database structures that represent them. (This connection will become clearer in the next section.) This in turn makes it relatively easy to write programming language tools that manipulate abstract syntax representations of programs.

## 4.3.2  Active Data

Access to shared data by itself is not enough to support an integrated environment; there must also be some way to coordinate tool invocation and the interactions among tools. In Gandalf environments the basis for this is active data. Active data refers to a triggering mechanism whereby changes made to an object by one tool cause the invocation of other tools in the environment. This is accomplished by allowing any tool to register its interest in objects of a particular type by associating a procedure, called a daemon or action routine, with that type. When an object is manipulated daemons associated with its type are activated.

Suppose, for example, that a project management tool in a software development environment would like to annotate each newly created module with a creation date. To do this the tool implementor would register a daemon with the create operation on objects of type module. The code for that daemon would contain actions to set a timestamp attribute of the object passed to it. (We will see an example of daemon code below.)

The association of daemons with types of objects leads to a form of control in which tools are invoked implicitly rather than explicitly. Thus tools are activated in appropriate ways as side effects of creating and modifying data. In this way tools can cooperate with each other in producing data with desirable properties, while at the same time a tool need not know about the existence of the other tools in the environment.[3]

Further, this design of active data gives tools considerable flexibility in determining the granularity and frequency of user interaction. Consider constructing a tool that checks the validity of a mail message destination field in a mail environment. The tool might check each recipient as it is created and added to the mail destination field. Alternatively, it might associate a daemon with the exit action on the list of recipients, causing it to be invoked when the user finishes constructing the list of recipients. Or, it could associate its daemon with the send action for the mail message, causing it to be invoked when the message is mailed.

Although daemons are the primary mechanism for active data, another design called action equations [19] was developed although never fully implemented. Action equations extend attribute equations [28] to handle history-sensitive properties of an environment, such as program interpretation, run-time support, and language-oriented debugging.

### 4.3.3  Views

As environments based on shared data grow larger, the description of object representations as a single system of types becomes increasingly difficult to manage. Different tools may be interested in different aspects of the common data. For example, a program type checker may be interested in the types of variables and expressions, a program editor in the source lines, and a documentation tool in the comments. Worse, different tools may even prefer that the data be structured differently. As a result, a representation satisfying the constraints imposed by all the tools can be extremely difficult to create, understand, or modify.

The Gandalf Project developed an approach that addresses this problem by allowing the description of the shared data to be factored into the individual tools [11]. Tools define their own "views" of the datatypes they use. These views are later integrated by describing how information is shared among tools and what invariants must be maintained among different views of the same data.

---

[3]Tools may also be invoked explicitly through procedure calls. In a mail environment, for example, a mailing tool might provide a "mail" command for sending a mail message. This could be invoked by a user or as a procedure call by other tools. Similarly, a software development environment might provide a "system build" command.

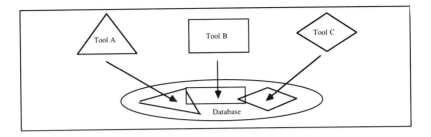

**EXHIBIT 4.4**
Views.

Exhibit 4.4 illustrates this design as an extended version of the architecture shown in Exhibit 4.2. As in the simple shared-database model, tools cooperate through data sharing. However, using views each tool accesses the shared data in terms of a particular view of the database. In effect, each tool can treat its view as the "real" database. The database itself is a *synthesis* of those views. New tools can (in principle) be added to an existing environment simply by describing a new view of the shared data.

In our research we have found distinguishing among three kinds of views useful: instance-based, type-based, and dynamic views. An *instance-based view* is a "region" of the database tree that is visible to a particular tool. Typically, such regions overlap at a single object, called a *gate*, that connects the two portions of the database. (Gates in Mentor [6], and in some of our earlier work [22], are restricted to overlaps at a single object.) Exhibit 4.5 illustrates this idea. For example, one might choose to place the header and the body of a mail message in two different views. In the one view, the message header would appear to a user (or tool) as an atomic object. Moving the cursor "in" to the header (for example, by double-clicking on it with a mouse) would "open" the new view, exposing those portions of the tree. Similarly, in a programming environment a nested procedure definition might appear simply as a signature in one view; "opening" that definition would reveal the full definition of the procedure.

A *type-based view* is one in which several type definitions are "merged" to produce composite or synthesized type definitions. Each of the types that combine to define a resultant type of an object can be thought of as representing a "facet" of the object. Any tool manipulating an object does so in terms of one of those facets. (See Exhibit 4.6.) For example, a *proc-decl* object for a Pascal-like programming language might have both a *Code* and a *Semantics* view. In the *Code* view a *proc-decl* object might define the declarations as an ordered sequence. The *Semantics* view might treat the declarations as an unordered set

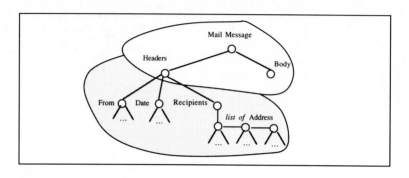

**EXHIBIT 4.5**
Gates.

(possibly represented as a hash-table). A tool manipulating a *proc-decl* object from the *Code* view would insert and remove declarations by manipulating a sequence, while a tool manipulating a *proc-decl* object from the *Semantics* view would treat the declarations interact with a set.

Given that the same object can represent data in distinct ways to different tools, there must be some mechanism for maintaining consistency among those representations. We developed the notion of "compatibility maps" to handle this problem. Briefly, a compatibility map defines a mapping between operations performed through one view and the effects it must have on the others. Compatibility maps act like daemons insofar as they are automatically invoked when changes are made to data. However, unlike daemons, compatibility maps are not a description of an individual tool's actions, but rather define the relation-

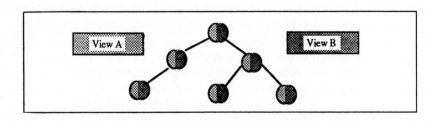

**EXHIBIT 4.6**
Type-based views.

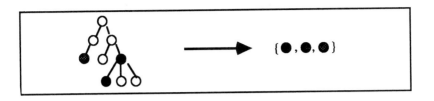

**EXHIBIT 4.7**
A dynamic view.

ship between types manipulated by different tools. For the above example, a compatibility map would define the meaning of operations on sets in terms of those on sequences (and vice versa). Compatibility maps can be defined using a language, called Janus, which was specifically designed for "programming with views" [16].

A *dynamic* view, the third kind of view mechanism, serves the purpose of associative retrieval found in relational databases. A dynamic view is specified by indicating a pattern and a view context in which to apply the pattern. The result of the application is the collection of all objects in the view that satisfy the pattern. Dynamic views are automatically updated when the database changes. Exhibit 4.7 illustrates the basic ideas of dynamic views.

### 4.3.4  An Example

LOIPE [7,21], one of the environments we constructed, demonstrates some of the benefits of our approach to tool integration. LOIPE is an incremental programming environment for a minor variation of C. Our tool integration mechanisms allows LOIPE to achieve the performance of compiler-based systems while providing the feel of an interpretive programming environment, using incremental editing, linking, loading, and execution.

Every component of LOIPE—the incremental compiler, the linker, the loader, and the debugger—performs its operations in terms of a shared abstract syntax tree that represents the common information. The central part of the shared abstract syntax tree represents the individual declarations and statements in a program. The tree also includes objects that represent breakpoint "statements" and variable name and value pairs for monitoring.

Since all the tools in LOIPE manipulate programs, using a shared tree structure simplifies the writing of these tools in several ways. First, problems, such as "the debugger doesn't know about types," are avoided since the full range of information about a program is available in the shared tree. Second, providing a common and natural representation for programs decreases the number of situations in which programmers are tempted to define specialized data structures for a given tool. (The view mechanism does, however, allow programmers to do this in a disciplined way, when it is necessary.) Third, writing the tools is simplified since the shared information is already structured; individual tools never have to parse text. Not only does this decrease the work of the tool writer, but it also localizes decisions about the language syntax. In contrast, in a conventional environment like UNIX the compilers and the prettyprinters are required to have their own parsers for the same language.

The common shared tree representation allows the environment to provide the user with a uniform model for program editing, debugging, and execution. Specifically, the user edits the abstract syntax tree directly using a structure-oriented editor. Some editing operations cause daemons to be fired. In this way most of operations on programs are invoked implicitly. For instance, procedures are incrementally compiled in LOIPE when a procedure is modified and then exited.

Several operations, such as run, are invoked explicitly. When run is invoked, any modified procedures are implicitly compiled, the entire program is implicitly linked and loaded, and then it is run. Breakpoints are handled by augmenting the abstract syntax of programs. The user then explicitly sets a breakpoint by inserting a breakpoint statement into a program. Using this approach, the programmer sets a breakpoint and makes changes in the program in an identical way, by modifying the tree representation of the program. This approach frees the programmer from having to select a specific tool (such as a debugger or compiler) based on a largely arbitrary classification of development activities.

Different tools in LOIPE have different views of the database. For instance, the structure-oriented editor manipulates the program's abstract syntax tree. The linker and loader, however, need some additional data structures (and, in fact, don't need to see everything the editor does, such as comments). In particular, since linking and loading in LOIPE are incremental and indirect, every procedure call is made indirectly through an address vector, which allows the environment to update the body of a procedure without recompiling, relinking, or reloading its calling sites. Another instance of a LOIPE view is the debugging and monitoring window, which displays pairs of variable names and values. The list of names and values is defined as an independent structure from the shared program database. The names and values are managed through messages emitted from the compiler as traced values change.

Views make programming easier. The critical shared information is easily available, but specially tailored data structures can also be defined and manipulated. This style allows the programmer to focus easily on precisely the information need to define a given tool.

Several other LOIPE-like environments have been constructed in the Gandalf framework. The most notable of these is the Pascal environment built as part of the Gnome Project [10]. Environments for Ada and even Fortran have been constructed as well, although in some cases full run-time support was not completed.

## 4.4    Generating Integrated Environments

As described in the introduction, the goal of producing many task-specific environments leads to an interest in automating the process of developing an integrated environment. Thus from the outset, the Gandalf Project has taken as one of its primary challenges the problem of automating the generation of integrated environments. To meet this challenge Gandalf adopted a *generic approach* to integrated environments; the task-specific components of an environment are viewed as parameters to an environment framework that provides the basic infrastructure to support the architecture described in the previous section.

This generic approach is based on three observations. First, there are many common facilities needed by virtually all environments; these facilities can be implemented once and then reused. Second, specialized high-level languages can help an implementor to define the tools and datatypes that are specific to a particular environment. Third, both the reuse of common facilities and the description of task-specific components of an environment can be supported by an integrated environment specialized to handle the generation of other environments.

These observations have led to the environment generation paradigm illustrated in Exhibit 4.8. An implementor describes the task-specific aspects of an environment using special-purpose notations and tools developed for this purpose. These descriptions are then compiled into tables, which are in turn linked with a library of reusable components to produce an executable environment.[4] These activities all take place in the context of an environment, called the *Gandalf System*, that manages the generation process and guarantees that a well-formed environment is generated. This environment makes it relatively easy to use the specialized notations for describing tools and datatypes. It also takes responsibility for linking in the appropriate reusable libraries, checking the completeness of tool descriptions, and managing the evolution of environments as new tools are added and old tools are modified.

---

[4] Since these reusable components provide the interface through which tools interact to modify data and interact with the user, in earlier papers they are frequently referred to as the environment *kernel*.

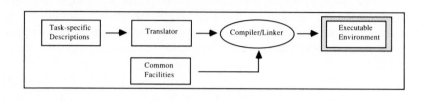

**EXHIBIT 4.8**
Generation of Gandalf environments.

### 4.4.1  The Common Facilities

In terms of supporting the architecture described in the previous section, there are two basic categories of common reusable components needed by all environments. The first category consists of user interface facilities. These include window management, menu support, help facilities, and formatting and display routines. The second category consists of facilities that support the Gandalf tool integration architecture: the shared database, the use of active data, and the management of views. In the area of database support, they handle low-level details of data storage, distribution, and concurrency. In addition, they define the interface used by tools to create, modify, transform, query, and traverse data. In the area of active data, they support the underlying triggering mechanisms that coordinate the invocation of tools. That is, they invoke appropriate daemons when changes to data occur. In the area of view management, they handle the updating of views and guarantee that tools manipulate objects through appropriate views.

The common facilities thus define a "support envelope" which greatly simplifies the definition of tools. On the one side, tools are insulated from representations of shared data through a uniform, high-level interface to the database. On the other side, tools are insulated from the complexities of user interface management through a framework that takes care of formatting, windowing, menus, event handling, screen update, etc. This has the additional benefit of providing a uniform interaction style for all the tools in the environment, as well as for all users of Gandalf-generated environments.

### 4.4.2  Formal Descriptions of Task-Specific Components

Even given a substantial base of common reusable components, the job of constructing an environment may still be rather difficult. The implementor must define the types of data structures to reside in the shared database, the actions of tools, the mappings between database objects and their displayed form, the structure and function of attributes, the relationships between views, specific help facilities, etc. To make this process manageable the Gandalf Project has developed a number of special-purpose, formal notations.

Special-purpose notations have several beneficial properties. First, they incorporate high-level facilities into a language, making it easier for a programmer to use those facilities. (For instance, a programming language with built-in notation for defining and manipulating sets encourages the use of sets in programs.) Second, relative to a general-purpose programming language, they constrain the class of computations, and thereby eliminate certain categories of illegal programs. (For example, some languages for parallel programming avoid certain classes of deadlocks by restricting the synchronization primitives that a programmer can use.) Third, they can raise the level of programming through declarative notations. (For example, it is generally easier to say *what* a computation should be doing than it is to say *how* it should be doing it.)

In the Gandalf System the three most important notations are those used to describe the task-specific aspects of an environment. Two of these are used to define the objects in the environment, and the third is used to define daemons. Objects are defined by first describing their abstract structure and then their concrete representations. The description of the abstract structure determines the legal types of objects to be stored in a database. Exhibit 4.9 shows part of such a description for a mail environment. As illustrated, this description resembles an abstract syntax definition and is often referred to as the "grammar" of the environment.[5]

The concrete representations of an object define the ways in which object instances will be displayed to the user. For each item in a grammar the implementor provides one or more "unparse schemes." Unparse schemes indicate indentation levels, where and how keywords should be displayed, how fonts are used, how lines are broken, etc. When multiple unparse schemes are associated with a grammar entry, instances of that datatype can be displayed in multiple ways. Exhibit 4.10 illustrates unparse schemes for the mail environment.[6] Notice that a mail message has two unparse schemes representing two (instance-based) views of a message. In one view, the header component is shown in elided form, but the body component is shown in full. In the other everything is fully displayed. Since the header component has been designated as a *gate*, double-clicking on it will automatically bring up the expanded view. Although

---

[5]The relationship between the productions in a grammar and traditional datatype definitions is roughly that nonterminal productions—such as MailMessage—define a record datatype, while terminal productions—such as MailBody—define primitive datatypes.

[6]The unparse notation has been considerably simplified for this example. In this exhibit the notation "@n" represents a newline, and "@+" represents an increase in indentation level. Text inclosed in quotes is printed as a literal.

---

<u>Grammar</u> Mail-Environment

   <u>View</u>:AbstractSyntax

       MailSystem  ::= <u>list of</u> MailBox
       MailBox     ::= name:BoxName
                  messages:<u>list of</u> MailMessage
       MailMessage:= header:Header
                  body:MailBody
       Header      ::= from:Address
                  to:<u>list of</u> Address
                  date:Date
                  subject:STRING
       MailBody   ::= TEXT
       . . .

<u>End</u> Mail-Environment

---

**EXHIBIT 4.9**
A grammar for a mail environment.

not shown here, the unparsing language is quite rich, allowing numerous options for windowing, conditional formatting, and elision [8].

    The daemons used by the tools in the environment are defined in a programming language called ARL (Action Routine Language). ARL is a procedural language with facilities built in for handling both the tree-oriented structures of a Gandalf database and the triggering mechanism that invokes a given dae-

---

<u>Grammar</u> Mail-Environment

   <u>View</u>:ConcreteSyntax

     MailSystem
          (1) 'Boxes:' boxes
     MailBox
          (1) name @n@+ messages
     MailMessage
          (1) 'Header: . . .' (<u>Gate</u> header) @n 'Contents:' @n@+ body
          (2) 'Header:" @n@+ header
     . . .

<u>End</u> Mail-Environment

---

**EXHIBIT 4.10**
Concrete syntax for a mail environment.

```
daemon AddressDaemon (node Address; trigger t)

case (t.TriggerKind)
    Create:
    Insert:
        { Check each newly-created address and each
          address inserted into the list. }

        { Perform checking after creation/insertion
          has occurred. }
        when isDone(t) =>
            if not CheckAddress (Address) then
                { RecordError stores an error message as
                  an attribute of the Address. }
                RecordError (Address, "Bad mail address.");
            end if

    ReportErrors:
        { Report all errors encountered at this node
          and its descendants. }
        begin
            node c;
            { If there is an error attribute of Address,
              report it. }
            if HasError (Address) then
                ReportError (Address)
            end if

            { Send the ReportErrors trigger to all children
              of Address, so they can report their errors.}
            visit c child of Address do
                trigger c with ReportErrors ;
        end;

end AddressDaemon;
```

**EXHIBIT 4.11**
An ARL daemon.

mon. Exhibit 4.11 shows part of a description for a daemon associated with the
to field of a mail message. The daemon checks the legality of the entries in
the list of destinations (using a routine, CheckAddress, not shown here). As
illustrated, this daemon is invoked when the user creates a new recipient for the
mail message. If an error is encountered it records the error with the recipient's
address. These errors can later be reported using the ReportErrors trigger.

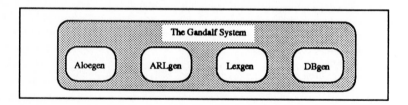

**EXHIBIT 4.12**
The Gandalf System.

### 4.4.3   The Gandalf System

The Gandalf System is itself a Gandalf environment specialized to the task of building other environments. It serves three primary functions. First, it supports the environment designer by providing language-based editors that understand the specialized notations outlined earlier. Second, it coordinates the generation process by checking the consistency and completeness of the tool descriptions and by linking the appropriate libraries to produce an executable environment. Third, it manages the evolution of an environment. In addition to these primary functions, the Gandalf System has forced us to make our tools reliable and useable, since it represents a bootstrapping of the system.

The Gandalf System can best be viewed as four cooperating subenvironments. (Exhibit 4.12.) Aloegen, the first subenvironment, provides a language-based editor for defining abstract and concrete syntax. Within this environment the implementor defines the types, attributes, and unparse schemes of the shared data in the environment. The second subenvironment supports the construction of tools written in ARL. Lexgen, the third subenvironment, defines lexical routines that are used to handle user input. DBgen, the fourth subenvironment, is used to fit the other pieces together.

The output of the Gandalf System is a task-specific environment consisting of a database and a set of daemons. In addition, the Gandalf System automatically produces a structure-oriented editor from the formal description of datatypes in the environment. This editor allows a user to create and manipulate structures stored in the database. Typically this editor is the focal point of user interaction with an environment. For example, in the mail environment, the output of the generation process would include a database for holding well-formed mailboxes, messages, routing tables, etc. When the user starts up the environment, a structure-oriented editor would be invoked. This editor would allow the user to browse through existing messages (by navigating through the database). New messages would be created by adding a new message to the database, which would appear as a message template to be filled out. Slots in the template can be chosen from a menu of legal values.[7] When the message is complete, the environment would invoke the appropriate daemon for mailing.

A serious problem for any system based on a database of persistent objects is that as an environment evolves, new representations may be required for its shared data. If care is not taken, stored databases can become unreadable. (For example, most people are familiar with file system conversion pains that arise when upgrading an operating system.) Hence, without some automated mechanism for evolving these databases, the practicality of an approach based on typed, persistent data is severely limited. To address this problem the Gandalf System includes a subenvironment, called TransformGen, which helps the environment builder manage changes to an existing environment [9]. Using TransformGen, changes to a grammar are semiautomatically translated into a program that transforms existing databases into a format compatible with the new grammar. For example, if the implementor decides to add a new component to an existing (nonterminal) type, the transformer will augment all instances of that type in an old database with a slot for that new component. In this case the implementor has several choices: he or she can indicate a default value to be inserted in the slot, leave the slot unfilled, invoke an arbitrary routine to calculate a new value, or have the transformation system interact with the user to supply a value.

Our experience is that the Gandalf System drastically reduces the time required to produce an integrated programming environment. In particular, minimal environments—consisting of a database and structure-oriented editor—can be constructed simply by describing the abstract and concrete syntax of a target language. For instance, it would take less than a half day to generate a syntax-directed environment for a programming language the size of Pascal. To add type checking to such an environment would take about a week. It is not surprising, therefore, that the Gandalf System has been popular as a rapid prototyping environment. It is significant, however, that the ability to generate prototype environments rapidly does not rule out the construction of production quality environments as well. Indeed, we have found that over time Gandalf environments typically evolve from prototypes into robust, efficient environments. A good case in point is the development of the Genie family of programming environments that are now sold commercially [10].

---

[7]When the structure-oriented editor manipulates objects that represent constructs in a programming language, the editor is sometimes referred to as a *language-based* or *syntax-directed* editor.

## 4.5  Conclusion

We now have extensive experience in constructing and using integrated task-specific software environments. This experience lets us look back and evaluate to what degree we have achieved our goals.

The project has made several contributions, and it has some shortcomings. Some of the contributions are original to the project; others were developed concurrently and independently, often in somewhat different form, by other projects. Some of the shortcomings are areas where we didn't follow through completely, in implementation, for instance. Others are fundamental shortcomings of our approach.

### 4.5.1  Contributions

We have made several contributions in the areas of tool integration and generating task-specific environments.

The combination of sharing structured data and implicitly invoking tools using active data is powerful. It would be difficult, for instance, to construct efficient compilation-based interactive programming environments (like LOIPE) in a conventional programming style such as that used in UNIX. The difficulties arise for at least two reasons: one, conventional tools cannot easily share fine-grained data (often because the tools live in separate address spaces); and two, conventional tools cannot pass control frequently, efficiently, and without direct user invocation. Sharing structured data using views makes the job of writing tools easier because key activities—like tree traversal and keeping different views consistent—are separated from rather than interleaved with the basic computations of the tools.

Perhaps the best indicator of the success of the task-specific approach lies in the Gandalf System, an environment we constructed to help design and construct Gandalf environments themselves. We found great leverage in identifying separate (but not entirely unrelated) tasks, such as database design and unparsing schemes. This decomposition was useful both to the users of the environment (i.e., the designers of new environments) and also to us as implementors of the Gandalf System; we were able to separate and largely isolate our decisions about how to represent and implement environment support subsystems.

Our work on TransformGen [9] is another contribution. By taking the unusual approach of "watching" the manipulation of the type definitions, which is possible largely because these definitions are manipulated structurally, TransformGen can identify simple relationships among old and new types in ways not possible by off-line differencing approaches. TransformGen is a nice example of using the 90-10 rule: it handles the 90% of the common cases that are relatively easy to manage, and it provides the environment designer hooks for handling the other 10% manually.

## 4.5.2  Shortcomings

Two key areas where we have nearly complete designs but only partial implementations are the view system and action equations. Undoubtedly, full implementations would provide additional insight into the technical problems associated with these mechanisms, and they would also permit us to gain experience with their design and use.

One fundamental problem with our approach is that we cannot easily integrate tools outside of the Gandalf Project. In one case where we did this, using the backend of the portable C compiler in LOIPE, the task wasn't easy; the primary difficulty was that the internal trees in Gandalf had to be translated to the trees expected by the C compiler. But our Ada editors, for instance, are used to ensure that users produce programs that are correct in terms of syntax and static semantics; however, to compile the programs, textual versions of the programs must be written to a file and then passed to a standard Ada compiler. It will be important to determine ways to share tools developed for use in different contexts.

## 4.5.3  Current and Future Topics

In addition to the areas that require implementation attention, we have ongoing efforts in several other areas. One area is support for the generation of distributed versions of our environments. Another is considering how to effectively segment the databases that the environments manipulate. A third is studying concurrency across multiagent environments, especially with respect to the kinds of long-term transactions that are common in environments. Yet another considers how to provide incremental parsing to lessen the restrictions of our structure-oriented user interface. A final area focuses on subclassing daemons to manage sharing and reuse. We are interested in pursuing several other areas as well, most notably the handling of graphical user interfaces.

## 4.5.4  Related Work

Research in environments can be categorized in many ways. One useful taxonomy identifies four different categories of environments [3].

    □ *Structure-based environments* include our work along with efforts like Pecan [24,25], the Cornell Synthesizer Generator [26,27], and Mentor [5].

This category focuses on mechanism rather than method. In particular, these efforts are more interested in defining what are good classes of environments than in defining good environments per se.

□ *Language environments* are language systems that have been extended with tools that make it easier to build and maintain programs and systems written in that language. Interlisp [32], Smalltalk-80 [13], Cedar [31], Fortran's Toolpack [23], and Ada's Rational [1] environments are examples of this category.

□ *Life-cycle support systems* are operating system extensions that handle common programming and software engineering tasks. ICL's CADES [30], the Bell Labs' Programmer's Workbench [4], Apollo's DSEE [20], and Atherton Technologies' Codesmith systems are instances of this approach.

□ *Software development methods* define intellectual means for constructing quality software. Jackson's JSP/JSD, Ross' SADT [29], Yourdon's SA/SD [33], and Gries' invariants [12] are examples of this approach. Only recently are several of these approaches providing tools to support software development.

Other efforts within the first category have important characteristics that distinguish them from the Gandalf work.

Emily [17] was perhaps the first in this category of environments. The structure-oriented user interface was modeled in terms of standard BNF, which led to two key problems. First, BNF combines abstract syntax with concrete syntax, which prohibits the definition of multiple visualizations through multiple unparse schemes, since the structure and the display (or parsing) information are bundled together. Second, BNF descriptions of most programming languages have many chain rules (such as $E \rightarrow T$ and $T \rightarrow F$), which are used to define precedence; in Emily, the user had to tediously expand each of these manually. Since Gandalf users directly create the abstract syntax, there is no need to infer precedence; instead, the Gandalf structure description language flattens the BNF hierarchy allowing, for example, an expression to be expanded directly into any legal operation (such as addition, multiplication, or function invocation). The benefits of this approach are not clear-cut, however, since it requires prefix input, which is not natural for some users and domains.

The Cornell Synthesizer Generator [27] is best known for its use of attribute grammars as the mechanism for describing the static semantics of the generated environment. Further, incremental attribute grammar evaluation algorithms are used to handle interactive editing required by the environment [28]. One hotly debated, and still unanswered question, is whether the daemon-based or the attribute grammar-based approach to defining semantics is better. There is more apparent freedom in the daemon-based style, but with such added flexibility comes some difficulties in managing some styles of semantics. The attribute grammar style is nicer theoretically, but some kinds of semantics (such as run-time) are harder to define than with daemons. A middle ground (such as action equations) may turn out to be most appropriate, assuming the full benefits of both approaches can be retained in practice.

In Mentor [5], one of the earlier systems in this category, users can collect information about an instance of a program by defining (in Gandalf terms) their own dynamic views. In contrast, only environment designers can define dynamic views in Gandalf. The critical question in selecting one approach over the other is in balancing the difficulty of defining a new dynamic view with the frequency with which users desire new views. The decision for us was clear, since the bulk of our experience is with novice users, who generally don't have the technical background needed to define new dynamic views in any situation.

Pecan [24] was one of the first environments to support multiple, concurrent graphical views on a given program. The central view was a structure-based editor, which was augmented by a flow chart view, a Nassi-Shneiderman diagram view, views of the symbol table and the run-time stack, etc. Pecan contrasts with Gandalf environments in at least two ways. First, Pecan effectively exploits bitmap workstations by displaying most or all of these views simultaneously. Second, in contrast to Gandalf environments, many of the views were read-only, with manipulations of the program taking place primarily through the editor; in addition, the graphical views are largely handcrafted, since generating graphics declaratively is an open question.

PSG [2] defines environments declaratively using an entirely denotational style. This contrasts with Gandalf's mixed procedural and declarative approach as well as with the Synthesizer Generator's attribute grammar approach. Although both the PSG and the Synthesizer Generator approach are declarative, the PSG style uses a kind of denotational semantics that makes defining run-time computations easier; still, however, it is not clear that defining run-time semantics declaratively is better than Gandalf's procedural style.

Several of these systems differ in how they handle editing program structures. In Gandalf, all editing is in terms of the structure of the program.[8] This structure is defined by the environment designer, who may decide to represent basic entities, such as expressions or even procedures, as text; however, in general, most Gandalf environments pushed the structural representation down to the expression level. In the Synthesizer Generator, the designer also decides which types of structure will be edited structurally and which will be edited textually; in general, expressions (indeed, entire assignment statements) are edited textually and parsed. In Mentor, users enter programs as text that is then incrementally parsed; after this, the operations are based on structure. In Pecan, the user can either type single lines as text that is incrementally parsed or can enter structural

---

[8] Kaiser and Kant defined a method for manipulating expressions at a token-level, which provides an intermediate level between editing structure and text [18].

commands. PSG provides a fully hybrid approach, where users can arbitrarily enter structural or textual commands, even in the midst of editing an expression.

Over time, we have refined our view of what is the best editing model. We have now defined an incremental parsing subsystem to provide textual operations in addition to the structure-based operations. We do not go as far as the PSG group, however, since we are concerned about the cost of arbitrary hybrid editing both for the implementor and also for the user. In general, we feel that structure-based editing is appropriate for large-grained structures (such as modules), but that text editing should also be supported for fine-grained structures (such as expressions and procedures).

These systems have influenced each other in a variety of ways. Pecan's graphical views, for instance, are desirable in many domains. Also, some form of incremental parsing seems to be a practical necessity, although the level at which it must be supported is not as clear. Finally, there seems to be general agreement that using declarative notations to describe an environment is beneficial, although there is still disagreement as to the degree to which existing notations are sufficient and practical for defining important kinds of environments.

Perhaps Gandalf's major influence on the other efforts has been in its generative, task-specific approach. Indeed, the last point above—the use of declarative descriptions—has arisen as people have pushed the idea of generating environments past our original syntax-based approach.

Our work in this area has also been influential in other ways. For instance, our work on the Gandalf Prototype, which combines the notions of LOIPE with support for programming-in-the-large and project management, has produced results in the general area of software development environments [15]. Gandalf environments have been used extensively in introductory programming courses too. In addition, some of the technology we have developed has been transferred to industrial sites; for instance, the VLSI (Very Large Scale Integration) chip design environment built at Siemens as part of the Esprit project, and the program inventory environment, based on manipulating module interfaces, constructed at Westinghouse. As a final note, many of the ideas in the Gandalf Project were developed independently, simultaneously, and in somewhat different forms by other research efforts. A good example is the development of direct-manipulation techniques. We are now in a position to look, with increased insight, at the confluences among these research efforts.

## 4.6   Acknowledgments

The many members of the Gandalf research effort laid the foundation for this chapter. In addition, Norman Delisle, William Griswold, Gail Harrison, Barbara Staudt Lerner, Richard Lerner, Mayer Schwartz, and Kevin Sullivan made numerous comments that allowed us to improve the chapter itself. We would especially like to thank Barbara for supplying the ARL daemon example.

# References

[1] J. E. Archer, Jr. and M. T. Devlin. Rational's experience using Ada for very large systems. *Proceedings of the First International Conference on Ada Programming Language Applications for the NASA Space Station*, NASA, pp. B2.5.1-B2.5.12, 1986.

[2] R. Bahlke and G. Snelting. The PSG system: From formal language definitions to interactive programming environments. *ACM Transactions on Programming Languages and Systems 8(4)*, pp. 547-576, 1986.

[3] S. A. Dart, R. J. Ellison, P. H. Feiler, and A. N. Habermann. Software development environments. *IEEE Computer 20(11)*, pp. 18-28, 1987.

[4] T. A. Dolotta, R. C. Haight, and J. R. Mashey. UNIX time-sharing system: the programmer's workbench. *The Bell Systems Technical Journal 57(2)*, 1978. Reprinted in D. R. Barstow, H. E. Shrobe, and E. Sandewall (eds.), *Interactive Programming Environments*, pp. 353-369, McGraw-Hill, 1984.

[5] V. Donzeau-Gouge, G. Huet, G. Kahn, and B. Lang. Programming environments based on structure editors: the mentor experience, INRIA Techical Report 26, 1980. Reprinted in D. R. Barstow, H. E. Shrobe, and E. Sandewall (eds.), *Interactive Programming Environments*, pp. 128-140, McGraw-Hill, 1984.

[6] V. Donzeau-Gouge, G. Huet, G. Kahn, B. Lang, and J. J. Levy. Document structure and modularity in Mentor. In *Proceedings of the ACM SIGSOFT/SIGPLAN Software Engineering Symposium on Practical Software Development Environments*, pp. 141-148, 1984.

[7] P. H. Feiler. *A Language-Oriented Interactive Programming Environment Based on Compilation Technology*, Ph.D. dissertation, Department of Computer Science, Carnegie Mellon University, Pittsburgh, PA, 1982.

[8] D. Garlan. Flexible unparsing in a structure editing environment. Carnegie Mellon University Technical Report CMU-CS-85-129, Carnegie Mellon University, Pittsburgh, PA, 1985.

[9] D. Garlan, C. W. Krueger, and B. J. Staudt. A structural approach to the maintenance of structure-oriented environments. In *Proceedings ACM SIGSOFT/SIGPLAN Software Engineering Symposium on Practical Software Development Environments*, 1987.

[10] D. Garlan and P. L. Miller. GNOME: an introductory programming environment based on a family of structure editors. In *Proceedings of the ACM SIGSOFT/SIGPLAN Software Engineering Symposium on Practical Software Development Environments*, pp. 65-72, 1984.

[11] D. Garlan. *Views for Tools in Integrated Environments*, Ph.D. dissertation, Department of Computer Science, Carnegie Mellon University, Pittsburgh, PA, 1987.

[12] D. Gries. *The Science of Programming*. Springer-Verlag, 1981.

[13] A. Goldberg. *Smalltalk-80: The Interactive Programming Environment*. Reading, MA: Addison-Wesley, 1984.

[14] M. A. Jackson. *System Development*. Englewood Cliffs, NJ: Prentice Hall International, 1983.

[15] A. N. Habermann and D. S. Notkin. Gandalf software development environments. *IEEE Transactions on Software Engineering SE-12(12)*, pp. 1117-1127, 1986.

[16] A. N. Habermann, C. Krueger, B. Pierce, B. Staudt, and C. Wenn. Programming with views. Carnegie Mellon University Technical Report CMU-CS-87-177, Carnegie Mellon University, Pittsburgh, PA, 1987.

[17] W. J. Hansen. User engineering principles for interactive environments. In D. R. Barstow, H. E. Shrobe, and E. Sandewall (eds.), *Interactive Programming Environments*, pp. 83-96, McGraw-Hill, 1984.

[18] G. E. Kaiser and E. Kant. Incremental parsing without a parser. *Journal of Systems and Software 5(2)*, pp.121-144, 1985.

[19] G. E. Kaiser. Incremental dynamic semantics for language-based programming environments. *ACM Transactions Programming Languages Systems 11(2)*, 1989.

[20] D. B. Leblang and R. P. Chase, Jr. Computer-aided software engineering in a distributed workstation environment. In *Proceedings of the ACM SIGSOFT/SIGPLAN Software Engineering Symposium on Practical Software Development Environments*, pp. 104-112, Pittsburgh, PA,1984. Appears as *Software Engineering Notes 9(3)*, 1984, and *SIGPLAN Notices 19(5)*, 1984.

[21] R. Medina-Mora and P. Feiler. An incremental programming environment. *IEEE Transactions on Software Engineering*, SE-7, pp. 472-482, 1981.

[22] D. Notkin. *Interactive Structure-Oriented Computing*. Ph.D. dissertation, Carnegie Mellon University, Pittsburgh, PA, 1984.

[23] L. J. Osterweil. Toolpack—an experimental software development environment research project. *IEEE Transactions on Software Engineering*, SE-9, pp. 673-685, 1983.

[24] S. P. Reiss. PECAN: program development systems that support multiple views. In *Proceedings of the 7th International Conference on Software Engineering*, IEEE Computer Society, 1984.

[25] S. P. Reiss. Graphical program development with PECAN program development systems. In *Proceedings of the ACM SIGSOFT/SIGPLAN Software Engineering Symposium on Practical Software Development Environments*, pp. 30-41, 1984.

[26] T. Reps and T. Teitelbaum. The synthesizer generator. In *Proceedings of the ACM SIGSOFT/SIGPLAN Software Engineering Symposium on Practical Software Development Environments*, pp. 42-48, 1984.

[27] T. Reps and T. Teitelbaum. *The Synthesizer Generator: A System for Constructing Language-Based Editors*. New York: Springer-Verlag, 1988.

[28] T. Reps. *Generating Language-Based Environments*. ACM doctoral dissertation award series, Cambridge, MA: MIT Press, 1983.

[29] D. T. Ross. Applications and extensions of SADT. *IEEE Computer 18(4)*, pp. 25-35, 1985.

[30] R. Snowden. An experience-based assessment of development systems. In W. E. Riddle and R. E. Fairley (eds.), *Software Development Tools*, Springer-Verlag, 1980.

[31] D. Swinehart, P. Zellweger, R. Beach, and R. Hagmann. A structural view of the Cedar programming environment. *ACM Transactions Programming Languages Systems 8(4)* pp. 419-490, 1986.

[32] W. Teitelman and L. Masinter. The Interlisp programming environment. *IEEE Computer 14(4)* pp. 25-34, 1981. Reprinted in Barstow, H. E. Shrobe, and E. Sandewall (eds.), *Interactive Programming Environments*, pp. 83-96, McGraw-Hill, 1984.

[33] E. Yourdon and L. L. Constantine. *Structured Design: Fundamentals of a Discipline of Computer Program and Systems Design*. New York: Yourdon Press, 1979.

# 5

---

# Tools for Experiments on Algorithms

Jon Louis Bentley

This chapter presents two case studies in the experimental analysis of algorithms. A small experiment on binary search trees examines their performance under random insertions, and compares that to their behavior on real text files. A large study investigates heuristics for the geometric Traveling Salesman Problem (TSP). The software tools used for these experiments are available on UNIX systems, but the underlying techniques can be applied in any software environment.

---

## 5.1   Introduction

Mathematical analysis is an effective technique for understanding the behavior of some algorithms. It is not, however, the only method for the task. Experiments provide another tool for learning about algorithms; they can guide theory, test hypotheses, help to make implementation choices, and provide insight.

This chapter examines the experimental analysis of algorithms with an emphasis on the software tools that aid the task. Section 5.2 describes experiments on binary search trees, and Section 5.3 describes the techniques used to con-

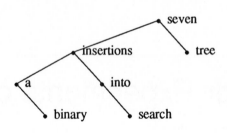

**EXHIBIT 5.1**
Seven insertions into a binary search tree.

duct those experiments. Section 5.4 sketches experiments on the TSP, with an emphasis on the tools. Finally, conclusions are offered in Section 5.5.

## 5.2    A Small Case Study: Binary Search Trees

Binary search trees (BSTs) are a convenient data structure for representing elements from an ordered set. They provide efficient implementations of insertion, searching, predecessor, successor, and enumeration of the set in sorted order (traversal). Exhibit 5.1 shows a BST after inserting the seven words in the title of the exhibit, in that order.

There are many kinds of "balanced" BSTs in which the nodes are reorganized to ensure that all operations on the tree are relatively efficient. In this section we will consider the efficiency of standard BSTs in which no special attempts are made to balance the tree and the $N$ elements stay in the positions in which they are inserted. In Exhibit 5.1, the cost of searching for "seven" is 1 comparison, the cost of "tree" is 2 comparisons, etc. The expected cost of a successful search in a given BST is defined to be the sum of the search costs of all nodes divided by $N$. Exhibit 5.2 shows that in the best of all worlds, the elements may happen to form a perfectly balanced BST. In this particular 15-node tree, the maximum search cost is 4; in a perfectly balanced $N$-node BST, the average search cost is about $log_2 N$. On the other hand, Exhibit 5.3 shows that in the worst case, BSTs can degrade to linear search with an expected cost of roughly $N/2$.

Neither extreme is likely to occur in practice, and we are more interested in what happens on the average. But what does "average" mean? We'll make the simple assumption that each input permutation is equally likely to occur;

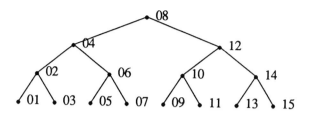

**EXHIBIT 5.2**
A balanced BST.

this is equivalent to assuming that each input is a real number independently chosen from a continuous distribution. Knuth [13] mathematically analyzes the expected search cost under this distribution.

Our goal now is to study experimentally the expected search cost. My first step in this endeavor was to examine a movie of the growth of a single random binary search tree with 200 nodes. An algorithm animation system allowed me to run a movie showing the tree's growth, pause with a mouse click, proceed backwards or forwards, go faster or slower, etc. This chapter cannot present the interactive session, so we'll have to settle for "stills" from the movie produced by the animation system. Exhibit 5.4 shows the BST after 25, 50, and 100 random insertions; Exhibit 5.5 shows the final tree with 200 nodes. The BST is certainly not perfectly balanced, but it appears to be closer in shape to the balanced tree in Exhibit 5.2 than to the linear tree in Exhibit 5.3. The average search cost over the 200 nodes in the tree is 8.44, which is much closer to $log_2 200 \approx 7.65$ than to $N/2 = 100$. This single anecdote gives us hope that

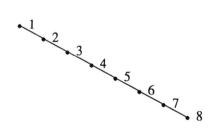

**EXHIBIT 5.3**
A linear BST.

**EXHIBIT 5.4**
A random tree after 25, 50, and 100 insertions.

the average search cost in a random BST might be close to the search cost in a perfectly balanced tree.

Our next step is to perform a simple experiment. Exhibit 5.6 reports the average search costs in 200 random trees with values of $N$ spread evenly between 50 and 20,000 on a logarithmic scale. Because we hope that the search cost grows roughly as $log\ N$, we choose to make the $x$-axis logarithmic and the $y$-axis linear. The data indeed appear to lie near a straight line. We are, therefore, justified in fitting the data to a function of the form $A\ log_2\ N\ +\ B$; a least-squares regression gives $A = 1.369$ and $B = -1.632$, with 95% confidence intervals of 0.032 and 0.32, respectively. The residuals in the bottom part

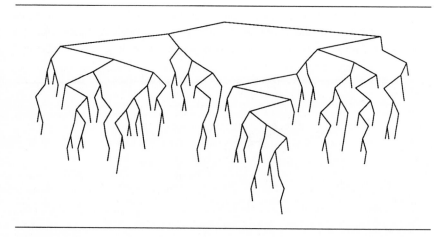

**EXHIBIT 5.5**
The tree after 200 insertions.

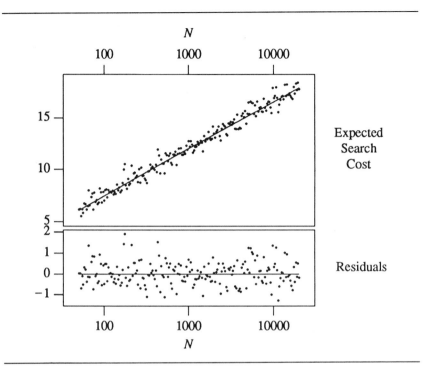

**EXHIBIT 5.6**
Search cost as a function of tree size.

of the graph are the average search costs minus the fit $1.369 log_2 N - 1.632$; their well behaved distribution underlines the appropriateness of the model.

This experiment has indeed led us in the proper direction. Knuth [13] shows that the expected search cost in a random $N$-node BST is $2(1 + 1/N)H_N - 3$ (where $H_N = 1 + 1/2 + 1/3 + ... + 1/N$), or approximately $1.386\ log_2 N - 1.85 + O((log\ N)/N)$. Thus, the cost of searching a random tree is only about 40% more than that of searching a perfectly balanced tree. It is hard, but not impossible, to design an experiment to lead to the wrong asymptotic growth of BSTs. My first silly experiment varied $N$ from 1 to 16 and measured three trees at each value; the function $0.20N + 1.27$ was a fair fit to the resulting data. A second experiment built one tree for $N$ in 1000..1050; the expected search cost was nicely modeled by the constant 12.07. Neither of these experiments achieved what our first did: an asymptotic view of the algorithm.

But is this mathematical abstraction an accurate model of the real world? Some data sets represent exactly the worst case. Consider, for instance, a spelling program that reads the words in a dictionary in sorted order. As a more typical

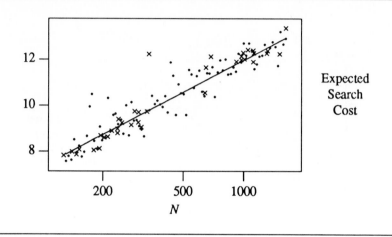

**EXHIBIT 5.7**
An experiment on search cost.

model of input text, the next experiment built 38 trees by processing 38 text files, files that make a book (specifically [4]). For each file, a tree was built by inserting the words of the file in order (where a word is defined as a longest alphanumeric string, with upper case letters mapped to lower case). Before reading on, think for a minute about the shape of trees built from text files.

> Please stop and think now.

Before I ran the experiment, I had strong expectations about its outcome. I guessed that most of the files would behave just slightly worse than random text; after all, there was no reason to expect the text to occur in sorted order (always being careful does ensure failing globally happens infrequently). Further reflection showed, though, that one file might provide exactly the worst case: the index of a book is useful precisely because it is sorted. I therefore expected to see that most files were close to uniform, while one was particularly expensive.

Exhibit 5.7 graphically describes the results of the experiment. The dots plot the random experiments from Exhibit 5.6, the crosses plot the text files, and the line is Knuth's function of $1.386 \ log_2 \ N \ - \ 1.85$. I was surprised to observe that the text files seemed to perform, if anything, slightly better than the random files. I was pretty sure that the outlier near $N = 400$ was the index.

Exhibit 5.8 zooms in on the part of Exhibit 5.7 with $N$ in the range 250..1000, and plots the name of the file instead of a cross. I was shocked to observe that the extreme outlier was not the index, but rather the preface.

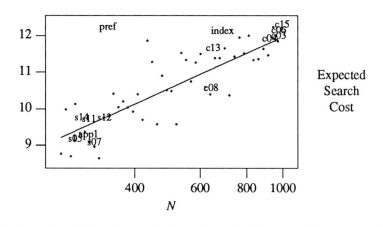

**EXHIBIT 5.8**
Details of Exhibit 5.7.

When I examined the file, I found that its first line was the Troff barbarism `.af zz i`, which helps to print page numbers as roman numerals. Thus the first word inserted into the tree was "af", the second was "zz", and the third was "i". Since the lion's share of words fall between "af" and "zz", those two nodes at the top of the tree add two comparisons for every later node. An animation showed that the rest of the tree looks like a typical random BST. If one lowers the $y$-value of the preface by two in Exhibit 5.7, it falls nicely into the cluster of points.

But what happened to the index? The real index was saved by 20 lines of (commented) formatting and title text that contains 100 words in relatively random order. Those words formed a starting stree into which the subsequent sorted words gracefully fell. To capture the flavor of the index as readers see it, I built a "tuned" index that removes the title, formatting information, and page numbers. The first few lines in the resulting file were:

```
Adams, J. L.
Aho, A. V.
Alexander
Algol
algorithm design
algorithms: see searching, sorting
algorithms, analysis of
```

Exhibit 5.9 shows the search tree after 30 insertions. Although the first words on the line do indeed occur in sorted order, later text forms a more

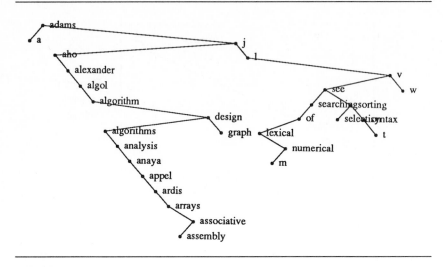

**EXHIBIT 5.9**
The Index BST after 30 insertions.

balanced tree to the right. (Notice that the simple pictorial representation leads to two ugly overprintings in that exhibit.) Exhibit 5.10 shows the shape of the final tree: there are several long spines to the left, but they become less frequent to the right of the tree. After $N = 373$ distinct words have been inserted, the average search cost is 14.98, or about $1.75 log_2 N$.

To summarize this section, here are some of the facts we have learned about nonbalanced binary search trees.

□ In the worst case, BSTs can degrade to sequential search. Some data sets that arise in practice, such as sorted dictionaries, realize this worst case.

□ On the average, random inputs have a search cost only about 40% worse than perfectly balanced trees. Most of the text files we studied behave very much like random inputs.

□ For files that are clearly not random, a slight trace of randomness seems to outweigh a lot of sortedness.

All in all, I'd feel pretty comfortable using nonbalanced BSTs as a data structure for processing text files like these.[1] How would binary search trees perform

[1] When I was an undergraduate, I wrote a program that used a BST to prepare the index of names for the college yearbook. The input data was on punched cards in several different formats that prohibited sorting by a card sorter. I knew that the input contained many long sorted runs (the names in a group photograph appeared adjacently in sorted

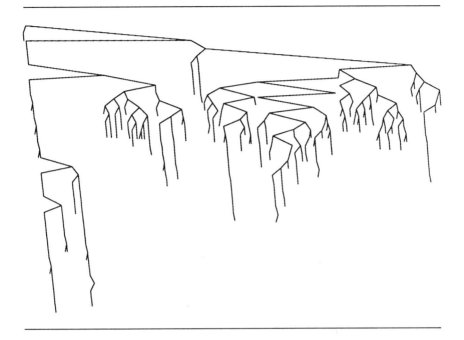

**EXHIBIT 5.10**
The final Index BST.

for your text files? The next section describes how you might perform similar experiments to answer the question.

Our first experiment on BSTs follows and supports Knuth's mathematical analysis of expected search cost. Sometimes, though, experiment leads theory: Eppinger's [11] empirical study of the expected search cost in BSTs with deletions and insertions led the way for later mathematical analysis.[2] Experiments are, however, the primary tool for showing how mathematical abstractions relate to reality. The anecdotal experiments described by animations are helpful in giving insight into why binary search trees behave as they do.

If experiments are useful, why aren't they conducted more frequently?

order) that I feared would cause the BST to degrade to linear search. I therefore used the randomizing algorithm of shuffling the deck of several thousand cards to appear in a random order. If I had to solve the problem now, I would stack the first 100 or so cards to form a well balanced starting tree, and let later cards fall as they may into that tree.

[2]Previous experimenters observed that the average search cost decreases in trees after repeated insertion/deletion pairs. Eppinger ran larger experiments and observed that the search cost initially decreases and then later increases, and finally reaches an asymptotic state (after roughly $N^2$ pairs) that is greater than the original search cost.

Most programmers believe that experiments are very costly. The experiments in this section, though, were relatively inexpensive: the program, animations, experiments, and analyses together took only a few hours.

## 5.3     The Tools Behind the Scenes

In this section we'll study the tools that were used in the experiments in Section 5.2. This section is not intended as a tutorial introduction to the various tools; rather, it shows how experiments can be conducted easily.

### 5.3.1     Algorithm Animation

The trees in Section 5.2 were drawn by the Anim animation system described by Bentley and Kernighan [8]. That system was designed to produce primitive output with little effort; programmers can animate a typical program in an hour or two with a few dozen lines of code. Brown and Sedgewick [9] describe a system that produces more sophisticated output, but is more difficult to use.

The computation depicted in Exhibit 5.1, for instance, was described by a "script" file named `bst1.s` , written by the `bst` program that we'll see in the next subsection. The file begins with this text:

```
#stat distinct_ipl_total 7 19 7
text ljust 6 -1 "  seven"
text 6 -1 bullet
click insert
line 6 -1 3 -2
text ljust 3 -2 "  insertions"
text 3 -2 bullet
click insert
```

The first line in the file is a comment because its first character is the sharp sign # ; it notes that of the 7 total words inserted, there were 7 distinct words, and the sum of search costs for the 7 words is 19 (hence the average search cost is $19/7 = 2.71$). The second line describes the left-justified text "seven" (preceded by two blanks) at Cartesian coordinates $(6, -1)$, and the third line puts a bullet at that position; these two statements together draw a labeled node. The fourth line is a click statement that marks the insertion of the first node. The next four statements insert the second node: a line connects it to its parent, two text statements draw the node, and the click statement marks the event. These lines were written by five different print statements in the program.

The script file can be interpreted by several programs. One Movie program allows one to study the computation in an interactive session controlled by a mouse and a keyboard; another Movie program prepares a more elegant animation suitable for presentation as a videotape. The Stills program was used to include Exhibit 5.1 in a Troff document by a description (roughly) like this:

```
.begin stills
file      bst1.s
frameht   1.1
framewid 2
print     final
.end
```

The first and last lines delimit the description; the second line names the script file, the third and fourth lines give the size of the picture, and the fifth line states that the final picture should be printed.

## 5.3.2  The Program

The workhorse program for the experiments is named bst . The script file bst1.s was produced by the command

```
bst -s <bst1.text >bst1.s
```

where bst1.text contains the text "seven insertions into a binary search tree", one word per line. The -s flag requests that the strings be printed as part of the animation (the default is to print the skeleton trees without text). The -v flag requests that only the statistical values be printed and no animation be produced (this was used for the larger experiments). The -n*number* flag states that *number* is the maximum number of nodes allowed in the tree (the program stops reading the file when that number is reached—it was used to produce Exhibit 5.9).

The bst program was written in about 120 lines of C. It reads the input file and inserts each word (one word per line) into the BST; it also inserts the new word at the end of a linked list. At the end of the file, it traverses the tree to calculate statistics and positions at which the various nodes are to be printed (the $I^{th}$ smallest word is printed at $x$ position $I$, the $y$ value of a node is the negative of its depth in the tree). If the animation is requested, the program then traverses the linked list and writes the script file. Simpler renditions of binary search trees can be prepared more easily; Bentley and Kernighan [8] present a 17-line Awk program to produce similar script files.

## 5.3.3  Supporting Programs

The bst program has simple input and output. Performing the experiments in Section 5.2 required the services of several additional programs. The one-line

UNIX Shell script wordify prepares text files for bst by translating uppercase to lowercase, removing nonalphanumeric characters, and placing one word per line. Thus the script file bst1.s could have been made by this command:

```
echo Seven insertions into a binary search tree. |
    wordify | bst -s >bst1.s
```

The command genfloat 10 generates 10 random floating point numbers between 0 and 1, one number per line; the program is implemented in 4 lines in the Awk language described by Aho, Kernighan and Weinberger [2]:

```
BEGIN { srand(); n = int(ARGV[1]+.5)
        for (i = 1; i <= n; i++)
                print rand() + .0001*rand()
      }
```

(The two calls to rand avoid problems inherent in 15-bit random numbers.) The 200-node tree in Exhibit 5.5 was made by the pipeline

```
genfloat 200 | bst >bst4.s
```

The data on 200 random trees described in Exhibit 5.6 was generated by this Awk program:

```
BEGIN { lo = log(50); hi = log(20000); inc = (hi-lo)/200
        for (x = lo; x <= hi; x += inc)
            system("genfloat " exp(x) " | bst -v")
      }
```

The loop generates 200 values evenly spaced between 50 and 20,000 on a log scale. At each value it passes to the UNIX system a command that generates the appropriate number of random floats, then pipes it through bst with the -v flag to print only the values (and no animations). The resulting data file, bst.e1.d , starts with these lines:

```
#stat n_ipl_words 50 305 50
#stat n_ipl_words 52 321 52
#stat n_ipl_words 53 290 53
#stat n_ipl_words 55 338 55
#stat n_ipl_words 56 323 56
```

Section 3.2 of Crowder, Dembo, and Mulvey's [10] paper on describing computational experiments has the title "Reproducibility." They state (in italics) that "an absolute, reasonable, and scientifically justifiable criterion should be that the authors themselves be able to replicate their experiments." The tools described in this chapter make it easy to reproduce experiments.

### 5.3.4 Data Analysis

The graphs in Section 5.2 were prepared by the Grap program described by Bentley and Kernighan [7]. The data points in the top panel of Exhibit 5.6, for instance, were plotted by a Grap program like this:

```
.G1
coord log x
label top "N"
label right "Expected" "Search" "Cost"
copy "bst.e1.d" thru { dot at $3, $4/$3 }
.G2
```

The first and last lines delimit the Grap input, the `coord` statement renders the $x$-coordinate on a logarithmic scale, and the two `label` statements label the axes. The `copy` statement places a dot in the graph for each line in the file.

The regression line plotted in Exhibit 5.6 was computed by this command:

```
$ awk '{print $3, $4/$3}' bst.e1.d |
        l2fit -lx 'a*log(x)/log(2.0) + b'
1.36917 -1.63241
$
```

The Awk command produces a file in which each line contains a value of $N$ followed by the expected search cost. That file is piped through the L2fit program for performing least-squares fitting described by Bentley, Fernandez, Kernighan and Schryer [6]. The optimal values of $A$ and $B$ appear on the standard output in alphabetical order; as a side effect, L2fit produces a one-page output file that plots the data points, fitted function, residuals, confidence intervals, etc.

## 5.4 A Large Case Study: The Traveling Salesman Problem

The binary search trees in Section 5.2 were a finger exercise, an evening's diversion to illustrate the tools in Section 5.3. In this section we'll study a more substantial example: a set of experiments on the TSP that represents about six months of effort spread over a period of a year and a half. We'll start with a brief glimpse of the experiments, and then turn to the tools behind them.

### 5.4.1 The Problem

These experiments deal with traveling salesman problems in which we are to compute a short path through a set of $N$ points in the plane. The left path in Exhibit 5.11, for instance, is constructed by an approximate version of Christofides'

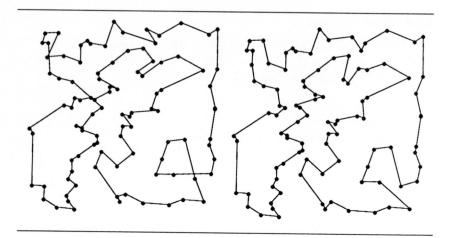

**EXHIBIT 5.11**
A CH tour through 100 points, then 2-Opting.

Heuristic (CH) through 100 points uniformly distributed over the unit square; the right path is that tour after improvements by the two-opting (2-Opt) heuristic. The first tour has length 8.76, while the second tour's length is decreased to 8.31 (an improvement of about five percent). Mathematical analysis shows that the CH tour is never more than 50% longer than the optimal tour through a set, and can be implemented in time roughly proportional to $N^3$. Experiments, however, indicate that on uniform point sets, approximate CH tours are usually within 15% of optimal and can be computed in $O(N \ log \ N)$ time.

Bentley [5] describes experiments on a dozen different starting heuristics and several forms of improvements by local optimizations. The analysis of tour length on uniform data sets is similar to the analysis of BSTs: probabilistic analysis shows that many heuristics have length proportional to $\sqrt{N}$, and regressions like Exhibit 5.6 show that a fit of the form $A\sqrt{N} + B$ accurately describes the data. The first step in the analysis of computational cost is to identify the parameters to study, such as the number of searches made by the algorithm and the number of nodes visited by each search. Techniques of exploratory data analysis helped to sleuth out the forms of the various functions, and regressions then computed parameters. Experiments on central processing unit (CPU) time showed that it was accurately predicted by the more abstract parameters. (CPU time is hard to measure accurately and varies widely among hardware and software implementations.)

Although most of the algorithms have experimentally observed run times of $O(N \ log \ N)$ on uniform point sets, I was not able to prove worst-case bounds tighter than $O(N^2)$. To gain insight into the performance of the algorithms on nonuniform data sets, an experiment studied 10 nasty distributions, such as normal data, clusters of normals, and points on a horizontal line, diagonal line, and the edge of a circle. The distributions were chosen both to model data sets that arise in particular applications, and because they serve as worst-case inputs in papers on the analysis of geometric algorithms.

Exhibit 5.12 uses a cluttered graph to describe the results of one such experiment. It shows one cost of 2-opting a CH tour: the number of nodes visted per search in the key data structure, a multidimensional binary search tree (which generalizes standard BSTs to geometric searching problems). The circles show the benchmark performance on uniform data, and the numbers plot the growth on the 10 ugly distributions. The 10 distributions fall into three groups: linear distributions 1, 2, 5, and 6 (with the points along lines and circles) are about 50% faster than uniform data; clustered distributions 3, 4, 7, 8, and 9 are up to 30% slower than uniform; distribution 10—which has the points spread uniformly over the plus sign "+"—starts off substantially slower than uniform, but becomes faster near $N = 1000$ (the value at which a certain algorithmic speedup is first invoked). This heuristic seems to be somewhat robust for nonuniform data; a 30% slowdown isn't terrible. Other heuristics are quite robust and experience just a few percent slowdown, while yet others fall to pieces with slowdowns of orders of magnitude.

While I was building the program, I tried well over 50 algorithmic variations intended to improve performance. I was not able to analyze the effects mathematically, so I had to resort to experiments. Exhibit 5.13 is the result of an experiment comparing "true" and "approximate" 2-opting on CH tours. I hoped that the approximate version would be significantly faster than the true version, but I feared that it would result in substantially longer tours. The experiment built 20 uniform point sets of size $N = 10,000$, and applied both versions of 2-opting to each set. Exhibit 5.13 reports the result of each experiment as two points connected by a line: the left point plots the CPU time and length of the approximate version, while the right point gives that information for the true version.

This messy graph contains several messages. The run time of approximate 2-opting is faster and more predictable than the true 2-opting. The tours made by the true version are usually a tad shorter than the approximation tours, but not always, and the variation from one tour to another is greater than the difference due to algorithm type.

## 5.4.2  The Program

The primary program for this experiment is written in 6000 lines of C++ (see [15]). It implements a dozen different starting heuristics and three kinds of local optimizations. It also contains a wide variety of supporting code for set algo-

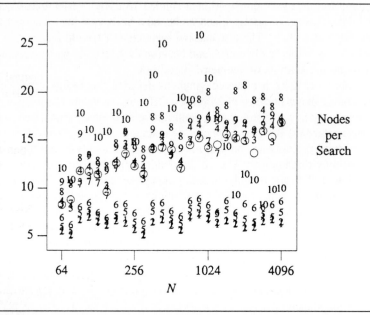

**EXHIBIT 5.12**
CH+2-Opting on 10 ugly distributions.

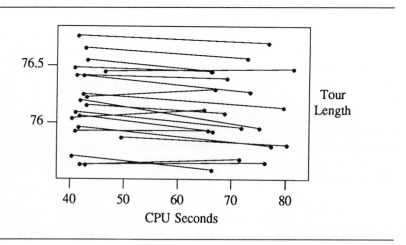

**EXHIBIT 5.13**
Tradeoff of time and tour length.

rithms (linked lists, selection, heaps), graph algorithms (building and maintaining graphs and computing Eulerian circuits), and geometric algorithms (multidimensional binary search trees, minimum spanning trees, matching).

The program is controlled by input described in a little language (see Column 9 of [4]). Exhibit 5.11, for instance, was generated by this input:

```
n 100
seed 1
distrib uni
detail 50
tour ch
touropt 2opt
```

The first three lines describe the input: $N$ is 100, 1 is the seed for the random number generator, and the points are from a uniform distribution. The last two lines state that the tour is built by Christofides' heuristic and then optimized by 2-opting. The detail controls the level of detail in the output of the program. At 0, the program performs its task silently; at 10, it writes a summary of key statistics; at 50 and above, it produces a movie using Anim.

The simplest possible movie is made by assigning 50 to detail. It shows each edge as it is added to and deleted from the tour; at this detail, it is interesting to watch a tour of several hundred points being constructed and then optimized. As the level of detail increases to 100, the movie contains additional views of the algorithm and records more interesting events. At level 60, for instance, one also sees the multidimensional binary search trees that support the algorithms. At level 100, the movie contains separate views of all supporting data structures and describes all events in excruciating detail, down to each node visited in all search trees. This level is appropriate for debugging a run on a dozen-city tour.

The Anim animations played a key role throughout the evolution of the program. I first executed the program when it was a couple of hundred of lines long. At that time, it could read the input and construct and draw a random point set. As I added each new operation to the code, I tested and debugged it by watching animations. The movies therefore provided the vast majority of the scaffolding of the program (but later versions also used a large regression test). The original animations all took place in the plane; to debug algorithms in $K$-dimensional space, I built a simple preprocessor for Anim in about 50 lines of Awk that allowed me to see three-dimensional movies with a stereo viewer. After adding a couple dozen lines of code to the program, I was able to study the algorithms working in three-space.

The program can read problems from an input file or generate random data from eleven different distributions. This allows the program to be used for production runs and for experiments on classic TSP problems from the literature, such as Kernighan and Lin's popular 318-city problem. (Good taste dictates that all inputs should be read from a file and that random inputs should be produced by a supporting program, but the input/output time required to read huge problems was significantly greater than the time required by some of the TSP heuristics.)

Before I put much faith in my experiments, I had to have a great deal of confidence that the 6,000-line program was correct. Watching the movies allowed me to see the program at work. The program is littered with about 100 assert statements that ensure that the program status conforms to my expectations. Regression tests warn me when the behavior changes, and the growth of statistical quantities gives me a broader view of the program. These various views help to convince me that the program behaves as I hope.

### 5.4.3  Instrumenting The Program

My first tools for instrumenting the program were the profilers provided by the C++ environment. During the development of the program I always ran it with a profiler that gave me counts and approximate CPU times for each procedure; these led me to the hot spots as I tuned the code. For a more detailed view, I used a more expensive profiler that recorded the number of times that each line of source code was executed.

My primary instrumentation tool, however, was built into the program using the techniques of "self-describing data" described in Column 4 of [4]. When the detail is set to 10, for instance, the program produces this output on a million-city run:

```
#default seed 587542180
#default distrib uni
      ...
#default cachedist 0
#input n   1000000
#input seed  225
#input distrib  uni
#input detail   10
#input showprog 1
#input tour   mf
#begin mftour
#begin kd.build
#stat kd.build kdnodes     524287
#stat kd.build cpusecs 257.083326
#end kd.build
#stat mftour distcalcs   1000000
#stat mftour distsqrds   26898048
#stat mftour nnsrchs    2595058
#stat mftour kdnnnodes   37597418
#stat mftour kdnndists   23771540
#stat mftour edgeadds    1000000
#stat mftour tourcost 809.76444
#stat mftour pqswaps    46068623
```

```
#stat mftour cpusecs 1704.60008
#end mftour
```

All of these lines begin with the sharp sign # to mark them as comments
when they are mixed with Anim input. The `default` lines give the default
values of various parameters (about 40 altogether). The `input` lines echo the
input as it is read. The defaults and inputs together allow any experiment to
be reproduced. The `begin` and `end` lines bracket key operations (notice that
they may be nested). The `stat` lines give the statistics as name-value pairs;
the `mftour` used 1,000,000 distance calculations, 26,898,048 squared distance
calculations, etc. This output is easy to read, both for human browsers and for
analysis by programs.

The program produces these statistics through a set of instrumentation functions. The start of the multifragment (or MF) tour heuristic contains this statement:

```
STATS(10, "mftour")
```

It states that statistics are to be gathered under this name if `detail` is 10 or
greater. (The implementation of `STATS` uses a C++ destructor—which is called
automatically when the block is exited—to print the statistics.) Other routines
collect statistics; here is a function from the C++ class `tour`:

```
void tour::addedge(int i, int j)
{       inc(EDGEADDS);
        inc(TOURCOST, dist(i, j));
        ANIM(50, "edge")
                ptset->drawline(i, j, "tour", "");
        MINA
}
```

When an algorithm adds an edge between two points, it modifies its data structures and then calls `addedge`. That function uses the overloaded function `inc`
to increment the number of edge adds and the tour cost. If the level of detail is
at least 50, the statements bracketed by `ANIM` and `MINA` draw an edge and give
the event the click name "edge".

I used the program to solve a number of large TSPs; some million-city
problems required several hours on a VAX-8550. I made these large runs after
midnight on a lightly loaded machine; several times, though, other large jobs
caused my computation to page thrash and make little progress. To follow the
progress of the computation I therefore added another instrumentation facility.
The input language therefore supports a new statement of the form `showprog`
`10000`, which states that progress is to be reported every 10,000 steps. The key
loop in the MF routine then begins like this:

```
for (i = 0; i < n-1; i++) {
        progress(i, "mftour main loop");
        ...
```

Every specified number of steps, the `progress` function prints a line giving the descriptive text, the value of the parameter, the CPU time since the last progress report, and the total CPU time so far. This mechanism also gave me insight into the performance of some algorithms: the CPU times showed that operations near the beginning of one algorithm were more expensive than later operations; given the experimental clue, it was easy to deduce why the algorithm behaved this way.

### 5.4.4  The Experiments

Our discussion so far has dealt with a single run of the program. In this subsection we will consider performing a set of experiments and analyzing the resulting data. The experiments used several supporting programs of general utility. One is a macro processor with all the typical functions: definition of text strings, replacement of defined text, file inclusion, conditional expansion, etc. Another is a "cross-product generator" program sketched in Problem 8 in Section 4.5 of [4]. Given this input file

```
[1 2] constant [a b]
```

the generator produces this output file:

```
1 constant a

1 constant b

2 constant a

2 constant b
```

Each list in brackets in the input is expanded in the output; if the input has three bracket lists with $I$, $J$, and $K$ elements, there will be $I \times J \times K$ items in the output file, each separated by a blank line.

With these tools in hand, we can examine the description of the experiments. The experiment shown in Exhibit 5.12, for instance, was described by a file that begins something like this:

```
@default NLB 64
@default NUB 4096
@default TNAME ch
@default ONAME 2
    ...
n [mulseq @NLB@ @NUB@ 2]
distrib [uni annulus arith ball clusnorm ... spokes]
detail 10
tour @TNAME@
touropt @ONAME@opt
```

The @default statements are interpreted by the macro processor; their values can be overridden by later or previous @define statements. The later text is interpreted by the cross-product generator. The distribution names following the distrib statements are a straightforward list. The n values are expanded as a "multiplicative sequence" starting at 64 and going to 4096, multiplied by 2 at each step.

Each of the experiments in the cross product is fed to the main program, which produces the name-value pairs shown earlier. Individual experiments are separated by blank lines, with redundant default lines removed for data compression. An Awk program, which is part of the description file, next builds a file in a form that is more easily processed by analysis tools. Grap and L2fit then prepare extensive summaries of interesting variables.

This file deals with the particular heuristic CH, given as the @default definition of TNAME; the name of the file is ch.exper.in. We could apply the same file to any other heuristic. For instance, we could study the MF heuristic by a file like this:

```
@define TNAME mf
@include ch.exper.in
```

This mechanism makes it easy to perform related sets of experiments.

As I built the program I conducted a series of pilot experiments to measure the performance of each algorithm as it was constructed. These experiments led me away from ineffective algorithms and toward more promising approaches. I also learned about appropriate quantities to measure and functional forms for later regressions. After the program became stable and I had performed several rounds of pilot experiments, I conducted the experiments for the final work. Each of the dozen sections in the paper is represented by a subdirectory. In addition to the on-line descriptions and summary databases in each subdirectory, I kept the Grap and L2fit output in a laboratory notebook. Although a particular section of the paper might explicitly contain only two or three graphs, the content is supported by a few dozen graphs and statistical regressions that convince me that there are no surprises lurking in the algorithms or their C++ implementations.

## 5.4.5   An Alternative Environment

David Johnson [12] has led an experimental team that since 1983 has conducted extensive experiments on a variety of problems in combinatorial optimization, including the TSP. Even though he and I live on the same software system, the experimental environment in which Johnson has worked was built around a different set of tools. While the tools were different, however, the underlying purposes were quite similar.

□ *Programming Language.* When Johnson started his experiments, C was the natural choice of programming language. By the time I implemented my program in the spring of 1988, C++ offered a stable language with more support for subtle data structures.

□ *Instrumentation.* Johnson instruments his program almost exclusively through the use of the procedure-time profiler invoked by the UNIX system command `cc -p`.

□ *Analysis Tools.* Johnson analyzes his data sets and prepares graphical displays of data in the S environment described by Becker, Chambers and Wilks [3].

□ *Algorithm Animation.* Johnson animates his algorithms with a system called GraphDraw that he and Linda Altounian built for the task.

Johnson and I have used the two programs to check one another, both on individual data sets and in sets of experiments.

## 5.5  Conclusions

The two case studies in this chapter have touched on several important points in the experimental analysis of algorithms. Unfortunately, there are many important ideas completely ignored by this chapter. McGeoch [14] discusses a number of additional techniques in her thesis, and illustrates them with four detailed case studies. For instance, she describes how "shortcuts" allow one to combine mathematical proofs with experiments to analyze part of an algorithm and simulate the remainder; this can reduce simulation cost while increasing experimental accuracy.

Even though much ground was left uncovered, these two case studies have allowed us to touch on most of the fundamental issues in the field. The important point are summarized in these "Ten Commandments for Experiments on Algorithms":

1. *Don't experiment when you should think; don't think when you should experiment.*

   It is foolish to conduct extensive experiments when the issue can be decided by a simple proof; it is equally foolish to labor over a proof of a "theorem" that a simple simulation can show is false. Whenever possible, use theory and experiment together to support one another.

2. *Define the goal of your experiment.*

   Start with narrow goals to achieve well-defined results, but keep your eyes open for surprises. Our first experiment on binary search trees determined the expected cost of searching under a mathematical model; our second experiment on BSTs studied the trees resulting from typical text files. The TSP experiments tested the efficacy of heuristics, their expected computational costs, and the relative merits of many variations. Measure quantities that can be precisely observed; be wary of CPU times.

3. *Write your workhorse program well.*

   Build the experiments around, not into, your program. Use a single program for animations, experiments, and production runs; the various views of the computation can help to identify bugs. Using separate programs guarantees more work and more bugs. Little languages provide a graceful interface to large programs; a "detail" knob allows one to control the quantity of output. Time and space performance are often important for conducting statistically significant simulations.

4. *Instrument your program.*

   Use profilers. Augment your programs with routines to gather and print key statistics. Keep the instruments in the production version; a temperature gauge is a critical part of an automobile.

5. *Animate your algorithms.*

   Movies are useful for testing, debugging, tuning, and teaching. Simple movies can be simple to make, and effective across many problem domains.

6. *Plan your experiments.*

   Start with pilot studies to determine what to measure and how many samples to take. Describe your experiments so you can vary them easily. If your aim is to gain insight into asymptotic performance, make sure that your experiments go to asymptopia.

7. *Your experimental results form a database; treat it with respect.*

   Data from experiments should at least be stored as an orderly set of files. Keep the ability to reproduce any particular experiment so you can track down interesting anomalies. Keep a laboratory notebook (electronic or paper) of your progress.

8. *Use the tools of data analysis.*

   Many data sets can be analyzed with the simple tools of graphical displays of data and least-squares curve fitting. More advanced tools can solve more interesting problems.

9. *Put the pictures in the paper.*

   Whether you're writing program documentation, user manuals, lecture notes, or learned papers, include animations, graphs, and other explanatory pictures.

**10.** *Keep a kit full of sharp tools.*

When I perform experiments, I write programs in C++, instrument them with profilers and well-tested routines, animate them with Anim, store the results on a UNIX file system, manipulate them with Awk programs, use Grap and L2fit for data analysis, control experiments with a set of tools, and document the results in Troff. Collect a set of tools that are comfortable and effective for you to use.

## 5.6   Acknowledgments

I am grateful for the helpful comments of Rick Becker, David Johnson, Brian Kernighan, Tom Szymanski, and Chris Van Wyk.

## References

[1] A. V. Aho, J. E. Hopcroft, and J. D. Ullman. *The Design and Analysis of Computer Algorithms.* Reading, MA: Addison-Wesley, 1974.

[2] A. V. Aho, B. W. Kernighan, and P. J. Weinberger. *The Awk Programming Language.* Reading, MA: Addison-Wesley, 1988.

[3] R. A. Becker, J. M. Chambers, and A. R. Wilks. *The New S Language.* Wadsworth & Brooks/Cole, 1988.

[4] J. L. Bentley. *More Programming Pearls: Confessions of a Coder.* Reading, MA: Addison-Wesley, 1988.

[5] J. L. Bentley. Experiments on traveling salesman heuristics. In *Proceedings of the First ACM-SIAM Symposium on Discrete Algorithms.* San Francisco, CA, January 22-24, 1990, pp. 91-99.

[6] J. L. Bentley, M. F. Fernandez, B. W. Kernighan, and N. L. Schryer. Simple Interfaces for Numerical Subroutines Using Unix Tools. AT&T Bell Laboratories Computing Science Technical Report, September 1990.

[7] J. L. Bentley and B. W. Kernighan. GRAP—A language for typesetting graphs: Tutorial and user manual. In *Unix Research System Papers, Tenth Edition Volume II,* Philadelphia, PA: Saunders College Publishing, 1990, pp. 109-146.

[8] J. L. Bentley and B. W. Kernighan. A system for algorithm animation: Tutorial and user manual. In *Unix Research System Papers, Tenth Edition Volume II,* Philadelphia, PA: Saunders College Publishing, 1990, pp. 451-475.

[9] M. Brown and R. Sedgewick. Techniques for algorithm animation. *IEEE Software,* pp. 28-39, January, 1985.

[10] H. Crowder, R. S. Dembo, and J. M. Mulvey. On reporting computational experiments with mathematical software. *ACM Transactions on Mathematical Software 5(2),* 1979, pp. 193-203.

[11] J. L. Eppinger. An empirical study of insertion and deletion in binary search trees. *Communications of the ACM 26(9),* pp. 663-669, 1983.

[12] D. S. Johnson. Local optimization and the traveling salesman problem. In *Proceedings Seventeenth Colloquium on Automata, Languages and Programming*, pp. 446-461. Springer-Verlag, 1990.

[13] D. E. Knuth. *The Art of Computer Programming, Volume Three: Sorting and Searching*. Reading, MA: Addison-Wesley, 1973.

[14] C. C. McGeoch. Experimental Analysis of Algorithms. Ph.D. Thesis, Computer Science Department, Carnegie Mellon University Technical Report CMU-CS-87-124, Carnegie Mellon University, Pittsburgh, PA, 1986.

[15] B. Stroustrup. *The C++ Programming Language*. Reading, MA: Addison-Wesley, 1986.

# 6

---

# Tools and Rules for the Practicing Verifier

Zohar Manna and Amir Pnueli

The chapter presents a minimal proof theory that is adequate for proving the main important temporal properties of reactive programs. The properties we consider consist of the classes of *invariance*, *response*, and *precedence* properties. For each of these classes we present a small set of rules that is complete for verifying properties belonging to this class. We illustrate the application of these rules by analyzing and verifying the properties of a new algorithm for mutual exclusion.

---

## 6.1 Introduction

In this chapter we present a minimal proof theory that is adequate for proving interesting properties of concurrent programs. The simple theory is illustrated by a single example, which is a new and interesting algorithm for mutual exclusion [10].

There are several points we would like to demonstrate in this chapter. The first and main point is that a very little general (temporal) theory is required to handle the most important properties of concurrent programs. The types of properties, on which a practicing verifier (hoping that such a position will eventually become a standard in any quality assurance team) typically spends most

of his or her time, usually fall into two or three simple classes. By presenting
a simple but complete set of rules for verifying properties belonging to each
of these classes, we provide the practicing verifier with precisely the tools he
or she needs. This pragmatic approach can be nicely complemented by a more
theoretical presentation of a comprehensive theory of a language of specification
(temporal logic would have been our choice), its power to express a wide spectrum of program properties, and a comprehensive proof theory and investigation
of its completeness (e.g., [6]). However, it may be an educational mistake to
require the study of such a comprehensive approach as an essential requisite for
the pragmatic application of the verification tools that result from the general
theory.

Consequently, the approach we take in this chapter is to circumvent the
general theory of temporal logic and proceed as directly as possible to the
introduction of the classes of properties that are most frequently verified, and to
the proof rules that are appropriate for their verification.

There are three classes of properties we consider in this chapter, and believe
to cover the majority of properties one would ever wish to verify.

□ *Invariance.* An invariance property refers to an assertion $p$, and requires
that $p$ is an invariant over all the computations of a program $P$, i.e., all the
states arising in a computation of $P$ satisfy $p$. In temporal logic notation,
such properties are expressed by $\Box p$, for a state formula $p$.

□ *Response.* A response property refers to two assertions $p$ and $q$, and requires
that every $p$-state (a state satisfying $p$) arising in a computation is eventually
followed by a $q$-state. In temporal logic notation this is written as $p \Rightarrow \Diamond q$.
In the Unity notation [2] this property is called a *leads-to* property and is
written as $p \mapsto q$.

□ *Precedence.* A simple precedence property refers to three assertions $p$, $q$,
and $r$. It requires that any $p$-state initiates a $q$-interval (i.e., an interval all
of whose states satisfy $q$) that either runs to the end of the computation
or is terminated by an $r$-state. Such a property is useful in order to express the restriction that, following a certain condition, one future event
will always be preceded by another future event. For example, it may express the property that from the time a certain input has arrived, there
will be an output before the next input. Note that this does not guarantee
that the output will actually be produced. It only guarantees that the next
input (if any) will be preceded by an output. In temporal logic, this prop-
erty is expressed by $p \Rightarrow (q \, \mathsf{U} \, r)$, using the *unless* operator (weak *until*)
$\mathsf{U}$. More complex precedence properties refer to a sequence of assertions
$q_0, \ldots, q_{m-1}$ and replace the requirement of a single $q$-interval, by a requirement of a succession of a $q_0$-interval, followed by a $q_1$-interval, $\ldots$,
followed by a $q_{m-1}$-interval.

According to the classification of properties discussed by Alpern and Schneider [1], the invariance and precedence properties are *safety* properties, while the response properties are *liveness* properties. Referring to the classification of properties discussed by Manna and Pneuli [6], the response properties defined here are a special case of the *responsiveness* class defined there (which allows $p$ and $q$ to be *past* formulae rather than assertions). The class of precedence properties and proof rules associated with it have been introduced first by Manna and Pneuli [4].

We refer the reader to Manna and Pneuli [7] for a top down approach, which attempts to present the most general proof rules that cover as many properties as possible. Here, however, we take the opposite approach of presenting rules that are closely tailored for the restricted classes that are most frequently needed. This reduction in generality is justified only if we can demonstrate a gain in the convenience and efficacy of using those rules for verifying properties that fall in these classes. This brings us to the second point we wish to make in this chapter.

The chapter contains no new theoretical results. Rather, it recommends the adoption of a set notation for expressing the control state of a system with an unbounded, and even dynamic, set of processes, within the framework of old and tried proof methods, such as those set forth by Lamport [3] and Manna and Pneuli [5] and also by Pneuli and Zuck [9] where this set notation has been introduced for the analysis of probabilistic algorithms.

The algorithm we have chosen to verify is an ideal example for demonstrating the acute need for formal verification of concurrent programs, as well as the style and level of verification that is currently possible. We refer the reader to Szymanski [10] for some of its important features, such as using single-writer bounded shared variables and enjoying the property of *linear* delay. These features make this algorithm a significant improvement over most of its predecessors.

Although the algorithm appears to be quite simple and innocuous, the only way we could convince ourselves of its correctness was to construct the formal proof outlined in this chapter. Szymanski [10] presented an informal proof, which is as convincing as informal proofs can be. In fact, our formal proof derives its main ideas from a formalization of his informal arguments. However, if the question of correctness is crucial, such as having to decide whether to include this algorithm as a contention-resolving component in a hardware chip, we see no way but to carry out a formal verification.

We have learned two lessons from carrying out this verification exercise. The less encouraging lesson is that it requires a non-negligible deal of creativity and dexterity in manipulating logical formulae to come up with the appropriate set of auxiliary assertions (and other constructs needed for the proof). This is so even if the correct intuition is given and all that is required is to formalize that intuition. The more encouraging lesson is that, once the appropriate constructs have been found, the rest of the verification process, which requires the construction of the verification conditions (proof obligations) and proving their validity, can to a large extent be automated. It is not that we have come up with a surprisingly new automatic theorem prover. But inspection of the kinds of assertions generated for a proof of an algorithm like the one we study here, convinced us that for a large and interesting class of algorithms all these assertions belong to a decidable class.

## 6.2   Programs and Computations

The basic computational model we use to represent programs is that of a *fair transition system*. In this model, a program $P$ consists of the following components.

- $V = \{u_0, \ldots, u_{n-1}\}$—A finite set of *state variables*. Some of these variables represent *data* variables, which are explicitly manipulated by the program text. Other variables are *control* variables, which represent, for example, the location of control in each of the processes in a concurrent program. We assume each variable to be associated with a domain, over which it ranges.

- $\Sigma$—A set of *states*. Each state $s \in \Sigma$ is an interpretation of $V$, assigning to each variable $y \in V$ a value over its domain, which we denote by $s[y]$.

- $\mathcal{T}$—A set of *transitions*. Each transition $\tau \in \mathcal{T}$ is associated with an assertion $\rho_\tau(V, V')$, called the *transition relation*, which refers to both an unprimed and a primed version of the state variables. The purpose of the transition relation $\rho_\tau$ is to express a relation between a state $s$ and its successor $s'$. We use the unprimed version to refer to values in $s$, and the primed version to refer to values in $s'$. For example, the assertion $x' = x + 1$ states that the value of $x$ in $s'$ is greater by 1 than its value in $s$.

- $\Theta$—The *precondition*. This is an assertion characterizing all the initial states, i.e., states at which the computation of the program can start. A state is defined to be *initial* if it satisfies $\Theta$.

We define the state $s'$ to be a *$\tau$-successor* of the state $s$ if

$$\langle s, s' \rangle \models \rho_\tau(V, V'),$$

where $\langle s, s' \rangle$ is the joint interpretation that interprets $x \in V$ as $s[x]$ and interprets $x'$ as $s'[x]$. Following this definition, we can view the transition $\tau$ as a function

$\tau : \Sigma \mapsto 2^{\Sigma}$, defined by

$$\tau(s) = \{s' \mid s' \text{ is a } \tau\text{-successor of } s\}.$$

We say that the transition $\tau$ is *enabled* on the state $s$ if $\tau(s) \neq \phi$. Otherwise, we say that $\tau$ is *disabled* on $s$. We say that a state $s$ is *terminal* if all the transitions $\tau \in T$ are disabled on it. The enabledness of a transition $\tau$ can be expressed by the formula

$$En(\tau) : (\exists V')\rho_{\tau}(V, V'),$$

which is true in $s$ iff $s$ has some $\tau$-successor.

Assume a program $P$ for which the above components have been specified. Consider

$$\sigma : s_0, s_1, s_2, \ldots,$$

a finite or infinite sequence of states of $P$.

We say that the transition $\tau \in T$ is enabled *at position* $k$ of $\sigma$ if $\tau$ is enabled on $s_k$. We say that the transition $\tau$ is *taken* (completed) at position $k + 1, k = 0, 1, \ldots$, if $s_{k+1}$ is a $\tau$-successor of $s_k$. Note that several different transitions can be considered as taken at the same position.

The sequence $\sigma$ is defined to be a *computation* of $P$ if it satisfies the following requirements:

☐ *Initiality*   $s_0$ is initial, i.e., $s_0 \models \Theta$.

☐ *Consecution*   For each $j = 0, 1, \ldots$, the state $s_{j+1}$ is a $\tau$-successor of the state $s_j$, i.e., $s_{j+1} \in \tau(s_j)$, for some $\tau \in T$.

☐ *Termination*   Either $\sigma$ is infinite, or it ends in a state $s_k$ that is terminal.

☐ *Justice*   For each transition $\tau \in T$, it is not the case that $\tau$ is continually enabled beyond some position $j$ in $\sigma$ (i.e., $\tau$ is enabled at every position $k \geq j$) while $\tau$ is not taken beyond $j$.

For a program $P$, we denote by $Comp(P)$ the set of all computations of $P$. We say that a state $s$ is *P-accessible* if it appears in some computation of $P$. Clearly, any $\tau$-successor of a $P$-accessible state is also $P$-accessible.

We assume an underlying assertional language, which contains the predicate calculus and interpreted symbols for expressing the standard operations and relations over some concrete domains. We refer to a formula in the assertional language as an *assertion*.

For an assertion $p$ and a state $s$, such that $p$ holds on $s$, we say that $s$ is a *p-state*. For a computation $\sigma : s_0, s_1, \ldots$, such that $s_j$ is a $p$-state, we call $j$ a *p-position*.

### 6.2.1  Set Notation

We introduce the following notation to facilitate a compact representation of sets of natural numbers.

A *set specification* consists of a list of one or more *set specifiers*, where each specifier is either a single natural number, or an *interval specifier* of the form $a..b$, for $a \leq b$, natural numbers. The set defined by the interval specifier $a..b$ consists of all the integers not smaller than $a$ and not larger than $b$, i.e.,

$$\{a..b\} \;\; = \;\; \{m \mid a \leq m \leq b\}$$

The set defined by a list of specifiers is the union of the sets defined by the individual specifiers. Thus, the set specified by $\{1, 3..5, 7\}$ consists of the natural numbers

$$\{1\,,\,3\,,\,4\,,\,5\,,\,7\}.$$

In the following, we define on several occasions a family of sets $A_a$ indexed by natural numbers. These definitions immediately extend to define sets indexed by general set specifications as follows:

$$A_{sp_1,\ldots,sp_k} \;\; = \;\; \bigcup_{a \in \{sp_1,\ldots,sp_k\}} A_a.$$

Thus, $A_{1,3..5,7}$ is given by

$$A_1 \cup A_3 \cup A_4 \cup A_5 \cup A_7.$$

---

## 6.3   The Program as a Fair Transition System

The program we wish to study can be given as

$$\textbf{MUTEX} :: \left[ \begin{array}{c} flag: \textbf{array}[0..n-1] \textbf{ of } 0..4 \textbf{ where } flag[0..n-1] = 0 \\ P[0] \parallel P[1] \parallel \ldots \parallel P[n-1] \end{array} \right]$$

Each process $P[i], i = 0, \ldots, n-1$ of the program is given by

**local** $j$ : $[0..n-1]$ **where** $j = 0$

$\ell_0$: **loop forever do**
    **begin**
        $\ell_1$ : Non Critical
        $\ell_2$ : $flag[i] := 1$
        $\ell_3$ : **wait until** $\forall j : 0 \leq j < n : (flag[j] < 3)$
        $\ell_4$ : $flag[i] := 3$
        $\ell_5$ : **if** $\exists j : 0 \leq j < n : (flag[j] = 1)$ **then**
            **begin**

$\ell_6$: $flag[i] := 2$
$\ell_7$: **wait until** $\exists j : 0 \le j < n : (flag[j] = 4)$
   **end**
$\ell_8$ : $flag[i] := 4$
$\ell_9$ : **wait until** $\forall j : 0 \le j < i : (flag[j] < 2)$
$\ell_{10}$: Critical
$\ell_{11}$: **wait until** $\forall j : i < j < n : (flag[j] < 2 \ \vee \ flag[j] > 3)$
$\ell_{12}$: $flag[i] := 0$
  **end**

Below, we identify the four components of a fair transition system, namely, state variables, states, transitions, and precondition, for the **MUTEX** program. This identification enables us to view the program as a fair transition system, and apply to it the verification methods that will be later presented for a general fair transition system.

□ $V$—The state variables are given by

$$L_0, \ldots, L_{12}, \quad flag[0], \ldots, flag[n-1], \quad j_0, \ldots, j_{n-1}.$$

The variables $L_0, \ldots, L_{12}$, are control variables that range over subsets of $\{0, \ldots, n-1\}$. At any state of the computation, $L_k$, for $k = 0, \ldots, 12$, contains the indices of all the processes that currently are ready to execute the statement labeled $\ell_k$. Variables $flag[0], \ldots, flag[n-1]$ naturally represent the current values of the corresponding program variables. The variables $j_0, \ldots, j_{n-1}$ represent the current values of the local variable $j$ of the processes $P[0], \ldots, P[n-1]$, respectively. As we will see below, we assume that a compound test, such as $\forall j : 0 \le j < n : (flag[j] < 3)$, is performed by several atomic tests, each checking the current value of $flag[j]$ for some $j$. The variable $j_i$ indicates that the next flag value to be tested by $P[i]$ is $flag[j_i]$.

□ $\Sigma$—The states consist of all the possible assignments to the state variables of values in their respective domains.

□ $\Theta$—The precondition is given by the assertion

$$\Theta \quad : \quad (L_0 = \{0, \ldots, n-1\}) \wedge (L_{1..12} = \phi) \wedge \bigwedge_{i=0}^{n-1} \Big( (flag[i] = 0) \wedge (j_i = 0) \Big)$$

Thus, at the initial state of the program, all processes reside at the location $\ell_0$, and the values of $flag[0], \ldots, flag[n-1]$ and of $j_0, \ldots, j_{n-1}$ are all zero.

To express the movement of control effected by the transitions, we introduce the following abbreviations:

$$move(i, k, m) \quad : \quad (L'_k = L_k - \{i\}) \wedge (L'_m = L_m \cup \{i\})$$
$$stay \quad : \quad \bigwedge_{k=0}^{12} (L'_k = L_k)$$

Clearly, $move(i, k, m)$ describes the movement of control within process $P[i]$ from $\ell_k$ to $\ell_m$, while $stay$ describes the case that the control does not move in any of the processes.

Note that the movement of control from $\ell_k$ to $\ell_m$ is represented by claiming that the new value of the set $L_k$, which contains the indices of all the processes that currently reside at $\ell_k$, equals its old value minus the process $i$ that has moved away. Similarly, $L_m$ is updated by the addition of $i$.

### 6.3.1   The Transitions

Before presenting the actual transitions corresponding to the **MUTEX** program, we present a general approach to the assignment of transitions to compound tests, such as the tests appearing in statements $\ell_3, \ell_5, \ell_7, \ell_9$, and $\ell_{11}$ of the program. These tests all perform a check of whether a certain condition $p(j)$ holds for all or some $j = 0, \ldots, n - 1$. We do not consider the interpretation of such tests as *atomic*, assuming them to be fully completed by a single transition, as a realistic representation of what really happen in concurrent systems. Instead, we consider them as *molecular* [9], and assign a separate transition to the check of $p(j)$ for each individual $j$. We refer the readers to Manna and Pneuli [8] for an analysis of the same program under the assumption of atomic compound tests, as well as a comparison of several versions of molecular compound tests.

There are three types of compound tests that appear in the **MUTEX** program. We discuss each of them separately. To represent an intermediate situation in the performance of a compound test by the process $P[i]$, we use the state variable $j_i$ that points at the next value of $j$, for which $p(j)$ should be tested. In the representation we consider here, $j_i$ is initiated at 0 and incremented by 1 to get to the new index to be tested. Consequently the value $j_i = n$ indicates the completion of the compound test.

In Manna and Pneuli [8] we also consider other orders in which the range $0..n - 1$ can be scanned, and study the effect the different scanning orders may have on the behavior of the program. In fact, we show there that the program is correct if we follow an *ascending* scanning order, which is the one adopted here, and is incorrect for any other scanning order.

In defining the transition relation $\rho_\tau$ corresponding to the transition $\tau$, we adopt the following convention. We present a *compact transition relation* $R_\tau$, which contains the conditions under which $\tau$ is enabled and the effect $\tau$ has on the variables it may modify. The full transition relation $\rho_\tau$ is given by a conjunction of $R_\tau$ with a list of clauses $u' = u$ for each variable $u$ whose primed version does not appear in $R_\tau$, i.e., a variable that is obviously preserved by $\tau$.

Assume that the following compound test appears in the program for the process $P[i]$, for some predicate $p(j)$ which depends on $j$.

$\ell_r$: **wait until** $\forall j : (0 \leq j < n) : p(j)$
$\ell_s$:

With this statement we associate the transition $\tau_r[i]$, whose compact transition relation is given by

$$R_r[i] : (i \in L_r) \wedge \left( \begin{array}{l} \left[ (j_i = n) \wedge move(i,r,s) \right] \\ \vee \quad \left[ (j_i < n) \wedge p(j_i) \wedge stay \wedge (j_i' = j_i + 1) \right] \\ \vee \quad \left[ (j_i < n) \wedge \neg p(j_i) \wedge stay \wedge (j_i' \leq j_i) \right] \end{array} \right)$$

The first clause of this formula corresponds to the case that the compound test has terminated, as is identified by $j_i = n$. This means that for each $j = 0, \ldots, n-1$, we have encountered a state in which $p(j)$ was true. By no means is it implied that there ever was a state in which $p(j)$ held for all $j = 0, \ldots, n-1$ at the same time.

The second clause of this transition corresponds to the case that $j_i$ is still in the range $0, \ldots, n-1$ and $p(j_i)$ is found to be true. In this case, $j_i$ is stepped up, but control still remains at $\ell_r$.

The third clause corresponds to the case that $p(j_i)$ is found to be false. Several strategies are possible at this point. Some implementations may decide to restart the testing cycle from the beginning and consequently reset $j_i$ to 0 on detecting a false $p(j_i)$. Other implementations leave $j_i$ as it is and will try again to test $p(j_i)$ until it is found to be true. The clause presented above is general enough to cover both these strategies by requiring only that $j_i$ does not increase. Obviously, if we prove the program to be correct under this more general representation, the results will hold, in particular, for the two specific implementations we have described above.

Next, let us consider a statement of the form

$\ell_r$: **wait until** $\exists j : (0 \leq j < n) : p(j)$
$\ell_s$:

With this statement we associate the transition $\tau_r[i]$, whose compact transition relation is given by

$$R_r[i] : (i \in L_r) \wedge \left( \begin{array}{l} \left[ p(j_i) \wedge move(i,r,s) \right] \\ \vee \quad \left[ \neg p(j_i) \wedge stay \wedge (j_i' = (j_i + 1) \bmod n) \right] \end{array} \right)$$

The first clause of this formula corresponds to the case that $p(j_i)$ is found to hold. In this case, the process $P[i]$ moves on to $\ell_s$.

The second clause corresponds to the case that $p(j_i)$ does not hold. In this case $P[i]$ remains at $\ell_r$ and $j_i$ is stepped to its next value. The incrementation of $j_i$ is done modulo $n$, so that the value following $n-1$ is again 0.

Finally, let us consider the statement

$$\ell_r : \text{if } \exists j : (0 \leq j < n) : p(j)$$
$$\text{then } [\ell_s : \ldots]$$
$$\text{else } [\ell_t : \ldots]$$

With this statement we associate the transition $\tau_r[i]$, whose compact transition relation is given by

$$R_r[i] : \ (i \in L_r) \wedge \left( \begin{array}{l} \big[(j_i = n) \wedge move(i, r, t)\big] \\ \vee \ \big[(j_i < n) \wedge p(j_i) \wedge move(i, r, s)\big] \\ \vee \ \big[(j_i < n) \wedge \neg p(j_i) \wedge stay \wedge (j_i' = j_i + 1)\big] \end{array} \right)$$

The first clause of this formula corresponds to the case that the search for a $j$ that satisfies $p(j)$ has been completed, apparently without finding such a $j$. Consequently, the result of the compound test is *false*, and we proceed to the **else** clause.

The second clause of the formula corresponds to the case that the current value of $j_i$ satisfies $p(j_i)$. This means that the test is successful, and we proceed to the **then** clause.

The third clause of the formula corresponds to the case that the current value of $j_i$ does not satisfy $p(j_i)$. We therefore step $j_i$ to its next value and stay in place.

Having considered the general form of the transitions associated with the three types of molecular tests we have in our program, we proceed to present the transitions for the program.

We recall that according to our set notations

$$L_{i_1, i_2, \ldots, i_m} \ = \ L_{i_1} \cup L_{i_2} \cup \ldots \cup L_{i_m}$$
$$L_{i..k} \ = \ L_i \cup L_{i+1} \cup \ldots \cup L_k \qquad \text{for } i < k$$

Below, we list the transitions associated with the process $P[i]$. For each such process there exist one or more transitions corresponding to each statement. For the statement labeled by $\ell_r$ we denote the corresponding transition by $\tau_r[i]$ and the associated compact transition relation by $R_r[i]$.

□ $R_0[i] : (i \in L_0) \wedge move(i, 0, 1)$

This transition corresponds to the case that $P[i]$ is at $\ell_0$ and moves inside the **loop** statement.

□ $R_1[i] : (i \in L_1) \wedge \big(stay \vee move(i, 1, 2)\big)$

This compact transition relation consists of two clauses representing a non-deterministic choice. The first clause corresponds to the case that the process $P[i]$ decides to remain in its non-critical section for awhile longer.

The situation that, from a certain point on, a process remains forever in its non-critical section (which we want to include) is represented by this process consistently choosing this clause of the transition relation from that point on. The second clause of the compact transition relation corresponds to the case that $P[i]$ decides to quit its non-critical section and move from $\ell_1$ to $\ell_2$.

□ $R_2[i] : (i \in L_2) \wedge move(i, 2, 3) \wedge (flag'[i] = 1) \wedge (j'_i = 0)$

This transition corresponds to the case that the process $P[i]$ moves from $\ell_2$ to $\ell_3$ while setting $flag[i]$ to 1. According to our convention, $flag'[k] = flag[k]$ for all $k \neq i$. Note that since $\ell_3$ performs a molecular test, we reset $j_i$ to 0 on entering $\ell_3$ as preparation for the compound test to be performed at $\ell_3$.

□ $R_3[i] :$

$$(i \in L_3) \wedge \left( \begin{array}{l} \phantom{\vee} \left[(j_i = n) \wedge move(i, 3, 4)\right] \\ \vee \ \left[(j_i < n) \wedge (flag(j_i) < 3) \wedge stay \wedge (j'_i = j_i + 1)\right] \\ \vee \ \left[(j_i < n) \wedge (flag(j_i) \geq 3) \wedge stay \wedge (j'_i \leq j_i)\right] \end{array} \right)$$

The first clause of this compact transition relation corresponds to a successful termination of the test, as a result of which, $P[i]$ moves to $\ell_4$. The second clause corresponds to the case that the next tested value of $j_i$ satisfies $flag[j_i] < 3$, as a result of which, $j_i$ is incremented to its next value. The last clause corresponds to the case that a tested $flag[j_i]$ is found to be greater or equal to 3. In this case, we allow resetting $j_i$ to any value not exceeding its current value.

□ $R_4[i] : (i \in L_4) \wedge move(i, 4, 5) \wedge (flag'[i] = 3) \wedge (j'_i = 0)$

Process $P[i]$ moves to $\ell_5$ while setting $flag[i]$ to 3 and resetting $j_i$ to 0.

□ $R_5[i] :$

$$(i \in L_5) \wedge \left( \begin{array}{l} \phantom{\vee} \left[(j_i = n) \wedge move(i, 5, 8)\right] \\ \vee \ \left[(j_i < n) \wedge (flag[j_i] = 1) \wedge move(i, 5, 6)\right] \\ \vee \ \left[(j_i < n) \wedge (flag[j_i] \neq 1) \wedge stay \wedge (j'_i = j_i + 1)\right] \end{array} \right)$$

The first clause of the compact transition relation corresponds to the case that the test has terminated unsuccessfully, and consequently $P[i]$ moves to $\ell_8$. The second clause represents the case that $flag[j_i] = 1$. Consequently, $P[i]$ moves to $\ell_6$. The last clause corresponds to the case that the current value of $j_i$ does not satisfy $flag[j_i] = 1$. Consequently, the process stays in the test and steps $j_i$ to the next value.

□ $R_6[i] : (i \in L_6) \wedge move(i, 6, 7) \wedge (flag'[i] = 2) \wedge (j'_i = 0)$

Set $flag[i]$ to 2 and $j_i$ to 0.

□ $R_7[i]$ :

$$(i \in L_7) \wedge \left( \begin{array}{l} \left[ (flag[j_i] = 4) \wedge move(i, 7, 8) \right] \\ \vee \quad \left[ (flag[j_i] \neq 4) \wedge stay \wedge (j'_i = (j_i + 1) \bmod n) \right] \end{array} \right)$$

The first clause of the compact transition relation represents the case that $flag[j_i]$ equals 4. In that case the search has terminated and $P[i]$ moves to $\ell_8$. The second clause corresponds to the case that $flag[j_i]$ does not equal 4. In that case the search continues by stepping $j_i$ to its next value.

□ $R_8[i] : (i \in L_8) \wedge move(i, 8, 9) \wedge (flag'[i] = 4) \wedge (j'_i = 0)$

Process $P[i]$ moves from $\ell_8$ to $\ell_9$ while setting $flag[i]$ to 4 and $j_i$ to 0.

□ $R_9[i]$ :

$$(i \in L_9) \wedge \left( \begin{array}{l} \left[ (j_i = i) \wedge move(i, 9, 10) \right] \\ \vee \quad \left[ (j_i < i) \wedge (flag[j_i] < 2) \wedge stay \wedge (j'_i = j_i + 1) \right] \\ \vee \quad \left[ (j_i < i) \wedge (flag[j_i] \geq 2) \wedge stay \wedge (j'_i \leq j_i) \right] \end{array} \right)$$

The first clause of the compact transition relation represents a successful completion of the test, which runs for $j_i$ ranging from 0 to $i-1$. $P[i]$ moves to $\ell_{10}$. The second clause represents the case that $j_i < i$ and the current $j_i$ satisfies $flag[j_i] < 2$. Consequently, the process increments $j_i$. The last clause represents the case that the current $j_i$ does not satisfy $flag[j_i] < 2$.

□ $R_{10}[i] : (i \in L_{10}) \wedge move(i, 10, 11) \wedge (j'_i = i + 1)$

The activity of the process inside the critical section is represented by the single transition that moves from $\ell_{10}$ to $\ell_{11}$. This represents the commitment that, differently from the non-critical section, the activity within the critical section must always terminate. Note that on moving to $\ell_{11}$ we reset $j_i$ to $i + 1$ to initialize the search at $\ell_{11}$ to start from that value.

□ $R_{11}[i] : (i \in L_{11}) \wedge$

$$\left( \begin{array}{l} \left[ (j_i = n) \wedge move(i, 11, 12) \right] \\ \vee \quad \left[ (j_i < n) \wedge (flag[j_i] < 2 \vee flag[j_i] > 3) \wedge stay \wedge (j'_i = j_i + 1) \right] \\ \vee \quad \left[ (j_i < n) \wedge (2 \leq flag[j_i] \leq 3) \wedge stay \wedge (j'_i \leq j_i) \right] \end{array} \right)$$

The first clause of this compact transition relation corresponds to a successful termination of the test. Consequently, $P[i]$ moves to $\ell_{12}$. The second clause corresponds to the case that $j_i < n$ and $flag[j_i] < 2 \vee flag[j_i] > 3$. Consequently, process $P[i]$ moves to the next value of $j_i$. The third clause corresponds to the case that $2 \leq flag[j_i] \leq 3$, and therefore $j_i$ is reset to any value not exceeding its current value.

□ $R_{12}[i] : (i \in L_{12}) \wedge move(i, 12, 0) \wedge (flag'[i] = 0)$

Process $P[i]$ moves from $\ell_{12}$ to the location at which the main loop restarts another execution of its body, while resetting $flag[i]$ to 0.

## 6.4 Invariance Properties

For an assertion $p$, we say that $p$ is (generally) *valid*, and write $\models p$, if $p$ is true on all possible states. All the known tautologies and theorems of the predicate calculus are obviously valid.

We say that the assertion $p$ is *valid over the program* $P$ (also described as being *P-valid*), and write $P \models p$, if $p$ holds over all the $P$-accessible states.

Clearly, if the assertion $p$ is $P$-valid, it is an *invariant* property of the program $P$. That is, it holds over all the states that can arise in any computation of the program $P$.

In this section we present several proof rules that are adequate for proving the invariance of an assertion $p$ over a program $P$, i.e., proving $P \models p$.

We will illustrate these rules by proving the main properties of the program **MUTEX**. To facilitate the expression of properties for this program, we introduce the following notation:

$$
\begin{aligned}
N_i &= |L_i| \\
N_{i_1, i_2, \ldots, i_m} &= |L_{i_1, i_2, \ldots, i_m}| &= N_{i_1} + N_{i_2} + \cdots + N_{i_m} \\
N_{i..k} &= |L_{i..k}| &= N_i + N_{i+1} + \cdots + N_k \qquad \text{for } i < k
\end{aligned}
$$

The main invariance property of the program **MUTEX** can be expressed by the assertion $N_{10} \leq 1$. This assertion limits the number of processes that can be concurrently executing at $\ell_{10}$, which corresponds to the critical section, to be at most 1. Thus we have to prove

$$P \models (N_{10} \leq 1)$$

for the **MUTEX** program.

Since most of our reasoning is done within the $P$-validity framework, we omit the prefix "$P \models$" and simply write $p$ to mean $P \models p$. The only exception to this convention are rules that deal at the same time with both general and $P$-validity, such as the **IMP** rule presented below.

**IMP**

(Import) rule:    $(\models p) \vdash (P \models p)$.

This rule states that if the assertion $p$ is generally valid, it is in particular $P$-valid. It is used to import general validities into the $P$-validity framework.

**MP**

(Modus Ponens) rule:    $\{p \rightarrow q, p\} \vdash q$.

This rule infers the $P$-validity of $q$ from the $P$-validity of $p \rightarrow q$ and $q$.

The above two auxiliary rules are independent of the particular program analyzed. The following **INV** rule refers to the elements of the program, and is the main working tool for establishing invariance properties.

The rule uses a special case of a particular formula, to which we refer as the *verification condition* of the transition $\tau$, relative to the assertions $p$ and $q$. This formula has the form

$$(p \wedge \rho_\tau) \rightarrow q'.$$

In this formula, $\rho_\tau$ is the transition relation corresponding to $\tau$, and $q'$, the *primed version* of the assertion $q$, is obtained from $q$ by replacing each variable occurring in $q$ by its primed version. Let $s$ and $s'$ be two states. Since $\rho_\tau$ holds over the joint interpretation $\langle s, s' \rangle$ iff $s'$ is a $\tau$-successor of $s$, and $q'$ states that $q$ holds over $s'$, it is not difficult to see that

> If the verification condition $(p \wedge \rho_\tau) \rightarrow q'$ is $P$-valid, then every $\tau$-successor of a $p$-state is a $q$-state.

The **INV** rule is given by

> **INV**     I1.   $\varphi \rightarrow p$
>
> I2.   $\Theta \rightarrow \varphi$
>
> I3.   $(\varphi \wedge \rho_\tau) \rightarrow \varphi'$     for every $\tau \in T$
> _____
>
> $p$

The **INV** rule uses an auxiliary assertion $\varphi$ which, by premise I2, holds initially, and by premise I3 is propagated from each state to its successor. This shows that $\varphi$ is an invariant of the program, that is, it holds continuously over all computations of $P$. Since, by I1, the assertion $\varphi$ implies $p$, it follows that $p$ is also an invariant of the program.

**Example** Consider the trivial program with a single state variable $x$, the precondition $x = 0$, and a single transition $\tau$ whose transition relation is given by $\rho_\tau : x' = x + 1$. Observe that this program has a single infinite computation, given by

$$\langle x : 0 \rangle, \langle x : 1 \rangle, \langle x : 2 \rangle, \ldots.$$

We wish to prove for this program the trivial invariance property

$$x \geq 0.$$

To prove this property, we use the **INV** rule with $p = \varphi : (x \geq 0)$. The rule requires showing the validity of the following three premises:

I1. $(x \geq 0) \rightarrow (x \geq 0)$

I2. $(x = 0) \rightarrow (x \geq 0)$

I3. $\big( (x \geq 0) \wedge (x' = x + 1) \big) \rightarrow (x' \geq 0)$

Clearly all the three premises are generally valid, which establishes the invariance of $x \geq 0$.

We proceed to establish several invariants for the program **MUTEX**, which together will yield the desired result.

## 6.4.1  Simple Invariants

First, we establish a list of invariants that connect for each $i = 0, \ldots, n-1$ the location of $P[i]$ with the value of $flag[i]$. To facilitate the expression of these invariants, we define

$$F_k = \{i \mid 0 \leq i < n , \; flag[i] = k\}.$$

Thus, $F_k$, for $k = 0, \ldots, 4$, denotes the set of indices $i$ such that $flag[i] = k$. We also recall the abbreviations

$$
\begin{aligned}
F_{i_1, i_2, \ldots, i_m} &= F_{i_1} \cup F_{i_2} \cup \ldots \cup F_{i_m} \\
F_{i \ldots k} &= F_i \cup F_{i+1} \cup \ldots \cup F_k \qquad \text{for } i < k
\end{aligned}
$$

Using these notations, the invariants relating the location of processes to their $flag$ values can be expressed as relations between $F_k$ and $L_r$ for various values of $r$ and $k$.

$$
\begin{array}{llrcl}
\text{IF0.} & F_0 & = & L_{0..2} \\
\text{IF1.} & F_1 & = & L_{3,4} \\
\text{IF2.} & F_2 & \subseteq & L_{7,8} \\
\text{IF3.} & F_3 & \subseteq & L_{5,6,8} \\
\text{IF4.} & F_4 & = & L_{9..12} \\
\text{IL5.} & L_5 & \subseteq & F_3 \\
\text{IL6.} & L_6 & \subseteq & F_3 \\
\text{IL7.} & L_7 & \subseteq & F_2 \\
\text{IL8.} & L_8 & \subseteq & F_{2,3}
\end{array}
$$

The invariants IF0,...,IF4 restrict the locations at which $P[i]$ can reside when the value of $flag[i]$ is $0, \ldots, 4$, respectively. For example, the invariant IF4 claims that the value of $flag[i]$ is 4 iff $P[i]$ is at one of the locations $\ell_9, \ldots, \ell_{12}$. The invariants IL5,...,IL8 restrict the value of $flag[i]$ while $P[i]$ is at the locations $\ell_5, \ldots, \ell_8$, respectively. For example, the invariant IL8 claims that when $P[i]$ is at $\ell_8$ its flag value must be 2 or 3. This is the only location in the program in which the value of the flag is not uniquely determined.

Let us see, for example, how an invariant such as IF1 is established. To prove $F_1 = L_{3,4}$, we actually prove

$$(i \in F_1) \leftrightarrow (i \in L_{3,4}),$$

for every $i = 0, \ldots, n - 1$. We apply the **INV** rule with $p = \varphi$ : $(i \in F_1) \leftrightarrow (i \in L_{3,4})$. There are three premises to verify.

Premise I1 is trivial since $\varphi = p$ for our case. Premise I2 requires showing that $\Theta$ implies $F_1 = L_{3,4}$. It is not difficult to see that $\Theta$ actually implies $F_1 = L_{3,4} = \phi$, since initially there are no processes whose flag value is 1, and there are no processes residing at either $\ell_3$ or $\ell_4$.

The premise that requires more attention is premise I3. Here we are called for writing a separate implication of the form $(\varphi \wedge \rho_\tau) \rightarrow \varphi'$, for every transition $\tau$ in the program. There are some simple heuristics that let us discard immediately many transitions as automatically guaranteed to preserve $\varphi$. The simplest and most effective one is

> All transitions that do not modify any of the variables on which $\varphi$ depends are guaranteed to preserve $\varphi$.

This heuristic leads immediately to the conclusion that, for the assertion $F_1 = L_{3,4}$, we should only be concerned with the following transitions that we consider one by one (we represent the transitions by the unique locations with which they are associated):

$\ell_2[i]$—The transition relation for this transition implies $(i \in L_3') \wedge (i \in F_1')$, since it causes $P[i]$ to move to $\ell_3$ and sets $flag[i]$ to 1. Consequently, it implies $\varphi'$.

$\ell_3[i]$—Even though this transition can potentially modify both $L_3$ and $L_4$, it does it in a way that preserves $L_{3,4}$. Consequently, the transition relation implies $(F_1' = F_1) \wedge (L_{3,4}' = L_{3,4})$, which ensures that $\varphi$ is preserved.

$\ell_4[i]$—The corresponding transition relation implies $i \notin F_1'$ (the transition sets $flag[i]$ to 3), and $i \notin L_{3,4}'$ (the transition leaves $\ell_4$). Consequently, $\varphi'$ is established, as both sides of the equivalence become false.

It is clear that these are the only transitions that modify any of the variables on which $\varphi$ depends.

We conclude that $(i \in F_1) \leftrightarrow (i \in L_{3,4})$ is an invariant assertion, and therefore so is $F_1 = L_{3,4}$.

## 6.4.2 Proving Mutual Exclusion

Having prepared the machinery for proving invariance properties, we may proceed to establish the main invariance property of the **MUTEX** program, namely, that of mutual exclusion.

We refer the reader to [10] for a detailed explanation of the basic ideas on which the **MUTEX** program is based. Here we extract just the main observations. The tortuous path a process has to follow on its way from the non-critical section at $\ell_1$ to the critical section at $\ell_{10}$, can be partitioned into several segments. We refer to the location $\ell_4$ as the *doorway*, to the section $\ell_{5..7}$ as the *waiting room* and to the section $\ell_{8..12}$, which contains the critical section as the *inner sanctum*.

The basic claims on which mutual exclusion is based are the following:

C1. Whenever a process enters an empty inner sanctum, i.e., $L_{8..12}$ changes its value from empty to non-empty, the doorway is locked, i.e., $L_4 = \phi$. The doorway remains locked until the last process leaves the inner sanctum. This implies the invariant

$$A_0 \quad : \quad (L_{8..12} \neq \phi) \rightarrow (L_4 = \phi),$$

which claims that if $L_{8..12}$ is non-empty then $L_4$ must be empty. If we believe this to be a true invariant, then the fact that $L_{8..12}$ is non-empty should prevent any new processes coming to $\ell_3$ to cross over into $\ell_4$. The only thing that can prevent processes from crossing over is if $flag[j]$ of some process equals 3 or 4. Thus, we must also have

$$A_1 \quad : \quad (L_{8..12} \neq \phi) \rightarrow (L_{8..12} \cap F_{3,4} \neq \phi).$$

Note that we require that one of the processes in $\ell_{8..12}$ has a flag value of 3 or 4. This is because a flag value of 3 which is held by a process at $\ell_{5,6}$ is unstable in the sense that it may very soon change to 2 again, by the statement at $\ell_6$.

C2. If a process $i$ is at $\ell_{10..12}$, then it must be the minimal (having the least index) of all the processes in $\ell_{5..12}$. This is expressed by the invariant

$$A_2 \quad : \quad \Big((k < i) \land (i \in L_{10..12})\Big) \rightarrow (k \notin L_{5..12}).$$

C3. If some process is at $\ell_{12}$, then all the processes in $\ell_{5..12}$ must have a flag value of 4. This is expressed by the invariant

$$A_3 \quad : \quad \Big((i \in L_{12}) \land (k \in L_{5..12})\Big) \rightarrow (k \in F_4).$$

Thus, as soon as a process enters the inner sanctum the doorway gets locked. This leaves the processes in the waiting room and the inner sanctum isolated from the rest of the processes and lets them compete for the entry to the critical section. By claim C2., only one process at a time can reside in the region $\ell_{10..12}$ which includes the critical section—the process whose index is minimal among all the processes in $\ell_{5..12}$. It follows that mutual exclusion is maintained.

If we were working in a framework such that the compound tests are considered atomic, then the conjunction

$$\varphi_0 \quad : \quad A_0 \land A_1 \land A_2 \land A_3$$

could have been shown to be invariant from which, by $A_2$, mutual exclusion would have followed.

Unfortunately, we have to deal with molecular tests, which require an extension to the above list of invariants. Consider any region of consecutive locations that is mentioned in one of the previous invariants, and that is preceded by a compound test. For example, $\ell_{10..12}$ is such a region, where the relevant compound test is the one at $\ell_9$. The assertion $A_2$ states that if $k < i$ and $i$ belongs to $L_{10..12}$, then $k$ cannot be in $L_{5..12}$. In the atomic case, one of the considerations used in proving this assertions is that $P[i]$ cannot pass the atomic test at $\ell_9$ if $k < i$ is anywhere at $\ell_{5..12}$. This is because the simple invariants connecting flag values to locations imply that $flag[k] \geq 2$ while $P[k]$ is at $\ell_{5..12}$.

In the molecular case, the test at $\ell_9$ is not passed in one step. Process $P[i]$ may reside at $\ell_9$ for several steps, checking the values of $flag[j_i]$ for various values of $j_i$. The important question concerning $k$, is whether $P[i]$ has already tested the value of $flag[k]$. This can be observed by checking whether $j_i > k$. If $j_i$ is greater than $k$, then we know that the value of $flag[k]$ has already been tested and found satisfactory, i.e., smaller than 2.

Consequently, to adapt the assertion $A_2$ to the molecular case, we should replace the simple region reference $i \in L_{10..12}$, appearing there, by the extended reference $i \in L_{10..12} \lor (i \in L_9 \land j_i > k)$. By applying such range extensions to the assertions $A_0, \ldots, A_3$, we obtain the following assertions:

$$B_0 : \quad (i \in L_5 \land j_i > k) \quad \rightarrow \quad \neg\left[(k \in L_4) \lor (k \in L_3 \land j_k > i)\right]$$

$$B_1 : \quad (i \in L_{8..12}) \quad \rightarrow \quad \exists r : \left(r \in L_{8..12} \cap F_{3,4}\right) : \neg\left[(k \in L_4) \lor (k \in L_3 \land j_k > r)\right]$$

$$B_2 : \quad \left[(k < i) \land \left(i \in L_{10..12} \lor (i \in L_9 \land j_i > k)\right)\right] \quad \rightarrow \quad (k \notin L_{5..12})$$

$$B_3 : \quad \left[\left(i \in L_{12} \lor (i \in L_{11} \land j_i > k)\right) \land \left(k \in L_{5..12}\right)\right] \quad \rightarrow \quad (k \in F_4)$$

Assertions $B_0$ and $B_1$ refine together assertions $A_0$ and $A_1$ to the molecular case. The basic idea is to show for any $k$ that if $P[i]$ is either at $\ell_{8..12}$ or at $\ell_5$ with $j_i > k$, i.e., having already checked $flag[k]$, then $P[k]$ cannot be at $\ell_4$, and if it is at $\ell_3$, then its $j_k$ value is below some $r$ that blocks it from proceeding into $\ell_4$ by having $flag[r] > 2$. If $P[i]$ is at $\ell_5$, we can take $r$ to be $i$ itself. If $P[i]$ is at $\ell_{8..12}$, we can only claim the existence of such a blocking $r$, such that $P[r]$ is also at $\ell_{8..12}$ and $flag[r] > 2$.

We form now the conjunction

$$\varphi \quad : \quad B_0 \land B_1 \land B_2 \land B_3$$

and claim that it is an invariant of the program **MUTEX**.

It is beyond the scope of this chapter to consider all the transitions and show that each preserves $\varphi$. We will, however, consider some of the more interesting cases.

Consider, for example, what transitions may possibly affect the assertion $B_1$. A critical transition of $P[i]$ is the one that moves from $\ell_5$ to $\ell_8$. However, due to $B_0$, the right-hand side of the implication of $B_1$ will hold after the transition with $r = i$ and (due to IL5) $flag[i] = 3$. Another potentially critical transition of $k$ is the one that increases $j_k$ beyond $r$. However, due to $flag[r] > 2$, such a transition is disabled. For this argument to hold it is essential that the indices $j$ in $\ell_3$ are scanned in increasing order.

Lastly, we consider the transition of $P[r]$ from $\ell_{12}$ to $\ell_0$, while resetting its flag value to 0. There are two possibilities. If $r$ is the last process in $\ell_{8..12}$, then after the transition $L_{8..12}$ will become empty, causing $B_1$ to hold trivially. If $r$ is not the last, there exists another process, say $P[t]$ in $\ell_{8..12}$. Then, due to $B_2$, which states that $r$ is the minimal process in $\ell_{8..12}$, $r$ must be smaller than $t$. Therefore if $j_k \leq r$, it is also $\leq t$. Due to $B_3$, $flag[t]$ equals 4. Consequently, after the transition, $B_1$ still holds if we use $t$ as a substitute for $r$.

## 6.5   Response Properties

Next to be considered is the class of *response* properties. The typical response property is expressed by the formula

$$p \Rightarrow \Diamond q,$$

for assertions $p$ and $q$. A sequence of states $\sigma$ is said to satisfy the response formula $p \Rightarrow \Diamond q$ if every $p$-position $i \geq 0$, is followed by a $q$-position $j \geq i$. Such a response formula is said to be valid over the program $P$ (also called $P$-valid), denoted by $P \models (p \Rightarrow \Diamond q)$, if all the computations of $P$ satisfy the formula. This means that every occurrence of (a state satisfying) $p$ in the execution of $P$, is followed by an occurrence of $q$. We will often omit the prefix $P \models$ when stating the validity of a response formula over $P$.

The temporal logic adepts will recognize $\Rightarrow \Diamond$ as the combination of the two operators $\Rightarrow$ and $\Diamond$ (e.g., [6]). However, for our purpose here it suffices to view it as a single binary temporal operator, whose semantics has been defined above. It is very similar to the *leads-to* operator of $Unity$ ([2]).

The following axioms and rules identify the basic properties of the *response* operator $\Rightarrow \Diamond$.

**RFLX**

(Reflexivity) axiom:

$$p \Rightarrow \Diamond p$$

This axiom expresses the fact that every $p$-position is trivially followed by a $p$-position, namely itself.

**TRNS**

(Transitivity) rule:

$$\{p \Rightarrow \Diamond q \,,\; q \Rightarrow \Diamond r\} \quad \vdash \quad p \Rightarrow \Diamond r$$

This rule states the transitivity of the *response* operator. It claims that if every $p$-position is followed by a $q$-position, and every $q$-position is followed by an $r$-position, then certainly every $p$-position must be followed by an $r$-position.

**MON**

(Monotonicity) rule:

$$\{p \Rightarrow \Diamond q \,,\; \tilde{p} \rightarrow p \,,\; q \rightarrow \tilde{q}\} \quad \vdash \quad \tilde{p} \Rightarrow \Diamond \tilde{q}$$

This rule allows us to replace in a valid response formula the antecedent $p$ by a *stronger* assertion $\tilde{p}$, and the consequent $q$ by a *weaker* assertion $\tilde{q}$, and obtain another valid formula.

**DISJ**

(Disjunction) rule:

$$\{p \Rightarrow \Diamond r \,,\; q \Rightarrow \Diamond r\} \quad \vdash \quad (p \vee q) \Rightarrow \Diamond r$$

This rule combines the two response formulae, $p \Rightarrow \Diamond r$ and $q \Rightarrow \Diamond r$, into the formula $(p \vee q) \Rightarrow \Diamond r$. It allows us to prove the last formula by separately considering the case that $p$ holds and the case that $q$ holds. In this way it supports proof by cases.

### 6.5.1  The Basic Response Rule

The axiom and three rules listed above are independent of the particular program analyzed, and describe the basic properties of the response operator. We now present a rule that enables us to establish the validity of a response formula over a program.

The rule singles out a particular transition $\tau_h$, to which we refer as the *helpful* transition. It can establish response formulae $p \Rightarrow \Diamond q$, such that a single activation of the transition $\tau_h$ is sufficient to achieve $q$. We therefore refer to this rule as the *basic* or *single step* response rule.

**RESP**   R1.  $p \rightarrow (q \vee \varphi)$
　　　　　R2.  $(\rho_\tau \wedge \varphi) \rightarrow (q' \vee \varphi')$　　for every $\tau \in T$
　　　　　R3.  $(\rho_{\tau_h} \wedge \varphi) \rightarrow q'$
　　　　　R4.  $\varphi \rightarrow \big(q \vee En(\tau_h)\big)$
　　　　　_____
　　　　　$p \Rightarrow \Diamond q$

Premise R1 ensures that $p$ implies $q$ or $\varphi$. Premise R2 states that any transition of the program, either leads from $\varphi$ to $q$, or preserves $\varphi$. Premise R3 states that the helpful transition $\tau_h$ leads from $\varphi$ to $q$. Premise R4 ensures that $\tau_h$ is enabled as long as $\varphi$ holds and $q$ does not occur.

It is not difficult to see that if $p$ happens, say at position $i \geq 0$, but is not followed by a $q$, then $\varphi$ must hold continuously beyond this position, and the helpful transition $\tau_h$ is never taken beyond $i$. The latter fact follows from premise R3, which states that taking $\tau_h$ from a $\varphi$-state immediately leads to a $q$-state, contradicting the assumption that $q$ never happens beyond $i$. However, due to R4, this means that $\tau_h$ is continuously enabled but never taken beyond position $i$, which violates the requirement of justice for $\tau_h$.

## 6.5.2  Example

We will illustrate the application of this rule on the following program:

$$\textbf{out } x, y : \textbf{ integer where } x = 0 \, , \, y = 0$$

$$P_1 :: \begin{bmatrix} \ell_0 : \textbf{ while } x = 0 \textbf{ do} \\ \quad [\ell_1 : y := y+1] \\ \ell_2 : \end{bmatrix} \quad \| \quad P_2 :: \begin{bmatrix} m_0 : x := 1 \\ m_1 : \\ \quad \cdots \end{bmatrix}$$

This program consists of two processes, $P_1$ and $P_2$. Process $P_1$ continuously increments $y$ while waiting for $x$ to become non-zero. Process $P_2$ consists of a single statement, assigning 1 to $x$.

The response property we wish to establish for this program is that of termination. It can be expressed by the formula

$$(at\_\ell_0 \wedge at\_m_0) \Rightarrow \Diamond (at\_\ell_2 \wedge at\_m_1),$$

which states that the event of being at the beginning of the program $(at\_\ell_0 \wedge at\_m_0)$ is eventually followed by the event of being at the end of the program $(at\_\ell_2 \wedge at\_m_1)$.

This property is established by a sequence of lemmas, each applying one of the rules presented above.

**Lemma 1 ($x$ eventually set to 1)**

$$(at\_\ell_0 \wedge at\_m_0) \Rightarrow \Diamond (at\_\ell_{0,1} \wedge at\_m_1 \wedge (x = 1))$$

This lemma claims that eventually the variable $x$ is set to 1 by the process $P_2$, which then moves to $m_1$. When this happens, process $P_1$ is still executing within the loop region $\ell_{0,1}$.

To prove the lemma we choose

$$p \quad : \quad at\_\ell_0 \wedge at\_m_0$$
$$\varphi \quad : \quad at\_\ell_{0,1} \wedge at\_m_0 \wedge (x = 0)$$
$$\tau_h \quad : \quad \tau_{m_0}$$
$$q \quad : \quad at\_\ell_{0,1} \wedge at\_m_1 \wedge (x = 1)$$

and apply the **RESP** rule.

It is not difficult to see that $p$ implies $\varphi$, provided we prove first the obvious invariant $at\_m_0 \to (x = 0)$. It is also clear that taking $\tau_{m_0}$ from a $\varphi$-state leads to a state satisfying $q$, and taking any other transition, i.e., $\tau_{\ell_0}$ or $\tau_{\ell_1}$, preserves $\varphi$. Obviously $\varphi$ implies that $\tau_{m_0}$ is enabled.

**Lemma 2 (From $\ell_0$ to $\ell_2$)**

$$\big(at\_\ell_0 \wedge at\_m_1 \wedge (x = 1)\big) \Rightarrow \Diamond (at\_\ell_2 \wedge at\_m_1)$$

Follows from the **RESP** rule, by taking $\varphi = p$ and $\tau_h = \tau_{\ell_0}$.

**Lemma 3 (From $\ell_1$ to $\ell_0$)**

$$\big(at\_\ell_1 \wedge at\_m_1 \wedge (x = 1)\big) \Rightarrow \Diamond \big(at\_\ell_0 \wedge at\_m_1 \wedge (x = 1)\big)$$

Follows from the **RESP** rule, by taking $\varphi = p$ and $\tau_h = \tau_{\ell_1}$.

**Lemma 4 (From $\ell_1$ to $\ell_2$)**

$$\big(at\_\ell_1 \wedge at\_m_1 \wedge (x = 1)\big) \Rightarrow \Diamond (at\_\ell_2 \wedge at\_m_1)$$

Follows by transitivity (rule **TRNS**) from Lemma 3 and Lemma 2.

**Lemma 5 (From $\ell_{0,1}$ to $\ell_2$)**

$$\big(at\_\ell_{0,1} \wedge at\_m_1 \wedge (x = 1)\big) \Rightarrow \Diamond (at\_\ell_2 \wedge at\_m_1)$$

Follows by the **DISJ** rule from Lemma 4 and Lemma 5, using the equivalence

$$\big(at\_\ell_{0,1} \wedge at\_m_1 \wedge (x = 1)\big) \equiv$$
$$\Big(\big(at\_\ell_0 \wedge at\_m_1 \wedge (x = 1)\big) \vee \big(at\_\ell_1 \wedge at\_m_1 \wedge (x = 1)\big)\Big).$$

**Lemma 6 (From $\{\ell_0, m_0\}$ to $\{\ell_2, m_1\}$)**

$$(at\_\ell_0 \wedge at\_m_0) \Rightarrow \Diamond (at\_\ell_2 \wedge at\_m_1)$$

This lemma, which establishes the termination property, follows by the **TRNS** rule from Lemma 1 and Lemma 5.    ◢

### 6.5.3 The Well-Founded Rule for Response

The basic response rule supports the proof of response properties that are established by a *single* helpful step. As we have seen, even the simple example above requires several helpful steps to achieve its goal, i.e., termination. When the number of helpful steps required is small and fixed we can use a sequence of lemmas, each considering a single helpful step, and then combine their results by transitivity and case splitting. However, for the case that a large and a priori unknown number of helpful steps is required, we introduce below a more powerful rule that uses well-founded induction to combine the helpful steps.

We define a *well-founded (embedded) structure* $(\mathcal{A}, \mathcal{B}, \succ)$ to consist of the following components:

- $\mathcal{A}$—A set of elements.

- $\mathcal{B}$—A subset of $\mathcal{A}$.

- $\succ$—A binary relation on $\mathcal{A}$, whose restriction to $\mathcal{B}$ is *well founded*. That is, there does not exist an infinite sequence of elements of $\mathcal{B}$; $\beta_0, \beta_1, \ldots$, such that

$$\beta_0 \succ \beta_1 \succ \ldots.$$

A typical example of a well-founded embedded structure is $(\mathcal{I}nt, \mathcal{N}at, >)$, where $\mathcal{I}nt$ are the integers (including the negative ones), $\mathcal{N}at$ are the natural numbers (including 0), and $>$ is the *greater than* relation. Clearly, $>$ is defined over all the integers but is well founded only over the natural numbers.

Given two well-founded structures, $(\mathcal{A}_0, \mathcal{B}_0, \succ_0)$ and $(\mathcal{A}_1, \mathcal{B}_1, \succ_1)$, we can form their *lexicographical product* $(\mathcal{A}, \mathcal{B}, \succ)$, defined by

- $\mathcal{A}$ is defined as $\mathcal{A}_0 \times \mathcal{A}_1$, i.e., the set of all pairs $(\alpha_0, \alpha_1)$, such that $\alpha_0 \in \mathcal{A}_0$ and $\alpha_1 \in \mathcal{A}_1$.

- $\mathcal{B}$ is defined as $\mathcal{B}_0 \times \mathcal{B}_1$.

- $\succ$ is defined to hold between $(\alpha_0, \alpha_1) \in \mathcal{A}$ and $(\alpha_0', \alpha_1') \in \mathcal{A}$ iff

$$(\alpha_0 \succ \alpha_0') \vee \left[(\alpha_0 = \alpha_0') \wedge (\alpha_1 \succ \alpha_1')\right].$$

It is not difficult to prove that the lexicographical product of two well-founded structures is also a well-founded structure.

For $\succ$, an arbitrary binary relation over $\mathcal{A}$, we define its *reflexive extension* $\succeq$ to hold between $\alpha, \alpha' \in \mathcal{A}$ if either $\alpha = \alpha'$ or $\alpha \succ \alpha'$.

The following rule uses several *intermediate* assertions that hold at the positions lying between the position satisfying $p$ and the position satisfying the goal $q$. We denote these assertions by $\varphi_i$, where $i$ ranges over some finite index set $\mathcal{I}$, and denote their disjunction by $\varphi = \bigvee_{i \in \mathcal{I}} \varphi_i$. Each intermediate assertion $\varphi_i$ is associated with a transition $\tau_i \in \mathcal{T}$, which is identified as *helpful* for $\varphi_i$.

The rule also requires the identification of a *distance function* $\delta_i$ for each $i \in \mathcal{I}$. These functions map the states into the set $\mathcal{A}$ of a well-founded structure $(\mathcal{A}, \mathcal{B}, \succ)$. The intended meaning of these functions is that they measure the distance of the current state from the closest state that satisfies the goal $q$ of the formula $p \Rightarrow \Diamond q$, which is the conclusion of the rule. We refer to the value of the distance function $\delta_i$ at a state satisfying $\varphi_i$ as the *i-rank* of that state or simply as the *rank* of the state if $i$ is understood from the context.

Assuming that these constructs have been identified, the following rule establishes the $P$-validity of the formula $p \Rightarrow \Diamond q$.

---

**WELL**  W1.  $p \rightarrow (q \vee \varphi)$

The following premises should hold for each $i \in \mathcal{I}$

W2.  for every $\tau \in \mathcal{T}$

$$(\rho_\tau \wedge \varphi_i) \rightarrow \left( q' \vee \bigvee_{j \in \mathcal{I}} \left[ \varphi'_j \wedge (\delta_i \succ \delta'_j) \right] \vee \left[ \varphi'_i \wedge (\delta_i = \delta'_i) \right] \right)$$

W3.  $(\rho_{\tau_i} \wedge \varphi_i) \rightarrow \left( q' \vee \bigvee_{j \in \mathcal{I}} \left[ \varphi'_j \wedge (\delta_i \succ \delta'_j) \right] \right)$

W4.  $\varphi_i \rightarrow \left( q \vee (En(\tau_i) \wedge (\delta_i \in \mathcal{B})) \right)$

$$p \Rightarrow \Diamond q$$

---

Premise W1 requires that $p$ implies that either $q$ already holds or the intermediate assertion $\varphi$ (i.e., one of the $\varphi_i$'s) holds. Premise W2 requires that taking any transition from a $\varphi_i$-state results in a next state that either satisfies $q$ or satisfies $\varphi_j$, for some $j \in \mathcal{I}$, and has a ($j$-) rank lower than that of the original state or satisfies $\varphi_i$ and has an equal rank. Premise W3 requires that taking the *helpful* transition $\tau_i$ from a $\varphi_i$-state, results in a next state that either satisfies $q$ or satisfies some $\varphi_j$ with a lower rank. Premise W4 requires that any state $s$ satisfying $\varphi_i$ either satisfies $q$ or is such that $\tau_i$ is enabled on it, and the $i$-rank of $s$, $\delta_i(s)$ assumes a value in $\mathcal{B}$.

Assume that all the four premises hold. Consider a computation $\sigma$ and a position $m$ that satisfies $p$. We wish to prove that some later position satisfies $q$. Assume to the contrary that all positions later than $m$ (including $m$ itself) do not satisfy $q$. By W2 each of these positions must satisfy some $\varphi_j$ and, according to W4, the value of $\delta_j$ for this position, to which we refer as the rank of the position, lies within $\mathcal{B}$. By W2, the value of $\delta_j$ can either decrease or remain the same. By the assumption that $\succ$ is well founded over $\mathcal{B}$, the value of $\delta_j$ can actually decrease only finitely many times. Therefore, there must exist some position $k \geq m$, beyond which $\delta_j$ never decreases.

Assume that $\varphi_i$ is the assertion holding at position $k$. Since $q$ is never satisfied and $\delta_j$ never decreases beyond position $k$, it follows (by W2) that $\varphi_i$ holds continually beyond $k$. By W3, $\tau_i$ cannot be taken beyond $k$, because that would have led to a position satisfying $q$ or to a decrease in $\delta$. By W4, $\tau_i$ is continually enabled beyond $k$ yet, by the argument above, it is never taken. This violates the requirement of justice for $\tau_i$. It follows that if all the premises of the rule hold then $p \Rightarrow \Diamond q$ is $P$-valid.

In many cases, we may use the same ranking function $\delta$ for all $i \in \mathcal{I}$. We refer to these as the case of *uniform* ranking function. In these cases it is possible to use a simpler form for the premises W2 and W3, which is given by

W2.   for every $\tau \in \mathcal{T}$

$$(\rho_\tau \wedge \varphi_i) \rightarrow \left(q' \vee [\varphi' \wedge (\delta \succ \delta')] \vee [\varphi'_i \wedge (\delta = \delta')]\right)$$

W3.   $(\rho_{\tau_i} \wedge \varphi_i) \rightarrow \left(q' \vee [\varphi' \wedge (\delta \succ \delta')]\right)$

### 6.5.4  Proving Accessibility

The main response property one usually wishes to prove for mutual exclusion programs is that of *accessibility*, by which whenever a process departs from its non-critical section it is guaranteed to eventually reach the critical section. In our case we will prove a stronger property that implies accessibility. The property we will prove is

$$(u \notin L_1) \Rightarrow \Diamond (u \in L_1).$$

This property, to which we refer as the *homing* property, states that from any location away from the non-critical section, each process $P[u]$ is guaranteed to home back to the non-critical section. Since in our case, when a process just departs from $\ell_1$ it can return to $\ell_1$ only via the critical section, the homing property implies accessibility. It also guarantees that processes do not get stuck in any of the locations following the critical section, such as $\ell_{11}$. The way we establish the homing property is by a sequence of lemmas, each showing that a process cannot get stuck in any location, except perhaps in the non-critical section. The lemmas corresponding to locations that involve no tests, such as $\ell_0, \ell_2, \ell_4, \ell_6, \ell_8, \ell_{10}$, and $\ell_{12}$, are trivial and will be omitted. We will concentrate on the testing locations.

The well-founded structures that we will use are either $(\mathcal{I}nt, \mathcal{N}at, >)$ or the lexicographic products of such structures.

**Lemma 1 (Not Stuck at $\ell_{9..12}$)**

$$(u \in L_{9..12}) \Rightarrow \Diamond (u \in L_0)$$

This lemma states that if the process $P[u]$ is anywhere within $\ell_{9..12}$, it will eventually return to $\ell_0$.

To prove this lemma, we prove first two auxiliary lemmas.

**Lemma 1.1 (Evacuation of the Waiting Room)**

$$(u \in L_{9..12}) \Rightarrow \Diamond \left((u \in L_0) \vee [(u \in L_{9..12}) \wedge (L_{5..8} = \phi)]\right)$$

This lemma states that if $P[u]$ is currently at $\ell_{9..12}$ then either it will reach $\ell_0$ or, prior to that, the computation will reach a state in which $P[u]$ is still at $\ell_{9..12}$, but the waiting room $\ell_{5..8}$ is empty.

To prove this lemma we use the following intermediate assertions, uniform distance function, and helpful transitions:

$$\varphi_{(k,i)} \quad : \quad (u \in L_{9..12}) \wedge (L_{5..8} \neq \phi) \wedge (i \in L_k)$$

$$\delta \quad : \quad \left( 4 \cdot N_5 + 3 \cdot N_6 + 2 \cdot N_7 + N_8 \, , \, \sum_{r : r \in L_5} (n - j_r) + \sum_{r : r \in L_7} ((u - j_r) \bmod n) \right)$$

$$\tau_{(k,i)} \quad : \quad \tau_k[i]$$

for $k \in \{5..8\}$ and $i \in \{0..n-1\}$. Thus, we use for the index set $\mathcal{I}$ the set

$$\mathcal{I} \quad : \quad \left\{ (k,i) \mid k \in \{5..8\} \, , \, i \in \{0..n-1\} \right\}$$

Let us convince ourselves that taking any helpful transition decreases the distance function. Clearly a movement of process $P[i]$ from any location in the range $\ell_{5..8}$ to any other location decreases the first component of $\delta$. For example, a movement of $P[i]$ from $\ell_6$ to $\ell_7$, removes $i$ from $L_6$, where it has a weight of 3, and adds it to $L_7$ with a weight of 2. Consequently, the net change in the first component is $-1$.

Next, let us consider a transition that involves a compound test. Consider, for example, a transition of process $P[i]$ which currently resides at $\ell_5$. According to $R_5[i]$ there are three possibilities. The first possibility is that $P[i]$ moves from $\ell_5$ to $\ell_8$, decreasing $\delta$ by $(3,0)$, i.e., 3 in the first component and 0 in the second component. The second possibility is that $P[i]$ moves from $\ell_5$ to $\ell_6$, decreasing $\delta$ by $(1,0)$. The last possibility is that $j_i$ increases by 1, decreasing $\delta$ by $(0,1)$, due to the summand $n - j_i$ appearing in the second component of $\delta$.

A somewhat more subtle argument is needed for the consideration of the transitions $\tau_7[i]$. Here there are two possibilities. Either $P[i]$ moves from $\ell_7$ to $\ell_8$, or $j_i$ is incremented modulo $n$. In the first case $\delta$ decreases by $(1,0)$. In the second case, we have to show that $((u - j_i) \bmod n)$ decreases. First, we observe that, since $u \in L_{9..12}$, $flag[u] = 4$, and therefore the test at $\ell_7$ cannot fail for $j_i = u$. We conclude that the second possibility exists only if $j_i \neq u$. In that case we rely on the property of the integers, by which if $0 \leq j_i, u < n$ and $j_i \neq u$, then

$$((u - j_i) \bmod n) > ((u - (j_i + 1)) \bmod n).$$

It follows that, in the second case, $\delta$ decreases by $(0,1)$.

Next let us show that any non-helpful transition either establishes $u \in L_0$, or at least preserves $\varphi_{(k,i)}$ and $\delta$. Clearly, this is true for $\tau_{12}[u]$. The only other transitions that may be suspected of falsifying $\varphi_{(k,i)}$ or increasing $\delta$ are those that may cause new processes to join $\ell_{5..8}$. However, due to the assumption $u \in L_{9..12}$ and the invariant $B_1$, there are no processes at $\ell_4$, and therefore, no new processes can join $\ell_{5..8}$.    ◢

**Lemma 1.2 (Progress within the Inner Sanctum)**

$$[(u \in L_{9..12}) \wedge (L_{5..8} = \phi)] \Rightarrow \Diamond (u \in L_0)$$

This lemma claims that if now there is no process within the range $\ell_{5..8}$ then process $u$ will eventually proceed to $\ell_0$. Of course, for that to happen, all the processes with lower indices must arrive to $\ell_{10}$ first and depart via $\ell_{12}$.

To prove the lemma we use the following intermediate assertions, uniform distance function, and helpful transitions:

$$\varphi_{(k,i)} \quad : \quad (u \in L_{9..12}) \wedge (L_{5..8} = \phi) \wedge (i \in L_k) \wedge (i = min_4)$$

$$\delta \quad : \quad \left( 4 \cdot N_9 + 3 \cdot N_{10} + 2 \cdot N_{11} + N_{12} \, , \, n - j_{min_4} \right)$$

$$\tau_{(k,i)} \quad : \quad \tau_k[i]$$

for $k \in \{9..12\}$ and $i \in \{0..n-1\}$, and where $min_4$ is defined to be the minimal element of $F_4 = L_{9..12}$, if that set is not empty, and 0 otherwise. In the case that $L_{9..12}$ is not empty, $min_4$ denotes the minimal index among all the processes currently residing at $\ell_{9..12}$ and (consequently) having a *flag* value of 4.

It is not difficult to see that the process with the minimal index is always enabled and causes a decrease in the value of the distance function, whatever transition in $\ell_{9..12}$ it takes.                                                                          ◢

We may now return to the proof of Lemma 1. We proceed as follows:

1. $(u \in L_0) \Rightarrow \Diamond (u \in L_0)$                                                  by **RFLX**

2. $\left( (u \in L_0) \vee \left[ (u \in L_{9..12}) \wedge (L_{5..8} = \phi) \right] \right) \Rightarrow \Diamond (u \in L_0)$

   by **DISJ**, 1., and Lemma 1.2.

3. $(u \in L_{9..12}) \Rightarrow \Diamond (u \in L_0)$          by **TRNS**, Lemma 1.1, and 2.

This concludes the proof.                                                                          ◢

**Lemma 2 (Not Stuck at $\ell_7$)**

$$(u \in L_7) \Rightarrow \Diamond (u \in L_8)$$

To prove this lemma, we establish first an additional invariant, using the **INV** rule.

$$B_4 : \quad (L_{6,7} \neq \phi) \rightarrow (L_{3..5} \cup L_{8..12} \neq \phi)$$

This invariant guarantees that if there is some process in the region $\ell_{6,7}$, then there is also some process in $\ell_{3..5}$ or in $\ell_{8..12}$. It is not difficult to show that the assertion $B_4$ holds initially and is preserved by any transition. In particular, we may rely on $B_3$ to show that no process can leave $L_{8..12}$ while $L_{6,7}$ is non-empty.

Then we prove two auxiliary lemmas.

**Lemma 2.1 (Entering $\ell_{9..12}$)**

$$(u \in L_7) \Rightarrow \Diamond \Big( (u \in L_7) \wedge (L_{9..12} \neq \phi) \Big)$$

Note that due to the invariant IF4, the set $L_{9..12}$ is precisely the set $F_4$, i.e., all the processes in this region have a $flag$ value of 4. To prove the lemma, we use the following intermediate assertions, distance functions, and helpful transitions:

$$
\begin{array}{lll}
\varphi_{(3,i)} & : & (u \in L_7) \wedge (L_{9..12} = \phi) \wedge (L_{4..6,8} = \phi) \wedge (i \in L_3) \\
\delta_{(3,i)} & : & \Big( 5 \cdot N_{0..3} + 4 \cdot N_4 + 3 \cdot N_5 + 2 \cdot N_6 + N_8 \,,\, n - j_i \Big) \\
\tau_{(3,i)} & : & \tau_3[i] \\
& & \text{For each } k \in \{4..6, 8\} \\
\varphi_{(k,i)} & : & (u \in L_7) \wedge (L_{9..12} = \phi) \wedge (i \in L_k) \\
\delta_{(k,i)} & : & \Big( 5 \cdot N_{0..3} + 4 \cdot N_4 + 3 \cdot N_5 + 2 \cdot N_6 + N_8 \,,\, n - j_i \Big) \\
\tau_{(k,i)} & : & \tau_k[i]
\end{array}
$$

where $i$ ranges over $\{0..n - 1\}$.

As we see, the index set $\mathcal{I}$ is partitioned into the two subsets $\{(3, i) \mid i \in \{0..n - 1\}\}$ and $\{(k, i) \mid k \in \{4..6, 8\}, i \in \{0..n - 1\}\}$. The transitions corresponding to the first subset are considered helpful (as we see from $\varphi_{(3,i)}$) only when $L_{4..6,8}$ is empty. This is necessary because $P[i]$ is guaranteed to progress when it is at $\ell_3$ only if $L_{4..6,8}$ is empty. Otherwise, the test at $\ell_3$ may cause $j_i$ to decrease, or at least not to increase. The invariant $B_4$ is used to establish the premise

$$(u \in L_7) \rightarrow \bigvee_{(k,i) \in \mathcal{I}} \varphi_{(k,i)}.$$

Essential to the proof is the observation that some process can move from $\ell_7$ to $\ell_8$ only if $L_{9..12}$ is already non-empty.    ⌐

**Lemma 2.2 (Escaping $\ell_7$)**

$$\Big( (u \in L_7) \wedge (L_{9..12} \neq \phi) \Big) \Rightarrow \Diamond (u \in L_8)$$

To prove this lemma, we use the following single intermediate assertion, single distance function, and single helpful transition:

$$
\begin{array}{lll}
\varphi_u & : & (u \in L_7) \wedge (L_{9..12} \neq \phi) \\
\delta & : & (min_4 - j_u) \bmod n \\
\tau_u & : & \tau_7[u]
\end{array}
$$

It is not difficult to see that when $L_{9..12} \neq \phi$, $flag[min_4] = 4$, and therefore $P[u]$ will find $flag[j_u] = 4$, at the latest, when $j_u = min_4$.    ⌐

We may now return to the proof of Lemma 2. By transitivity, we may combine the results of Lemma 2.1 and Lemma 2.2 to obtain

$$(u \in L_7) \Rrightarrow \Diamond (u \in L_8),$$

as claimed by Lemma 2.                                                                                    ◢

**Lemma 3 (Not Stuck at $\ell_5$)**

$$(u \in L_5) \Rrightarrow \Diamond (u \in L_{6,8})$$

This lemma is easily proven by taking

$$\begin{aligned}
\varphi_u &: \quad u \in L_5 \\
\delta &: \quad n - j_u \\
\tau_u &: \quad \tau_5[u]
\end{aligned}$$

Progress in the execution of the compound test at $\ell_5$ is guaranteed independently of the flag values encountered.                                                                                    ◢

**Lemma 4 (Not Stuck at $\ell_3$)**

$$(u \in L_3) \Rrightarrow \Diamond (u \in L_4)$$

We define the following sets of process indices

$$\begin{aligned}
L_5(j > F_1) &: \quad \{ r \mid r \in L_5 \,,\, j_r > F_1 \} \\
Block_3 &: \quad L_{8..12} \cup L_5(j > F_1)
\end{aligned}$$

where the inequality $j_r > F_1$ is defined to hold if $F_1$ is non-empty and $j_r$ is greater than any element of $F_1$. Consequently, if $F_1$ is empty, then so is $L_5(j > F_1)$. Note that by the invariant $B_0$ it follows that if $L_5(j > F_1)$ is not empty, then $L_4 = \phi$, which implies $F_1 = L_3$.

The set $Block_3$ represents the set of processes that may potentially block the progress of any processes currently at $\ell_3$ (including $P[u]$). Note that we have to add to $\ell_{8..12}$ also the processes that are in $\ell_5$ and have already checked $flag[j]$ for all $j \in F_1$. This is because such processes may potentially move to $\ell_8$. On the other hand, processes that are in $\ell_5$ but have not checked $flag[j]$, for some $j \in F_1$, can only move to $\ell_6$.

We prove the following auxiliary lemmas.

**Lemma 4.1**

$$(u \in L_3) \Rrightarrow \Diamond \Big( (u \in L_4) \vee \big[ (u \in L_3) \wedge (L_5(j > F_1) = \phi) \big] \Big)$$

This lemma states that if $P[u]$ is currently at $\ell_3$ then either it will reach $\ell_4$, or prior to that, the computation will reach a state in which $P[u]$ is still at $\ell_3$, but no process $P[i]$ is currently at $\ell_5$ with $j_i > F_1$.

To prove the lemma, we use

$$\begin{aligned}
\varphi_i &: \quad (u \in L_3) \wedge (i \in L_5(j > F_1)) \\
\delta_i &: \quad (|L_5(j > F_1)| \, , \, n - j_i) \\
\tau_i &: \quad \tau_5[i]
\end{aligned}$$

for $i \in \{0..n-1\}$. Thus the relevant processes are those that are at $\ell_5$ and have already checked $flag[j]$ for every $j \in F_1$. Note that no new processes can join $L_5(j > F_1)$ since any process checking $flag[j]$, for some $j \in F_1$ proceeds immediately to $\ell_6$. ⌐

**Lemma 4.2**

$$\left((u \in L_3) \wedge (L_5(j > F_1) = \phi)\right) \Rightarrow \Diamond \left((u \in L_4) \vee \left[(u \in L_3) \wedge (Block_3 = \phi)\right]\right)$$

This lemma establishes that if $P[u]$ does not reach $\ell_4$, then at least the set $Block_3$ becomes empty. To prove the lemma, we use

$$\begin{aligned}
\varphi_{(7,i)} &: \quad (u \in L_3) \wedge (L_5(j > F_1) = \phi) \wedge (i \in L_7) \wedge (L_{9..12} \neq \phi) \\
\delta_{(7,i)} &: \quad \Big(8 \cdot N_5 + 7 \cdot N_6 + 6 \cdot N_7 + 5 \cdot N_8 + 4 \cdot N_9 + 3 \cdot N_{10} + 2 \cdot N_{11} + N_{12} \, , \\
&\qquad\qquad\qquad\qquad\qquad\qquad\qquad\qquad\qquad\qquad ((min_4 - j_i) \bmod n)\Big)
\end{aligned}$$

For each $k \in \{5, 6, 8\}$

$$\begin{aligned}
\varphi_{(k,i)} &: \quad (u \in L_3) \wedge (L_5(j > F_1) = \phi) \wedge (i \in L_k) \wedge (L_{8..12} \neq \phi) \\
\delta_{(k,i)} &: \quad \Big(8 \cdot N_5 + 7 \cdot N_6 + 6 \cdot N_7 + 5 \cdot N_8 + 4 \cdot N_9 + 3 \cdot N_{10} + 2 \cdot N_{11} + N_{12} \, , \, n - j_i\Big)
\end{aligned}$$

For each $k \in \{9..12\}$

$$\begin{aligned}
\varphi_{(k,i)} &: \quad (u \in L_3) \wedge (L_5(j > F_1) = \phi) \wedge (i \in L_k) \wedge (L_{5..8} = \phi) \wedge (i = min_4) \\
\delta_{(k,i)} &: \quad \Big(8 \cdot N_5 + 7 \cdot N_6 + 6 \cdot N_7 + 5 \cdot N_8 + 4 \cdot N_9 + 3 \cdot N_{10} + 2 \cdot N_{11} + N_{12} \, , \, n - j_i\Big)
\end{aligned}$$

for $i \in \{0..n-1\}$. The overall range of $k$ in the index set $\{(k,i)\}$ used in this lemma is $\{5..12\}$, and as usual $\tau_{(k,i)} = \tau_k[i]$.

Note that since $L_{8..12} \neq \phi$, no new processes can enter $\ell_5$. ⌐

**Lemma 4.3**

$$\left[(u \in L_3) \wedge (Block_3 = \phi)\right] \Rightarrow \Diamond (u \in L_4)$$

Note that when $Block_3$ is empty it cannot become non-empty as long as $P[u]$ stays at $\ell_3$ with a $flag$ value of 1. At most, processes can accumulate at $\ell_7$. Consequently, we use the following constructs:

$$\varphi_{(3,i)} \quad : \quad (u \in L_3) \wedge (Block_3 = \phi) \wedge (i \in L_3) \wedge (L_{4..6} = \phi)$$

$$\delta_{(3,i)} \quad : \quad \left(4 \cdot N_{0..3} + 3 \cdot N_4 + 2 \cdot N_5 + N_6 \ , \ n - j_i\right)$$

For each $k \in \{4..6\}$

$$\varphi_{(k,i)} \quad : \quad (u \in L_3) \wedge (Block_3 = \phi) \wedge (i \in L_k)$$

$$\delta_{(k,i)} \quad : \quad \left(4 \cdot N_{0..3} + 3 \cdot N_4 + 2 \cdot N_5 + N_6 \ , \ n - j_i\right)$$

for $i \in \{0..n-1\}$.

Note that when $L_{4..6}$ is empty, any transition $\tau_3[i]$ is helpful.     ◢

It is not difficult to combine the results of Lemmas 4.1, 4.2, and 4.3, using reflexivity, disjunction, and transitivity, to obtain the result of Lemma 4, namely,

$$(u \in L_3) \Rightarrow \diamondsuit (u \in L_4)$$

◢

This concludes the proof of the homing property for the **MUTEX** program.

## 6.6  Precedence Properties

Next, we consider properties that are expressed by the formula

$$p \Rightarrow q_0 \, \mathsf{U} \ldots \mathsf{U} q_{r-1} \, \mathsf{U} q_r,$$

for any $r > 0$. Adepts in temporal logic will recognize this formula as a nested *unless* formula. For our purposes here, it suffices to consider it as a temporal operator of $r + 2$ arguments.

To define the semantics of this operator, we deal with *half-open intervals* of the form $[i..j)$, for $i \leq j$. Such an interval consists of all the positions $k$, such that $i \leq k < j$. Note that if $i = j$, the interval is empty. For the two intervals $[i..j)$ and $[j..k)$, we say that the second interval is adjacent to (or follows) the first and observe that their union is also a half-open interval, given by $[i..k)$. For infinite computations, we allow also intervals of the form $[i..\omega)$ for an integer $i$ and the interval $[\omega, \omega)$, which by definition is empty.

Given a computation $\sigma : s_0, s_1, \ldots$ , we say that the interval $[i..j)$ is a *p-interval* if for every $k \in [i..j)$, $s_k$ satisfies $p$. By definition, an empty interval is a p-interval for every assertion $p$.

A computation $\sigma$ is said to satisfy the *precedence* formula $p \Rightarrow q_0 \, \mathsf{U} \ldots \mathsf{U}$ $q_{r-1} \, \mathsf{U} q_r$ if for every p-position $i$ there exists a sequence of positions $i = i_0 \leq i_1 \leq \ldots \leq i_r \leq |\sigma|$, such that $[i_0..i_1)$ is a $q_0$-interval, $\ldots$, $[i_{r-1}..i_r)$ is a $q_{r-1}$-interval, and finally, if $i_r < |\sigma|$, then $i_r$ is a $q_r$-position. That is, it requires that any p-position initiates a $q_0$-interval, which is followed by a succession of $q_1, \ldots, q_{r-1}$-intervals, where the $q_{r-1}$-interval either extends to the end of the computation or is terminated by a $q_r$-position. Note that this definition allows some of the intermediate intervals to be empty, and any of them to extend to the end of the computation $|\sigma|$ (which may also be $\omega$), and this forces all the succeeding intervals to have the form $[|\sigma|..|\sigma|)$, and therefore to be empty.

The precedence formula $p \Rightarrow q_0 \, \mathsf{U} \ldots \mathsf{U} q_{r-1} \, \mathsf{U} q_r$ is said to be $P$-valid if it satisfied by all computations of the program $P$.

Let us see how the property of *linear wait* as claimed in [10] for the **MUTEX** program, can be expressed by a precedence formula. Consider the precedence formula

$$[(u \in L_3) \wedge (v \in L_{1,2})] \Rightarrow (v \notin L_{10}) \, \mathsf{U} (v \in L_{10}) \, \mathsf{U} (v \notin L_{10}) \, \mathsf{U} (u \in L_{10})$$

This formula considers the question of how many times the process $P[v]$ can *overtake* the process $P[u]$ on its way to the critical section. It considers a starting position in which $P[u]$ has already made public its intention to proceed to the critical section (by setting $flag[u]$ to 1), while $P[v]$ has not done so yet. In this starting position $P[u]$ is somewhat ahead of $P[v]$. The precedence formula predicts that, following such a position, there will be an interval in which $P[v]$ is not critical (i.e., not in the critical section $\ell_{10}$), followed by an interval in which $P[v]$ is critical, followed by an interval in which $P[v]$ is again non-critical, followed by a position in which $P[u]$ is critical. Consequently, it claims that between the starting position and the entry of $P[u]$ to the critical section, there can be at most one visit of $P[v]$ to the critical section. Note that the interval of $P[v]$ being critical can also be empty. This is why we say *at most* once. Note that this property does not guarantee that $P[u]$ will eventually get to the critical section, because any of the preceding intervals may extend to the end of the computation. In Manna and Pneuli [4] this property is called 1-*bounded overtaking*.

First let us consider two rules that characterize some of the basic properties of the precedence operator.

**MON**   (*Monotonicity*)

$$p \Rightarrow q_0 \, \mathsf{U} \ldots \mathsf{U} q_{r-1} \, \mathsf{U} q_r$$

$$\underline{\tilde{p} \to p, \quad q_0 \to \tilde{q}_0, \ldots, q_r \to \tilde{q}_r}$$

$$\tilde{p} \Rightarrow \tilde{q}_0 \, \mathsf{U} \ldots \mathsf{U} \tilde{q}_{r-1} \, \mathsf{U} \tilde{q}_r$$

This rule allows us to replace in a valid precedence formula the antecedent $p$ by a *stronger* assertion $\tilde{p}$, and the assertions $q_0, \ldots, q_r$ appearing in the consequent by *weaker* assertions $\tilde{q}_0, \ldots, \tilde{q}_r$, and obtain another valid formula.

For the next rule we introduce the following notations

$$\begin{aligned} q_{i_1, i_2, \ldots, i_m} &= q_{i_1} \vee q_{i_2} \vee \ldots \vee q_{i_m} \\ q_{i..k} &= q_i \vee q_{i+1} \vee \ldots \vee q_k \qquad \text{for } i < k \end{aligned}$$

**TEL**

(Telescoping) rule:

For each $i = 0, \dots, r - 1$

$$p \Rightarrow \cdots q_i \, \mathsf{U} \, q_{i+1} \cdots \quad \vdash \quad p \Rightarrow \cdots q_{i,i+1} \cdots$$

For the case of $i < r - 1$, this rule allows us to replace (telescope) the prediction of a $q_i$-interval followed by a $q_{i+1}$-interval, by the prediction of a single $(q_i \vee q_{i+1})$-interval (i.e., a $q_{i,i+1}$-interval). For the end case of $i = r - 1$, the rule allows us to replace the prediction of a $q_{r-1}$-interval followed by a $q_r$-position, by the prediction of a $(q_{r-1} \vee q_r)$-position (i.e., a $q_{r-1,r}$-position).

The next rule is the main proof rule for establishing precedence properties of a given program.

$$
\begin{array}{ll}
\textbf{PREC} & \text{R1.} \quad p \to q_{0..r} \\
& \textit{For each } i{=}0,\dots,\text{r-1, and each } \tau \in \mathcal{T} \\
& \text{R2.} \quad (q_i \wedge \rho_\tau) \to q'_{i..r} \\
\hline
& \quad p \Rightarrow q_0 \, \mathsf{U} \dots \mathsf{U} \, q_{r-1} \, \mathsf{U} \, q_r
\end{array}
$$

## Proving Bounded Overtaking

We are now ready to prove the property of 1-bounded overtaking, or linear wait, for the program **MUTEX**.

For our case, we take $r = 6$ and define as follows:

$$p : (u \in L_3) \wedge (v \in L_{1,2})$$

The assertion $q_0$ is given by

$$q_0 : (u \in L_3) \wedge (Block_3 \neq \phi) \wedge (v \in L_{1..3})$$

where $Block_3$ is as defined before, i.e., $Block_3 = L_{8..12} \cup L_5(j > F_1)$.

The assertions $q_1, \dots, q_6$ are given by

$$
\begin{aligned}
q_1 \quad &: \quad (u \in L_{3,4}) \wedge (Block_3 = \phi) \wedge \left( (v \in L_{1..4,6,7}) \vee \left[ (v \in L_5) \wedge (j_v \leq u) \right] \right) \\
q_2 \quad &: \quad (u \in L_{5..7}) \wedge (L_{8..12} = \phi) \wedge (v \in L_{1..7}) \\
q_3 \quad &: \quad (u \in L_{5..9}) \wedge (L_{8..12} \neq \phi) \wedge (L_4 = \phi) \wedge (v \in L_{5..9}) \\
q_4 \quad &: \quad (u \in L_{5..9}) \wedge (L_{8..12} \neq \phi) \wedge (L_4 = \phi) \wedge (v \in L_{10}) \\
q_5 \quad &: \quad (u \in L_{5..9}) \wedge (L_{8..12} \neq \phi) \wedge (L_4 = \phi) \wedge (v \in L_{0..3,11,12}) \\
q_6 \quad &: \quad (u \in L_{10})
\end{aligned}
$$

It is beyond the scope of this chapter to check the second premise for $i = 0, \ldots, 5$ and all the transitions. We will, however, indicate in the table below what transitions $\tau_k[i]$ may lead from $q_f$ to $q_t$ for $f = 0, \ldots, 5$ and $t = 0, \ldots, 6$. Note that the same transition may lead from $q_f$ to two or more $q_t$'s. By observing that the only non-empty entries in this table correspond to $f \leq t \leq 6$, we are convinced that the second premise of the **PREC** rule is valid. In computing such successors, we may rely on any of the previously proven invariants.

| From | To: $q_0$ | $q_1$ | $q_2$ | $q_3$ | $q_4$ | $q_5$ | $q_6$ |
|------|-----------|-------|-------|-------|-------|-------|-------|
| $q_0$ | | $\tau_{0..12}$ | $\tau_{2,12}$ | | | | |
| $q_1$ | | | $\tau_{0..12}$ | $\tau_5[u]$ | | | |
| $q_2$ | | | | $\tau_{0..12}$ | $\tau_5$ | | $\tau_5$ |
| $q_3$ | | | | | $\tau_{0..12}$ | $\tau_9[v]$ | $\tau_9[u]$ |
| $q_4$ | | | | | | $\tau_{0..12}$ | $\tau_{10}[v]$ |
| $q_5$ | | | | | | | $\tau_{0..12}$ $\tau_9[u]$ |

We may conclude, by the **PREC** rule, that the precedence formula

$$p \Rightarrow q_0 \, \mathsf{U} \, q_1 \, \mathsf{U} \, q_2 \, \mathsf{U} \, q_3 \, \mathsf{U} \, q_4 \, \mathsf{U} \, q_5 \, \mathsf{U} \, q_6$$

is valid over the program **MUTEX**.

Next, we apply the monotonicity rule with $\tilde{p} = p$, $\tilde{q}_0 = \tilde{q}_1 = \tilde{q}_2 = \tilde{q}_3 : (v \notin L_{10})$, $\tilde{q}_4 : (v \in L_{10})$, $\tilde{q}_5 : (v \notin L_{10})$, and $\tilde{q}_6 : (u \in L_{10})$. This application is justified by observing that $\tilde{p} = p$, and getting easily convinced that $q_i$ implies $\tilde{q}_i$ for $i = 0, \ldots, 6$. The application yields the formula

$$p \Rightarrow \tilde{q}_0 \, \mathsf{U} \, \tilde{q}_1 \, \mathsf{U} \, \tilde{q}_2 \, \mathsf{U} \, \tilde{q}_3 \, \mathsf{U} \, \tilde{q}_4 \, \mathsf{U} \, \tilde{q}_5 \, \mathsf{U} \, \tilde{q}_6.$$

Observing that $\tilde{q}_0 = \ldots = \tilde{q}_3$, we may telescope the first four intervals together. This yields the formula

$$p \Rightarrow \tilde{q}_0 \, \mathsf{U} \, \tilde{q}_4 \, \mathsf{U} \, \tilde{q}_5 \, \mathsf{U} \, \tilde{q}_6,$$

which, when substituting the assertions standing for $p$ and $\tilde{q}_i$, leads to

$$[(u \in L_3) \wedge (v \in L_{1,2})] \Rightarrow (v \notin L_{10}) \, \mathsf{U} \, (v \in L_{10}) \, \mathsf{U} \, (v \notin L_{10}) \, \mathsf{U} \, (u \in L_{10}).$$

## 6.7 Acknowledgments

We gratefully acknowledge the help rendered by Rajeev Alur, Ed Chang, and Tom Henzinger who critically read various versions of this manuscript. Special thanks are due to Roni Rosner for his dedicated technical help and most helpful suggestions.

## References

[1] B. Alpern and F. B. Schneider. Defining liveness. *Info. Proc. Lett. 21*, 1985, pp. 181-185.

[2] K. M. Chandy and J. Misra. In *Parallel Program Design*. Reading, MA: Addison-Wesley, 1988.

[3] L. Lamport. Proving the correctness of multiprocess programs. *IEEE Trans. Software Engin. 3*, 1977, pp. 125-143.

[4] Z. Manna and A. Pnueli. Proving precedence properties: The temporal way. In *Proc. 10th Int. Colloq. Aut. Lang. Prog.*, Lec. Notes in Comp. Sci. 154, Springer, 1983, pp. 491-512.

[5] Z. Manna and A. Pnueli. Adequate proof principles for invariance and liveness properties of concurrent programs. *Sci. Comp. Prog. 32*, 1984, pp. 257-289.

[6] Z. Manna and A. Pnueli. The anchored version of the temporal framework. *Linear Time, Branching Time and Partial Order in Logics and Models for Concurrency* (J. W. de Bakker, W.-P. de Roever, and G. Rozenberg, eds.), Lec. Notes in Comp. Sci. 354, Springer, 1989, pp. 201-284.

[7] Z. Manna and A. Pnueli. Completing the temporal picture. *Proc. 16th Int. Colloq. Aut. Lang. Prog.*, Lec. Notes in Comp. Sci. 372, Springer, 1989, pp. 534-558.

[8] Z. Manna and A. Pnueli. An Exercise in the Verification of Multi-Process Programs. Technical Report, Stanford University, Stanford, CA, 1989. To appear in a book dedicated to E.W. Dijkstra.

[9] A. Pnueli and L. Zuck. Verification of multiprocess probabilistic protocols. *Distributed Computing 1*, 1986, pp. 53-72.

[10] B. K. Szymanski. A simple solution to Lamport's concurrent programming problem with linear wait. In *Proc. 1988 International Conference on Supercomputing Systems*, St. Malo, France, 1988, pp. 621-626.

# PART THREE

# Systems and Strategies

# 7

# Strongbox: A System for Self-Securing Programs

J. D. Tygar and Bennet S. Yee

## 7.1 Introduction

Security is a pressing problem for distributed systems. Distributed systems exchange data among a variety of users over a variety of sites, which may be geographically separated. A user who stores important data on processor $A$ must trust not just processor $A$ but also the processors $B, C, D, \ldots$ with which $A$ communicates. The distributed security problem is difficult, and few major distributed systems attempt to address it. In fact, conventional approaches to computer security are so complex that they actually discourage designers from trying to build a secure distributed system: A software engineer who wishes to build a secure distributed data application finds that he or she must depend on the security of a distributed database which depends on the security of a distributed file system which depends on the security of a distributed operating system kernel, etc. Under this design approach, security necessarily becomes a secondary concern since just making an (unsecure) distributed system work efficiently is a daunting task. And adding security raises the difficulty by an order of magnitude.

We propose a new model of security: *self-securing programs*. Self-securing programs are designed to run in environments where only a minimal number of assumptions are made about the security of the operating system kernel. Self-securing program run in a client-server model, use advanced authentication and fingerprinting techniques, and can guarrantee extremely high levels of security without requiring a secure kernel. We have built a system for constructing self-securing programs called Strongbox. We have made the use of Strongbox relatively transparent to programmers who write multithreaded servers. This allows existing servers to be retrofitted with security and allows programmers to separate security from other concerns. Strongbox provides facilities to protect the privacy of data and the integrity of data from alteration, and to implement quickly a variety of policy decisions about data protection.

Strongbox depends on two types of assumptions: one concerning the privacy process data space and one concerning cryptographic security. Clearly a protected process data space is requisite for security—otherwise an adversary could "spy" on a computation and break security. The cryptographic assumption is used to implement a new *zero-knowledge* authentication protocol. This protocol performs substantially better than previous authentication protocols, and includes facilities for key exchange. (Our method is faster than previously proposed zero-knowledge authentication protocols such as [8]. Moreover, our method can be *proven* not to leak any information about the keys we use—this stands in contrast to authentication protocols such as Needham and Schroeder's method [17,18].) Finally, our method of demonstrating that the security of our protocol differs from those suggested by Burrows, Abadi, and Needham [4] is that our proof technique does not suffer from the drawbacks observed in [12].

The current version of Strongbox does not yet address several secondary concerns including *traffic analysis* of data message exchange, communication by adjusting the use of system/network resources (the *covert channel* problem), or the availability of system components (the *denial of service* problem). Our future work will focus on these concerns, and some preliminary thoughts toward these problems are discussed in Section 7.8. However, Strongbox can be used in conjunction with any solution to these secondary concerns.

This chapter begins by discussing our goals for Strongbox—both functional and performance goals. In Section 7.2 we discuss the basic computational model that we assume for our system. In Section 7.3 we give a high level description of the methods used by Strongbox. Sections 7.4 and 7.5 present an overview of the architecture used in implementations that are built on top of Camelot, a distributed transaction system, and Mach, a UNIX-compatible distributed operating system, respectively. (More information about the Camelot implementation is given in [31].) In Section 7.6, we give performance figures and code size for these algorithms, and discuss issues of bootstrapping Strongbox. In Section 7.7 we give full descriptions of our new algorithms, and efficient implementation techniques for those algorithms.

### 7.1.1   Our Goals

The primary functional goals of Strongbox are to guarantee the integrity and privacy of data handled by it. Section 7.3 shows that the architecture of Strongbox protected data from modification or guaranteed that data messages will be protected by end-to-end encryption. In Section 7.7 we show that Strongbox's fingerprinting and authentication algorithms do not leak information. An additional functional goal of Strongbox is to provide programmers with a security library that can be easily used in a server or client. We do not expect programmers to master the subtleties of a delicate protection mechanism. We have structured our interface so that converting an existing client/server to be secure requires only a few simple modifications to the program text.

Security is typically expensive. It is not uncommon for secure versions of operating systems to run an order of magnitude slower than their insecure counterparts. We view this as completely unacceptable for real applications; we demand that the overhead for security, amortized over all computations, should use no more than 5% of the processor cycles, excluding encryption. We have strived to make our security routines extremely fast, and we give our performance figures in Section 7.6.

Another measure of effectiveness of security code is the size of the code. The smaller the code is, the less likely it is to contain errors and the easier it is to verify, whether by formal or other methods. Since our library isolates simple points of communication, we believe that we have met those goals.

## 7.2   Statement of Model

When designing a security system, it is important to keep the system model in mind. Strongbox is intended to be used within the Client-Server model where client programs running on the behalf of users invoke operations within servers using interprocess communication (IPC). In Strongbox, we restrict client/server interactions to remote procedure calls (RPCs)—access is controlled by servers at this level. It is necessary to make some assumptions about the rest of the system when building secure facilities. For example, if the system design assumes an insecure communication mechanism, then communication security must be provided by other means, such as cryptography, and one must make the assumption that the cryptosystem used can not be compromised by attackers. Since cryptosystems can always be broken by nondeterministic agents (who can simply guess the cleartext and the key and verify that the encryption function holds), if we adopt the practice of considering operations in P as tractable and operations in NP as intractable, then showing a secure cryptosystem exists is equivalent to showing P is different from NP, a well known open (and difficult) problem.

In building a security system, it is necessary to make some assumptions. We believe that these are the minimal assumptions needed to provide security. In addition to assumptions about physical security, we need to make a complexity assumption that some problem, such as factoring large integers or inverting the data encryption standard (DES), is intractable. We use this assumption in our authentication, key exchange, and encryption algorithms. (It is important to note that for our authentication algorithm, this weak assumption will allow us to authenticate processes while guaranteeing that no bits of information are leaked to either party or to an eavesdropper.) We also need to assume that our base operating system supports protected address spaces, including contents of virtual address spaces stored on a disk,[1] since without this assumption no privacy is possible between processes on a single host because no process can have secrets. For example, it is often assumed that the local host is physically secure, that it is configured properly so that there are no security holes outside of Strongbox's domain, i.e., the terminal lines from the user are not tapped, the central processing unit (CPU)/display are not bugged to leak information, etc. We do *not*, however, make any assumptions about the security of the network— so we assume that an adversary can eavesdrop a message, replay messages, inject his or her own messages, and prevent messages from being delivered. Since servers that do not use Strongbox are not offered any protection, we assume that application programs use our protection scheme uniformly and do not explicitly bypass protection mechanisms. We assume that our algorithms were implemented without error, and that the compiler produced correct object code for them.

The current version of Strongbox does not address issues of denial of service, covert channel analysis, or traffic analysis of messages (information revealed in the pattern of message transfers). Although we have not explicitly addressed these problems, we conjecture that they may be solved by extensions to the self-securing paradigm. For example, the Camelot transaction system [7] supports fault tolerance, and the Camelot version of Strongbox makes that fault tolerance secure. We believe that these fault-tolerant facilities might be extended to the security case to support protection against denial of service attacks. (For some theoretical contributions to these issues, see [14,24].)

A key scenario for Strongbox is the loosely coupled distributed systems case. In these systems, covert channel analysis may be considerably simplified by storing files/running processes of a single security level on each host. Interactions

---

[1] If we are implementing Strongbox on a paging operating system, we must depend on the security of the paging system. In some cases we can assist the security of the data stored by the pager by using a pager that encrypts as it pages. However, we still need to rely on the security of such a pager.

between security levels will take place over the communication network, which is a simpler object to examine for covert channels than an operating system on a single host. In addition, secure address spaces for processes will be easier to satisfy if all user-applications on the entire node are at the same level of security. This is a natural mode of operation for a loosely coupled network of workstations.

We are continuing to explore approaches such as these in ongoing research. Our current security code is publicly available.[2] We will continue to examine its performance in large applications.

## 7.3  Conceptual Solution

At the core of Strongbox are new routines for key exchange, authentication, and fingerprinting. End-to-end private key encryption protects the privacy and integrity of messages passed among clients, servers, and other system components. Because we do not make assumptions about the security of communications, it is necessary to encrypt our RPC messages; the encryption mechanism, however, is modular and can be easily omitted when appropriate. In particular, in situations where communication is secure or involves no sensitive data—but where operations on sensitive data may be requested—only authentication is required. Key-exchange is performed using a public key system equivalent to deciding quadratic residuosity, a variant of the algorithm described in [10]. In addition, Strongbox provides an authentication system that provides us with support for any user-supplied access control/authorization system. This authentication system differs from previous authentication and key exchange protocols, such as Needham-Shroeder [18] in that it can be proved to not leak any information that would allow eavesdroppers to masquerade as either party. The authentication algorithm is based on the idea of proving identity by having the authenticator prove that he or she has the solution to an *authentication puzzle* without revealing the solution itself. It is similar to the algorithm described in [8] in that it is also based on Rabin's observation about the square root operation, but it provides a level of security superexponential on the size of the puzzle.

Integrity of data or program text files is checked in Strongbox by using provably secure cryptographic checksums. These checksums, called *fingerprints*, are computed prior to storing data in the file system and are checked when the system retrieves data.

Below, we will first talk about the steady-state Strongbox system's operation

---

[2] For information on obtaining Strongbox, write to the authors at Carnegie Mellon University (CMU).

by describing the system components and their interactions with a client when that client is started. Next, we will describe what happens when Strongbox is booted, the assumptions we make about the operator's role, etc.

### 7.3.1  Strongbox System Components

On each host, two servers are essential to Strongbox's operation. The first is the *White Pages* server which maintains the database containing Strongbox key exchange information and authentication puzzles. The second server is the *secure loader*. The secure loader is a user-level program that uses Operating System primitives to load the run-time image of Strongbox servers and clients after verifying their fingerprints. Instead of using a loader within the kernel after verifying the fingerprint, Strongbox must first read the program text into memory, verify the fingerprint, and load the new task with the text from memory. This procedure avoids the possibility of an attacker changing the executable file just after the fingerprint check but before the kernel can load the task. Exhibit 7.1 shows the relationships among the various system components in the Camelot implementation of Strongbox, which is discussed in Section 7.4. The same relationships hold for these servers in the vanilla implementation of Strongbox, modulo the absence of Camelot (discussed in Section 7.5).

We now consider the typical interactions of a secure client with secure Strongbox servers that it uses, the White Pages server, and the secure loader. To start the first secure client running, a user requests the secure loader to start a new client. The user authenticates his or her identity to the secure loader by a standard password mechanism. After the authentication completes, the secure loader will create a new task, load the task's address space with the fingerprint-checked program text, initialize the task's registers, and start the task running. The secure loader gives the task a seed for its random number generator and the puzzle solution for a new, randomly created authentication puzzle.[3]

After the secure client is bootstrapped, it runs on the behalf of the user and interacts with the user using its standard input and standard output streams. The White Pages server $WP$ maintains a database of servers and client names along with their key exchange information and authentication puzzles. When the client $C$ needs to make an RPC with a secure server $S$, it must first contact a $WP$ to obtain $S$'s published key exchange information and authentication puzzles. If $S$ is on the local host, the client will ask the local $WP_{local}$, and it will not need to authenticate the identity of $WP_{local}$ (we assume that the local host was booted securely; see Section 7.3.2). The more interesting case occurs when $S$ is on a remote host. In that case, we may either run an authentication with

---

[3] In Mach, this is done by using an RPC via the task's bootstrap port. This RPC is local to the host and does not appear over the network.

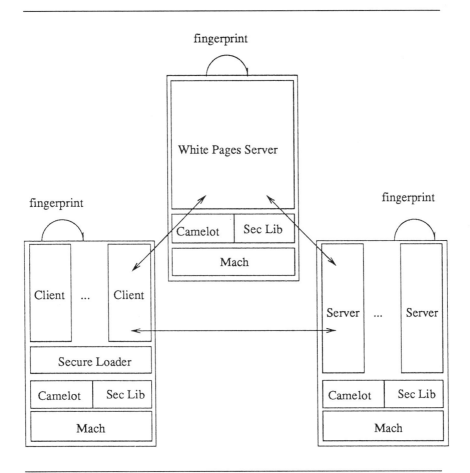

**EXHIBIT 7.1**
Strongbox architecture—Camelot implementation. In this figure, we show
how Strongbox interacts with other system components. Each of the large
boxes denotes a computer. The client, server, and White Pages server are
shown as running on different machines; this is not a requirement of
Strongbox, however, so they may all reside on the same computer. The lines
among the client, server, and White Pages server boxes denote
communication that may be visible on the communication network. Within
each computer, the smaller boxes denote the major software components:
the Mach operating system kernel, the Security Library which is used by
every secure server or client, the White Pages server, the secure loader, and
the secure clients and servers. The curved arrows denote the fingerprint
operation which verifies that none of the files have been corrupted.

the remote White Pages server $WP_{remote}$ directly and obtain $S$'s puzzle, or we may ask our $WP_{local}$: $WP_{local}$ will forward our request to $WP_{remote}$ after performing the appropriate key exchange and authentication steps to establish a secure channel and verify $WP_{remote}$'s identity. The standard routine supplied by Strongbox uses the latter method. After $C$ obtains $S$'s key exchange data and authentication puzzle, $C$ invokes the key exchange routine to establish a secure channel, perform an authentication, and obtain an authentication token from $S$. The authentication performed is symmetrical:[4] the client is assured that it is communicating with the right server, and the server is assured of the identity of the client (and that of the user) and may control access based on that identity. It is only after $C$ has obtained an authentication token that it can call the remote procedure at $S$; the authentication token is used in all subsequent requests to this server, therefore depending on the life time of the client, the cost of key exchange, and the cost of authentication, already low, may be amortized over many RPC operations.

## 7.3.2  Booting Strongbox

To run securely, Strongbox must be booted in a secure fashion. We assume that the Strongbox host is physically secure and that a trusted operator boots the machine. How do we validate the integrity of the host? The same solution that we used to verify the integrity of data files and program text when Strongbox is running can be applied to the operating system kernel and system utilities: simply maintain a list of fingerprints for the system components and verify their correctness at boot time, where a copy of the fingerprint code is placed in the boot read-only memory (ROM) to deter tampering. The fingerprint list is kept secret, and the operator must enter a decryption key to initiate the boot sequence. Along with using encryption, the list of fingerprints of the system modules may itself be fingerprinted; if desired, each host my use a distinct encryption key and a different system fingerprint key. Since the puzzle for the White Pages server is common to *all* White Pages servers, the solution, which is compiled into the binary of the server, must also be kept secret via encryption. The server binary can be handled just like the fingerprints. Note that the plaintext version of the binary need not ever reside in the file system: we can decrypt entirely in main memory and then run the server directly.

Currently, a single puzzle/solution pair is used for all White Pages servers. To avoid the problem of a single untrustworthy site causing problems, multiple puzzle/solution pairs may be employed. This strategy means that we must use a

[4] The server, symmetrically, asks a White Pages server for $C$'s puzzle, and two rounds of authentication, one proving the identity of $C$ to $S$ and the other proving the identity of $S$ to $C$, are run simultaneously.

quorum consensus protocol [9]: to look up the puzzle of a White Pages server $WP_a$, we ask, after establishing a secure channel and authenticating, $n$ servers $WP_1, \cdots, WP_n$ for $WP_a$'s puzzle $P_a$. For the $n$ replies, if $k$ or more of them are identically $P$, then $P$ will be accepted as $P_a$. We are simply assuming that an adversary can not break into $k$ or more hosts. Note that this means that each site must maintain locally the current puzzles of at least $n$ remote $WPs$. This slightly complicates the interface to the White Pages server, since site operators must be able to install new puzzles for remote $WPs$ manually. $WP$ puzzle updates need not be entirely manual, however: quorum consensus can also be used to propagate puzzles once $k$ $WPs$ are updated. We may omit the key exchange and authentication step when we contact our $n$ servers if we are assuming reliable communications and wish only to make sure that information about site security failures are propagated.

## 7.4  Camelot Implementation

We initially implemented a Strongbox interface to work with the Camelot distributed transaction system. Camelot extends the usual programming model [2] to include the *transaction* abstraction for persistent memory objects. Before we describe our implementation for Camelot, we first give an overview of Mach and Camelot.

### 7.4.1  Mach/Camelot Overview

The Mach operating system [1,26] provides the basic services needed to support the client server model for which Strongbox was designed. Mach is upward compatible with 4.3 BSD UNIX, but provides additional primitives for supporting multithreaded processes (called tasks), location transparent intertask communication, and efficient virtual memory. Mach is also relatively machine-independent, running on a variety of uniprocessors and multiprocessors including the IBM RT/PC, Sun 3, Sun 4, DEC VAX and Pmax, Encore Multimax, and the NeXT workstation. The work reported in this chapter was done primarily on Mach running on RT/PCs and Vaxs.

The Mach Interface Generator (MIG) is Mach's RPC stub generator [15]. MIG accepts a syntactic specification for procedure headers (written in a Pascal-like syntax), and generates libraries for calling and dispatching RPCs. These libraries link into the executable image of both clients and servers. The client library contain RPC procedure stubs that copy input arguments into a Mach message, send the message to the server, and unpack the reply message contents into output arguments. The server library contains a demultiplexing routine that, given a message sent by some client, figures out from the message ID in the header the RPC to which the message corresponds, unpacks the arguments appropriately, and calls the service routine with the unpacked arguments. When the service routine completes, the demux routine packs the output arguments into a reply message and sends that message back to the client.

Another detail of Mach IPC that is important to Strongbox is the message format. Each IPC message has a fixed header followed by a variable data part. The variable data part of a message is an array of data descriptors and data. The data descriptor is a structure containing the size and type of the next datum. MIG places arguments in the message in the order of declaration, so by constraining the RPC declaration we can be sure of the argument's location in a message. In particular, this is how Strongbox extracts the authentication token from generic RPC requests.

The Camelot distributed transaction facility is layered on Mach and MIG. It provides mechanisms for constructing reliable distributed programs that access shared data [6,28]. Camelot simplifies the handling of network, processor, and software failures; performs synchronization of concurrent programs; manages storage resources; and reduces the complexity of invoking and building shared databases.

The most important abstraction provided by Camelot is the transaction, a collection of operations bracketed by two markers: BEGIN_TRANSACTION and END_TRANSACTION. Transactions provide three properties that reduce the amount of attention that a programmer must pay to concurrency issues and failures [11,29]:

□ *Failure atomicity*. Failure atomicity ensures that if a transaction's work is interrupted by a failure, any partially completed results will be undone. A programmer or user can then attempt the work again by reissuing the same or a similar transaction.

□ *Permanence*. If a transaction completes successfully, the results of its operations will never be lost, except in the event of catastrophes. Systems can be designed to reduce the risk of catastrophes to any desired probability.

□ *Serializability*. Transactions are allowed to execute concurrently, but the results will be the same as if the transactions executed serially. Serializability ensures that concurrently executing transactions cannot observe inconsistencies. Programmers are therefore free to cause temporary inconsistencies during the execution of a transaction knowing that their partial modifications will never be visible.

The properties of transactional memory is exploited in the Camelot version of Strongbox to simplify the structure of the servers.

## 7.4.2  Camelot Strongbox

Camelot entities are divided into two classes, clients and servers; typically, clients initiate operations at servers via RPCs, though a server may act as a client of a second server as well. Instead of using the MIG-generated RPC stub routines directly, the RPCs were performed by wrapping the RPC request in a C preprocessor macro—Camelot does not allow "raw" RPCs because it must keep track of transaction IDs, etc. Since the IPC among Camelot entities are so highly constrained, we were able to engineer the integration of Strongbox so that modifying an insecure Camelot server or client is as painless as possible. Using Strongbox usually involves changing the macro invocations to use Strongbox-style macros that hide additional Strongbox bookkeeping along with the Camelot bookkeeping.

In the Camelot library, the SERVER_CALL macros handled the transactional bookkeeping for invoking a RPC[5]. Servers never receive RPC requests directly; rather, a Camelot supplied routine receives the incoming request and perform some preprocessing prior to invoking the MIG generated demultiplexing routine. Instead of using the SERVER_CALL macro for performing RPCs, we require that the SEC_SERVER_CALL macro be used instead.

The secure RPC macro hides a bit more detail than the nonsecure version—in addition to the extra input parameters already hidden by SERVER_CALL (e.g., the current transaction ID), it hides another argument, an authentication token,[6] which will also be sent along with the "normal" RPC parameters. Prior to performing the actual RPC request, the secure macro performs Strongbox book-keeping such as looking up the token associated with the server. If there are no valid tokens or if the RPC request is denied for some other reason (e.g., the token expired or the server restarted), the macro automatically runs the key exchange and authentication protocols to obtain a valid token. By adding cached tokens to the RPC parameters and obtaining new tokens when needed automatically, the token management is completely transparent to the application. Hiding all this activity from the interface is desirable for simplifying the task of converting existing non-secure Camelot applications to use Strongbox. Another Strongbox macro, SEC_CAP_SERVER_CALL, allows the programmer to supply a capability token as a parameter of the RPC, thus enabling the program to explicitly manage its tokens.

On the server side, we hide Strongbox-related activities by providing a cover routine for demultiplexing incoming RPC requests. To handle the RPC de-multiplexing, Camelot servers normally gives the name of the demux procedure

---

[5] This applies to both servers and clients.

[6] These tokens are *capabilities* that could be transferred among programs. We do not make any distinction between authentication tokens and capabilities: in particular, a successful authentication for group membership just results in a new capability in addition to the old one rather than a modification to the data entry associated with the old token.

generated by MIG to the Camelot library via the START_SERVER macro. Strongbox provides the SEC_START_SERVER macro to be used in lieu of START_SERVER
macro, which substitutes in a special predemux procedure that implements access control. Since all initial segments of Strongbox RPC message bodies contain a capability token and all RPC headers contain the RPC request ID, we
easily provide coarse-grained access control at the RPC entry-point level. The
access control routine consults a simple, per-server authorization database (implemented using Camelot's recoverable memory objects) implemented with a
library provided with the Camelot version of Strongbox to decide whether to
grant access to a particular RPC routine. If access is denied, the access controller
would just abort the transaction; if access is permitted, the access controller invokes the normal demux procedure. By performing access control before the
service routines are invoked, we eliminate the need to extensively change the
sources for the service routines. This method is somewhat inflexible, however,
and does not extend well to provide finer-grained access control; a simpler
mechanism is used in the vanilla version of Strongbox described in the next
section.

Why are the authentication tokens unforgeable? When the network is insecure, the Strongbox RPC library encrypts all traffic between clients and servers.
The encryption used is based on using a cryptographically secure random number generator (see [3]) as a source of random bits for a one-time pad,[7] so
multiple encryptions of the same data results in different ciphertext: replay-
ing an encrypted token from a message will not aid in spoofing subsequent
messages. There is a caveat: the message header and the type information for
the data fields cannot be encrypted because they are interpreted by the kernel,
and a small integer (part of the token) must remain visible within the message. The integer identifies the secure channel to which the message belongs so
Strongbox will decrypt the message with the appropriate key. This means that,
in its current form, RPC communication is not protected against simple traffic
analysis.

The authorization database that the access control routine consults is maintained within the server. In particular, Camelot's recoverable memory is used,
simplifying the issues of saving and restoring this database. Because the memory
is transactional, once we commit modifications to the authorization database, the
change is permanent—the server may be arbitrarily crashed and restarted without fear of damage to the database. We assume that the underlying Camelot
core servers are secure, and that the transactional logging of the values of the
recoverable memory is performed in a secure fashion.[8] When a secure Camelot
server initially starts up, it performs a once-only transaction that initializes its

---

[7] The generator is based on the assumption that inverting DES is intractable.

[8] The Camelot log must be encrypted so no data can be leaked and fingerprinted so no
data can be modified, or the logging must be to a secure device.

recoverable memory. At this time, the Strongbox server initializes its authorization database to allow an administrative user to access Strongbox-provided authorization handling RPCs. All other access permissions are derived from the administrative user.

## 7.5   Vanilla Implementation

The "vanilla" implementation of Strongbox runs directly on Mach. There are a few differences between the Camelot implementation of Strongbox and the vanilla implementation. This section will describe these differences.

The overall architectures of the two implementations are the same. The main observations are that, without the transactional abstraction provided by Camelot, writing large servers become more complex. Depending on system reliability, a server has several strategies to prevent corrupting its database if the node crashes: it may simply checkpoint its database periodically; it may maintain its database entirely on disk, using main memory as a write-through cache; or it may log changes prior to modifying values so it can reconstruct its database from the log. Furthermore, Strongbox places no trust in the filesystem; if a server is to share that assumption, it must encrypt its database when writing it out to disk. For this purpose, Strongbox provides a routine for using DES in block chaining mode to encrypt contiguous blocks of memory.

In the vanilla version of Strongbox, the access control is no longer at the RPC level. We simply provide a standardized interface between the authentication routines and any authorization mechanism (perhaps provided as library) that the programmer wishes to use. All Strongbox servers' service routines take an authentication token as an argument—as before, its placement in the argument list is constrained so that encryption can be used to establish a secure channel. Unlike the Camelot implementation, however, access is not controlled at the RPC entry point, and the programmer must explicitly control access.

Typically the programmer implements access control by placing queries to authorization routines at appropriate places within the service routine with the authentication token and name of the operation/suboperation as parameters. The authentication routines provide the ability to map from the authentication tokens to client/user names as strings or internal ID numbers, so the authorization routines can use these identifiers as indices into its access control database. Finer grained protection such as that needed by a file server may need authorization routines that allow object identifiers as well. Where the access control matrix for the previous case was indexed by the tuple $user \times operation$, here it is indexed by the triplet $user \times operation \times object$.

## 7.6   Performance and Implementation Issues

This section gives timing figures for our implementations of the authentication algorithm and fingerprinting algorithm described in Section 7.3. Our timing figures are for an IBM RT/APC, which is a reduced instruction set computer (RISC) running at 4 MIPS.

An IBM RT/APC requires 105 milliseconds (mS) to perform (one-way) authentication in addition to the RPC overhead. To perform the authentication, the client invokes two RPCs. The overhead for performing an RPC is approximately 35 mS [30]. We have a software implementation of DES that works at a rate of 220 encryptions per second.

An IBM RT/APC achieves a fingerprinting rate of over 880 KBytes/sec. The fingerprinting routine uses a 65536 ($2^{16}$) entry table of precomputed partial residues to achieve this speed. Another implementation which uses a 256-entry table achieves a fingerprinting rate of 710 Kbytes/sec. The residue table initialization algorithm is described in Section 7.7.2. For the large table, the time required is approximately 1 sec; the time for the small table is negligible.

The trade-off in data size and speed between the two versions of fingerprint implementation indicates using the smaller version for most cases. The large table version is useful where the same irreducible polynomial is used for a large amount of data; the small version wins out when the irreducible is changed often, or where there are tight memory requirements.

While not a requirement when implementing security code, smaller code size is desirable. When the code is smaller, the system is easier to verify and is less likely to contain bugs. The key exchange routines consists of 80 lines of C code, not including comments. The authentication routines consists of 75 lines of C code, not including comments. Both the key exchange and the authentication code are written on top of a library of routines for calculating with arbitrarily large integers. The fingerprinting code consists of 211 lines of C code, not including comments. Our total core routines are relatively small: 366 lines of C code.

## 7.7   Algorithms and Analysis

This section discusses and analyzes the key algorithms in Strongbox. **Warning**: The material in this section is substantially more difficult than the rest of the chapter. A casual reader may wish to skip it. The notation used is standard from number theory and algebra (groups, rings, and fields). Primes needed in the key exchange algorithm, the authentication algorithm, and the two merged exchange/authentication algorithms may be generated using known probabilistic algorithms such as the one given by Rabin in [22].

### 7.7.1  Description of Algorithms

Before we launch into the description of our algorithms, let us define some terms that will be used throughout this section.

A number $M$ is said to be a *Blum modulus* when $M = P \cdot Q$, and $P$, $Q$ are primes of the form $4k + 3$. Moduli of this form is said to have the *Blum* property. As we will see later, Blum moduli have special number theoretic properties that we will make use of in our protocols.

A value is said to be a *nonce* value if it is randomly selected from a set $S$ and is used once in a run of a protocol. The nonce values that we will use are usually selected from a ring $\overset{*}{M}$, where $M$ is a Blum modulus.

Key Exchange.   End-to-end encryption of communication channels is mandatory when the security of the channels is suspect. To do this efficiently, we use private-key encryption coupled with a public-key encryption algorithm used for key exchange. We will first describe the public-key algorithm.

What properties do we need in a public-key encryption algorithm? Certainly, we want assurances that inverting the ciphertext without knowing the key is difficult. To show that inverting the ciphertext is difficult, often we show that breaking a cryptosystem is equivalent to solving some other problem that we believe to be hard. For example, Rabin showed that his encryption algorithm is equivalent to factoring large composite numbers, which number theorists believe to be difficult. Unfortunately, Rabin's system is brittle, i.e., if the agents can be made to decrypt ciphertext chosen by an attacker, it is easy to subvert the system, divulging the secret keys. The RSA encryption algorithm, while believed to be strong, has not been proven secure. Chor [5] showed that if an attacker can guess a single bit of the plaintext when given the ciphertext with an accuracy of more than $1/2 + \epsilon$, then the attacker can invert the entire message. Depending on your bias, this could be interpreted to mean either that RSA is strong in that not a single bit of the plaintext is leaked, or that RSA is weak in that all it takes is one chink in its armor to break it. The public-key cryptosystem used in Strongbox is based on the problem of deciding quadratic residuosity, another well-known problem in number theory that is believed to be difficult.

When a connection is initially established between a client and a server, the two exchange a secret, randomly generated DES key using a public key encryption system. Because private key encryption is relatively cheap, we use the DES key to encrypt all other traffic between the client and the server.

Our public key system works as follows: All entities in the system have published via the White Pages server their moduli, $M_i$, where $M_i$ is a Blum

moduli. The factorization of $M_i$, of course, is known only to the entity corresponding to $M_i$ and is kept secret.

Now, observe that Blum moduli have the property that the multiplicative
group $_{M_i}^*$ has $-1$ as a quadratic nonresidue.[9] To see this, let $L(a, p)$ denote the
Legendre symbol, which is defined as

$$L(a, p) = \begin{cases} 1 & \text{if } a \text{ is a quadratic residue, i.e., if } \exists x : x^2 \equiv a \pmod{p} \\ -1 & \text{otherwise} \end{cases}$$

where $p$ is prime and $a \in _p^*$. Now, we are going to use two important identities
involving the Legendre symbol: [10]

$$L(-1, p) = -1^{(p-1)/2} \tag{7.1}$$

$$L(m \cdot n, p) = L(m, p) \cdot L(n, p) \tag{7.2}$$

When $p = 4k + 3$, from (7.1) we have $L(-1, p) = -1^{2k+1} = -1$, so $-1$ is a
quadratic nonresidue. Further, it is easy to randomly generate random quadratic
residues and nonresidues: simply chose a $r \in _{M_i}^*$ randomly [11] and compute
$r^2 \bmod M_i$. If we wanted a quadratic residue, use $r^2 \bmod M_i$; if we wanted a
quadratic nonresidue, use $-r^2 \bmod M_i$.

We have established that, given $n = p \cdot q$ where both $p$ and $q$ are of the
form $4k + 3$, it is easy to generate random quadratic residues and quadratic
nonresidues. Next, we need to note another property of quadratic residues that
will enable us to decode messages. The important property of the Legendre
symbol is that it can be efficiently computed using a simple algorithm similar
to the Euclidean algorithm for computing the $gcd$. Note that this likewise holds
for the generalization of the Legendre symbol, the Jacobi symbol, defined by
$J(n, m) = \prod_i L(n, p_i)$ where $m = \prod_i p_i$, where the $p_i$'s are the prime factors
of $m$. The value of the Jacobi symbol can be efficiently calculated *without*
knowing the factorization of the numbers.

Suppose a client wants to establish a connection to the server corresponding
to $M_i$. The client first randomly choses a DES key $k$, which will be sent to the
server using the public key system. The client then decomposes the message into
a sequence of single bits, $b_0, b_1, \ldots, b_m$. Now, for each bit of the message $b_j$,
we compute $x_j \equiv -1^{b_j} r_j^2 \pmod{M_i}$ where $r_j$ are random numbers (nonce

---

[9] $_n^*$ denotes integers modulo $n$ relatively prime to $n$ considered as a group with multiplication as the group operator

[10] See [19] for a list of identities involving the Legendre symbol.

[11] We can actually just chose $r \in _{M_i}$ and not bother to check that $r \in _{M_i}^*$. If $r \notin _{M_i}^*$,
this means that $GCD(M_i, r) \neq 1$ and we've just found a factor of $M_i$. Since factoring
is difficult, this is an highly improbable event.

values). The receiver $i$ can compute $b_j = L(x_j, P_i)$ to decode the bit stream since he or she knows the factorization of $M_i$. Note that while the Jacobi symbol, the generalization of the Legendre symbol, can be quickly computed without knowing the factorization of $M_i$, it does not aid the attacker. We see from

$$
\begin{aligned}
J(-r^2, M_i) &= J(-1, M_i)J(r^2, M_i) \\
&= J(-1, P_i)J(-1, Q_i)J(r^2, M_i) \\
&= -1 \cdot -1 \cdot J(r^2, M_i) \\
&= J(r^2, M_i) \\
&= 1
\end{aligned}
$$

that quadratic nonresidues formed as residues modulo $M_i$ of $-r^2$ will also have 1 as the value of the Jacobi symbol.[12]

When receiver has decoded the bit sequence $b_j$ and reconstructed the message $m_i$, he installs $m_i$ as the key for DES encryption of the communication channel. From this point on, DES is used to encrypt all Strongbox managed RPC traffic between the client and the server.

Authentication.    Whether or not our communication channels are secure against eavesdropping or tampering, some form of authentication is needed to verify the identity of the party with whom we are establishing communication. Even if our physical network links are secure, we still need to use authentication: we can not simply trust the nameservers because to look up the communication ports of remote servers we must ask a nameserver on a remote machine. Since we make no assumptions about the network name servers, even the identity of a remote host is suspect. Thus on top of the existing Mach nameserver, Strongbox provides a White Pages server that maintains authentication information (in addition to key exchange moduli when applicable) and is itself an authenticated agent. For the purposes of this discussion, the role of the White Pages server is to serve as a repository of *authentication puzzles*. Authentication is based on having the authenticator proving that he or she can solve the published puzzle without revealing the solution.

Strongbox uses an authentication protocol derived from Rabin's observation about the square root operation: if one can extract square roots modulo $n$ where $n = p \cdot q$, $p$ and $q$ primes, then one can factor $n$. Another authentication protocol derived from Rabin's work is the Feige-Fiat-Shamir (FFS) authentication algorithm. Both our protocol and FFS are *zero-knowledge authentication protocols*. Unlike FFS, our protocol provides superexponential security factor. And in contrast to Needham and Schroeder's authentication protocol[18], zero-

---

[12] Some cryptographic protocols, such as RSA, leak information through the Jacobi symbol. In RSA, plaintext and corresponding ciphertext always have the same value for their Jacobi symbols. If only a limited number of messages or message formats are used, attackers can easily gather statistical information on the distribution of messages.

knowledge authentication protocols require no central authentication server and thus there is no single point of failure that would cripple the entire system.

What do we mean when we say the authentication is *zero-knowledge*? By this we mean that the entire authentication session may be open—eavesdroppers may listen to the entire authentication exchange, and nobody will gain any information at all that would enable them to later masquerade as the authenticator; furthermore, both ends of the protocol may be simulated by any entity even though they have no knowledge of the secrets known only to the authenticator. We will see how this is possible in Section 7.7.2.

Let's see how Strongbox authentication works. After establishing a secure communication channel with the remote entity, we query the White Pages server for the corresponding authentication puzzle. These authentication puzzles are randomly generated and can be solved only by their owners who knows their secret solutions. In the protocol, however, the remote entity is not asked to exhibit a solution to their puzzles, but rather is asked to show a solution to a randomization of their puzzle. Our puzzles are again based on quadratic residuosity—this time not on deciding residuosity but on actually finding square roots.

Whenever a new entity is created, an authentication puzzle/solution pair is created for it in an initial, once-only preparatory step—the puzzle is published in the local White Pages server, and the solution is given to the new task. The puzzle consists of a modulus $M_i = p_i \cdot q_i$ and the vector

$$\vec{V_i} = (v_{i,1}, v_{i,2}, \ldots, v_{i,n-1}, v_{i,n})$$

where $p_i$ and $q_i$ are primes, and each $v_{i,j}$ is a quadratic residue in $\overset{*}{\mathbb{Z}}_{M_i}$. The authentication modulus is distinct from the key exchange modulus; in our authentication algorithm, it is not necessary for anyone to know the factors $p_i$ and $q_i$, and in fact a single modulus can be used for all authentication puzzles. The secret solution is the vector

$$\vec{S_i} = (s_{i,1}, s_{i,2}, \ldots, s_{i,n-1}, s_{i,n})$$

where $s_{i,j}$ are roots of the equations $x^2 \equiv 1/v_{i,j} \pmod{M_i}$. Generating a new solution/puzzle pair is simple: we chose random $s_{i,j} \in \mathbb{Z}_{M_i}$ to form the solution vector, and then element-wise squaring and then inverting $\vec{S_i}$ modulo $M_i$ to form the puzzle $\vec{V}$.

Suppose a challenger $\mathcal{C}$ wants to authenticate $\mathcal{A}$'s identity. $\mathcal{C}$ first randomly choses a boolean vector $\vec{E} \in \mathbb{Z}_2^n$:

$$\vec{E} = (e_1, e_2, \ldots, e_{n-1}, e_n)$$

where $\vec{E} \circ \vec{E} = \lfloor \frac{n}{2} \rfloor$, and $\phi \in S_n$ a permutation.[13] We can represent $\phi$ as a

[13] $S_n$ denotes the symmetric group of $n$ elements.

number $\varphi$ from 0 to $n! - 1$ which represents elements of $S_n$ under a canonical numbering.[14]

The pair $(\vec{E}, \phi)$ is the *challenge* that $\mathcal{C}$ will use to query $\mathcal{A}$. Now, $\mathcal{C}$ encodes $\vec{E}$ and $\varphi$ as follows:

$$\vec{C} = (c_1, c_2, \ldots, c_{n-1}, c_n)$$

where

$$c_i = \begin{cases} -1^{e_i} t_i^2 \bmod M_{pub} & \text{if } 1 \le i \le n \\ -1^{\varphi_i} t_i^2 \bmod M_{pub} & \text{otherwise} \end{cases}$$

where $\varphi_i$ denotes the $i^{th}$ bit of $\varphi$ and $t_i$ are nonce values from $\overset{*}{M_{pub}}$, $M_{pub}$ a Blum modulus, i.e. $M_{pub} = P_{pub} Q_{pub}$, where $P_{pub} \equiv Q_{pub} \equiv 3 \pmod 4$, which is used by all entities in this initial round. The values of $P_{pub}$ and $Q_{pub}$ are secret and may be forgotten after $M_{pub}$ was generated.

$\mathcal{C}$ sends the encoded challenge, $\vec{C}$, to $\mathcal{A}$.

When $\mathcal{A}$ receives $\vec{C}$, $\mathcal{A}$ computes the nonce vector

$$\vec{R} = (r_1, r_2, \ldots, r_{n-1}, r_n)$$

where $r_j$ are randomly chosen from $\overset{*}{M_i}$, and the vector

$$\vec{X} = (x_1, x_2, \ldots, x_{n-1}, x_n)$$

where $x_j \equiv r_j^2 \pmod{M_i}$. The authenticator sends $\vec{X}$, called the *puzzle randomizer*, to the challenger $\mathcal{C}$, keeping the value of $\vec{R}$ secret. As we will see in Section 7.7.2, $\vec{X}$ is used to randomize the puzzle in order to keep the solution from being revealed.

$\mathcal{C}$ responds to the puzzle randomizer with $\vec{T} = (t_1, t_2, \ldots, t_{n-1}, t_n)$ of nonce values used to compute $\vec{C}$. With $\vec{T}$, $\mathcal{A}$ computes the exponents to $-1$ in $c_i$ and thus reconstruct $\vec{E}$ and $\phi$.

In response to the decoded challenge, $\mathcal{A}$ replies with

$$\vec{Y} = (y_1, y_2, \ldots, y_{n-1}, y_n)$$

where $y_j \equiv r_{\phi(j)} \cdot s_{i,j}^{e_j} \pmod{M_i}$. $\vec{Y}$ is the *response*. To verify, the challenger checks that $\forall j : x_{\phi(j)} \equiv y_j^2 \cdot v_{i,j}^{e_j} \pmod{M_i}$ holds.

**Authentication and Secret Agreement.**   Instead of running key exchange and authentication as separate steps, we have a merged protocol that performs secret

---

[14] Note that this numbering provides a way to randomly choose $\phi$: since $\varphi$ requires $\log(n!)$ bits to represent, we can simply generate $\lceil \log(n!) \rceil$ random bits and use it as a number from 0 to $2^{\lceil \log(n!) \rceil} - 1$. If the number is greater than $n! - 1$, we try again. This procedure terminates in an expected two tries, so on average we expend $2\lceil \log(n!) \rceil$ random bits.

agreement and authentication at the same time. The protocol performs *secret agreement* rather than key exchange: after the protocol completes, both parties will share a secret, but that secret is a random value; neither party in the protocol can control the final value of this secret. This merged protocol has the advantage of eliminating an RPC,[15] but requires that the authentication security parameter $n$ (the puzzle size) be at least $2m$, where $m$ is the number of bits in a session key. We did not use this protocol because $n = 2m$ would have provided an unnecessarily high level of authentication security and we did not want to expend too many cryptographically secure random bits.

Our merged protocol goes as follows:

As in the normal key exchange protocol, each entity $i$ in the system calculate a Blum modulus $M_i = P_i Q_i$, with $P_i$ and $Q_i$ primes of the form $4k + 3$. $i$ keeps the values of $P_i$ and $Q_i$ secret and publishes $M_i$. $i$ also generates a random puzzle by first generating the desired solution vector

$$\vec{S_i} = (s_{i,1}, s_{i,2}, \cdots, s_{i,n})$$

where the elements of $\vec{S_i}$ are computed by $s_{i,j} = z_{i,j}^2$, where $z_{i,j}$ a random number from $\overset{*}{M_i}$. Then, $i$ publishes the puzzle vector

$$\vec{V_i} = (v_{i,1}, v_{i,2}, \cdots, v_{i,n})$$

with $v_{i,j} = 1/s_{i,j}^2$. With both $M_i$ and $V_i$ are published, $i$ is ready to authenticate and exchange keys.

When the challenger $C$ wishes to verify $A$'s identity and obtain a session key from $A$, first $C$ chooses a challenge $(\vec{E}, \phi)$ as before, with $\vec{E} \in \overset{n}{2}$ such that $\vec{E} \circ \vec{E} = \lfloor \frac{n}{2} \rfloor$, and permutation $\phi \in S_n$. Just as in the vanilla authentication protocol, $C$ encodes $\vec{E}$ and $\phi$

$$\vec{C} = (c_1, c_2, \ldots, c_{n-1}, c_n)$$

where

$$c_j = \begin{cases} -1^{e_j} t_j^2 \bmod M_{pub} & \text{if } 1 \leq i \leq n \\ -1^{\varphi_j} t_j^2 \bmod M_{pub} & \text{otherwise} \end{cases}$$

where $\varphi_j$ denotes the $j^{th}$ bit of $\varphi$, the canonical numbering of $\phi$ in $S_n$, and $t_j$ are nonce values from $\overset{*}{M_{pub}}$, $M_{pub}$ a Blum modulus. $C$ sends $A$ the encoded challenge $\vec{C}$. Let $\vec{T}$ denote the vector of nonce values used to generate $\vec{C}$.

$A$ computes a puzzle randomizer $\vec{R}$

$$\vec{R} = (r_1, r_2, \ldots, r_{n-1}, r_n)$$

---

[15] The key exchange and the authentication messages from the original two protocols could be "piggybacked" to eliminate this extra RPC as well since the initial message of the authentication need not be encrypted.

by randomly choosing the nonce vector

$$\vec{W} = (w_1, w_2, \ldots, w_{n-1}, w_n)$$

The values $w_j$ are chosen from $^*_{M_a M_c}$, where $M_a$ is the published modulus of $A$ and $M_c$ is the published modulus of $C$. The value of $\vec{R}$ is obtained by setting $r_j = w_j^2 \bmod {M_a M_c}$. Next, $A$ computes the puzzle randomizer $\vec{X}$ from $\vec{R}$ as before, setting $x_j = r_j^2 \bmod {M_a M_c}$, and sends $\vec{X}$ to $C$.

Now, $C$ reveals the challenge $(\vec{E}, \phi)$ by sending $A$ the vector $\vec{T}$; in response, $A$ sends $\vec{Y}$ with

$$y_j = -1^{b_j} \cdot r_{\phi(j)} \cdot s_{a,j}^{e_j} \bmod (M_a M_c^{1-e_j})$$

where $b_j$ is a random bit that is used as a bit in the key when $e_j = 0$.

To verify $A$'s identity, $C$ checks that

$$\forall j : x_{\phi(j)} = y_j^2 v_{a,j}^{e_j} \bmod M_a$$

holds. There are $\lceil \frac{n}{2} \rceil$ usable key bits transferred, and they correspond to those $y_j$ for which $e_j = 0$. To extract, $C$ computes the Legendre symbol $L(y_j, P_c)$ to determine whether $y_j$ is a quadratic residue. If $y_j$ is a quadratic residue, then $b_j = 0$; otherwise, $b_j = 1$.


Practical Authentication and Secret Agreement.    In this section, we present another protocol for simultaneous authentication and secret agreement that also requires two rounds of interaction but requires many fewer random bits. Furthermore, the message sizes are smaller, thus making this protocol more practical.

Each agent $A$ who wishes to participate in the protocol generates a modulus $M_a$ with secret prime factors $P_a$ and $Q_a$. Each agent also generates a vector of secret numbers

$$\vec{S}_a = (s_{a,1}, s_{a,2}, \cdots, s_{a,n})$$

where $s_{a,i} \in {}^*_{M_a}$. From this $\vec{S}_a$, $A$ computes

$$\vec{V}_a = (v_{a,1}, v_{a,2}, \cdots, v_{a,n})$$

where $v_{a,i} = 1/s_{a,i}^4$. Published for all to use is a modulus $M_{pub}$; the two prime factors of $M_{pub}$, $P_{pub}$ and $Q_{pub}$, are kept secret.

Now, suppose a challenger $C$ wishes to verify the identity of an authenticator $A$. Assume they have published their moduli $M_c$ and $M_a$, respectively, and that $C$'s puzzle vector $\vec{V}$ has also been published. First, $C$ chooses a bit vector

$$\vec{E} = (e_1, e_2, \cdots, e_n)$$

where $\vec{E} \circ \vec{E} = \frac{n}{2}$, and a permutation $\phi \in S_n$. The pair $(\phi, \vec{E})$ is the challenge that $C$ will use later in authentication. Let $\zeta = \binom{n}{\frac{n}{2}}$, the number of possible vectors $\vec{E}$. Encode both as two numbers using mappings $f:\{\vec{E}\} \leftrightarrow \zeta$ and $g: S_n \leftrightarrow n!$. Let $E = g(\phi) \cdot \zeta + f(\vec{E})$ the combined encoding for the two parts of the challenge,[16] and let $C = E^2 \bmod M_{pub}$. The value $C$ is used to commit $\mathcal{C}$'s challenge to $\mathcal{A}$. $\mathcal{C}$ sends $C$ to $\mathcal{A}$.

In response, $\mathcal{A}$ generates a puzzle randomizer by choosing

$$\vec{R} = (r_1, r_2, \cdots, r_n)$$

where each $r_i$ is a nonce value chosen from $M_a M_c$. $\mathcal{A}$ creates the puzzle randomizer vector $\vec{X}$ from this by setting

$$\vec{X} = (x_1, x_2, \cdots, x_n)$$

where $x_i = r_i^4$. $\mathcal{A}$ sends $\vec{X}$ to $\mathcal{C}$.

When $\mathcal{C}$ receives the puzzle randomizer, $\mathcal{C}$ replies by revealing the challenge by sending $E$ to $\mathcal{A}$.

$\mathcal{A}$ verifies that this $E$ encodes the challenge that corresponds to the challenge commitment value $C$ by checking that $C = E^2 \bmod M_{pub}$. If the encoding is correct, $\mathcal{C}$ extract the challenge tuple $(\phi, \vec{E})$, and computes

$$\vec{Y} = (y_1, y_2, \cdots, y_n)$$

where $y_i = r_{\phi(i)}^2 s_i^{2e_i} \bmod M_a^{e_i} M_c^{1-e_i}$, and

$$\vec{W} = ((z_{j_1}, E_{r_{\phi(j_1)}}(z_1)), (z_{j_2}, E_{r_{\phi(j_2)}}(z_2)), \cdots, (z_{\frac{n}{2}}, E_{r_{\phi(j_{\frac{n}{2}})}}(z_{\frac{n}{2}})))$$

where $z_i$ are nonce values used for a family of secret key encryption functions $\mathcal{F} = \{E_k()\}$, and $j_k$ are the $\frac{n}{2}$ indices where $e_{j_k} = 0$. $\mathcal{A}$ sends $\vec{Y}$ and $\vec{W}$ to $\mathcal{C}$ in response.

$\mathcal{C}$ verifies that

$$\forall i: y_i^2 v_i^{e_i} = x_{\phi(i)} \bmod M_a^{e_i} M_c^{1-e_i}$$

If each $y_i$ passes this test, $\mathcal{C}$ then examines the values of $y_i$ for which $e_i = 0$: since

$$y_i = r_{\phi(i)}^2 \bmod M_c$$

and $\mathcal{C}$ knows the factorization of $M_c$, $\mathcal{C}$ can extract the four square roots of $y_i$ (mod $M_c$), one of which was the original $r_{\phi(i)}$ chosen by $\mathcal{C}$.[17] To disambiguate and choose among the roots of $y_i$, $\mathcal{C}$ uses the $i$-th element of $\vec{W}$ to find the value that satisfies the encryption. This assumes that $\mathcal{F}$ is immune from known plaintext attacks. Alternatively, instead of having to send $\vec{W}$, if there is enough redundancy in the data that we wish to encrypt, $\mathcal{A}$ can just use the shared secret

---

[16] If $|E| \not\approx |M_{pub}|$, extra random pad bits may be necessary.

[17] Either Berlekamp's algorithm or that of Adelman, Manders, and Miller will do.

values to form a key and start using it. $C$ tries the four possible decryptions and determines which key is valid using the redundancy in the data. This alternative assumes that having some redundancy in the plaintext will not compromise the encryption system.

Fingerprints.    Next, we describe the Karp-Rabin fingerprinting algorithm, which is crucial to Strongbox's ability to detect attackers or security problems in the underlying system. The key idea is this: associated with each file—in particular, every trusted program generated by trusted editors/compilers/assemblers/linkers/ etc.—is a *fingerprint* which, like a normal checksum, detects any modifications to the data. Unlike normal checksums, however, fingerprints are parameterized by the irreducible polynomial[18] used and the likelihood of an attacker forging a fingerprint without knowing the irreducible polynomial is exponentially small on the degree of $p$.

In Strongbox, we chose random irreducible polynomials $p$ from $_2[x]$ of degree 31 by the algorithm due to Rabin [20,16,23].

Let us visualize the fingerprinting operation. We take the irreducible polynomial $p(x)$, arrange the coefficients from left to right in decreasing order, i.e., with the $x^{31}$ term of $p(x)$ at the leftmost position, and scan through the input bit stream from left to right. If the bit in the input opposite the $x^{31}$ term is set, we exclusive-or $p(x)$ into the bit stream.[19] As we scan down the bit stream all coefficients to the left of the current position of $x^{31}$ term of $p(x)$ will be zeros. When we reach the end of the bit stream, i.e., the $x^0$ term of $p(x)$ is opposite the last bit of the input stream, we will have computed $f(x) \bmod p(x) = \varphi(f(x))$.

### 7.7.2   Analysis of Algorithms

Key Exchange.    The correspondence between the problem of deciding quadratic residuosity and the protocol is direct. For a detailed analysis, see [10].

Authentication.    What are the chances that a system breaker $B$ could break the authentication? First, we assume that the modulus $M_i$ is sufficiently large so that factoring it is impractical. Now, consider what $B$ must do to pose as $A$.

Let us first look at a simpler authentication system to gain intuition. The puzzle and the secret solution is $v$ and $s$ where $v = 1/s^2$; the puzzle randomizer

---

[18] A polynomial $p(x) \in F[x]$ ($F$ a field) is said to be *irreducible* if $f(x) \in F[x]$: $f(x) \mid p(x), 0 < \deg f < \deg p$, i.e., the only divisors are $p$ and nonzero elements of $F$ (the units of $F[x]$). This is analogous to primality for integers.

[19] Exclusive-or is equivalent to addition/subtraction mod 2. In particular, when we pairwise exclusive-or the coefficient bits with the input stream in this fashion, we are subtracting $p(x) \cdot x^k$, where $k$ is the distance from the leftmost bit of our irreducible to the rightmost bit in the input stream.

is $x = r^2$, $r$ known only to the authenticator; the challenge is $e \in Z_2$; and the response is $y = r \cdot s^e$. All calculations are done modulo $M$.

We claim that a system breaker $B$ has exactly a $\frac{1}{2}$ chance of foiling this authentication procedure and masquerading as $\mathcal{A}$. The best $B$ can do to masquerade as $\mathcal{A}$ is to try to guess the value of $e$: (1) $B$ guesses $e = 0$, and randomly generate $r$ and $x$ according to the protocol: $B$ choses $r$ randomly from $_M$, and and set the randomizer $x$ to be $r^2$; (2) $B$ guesses $e = 1$, and simply generates a random $t \in {}^*_{M_i}$ and set the randomizer $x$ to be $t^2/v$. The randomizer $x$ chosen is sent to $C$.

Now, let us examine what are the possible outcomes for each of his guesses. Consider case (1): If $B$ guessed the challenge correctly, the reply is just $y = r$ and $B$ would pass the verification; on the other hand, if $B$ guessed it incorrectly, he or she is revealed since $B$ can not produce $y = r \cdot s$. Consider case (2): If $B$ guessed the challenge correctly, the reply is just $y = t$ and $B$ would pass the verification; on the other hand, if $B$ guessed incorrectly, he or she is revealed since $B$ cannot produce $y = \sqrt{x} = t \cdot s$.

Now, since $C$ chose $e$ uniformly from $_2$, so in each case there is a $\frac{1}{2}$ chance of being revealed. Thus, regardless of the method by which $B$ guessed $e$, $B$ can do no better than pass with a probability of $\frac{1}{2}$.

What must $B$ do in the full version of the authentication? $B$ must essentially guess $\vec{E}$ and $\phi$ to pass the challenge. Note that while

$$\left| \{ (\vec{E}, \phi) : \vec{E} \in {}^n_2, \vec{E} \circ \vec{E} = \lfloor \tfrac{n}{2} \rfloor, \phi \in S_n \} \right| = \binom{n}{n/2} n!,$$

the security factor (the inverse of the probability of breaking the system) is slightly smaller: $B$ does not have to guess all of $\phi$ but only those values selected by the 1 entries in $\vec{E}$. Our authentication system provides, for puzzles of $n$ numbers, a probability of an attacker breaking the authentication system of

$$
\begin{aligned}
P &= \frac{1}{\binom{n}{n/2} n! / \frac{n}{2}!} \\
&= \frac{(n/2)! \, t^3}{n!^2} \\
&\approx \frac{\left(\frac{2\pi n}{2}\right)^{\frac{3}{2}} \left(\frac{n}{2e}\right)^{\frac{3n}{2}}}{(2\pi n)\left(\frac{n}{e}\right)^{2n}} \\
&= \frac{\sqrt{2\pi n} \; e^{\frac{n}{2}}}{2^{\frac{3}{2}(n+1)} \, n^{\frac{n}{2}}} \\
&= \frac{\sqrt{\pi} \; e^{\frac{n}{2}}}{2^{\frac{3}{2}n+1} \, n^{\frac{n-1}{2}}}
\end{aligned}
$$

using the Stirling's approximation of $n! \approx \sqrt{2\pi n}(\frac{n}{e})^n$, which shows that $P$ is clearly superexponentially small. By using longer vectors or multiple vectors (iterating) the security factor can be made arbitrarily high. Note that since the security factor is superexponential on $n$, the puzzle size, and only multiplicative when the protocol is iterated, increasing puzzle size is usually preferable: If $n'$,

the new size of the puzzle, is $2n$, then the probability of successfully breaking
the system becomes

$$P' \approx \frac{\sqrt{\pi 2n}\, e^n}{2^{3n+1}(2n)^n}$$

$$= \frac{\sqrt{2\pi n}\, e^n}{2^{\frac{3n}{2}+1} 2^{\frac{3n}{2}} 2^n n^n}$$

$$= \frac{2\sqrt{2}(\pi n) e^n}{2^{\frac{3n}{2}+1} 2^{\frac{3n}{2}+1} 2^n \sqrt{\pi n}\, n^n}$$

$$= \frac{P^2}{2^{n-\frac{3}{2}}\sqrt{\pi n}}$$

If, on the other hand, we simply run the protocol twice, we would only obtain
$P' = P^2$. Iterating, on the other hand, has the advantage of making the security
factor $(1/p)$ flexible: applications at different security levels can easily negotiate
the desired security of the connection.

How did we arrive at the expression for $P$? $1/P$ simply measures is the
number of equiprobable random states visible to the attacker. First, note that
$\binom{n}{n/2}$ is the number of different $\vec{E}$ where $\vec{E} \circ \vec{E} = \lfloor \frac{n}{2} \rfloor$ (i.e., the number of 1
bits in $\vec{E}$ is $\lfloor \frac{n}{2} \rfloor$). The $n!/(n-i)!$ term gives the number of ways of chosing $i$
objects from $n$ without replacement, which is what the projection, as specified
by the 1 values in $\vec{E}$, of the permutation $\phi$ gives us.

Why do we restrict $\vec{E}$ to have $\lfloor \frac{n}{2} \rfloor$ 1 bits? If $e = \vec{E} \circ \vec{E}$ can take only
any value, then there are $\sum_{k=0}^{n} \binom{n}{k} \frac{n!}{(n-k)!}$ different states visible to $B$, *not all
of which are equiprobable* if $\vec{E}$ and $\phi$ are chosen uniformly from $\frac{n}{2}$ and $S_n$. In
particular, the state corresponding to $e = 0$ is most probable,[20] with a likelihood
of $2^{-n}$, and our protocol would no longer provide superexponential security.

Our protocol provides superexponential security as long as the moduli remain unfactored. Please note that since there is an exponential time algorithm for
factoring, it is always possible to break our system in the minimum of the time
for factoring and our superexponential bound. Thus we can scale our protocol
in a variety of ways.

The authentication protocol not only provides superexponential security
when the moduli cannot be factored, but is also zero knowledge. The encoded
challenge vector, $\vec{C}$, performs *bit commitment*, forcing $C$ to choose the challenge
values prior to $A$ choosing the puzzle randomizer. This means that $\vec{E}$ and $\phi$ can
not be a function of $\vec{X}$, and thus the protocol can be simulated by an entity that
does not have knowledge of any of the secrets. Any entity $S$ can simulate both

---

[20] To see this, note that all vectors $\vec{E}$ are equiprobable with probability $2^{-n}$, and $e$
determines how many values in the permutation $\phi$ matters: the probability $2^{-n}$ is evenly
divided among the $\frac{n!}{(n-e)!}$ visible states of $\phi$, with each state having a probability of
$\frac{(n-e)!}{2^n n!}$.

sides of the protocol—$S$ can choose random $\vec{E}$, $\phi$, and, knowing their values, construct vectors $\vec{X}'$ and $\vec{Y}'$ that will pass the verification step:

$$y_j = r_{\phi(j)}, x_j = r_j^2 \qquad\qquad \text{if } e_j = 0$$
$$y_j = r_{\phi(j)}, x_j = r_j^2 \cdot v_{i,\phi^{-1}(j)} \quad \text{if } e_j = 1$$

Note that our model differs slightly from the usual model for zero knowledge interactive proofs in that here both the prover and the verifier are assumed to be polynomial time (and that factoring and quadratic residuosity are not in polynomial time); if the prover is assumed to be infinitely powerful as in the usual model, the prover can simply factor the moduli used in the bit commitment phase of our protocol. Other bit commitment protocols may be used instead; e.g., a protocol based on the discrete log problem [27] could be used that would require more multiplications but use fewer random bits.

**Merged Authentication and Secret Agreement.**   Like the vanilla authentication algorithm, the merged authentication and key exchange algorithm reveals no information assuming that factoring and deciding quadratic residuosity are difficult.

What did we change from the original zero knowledge authentication? The modification is to use $M_a M_c$ as the modulus for the nonce vectors, and to use quartic residues instead of quadratic residues for the puzzle randomization vector $\vec{X}$.

No information is leaked. When $e_j = 1$, we know that

$$
\begin{aligned}
y_j &= -1^{b_j} \cdot r_{\phi(j)} \cdot s_{a,j} \bmod M_a \\
&= -1^{b_j} \cdot w_{\phi(j)}^2 \cdot z_{a,j}^2 \bmod M_a \\
&= -1^{b_j} \cdot (w_{\phi(j)} z_{A,j})^2 \bmod M_a
\end{aligned}
$$

so $y_j$ looks like the square of a random number, possibly negated, in $\overset{*}{M_a}$. The challenger $\mathcal{C}$ or an eavesdropper could have generated this without $\mathcal{A}$'s help. Note that the reason that this value is computed modulo $M_a$ is because $s_{a,j}$ is the residue modulo $M_a$ of a random square; if we computed $y_j$ modulo $M_a M_c$, would have no guarantees as to whether $s_{a,j}$ would be a quadratic residue.

When $e_j = 0$, we have

$$
\begin{aligned}
y_j &= -1^{b_j} \cdot r_{\phi(j)} \bmod M_a M_c \\
&= -1^{b_j} \cdot w_{\phi(j)}^2 \bmod M_a M_c
\end{aligned}
$$

This is just the square of a random value, possibly negated, in $_{M_a M_c}$. The challenger $\mathcal{C}$ or any eavesdropper could have generated this without $\mathcal{A}$'s help as well.

This proves that one atomic round of the authentication leaks no information. As with the vanilla authentication, the vectors $\vec{C}$ and $\vec{T}$ provide bit commitment, forcing the challenge $(\vec{E}, \phi)$ to be independent of $\vec{X}$, thus running the atomic rounds in parallel rather than in serial has no impact on the proof of zero knowledge.

Might some system breaker $B$ compromise the authentication? To do so, $B$ must guess the values of $\vec{E}$ and $\phi$ just as in the vanilla authentication protocol. The probability of somebody breaking the authentication is superexponentially small as before (see Section 7.7.2).

The bits of the session key transferred only when $e_j = 0$. When $e_j = 1$, $C$ cannot determine the quadratic residuosity of the element $y_j$ since we assume that quadratic residuosity is hard without the factorization of $M_a$. When $e_j = 0$, on the other hand, $C$ can easily determine the quadratic residuosity of $y_j$ by simply evaluating the Legendre symbol $L(y_j, P_c)$.

**Practical Authentication and Secret Agreement.** Assuming that factoring is intractable, the protocol is zero knowledge. In particular, breaking the protocol is equivalent to factoring: any system breaker $B$ who has a strategy that allows $B$ to masquerade as $A$ can trivially adapt the strategy to factor the various moduli in the system.

Let us examine how this authentication/secret agreement protocol differs from the previous one. Instead of using the quadratic residuosity decision problem to do bit commitment, this protocol uses the Rabin function, removing the requirement that the moduli have the Blum property. Since we assume that neither $A$ nor $C$ can factor, neither of them can extract the square root of an arbitrary number mod $M_{pub}$. In particular, $A$ has no way of getting the encoding $E$ from the commitment value $C$; the only way $A$ finds out the value of $C$ (and thus the value of $(\phi, \vec{E})$) is for $C$ to reveal $C$. The challenge commitment works as before.

The analysis for the authentication properties are identical to that for the previous protocols, so we elide that here. (See Section 7.7.2.) What about the zero-knowledge property?

When $e_j = 1$, we know that

$$
\begin{aligned}
y_j &= r_{\phi(j)}^2 \cdot s_{a,j}^2 \bmod M_a \\
&= (r_{\phi(j)} \cdot s_{a,j})^2 \bmod M_a
\end{aligned}
$$

so $y_j$ looks like the square of a random number in $\overset{*}{M_a}$. The challenger $C$ or an eavesdropper could have generated this without $A$'s help. Note that the reason that this value is computed modulo $M_a$ is because $s_{a,j}$ is the residue modulo $M_a$ of a random square; if we computed $y_j$ modulo $M_a M_c$, we would have no guarantees as to whether $s_{a,j}$ would be a quadratic residue.

When $e_j = 0$, we have

$$
y_j = r_{\phi(j)}^2 \bmod M_c
$$

This is just the square of a random value in $M_c$. The challenger $C$ or any eavesdropper could have generate this without $A$'s help as well.

In both cases, a simulator $S$ who pretends to be $A$ and is able to control the coin flips of $C$ can easily produce a run of the protocol where the message traffic is indistinguishable from that of an actual run. Since $S$ can simulate protocol without the secret known only to $A$, the protocol is zero knowledge.

Fingerprints.   Choosing random irreducible polynomials is equivalent to chosing random homomorphisms $\varphi: {}_2[x]\ GF(2^{31})$, where $\ker \varphi = (p(x))$, $p(x)$ the irreducible polynomial. To be precise, $\varphi$ identifies the indeterminate $x$ with $u$, a root of the irreducible polynomial in the field $\tilde{{}_2}$, the algebraic closure of ${}_2$, i.e., $\varphi: {}_2[x]\ {}_2(u) \cong GF(2^{31})$. There are exactly $(2^{31} - 2)/31$ such homomorphisms. To compute the fingerprint of a file, we consider the contents of the file as a large polynomial in ${}_2[x]$: take the data as a string of bits $b_n, b_{n-1}, \ldots, b_1, b_0$, and construct the polynomial $f(x) = \sum_{i=0}^n b_i x^i$. The fingerprint is exactly $\varphi(f(x))$.

Now if a polynomial of degree $l$ can have at most $l/\deg p = l/31$ divisors of degree $\deg p = 31$. Any two distinct polynomials $f_1(x)$ and $f_2(x)$ will have the same residue if $(f_1 - f_2)(x) \equiv 0 \pmod{p(x)}$. The number of polynomial divisors of $(f_1 - f_2)(x)$ is at most $l/31$, so the probability that a random irreducible polynomial giving the same residue for $f_1(x)$ and $f_2(x)$ is $\frac{l/31}{(2^{31}-2)/31} = l/(2^{31} - 2)$. For a page of memory containing 4 kilobytes of data ($l = 2^{15}$, or 32 kilobits), this is less than 0.002%.

We speed up this computation efficient by precomputing a table $T$, when given $\varphi$, of residues of small polynomials. We initially describe the algorithm for arbitrary sized $p(x)$; optimizations specific to $\deg p = 31$ will be described afterward.

Let $T$ be the table of residues $\varphi(g(x) \cdot x^{\deg p})$ where $\deg g(x) < k$. We examine $k$ bits from the input stream at a time instead of one at a time. View $f(x)$ now as

$$f(x) = \sum_{i=0}^{\lceil \frac{n}{k} \rceil} a_i(x) x^{i \cdot k}$$

where $\deg a_i(x) < k$. The algorithm to compute the residue $r(x) = f(x) \bmod p(x)$ becomes the code shown in Exhibit 7.2.

Now, let us consider what further size-specific optimizations are possible. Since $\deg p = 31$, $p(x)$ fits exactly into a 32-bit word. Furthermore, since word at a time operations work on 32 bits at a time, by packing the coefficients as bits in a word we can perform some basic operations on the polynomials as bit shifts and exclusive-ors: multiplication by $x^k$ is a left-shift by $k$ bits; addition or subtraction of two polynomials is just exclusive-or. Of course, since we are dealing now with fixed size machine registers, we must take care not to overflow.

```
r(x) = 0;
for (i = ⌈ⁿ⁄ₖ⌉; i ≥ 0; --i) {
    r'(x) = r(x) · xᵏ + aᵢ(x);
    r(x) = r'(x) mod p(x);
}
```

**EXHIBIT 7.2**
Fingerprint residue calculation. The operation $r'(x) \bmod p(x)$ is performed by decomposing $r'$ into $g(x) \cdot x^{\deg p} + h(x)$, where $\deg g < k$ and $\deg h < \deg p$, finding $r''(x) = g(x) \cdot x^{\deg p} \bmod p(x)$ from $T$, and setting $r(x) = r''(x) + h(x)$.

In Strongbox, we have two versions of the fingerprinting code, one for $k = 8$ and the other for $k = 16$, both of which used irreducible polynomials of degree 31. Because we want to read the input stream a full 32-bit word a at time, we modified the algorithm slightly: instead of $T$ being a table of $\varphi(g(x) \cdot x^{\deg p})$, $T$ contains $\varphi(g(x) \cdot x^{32})$; the corresponding decomposition of $r'(x)$ becomes $r'(x) = g(x) \cdot x^{32} + h(x)$ where $\deg g < k$ and $\deg h < 32$. While the residues $\varphi(g(x) \cdot x^{32})$ require only 31 bits to represent, $T$ is kept as a simple table of machine words of size $2^k$ words, indexed by $g(2)$, viewing $g(x)$ as a map $g: {}_2[x] \leftrightarrow$ (this is just using the coefficient bits, which are packed in a machine word anyway, as an integer). The result of the loop, $r(x)$, is either the residue $R(x) = f(x) \bmod p(x)$ or $R(x) + p(x)$, and we must fix up the result:

$$\varphi(f(x)) = \begin{cases} r(u) & \text{if } \deg r(x) < 31 \\ (r - p)(u) & \text{otherwise} \end{cases}$$

By shifting 8 or 16 bits at a time, we eliminate the need for looping code to break up 32-bit input words into the appropriate sizes, as illustrated by the code in Exhibit 7.3 for $k = 16$.

For the case where $k = 16$, the initialization of $T$ could be time consuming if the simple brute force method is used. Instead of calculating each of the $2^{16}$ entries directly, we first compute the table $T'$ for $k = 8$, size 256, and then $T$ is bootstrapped from $T'$ in the obvious manner: for each entry in $T$, we simply use its index $g(x)$, decompose it into $g(x) = g_{hi}(x) \cdot x^8 + g_{lo}(x)$ where $\deg g_{hi} < 8$ and $\deg g_{lo} < 8$, and compute $T'[T'_{hi}(g_{hi}) \oplus g_{lo}] \oplus T'_l o(g_{hi}) \cdot x^8$ as the table entry.

If a higher security level is required, multiple fingerprints can be taken on the same data, or polynomials of higher degree may be used. The speedup techniques extend well to handle $\deg p(x) = 61$, the next prime[21] close to a multiple

---

[21] While Rabin's algorithm for finding irreducible polynomials do not require that the degree be prime, using polynomials of prime degree makes counting irreducibles simpler.

```
fp_mem(a,nwords,p,table)
unsigned long *a, p, *table;
int           nwords;
{
        unsigned long   r, rlo, rhi, a_i;
        int             i;

        r = 0;
        for = (i = 0; i < nwords; i+{}+) {
                a_i = a[i];
                rhi = r >> 16;
                rlo = (r << 16) ^ (a_i >> 16);
                r = rlo ^ table[rhi];
                rhi = r >> 16;
                rlo = (r << 16) ^ (a_i & ((1 << 16)-1));
                r = rlo ^ table[rhi];
        }
        if (r >= 1 << 31) r ^= p;
        return r;
}
```

**EXHIBIT 7.3**
Fingerprint calculation (C code). This C code shows how using a
precomputed table of partial residues can speed up fingerprint calculations.
Unlike the actual code within Strongbox, it omits loop unrolling, forces
memory to be aligned, and may perform unnecessary memory references.

of word size, though the number of working registers required (if implementing
on a 32-bit machine) doubles. Our current implementation is largely limited by
the main memory bandwidth for reading the input data and the table (note that
the table for $k = 8$ can easily fit in most caches) and having to use main memory
to store intermediate results would decrease performance dramatically.

## 7.8   Future Work

We have shown that the Strongbox system allows one to realize self-securing
programs—programs that can be run securely in environments that provide only
minimal security. We have provided algorithms that substantially outperform
existing algorithms. We have implemented our system in two different environments: the distributed transaction system Camelot, and the distributed operating
system Mach.

What directions are next for the theory of self-securing programs? In addition to considering implementing Strongbox in other environments and putting more sophisticated access control mechanisms (such as those suggested in [21]), we are continuing to consider basic research issues related to self-securing programs. We are pursuing two possible avenues for the future evolution of Strongbox: attacking the denial of service problem and using secure coprocessors in conjunction with Strongbox.

### 7.8.1    The Denial of Service Problem

Traditionally the concerns of availability and security have been thought to be contradictory [25]. To see one reason why, consider the use of *replication* to provide high availability. When we attempt to to guarantee a distributed system's availability the following problem arises: the larger the number of independently failing components, the smaller the likelihood they will all be working simultaneously, and the smaller the likelihood the system will be accessible when needed.

This well-known phenomenon is typically addressed by designing distributed systems to be *fault-tolerant*, i.e., able to function correctly in the presence of some number of failures. In particular, the availability of long-lived data can be enhanced by storing the data redundantly at multiple sites, a technique commonly known as *replication* [9,13].

But this physical distribution of security also makes security more difficult. When repositories for data are physically distributed it is more difficult to ensure that each one is physically secure. As the number of sites increases, so does the number of ways in which the secrecy and integrity of the data can be compromised.

In [14] we have proposed that we describe and analyze several encryption-based secrecy protocols that, for a given threshold value $t$, ensure that an adversary cannot ascertain the object's state by observing the contents of fewer than $t$ repositories. We then extend these protocols to guarantee integrity, ensuring that the object's state cannot be altered by an adversary who can modify the contents of fewer than $t$ repositories.

Our method successfully provides full file system security simultaneously with high availablity. We would like to develop techniques that provide other availability concerns.

### 7.8.2    Secure Coprocessors

One assumption we built on was the security of process space. But building this into existing systems can be quite difficult: in fact it is often impossible to even promise physical security of memory in a distributed systems. As a result, there are just some things that we can't trust in a distributed system, and some problems that are partially solved by ad hoc approach.

In Strongbox, we use authentication protocols to provide security. But our authentication protocols, like all known authentication protocols, use some sort of key. The possession of this key is accepted as prima facie evidence of identity. However, it is usually impossible to establish all the necessary patterns of trust because the authentication key management requires certain assumptions about physical security that do not hold in general. To see this, consider the management of a key used to establish the identity of a client machine to a server. At some point in the authentication, a key must be present somewhere. (This key might be formed by combining keys from several different sources.) The key could be stored in the client machine itself, or it could be held by the user, or it could be stored in some auxiliary device (such as a "smartcard") used by the user. Suppose the key is stored in the client machine. Then it becomes vulnerable to physical attack. If the user is able to physically read memory or to load new system software that will allow him to examine any memory location, then he can find the value of the key. On the other hand, if the user, or an auxiliary device held by the user, holds the value of the key then it remains to be seen how the user can trust the integrity of the client machine. The client machine may be running bogus software. Even an attempt to take a cryptographic checksum of the client machine will not prove the trustworthiness of the machine, since it is easy to create a pair of system software: one trustworthy and used for generating cryptographic checksums, the other untrustworthy and actually executed on the client machine.

Recently, a new architecture, called a secure coprocessor, has been proposed [32,33]. A *secure coprocessor* is a processor and memory that is tightly coupled with the client machine, and that is physically protected. The physical protection can take various forms, but at the least we need a guarantee that the memory of the secure coprocessor is safe from attack. Any attempt to actually physically access the memory of the machine results in the memory being erased.

The secure coprocessor consists of a Central Processing Unit (CPU), some memory, and often some special encryption hardware. The secure coprocessor is realized as a board that is added on the bus of an existing workstation and that can work in tandem with the regular processor on that workstation. Attempts to penetrate the secure coprocessor result in total memory loss. Thus a secret that is stored on a secure coprocessor will remain secret, unless the secure coprocessor itself reveals the secret. Traces of computation on the secure coprocessor, as well as intermediate values generated by that computation, also remain secret. New software can be stored on the secure coprocessor only by using previously established protocols; the secure coprocessor can accept or reject the new software. This architecture raises exciting possibilities for providing trust in systems.

The question of authenticating identity becomes much simpler, since authentication can be performed, using standard techniques, among the user, the physically secure coprocessor, and the server. An initial key can be established at the time the secure coprocessor is manufactured; and this key can be used for future authentications. Any keys used for encryption can be held in the secure coprocessor. Secure software that is loaded on the client machine can be trusted by locating particular portions of the secure software on the coprocessor.

Indeed, it seems that secure coprocessor used with a system such as Strongbox could provide a large number of novel applications in computer security.

## 7.9  Acknowledgments

We are deeply indebted to Alfred Spector for many discussions about the Camelot implementation of Strongbox. Alfred actively participated in the design phases of that implementation, and provided the facilities for us to integrate Strongbox into Camelot. Section 7.4.1 of our chapter is based on a description prepared by Alfred Spector. We would also like to thank James Aspnes for a helpful late night discussion.

This research was sponsored by the Defense Advanced Research Projects Agency under Contract No. F33615-87-C-1499 and by a National Science Foundation Presidential Young Investigator Award, Contract No. CCR-88-58087.

The views and conclusions contained in this chapter are those of the authors and should not be interpreted as representing the official policies, either expressed or implied, of the Defense Advanced Research Projects Agency, the National Science Foundation, or the U. S. Government.

## References

[1] M. Accetta, R. V. Baron, W. Bolosky, D. B. Golub, R. F. Rashid, A. Tevanian, Jr., and M. W. Young. Mach: A new kernel foundation for UNIX development. In *Proceedings of Summer Usenix*, 1986.

[2] J. J. Bloch. The camelot library: A c language extension for programming a general purpose distributed transaction system. In *Proceedings of the Ninth International Conference on Distributed Computing Systems*, 1989.

[3] M. Blum and S. Micali. How to generate cryptographically strong sequences of pseudo-random bits. *SIAM Journal on Computing*, 13(4):850-864, 1984.

[4] M. Burrows, M. Abadi, and R. Needham. A logic of authentication. In *Proceedings of the Twelfth ACM Symposium on Operation Systems Principles*, 1989.

[5] B. Z. Chor. *Two Issues in Public Key Cryptography: RSA Bit Security and a New Knapsack Type System*. ACM Distiguished Dissertations. Cambridge, MA: MIT Press, 1986.

[6] J. L. Eppinger, L. B. Mummert, and A. Z. Spector. *Guide to the Camelot Distributed Transaction Facility including the Avalon Language*. Englewood Cliffs, NJ: Prentice-Hall, 1989.

[7] J. L. Eppinger and A. Z. Spector. Transaction processing in UNIX: A camelot perspective. *Unix Review*, 7(1):58-67, 1989.

[8] U. Feige, A. Fiat, and A. Shamir. Zero knowledge proofs of identity. In *Proceedings of the 19th ACM Symposium on Theory of Computing*, pp. 210-217, 1987.

[9] D. K. Gifford. Weighted voting for replicated data. In *Proceedings of the Seventh Symposium on Operating System Principles*, pp. 150-162. ACM, 1979.

[10] S. Goldwasser and S. Micali. Probabilistic encryption and how to play mental poker keeping secret all partial information. In *Proceedings of the Fourteenth Annual ACM Symposium on Theory of Computing*, 1982.

[11] J. N. Gray. A transaction model. Technical Report RJ2895, IBM Research Laboratory, San Jose, California, 1980.

[12] N. Heintze. A critique of Burrows', Abadi's, and Needham's *a logic of authentication*. Carnegie Mellon University Technical Report, Carnegie Mellon University, Pittsburgh, PA, 1990.

[13] M. P. Herlihy. General quorum consensus: A replication method for abstract data types. Technical Report CMU-CS-84-164, Carnegie Mellon University, Pittsburgh, PA, 1984.

[14] M. P. Herlihy and J. D. Tygar. How to make replicated data secure. In *Advances in Cryptology, CRYPTO-87*. Springer-Verlag, 1987. To appear in *Journal of Cryptology*.

[15] M. B. Jones, R. P. Draves, and M. R. Thompson. MIG—the Mach interface generator. Mach Group document, Carnegie Mellon University, Pittsburgh, PA, 1987.

[16] R. M. Karp and M. O. Rabin. Efficient randomized pattern-matching algorithms. Technical Report TR-31-81, Aiken Laboratory, Harvard University, 1981.

[17] R. M. Needham. Using cryptography for authentication. In S. Mullender (ed.), *Distributed Systems*. New York: ACM Press and Addison-Wesley Publishing Company, 1989.

[18] R. M. Needham and M. D. Schroeder. Using encryption for authentication in large networks of computers. *Communications of the ACM*, 21(12):993-999, 1978. Also Xerox Research Report, CSL-78-4, Xerox Research Center, Palo Alto, CA.

[19] I. Niven and H. S. Zuckerman. *An Introduction to the Theory of Numbers*. Wiley, 1960.

[20] M. Rabin. Fingerprinting by random polynomials. Technical Report TR-81-15, Center for Research in Computing Technology, Aiken Laboratory, Harvard University, May 1981.

[21] M. Rabin and J. D. Tygar. An integrated toolkit for operating system security (revised version). Technical Report TR-05-87R, Center for Research in Computing Technology, Aiken Laboratory, Harvard University, 1988.

[22] M. O. Rabin. Probabilistic algorithm for testing primality. *Journal of Number Theory*, 12:128-138, 1980.

[23] M. O. Rabin. Probabilistic algorithms in finite fields. *SIAM Journal on Computing*, 9:273-280, 1980.

[24] M. O. Rabin. Efficient dispersal of information for security and fault tolerance. Technical Report TR-02-87, Aiken Laboratory, Harvard University, Apr 1987.

[25] B. Randell and J. Dobson. Reliability and security issues in distributed computing systems. In *Proceedings of the Fifth IEEE Symposium on Reliability in Distributed Software and Database Systems*, pp. 113-118, 1985.

[26] R. F. Rashid. Threads of a new system. *Unix Review*, 4(8):37-49, 1986.

[27] A. W. Schrift and A. Shamir. The discrete log is very discreet. In *Proceedings of the 22nd ACM Symposium on Theory of Computing*, pp. 405-415, May 1990.

[28] A. Z. Spector. Distributed transaction processing and the Camelot system. In Yakup Paker et al. (ed.), *Distributed Operating Systems: Theory and Practice*, Nato Advanced Study Institute Series—Computer and Systems Sciences, pp. 331-353. Springer-Verlag, 1987. Also available as Carnegie Mellon Report CMU-CS-87-100, 1987.

[29] A. Z. Spector and P. M. Schwarz. Transactions: A construct for reliable distributed computing. *Operating Systems Review*, 17(2):18-35, 1983. Also available as Technical Report CMU-CS-82-143, Carnegie Mellon University, 1983.

[30] A. Z. Spector, D. Thompson, R. Pausch, J. L. Eppinger, R. Draves, D. Duchamp, D. S. D.iels, and J. J. Bloch. Camelot: A distributed transaction facility for Mach and the internet—an interim report. Technical Report CMU-CS-87-129, Carnegie Mellon University, Pittsburgh, PA, 1987.

[31] J. D. Tygar and B. S. Yee. Strongbox. In J. L. Eppinger, L. B.Mummert, and A. Z. Spector (eds.), *Guide to the Camelot Distributed Transaction Facility including the Avalon Language*. Englewood Cliffs, NJ: Prentice-Hall, 1991.

[32] S. H. Weingart. Physical security for the $\mu$abyss system. In *Proceedings of the IEEE Computer Society Conference on Security and Privacy*, pp. 52-58, 1987.

[33] S. R. White and L. Comerford. Abyss: A trusted architecture for software protection. In *Proceedings of the IEEE Computer Society Conference on Security and Privacy*, pp. 38-51, 1987.

# 8

# The Role of Distributed State

John Ousterhout

Distributed state offers the potential for improving the performance, coherency, and reliability of distributed systems. Unfortunately, distributed state also introduces consistency problems, crash sensitivity, time and space overheads, and complexity; these problems make it difficult to achieve the potential benefits. This chapter describes the advantages and disadvantages of distributed state, and presents the NFS and Sprite file systems as examples of different tradeoffs. It does not appear possible to achieve all the advantages of distributed state and also avoid all the problems; rather, system designers must make compromises based on the needs of their individual environments.

## 8.1 Introduction

*Webster's New World Dictionary* defines *state* as "a set of circumstances or attributes characterizing a person or thing at a given time" [4]. State plays a fundamental role in all computer systems. One way of characterizing *computation* is to define it as a set of operations applied to an initial state in order to produce some (presumably more interesting) final state. In this interpretation, *programming* is the act of invoking and organizing state transitions. *State*

199

includes all of the observable properties of a program and its environment, including instructions, variables, files, and input/output (i/o) devices. Without state there would be no computers or computation; many of the recent advances in computer science have occurred because state (in the form of main memory and disk storage) has become cheaper and more plentiful.

In a distributed system, such as a network of workstations and servers, the overall state of the system is partitioned among several machines. The machines execute concurrently and mostly independently, each with immediate access to only a piece of the overall state. To access remote state, such as a memory location or device on a different machine, the requesting (or "client") machine must send a message to the machine that contains the state (called the "server" for the request). Many of the interesting issues in distributed systems stem from two properties of their state: first, some state must be accessed in a different fashion than other state; and second, if one machine in the system crashes, it causes some *but not all* of the overall state to be lost.

For this chapter I will focus on *distributed state*, which I define loosely as "information retained in one place that describes something, or is determined by something, somewhere else in the system." Some examples of distributed state are

- A small table kept on each host to associate network addresses with the textual names of other hosts.

- A sequence number kept on a host to identify the most recent byte of data received from some other host.

- A block of a file cached in the main memory of one host even though the file is stored on a disk attached to a different machine.

- A table kept on a file server to keep track of the workstations that are caching a particular file.

Only a small fraction of all the state in a distributed system is distributed state: information that describes something on one machine and is only used on that machine (e.g., saved registers for an idle process) is not distributed state, by my definition.

The act of building a distributed system consists of making tradeoffs among various alternatives for managing the distributed state. This chapter is a discussion of some of the alternatives and their implications. Section 8.2 describes the potential benefits offered by distributed state, and Section 8.3 then shows why it is difficult in practice to achieve the benefits. Sections 8.4 and 8.5 use two network file systems as case studies to illustrate the tradeoffs in managing distributed state. Finally, Section 8.6 concludes with the opinion that there is no perfect solution to managing distributed state: each system designer must choose a particular approach (which will necessarily have both advantages and disadvantages) based on the needs of his or her particular environment.

## 8.2   Why Is Distributed State Good?

Distributed state can be used to provide three benefits in a distributed system: performance, coherency, and reliability. Distributed state improves performance because it makes information available immediately; there is no need to send a message to a remote machine to retrieve the information. For example, a local table containing name-to-address mappings makes it unnecessary to contact a central name server each time a textual name must be mapped to its corresponding address. Or, if a machine caches a remote file in its main memory then the file can be read without rereading the file from disk and potentially without even contacting the server to which the disk is attached.

The second potential advantage of distributed state is coherency. For machines (or people) to work together effectively, they must agree on common goals and coordinate their actions. This requires each party to know something about the other. For example, if a host keeps a sequence number identifying the most recent byte of data it has received from some other host, and if each arriving packet contains a sequence number identifying the first byte of data in that packet, then the receiver can compare sequence numbers to detect when packets are duplicated or arrive out of order. Without the sequence number there would be no way to detect these common error conditions, and it would be much more difficult for machines to communicate. Another example is the one from above, where a file server keeps a table of file usage: if one workstation is about to write a file that is cached on several other workstations, the file server can notify the other workstations so that they don't use "stale" data from their caches.

The third potential advantage of distributed state is reliability. If a particular piece of information is replicated at several sites in a distributed system and one of the copies is lost due to a failure, then it may be possible to use one of the other copies to recover the lost information. For example, if a file server crashes but a workstation has one of its files cached, it might be possible for the workstation to make the file available to the rest of the system while the server reboots; after the server has rebooted it could reclaim jurisdiction over the file.

## 8.3   Why Is Distributed State Bad?

Unfortunately, the benefits of distributed state listed above are only *potential* benefits; in practice they are difficult to achieve. The following subsections describe four problems introduced by distributed state: consistency, crash sensitivity, time and space overheads, and complexity.

## 8.3.1 Consistency

The first problem with distributed state is consistency: if the same piece of information is stored at several places and one of the copies changes, what happens to the other copies? If the other copies are not updated then incorrect decisions may be made with the out-of-date information. Even if the other copies are eventually updated, there will be a window of time when the copies are inconsistent and this could cause the system to behave incorrectly. Approaches to the consistency problem fall into three classes.

□ *Detect stale data on use.* In some situations it is easy to detect attempts to use out-of-date information. In these cases, there is no need to update all the copies when one changes. If an attempt is made to use stale information, its staleness will be noticed and a fresh copy of the information can be fetched. As pointed out by Lampson [6], the name-to-address map is an example of this approach. Suppose that there is a change in the address corresponding to a given name. If each message contains the name of the desired host as well as its address, then message recipients can verify that each incoming packet has the correct name. If a machine attempts to use an out-of-date address this fact will be detected (either as a timeout or as an error return from the machine with the erroneous address), at which point the sender can contact a central name server to refresh its name-to-address mapping. This form of distributed state is sometimes called *hints* to reflect the fact that it need not always be correct.

□ *Prevent inconsistency.* The second approach is to mask the window of inconsistency, either by eliminating all but one copy of the information before each modification, or by preventing access to the out-of-date copies until they are updated. For example, in the Sprite system if a file is being modified by one workstation while being read by another workstation, then neither is allowed to cache the file; all read and write operations are passed through to the server and applied to its single copy of the file [8]. In Locus, it is possible for a file to be replicated on different disks attached to different servers [12]. If the file is modified, the changes are applied initially to a single copy of the file and then propagated to the other copies. During the propagation period all accesses to the file are directed to the one up to date copy.

□ *Tolerate inconsistency.* In some situations the errors caused by stale state information may not do any harm, so they can be tolerated during a brief period while the copies are updated. For example, in a distributed game it may be acceptable for there to be slight delays between when one player moves and another player perceives that move. Another example is the Grapevine mail system, where it can take several minutes for certain changes in configuration (such as the addition of a new user) to become visible everywhere in the system [2]. In general, users have a very low tolerance for inconsistencies of any sort (they tend to complain that the system is broken); fortunately, in the Grapevine case the inconsistencies are almost never noticed by anyone except system administrators.

## 8.3.2  Crash Sensitivity

The second problem with distributed state is crash sensitivity. In principle, distributed state should enhance the reliability of a system: if one machine fails then another should be able to take over its function. However, this only works if the replacement machine can reconstruct the state that had existed on the failed machine at the time of its failure. If the replacement machine cannot recreate the exact state of the failed machine then it will not be able to take over in a seamless fashion and the failure of the primary machine will be visible to other parts of the system.

In practice it is rare for state to be fully replicated (but see [2,12,14] for examples where it is). More commonly, each of the several distributed components has a different piece of the overall state, so that the failure of any component makes the entire system unusable. This sort of a distributed system is less reliable than a centralized system with only one component to fail. Most network file systems fall into this category: users invariably manage to spread essential files across all of the system's file servers, so that no one can get any work done if any file server is down. In the worst case, the entire system has to be reinitialized when any component fails. In a slightly better scenario a crash on one file server "only" prevents people from working while the machine is down; activity resumes normally (without the need to restart other machines or programs) when the failed machine reboots.

If state is to be fully replicated in order to mask failures, several difficult problems must be resolved, including the following:

- □ The communication protocols must be designed in a way that redirects message traffic to the replacement machine after the failure of the primary machine.

- □ A failure may occur during the window of inconsistency when one replica has been modified but the others have not yet been modified. The communication protocols must be able to determine which copies have been updated, and the out-of-date copies must be brought back into consistency without waiting for the failed machine to reboot.

- □ When the failed machine eventually restarts, it must be able to use the replicas to bring its state into consistency with its replicas (the state could have changed substantially while the machine was down). In some cases the revived machine may be able to collect a complete snapshot of the state from a replica. In other cases (e.g., where the state involved is a large replicated file system) it may be too expensive to copy the entire state to the reviving machine; the backup machine may have to keep a record of changes and "replay" them for the reviving machine. Finally, the catching-up of the reviving machine must be synchronized with its participation in new requests made by clients.

All of these problems are solvable, but the solutions tend to be complex or inefficient, particularly if they are implemented in a general-purpose fashion. Some of the most successful approaches use information about a particular problem domain to implement replication for that domain. See [1,2,3,12,14] for examples of the use of replication.

### 8.3.3  Time and Space Overheads

The third problem with distributed state is that it introduces overheads, both in time and in space. The time overheads are incurred mainly in maintaining consistency. Either the consistency of distributed state must be checked every time the state is used (e.g., by contacting a file server to see if a cached copy of a file contains the most recent version), or some party must keep track of the distributed copies and notify each owner of a copy when the state changes (e.g., the file servers in the Andrew file system (AFS) perform this function [5]). If replicated copies are to be kept up to date then each update must be reflected in each of the copies. This overhead can make replicated updates substantially more expensive than nonreplicated ones.

The most obvious source of space overhead is the storage needed for distributed copies of the same state (e.g., a single file may be cached on many workstations). However, there may be other space overheads to keep track of the distributed copies so that they can be kept consistent. In some environments, such as the Sprite file system, the space required for consistency-related information can be substantial.

The overhead problems are closely related to the degree of sharing and rate of modification. If information is not widely shared, then there need not be many copies of the information and it will not take much time to keep them all consistent. If there are many copies, then the space overhead increases. If shared information is updated frequently, then consistency actions will be invoked more frequently. At some point the cost of maintaining consistency becomes higher than the cost of communicating with a central server on each use; when this occurs, performance can be improved (and the system can probably be simplified) by reverting to a centralized approach to state management.

### 8.3.4 Complexity

The final problem with distributed state is complexity. Without distributed state there is no need to deal with consistency (it isn't a problem), nor is there any possibility of masking failures (one of the best things about a centralized system is that the whole system stops whenever any component stops). Distributed state makes a system substantially more complicated. The complexity makes it harder to debug the system and thereby reduces the reliability advantages offered by distributed state. Complexity also makes it harder to tune the system's performance (system implementors spend more time "getting it right" and less time "making it fast"), thereby reducing the performance advantage offered by the distributed state.

## 8.4    Case Study #1: The NFS File System

To illustrate some of the issues in managing distributed state, this section and the next describe two network file systems: NFS and Sprite. NFS is a commercial product; it was originally developed by Sun Microsystems but it has become a de facto standard supported by almost all workstation vendors [13]. The Sprite file system was developed in a research project at the University of California at Berkeley [8,10]. Both systems use a client-server model with caching, as shown in Exhibit 8.1: files are stored on disks attached to server machines, and clients make requests of the servers in order to access the files. Each system defines a particular set of possible requests, which represents a particular set of tradeoffs among the advantages and disadvantages inherent in distributed state. As a consequence, each system ended up with a corresponding set of good and bad properties; the strengths and weaknesses of the two systems are almost opposites.

The NFS design was optimized for simplicity and robustness, with performance a secondary goal. Simplicity and robustness were achieved by using a *stateless* protocol with *idempotent* operations. The term "stateless" means that file servers need not retain any information in their main memories. All essential information about the file system, such as the contents of files, must be kept on disk. As part of servicing each client request, the server must write any modified information to disk, so that future requests can be serviced even if the contents of the server's memory are lost (in a server crash, for example). Servers may cache disk blocks and other information in their main memories to improve performance, but the system must not depend on this information to function correctly. The term "stateless" is something of a misnomer, in that (1) it only applies to servers, (2) it only applies to the servers' main memories, and (3) it permits state in the main memories as long as that state is also on disk.

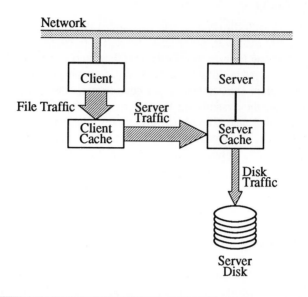

**EXHIBIT 8.1**
A network file system. File blocks are cached in the main memories of
servers (machines with disks) and clients (machines without disks). When a
process on a client machine attempts to read a file ("File Traffic"), the
information is retrieved from the client's cache if it is present. If the desired
information is not in the client's cache, the client issues a network request to
the file server ("Server Traffic"); the server retrieves the information from its
own cache (reading it from disk if it wasn't already in the cache) and returns
the information to the client.

The second important characteristic of NFS is that almost all of its operations are idempotent. An *idempotent operation* is one that can be executed
many times with the same overall effect as if it were executed only once. Some
examples of idempotent NFS operations are

□ *read(fileId, position, count)*: given an identifier for a file and a byte position
within that file, return *count* bytes starting at that position. Note that this
operation would not be idempotent if the position were not specified by
the client as part of the operation but instead were kept on the server and
incremented by *count* as part of each read request.

□ *write(fileId, position, count, data)*: given an identifier for a file and a byte
position within that file, replace *count* bytes with data supplied by the
client.

□ *lookup(fileId, name)*: given an identifier for a file (which must be a directory) see if a particular name exists as an entry in that directory. If so, return the identifier for that file and its attributes (which include last-modified time, permissions, size, etc.). The identifier may be used by the client in later operations such as *read* and *write*.

Although almost all of the NFS operations are idempotent, there are a few nonidempotent operations, such as:

□ *mkdir(fileId, name, attr)*: given an identifier for a directory, create a subdirectory in that directory with a given name and attributes. This operation is not idempotent because it returns an error if the given name is already present in the directory. Invoking it multiple times will result in success on the first invocation and failure on the second and later invocations.

In NFS, distributed state is kept almost exclusively on the clients. Servers do not store any information about their clients except for a list indicating which clients are allowed to access which disk partitions. Servers need not keep track of which files are currently in use or which clients are using which files. In fact, NFS servers *cannot* keep track of this information: there are no "open" or "close" requests to indicate when clients start and stop using files. NFS clients do keep distributed state, however. This state includes the following:

1. File identifiers, returned by the *lookup* request and used in other requests, such as *read*.

2. File data, returned by *read* operations and cached on clients to eliminate server requests if the information is reused.

3. File attributes, returned by *lookup* and other requests.

4. Name translations (results of recent calls to *lookup*), cached on clients in order to bypass future calls to *lookup* for the same *fileId*s and *name*s.

Of this information, only the file identifiers are necessary for the system to function; the other information is cached in order to reduce the number of calls to file servers.

## 8.4.1  Advantages of NFS

Perhaps the greatest advantage of the NFS protocol is the ease with which it handles server crashes. If a server crashes, client requests will not be answered; the clients will detect the timeouts and simply retry their requests until eventually the server reboots and the requests succeed. Clients need not take any special action to handle server crashes since the retry mechanism is already required to handle lost packets. All important server state is on disk so nothing is lost during the crash (unless the disk was corrupted, which rarely happens). If the server crashes after completing an operation but before sending a response back to the client, then the client will reissue the request after the server reboots, but this causes no problem for idempotent operations. To users on client machines, the server crash appears as a delay during which some processes are suspended, but when the server reboots all existing processes continue normally and seamlessly.

In NFS there is not enough replicated state to permit access to a server's files while it is down, and this is a disadvantage (which, by the way, is shared by almost all network file systems; the best-known counter example is Locus [12]). But NFS has the important property of allowing client machines to survive server crashes without rebooting; the crash results only in delay, not in loss of state.

Another advantage of the NFS protocol is its simplicity, which stems directly from the stateless nature of the protocol. For example, crash recovery is handled without special code on either the client or server. The stateless protocol results in a small set of operations with simple interactions between clients and servers; this makes it easy to build NFS clients and servers. Although most implementations of NFS have been made in variants of the UNIX operating system, there are also exist NFS implementations for other systems, such as Microsoft's MS-DOS for the IBM PC.

## 8.4.2   Disadvantages of NFS

Unfortunately, statelessness is also a source of problems in NFS. The NFS protocol suffers from three major weaknesses: performance, consistency, and semantics. The greatest problem with NFS is its performance, which is limited by the stateless protocol. Whenever a client issues a write request, the server must guarantee that all modified data are safely on disk before the write returns. Not only must the file's data be written to disk, but the file's descriptor must also be flushed along with any index blocks that have changed. This results in two or three disk transfers for every block of file data. When a large file is written, each block of the file will result in a separate write request, so the file's descriptor and index blocks will be written to disk over and over. As a result, NFS clients cannot typically achieve write bandwidths greater than about 60 Kbytes/sec. In contrast, UNIX systems with local disks can usually achieve write bandwidths of 500-1,000 Kbytes/sec.

Nonvolatile memory may make it possible to alleviate some of the performance problems caused by statelessness. For example, Legato Systems offers an NFS accelerator that uses a small nonvolatile memory unit as a write buffer for the disk. The cache has a much faster access time than the disk. When descriptors and index blocks are repeatedly written, as described above, the writes are made to the nonvolatile memory. Only a single disk write will be necessary when the information ages out of the cache. Because the cache is nonvolatile, it can survive server reboots just as well as the disk. However, nonvolatile memory does not eliminate all of the performance problems with NFS: NFS still requires extra i/o operations to the cache, and it also requires additional server traffic as described below.

The second problem with NFS is consistency. Consistency problems arise because servers do not keep track of which clients are using which files. If one client modifies a file, there is no way for the server to notify other clients that have cached the old contents of the file; it is up to the other clients to find out on their own. This is achieved by polling. Whenever a file is accessed on a client, the client checks to see how recently the attributes for the file were fetched from the server. If the attributes are more than a few seconds old, the client refetches them. If the last-modified-time in the new attributes does not match the last-modified-time in the client's old copy of the attributes, then the client invalidates its cached data for the file. Similarly, cached name translations are also invalidated when they become more than a few seconds old. This approach ensures that each client eventually receives up to date information, but it permits windows of inconsistency where stale data may be used. Because of this, NFS cannot be used for certain applications where consistency is required, and it occasionally produces counter intuitive behavior.

The consistency issue also impacts the performance of NFS systems. For example, the polling approach described above results in extra server traffic. Even worse, NFS uses a *write-through-on-close* policy to reduce windows of inconsistency. Whenever a file is closed on a client machine, the client immediately transmits modified data for the file back to the server. The close operation does not complete until the data are safely on the server's disk. This approach is necessary in order to make the file's new data available to other clients as quickly as possible; if the new data are not returned to the server, then other clients will have no way of knowing that the file has changed.

Write-through-on-close has two unpleasant consequences. First, it delays the closing process until the data are written to disk. Second, it results in unnecessary load on the server and the disk. Many files are deleted or overwritten shortly after they are created [9]; if new data were retained for a while on the client before transmitting it to the server, much of the new data would be deleted and would never need to be transferred to the server or disk at all. Unfortunately, the statelessness of NFS requires that new data be returned immediately to the server to reduce consistency problems, and the only way to return data to the server is with the write operation, which forces data to be written on disk.

The third problem with the NFS approach is that it introduces semantic difficulties. Statelessness and idempotency impose constraints that make it impossible or expensive to implement certain features. When a conflict occurs between a particular feature and statelessness or idempotency, there are two choices: don't implement the feature, or violate the goals of statelessness and idempotency. NFS uses both approaches. For example, file locking requires the server to keep track of which files are locked; the stateless model prohibits servers from keeping lock information solely in memory. Locks could have been implemented by writing the lock information to disk, but that would have made locking slow. The NFS designers decided not to provide locking at all (it was later provided by a separate network service). Another example of a semantic conflict is the *mkdir* operation described above. This operation is nonidempotent by definition, but had to be included in the protocol anyway. As a result, server crashes (or even lost packets) can produce unexpected behavior. For example, a *mkdir* could be processed by the server successfully, but if the response packet is lost the client will retry; the retry will fail because the file now exists.

### 8.4.3   NFS Summary

The best features of NFS are its simplicity and robustness; because of them, NFS is an overwhelming commercial success and a de facto standard. The semantic difficulties in NFS do not often arise in practice (e.g., sharing of a single file within a period of a few seconds is uncommon, so the windows of inconsistency are not usually noticed). Even NFS's performance problems have not been a problem on slower workstations that are limited more by Central Processing Unit (CPU) speed than disk speed. However, newer workstations with CPU speeds of 10 MIPS or more are severely hampered by NFS's "flush-to-disk" approach. It seems likely that changes will have to be made in the NFS protocol to improve its performance for the even faster workstations of the future.

## 8.5   Case Study #2: The Sprite File System

The Sprite file system appears on the surface much like NFS. It uses a client-server model, clients use a request-response protocol to communicate with the servers, the actual requests bear quite a bit of surface similarity to those in NFS, and clients keep many of the same kinds of distributed state as in NFS. However, Sprite manages the distributed state of the file system in a different fashion than NFS. The result is a system with almost totally opposite strengths and weaknesses: Sprite provides high performance and clean semantics, but it is more complex and faces more difficult crash recovery problems.

The protocol between clients and servers is definitely not stateless in Sprite; we call it "stateful" for lack of a better term. Three additional pieces of distributed state are kept in Sprite:

1. Servers keep information in their main memories about which workstations are reading or writing which files. This requires clients to notify servers

whenever files are opened or closed, but allows the servers to enforce consistency as described below.

2. Servers retain modified file blocks in their main memories, and do not write that information back to disk until it has aged for 30 seconds.

3. Clients also retain modified file blocks in their main memories; they do not pass new information back to servers until it has aged for 30 seconds or until the information is needed by some other client. If a client has dirty blocks for a file, the server's state information reflects this.

In contrast to NFS, Sprite does not keep name translation information on clients. For servers to maintain the state described above, clients must already contact servers whenever they open or close a file; in Sprite, the clients pass the entire multilevel file name to the server and let the server handle the name lookup.

### 8.5.1  Advantages of Sprite

By retaining additional state, the Sprite file system provides substantially better consistency and performance than NFS. Consistency is improved because Sprite file servers can use their state information to prevent stale data from being used. If a file is ever open simultaneously on several clients and at least one of them is writing the file, then the server notifies each of the clients and insists that they not cache the file; all read and write operations must be passed through to the server, where they are applied to a single copy of the file in the server's cache. If a client has a cached copy of a file, but the file isn't open on that client, then the client will not be notified if other clients modify the file; stale data will remain in its cache. However, these data cannot be used until the file is opened. When the client makes an open request to the server, the server returns a version number for the file. This version number will not match the version associated with the stale data, so the file will be purged from the client's cache. Thus Sprite provides "perfect" file consistency: each read operation is guaranteed to return the most recently written data for that file, regardless of where and when the file is read and written.

Sprite's stateful approach also allowed file locking to be implemented easily, using the main memory of the server to record who owns which locks. Overall, the behavior of the Sprite file system as seen by users is identical to the behavior of a file system running on a single timeshared UNIX machine.

The second advantage of the Sprite file system, performance, is even more noticeable. Much of Sprite's performance is due to the way it handles consistency. Since the servers keep track of which clients are using which files, clients need not return modified file data to servers immediately. If some other client opens the file, then the server will retrieve the dirty data from the client

| Machine Type | Sprite (secs.) | NFS (secs.) | NFS Slowdown (%) |
|---|---|---|---|
| Sun-3/75 | 439 | 635 | 44 |
| Sun-4/280 | 184 | 270 | 46 |
| DECstation 3100 | 127 | 269 | 111 |

**EXHIBIT 8.2**
A performance comparison of the NFS and Sprite file systems on a modified
version of the Andrew benchmark devised by M. Satyanarayanan. The Sprite
column gives the elapsed time for a diskless client to complete the
benchmark when both the client and server machines were running Sprite.
The NFS column gives the elapsed time when both the client and server ran
a vendor-supplied version of Ultrix or SunOS with all (or almost all) file
accesses made remotely using NFS. The NFS Slowdown column indicates
how much slower NFS was than Sprite. In each case the server machine
was the same type as the client machine.

that modified it. When servers eventually do receive information from clients,
they do not force it immediately to disk, nor do they write the file descriptor
and index blocks to disk every time a data block is written to disk. If the new
data survive for 30 seconds, then these data will be written to disk, and the
corresponding file descriptor and index blocks will be written to disk *once*.

Sprite's approach has two performance advantages. First, clients need not
wait for information to be written to disk when they close files. They can continue processing immediately; if the data eventually need to be passed back to
the server, a background kernel process does it. The second advantage is that
some new data are deleted or overwritten before being passed back to the server,
so the overhead of communicating with the server is never incurred. Measurements of our Sprite network indicate that only about 50% of newly written data
are ever returned to the file server [15]. Exhibit 8.2 compares the performance
of Sprite and UNIX/NFS for a file-intensive benchmark. On identical hardware
configurations, the benchmark ran 45% to 110% slower under UNIX/NFS than
under Sprite. Nelson's dissertation shows that most of the performance difference is due to the difference in writing policy between the two systems [7].

### 8.5.2  Disadvantages of Sprite

Unfortunately, the stateful approach used in Sprite has disadvantages as well
as advantages. The section below discusses four problems we had to face in
Sprite: complexity, recovery, performance, and space overhead. First, Sprite's
file system is more complex than that of NFS. Most of the complexity is as-

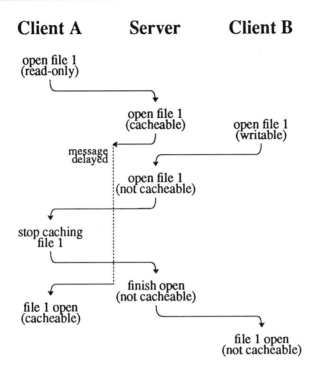

**Client A**        **Server**        **Client B**

open file 1
(read-only)

open file 1
(cacheable)
open file 1
(writable)

message
delayed

open file 1
(not cacheable)

stop caching
file 1

finish open
(not cacheable)

file 1 open
(cacheable)

file 1 open
(not cacheable)

**EXHIBIT 8.3**
A race condition in managing cache coherency, which occurred in an early version of Sprite. Client A opens a file for reading; since A is the only client using the file, the server responds with an indication that the file is cacheable. Then client B opens the same file for writing. At this point the server decides that the file cannot be cached safely, and it sends a message to A indicating this fact. Unfortunately, the response to A's earlier open request may have been delayed (e.g., because the response packet was lost and had to be retransmitted after a timeout), so that the "don't cache" request arrives at A before the open response. When the open response eventually arrives at A, it causes A to cache the file, which is unsafe. The race condition was eliminated by keeping extra state on the client.

sociated with managing the server's state. The initial implementation suffered from subtle race conditions (see Exhibit 8.3, for example) and network-wide deadlocks involving several clients and servers. Although we have gradually eliminated these problems, it has been difficult both to isolate the problems and to find simple solutions for them.

The second, and greatest, problem with the Sprite approach is recovery. Much volatile information is kept in the main memories of clients and servers, and all of this information can potentially be lost in a crash. Fortunately, when Sprite machines crash they attempt to flush their file caches (to disk in the case of servers; to servers in the case of clients). This approach almost always works except for power failures, so file data are almost never lost (and when information is lost, it is confined to information written in the last minute).

Unfortunately, when a server reboots it loses its information about file usage. Thus it no longer knows which clients are using which files, so it may not be able to enforce consistency for files that are already open. In the original version of Sprite, all files open at the time of a server crash were forcibly closed when the server rebooted. This caused all work in progress to be lost, including shells and window systems; most users found it easiest to reboot their workstations in order to restore their execution environment. We very quickly decided that this approach was intolerable.

Fortunately, we discovered that distributed state was not just the cause of the recovery problem, but also the solution. By adding slightly to the state kept by clients about their files, it became possible for servers to recreate all their usage information after rebooting. A new operation was added to the Sprite protocol: *reopen*. When a server reboots, each client reopens all of its files by passing the server a copy of its state information (including information such as which files are open for reading or writing, which are locked, etc.). This allows the server to reconstruct its state so that it can continue to guarantee consistent access to files, and so that locks are not broken when servers reboot. Our experience is that this provides an effect almost identical to NFS: files are not accessible while a server is down, but when servers reboot the clients can continue operation without any loss of state.

Of course, Sprite's approach to recovery is more complicated than the NFS approach where there are no special recovery actions at all. It has also introduced another performance problem. Clients typically have several hundred files open on each of several servers. When a server reboots, all of the clients simultaneously attempt to reopen their files. Our current system contains about 40 machines, and the recovery traffic from these machines is so intense that we refer to it as a *recovery storm*. The recovery storms overload the servers to the point where they cannot respond to requests in a timely fashion. Some operations time out, causing clients to think the server has crashed, whereupon they reinitiate their file reopening from the beginning. As a result, most clients have to attempt recovery several times before successfully reopening all their files. If the system is to scale from its current size of 40 machines to 400, techniques will have to be found to deal with the contention induced by recovery. We are currently exploring a variety of approaches in the low-level communication protocol and in the file system. Although we expect to solve the problem, the solution will undoubtedly add more complexity.

A third potential problem with Sprite's approach is its requirement that each open and close be reflected through to the file's server. In contrast, NFS clients never contact servers during closes except to write new data; during opens, an NFS client need not contact the server as long as it has up to date attributes cached for the file. It would be possible to extend the Sprite mechanism so that clients cache naming information and need not contact the servers on every open or close; the Andrew file system already implements such a mechanism [5]. However, such a mechanism would add to the distributed state, thereby increasing the complexity of clients and servers (particularly because the cached naming information would have to be kept consistent). In addition, the performance benefit would be partially offset by server traffic to fill the clients' name caches and keep them consistent. Our performance measurements indicate that name caching would reduce server loading but would have relatively little effect on the performance of clients. Since server loading is not a major limitation in our environment we haven't implemented name caching (yet).

The last, and least important, problem with Sprite's approach is the space overhead for the servers' file state. A file server needs several hundred bytes of storage for each open file to keep track of the file's usage, and may have many thousand files open at once. As a result, the storage required for file state grossly exceeded our initial estimates, causing internal memory limits in the Sprite kernel to be exceeded. We solved the problem by increasing the internal limits, but we were surprised at how much space the state occupies. In typical configurations, a Sprite file server will use most of its memory (10 to 100 Mbytes) for caching file data, and the usage state information typically occupies about 15% to 20% as much space as the file data (many megabytes in larger configurations). Furthermore, we expect the usage information to increase as the number of client workstations increases. If the system increases in size by another order of magnitude, the size of the file usage information could potentially become a problem.

### 8.5.3  Sprite Summary

Our main goals in Sprite were to achieve high performance and timesharing semantics; those goals have been met. A secondary goal was to achieve reliability comparable to NFS. That goal has also been met, although it was not met in the initial version of the system. Unfortunately, meeting the goals has resulted in a system substantially more complicated than NFS and has introduced some scaling problems that have not yet been completely resolved.

## 8.6    Conclusions

I do not believe there is a "perfect" solution to the problems associated with distributed state. The simpler solutions, like NFS, are likely to have performance problems, and the faster solutions, like Sprite, tend to be more complicated and to present more difficult recovery problems. Systems that are more fault-tolerant tend to have even greater performance or complexity problems. In striving for some of the potential advantages of distributed state, system designers must necessarily embrace some of the disadvantages as well. The exact choice among the various options should reflect the needs of the environment being designed for: in some environments performance may be less important than the ability to survive machine failures, and vice versa.

Based on my experience with the NFS and Sprite file systems, I do not believe that the stateless model can meet the needs of high-performance worksta-tions of the future. A stateless approach will limit the performance of the system to the performance of disks; unfortunately, disk performance is not improving at anywhere near the rate of processor performance. Nonvolatile memory of-fers some hope for performance improvement, but I think the best solution is a change to more stateful protocols.

On the other hand, distributed state almost always introduces complexity and fragility, so system designers should attempt to reduce distributed state as much as possible. The less state, the better. In Sprite, I suspect that we may have been a little too eager to embrace state, and that a careful redesign of the system could reduce the amount of state we have to maintain.

Finally, the best approach to dealing with failures is to merge recovery with normal operation so that there is nothing special to do during recovery. NFS achieves this quite nicely through its combination of statelessness and idempotency. Recovery happens so infrequently that is is very difficult to debug special-case recovery code: it is hard to invoke the code under test conditions, and the code is hardly ever executed under real-life conditions. This means that there is a good chance that the code will not work when it is needed. On the other hand, if the recovery code and regular-case code are the same, the recovery code will be exercised constantly during everyday operation of the system so it is likely to work correctly when needed.

## 8.7    Acknowledgments

Mendel Rosenblum, Ken Shirriff, and Brent Welch made helpful comments that improved the presentation of this chapter.

# References

[1] J. Bartlett. A NonStop Kernel. *Proceedings of the 8th Symposium on Operating Systems Principles. Operating Systems Review 15(5)*, 1981, pp. 22-29.

[2] A. D. Birrell, et al. Grapevine: An Exercise in Distributed Computing. *Communications of the ACM 25(4)*, 1982, pp. 260-274.

[3] A. Borg, et al. Fault Tolerance Under UNIX. *ACM Transactions on Computer Systems 7(1)*, 1989, pp. 1-24.

[4] D. Guralnik, Ed. in Chief. *Webster's New World Dictionary*, Second College Edition, Simon & Schuster, 1982.

[5] J. Howard, et al. Scale and Performance in a Distributed File System. *ACM Transactions on Computer Systems 6(1)*, 1988, pp. 51-81.

[6] B. Lampson. Hints for Computer System Design. Proceedings of the 10th Symposium on Operating Systems Principles. *Operating Systems Review 17(5)*, 1985, pp. 33-48.

[7] M. Nelson. *Physical Memory Management in a Network Operating System*. Ph.D. dissertation, technical report UCB/CSD 88/471, Computer Science Division, University of California at Berkeley, 1988.

[8] M. Nelson, B. Welch, and J. Ousterhout. Caching in the Sprite Network File System. *ACM Transactions on Computer Systems 6(1)*, 1988, pp. 134-154.

[9] J. Ousterhout, et al. A Trace-Driven Analysis of the UNIX 4.2 BSD File System. In *Proceedings of the Tenth Symposium on Operating Systems Principles*, 1985, pp. 15-24.

[10] J. Ousterhout, et al. The Sprite Network Operating System. *IEEE Computer 21(2)*, 1988, pp. 23-36.

[11] J. Ousterhout. Why Aren't Operating Systems Getting Faster as Fast as Hardware? Technical note TN-11, DEC Western Research Laboratory, Palo Alto, CA, 1989.

[12] G. Popek, and B. Walker (eds.). *The LOCUS Distributed System Architecture*. Cambridge, MA: MIT Press, 1985.

[13] R. Sandberg. Design and Implementation of the Sun Network Filesystem. In *Proceedings of the USENIX 1985 Summer Conference*, 1985, pp. 119-130.

[14] M. Satyanarayanan, et al. *Coda: A Highly Available File System for a Distributed Workstation Environment*. Technical report CMU-CS-89-165, School of Computer Science, Carnegie Mellon University, Pittsburgh, PA, 1989.

[15] B. Welch. *Naming, State Management, and User-Level Extensions in the Sprite Distributed File System*. Ph.D. dissertation, University of California at Berkeley, Berkeley, CA, 1990.

# 9

# Large-Scale Hardware Simulation: Modeling and Verification Strategies

Douglas W. Clark

Simulation is a critically important phase of modern computer hardware design. Lacking practical formal methods for proving complex systems correct, designers must run tests on simulation models to demonstrate correctness before chips and boards are fabricated. Using a large-scale model, such as an entire central processing unit (CPU), at a low level of representation, such as the logic gate level, is an efficient way to uncover the inevitable bugs in a complex design. Testing efforts should aim at finding these bugs rather than passing a fixed set of tests. Random generation of automatically checked tests effectively applies computing power to the debugging process. Simulation "demons," which run alongside a test, help to find difficult bugs in the interactions of subsystems. The methodological ideas discussed in this chapter have been used in several large projects at Digital.

## 9.1   Introduction

Simulation is an indispensable technique in modern computer design. In the days of computers made entirely from off-the-shelf small- and medium-scale

219

integrated circuits it was possible to build a hardware prototype and "debug it into existence," but nowadays the use of highly integrated custom and semicustom components makes this practically impossible. These components severely constrain hardware prototype debugging because it typically takes a long, and sometimes very long, time to get a new version of a part once a bug is discovered. Repeated re-fabrication of parts can delay a project beyond its economic justification. It is therefore critically important to assure the correctness of complex integrated-circuit designs *before* physical fabrication. Simulation makes this possible.

In this chapter I will present a set of opinions and recommendations based on Digital's experience with several large VAX system developments. Methodological recommendations would ideally be validated by controlled scientific experiment: one could imagine setting up two independent teams with the same charter—design a computer system with specified cost, performance, and development schedule—but with different simulation methodologies. Unfortunately, in the real world, with real constraints, such an experiment would not be practical. So my views here come not from any systematic evaluation of competing methodologies, but rather from real-world experience.

My subject in this chapter is assuring the logical or functional correctness of a newly designed computer system's hardware. I will not address the companion problem of *timing verification*, for which modern techniques (e.g., [10]) can guarantee correctness. No such guarantee is (as yet) possible in establishing the logical correctness of a complex system, although some progress has been made with simple designs (e.g., [2,8]). So the term *simulation* in this chapter will mean logical simulation only.

There are two fundamental challenges to the effective simulation of complex computer hardware. First is the challenge of speed: simulations are orders of magnitude slower than real hardware, so it is extremely important for simulation to be efficient. Second is the challenge of correctness: since formal methods are not yet practical for verifying the correctness of an entire computer system, some testing scheme must be used to verify, or attempt to verify, the design. To deal with the twin challenges of speed and correctness, I advocate in this chapter two basic methodological approaches: first, the use of large-scale models using a detailed representation of the logic; and second, a testing strategy that is organized around bugs found rather than tests passed.

The next section of this chapter argues that computer simulations should use large models—e.g., of an entire CPU or even an entire system—at a low level of representation—e.g., the level of individual gates and latches. This approach might seem to exacerbate rather than mitigate the problem of simulation speed, but I will try to show that it is the most efficient use of the available resources: computer power, designers' time, and project schedule.

Section 9.3 considers two testing strategies that attempt to show the correctness of a design. The traditional method, which I call *test-centered*, relies on a fixed list of tests that exercise the design thoroughly. I will argue that this is the wrong way to test a model and advocate instead a more flexible *bug-centered* strategy, which focuses on design bugs and their removal.

In Section 9.4 several ideas concerning random testing are presented, including the use of simulation *demons*. The conclusion summarizes this chapter's recommendations.

## 9.2   Levels of Modeling and Representation

In computer system design there is a natural hierarchy determined by physical boundaries: the system may be composed of several cabinets, each of which contains printed-wiring boards, on which sit a number of integrated-circuit chips. Complex chips will contain further levels of hierarchy. The physical (and often logical) hierarchy is a convenient and natural way to organize the design work and the implementation. Specifications and models can be created at a high level, then decomposed into smaller units and parcelled out to the design team for further decomposition or for detailed logic design. At higher levels, descriptions can have various degrees of precision and formality, but at the bottom level— the level communicated to the factory—the requirement is a rigid and exact definition of the actual hardware in all its details. Computer-Aided Design (CAD) tools integrate elements from various levels in the hierarchy for timing analysis and logical simulation.

It is common practice to carry this hierarchical viewpoint into the effort of simulating a system design. In the specification phase of a project, the designers write behavioral models of the hardware for which they were responsible. (A *behavioral* model is a simulatable representation whose input-output behavior mimics that of the ultimate hardware, but within which hardware detail is suppressed.) At each hierarchical level, these models might be expressed as interconnections of lower-level components, on down to the level of actual circuits. The simulation objective would then be to show that each decomposition was correct—that each component was logically equivalent to its implementation at the next lower hierarchical level. For example, input-output test patterns for a very large scale integration (VLSI) chip could be captured from its behavioral model and used to test the detailed hardware model as it was developed. A low-level description of one chip could be simulated with behavioral descriptions of other chips in a "mixed-mode" simulation [9,11,13]. Execution efficiency might be obtained through independent simulation of parts of the design, driven either by captured patterns, or by direct simulation in the mixed-mode model, since behavioral models are faster than gate-level models as a rule.

I believe that this top-down, hierarchical approach is the wrong way to simulate computer systems. I advocate instead simulating a single integrated large-scale model based on a complete detailed representation of the logic. The most familiar and still quite widely used representation level is that of logic gates and latches, but computer designers increasingly use various kinds of automatic sythesis methods that elevate somewhat the level of logical description [14]. I will use the phrase "gate level" to mean the lowest level of description used by the logic designers, which should be the *highest* level that can convincingly be shown to be logically equivalent to the circuits actually fabricated.

The hierarchical approach requires extra designer time, exposes the design to late discovery of subtle bugs, and hence can delay the project schedule. Before discussing these effects, let me point out three characteristics of most (industrial) development environments that strongly affect methodological decisions:

1. *Designer time* is the single most precious resource in the entire effort,

2. *Computational resources*—compute cycles, memory, disks—are plentiful, relative to designer time,

3. *Project schedule* is the most important constraint.

These factors mean that project managers should be willing to make tradeoffs of computing resources for designer resources, and that they should want to use calendar time as efficiently as possible.

The first problem with the top-down, hierarchical, mixed-mode approach is that engineers must create and maintain behavioral models with detailed interface specifications, in addition to doing the actual logic design. Development projects should instead substitute computer power for this extra design effort: gate-level models (or the equivalent) should be the only simulatable description of the design. This allows logic design to begin sooner and frees the designer from the responsibility of maintaining two or more models of the same piece of logic.

Another problem with the hierarchical approach is the difficulty of independently simulating separate parts. Unless there is an accurate set of good input-output patterns captured from a higher-level model, the designer must somehow generate inputs and check outputs of the designer's part of the logic. At many levels these "test vectors" can be quite inscrutable and very large. Furthermore, it is easy to see how two designers of interacting pieces of logic might have subtle differences in their understandings of the interface, each believing their design to be correct. An integrated behavioral model can take care of these difficulties only if it is exquisitely detailed: more time, more effort!

A third problem with this approach is accuracy: how can the designer be sure that the logic matches its behavioral description in every detail? And a fourth problem is the sacrifice of partitioning flexibility, about which more below.

Gate-level models of the entire CPU or system address all of these problems. By "system" I mean a substantial collection of hardware: my own group has used models that include multiple CPUs, main memory boards and buses, input/output (i/o) adapters, i/o buses, simplified models of i/o devices, and even a console interface. Our goal has been to simulate together all of the new hardware the group is designing.

Gate-level models are derived directly from the designers' own specification of the logic (remember that this is sometimes in the form of Boolean equations or other abstract descriptions—one need not draw actual logic gates for everything). Hence there is no possibility of the simulation model disagreeing with the actual design. With multiple-model methods there is always this risk. "If you want two things to be the same," observed one of our engineers, "then only have one thing."

But what about the problem of speed? It is certainly true that a large-scale, gate-level model will run much more slowly than an abstract behavioral model. When will this be a problem? A simulation model is fast enough when it is turning up bugs at least as fast as they can be fixed by the designers. Conversely, a model is too slow only when it becomes the bottleneck in the debugging process. But when during the project is this likely to happen? Digital's VAX experience [3,4] strongly suggests that it is likely to happen when the bugs are subtle and difficult, requiring complicated stimulus, intensive subsystem interaction, and the simultaneous occurrence of unusual events. And it is precisely then that the big, detailed model is most needed, for only it expresses the exact logical behavior of the system under these extreme conditions.

Gate-level simulation of a large-scale model can be thought of as a brute-force substitution of processing power and main memory capacity for designers' brain power and time [15]. In the industrial environment it is usually easier to apply more computer power than more brain power to this problem.

Partitioning flexibility is lost to some degree in the hierarchical approach. Early specification of the behavior and interfaces of the parts makes it relatively more cumbersome to change the location of some piece of functionality. The brute approach of a single gate-level model allows more flexibility. Not only can changes be made more quickly, but knowing in advance that one will simulate (and timing-verify) this way allows the designers to adopt a looser attitude toward interface definitions, which in turn enables them to start the detailed design work earlier [15]. (Of course, more formal up-front interface design can improve the initial quality of the interface; this benefit is outweighed in my view by the disadvantages of this approach.)

Partitioning flexibility is also important when timing or other physical or electrical design considerations (pins, power, area) force repartitioning. Pure top-down methods may not even be able to express these constraints at higher levels. In some cases, too, when working with advanced technology, physical and electrical parameters can change late in the game; when this happens easy repartitioning is quite valuable.

An extraordinary advantage of a CPU-level (or higher-level) model, whether represented behaviorally or at the gate level, is that it is essentially a very slow computer, and its stimulus is an ordinary computer program. Numerous benefits follow. First, no knowledge of the hardware details is required for a person to run a test program on a simulated CPU. This greatly enlarges the population of competent model testers. Hardware expertise is only required when a test program goes astray. Another benefit is that (for existing instruction-set architectures) there is a ready standard of comparison and a plentiful supply of already written test programs: any program that doesn't run for very long is a candidate. A third benefit is that a program can check its own answers. The problem of checking the output of a simulation is quite serious, the more so when the volume of tests is large, as it must be for the systems under discussion. Inevitably one needs some other model against which to compare the output. A self-checking program in essence computes some value in two different ways, checking for internal architectural consistency rather than using a separate model for comparison. This procedure will not catch all bugs, of course.

A final advantage of big-model simulation comes from the empirical observation that in using these models, designers often discover bugs in parts of the logic other than the ones they are testing. As I will argue in the next section, these serendipitous bug discoveries should be highly valued.

The orderly construction of a large model will clearly entail *some* simulation of its lower-level parts; I do not mean to prohibit small models absolutely. Indeed, too-early use of a large-scale model can be a very inefficient way to find simple bugs in small components. A modest amount of independent simulation of smaller units should be done to assure basic functionality before integration into a larger model.

Neither do I mean to imply that large-scale models should represent logic at a level of detail *finer* than that used by the designers. At some point, trusted translation tools transform the designers' logical description into an exact physical specification of the circuits. Simulation of individual transistors and the like is certainly required to certify the logical components used by the designers, but it can safely be done in the small. When logic synthesis is used, the correctness of the translation must be rigorously established if a higher-level representation is to be simulated.

One way to think about my dual recommendations is the following. Simulation of large-scale models attacks bugs in the *design* of a system, whereas simulation using low-level representation attacks bugs in the *implementation* of that design. (Things are not quite this pure, of course.) A big model, even if composed of abstract behavioral elements, can uncover design flaws: e.g., the bus protocol handles a certain case improperly. Gate-level simulation, even of small pieces of the design, can uncover implementation flaws: e.g., these three gates do not express the designer's intent. Together, these approaches constitute a powerful method for doing both at once, a method that efficiently uses the available resources of designer effort, computer power, and calendar time.

## 9.3  Passing Tests Versus Finding Bugs

So we can now imagine a large-scale model based directly on the designers' lowest-level specification of the design. It can simulate, albeit at a somewhat slower speed, anything the real machine could do. In the design lurk some unknown number of bugs. How best to find them? In this section I will explore two possible approaches and then discuss the question of knowing how much simulation is enough. (Much of the material in this section is drawn from an earlier report [4].)

Efficient simulation is important because simulation is expensive. In 1 CPU development project at Digital [5], the simulation ratio, i.e., the ratio of the speed of the real machine to the speed of its system-level simulation, was 300 million to one. That means that to simulate just 1 second of target machine time, the simulation model would have to run around the clock for *10 years*.

The traditional or *test-centered* approach to simulation works as follows. A (long) list of tests is created, one for each identifiable function of the system; these tests should ideally "cover" the design, that is, exercise all of its parts in a balanced way. The tests are then simulated on the model. When tests fail, bugs are uncovered and repaired. Progress is measured against the list: the number of tests that pass is a measure of the goodness of the design. When all the tests pass, the design is regarded as correct, and parts can be released for fabrication.

This approach has several attractive features. It provides a definite plan of attack (the list), which allows a rational allocation of human and computational resources to the simulation task. It provides a clear measure of progress: how many tests pass? The remainder are a measure of the work left to do. And finally, the test-centered approach provides an unambiguous ending criterion: when all the tests run correctly, simulation is complete and hardware fabrication can begin.

So what is wrong with this attractive approach? Simply this: passing all the tests on the list does not demonstrate that any other single test will be able to pass. In essence this approach guarantees that fabricated hardware will pass exactly—and perhaps *only*—those tests on the list.

The test-centered approach simply has the wrong focus, for no amount of testing can guarantee the perfect correctness of a design. As Dijkstra said in another context, "testing can be used to show the presence of bugs, but never to show their absence!" [7] A computer system is just too complex to test completely. Although any computer is in principle just a huge finite-state machine with a finite number of possible programs that could ever be run, the number of states and state-transitions and programs might as well be infinite. Exhaustive testing is out of the question, and furthermore there is no representative subset of tests that, if passed, will demonstrate perfect correctness. We can aspire to test only a tiny fraction of the system's entire behavior.

Happily, we only need to test a tiny fraction to find all the bugs. The trick is to test the *right* tiny fraction! When simulation begins there is some unknown number of bugs in the design; let $B$ be the number. (Digital's experience suggests that for VAX designs $B$ is on the order of one thousand.) There is a huge but finite number of test programs that could be run. Every bug can be exposed by at least one test, and some tests expose multiple bugs. In principle, no more than $B$ tests need to be simulated to remove all the bugs (neglecting any new bugs that might be introduced in the repair process). There are, of course, many many sets of $B$ or fewer tests, each capable of doing this. The strategic objective of system simulation should be obvious: minimize the number of tests run while maximizing the chance that some one of these special sets of $B$ tests is among the ones actually run. There is little reason to think that any fixed list of tests constructed *a priori* will contain one of the desired sets.

"Regression testing" is a particularly wrong-headed example of the test-centered approach. It means rerunning old tests after a change or bug-repair to the design, in order to make sure the design has not "regressed" or lost any abilities it once had. A particularly slavish adherence to this idea would have *all* old tests rerun after *every* design change.

If testing were free this might be all right, but in the hardware simulation environment, testing is far from free. If the tester asked, "What test is most likely to uncover a design bug?" the answer would almost never be one of the tests in the regression suite. A test that has passed before is highly likely to pass again. Looking for new tests to uncover new bugs is what the bug-oriented tester would do. Regression testing is a way to get good tests, not a bug-free design; it may also encourage a false sense of confidence in the design's correctness.

"Design verification" is the traditional name for the phase of a project devoted to demonstrating the correctness of a fully specified design. But it should be self-evident that any design is most certainly *not* correct when this activity starts and possibly even when it ends. How can an incorrect design be "verified"? Perhaps a better name for this phase of a project would be *design falsification*. The object should not be to show that the design works (for it surely doesn't), but to show exactly how it does not.

In other words, the object should be to find bugs, not to pass tests. Design verification is a gradually developing side effect of the process of design falsification: as falsification becomes more and more difficult, the design comes closer and closer to being correct. Testing and debugging should be oriented around the bugs themselves; hence the notion of *bug-centered* simulation. To find a bug it is best to be looking for one. Passing a test—getting the intended result—does not advance this effort one bit.

Indeed, following Myers, who made this observation in the context of software testing [12], we should call such a test a *failure*. If a test gets an incorrect result and thereby uncovers a bug, we should call it a success. This apparently backward way of looking at things is very useful, especially in the hardware simulation environment, where testing is so costly.

A focus on bugs will orient testing away from rigid procedures intended for thorough functional coverage, and toward a flexible approach that applies tests in areas most likely to contain bugs. These include especially

□ Areas of unusual logical complexity.

□ Interfaces between parts designed by different people or groups.

□ Parts of the design that deal with rarely-exercised functionality (for example, error-detection circuits).

□ Parts of the design that, paradoxically, have already yielded many bugs.

Rather than follow a fixed list of test cases, testing efforts should adapt to the empirical situation: testing methods that do not find bugs should be abandoned in favor of methods that do.

Underlying these efforts should be a fundamentally positive attitude toward bugs. Unfortunately it is more natural for design engineers (and their managers!) to see a bug as a defect or a failure. Particularly in times of schedule pressure it is difficult to imagine that finding a bug is a good thing. It is quite understandable that an engineer might be ashamed of a bug, or try to deny it, or hope that its true location is in someone else's logic, or concentrate on portions of the design that function correctly rather than ones that don't.

The design engineer wants to show that the design works; it is quite unnatural to take pleasure in a demonstration that it really doesn't. Yet this is exactly the attitude that engineering management should encourage. Finding a bug should be a cause for celebration. Each discovery is a small victory; each marks an incremental improvement in the design. A complex design always has bugs. The only question is whether they are found now or later, and *now is always better*.

One way to deal with the natural tendency of a design engineer to resist bugs is to give the testing job to somebody else. In one group at Digital [3] a team separate from the designers helps build simulation models and then creates and runs tests. A similar arrangement is also common in software companies, where the Quality Assurance department or its equivalent is in charge of testing. (Such groups have the luxury of running their tests at full speed, of course.) But having a separate testing team is no guarantee of success: such a team might fall into the test-centered trap itself.

It is quite difficult to predict which testing methods will in fact find bugs. Planning for the design falsification phase of a project is hampered by this fact and by the uncertainty over how many bugs there are. (One Digital engineering manager called this project phase the "Twilight Zone"!) The bug-centered approach urges flexibility in testing. Whatever the plan says, the design or testing team must be prepared to abandon methods that do not find bugs and in their place expand and promote methods that do.

A bug is an opportunity to learn about the design, and can lead the designer to other bugs (called "cousin bugs" by Sherwood [3]). On finding a bug, the designer or debuger should try to generalize in various ways by asking questions like these:

☐ Is this bug an instance of a more general problem?

☐ Does this same bug occur in any other parts of the design?

☐ Can the same test find more bugs? Are there any enhancements to the test suggested by this bug?

☐ Does this bug mask some other bug?

☐ What other similar tests could be run?

☐ Why was it not caught earlier? Is there a coverage hole, or is a new test needed?

☐ How did it get into the design? Was it, for example, due to designer misconception, an ambiguity or error in a design specification, a failure of some CAD tool? (Beware of assigning blame, however.)

The bug-centered strategy, which sometimes goes by the shorthand phrase "bugs are good" at Digital, is slowly taking hold within the company. There remain, however, many groups that operate in a test-centered way, running and rerunning their regression tests. The attachment these groups have to the traditional approach comes largely from its clear endpoint: when all the tests pass, testing is done. There may still be bugs, of course, but the management milestone has been met. How can a bug-centered group decide that enough testing has been done? And how can its progress be measured?

To measure progress, bug-centered testers should not count the number of tests passed, but should instead watch the *bug discovery rate*. In several projects my group has used a low-overhead but high-visibility bug-counting method. Engineers simply marked a centrally posted sheet with a tick-mark for each bug they found. Elaborate, comprehensive, computer-aided bug reports were explicitly *not* used, because we felt that the attendant visibility and overhead would discourage candid reporting, particularly of bugs found by their own creators. The bug tallies were updated weekly, and a plot of the rate centrally displayed.

Fabrication release decisions should not be made until this rate drops to a level low enough to establish confidence in the design. With a steady (or increasing!) rate of bug discovery, there is no evidence that the end might be near—none whatever. It is necessary that the rate decline in the face of determined, creative, flexible bug-finding attack. Ideally one would wait until the rate was actually zero for some considerable time. What exactly a "low" rate means is determined by the parameters of the fabrication process and the economics of the project. Low might mean very very low if the fabrication time is long, or cost high. A higher value of "low" can be tolerated if quick turnaround of new designs is available. In designs that contain a number of separately manufactured pieces, one can try to release first those pieces that have been bug-free the longest. Release decisions are in the end a question of judgment and risk: experience with prior projects, confidence in the design, and willingness to take risks with remaining bugs will determine when designs are released. There can be few hard and fast rules in this area.

One rule does seem clear, however: one should not release logic that has *never* been tested! It is important to do some kind of *coverage measurement* during simulation [11]. (The well studied area of *fault coverage* is not what I mean here. Fault coverage addresses the ability of a test to uncover physical failure of the implementation, not the design flaws we are discussing.) For example, one simple measurement is to record which signals have taken on both logical 0 and 1 values at some point during some test. Now, of course, mere coverage does not show correctness. A fully exercised design can still have bugs, so the temptation to stop simulating once some desired level of coverage is reached must be firmly resisted. But a lack of coverage of some piece of logic means that any bugs that might be there have certainly not been found. Coverage measurement should be thought of as a way to find *un*covered logic, rather than as a way to establish confidence in covered logic. Uncovered logic needs new tests.

When the bug discovery rate finally does fall off, it is important to investigate the reason. It may be that there are in fact very few bugs left in the design. But it may also be that the particular testing methods then in use are faltering. If this is so, new methods, perhaps more intensive or complex ones, should be quickly brought to bear. We do not want the bug rate to decline slowly; we would much prefer a precipitate drop from a high rate when there are in fact very few bugs left.

## 9.4  Random Testing

When the space of possible behaviors is too vast to test exhaustively (as is obviously the case for computer systems), some method must guide the selection of tests. One way to do this is *directed testing*, in which some human intention controls the selection. This is an important method for areas of the design with a high *a priori* chance of yielding bugs, but if used universally, it leaves open the possibility that unselected tests might reveal bugs. And of course it is quite likely that some behavior not fully considered by the designers, and hence not exercised by the chosen tests, might yield a bug.

Put the other way, any design bug that does show up after fabrication is proof that some important test was never simulated.

The method I advocate for dealing with the problem of a huge space of behaviors is to sample randomly (really pseudo-randomly) from one or more sets of possible tests. A random selection can pick any test with some probability, and the longer a random test-selector runs, the more likely it is that any particular test will be found.

Sometimes it is desirable to have a completely unbiased selection, so that all tests (from some specified set) are chosen with equal probability. This is clearly the right thing to do if one has absolutely no idea where the bugs might be. Sometimes, however, it may be important to bias the selection in some known way. This bias enables the tester to focus on a particular subset of the test space. (I use terms like "space" and "probability" and "bias" here with conscious informality. No one would actually define the "space" of possible behaviors or enumerate all possible test programs. The ideas become clearer when expressed in this language, but in actual application the details behind the suggestive terminology are never worked out.) For example, to test the floating point logic one might want to bias the selection of input data toward numerical boundary conditions of various kinds. Or perhaps at the beginning of simulation one might bias the selection toward very simple tests, leaving the more complex choices until bugs in the basic functionality had been found.

What must never be done, however, is to bias the selection is such a way that some important subspace of possible tests is sampled with probability zero!

Random testing implies that a huge volume of tests will be simulated (and also that you'd better have a fearsome computing armamentarium to run the simulations). This in turn has two consequences: first, the tests must be auto-matically generated; and second, the results of each test must be automatically checked. Manual generation and checking are simply out of the question unless the hardware is trivial and the volume of testing small.

An example of an automatic random tester is the AXE architectural ex-erciser used at Digital to test VAX implementations, both in simulation and in real hardware [1,6]. The strict level of architectural compatibility demanded of VAX family members—essentially this: that all legitimate programs must get the same answer on all VAXes without recompiling—yields a ready standard of comparison.

AXE compares two VAX implementations by generating random instruc-tions, running them on both implementations, and noting any differences in the results. It makes a random choice of opcode, picks some random operand spec-ifiers, drops random data into random locations in memory, and arranges for a random selection of architectural impediments such as page faults, arithmetic exceptions, traps, and the like. AXE's random choices can be constrained by the user in various ways; the user might want AXE to pick only certain opcodes, for example. The "case" AXE generates is run on the target machine (a simulation model) and on a known standard VAX (usually the simulation engine itself) and the results are compared in detail. AXE looks at the instruction's actual result, of course, but also checks all register contents, condition codes, relevant memory locations, and the correct handling of any exceptions the case provoked.

AXE, originally developed to certify new hardware, is now also used in every VAX CPU simulation. It has proven to be an excellent bug-finder and is being enhanced to generate multiple-instruction cases.

When the designers suspect that some parts of the system are more likely than others to contain bugs, they can focus testing by biasing the random test selection, as discussed above. Another way to focus is to use a simulation *demon*. A demon is an autonomous source of interference in a simulation. A common type of demon takes the place of one system component while another, usually a CPU, runs a test. The idea is that by generating extra functional interactions, a demon can flush out lurking bugs. It can be implemented as a simple behavioral (i.e., not gate-level) simulation of a system component, with its own source of stimulus.

A *Hamming demon*, for example, might randomly drop bad bits into data fetched out of an ECC-protected memory by a simulated CPU. A *bus demon* might generate random (but legitimate) bus transactions while the connected CPU runs a self-checking test that also uses the bus.

Some demons are useful because they bias the random selection of system-level test cases in the direction of high subsystem interaction. Experience teaches that system bugs often occur in these interactions, which lack the architectural clarity of specification found in, say, floating point hardware or caches or instruction sets. Other demons, like the Hamming demon, force error conditions at unplanned times, another traditional source of bugs.

A demon, in this formulation, does not check its own answers. Instead it relies on the self-checking test running in the CPU to be affected by any bug it turns up. This will not always happen. A thorough check of all the outcomes of a demon's interference might find a failure not visible to the particular test running in the CPU. In some simulation environments, intensive checking of this kind may well be advisable.

Demons can themselves generate random activity, or use a particular type of stimulus generated according to some fixed scheme, since the desired randomness can come from the main self-checking test.

Here are some examples of demons that have been used over roughly the last 6 years in various VAX simulation efforts. All assume that a self-checking test (often AXE) is running on one processor, and that any errors will be reflected in some failure of the check.

1. *System bus demon*. In shared-memory multiprocessors there are several

players on the main system bus: processors, memories, and i/o adapters. Several projects have used bus demons to take the place of one or more of these players and increase the level of bus traffic in the simulation.

2. *i/o bus demon.* Here the demon sits on a simulated i/o bus pretending to be some sort of i/o device.

3. *Clock demon.* One project used a clock demon to turn off non-memory clocks at random times and for random intervals, mimicking what would happen when actual hardware clocks were stopped and restarted from the system console. (Memory clocks were needed to prevent volatile DRAMs —dynamic random access memories—from forgetting.)

4. *Stall demon.* Stalls occur when one part of the computer can't make progress due to a lack of response from, or contention against, some other part. A typical implementation is to block the clocks of the first part while letting the second part proceed until the original reason for stalling is removed. A common example: the first part is the processor, the second part is the cache, and the processor stalls during a cache miss. A stall demon drops in stalls of random (but legitimate) duration at random (legitimate) times.

5. *Error demon.* Some projects have used demons that randomly cause hardware errors in the simulation model. Things like single-bit errors in ECC-protected memory should be transparent, while more serious errors in less protected domains may have more serious consequences. Sometimes such consequences (operating-system intervention, for example) must be checked by more serious methods too.

There is no reason not to run multiple demons simultaneously. When simulation is turning up few bugs, the use of more and nastier demons may expose especially obscure bugs.

---

## 9.5   Conclusion

In this chapter I have presented a set of recommendations concerning computer hardware simulation. Methodological ideas, especially those involving big projects with real-world constraints, cannot easily be subjected to rigorous scientific scrutiny. I can claim only logic and experience as supports for my prescription, which in barest essence is this:

☐ Simulate the lowest level of representation used by the logic designers (e.g., the gate or logic equation level).

□ As soon as the basic functionality of the system parts has been tested independently, integrate the parts into a large-scale model such as a CPU or even an entire system. Use this model for most simulation.

□ Remember that *bugs are good:* organize the effort around finding the bugs rather than passing the tests.

□ Use randomly selected, automatically generated, automatically checked or self-checking tests.

□ Use simulation demons to focus stimulus on subsystem interactions, a traditional source of difficult bugs.

□ Measure coverage of the logic during simulation and add tests or test methods for areas that lack good coverage. Do *not* stop simulating when some predetermined coverage level is reached.

□ Release designs for fabrication only when the bug discovery rate is low (despite determined efforts to raise it), and *not* when some preconceived list of tests is passed.

□ Do not stop simulating just because the parts have been released! Simulation is *never* done. A bug found during fabrication is one less bug to find in the prototype.

In a sense one could say that the reason we do extensive simulation of computer system hardware is that we don't know any better. We would much prefer to have the ability to produce bug-free designs to begin with, or to have formal proof methods capable of verifying big systems, or to have rigorous testing regimes that could certify correctness. We can certainly hope that the increasing use of logic synthesis techniques [14] will result in designs with fewer bugs. We can also hope that hardware verification methods of various kinds [2,8] will be able to handle ever-larger and more complex structures. But for the present, simulation is our lot, and we need to do it well.

## 9.6  Acknowledgments

I am grateful to many Digital colleagues who have advised me and/or worked with me on the simulation phase of several CPU projects. Among them I acknowledge particularly Pete Bannon, Debbie Bernstein, Tom Eggers, Jim Keller, Kevin Ladd, Will Sherwood, Bob Stewart, and Neil Wilhelm. Helpful comments on an early draft of this chapter were offered by Dileep Bhandarkar, Jim Finnerty, Paul Kinzelman, Richard McIntyre, and Will Sherwood.

# References

[1] D. Bhandarkar. Architecture Management for Ensuring Software Compatibility. *IEEE Computer*, pp. 87-93, February, 1982.

[2] R. E. Bryant. A Methodology for Hardware Verification Based on Logic Simulation. Technical Report CMU-CS-87-128, Department of Computer Science, Carnegie-Mellon University, Pittsburgh, PA 1987.

[3] R. E. Calcagni and W. Sherwood. VAX 6000 Model 400 CPU Chip Set Functional Design Verification. *Digital Technical Journal 2(2)*, pp. 64-72, Digital Equipment Corp., Maynard, MA, 1990.

[4] D. W. Clark. Bugs are Good: A Problem-Oriented Approach to the Management of Design Engineering. *Research-Technology Management 33(3)*, pp. 23-27, 1990.

[5] D. W. Clark. Pipelining and Performance in the VAX 8800. In *Proc. Second International Conference on Architectural Support for Prog. Lang. and Op. Syst.*, pp. 173-177, ACM/IEEE, Palo Alto, CA, 1987.

[6] J. W. Croll, L. T. Camilli, and A. J. Vaccaro. Test and Qualification of the VAX 6000 Model 400 System. *Digital Technical Journal 2(2)*, pp. 73-83, Digital Equipment Corp., Maynard, MA, 1990.

[7] E. W. D. Dijkstra. Notes on Structured Programming. In Dahl, Dijkstra, and Hoare (eds.), *Structured Programming*. p. 6, New York: Academic Press, 1972.

[8] W. A. Hunt, Jr. *FM8501: A Verified Microprocessor*. Ph.D. thesis, Institute for Computing Science, University of Texas at Austin, Austin, TX, Technical report 47, 1986.

[9] M. A. Kearney. DECSIM: A Multi-Level Simulation System for Digital Design. In *Proceedings of the International Conference on Computer-Aided Design*, New York: IEEE, 1984.

[10] T. M. McWilliams. Verification of Timing Constraints on Large Digital Systems. In *17th Design Automation Conference*, pp. 139-147, ACM/IEEE, 1980.

[11] M. Monachino. Design Verification System for Large-Scale LSI Designs. *IBM Journal of Research and Development 26(1)*, pp. 89-99, IBM Corporation, Armonk, NY, 1982.

[12] G. J. Myers. *The Art of Software Testing*. New York: John Wiley and Sons, 1979.

[13] Samudrala, et al. Design Verification of a VLSI VAX Microcomputer. In *Proceedings MICRO-17*, ACM/IEEE, 1984.

[14] D. E. Thomas, et al. *Algorithmic and Register-Transfer Level Synthesis: The System Architect's Workbench*. Boston: Kluwer Academic Publishers, 1990.

[15] N. Wilhelm. Personal communication, 1986.

# 10

# Heterogeneous Multicomputers

H. T. Kung

Heterogeneous multicomputers, capable of simultaneously providing different types of computing resources to meet application needs, are expected to be the mainstream high-performance computing environment of the 1990s. Heterogeneous multicomputers can speed up both computation and input/output (i/o), and can possess a large amount of memory. Moreover, they can take advantage of advances and infrastructures of existing computer architectures, while providing a graceful way of migrating the environment to incorporate new architectures.

High-speed networks are the key technology enabling high-performance heterogeneous multicomputers. Rapid progress is being made in this area, as demonstrated by the Nectar system under development at Carnegie Mellon University. Using high-bandwidth and low-latency networks such as Nectar, heterogeneous multicomputers can sustain the communication bandwidth required by nodes operating at high speed and allow concurrent processing of small-grain computations at different nodes.

## 10.1   Introduction

Future high-performance computing needs will require more than just vector supercomputers or massively parallel architectures. A complementary and some-

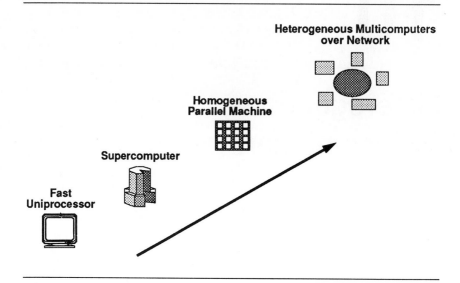

**EXHIBIT 10.1**
Evolution of high-performance computing systems.

times much smarter approach is to use *heterogeneous multicomputers* capable of simultaneously providing a variety of computer architectures to meet different needs of an application. For example, we envision such a heterogeneous environment including both conventional supercomputers and parallel computers. The parallel computers may handle parts of the application that are parallelizable while the supercomputers can deal with those parts that are vectorizable. The environment could also include workstations, graphics displays, i/o systems, and application-specific computer systems.

Exhibit 10.1 illustrates the evolution of high-performance computing systems, starting from fast uniprocessors to supercomputers and homogeneous parallel computers. To be able to use a large number of processing nodes, scalable parallel computers will mainly be network-based, distributed-memory multicomputers [11]. Most of today's multicomputers are "homogeneous" [2,3,4,8,12] in the sense that such a system is made of one single processor type. However, to achieve the next level of performance, multicomputers will need to explore multiple levels and forms of parallelism, and allow "heterogeneous" processing nodes whenever appropriate. This chapter argues that heterogeneous multicomputers are the next step in the evolution of high-performance computing systems.

Key scientific advances required for realizing high-performance heterogeneous multicomputers are in high-bandwidth and low-latency networks for intersystem communication. For this, very high-speed computer networks are being developed. Taking advantage of the recent phenomenal progress in fiber-optics technology, these new networks will be orders of magnitude faster than current ones and will allow heterogeneous multicomputers to be constructed using local area or even wide area networks.

The Nectar project [1] at Carnegie Mellon is one of the first attempts in building these very high-speed networks. Nectar uses fiber-optic links, large crossbar switches, and dedicated network coprocessors. A prototype system employing 100 megabits per second (Mb/s) links has been operational since early 1989. As of spring 1990 the system has 26 hosts, and is readily extendible to 32 hosts. In addition, a 26 km Nectar connection to a Westinghouse facility, which hosts the CRAY Y-MP of the Pittsburgh Supercomputing Center, is operational.

With a competitively selected industrial partner, Carnegie Mellon is designing the next-generation Nectar using 1 gigabit per second (Gb/s) or higher speed fiber links. This new system will be able to interface with systems supporting the 800 Mb/s HIgh-Performance Parallel Interface (HIPPI) ANSI standard, and with telecommunication networks supporting SONET/ATM standards.

In Section 10.2 we describe heterogeneous multicomputers and provide further motivations. Section 10.3 briefly describes Nectar as an existing example of heterogeneous multicomputers. A summary of advantages of heterogeneous multicomputers is given in Section 10.4. Section 10.5 shows an analysis of how high-speed networks such as Nectar enable high-performance distributed solutions over heterogeneous multicomputers. The chapter ends with some concluding remarks in Section 10.6.

## 10.2  Heterogeneous Multicomputers

This section describes heterogeneous multicomputers and motivates the need for them from applications viewpoints. A *heterogeneous multicomputer* is a network-based computing environment allowing two or more different kinds of computing resources cooperating on a single application. Exhibit 10.2 depicts the concept of a heterogeneous multicomputer whose nodes are various kinds of processors or devices. Note that in addition to conventional high-performance processors, the system can include i/o nodes, special-purpose processors, and terminals for user interface.

Prior approaches in high-performance computing architectures have been developments of fast scalar or vector processors and homogeneous parallel machines. Each of these machine types is optimized for certain kinds of computations. For a computation that is highly parallelizable but requires only simple control, a massively parallel machine that can scale up easily with problem size is ideal. However, a parallel machine is fundamentally not suited for compu-

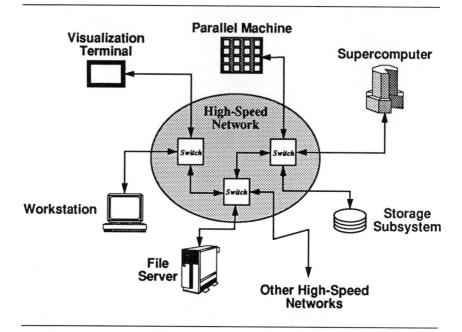

**EXHIBIT 10.2**
Heterogeneous multicomputer.

tations that are highly sequential; in this case fast scalar processors should be used. Similarly, while ideal for vector computations, vector machines are not cost-effective for highly sequential or parallel computations.

Heterogeneous multicomputers represent a new direction in high-performance architectures. By incorporating a variety of existing processors or devices as nodes, a heterogeneous multicomputer allows simultaneous use of the best suited architectures to carry out computations of different characteristics.

Consider, for example, a numerical simulation of a flying airplane. The simulation involves two interacting, large-grain computation tasks that need to be performed simultaneously. One task is the simulation of the aircraft body structure using implicit numerical methods on irregular, coarse meshes. The other task is the simulation of air fluid around the airplane using explicit numerical methods on regular, fine meshes. It turns out that the first task is suited to a vector machine while the second task is ideal for a parallel machine. Therefore the entire simulation requires a heterogeneous multicomputer equipped with both kinds of machines as nodes. The heterogeneity is inherent in the physical world to be simulated!

Heterogeneous multicomputers are useful for applications that require information processing at multiple, qualitatively different levels [1]. For example, a computer vision system may require image processing on its raw sensor input at the lowest level, and scene recognition using a knowledge base at the highest level. A speech understanding system has a similar structure, with low-level signal processing and high-level natural language parsing. The processing required by an autonomous robot might range from handling sensor inputs to high-level planning. At the lowest levels, these applications deal with simple data structures and highly regular number-crunching algorithms. The large amount of data at high rates often requires specialized hardware. At the highest levels, these applications may use complicated symbolic data structures and data-dependent flow of control. Specialized inference engines or database machines might be appropriate for these tasks. The very nature of these applications dictates a heterogeneous hardware environment, with varied instruction sets, data representations, and performance characteristics.

Heterogeneous systems are being pursued today in many high-performance computing installations for reasons including the ones given above. It is important, however, that this not be done in an ad hoc manner. We need to develop general and uniform hardware and software systems to incorporate different types of systems into the environment. The Nectar system, described in the next section, illustrates a general approach for constructing heterogeneous multicomputers.

## 10.3  The Nectar System at Carnegie Mellon

To demonstrate the feasibility of constructing high-performance heterogeneous multicomputers in a general way, we have been developing the Nectar system [1] at Carnegie Mellon since 1987. The Nectar system is a high-bandwidth, low-latency computer network for connecting high-performance hosts. Hosts are attached using powerful network coprocessors (CABs) that accelerate communication protocols. Therefore for Nectar a node is a CAB-host pair. The CAB can be on the same board as the host, or can be connected to the host via an external bus backplane. The Nectar network (Nectar-Net) consists of fiber-optic links and crossbar switches (HUBs). The Nectar system has a command set that supports circuit switching, packet switching, multihop routing, and multicast communication. Exhibit 10.3 gives an overview of the Nectar system.

### 10.3.1  Nectar Prototype

We have developed a 26-node *Nectar prototype* system to support early system

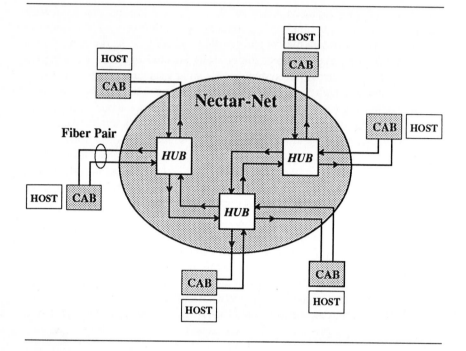

**EXHIBIT 10.3**
The Nectar system at Carnegie Mellon.

software and applications development. The prototype uses 100 Mb/s fiber links and 16 × 16 HUBs. The CAB is implemented as a separate board on the host VME backplane (Exhibit 10.4). Via its VME bus interface, the CAB can connect to its host and to other devices such as graphics boards. Each CAB has 1 megabyte of data memory, 512 kilobytes of program memory, and a central processing unit (CPU) based on a 20 MHz SPARC processor.

The CAB is connected to a HUB via a Fiber Port. For each direction (input and output), the Fiber Port contains the optoelectronics interface to a fiber line and a 4 kilobyte FIFO to buffer data and commands transferred over the fiber, and can support data rates up to 100 Mb/s. The CAB has a DMA controller to provide high speed transfers between the Fiber Port and the data memory, and between the data memory and the VME interface.

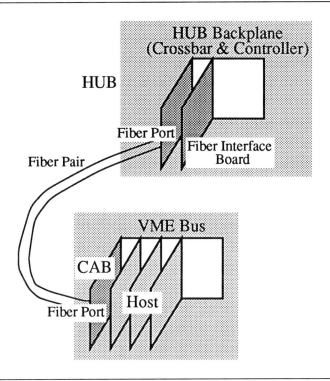

**EXHIBIT 10.4**
HUB and CAB in Nectar prototype.

## 10.3.2 Nectar Systems Software

Using the Nectar prototype, we have developed an extensive set of software for
the Nectar system. The CAB run-time system manages hardware devices such
as timers and DMA, supports multiprogramming (the threads package [6]), and
manages buffers (the mailbox module). The threads package, derived from the
Mach C Threads package, supports lightweight processes in a single address
space. Threads provide a low cost method of sharing the CAB CPU among
concurrent activities, which is important for communication protocol implementation. Mailboxes provide efficient management of buffer space in the CAB
memory and form the endpoints of communication between processes on hosts
or CABs. Mailboxes also provide synchronization between readers and writers.
For example, if a host process or CAB thread tries to read a message from an

empty mailbox, it will block; it will resume automatically when a message is placed in the mailbox, typically by a transport-layer software on the CAB.

The streamlined structure of the CAB software has made it possible for Nectar to achieve the goal of low communication latency. For the existing Nectar prototype, the latency is under 1 microsecond to establish a connection through a single HUB; under 100 microseconds for a message sent between processes on separate CABs; and under 175 microseconds between processes residing in separate workstation hosts. (The transmission latency over a fiber depends on the length of the fiber; the above figures do not include the fiber latency.)

The Nectar prototype achieves the low-latency inter-host communication in two ways. First, network interrupt handling and transport protocol processing are off-loaded from the host to the CAB, whose hardware and software are specifically designed for protocol processing. This increases communication performance and also frees up the host for application processing. Second, by directly manipulating buffers in CAB memory, host processes can bypass the host operating system when reading and writing messages. By doing this, host processes avoid the cost of system calls and of data copying between the host process and the host operating system.

In the area of protocol software, the CAB currently supports several transport protocols with different reliability/overhead trade-offs. The CAB implementation of the Internet standard protocol TCP is also available. The TCP throughput between two CABs is over 90 Mb/s for 16 kilobyte or larger packets, if the TCP checksum is turned off. This corresponds to the case when the TCP checksum is implemented in hardware (see Nectar Chip under Section 10.3.3 below).

### 10.3.3  Gigabit Nectar

To further develop the Nectar technology, Carnegie Mellon is working with a competitively selected industrial partner (Network Systems Corporation) to develop a *gigabit Nectar* system capable of sustaining 1 Gb/s or higher speed end-to-end communication. The system will be made of the following components:

□ *Nectar Chip*. This will be a 1 Gb/s or higher speed network communication chip for processing datalink protocols and for performing higher level functions such as TCP checksum computations and buffer memory management.

□ *Nectar Module*. The Nectar Chip together with other components such as serial/parallel conversion chips and optical/electrical conversion parts can form a useful system building block, called the *Nectar Module* here, for Gb/s or higher speed network communication. As depicted in Exhibit 10.5,

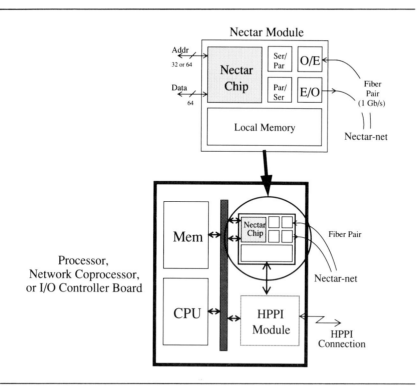

**EXHIBIT 10.5**
Nectar module as a system building block for high-speed network interface.

the Nectar Module could be used in a variety of processor boards, network coprocessor boards, and i/o boards such as disk controllers and frame buffers. Such a board can include an optional on-board HIPPI module. Via the HIPPI module the board can interface to any system supporting the 800 Mb/s HIPPI standard.

▢ *Gigabit CAB.* An example of a network coprocessor based on the Nectar Module is the gigabit CAB. It will have higher performance and a faster, cheaper implementation than the current prototype CAB. Using, for example, a 32 MHz Nectar Module and a 64-bit data bus, the gigabit CAB will support a 1 Gb/s full duplex fiber interface and the HIPPI interface.

▢ *Gigabit HUB.* This will be a crossbar switch with its controller and 1 Gb/s or higher speed Fiber Interface Boards. HIPPI interface will be supported.

□ *SONET/ATM Interface.* Some of the Fiber Interface Boards for the Gigabit HUB will have a SONET/ATM interface. This will allow the gigabit HUB to connect to future public network switching.

The gigabit Nectar system is scheduled to be operational in early 1992.

## 10.4   Advantages of Heterogeneous Multicomputers

Heterogeneous multicomputers such as Nectar offer substantial advantages in high-performance computing. The following summarizes some of these advantages:

1. *Architectures matched to applications.* A heterogeneous multicomputer can incorporate nodes specially selected to suit a given application. Furthermore, a user or a piece of software can choose systems with proper architectures from existing nodes to process different parts of the application. Thus, instead of fitting computations of different characteristics to a single architecture as in the case of using conventional computer systems, heterogeneous multicomputers support a new computation paradigm that matches architectures to different computational needs. Therefore performance gains can be obtained through optimal use of architectures by the application.

2. *Cooperative and simultaneous use of heterogeneous architectures.* Heterogeneous nodes in the multicomputer can collaboratively work on the same application at the same time. Concurrency of various levels and of different grain sizes can be exploited simultaneously. This is made feasible by high-bandwidth and low-latency networks (discussed in Section 10.5).

3. *High-speed i/o.* The underlying high-speed network of a heterogeneous multicomputer is inherently suited to support high-speed i/o to devices such as displays, monitoring stations, sensors, file systems, mass stores and interfaces to other networks. These i/o devices can be viewed as special-purpose nodes of the multicomputer. High-speed networks provide a key technology to speed up all these i/o devices substantially. For example, via such a network, disk arrays [9,7] can deliver very high data transfer rates to applications. With this and the capability of incorporating powerful computing nodes to fit application needs, heterogeneous multicomputers represent a balanced architectural approach capable of speeding up both computation and i/o in the same framework.

4. *Large memory accessible over network.* Over the underlying network of a heterogeneous multicomputer, applications can access a large amount of memory available in all the nodes. By combining memories from different

nodes, one can address memory-bound problems such as logic simulation of very large circuits. For example, we have ported the COSMOS simulator [5] onto the Nectar prototype to handle large circuits that are too large to be simulated on a single node. Being able to address problems of large sizes, applications have the opportunity to benefit fully from the computation and i/o capabilities of a heterogeneous multicomputer.

5. *Use of existing architectures.* By incorporating systems of existing architectures as nodes, a heterogeneous multicomputer can take advantage of rapid improvements of commercially available computers. In addition, it can use systems software and applications that are already in place with these existing computers. For example, at Carnegie Mellon we have been able to port a large solid modeling application (developed by the National Science Foundation sponsored Engineering Design Research Center on the campus) onto the Nectar prototype with a little effort. The porting was facilitated greatly by using as nodes those workstations on which the application had previously been developed.

6. *Incremental migration to new architectures.* A heterogeneous multicomputer provides a graceful environment for moving applications to new architectures such as special-purpose, parallel systems. That is, in the beginning an application can run only part of the computation on these new systems while using more conventional systems in the multicomputer to run the rest of the application. Thus the application can start using the new systems without having to move completely at once to the new environment. The application can increase its use of the new systems over time when more software and application code for the new environment is developed.

In summary, heterogeneous multicomputers offer a complete and balanced approach to high-performance computing. It provides powerful computing resources matched to applications needs. It can speed up both computation and i/o, and provide a large amount of memory. Moreover, it can take advantage of advances and infrastructures of existing architectures, while providing a graceful way of migrating the computing environment and applications to incorporate new architectures.

## 10.5  Effectiveness of Speed-High Networks in Distributing Computation

High-speed (i.e., high-bandwidth and low-latency) networks such as Nectar make high-performance heterogeneous computing, using nodes over a network, feasible for many applications. When nodes are slow or computation grains are large, it is not critical to use high-speed networks, because the computation time at a node is long and as a result delays due to network communication is relatively insignificant. However, to achieve high-performance computing, nodes need to be as fast as possible; and to allow high degrees of parallelism, computation grains need to be as small as possible. We show in this section that high-speed networks can sustain fast nodes and allow concurrent processing of small-grain computations at different nodes.

There are two objectives of using a high-speed network in distributing computations from a node (Master) to another node (Slave):

1. Use of the network's high-bandwidth communication to sustain the computation speed of the Slave.

2. Use of the network's low-latency communication to maximize the concurrent processing of the Master and the Slave, while keeping computation grains small.

In the following discussion we derive conditions for the network to meet these two objectives. To simplify the derivation, we make these assumptions:

1. The end-to-end network bandwidth between the Master and the Slave is *BDWH* Mb/s in each direction.

2. The end-to-end network latency between the two nodes is *LATN* microseconds.

3. Each of the two nodes can deliver *COMP* 64-bit million floating point operations per second (MFLOPS) for computation modules assigned to it. That is, the computation rate that each node can achieve for these computation modules is *COMP*. (Extending the analysis to allow the two nodes to process computations at different rates is straightforward.)

4. Each computation module requires *GRAIN* 64-bit floating-point operations to be performed. That is, the grain of each computation module is *GRAIN*.

5. The Slave, in executing computation modules assigned to it, performs $\alpha$ 64-bit floating-point operations for each 64-bit data input and for each 64-bit data output.

### 10.5.1   High-Bandwidth Networks Able to Sustain High-Speed Nodes

The minimum network bandwidth required to meet objective O1 depends on the values of *COMP* and $\alpha$. From assumptions A1, A3, and A5, it is easy to see

| COMP \ $\alpha$ | 10 | 100 | 1,000 |
|---|---|---|---|
| 10 | 64 | 6.4 | .64 |
| 100 | 640 | 64 | 6.4 |
| 1,000 | 6,400 | 640 | 64 |

Only case requiring more than 800 Mbits/s → (points to 6,400)

**EXHIBIT 10.6**
Minimum network bandwidth required (in # Mb/s).

that the network will be able to sustain the Slave's computation rate, provided that the network's bandwidth satisfies the following condition:

$$BDWH \geq 64 : COMP/\alpha. \tag{10.1}$$

Based on Eq. 10.1, Exhibit 10.6 displays the values of minimum $BDWH$ (in # Mb/s) for a set of values of $COMP$ and $\alpha$.

We see from Exhibit 10.6 that a high-speed network with $BDWH \geq 800$ Mb/s, such as the gigabit Nectar (see Section 10.3.3), will take care of all but one case where $COMP = 1,000$ and $\alpha = 10$. The exceptional case corresponds to the situation where the Slave performs severely i/o bounded computations at a high rate of 1,000 MFLOPS. This situation is rare because usually a node can realize very high computation rates only for compute intensive computations. For example, a systolic array achieves a very high computation rate because a large number of processors can be used to perform many operations for each input or output data item [10].

## 10.5.2  Low-Latency Networks Able to Allow Concurrent Processing of Small-Grain Computations

We describe a scheduling strategy to achieve the objective O2 of maximizing the time when both the Master and the Slave can work concurrently for the application. We partition the application into a sequence of computation modules, $M_1, M_2, \cdots$, whose computation grains satisfy

$$GRAIN \geq LATN : COMP. \tag{10.2}$$

| | Executing at Master | Shipping from Master to Slave | Executing at Slave |
|---|---|---|---|
| Period 1: | $M_2$ | $M_1$ | |
| Period 2: | $M_4$ | $M_3$ | $M_1$ |
| . | . | . | . |
| . | . | . | . |
| . | . | . | . |
| Period $i$: | $M_{2i}$ | $M_{2i-1}$ | $M_{2i-3}$ |
| . | . | . | . |
| . | . | . | . |
| . | . | . | . |

**EXHIBIT 10.7**
Scheduling strategy to maximize concurrent processing of Master and Slave.

This condition ensures that *GRAIN/COMP*, the time for either the Master or the Slave to process a computation module, is at least *LATN*. Therefore it is possible to overlap the network latency with the computation time at a node.

Viewing time as a sequence of *periods* of *GRAIN/COMP* microseconds, our scheduling strategy is that for each period $i$ ($i = 1, 2, \cdots$) we have the Master execute $M_{2i}$, while having the Slave execute $M_{2i-3}$ (for $i > 1$) and the network ship $M_{2i-1}$ from the Master to the Slave. Thus the Master and the Slave execute all even numbered and odd numbered computation modules, respectively. This situation is depicted in Exhibit 10.7. Since $GRAIN/COMP \geq LATN$, the Slave will start receiving $M_{2i-1}$ before period $i + 1$ begins.

Assume that the network's bandwidth is sufficient to sustain the computation rate of the Slave, i.e., the condition shown in Eq. 10.1 is satisfied. Then it is easy to see that the following holds:

**THEOREM 1**

Suppose that for each period the Master can identify at least two new independent computation modules whose grain sizes satisfy Eq. 10.2. Then after period 1, the Master can always work on one computation module while the Slave is working on another.

Note that in each period one of the new modules will be executed by the Master while another will be shipped to the Slave.

An implicit assumption in the scheduling strategy described above is that a new computation module to be executed by the Master cannot use results from the Slave that have not reached the Master. More precisely,

$$M_{2i} \text{ can depend on results of } M_{2j-3} \text{ only if } j \leq i - 2. \qquad (10.3)$$

Of course, $M_{2i}$ can depend on results of $M_{2j}$ for $j \leq i - 1$, since all even numbered computation modules are executed by the Master.

The conditions shown in Eqs. 10.2 and 10.3 represent the two restrictions imposed on our scheduling strategy due to network latency. In the following discussion we argue that these conditions are likely not restrictive in the practical use of high-performance heterogeneous multicomputers.

The degree of parallelism required in the application to satisfy condition 10.3 is modest, since the difference between $2i$ and $2j - 3$ can be as small as 7. Scheduling techniques for satisfying condition 10.3 are fundamentally not different from those typically used in scheduling computations on a parallel machine. Therefore existing scheduling methods can be used to satisfy condition 10.3.

For condition 10.2, consider Exhibit 10.8, which summarizes the minimum grain size for various values of *LATN* and *COMP*. As far as the minimum grain size is concerned, the most demanding case in Exhibit 10.8 is when $COMP = 1,000$ and $LATN = 100$. In this case each computation module needs to perform 100,000 floating point operations. Note that a typical computation on $n \times n$ matrices, such as matrix multiplication or matrix factorization, takes $\mathcal{O}(n^3)$ floating point operations. For $50 \times 50$ matrices, the computation will easily take 100,000 operations or more. Thus the matrices the Master can ship out for remote processing at a 1,000 MFLOPS Slave can be as small as $50 \times 50$ even in the most demanding case.

## 10.6  Concluding Remarks

This chapter elaborated on a vision of using high-speed networks to implement heterogeneous multicomputers for high-performance computing. All the technology required to implement the vision appears to be available, as exemplified by the Nectar approach being taken by Carnegie Mellon. Using high-bandwidth and low-latency networks such as Nectar, heterogeneous multicomputers can sustain the communication bandwidth required by nodes operating at high speed and allow concurrent processing of small-grain computations at different nodes. Some of the present challenges are to build computing and i/o nodes with gigabits

|  LATN COMP | 10 | 100 |
|---|---|---|
| 10 | 100 | 1,000 |
| 100 | 1,000 | 10,000 |
| 1,000 | 10,000 | 100,000 |

**EXHIBIT 10.8**
Minimum grain size required (in # floating point operations).

per second fiber interface and to develop software and applications for these systems. We expect that rapid progress will be made in these areas and that an exciting new era of high-performance computing induced by heterogeneous multicomputers will unveil in the near future.

## 10.7 Acknowledgments

Much of the views expressed in this chapter are shared by many members of the Nectar project at Carnegie Mellon. The research was supported in part by Defense Advanced Research Projects Agency (DOD) monitored by DARPA/CMO under Contract MDA972-90-C-0035; in part by the National Science Foundation and the Defense Advanced Research Projects Agency under Cooperative Agreement NCR-8919038 with the Corporation for National Research Initiatives, and in part by the Office of Naval Research under Contract N00014-90-J-1939. Views expressed in this chapter are those of the author alone.

## References

[1] E. A. Arnould, F. J. Bitz, E. C. Cooper, H. T. Kung, R. D. Sansom, and P. A. Steenkiste. The design of nectar: A network backplane for heterogeneous multicomputers. In *Proceedings of Third International Conference on Architectural Support for Programming Languages and Operating Systems (ASPLOS III)*, pp. 205-216. ACM, 1989.

[2] W. C. Athas and C. L. Seitz. Multicomputers: Message-passing concurrent computers. *Computer*, 21(8):9-24, August 1988.

[3] S. Borkar, R. Cohn, G. Cox, S. Gleason, T. Gross, H. T. Kung, M. Lam, B. Moore, C. Peterson, J. Pieper, L. Rankin, P. S. Tseng, J. Sutton, J. Urbanski, and J. Webb. iwarp: An integrated solution to high-speed parallel computing. In *Proceedings of Supercomputing '88*, pp. 330-339, Orlando, FL, November 1988. IEEE Computer Society and ACM SIGARCH.

[4] S. Borkar, R. Cohn, G. Cox, T. Gross, H. T. Kung, M. Lam, M. Lĕvine, M. Wire, C. Peterson, J. Susman, J. Sutton, J. Urbanski, and J. A. Webb. Integrating systolic and memory communication in iwarp. In *Conference Proceedings of the 17th Annual International Symposium on Computer Architecture*, pp. 70-81, May 1990.

[5] R. E. Bryant, D. Beatty, K. Brace, K. Cho, and T. Sheffler. Cosmos: A compiled simulator for mos circuits. In *Proceedings of the 24th Design Automation Conference*, pp. 9-16. ACM/IEEE, 1987.

[6] E. C. Cooper and R. P. Draves. C threads. Technical Report CMU-CS-88-154, Carnegie-Mellon University, Computer Science Department, 1988.

[7] D. A. Patterson, G. A. Gibson, and R. H. Katz. A case for redundant arrays of inexpensive disks (raid). In *Proceedings of ACM SIGMOD International Conference on Management of Data*, pp. 109-116, 1988.

[8] M, Homewood, et al. The ims t800 transputer. *IEEE Micro*, 7(5):10-26, 1987.

[9] R. H. Katz, J. K. Ousterhout, D. A. Patterson, P.M. Chen, A. Chervenak, R. Drewes, G. A. Gibson, E. K. Lee, K. Lutz, E. L. Miller, and M. Rosenblum. A project on high performance i/o subsystems. *ACM Computer Architecture News*, 17(17):24-31, 1989.

[10] H. T. Kung. Why systolic architectures? *Computer Magazine*, 15(1):37-46, January 1982.

[11] H. T. Kung. Network-based multicomputers: Redefining high performance computing in the 1990s. In *Proceedings of Decennial Caltech Conference on VLSI*, pp. 49-66, Pasadena, California, Cambridge, MA: MIT Press, 1989.

[12] C. L. Seitz. The cosmic cube. *Communications of the ACM*, 28(1):22-33, 1985.

# PART FOUR

# Artificial Intelligence

# 11

# Formulating the Problem-Space Computational Model

Allen Newell, Gregg Yost, John E. Laird,
Paul S. Rosenbloom, and Erik Altmann

## 11.1 Introduction

The *foundation paradigm* of computer science is the application of computational operations to data structures to perform semantically meaningful computations, as specified by a program. The great utility of this arrangement depends on the existence of programming languages that humans can use to specify the computations that perform tasks of interest. This utility is enhanced many-fold by the generality of these computations and the immense rapidity with which they can be carried out and their results communicated over large distances. But the basic paradigm is key—a human with a task that he or she can cast as a computation and express in a programming language that a computer can interpret and perform.

The revolutionary productivity of this paradigm—economically, socially, and intellectually—is apparent to us all. An important element in its success is situating the task in the mind of the human, without explicit representation in the paradigm. All that need exist to make the paradigm work is the program embodied in a program-language expression for some computer. The relation of the task to the program is a conceptual invention in the mind of the human user

255

that need never be made manifest. This was a great divide and conquer. Society could understand and automate one type of intellectual activity (instruction following) without automating another more difficult type (task definition). In the event, it has yielded immense rewards.

Immediately, of course, the enterprise commenced to understand and automate the bypassed intellectual activity. The intellectual agent that conceives a task, designs the algorithm, embodies it in programming-language expressions, and maintains the connection between task and interpretable structure should be realizable as a computational process. Conceivably, no such extension is possible—task creation cannot be automated in general. However, many indicators contravene this conservative reaction, among them the universality of computers and the successful psychological analysis of human task creation and task definition. Indeed, much progress has already occurred in this enterprise. In many limited, though interesting, ways, programs write other programs. These keep the basic paradigm of the human creating the task, but make the task be that of creating programs. More far reaching are the efforts in artificial intelligence (AI) to create intelligent agents that have the essential characteristic of creating and representing their own tasks and the operational structures to accomplish them.

The key question to be asked in opening up task creation to understanding and automation is how tasks are to be *formulated*. Before an agent can even begin on a task, that task must be given form. Enough elements of the task— givens, goals, constraints, resources, background, whatever—must be assembled in a way that permits processing to commence. This is exactly what the basic paradigm avoids—it leaps directly to accomplishment by a program, taking the formulation to be something already accomplished by the human.

The conundrum is that the agent must at once begin to do something—it must take steps to accomplish the task—yet it cannot know what to do at the beginning, because that would imply that the task was already accomplished in its essentials. This is exactly what the program provides—it lays out the steps to be done (possibly conditional on data in specified ways). But it never says how it was known to do just *these* steps rather than others. The problem for the agent is how to get started before knowing what to do.

For computer scientists, the immediate impulse for how to get something for nothing is to recurse—deciding the first step is just another task. Alas, the impulse is in vain. It is reminiscent of the old Pat-and-Mike story. Pat offered Mike a million dollars a year just to solve problems for him. That seemed to Mike a fantastic deal, and he accepted with alacrity. Knowing Pat to be a man of modest means, Mike said "Where will you find all that money to pay me?" "That," said Pat, "is your first problem."

What seems to be needed is the adoption of some kind of *framework* that permits bringing in all the considerations necessary to get a task sufficiently formulated to get off the ground. There is no magic, so the framework must be

1. **Operationality.** The framework must permit the agent to work, i.e., it must be grounded in some version of the basic paradigm, with data structures and operations.

2. **Scope.** The framework must be usable on the full range of tasks that the agent can attempt. The interest is at human scale, corresponding to the range of tasks humans cast into computer programs.

3. **Initialization.** The framework must not pose significant difficulties or require significant effort to get started formulating and attempting a task from whatever initial fragments exist. The point of a framework is to help get started.

4. **Openness.** The framework must easily admit the incorporation of whatever resources, knowledge, considerations and constraints the agent and the environment bring to the task, and in whatever form.

5. **Bias.** Frameworks will necessarily impose something of their own structure on how they are used. As with programming languages, they will make some things easy and other things hard. But a framework should inject as little bias as possible into how task accomplishment proceeds.

**EXHIBIT 11.1**
Criteria for a task-formulation framework.

adopted without knowledge of the specific task. Thus, the framework must be essentially domain independent. The best that can be hoped for is that it satisfy some very general criteria.

The criteria are described in Exhibit 11.1. The few task-formulation frameworks that have emerged as candidates to meet them are listed in Exhibit 11.2.[1] These frameworks all define an arena in which task accomplishment can proceed. With a cunning reminiscent of Pat, they all hire a hall before knowing what entertainment is to play.

It is difficult to evaluate such candidates abstractly. Each candidate does provide an operational computational framework that permits tasks to be formulated and work to commence. Likewise, most have an extremely broad scope. Indeed, most can, in some technical way, incorporate the others, so their scopes are all formally equivalent and computationally universal. The exceptions are

---

[1]There is no received list of candidates, so we may have missed some. Some other plausible candidates do not seem viable at the present time. Natural language and sensory images seem difficult to complete with appropriate operations in their own terms. Blackboard architectures [6] seem to specify too little of an entire framework. Production systems and object-oriented programming systems, although they make many things easier, remain within the foundation paradigm of humans doing the task formulation. Connectionist systems have not yet matured to a broad enough scope.

1. **Problem spaces.** A space of states with a set of operators on states, where a task is formulated as starting at an initial state and searching for a desired state.

2. **Logics.** A set of clauses that describes the task situation with rules of inference to derive new clauses, where a task is formulated as proving a given theorem from a set of axioms.

3. **Constraint satisfaction.** A set of variables of given (often discrete) ranges subject to a set of constraints of fixed types, where a task is formulated as finding the values of the variables that satisfy the constraints and (often) optimize various functions of the variables.

4. **Schemas.** A hierarchical attribute-value structure with values determined by inheritance hierarchies, defaults, constraints, and attached procedures, where a task is formulated as filling out the slots of a given schema.

5. **Programs.** A programming language, where a task is formulated as synthesizing a program to meet a specification on the inputs, outputs and behavior. The specification is given in some formal language.

6. **Plans.** A (large) data base of highly abstract variabilized procedures containing subgoals to be obtained by other plans, where a task is formulated as attaining a given partially instantiated plan.

7. **The big switch.** A (large) data base of programs with a big index on task-relevant features, where a task is formulated by sorting it through the index and applying whatever program is obtained.

**EXHIBIT 11.2**
Candidate frameworks for formulating tasks.

plans and the big switch, which depend on a pre-existing data base. These sacrifice scope for practicality, relying on the fact that the data bases can be built to cover the most frequently occurring tasks for an agent. They can of course be augmented by a capability for automatically adding to the data base, which then requires another framework to do the plan or program synthesis.

Initiation, in some sense the most important criteria, is even harder to assess. Within their scopes plans and the big switch are clearly built to be easy. The others have not been used extensively to formulate tasks in a context that requires going from nothing to something, i.e., from an environment that contains dispersed, fragmented, and hidden bits of knowledge, difficulties, and goal indications, to a formulated task. Instead, in the tradition of the basic paradigm, humans formulate the tasks within these frameworks. However, the intellectual efforts required for this are much less than to produce programs to do the specific tasks. The systems employing these frameworks—theorem provers and problem solvers—formulate for themselves the many subtasks that are needed to complete a task. Some work on initial formulation has occurred, of course, but only in simple situations.

Bias is a second-order concern, since the primary requirement is to be able to do something at all. But there is plenty of evidence that bias will be an issue. In AI this often shows up as the *representation problem*, namely, that much depends on the representation that is chosen for a task. Changing the representation (though staying within a framework) may make orders of magnitude differences in the effort required. A recent example showed up in the N-Queens task [19].[2] The best constraint-satisfaction and heuristic search programs solve on the order of the 1,000-Queens task. A shift to searching in the space of repairs of faulty but complete solutions has been able to solve the million-Queens task, limited only by space. Nonetheless, it will be a while before issues of bias become paramount in evaluating task frameworks.

It should be evident we are still at the stage of exploring each framework in its own terms to discover how it well works out. In fact, that is what we see happening. Research groups and subfields adopt one framework or another, in order to get on with their work. And indeed, each framework can be made to work reasonably well in limited situations.

Against this background, we wish to focus on the *problem-space* framework, the candidate listed at the top of Exhibit 11.2. Problem spaces have a long history in artificial intelligence (AI), growing out of the concept of heuristic search in a combinatorially expanding state space. Most early AI systems used a search space. Indeed, this was true of all the problem-solving systems described in *Computers and Thought* [7], the famous early compendium of AI research. The continuing central role of problem spaces can be traced through the major textbooks of the field [23,24,28,33,34]. However, the search space has seemed conceptually simple, and has not attracted theoretical attention. Its ubiquity is often noted, as is its entailment of combinatorial search. It has also been used to epitomize a paradigm era in AI (search-based) in contrast to other newer paradigms, e.g., knowledge-based [8]. But that is about all the attention it has garnered.

In fact, there is more to problem spaces than meets the eye. Our own involvement with problem spaces began with the Logic Theorist, our first AI system [27], moved though observing their centrality [20,26], demonstrating that they describe human problem-solving [25], extending them to routine as well as problematical situations [21], and taking them as the foundation of an architecture for general intelligence (Soar) [14]. New aspects of problem spaces have continued to emerge throughout, convincing us of their fundamental nature.

---

[2]Placing N queens on an N × N chessboard so that no Queen can capture any other Queen.

As they stand, problem spaces are incomplete as a task framework. They specify that search occurs in a space, but they leave open almost everything else—how to specify operators, how to specify the heuristics that guide search, how to specify detection of the desired state. In our work on Soar we combined problem spaces with a significant number of organizing principles in order to fashion a complete framework (production systems, preference-based decision making, universal subgoaling, and chunking to name the main ones). However, our continuing experience with Soar has moved us more and more toward treating the problem space as a self-contained level. In particular, it seems that users should view Soar as consisting entirely of problem spaces, whatever that might mean. The gradual emergence of a problem-space level as a way of describing Soar can be traced through our recent history (e.g., by comparing succeeding versions of its manuals).

To anyone grounded in computer science, this indicates that the problem space should be cast as a complete level, i.e., as a self-contained computational model. Doing so is not entirely straightforward, because of all the unspecified aspects mentioned above. The present chapter is our attempt at a complete formulation. This attempt will occupy the entire chapter, leaving little room to analyze and elaborate the formulation or to discuss its ramifications.

In Section 11.2 we lay out the general scheme of analysis in terms of computational models, and provide an overview of how we will proceed. Section 11.3 describes the *knowledge-level computational model* (KLCM), the first of the computational models we will need. Section 11.4, the main one, describes the *problem space computational model* (PSCM) in a sequence of three stages: defining the problem space, implementing the KLCM by means of problem spaces, and generating multiple problem spaces. Section 11.5 provides a brief discussion.

## 11.2  Computational Models and the Overall Scheme

To describe problem spaces we use the notion of *computational model*, which is just an articulation of the foundation paradigm stated at the beginning. A *computational model* is a description of a class of systems in terms of a set of operations on entities that can be interpreted in computational terms, to wit, that have a computational semantics. A computational model permits the description of particular systems. The description can be *complete* in that the system's structure, its behavior, and how the behavior is determined by its structure, can all be described without appeal to any constructs outside the computational model.

Such a framework is implicit in any discussion of computation, but becomes explicit when multiple models are under consideration. This occurs in

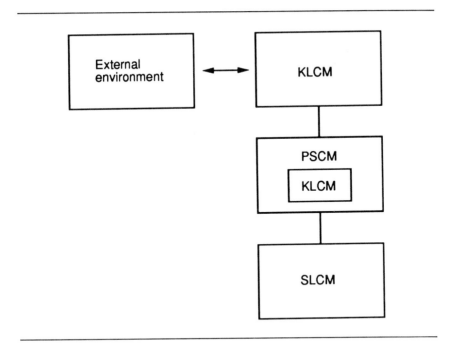

**EXHIBIT 11.3**
Computational models involved in defining problem spaces.

many places in computer science. One computational model is often specified or implemented within another, for example, the hierarchy of system levels that governs the way we construct computers, and also the programming-language systems that tower unendingly upward. As these examples illustrate, the bottom of a hierarchy can be a system without a computational interpretation—indeed, it must be if the hierarchy grounds the systems in the world of physics. Although completeness is of the essence, system levels are often realized only approximately. In programming systems, especially, higher levels often leave much to be described by the lower level, as in packages of subroutines. Computational models are also a standard device in the study of algorithms, where they provide the bases within which algorithms can be described and their computational costs assessed [1]. Turing machines and random-access machines are familiar computational models for these purposes. Computational models play a strong role in parallel computer systems, where simplified computational models of parallel computation are adopted for programming purposes, which are realized in an underlying, more complex hardware architecture. The LINDA computational model is a typical example [3].

Exhibit 11.3 shows the computational models needed to provide a formulation of problem spaces. At the top we define the KLCM. This will provide a model for a system capable of goal-oriented rational behavior, i.e., capable of intelligent action in interaction with an external environment. A knowledge-level (KL) system is implemented by a PSCM system, i.e., by a system described in the problem-space computational model. The PSCM describes a class of symbolic processing systems. However, it remains abstract in essential ways. Hence, a PSCM system must still be implemented in a symbol-level computational model (SLCM) of the standard kind, with memory, representations, and operations. Though the PSCM is defined as an autonomous level (as with any computational model), it is shaped by both the functional constraints of being suitable to realize KL systems to a useful approximation and the structural constraint of being physically realizable in a standard SLCM.

The abstract character of the PSCM shows up in some of its components being defined as KL systems. That is, certain aspects of a PSCM will not be defined by specific symbolic mechanisms and structures, but only by the knowledge they make available. This knowledge, of course, is not knowledge about the external task environment, which is the knowledge in the top KL system; rather, it is about the problem space. Nevertheless, the result is that the KLCM shows up in our analysis in two ways and plays two distinct roles.

## 11.3   The Knowledge-Level Computational Model (KLCM)

The notion of a KL system is already familiar in AI and expert systems [5,12,22, 29] and a closely corresponding notion of intentional systems is familiar in philosophy [4]. We use the simplest version sufficient for our purposes, which has a single goal, discrete errorless actions and perceptions, and a deterministic discrete environment.

Exhibit 11.4 records the essential definition. A *knowledge-level system* is defined as an *agent* behaving in an *environment (E)*. The agent is defined as a set of *actions (A)*, a set of *perceptual devices (P)*, a *goal (G)*, and a *body of knowledge (K)*. The environment is in one of a set of states at each instant of time, and the state changes with time. The agent interacts with the environment at various times by taking actions, which affect what next environment state occurs, and by using its perceptual devices, which acquire knowledge about the environment (adding to K). The state of the environment, the state of the agent, and the interactions determine the joint behavior over time of the environment and the agent. The goal is a preference function on behavior, i.e., the agent prefers some joint behaviors to others. The agent's knowledge is about the environment, the agent, and their joint behavior. The agent's behavior is determined by the *principle of rationality* that if the agent knows that one of its actions leads to a preferred situation according to its goal, than it will *intend* the preferred action, which will then occur if it is possible. In the application of this principle, the entire body of knowledge is brought to bear on determining the action. Knowledge once acquired continues to be available forever, the *principle of permanence*. The source of new knowledge is perception.[3] Thus, knowledge in the system grows with each perception and increases monotonically throughout the life of the system. The KLCM defines a class of systems, each situated in a specific environment and with specific actions, perceptual devices, goal, and initial knowledge.

This is a model of goal-directed behavior, because all actions intend to attain the goal of the agent. It is a model of rational behavior, because everything the agent knows serves the agent's interest. This is a narrow concept of rationality. It takes the goal of the agent as given, so there is no issue of whether the agent's goal is rational or not, in terms of any larger considerations (e.g., the agent's survival). What determines the agent's behavior is the agent's knowledge of its goal, rather than the objectively defined preference function. Thus, the only thing that distinguishes the agent's own goal from other things the system knows about is that the principle of rationality operates in terms of the agent's goal.

Actions must be intended rather than just taken. The agent's knowledge need not necessarily include whether an action is possible. Thus, the principle of rationality can determine an action to be taken that cannot in fact occur. In our simple model, where an action cannot produce an errorful result, this implies that no action on the environment then occurs. However, knowledge may be acquired about the situation that leads to different actions being determined subsequently.

Knowledge can be taken to be an abstract set of states with the properties necessary to fulfill the principles of rationality and permanence for the range of environments and goals that characterize the agent. At any moment, the agent's body of knowledge is one of these states and each act of perception changes the state of knowledge. To be in a given state of knowledge (including knowledge of the goal) is to determine the set of actions that move toward maximally preferred behaviors. Knowledge has certain general properties that hold whatever the content domain involved and there have been attempts to formally axiomatize it [9,10,12]. Two properties are needed here. First, knowledge is *about* something. Each knowledge state has associated with it a set of entities to which the content of the knowledge refers (often called its *ontology*). KL systems are often restricted to be about some specific set of entities, and hence have nothing

---

[3] Perception is taken to be equivalent to acquisition. Elaboration of the definition is required to accommodate that only a fraction of what is perceived generally becomes part of the long-term body of knowledge.

E:   An external environment
     Exists in some state at each time t
     The agent is an object in the environment

**The agent**

A:   A set of actions
     Can be evoked at time t
     May or may not be applicable, depending on state of E
     Affect state of E at next time t+1

P:   A set of perceptual devices
     Adds knowledge of E to K at time t
     This is the only source of new knowledge

G:   A goal

K:   A body of knowledge
     About the environment, goal, actions, perceptual devices

Principles of operation

Rationality: Take actions that know lead to attaining goal
      Take $A_t$ such that $K_t$ and $K(G)$ imply will-attain($A_t$, G)

Permanence: Knowledge once acquired is available ever after
      $P_t{:}K_t \rightarrow K_{t+1}$, where $K_{t+1}$ includes $K_t$

**EXHIBIT 11.4**
The definition of a knowledge-level (KL) system.

to say about any of the other things in the universe. Second, there is relation of *inclusion* on knowledge states. One state of knowledge can include another. So, when knowledge is added by perception, thus leading to a new knowledge state, the knowledge of the previous state is still available, because the new state includes the old.

At any specific moment, either no action, a unique action, or a set of actions may be intended. Intending no action or a unique action uniquely determines the behavior of the agent. However, intending a set of actions is indeterminate.

This can occur from multiple causes, e.g., knowledge can be incomplete so that the agent does not know which of several actions leads toward the goal; or any action of the set suffices so the agent does not need to resolve the indeterminacy. In any event, it is sufficient for our purposes to leave unresolved the possibility of indeterminism.

The KLCM specifies an agent without commitment to specific internal mechanisms. It is a description entirely in terms of the external environmental situation. True, both the agent's goals and knowledge are internal to the agent. However, both constructs are expressed entirely in terms of the external situation, so do not require positing structures and mechanisms internal to the agent. Despite this lack of internal mechanisms, the description of a KL system can be complete, so that behavior is completely determined by the internal state of the system, namely by its goals and knowledge, in conjunction with the state of the environment.

KL systems are useful for two distinct but equally important purposes. The first purpose is to describe systems capable of intelligent action. A sufficiently intelligent system must appear to the external world as a KL system. The more effectively a system realizes its goals, the more its behavior conforms entirely to the actual relations of means to ends in the external environment, and the less its behavior reflects any inner mechanisms or structure. To state the matter negatively, if some inner structural characteristic of a system determines some aspect of its external actions (so the action gives evidence that the system has the given internal characteristic), the system will fail to attain its goals when the environment demands a different characteristic. This is the basic argument through adaptation [32] and it applies to all adaptive agents, animal, human, or machine. It is what justifies taking a perfect KL agent as the appropriate model of an intelligent system—intelligence has done all it can do if it perfectly relates means to ends, subject to the knowledge available.

By way of example, Exhibit 11.5 shows a simple situation involving an intelligent system whose internal mechanisms we hardly know, namely a human. By viewing the human as a KL system, positing some knowledge and a goal, the human's behavior can be predicted. We have no idea how Louie has represented his knowledge that St. Louis is a city, the routes to get there, and what one does to travel those routes, nor how he processes these representations to actually call up an airline, get a ticket, call a taxi, go to the counter, or whatever. But it is a good prediction that Louie will indeed get there, if we have agreement from him to meet us (hence having evidence of his goals). There is no issue of design here, just prediction of a goal-oriented system's behavior.

The second useful purpose of KL systems is for design of computational systems. In design, systems are specified prior to determining the structures and mechanisms that meet their specifications. A KL description goes beyond specifying the inputs and outputs to provide necessary and sufficient conditions on what must be available internally, without committing to mechanism. In fact,

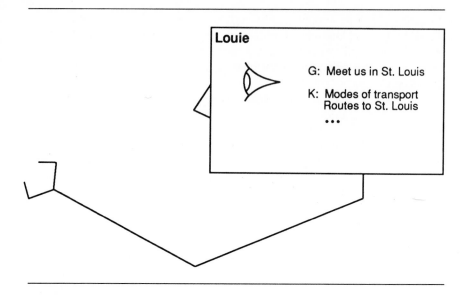

**EXHIBIT 11.5**
Example KL system: an intelligent system.

the knowledge level of description provides the maximal specification that can be given without making commitments to internal structure.

By way of example, Exhibit 11.6 shows a simple design specification for a data base application, in a form that is familiar to everyone in computer science. In particular, the various components are specified at disparate levels of detail. K is specified in general terms, leaving it to the programmer to choose how to structure the data base, given that the relevant database concepts are understood. P is specified in greater detail, partly as a convenient way to clarify the demands on K and A. Here, the behavior is taken for granted, and the primary issue is design of a system.

The same feature of KL systems underlies both uses, namely, the ability to work from a description given entirely in external terms. In the case of prediction, an internal system exists, but nothing is known about it. In the case of design, nothing internal exists to be described.

In the definition of problem spaces, KL systems will appear in both roles. The KL system at the top of Exhibit 11.3 is intended to be an intelligent system. Therefore, it is appropriately modeled as a KL system. On the other hand, the KL systems that are part of the PSCM are intended to perform specific functions, but to be specified in as general a manner as possible. Therefore they are also appropriately modeled as KL systems.

E:   Personal computer

G:   Prompt for a query, then respond to it

K:   A database relating townships, electoral districts, zip codes
     The ability to retrieve on each key

P:   Strings that represent queries
     Format:   "I ; Q"
          Where I is an index, of the form:
               "D = d"  or  "T = t"  or  "Z = z"
               Where:
                    d  is a district number
                    t  is a township
                    z  is a zip code
          and Q is a query, of the form:
               "D = ?"  or  "T = ?"  or  "Z = ?"
     Examples:
          Q1:  "D = d; Z = ?"
               (Given district number, what are all zip codes in it?)
          Q2:  "Z = z; D = ?"
               (Given zip code, what districts is it in?)

A:   Responses sent to the printer
     Examples (corresponding to above):
          R1:  List of zip codes
          R2:  List of districts

**EXHIBIT 11.6**
Example KL system: a design specification.

    That KL systems are an appropriate model for both rational behavior and design specification has important consequences. The enterprise of automating task formulation is driven by a mixture of motives. On the one hand, we want to be able to construct computer systems that formulate their own tasks. Not only do we want this for its own sake, in order to understand the nature of intellectual activity, but from an applications point of view we want to create devices that can face problematic situations without us around and still succeed. On the other hand, we still want to create systems where we can specify as much of the behavior as we care to and let the rest of the formulation happen within the system we are designing. The two faces of KL systems, toward rational behavior and toward design specification, match well these two different motivations for computational systems.

## 11.4    The Problem Space Computational Model (PSCM)

An agent described at the knowledge level must be realized by a system that has representations of the agent's body of knowledge, and processes that represent new knowledge from perception and determine the actions according to the principle of rationality. In short, KL systems are realized by symbol-level systems. For a sufficiently large and diverse body of knowledge and a sufficiently wide range of goals, no physically realizable system (whether a symbol-level system or any other) can do this in bounded time. This is simply another way of reading the results on undecidability for universal computing systems. Symbol-level systems can, of course, approximate such realizability. This is where the adoption of a framework comes in (see Exhibit 11.2). For us it means problem spaces.

### 11.4.1    Problem Spaces

The conceptual unit of the PSCM is the *problem space*, whose definition is given in Exhibit 11.7. A problem space consists of a space of *states (S)* and a set of *operators (O)*. Each operator is an effective procedure for a function from a subset of states to states. Thus, for each state there is a set of *applicable* operators, each of which, when applied to the state, produces a new state. Overall, the application of operators to states remains within the space.

A problem-space system generates *behavior* in a problem space, consisting of an indefinite sequence of *steps*, each a state-operator pair, $(s_i, o_i)$, where i indexes the sequence. At each step, the system is at some *current state* $s_i$. It first selects a *current operator* $o_i$ and then applies the operator to the current state $s_i$. If it succeeds (the operator is applicable to $s_i$), the current state for the next pair in the sequence (i+1) is the result, $s_{i+1} = o_i(s_i)$. If it fails (the operator is not applicable to $s_i$), then the system remains at state $s_i$, attempting to select an operator.

A problem space is a framework within which to attempt many tasks. A task is *formulated* in a problem space as starting at an *initial current state ($s_0$)* to produce a *desired state* in a specified set D, by the successive application of operators to the current state. The task is accomplished if, at some step, the current state is a desired state. Any applicable operator of the space can be used at any step to produce the next current state. Thus the requirement for task accomplishment is that a connected *path* of states and operators exist from the

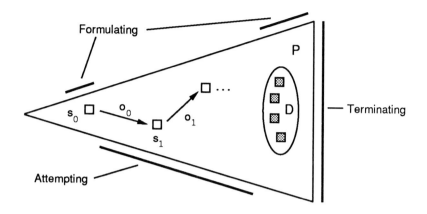

A problem space P is **defined** by:

S   A set of states

O   A set of operators on S
Each o in O is applicable to a subset $S_o$ of S
Each o realizes a function: $o:S_o \rightarrow S$
Applying o to a state in $S_o$ produces a new state in S

**Behavior** occurs in problem space P by consecutive steps:
The step at i starts with the system at current state $s_i$

Each step has two phases:
**Selecting:** The current operator $o_i$ is selected from O
**Applying:**  The operator $o_i$ is applied to $s_i$
If $o_i$ is applicable, the current state at i+1 is $o_i(s_i)$
If $o_i$ is not applicable, still remain at $s_i$

A task is **formulated** using a problem space by:
**Determining-space:** A problem space P is adopted
**Goal-setting:** A set of desired states D is adopted
**Initializing:** The state $s_0$ becomes the current state

A formulated task is **accomplished** by:
**Attempting:** Steps are taken in the space
**Independence principle:**  Any operator that can be applied,
may be applied
**Terminating:** The task attempt is terminated
If the current state $s_i$ is in D
If $s_i$ cannot be brought to be in D

**EXHIBIT 11.7**
Definition of a problem space.

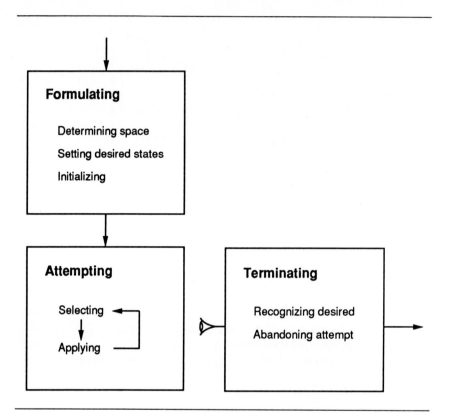

**EXHIBIT 11.8**
Problem space processes.

initial state to a desired state—and that the system traverse such a path, where it has access at any moment only to a single state (the current one). A given problem space can only be used for tasks that can be formulated in its terms; but given a task a problem space can be fashioned in whose terms the given task can be formulated.

For a problem-space system actually to behave, the states and operators must be represented and a set of processes adequate to imply Exhibit 11.7 must be carried out effectively. Exhibit 11.8 shows these processes in a simple flow diagram. The processes of formulating the task come first: determining the problem space, and then the desired states and the initial state. Then the processes of attempting the task occur: an unending loop of selecting the next operator, and applying it. Finally, there must be processes of terminating the task attempt: detecting the current state to be a desired state or terminating the attempt without accomplishing the task.

Terminating processes proceed concurrently with attempting processes and take the running results of the attempt as their input. Thus the process of determining if $s_i$ is in D must occur concurrently with select-operator for $s_i$. D itself is not given explicitly as part of the state, but is incorporated in the terminating process. This process can be said to *recognize* that $s_i$ is in D, in the sense of being an immediate action. Such a recognition must always exist. One could imagine an expensive test to determine if a state was in D. This could be embodied in an operator $o_D$ and applied to every state produced by any other operator. Thus, even states (say) would be the result of a task operator and odd states would contain an additional mark *yes* or *no*, which would be the result of $o_D$. It would still be necessary to recognize whether *yes* or *no* occurred on the state to convert this symbolized knowledge into the action to stop the attempt. Thus, the real set of desired states would be the set of all states marked *yes*.

The activities of Exhibit 11.8 may be encapsulated into four component processes by putting together those that use common knowledge and separating those with data dependencies: *formulate-task*, *select-operator*, *apply-operator*, and *terminate-task*. These processes require further specification. We will do this by making each a KL system (these are the KL systems internal to the PSCM in Exhibit 11.3). Exhibit 11.9 sets out for each its goal, actions, perceptions, and knowledge. The environment of these components is the internal computational environment of an agent, not the external environment of Exhibit 11.3. It is not specified yet, because we are just defining the problem space itself, but we can call it the *current context*. The impulse to formulate a task can be taken to have just arisen in this current context. But this impulse situation and all other aspects of the current context are not in terms of the problem space or its parts, since no problem space has yet come into existence.

The goal of formulate-task is to determine the problem space P, the set of desired states D, and the initial state $s_0$. Formulate-task is to be evoked at the point when a task is to be formulated, before any formulation has occurred. This contrasts with what might seem more natural, namely, to take the problem space as given. This would take the problem space as an input to formulate-task. However, all aspects of a task formulation—the problem space, desired set, and initial state—call on the same body of knowledge and are interrelated. Formulate-task has knowledge about the current context and perceptual access to it. In particular, it perceives the situation that gave rise to its evocation and it has knowledge about possible problem spaces that might be useful.

The goal of select-operator is to produce the operator to be applied to the current state that will lead to successful performance of the task. It operates in the context of each current state as it occurs. Select-operator generates the control knowledge for moving through the problem space. It has knowledge about the problem space (the states and operators), the task, and the relation

| | |
|---|---|
| Environment | The inner computational context of an agent. |
| **Formulate-task** | |
| Goal | To formulate a task by using a problem space |
| Actions | Produce P (the problem space), D, and $s_0$ |
| Perceptions | Of the current context and the impulse situation |
| Knowledge | About problem spaces and the current context |
| **Select-operator** | |
| Goal | To select $o_i$ to reach a state in D |
| Actions | Produce $o_i$ |
| Perceptions | Of $s_i$ |
| Knowledge | About P, $s_0$, and D |
| **Apply-operator** | |
| Goal | To apply $o_i$ to $s_i$ |
| Actions | Produce $o_i(s_i)$ |
| Perceptions | Of $o_i$ and $s_i$ |
| Knowledge | About the conditions of applicability of $o_i$ and the function $o{:}S \rightarrow S$ |
| **Terminate-task** | |
| Goal | To stop attempt if $s_i$ in D or if cannot succeed |
| Actions | Stop processing |
| Perceptions | Of P, D, $o_i$, and $o_i(s_i)$ for the current i |
| Knowledge | About the current context |

**EXHIBIT 11.9**
Knowledge-level specification of problem-space components.

between the two—exactly what it knows determines how effective it can be in selecting operators, hence how intelligent the processing can be.

The goal of apply-operator is to produce the next state by applying the operator. Operators are context-limited effective procedures, so that nothing besides the state and operator needs to be known to produce the result. Determining whether the operator is applicable is part of apply-operator and requires only the same knowledge.

The goal of terminate-task is to stop work in the problem space. It should stop the attempt as soon as the task is accomplished, i.e., on the first occasion when $s_i$ is a member of D. Success cannot be assured, of course, so terminate-task must also stop for other reasons as well. Terminate-task might come to know that the task cannot be accomplished, but there are indefinitely diverse other reasons, for instance, that time or some other resource has run out. These depend on aspects of the current context.

The reason for defining the component processes as KL systems is to characterize them as generally as possible, without regard to what processing must occur within them to accomplish their functions. Even with such an abstraction, these processes are limited by the knowledge they have available, especially the entities they can know about, and by their being goal-oriented.

Exhibit 11.10 provides a simple example of a problem-space system and its behavior. The system is a subset of a simple job-shop scheduler [18]. The task is to schedule a series of machining operations on a collection of objects. The customer supplies the objects and their desired characteristics, and also a time constraint in the form of a bound on how long the system has to satisfy the order.

From a description of the objects, formulate-task produces an initial state that contains the objects to be processed and their initial characteristics. Characteristics include shape, surface condition, and number of holes. The operators correspond to a particular machine operating on a particular object at a particular time. Interactions between operator preconditions and effects constrain the order in which operators can be executed. Select-operator has some knowledge of these constraints, and tries to select an operator that will prove to fit into a final schedule. Apply-operator also has knowledge of operator effects, which it uses to change the state when an operator has been selected. In particular, apply-operator updates the developing schedule with a new triple that ties an object to a time slot and a machine, and updates the characteristics of the object affected by the machine.

The behavior of the system is depicted at the bottom of the exhibit. Operator selection knowledge guides the system to apply the lathe to object B and the punch to object A, both during time slot 1. By scheduling early time slots first, the system attempts to maximize concurrency. After polishing B to bring it to its final state, the system tries to roll A, but because this heats the object the polisher cannot be used. The system backtracks from this failure by returning to the previous state. Backtracking is enabled by a history of states maintained by the system. From the previous state, the system first lathes and then polishes A. Terminate-task recognizes that this is a desired state, and the task halts with success.

A problem-space system is a partially specified symbol system. It is a symbol system because it describes the processing that is required to accomplish a task and because what it processes are representations. But it is only partially specified. The component processes are only determined up to KL systems. This

## System Specification

Name:            Job-shop-scheduler
State:
    Time slots:   1, 2, 3
    Objects:     A, B
    Schedule:    { (object$_i$, machine$_i$, timeslot$_i$) }
$s_0$:
    A: rough, triangular, no holes
    B: spherical, no holes, surface undetermined
D:
    A: cylindrical, polished, size 2 hole
    B: cylindrical, polished, no holes

Operators:
    Lathe (what when)
        Preconditions:        none
        Effects:              cylindrical, rough
    Punch (what when size)
        Preconditions:        unheated or rectangular
        Effects:              rough, hole
    Polish (what when)
        Preconditions:        unheated or rectangular
        Effects:              smooth
    Roll (what when)
        Preconditions:        none
        Effects:              cylindrical, hot, surface undetermined

Operator selection:
    Rule out all unhelpful operators
        Those that do not achieve a desired characteristic
    Punch before rolling
        Rolling heats the object so it cannot be punched
    Punch or lathe before polishing
        Punch and lathe leave an object rough
    Try earlier time slots first
    Choose randomly among undifferentiated candidates

## Behavior on the task

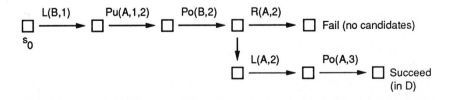

**EXHIBIT 11.10**
Example of a problem-space system.

suffices as far as determining the system's behavior is concerned, providing that an external notation exists in which to express the knowledge, for then the behavior can be derived. But the problem space must also be realized computationally. If only a small body of knowledge is involved this might be a detail, for any number of mechanisms could be used to realize the component KL systems. But problem spaces are intended to be used with arbitrarily large and rich bodies of knowledge. Then constructing the KL systems for the component becomes problematical.

There are two additional minor ways in which a problem-space system is only partially specified. One is the representation of the states and the operators that apply to them. The other is the operating structure of the current context, which permits the four components to execute, produce actions, and communicate with each other. These are left to be specified in the symbol-level computational model that supports the problem space. Any way of realizing these that meets the functional specification of a problem space with its four components will suffice. No critical implementation issues are hidden within these two aspects.

### 11.4.2   Implementation of a Knowledge-Level System

For those familiar with problem spaces for the last 30 years, the treatment to this point may seem a bit labored. We now enter upon new ground. The problem space has been described as an autonomous system level, without reference to adjacent levels (once a task is formulated in it). However, problem spaces are intended to implement KL systems.

Exhibit 11.11 shows how this occurs. The exhibit depicts a simple agent described as a KL system implemented by a problem space. The top panel depicts the agent's knowledge and goal embodied in the knowledge of the four components of the problem space: formulate-task (Ft), select-operator (So), apply-operator (Ao), and terminate-task (Tt). The middle panel depicts the operation of the agent's perception and action. The bottom panel indicates which parts of the problem space realize the various parts of the KL system. The situation is a simple reactive arc from perception through the KL system to action. This bypasses many issues of dynamic interaction with a concurrently dynamic and reactive environment, but it will suffice for this chapter.

The key to the implementation is the middle panel. KL perceptions are realized partly by formulate-task, which creates an initial state that corresponds to relevant aspects of the external environment, and partly by apply-operator, which generates the changes due to a KL-action operator. KL actions are realized by operators in the problem space. When an operator is applied, the corresponding

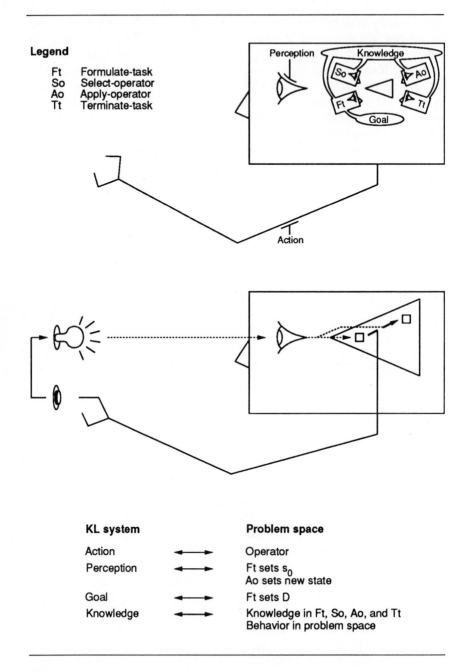

**Legend**

Ft    Formulate-task
So    Select-operator
Ao    Apply-operator
Tt    Terminate-task

| KL system | | Problem space |
|---|---|---|
| Action | ⟷ | Operator |
| Perception | ⟷ | Ft sets $s_0$<br>Ao sets new state |
| Goal | ⟷ | Ft sets D |
| Knowledge | ⟷ | Knowledge in Ft, So, Ao, and Tt<br>Behavior in problem space |

**EXHIBIT 11.11**
The problem-space implementation of a KL system.

external action occurs.[4] The new state produced by apply-operator in the problem space is the result of doing the KL action in the environment. Perception reflects those changes in the new state.

The agent's knowledge is embodied in the knowledge of the four problem space components. However, this latter knowledge is about the problem space, states, and operators; hence it cannot of itself be the knowledge of the agent, which is about the goal, actions, and environment. It becomes the agent's knowledge by means of the relationships just described. That is, states are about the external world because of KL perception; operators are about the external world because of KL actions; the desired states are about the goal of the KL agent because of formulate-task; and the means-ends knowledge of select-operator is about performing tasks in the environment because it links environment-referring operators on environment-referring states to descriptions of environment-referring desired states.

Behavior of the KL agent happens as follows. We imagine a changing environment, which is mostly irrelevant to the agent but which from time to time creates a situation relevant to the agent's goal. This external situation is perceived by formulate-task defining a set of states in this space to be desired states, expressing the agent's goal. Formulate-task also encodes the current external situation as an initial current state in the space. Select-operator proposes an operator to change this state. It knows something about the current state and the desired states and uses this knowledge to select an appropriate operator, which apply-operator then executes by the corresponding action, which affects the environment, which is then perceived, which then produces a new state, which becomes the current state. (If the action could not take place in the external world, then the operator was not applicable.) If the new state is a desired state, then both the agent's goal in the external environment and the task in the problem space have been accomplished and terminate-task lapses the agent back into inactivity. If the situation does not attain the goal and the current state is not desired, then another step is taken. This continues until the internal task and external goal are accomplished, or until terminate-task abandons the agent's attempt to attain its goal. After all, there is nothing in the nature of things to assure success. The agent remains quiescent until the environment again presents a situation in which the agent's goal is perceived as not satisfied. Thus, behavior in the problem space realizes the principle of rationality to the extent that the tasks formulated in it are accomplished.

This is a simplistic scenario. It even has some glitches. For instance, it assumes (unrealistically) that the environment changes autonomously until it provokes the agent, but then ceases autonomous change while the agent acts

---

[4] As discussed above, the action is actually only intended; whether it occurs depends on the state of the external world, which includes the state of the agent as object in that world.

upon it, even through multiple actions. However, the glitches are not worth fixing at this point. Our aim has been solely to show how a problem-space system implements or realizes a KL system. Putting the glitches to one side, what we get is a reactive agent that operates directly coupled to its environment, something like a Brooks critter [2].

### 11.4.3  Lack of Knowledge and Multiple Problem Spaces

The KL agent of Exhibit 11.11 is to be a rational goal-oriented agent. Implicit in this is the requirement for unlimited scope for the agent's knowledge and goal—problem spaces are to be a general implementation of KL agents. Though an unlimited KL agent cannot be perfectly realized, problem spaces are to be the symbol-level processing scheme to approximate pure knowledge-based behavior indefinitely closely.

Against this aspiration, the scheme of Exhibit 11.11 appears totally inadequate, well beyond any glitches. Suppose we take the system to be a reactive agent, analogous to a Brooks critter. Then the problem-space components (formulate-task, select-operator, apply-operator, terminate-task) are primitive processes that embody some fixed, limited knowledge of the environment. But we know that only extremely simple behavior can be so realized. Suppose, instead, we take the problem space in Exhibit 11.11 to be the arena to deal with really difficult tasks of goal attainment. Then we see that our example doesn't even permit any internal processing within the problem space to create and verify plans. Every internal operator executes as an external operator. What has happened to the problem space as a means for doing problem solving?

We can extend Exhibit 11.11 to take care of this latter difficulty. We add operators to the space whose application produces only an internal state. This provides for internal heuristic search before executing an external action. With a mechanism for saving states, this extends to planning and even the mixing of planning and execution. Some elaboration is required to provide for inner/outer correspondences, i.e., pairs of operators that produce the same internal change of state, but only one of which intends a KL action; and states that describe the same external situation, but with various modalities such as perceived, expected, imagined, or desired. Such elaboration, if done correctly, removes the glitches, permitting the external situation to change continuously and the state to be modified continuously by perception.

All the above, while essential and not entirely without interest, does not touch the essential difficulty—the component problem-space processes are themselves described only at the knowledge level. They remain without realization in terms of symbol-level mechanisms. It is not that *no* reduction has occurred in going from the KL agent to the problem space that realizes it, only that the reduction is small. Only if the components are simple enough to be realized by fixed mechanisms can the scheme of Exhibit 11.11 be taken to be operational. In terms of KL systems, we might describe this as the components having their knowledge *immediately available*. That is, if the components have knowledge immediately available, the system of Exhibit 11.11 is operational. We have not yet explored what is implied by knowledge being immediately available. Nevertheless, we can see that in some definite, if small, set of circumstances, reduction to symbol-level mechanisms can occur.

Now is the time to yield to the impulse to recurse. Let us be in a problem space with its four components: formulate-task, select-operator, apply-operator, and terminate-task. Let there be some symbol-level scheme that permits their implementation if the knowledge they contain is immediately available. Suppose, on the contrary, for some component, C, knowledge is not available. In this circumstance, let C's behavior be realized by means of a problem-space system, $P_C$. If appropriate knowledge becomes available, C will attain its goal, and behavior in the original problem space proceeds. $P_C$ has its own four components, each characterized as a KL system. The knowledge may be available for these components. But if not—if some knowledge is not available—then the lacking component is implemented by yet another problem-space system.

We have recursed. The recursion bottoms out when the knowledge required by a component of a problem-space system is immediately available. This aspect is the primitive mechanism, and remains undefined. For the moment, however, we should contemplate what has been attained. We now have a *multiple problem-space system*. This brings us a long ways toward having an adequate definition of a PSCM. Exhibit 11.12 gives its specifications. Not surprisingly, problem spaces are related as means to ends. However, the relationship between problem spaces is the general one of *lack of knowledge*. Whenever in a problem space there is a lack of knowledge, then another problem space is created that obtains that knowledge.[5] The generality of this relationship should be noted. For computer science, the natural relationship on which to establish a multiple problem-space system is operator implementation, i.e., procedure hierarchy. Not only does the present scheme encompass the additional functions of formulating tasks, selecting operators, and terminating tasks, but the means-ends linkage is defined by whatever lack of knowledge has occurred.

We now have a symbol-level process that operates to approximate a given KL system. Whenever knowledge is missing the system operates so as to acquire it. It ceases to set up processes to acquire more knowledge when its available knowledge suffices. It almost seems too good to be true—as if we really have gotten something for nothing, because we seem to have avoided forcing the system into definite representations and processes that would compromise the

---

[5]This includes conflicting knowledge, since the fundamental way of dealing with contradictions is by adding knowledge, e.g., explanations, determinations of what knowledge is in error, etc.

**A multiple problem-space system** consists of:

A KL system (EKL) situated in an external environment

A set of problem spaces PS: $\{P_\alpha\}$

Each component of $P_\alpha$ is a KL system

A top problem space (TPS) that implements EKL

Each $P_\alpha$ (except TPS) supports another space $P_\beta$ in PS

$P_\alpha$ implements a component of $P_\beta$

Components (hence their spaces) may have many supporting $P_\alpha$

The $P_\alpha$ that have no support are the primitive spaces of PS

The components of a primitive $P_\alpha$ have available knowledge

**EXHIBIT 11.12**
Multiple problem space system.

generality. Nevertheless, it certainly is the right shape for a symbol-level system that is supposed to implement a KL system, hence a rational goal-oriented agent.

Such systems are a little unwieldy to be laid out in full detail within the confines of a chapter. Nevertheless, Exhibit 11.13 shows a system, Browser-Soar [11], which operates through many different problem spaces (the triangles). The small circled numbers are the order in which the system generated the spaces. The task is one of using a browser[6] on an interactive computer system called cT. Browser-Soar is simulating a human using the browser at the workstation display, the whole being about a minute's worth of human behavior, although that is not relevant here. Almost all the relations among spaces in the exhibit are due to apply-operator. That is, the results of operators in the space are not immediately known, with the consequent need to go into a subproblem-space to implement the operator. However, in the upper part of the figure there is an operator that is proposed independent of what space the system is in, which acts as an interrupt from perceived information from the display; and in the lower right corner select-operator was unable to select any operator at all, so another problem space (back-up) had to be entered to change the situation to where an operator could be selected.

---

[6]A browser is an interactive tool that lets a user move from place to place in a data base by displaying a continuously changing accessing structure. Hypermedia are a type of browser.

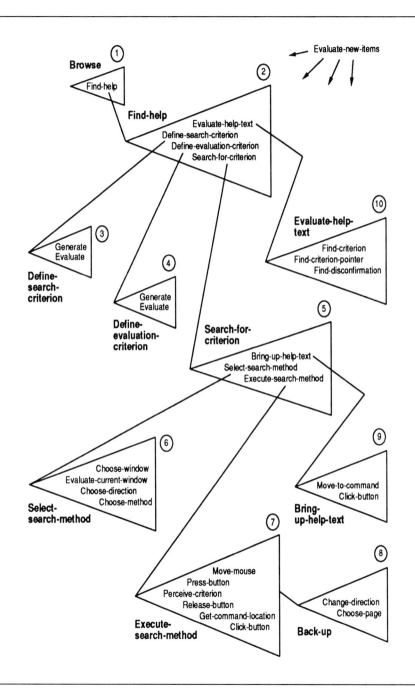

**EXHIBIT 11.13**
Problem-space trace of Browser-Soar.

Several aspects remain to be pinned down before the PSCM is defined. The first is available knowledge, which serves to ground the recursion of problem spaces. For the knowledge in a component to be available means both that a representation of the knowledge exists that determines the actions, given the goal of that component and the principle of rationality, and that the component will actually behave in accordance with it within some definite time. Although the symbol mechanisms that produce the behavior are not specified, they must operate as a primitive, finite mechanism—there can be no possibility of internal exponential problem-solving or of failing to reach a definite termination. Thus, if the knowledge of a component is available, the component will perform its function in some finite time, otherwise it will indicate that the knowledge is not available. Each component could have its own internal mechanisms, so each could have its own distinct time bound. However, we will assume there is a uniform *time constant* for the system, within which the bounds of all individual components fit. The available knowledge itself need not be adequate in terms of the goals of the system as a whole. Nothing guarantees that a system must be able to actually meet its goals, only that the system's capability to attain its goals can be expressed as knowledge about its goals, environment, and actions, so that limitations in the system's capability show up as limitations in knowledge, not as limitations in whether available knowledge can be brought to bear.

The second aspect demanding attention consists of some details of operation. Exhibit 11.14 shows a set of problem spaces as generated by a problem-space system. This is a dynamic trace, starting with the top problem space (TPS) and proceeding to P1, then P2, and finally to P5. Around each problem space (the triangles) cluster its four components. Most components have knowledge immediately available and respond immediately. Some, such as the apply-operator of TPS, require a problem space in order to perform (the double arrow). Expansion to a subproblem space occurs for formulate-task (at P5), select-operator (at P1), and apply-operator (at TPS, P1, and P3). However, no such expansion is possible for terminate-task, which operates as a concurrently acting recognizer, hence is never required to produce a result. Only part of the structure in Exhibit 11.14 exists at any one time. The trace of the active spaces is given at the right of the exhibit; it is a typical stack discipline.

The trace assumes that all components succeed, although they may require the support of processing in subspaces. Failure is also possible, since not all tasks can be accomplished. Failure is determined by terminate-task, which can stop an attempt in a problem space before the desired state is reached. This can cause the component being supported by the given problem space to fail (though it need not, because formulate-task could formulate another task using a different space). If a formulate-task fails then the component it supports fails. If a select-operator fails, then there is nothing more to do in the space and terminate-task stops the attempt (with failure, since the current state will not

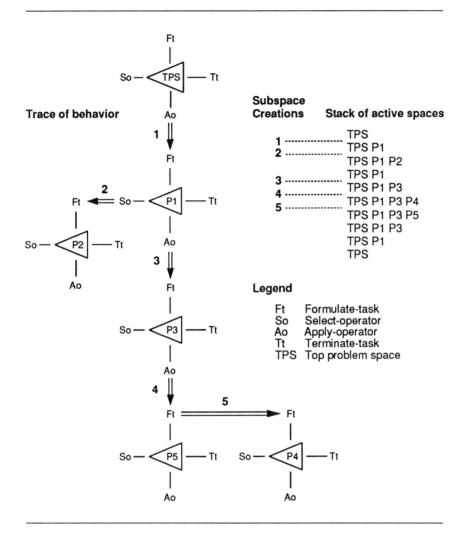

**EXHIBIT 11.14**
Details of PSCM operation.

be in D). If an apply-operator fails, this simply leaves the system at its current state, attempting to select an operator to apply.

The third aspect requiring attention is the possibility of unending operation. This occurs in two forms. One is infinite descent in the recursion of problem spaces because no knowledge is ever immediately available. The other is infinite search through a problem space because terminate-task never stops the proceedings, even though the task can never be accomplished. These infinities are to be avoided by the components having specific immediate knowledge, not by anything built into the PSCM structure. General default knowledge can avoid most of them. For example, let formulate-task know to fail if the component for which it is formulating a task is formulate-task and if it itself doesn't even know a problem space in which to cast this task. Then nothing is to be served by recursing further. This will avoid all infinite descent except loops.[7] For another example, let terminate-task have an upper bound on the number of steps it will permit in a problem space. This will avoid infinite search (though there are more task-sensitive ways to keep search under control).

We now have a complete performance system. Given available knowledge for some components of various problem spaces, the system will attempt to realize a KL system behaving in its external environment. The knowledge that this KL system will exhibit cannot be described simply as the union of the available knowledge of these components. Many (indeed, most) of these components do not have knowledge about the external environment of the top KL system, but rather possess knowledge about the internal computational environment; this knowledge is not included. However, the tasks attempted in all these internal problem spaces serve to generate knowledge in the components of higher spaces, which ultimately serve to generate knowledge in the top KL system. It is the immediately available knowledge in the top KL system plus the generated knowledge arising from the activity in all the problem spaces that forms the total knowledge of the top KL system.

## 11.5   Discussion

The formulation of the PSCM is now complete in its essentials. Many elaborations, issues, and questions should follow in its wake, but we will only be able to hint at them here. We will do that first. Then we will discuss briefly the PSCM as a task formulation, the issue raised as an opener. Finally, we will expand a little on the relation of the PSCM to Soar.

### 11.5.1   Elaborations, Caveats, and Missing Aspects

It is important not to take the *search view* of problem spaces (and the PSCM) exclusively, although that is the role it has played in AI. There is also the *control view*. The problem space is a *least-commitment* programming control

---

[7] Soar has an analogous default rule.

construct. It delays as long as possible determining what operations to execute, namely to the moment of execution. This arises from the complete separation of select-operator from apply-operator. Programming languages in general intermix control and application, thereby giving up flexibility (and buying efficiency). There is also the *error-recovery view*. Any error occurs in a context (the problem space) that permits recovery from error and the consideration of alternative behaviors. Furthermore, any failure of the system to have the knowledge to deal with errors leads to the formulation of tasks to gain that knowledge. Programming languages in general do not have the context available to recover from error and must settle for communicating the error to some appropriate intelligent agent. In sum, the PSCM incorporates many of the characteristics needed by an autonomous agent.

The problem space, as given in Exhibit 11.7, has no automatic state saving and advances entirely from the current state. Thus as it stands, it can perform none of the weak methods, such as depth-first search and means-ends analysis. In fact, state saving is important, but in our formulation of PSCM it is to be done by the task encoded in the PSCM rather than automatically by the PSCM. States can be saved in several ways, e.g., by having the current state incorporate related prior states, or by reconstructing past states from history descriptions stored in the current state, or by spreading the search across many problem spaces so each space stores a single state (Soar usually saves state this way).

The problem space is a form of generate and test, the most fundamental problem solving method of them all. Sequences of operators generate candidate states for testing by terminate-task. This identification helps to understand why many features of the PSCM are the way they are. Encapsulating more knowledge of a task in the operators and less in the desired state shifts knowledge from the test to the generator (almost always improving efficiency). The existence of multiple problem spaces, as opposed to a single large space, implies putting more knowledge in the generator. The independence principle of operator application guarantees that extensive memory of paths need not be maintained automatically to verify path constraints.

The definition of problem spaces sets no limits on the complexity or number of states or operators. There clearly are some limits, although it makes sense to consider them as additional specifications, rather than complicating the basic definition. For instance, operators can be finitely generated. Each state that becomes current must be a finite structure. The space can have an infinite number of states, since only the current state is present in the agent at one time, hence an infinite number of states need never be realized simultaneously.

The PSCM contains an implicit requirement for mechanisms of experiential learning in its implementation. A PSCM system faces the external environment as a KL system. As it performs a sequence of tasks, the problem spaces evoked generate knowledge, which is exhibited in the behavior of this KL system (indeed, that is what the problem spaces are for). According to the permanence principle, this knowledge should then be available ever after. But there is no guarantee the knowledge will be available on later tasks, even if it is relevant. The problem space may have no way of generating it again in the different circumstances. Thus the KL system appears inconstant, exhibiting knowledge on one occasion, then failing to exhibit it, then perhaps exhibiting it again. This condition may be viewed simply as a facet of the necessarily approximate nature of all implementations of KL systems. However, if it were required that the knowledge generated by a problem space for the KL system it implements becomes part of that KL system's immediately available knowledge, then the inconstancy would be ameliorated. The matter is not entirely simple, because the knowledge to be added is underdetermined by the KL system's performance—the KL system may induce beyond the minimum knowledge necessary for the task. Consequently, many different learning mechanisms may be able to fulfill this requirement, with varying characteristics. In any event, we see that the principle of permanence strongly implies that experiential learning be a feature of PSCM systems.

The PSCM must be implemented in a symbol-level computational model (recall Exhibit 11.3). This SLCM must provide an operational arena within which all the activities of the PSCM occur and intercommunicate. It must also provide the symbol-level mechanisms that realize all the sources of immediately available knowledge. We have not attempted to treat the SLCM in this chapter, since it does not affect the definition of the PSCM, just as long as the entire scheme is realizable. As for the latter, Soar provides a concrete and useful demonstration of an operational system organized along PSCM lines.

### 11.5.2   The PSCM as a Task Formulation Framework

The PSCM incorporates the complete act of task formulation in the formulate-task component. If formulate-task is primitive, it knows (immediately) what problem space, desired states, and initial state to put into effect. If formulate-task is not primitive, it formulates the task of determining the problem space, desired states and initial state—doing so, of course, in another problem space, namely, one for determining formulations (or more precisely, for determining whatever part of the formulation cannot be immediately produced). And if this latter formulation cannot be done immediately, this formulation task itself (i.e., how to formulate the task of formulating a problem space) can be formulated. In short, the PSCM is reflective enough to cast the formulation problem in its own terms.

The PSCM also incorporates the instigation of task creation—the going from nothing to something. Creation occurs at the moment when the system becomes dependent on a component that does not have the appropriate available knowledge. Thus the PSCM not only creates its own subtasks but determines the circumstances in which to do so. The temptation is to say the PSCM *decides* when to create a new task, but that is not correct. The PSCM creates a new task when it has to, because knowledge is unavailable to do what it wants to do. Positive knowledge is not required to initiate creating a task; the system itself does it autonomously.

Of the five general criteria for evaluating task frameworks mentioned in the introduction, three require little comment: operationality, scope, and bias. The PSCM is implementable with an appropriate symbol-level computational model (such as Soar) and is fully operational. The scope of PSCM is universal, which can again be seen from the Soar implementation, but is also apparent on its face given appropriate state saving. As for bias, not much can be said at this stage (as noted more generally at the beginning of this chapter).

A potentially interesting feature of PSCM with respect to openness is multiple problem spaces. Problem spaces can be created in response to whatever things are in the environment, reflecting their structure in such a way as to make their incorporation easy. That is, problem spaces invite the creation of special representations for special purposes. This contrasts with a framework such as logic that specifies the form of the representation, thus forcing the encoding of all external things into its own terms. We describe this feature only as potential, because there are as yet no substantial demonstrations of its use. Indeed, on the other side of the ledger, problem spaces do not seem to lend themselves to embodying declarative information (e.g., geographical information) and this is an active research issue in Soar.

With respect to initialization, problem spaces have the property of being almost indefinitely easy to formulate a task within. The space is simply made larger and larger until it is believed to encompass both the initial state and the projection of the desired states into the space. A price is to be paid for this, of course. As the space gets larger, the search for a desired state gets more expensive, in general, combinatorially so. Concomitantly, the test for the desired state can be left more and more to be the unassimilated and uninterpreted initial problem statement. This also increases the ease of task formulation. The corresponding price is the expense of detecting that the current state is a desired state. These costs can be very real. But the fundamental point is that at least by paying them, task formulation occurs and an attempt gets underway. Moreover paying a heavy price need only occur if no knowledge is available to use a smaller space or a less expensive goal test.

The formulation of tasks arises in a variety of contexts. At one extreme is the *autonomous* agent, which has its own high-level goals and concerns. It needs to formulate tasks in its encounters with its environment. This is (mostly) the situation with us humans. As we construct systems capable of task formulation, this will be the situation for many robotic systems. We have described the PSCM mostly as an autonomous agent. This flows naturally from the fact that the topmost level is a rational, goal-oriented KL agent.

At the other extreme is the *instrumental* agent, coupled to an autonomous agent. The autonomous agent wishes to formulate a task it has formulated only partially or perhaps has not formulated at all beyond some fragmentary goal statement. It wishes to use the instrumental agent to help in the formulation, getting the instrumental agent to formulate whatever does not seem critical, but reserving to itself the important parts of the formulation, including final review. This instrumental situation, of course, is the extension of the foundation paradigm of programming, described at the beginning of the chapter.

An indication of how this instrumental relation might develop is given by a hypothesis that has emerged in the Soar effort [36]. In attempting to realize a typical expert system within PSCM (i.e., using Soar as a PSCM system) it appears that no knowledge of methods needs to be provided. That is, starting from a specification of the task in English in entirely domain-oriented terms, it is necessary for the human knowledge engineer to: (1) map the parts of the spec (literally, in terms of short sections of text) into the elements of the PSCM (spaces, operators, desired states); (2) decide on the representation of the elements (in Soar's basic representation of attributes and values); and (3) determine the communication requirements for results between spaces and within spaces at different points in time. The rest takes care of itself, namely, the knowledge engineer does not have to design the methods to be used to accomplish the task or an executive system for carrying out the task. These are provided by the PSCM. This avoidance of method design is possible because (typically) expert systems explicitly specify how they want things done (not just what they want done), though in domain-oriented terms. The PSCM is able to capitalize on this characteristic of expert systems to make formulation easy. The domain-oriented structures are reflected directly in the PSCM structure. We are currently engaged in a major experimental effort to explore how robust our initial findings are, using a task-acquisition language, TAQL, that treats Soar as a PSCM [35].

Another indication of the power of PSCM for task formulation is that it provides for what might be called *goal programming*. The face that a PSCM system shows to the human is that of the top KL system. If the user can specify the goals desired, the knowledge available, and the actions whereby the goal is to be effected, this should be enough for the PSCM system to formulate the task of attaining the goal. More precisely, it provides the framework in which knowledge can be provided to do that formulation. Small experiments are underway in Soar that operate at about this level [13]. Soar is first given some general instructions, as shown in the sentences 1 to 4 of Exhibit 11.15. Then it is given a specific task in sentences 5 to 9, whereupon it answers *true*, as required. The form of the instructions is program-like, but it is a far cry from a program in a procedural language. The knowledge that the PSCM system has so it can formulate a task from the instructions is given in its knowledge of English, both syntax and semantics. But the entire act of task formulation occurs within the PSCM, including the comprehension of the specification and the creation of

---

Instructions:

1. Read four premises.
2. Then read a statement.
3. If the statement is true say "true".
4. Then stop.

The specific task:

5. A plate is left of a knife.
6. A fork is left of the plate.
7. A jug is above the knife.
8. The fork is below a cup.
9. The cup is left of the jug.

The system should answer:

10. True.

---

**EXHIBIT 11.15**
Simple instruction-taking (by Soar).

problem spaces to do the task. This experiment is quite rudimentary, but it gives a glimpse of how a PSCM might actually support task formulation.

### 11.5.3   The Role of Soar in the Development of the PSCM

Although, as noted in the introduction, problem spaces have been around for a long time, both in AI and in our own research, Soar has been the major catalyst in the formulation of the PSCM. Prior to Soar there were no multiple problem-space systems. Problem spaces remained a system-organizing principle rather than a complete system level (computational model). For one, much was missing in the notion of problem spaces, so it required completion in some way. But also problem spaces were seen as appropriate only for problematical situations requiring search. They provided a reduction to something nonproblematical, namely, the operators. Necessarily, then, operators should be specified in a more computationally effective way, i.e., in a standard programming language. This kept the problem space as a single level of organization, with the parts (the PSCM components) specified in another programming formalism.

The first break in this relatively fixed picture seems to have been the extension of problem spaces to be an organizing scheme for all goal-oriented activity, in what was called the *problem-space hypothesis* [21]. This was motivated largely by psychological concerns. It did, however, open the way for the construction of Soar as a multiple problem-space system [15]. This system developed a series of symbol-level mechanisms, first for combining problem spaces and production systems (the universal weak method), then for doing universal subgoaling and then for chunking. The result was a tightly integrated system that combined all these organizational constructs.

As Soar has evolved we have more and more come to separate a problem-space level from the set of symbolic mechanisms that supports it. This evolution has been driven by three forces. First, people seem to find Soar hard to understand and we keep changing the description to find ways to make the system clearer. Second, in designing a more general specification language for Soar we have moved toward the PSCM as the appropriate level of generality [36]. Third, in moving to a new implementation based on some low-level considerations (whether to copy states or modify them) we found we needed to describe a distinct problem-space level in order to understand the effects of the symbol-level changes [17]. All of this has moved us toward the PSCM, though still drawing on the symbol-level aspects of the Soar architecture to fill in the missing details.

The final ingredient in creating an autonomous PSCM has been our growing use of the knowledge level. Ever since the knowledge level was introduced as a system construct [22] it has provided a useful definition of an intelligent agent, namely one that closely approximates a KL system. We have continually tried to use the knowledge level as a way of organizing and understanding Soar [29,30,31]. This has had as a primary focus analyzing Soar as an agent in an external world (knowledge-level learning) and how close the mechanisms of Soar could be seen to support a knowledge-level description of that agent.

The present chapter takes the important step of creating the PSCM as a genuine systems level, independent of Soar. Soar has informed this effort at every point along the way and a direct mapping can be made between the constructs of the PSCM and Soar. As should be evident, Soar is the one system we can draw upon to illustrate a number of features of the PSCM. However, it would be wrong to think of the PSCM as simply Soar in disguise. A genuine act of abstraction has occurred, and multiple implementations of the PSCM are certainly possible. Indeed, in the Soar project we have had two quite distinct symbol-level implementations, Soar4 [16] and Soar5 [17], and expect additional ones to follow. As a final point of dependence of this PSCM effort on Soar, we are able to detect inadequacies in the PSCM by noting features of the Soar architecture that have no reflection in the PSCM. The primary example is the way Soar is able to make decisions at any level of the context at any time and to communicate freely among all active problem spaces. The PSCM described here does not seem to have this property, but to be a more classically stack-like structure.

## 11.6  Conclusion

We have attempted in this chapter to describe the PSCM, a computational model of multiple problem spaces. This task goes beyond simply having the concept of problem spaces around as an organizing principle for AI systems. It implies an act of abstraction to define a complete system structure in its own terms, i.e., without embedding it in another computational model. As it turns out, the PSCM requires another computational model, the knowledge level computational model (KLCM). However, this is not an implementation model for the PSCM, but one that is co-defined with it. The entire structure is grounded in a more conventional symbol-level computational model (SLCM), but one whose character is quite constrained. Most of what is novel in this effort comes from the use of the PSCM and KLCM to realize each other.

Although the PSCM is necessarily abstract, and properly so, this effort arises from extremely practical motivations. Generally stated, it is the need in computer science to extend the foundation paradigm to systems that formulate their own tasks. As such, this is an attempt to advance programming systems and languages as much as AI. It seeks to get work in programming systems to raise its sights from variations of the foundation paradigm, even those as rich as object-oriented programming, to organizations that permit computer systems to take on more of the total intellectual task of helping humans get their computational work done.

We started by describing the several task-formulation frameworks that have emerged as possibilities (see Exhibit 11.2). At this stage of understanding, none can be eliminated in favor of the others. We know too little about any of them in the face of realistic task formulation. We hope that these other frameworks will continue to be developed. We have been sufficiently encouraged by our work with the PSCM that we will continue to pursue it.

## 11.7  Acknowledgments

We would like to acknowledge the entire Soar research community, which has provided the environment in which the ideas of the PSCM have matured.

This research was supported in part by the Defense Advanced Research Projects Agency (DOD), and monitored by the Avionics Laboratory, Air Force Wright Aeronautical Laboratories, Aeronautical Systems Division (AFSC), Wright-Patterson AFB, Ohio 45433-6543 under Contract F33615-87-C-1499, ARPA Order No. 4976, Amendment 20; in part by DARPA under Contract

N00014-89-K-0155; in part by the National Aeronautics and Space Administration under Contract NASA Ames NCC2-517; in part by the Natural Sciences and Engineering Research Council of Canada and the Alberta Heritage Scholarship Fund; and in part by the Digital Equipment Corporation.

The views and conclusions contained in this chapter are those of the authors and should not be interpreted as representing the official policies, either expressed or implied, of the Defense Advanced Research Projects Agency, the National Aeronautics and Space Administration, the U.S. government, the Canadian Government, or the Digital Equipment Corporation.

# References

[1] A. V. Aho, J. E. Hopcroft, and J. D. Ullman. *The Design and Analysis of Computer Algorithms*. Addison-Wesley, Reading, MA, 1974.

[2] R. A. Brooks. A robust layered control system for a mobile robot. *IEEE Journal of Robotics and Automation*, RA-2:14-23, 1986.

[3] N. Carriero and D. Gelernter. How to write parallel programs: A guide to the perplexed. *ACM Computer Surveys*, 21:232-357, 1989.

[4] D. C. Dennett. *The Intentional Stance*. Bradford Books: MIT Press, Cambridge, MA, 1988.

[5] T. G. Dietterich. Learning at the knowledge level. *Machine Learning*, 1:287-316, 1986.

[6] *Blackboard Systems*, Addison-Wesley, Reading, MA, 1988.

[7] *Computers and Thought*, McGraw-Hill, New York, 1963.

[8] I. Goldstein and S. Papert. Artificial intelligence, language and the study of knowledge. *Cognitive Science*, 1:84-124, 1977.

[9] J. Hintikka. *Knowledge and Belief*. Cornell University Press, Ithaca, NY, 1962.

[10] J. Hintikka. *Logic, Language-games and Information*. Oxford, London, 1973.

[11] B. E. John, A. Newell, and S. Card. Browser-soar: A goms-like model of a highly interactive task, 1990 (in preparation).

[12] H. J. Levesque. Foundations of a functional approach to knowledge representation. *Artificial Intelligence*, 23:155-212, 1984.

[13] R. L. Lewis, A. Newell, and T. A. Polk. Toward a soar theory of taking instructions for immediate reasoning tasks. In *Proceedings Cognitive Science Eleventh Annual Conference, 1989*. Cognitive Science Society, 1989.

[14] J. E. Laird, A. Newell, and P. S. Rosenbloom. Soar: An architecture for general intelligence. *Artificial Intelligence*, 33:1-64, 1987.

[15] J. Laird, P. Rosenbloom, and A. Newell. *Universal Subgoaling and Chunking*. Kluwer Academic Publishers, Boston, MA, 1986.

[16] J.E. Laird, K.R. Swedlow, E.M. Altmann, C.B. Congdon, and M. Wiesmeyer. Soar 4.5 User's Manual. School of Computer Science, Carnegie Mellon University and Department of Electrical Engineering and Computer Science, University of Michigan, 1989. Unpublished.

[17] J.E. Laird, K.R. Swedlow, E.M. Altmann, and C.B. Congdon. Soar 5 User's Manual. School of Computer Science, Carnegie Mellon University and Department of Electrical Engineering and Computer Science, University of Michigan, 1989. Unpublished.

[18] S. Minton, J. G. Carbonell, C. A. Knoblock, D. R. Kuokka, O. Etzioni, and Y. Gil. Explanation-based learning: A problem solving perspective. *Artificial Intelligence*, 40:63-118, 1989.

[19] S. Minton, M. D. Johnston, A. B. Philips, and P. Laird. Solving large-scale constraint-satisfaction and scheduling problems using a heuristic repair method. In *Proceedings of IJCAI-90*. American Association of Artificial Intelligence, 1990 (in press).

[20] A. Newell and G. Ernst. The search for generality. In W. A. Kalenich, editor, *Proceedings of IFIP Congress 65*, pages 17-24, Spartan, Washington, DC, 1965.

[21] A. Newell. Reasoning, problem solving and decision processes: The problem space as a fundamental category. In R. Nickerson, ed., *Attention and Performance VIII*. Erlbaum, Hillsdale, NJ, 1980.

[22] A. Newell. The knowledge level. *Artificial Intelligence*, 18:87-127, 1982.

[23] N. Nilsson. *Problem Solving Methods in Artificial Intelligence*. McGraw-Hill, New York, 1971.

[24] N. Nilsson. *Principles of Artificial Intelligence*. Tioga, Palo Alto, CA, 1980.

[25] A. Newell and H. A. Simon. *Human Problem Solving*. Prentice-Hall, Englewood Cliffs, 1972.

[26] A. Newell and H. A. Simon. Computer science as empirical inquiry: Symbols and search. *Communications of the ACM*, 19(3):113-126, 1976.

[27] A. Newell, J. C. Shaw, and H. A. Simon. Empirical explorations of the logic theory machine: A case study in heuristics. In *Proceedings of the 1957 Western Joint Computer Conference*. Western Joint Computer Conference, 1957.

[28] E. Rich. *Artificial Intelligence*. McGraw-Hill, New York, 1983.

[29] P. S. Rosenbloom, J. E. Laird, and A. Newell. Knowledge-level learning in soar. In *Proceedings of AAAI-87*, Morgan Kaufman, Los Altos, CA, 1987.

[30] P. S. Rosenbloom, J. E. Laird, and A. Newell. The chunking of skill and knowledge. In B. A. G. Bouma and H. Elsendoorn, ed., *Working Models of Human Perception*, pp. 391-410. Academic Press, London, 1988.

[31] P. S. Rosenbloom, A. Newell, and J. E. Laird. Towards the knowledge level in soar: The role of the architecture in the use of knowledge. In K. VanLehn, ed., *Architectures for Intelligence*. Erlbaum, Hillsdale, NJ, 1990 (in press).

[32] H. A. Simon. Cognitive science: The newest science of the artificial. *Cognitive Science*, 4:33-46, 1980.

[33] J. Slagle. *Artificial Intelligence: The heuristic programming approach*. McGraw-Hill, New York, 1971.

[34] P. H. Winston. *Artificial Intelligence*. Addison-Wesley, Reading, MA, 1977.

[35] G.R. Yost and E.M. Altmann. Taql 3.0: Soar task acquisition system user's manual, 1989. School of Computer Science, Carnegie Mellon University, December, 1989, Unpublished.

[36] G. Yost and A. Newell. A problem space approach to expert system specification. In *Proceedings of IJCAI-89*. American Association of Artificial Intelligence, 1989.

# 12

# Why Can't We Model the Physical World?

Steve Shafer

For decades, computer scientists have been studying toy problems such as compiling computer programs, playing chess, designing parallel computers, and finding convex hulls. Now, under the impetus of robotics, computer scientists are trying to represent the physical world in computer hardware and software. It turns out, we can't do it—in fact, we can't even come very close. Every time we make a decision about how to represent the world, we necessarily partition the real-world states into equivalence classes of states with identical representations. We therefore lose the ability to reason about the differences among the states within each equivalence class. I call this "model aliasing" since it is a symbolic version of the "aliasing" phenomenon in signal processing. Model aliasing pervades all of computer science, e.g., roundoff error in floating point computations, or building paging strategies into an operating system. In most situations, we regard it as trivial; but when we try to represent the physical world, it's deadly. There's a related, inverse condition, which I call "model coherence," that helps to explain why model aliasing is trivial in many computer science areas but not in robotics. Model coherence underlies all abstraction in representations, e.g., loop invariants in program verification; it also helps indicate what would constitute an "adequate" representation of the physical world for a particular task. In this chapter, I introduce these concepts and illustrate them with some simple examples.

## 12.1  Something On My Mind

I've noticed a problem that crops up all the time in my research area, which is robot vision, and it seems to be endemic to all areas of robotics research. The problem, bluntly put, is that nobody knows how to represent anything. Of course, they don't come right out and say that—instead, they represent everything they are concerned with. It's just that the representations seem to simplify away all the interesting problems, so that the resulting robot systems can't do anything resembling a real task in a real environment. I never had this problem when I was learning about computer science—compilers and operating systems and Turing machines and such—so it seems rather remarkable that I can't get away from it in the domain of robotics. After all, it's just more software, isn't it, and that's where we computer scientists have our expertise. Don't we?

I don't believe this is just happening because all robotics researchers are dummies. There seems to be something about the physical world that makes representing it qualitatively more difficult than representing things like mere operating systems. But it's not easy to put it into words. Hopcroft noted the same problem in [4].

It bothers me that we don't have the vocabulary to talk about what makes a representation or an abstraction succeed or fail. As computer scientists, we ought to at least be able to talk about these things. I've come to believe that we just don't talk about this stuff enough in our usual computer science curricula. My guess is that it's because we hail from a tradition of symbolic logic and finite-state machines, but the physical world is full of continuous or nearly continuous functions, "medium-number" phenomena that defy simple symbolization, and state spaces with astoundingly huge numbers of parameters (dimensions).

In this chapter, I present a brief discussion of some of these issues centering on the dual concepts I call *model aliasing* and *model coherence*. There probably isn't a single new fundamental principle discussed here, just a new way of viewing the relevance of information theory and signal processing theory to problems in computer science. Yet, the issue of how to define appropriateness of representations seems to me an important aspect of our discipline, and since we don't usually talk about this stuff, I thought a little reflective essay on the topic would be appropriate on the occasion of our 25th anniversary.

## 12.2  Real Men Don't Need Continuous Functions

Let's start with a simple situation. Suppose we want to simulate someone falling off of a 20-story building onto the pavement below, as shown in Exhibit 12.1. Of

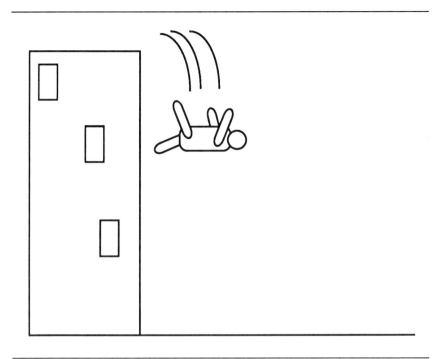

**EXHIBIT 12.1**
Bombs away!

course, it's pretty dull on the way down, so what we want is to capture the critical moment in all its glory. One way to do this is by an *event-driven simulation*, in which we use some equations to calculate when the impact will occur, skip all the time until then, and then calculate what happens at that moment. But that's not too satisfying, because the effect of the impact depends somewhat on how the arms and legs are wiggling on the way down. So, the event-driven approach loses too much information.

The alternative is a *clock-driven simulation*, in which we have a clock that ticks in some units, say once every second, and at each tick of the clock we evaluate all the state variables such as the position and velocity of all the limbs, the spin of the body, and so on. But wait! something very funny happens at the magic moment. At one tick of the clock, the body is in midair, hurtling inescapably toward impact; but at the next tick, it's sunk down below the ground. Somehow, we missed the exact moment of impact! Exhibit 12.2 shows this problem.

What happened is easy to understand—the moment of impact fell in be-

**EXHIBIT 12.2**
Missing the critical moment.


tween ticks of the clock. How can we fix this? One way is to run a little event-driven simulator in between the two critical clock-ticks, to figure out what happened in that interval of time. But we already know the problems of that approach. The other alternative is to run a clock-driven simulator with a finer grain of time-unit. That looks fine, until the critical moment comes again, and look! we still miss that moment. In fact, unless we are the beneficiary of a remarkable coincidence, no matter how finely we chop up the time-unit, and no matter how many people we drop off the roof, we will always miss the critical moment. Every time.

So, what's going on here? All the way down, no problem; but when the critical moment comes along, the simulation fails. Do we even have a vocabulary to describe this phenomenon? It turns out, there's a perfectly good vocabulary that explains it in an instant—but we don't teach it in computer science! It's the vocabulary of continuous function modeling, usually taught in the guise of signal processing, and one common form of this vocabulary uses Fourier transforms. In the Fourier transform, we model any function as a linear combination of sine waves of various wavelengths. The Fourier transform is the set of coefficients of these sine waves used to model the given function. Long wavelengths are called "low frequencies;" short wavelengths are "high frequencies." Whenever a function is sampled, as our clock-based simulation samples time, the sampling rate corresponds to a frequency called the Nyquist frequency, above which we have lost all information about the function. In other words, we can't model things that happen faster than our clock rate, as formalized by the Fourier representation. The clock rate determines a maximum frequency at which we can model things happening. So, the relatively gentle (low-frequency) flapping of arms and legs on the way down can be modeled easily, whereas the discontinuities at the moment of impact (which contain all frequencies) cannot be adequately calculated. This is called *aliasing*. Aliasing is a fundamental property of the representation of continuous information. Curiously, engineering students know all about aliasing, but I believe that many computer science students have never heard of it. We'll discuss that again later.

## 12.3  Aliasing, Aliasing Everywhere

But first, since we couldn't make our simulated person create a very satisfying splat, let's lower our sights a bit and simply try to punch him in the nose. So, we'll build a robot with a big fist, and we'll keep it cocked, and when we get close enough to his nose, we'll let fly! Just to keep things simple, we'll make the fist a simple cylinder, we'll move straight forward toward our hapless victim, and we'll ignore any little timing problems like those we saw above. Exhibit 12.3 shows the scenario.

Now, here's the problem. If we strike too soon, we'll miss, and the person will probably run away laughing. And if we approach too closely before striking, he may get suspicious and run away anyway. So, we want to strike just when we're in reach of the nose. We might have a little program like this:

```
repeat
        move forward
until distance-to-nose <= reach-of-arm;
punch;
emit laughing noise
```

Now, all of these things are simple enough, except the one called *distance-to-nose*. The problem is: how are we to represent the shape of the nose, so that we can calculate the distance to it?

Exhibit 12.4 shows some solutions that don't work. For example, suppose we represent the shape of the nose by a polyhedron. Then the polyhedron is a kind of approximation to the nose, but it doesn't conform exactly to the shape of the nose. And there's the problem: if it sticks out too far, say having one vertex

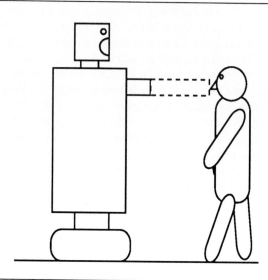

**EXHIBIT 12.3**
Rock'em, sock'em!

that pokes out in front, then our calculated distance to the nose is too short. So, we might strike too soon. But that's not all—there's yet another embarrassment in store, because even though we miss the nose in reality, *we hit it squarely in our representation*. In other words, in the world of our representational imagination, we actually hit the nose, and the victim ought to cry out! Won't we be surprised when we launch what we think is the telling blow, only to be met with a derisive snicker. And, we won't even know what went wrong. We can play it back in our representation a million times, and every time, we hit the nose right on the money. We can't even fix the problem by, say, always jiggling the frontmost vertex, because it's also possible that the nose sticks out further than the polyhedron and we are making the opposite mistake—there's no way to tell by examining the representation, because it's identical in both cases. Furthermore, these problems arise no matter what representation we use for the nose—polyhedra, spline surfaces, spherical harmonics, anything.

What's going on here? In the real world, things have huge numbers of parameters in their description. In other words, the world state space has an astounding number of parameters (dimensions). When we go to make a representation of the world state, we select a model system with a vastly smaller number of parameters. As a result, there's a many-to-one mapping from the *world space* of world states onto the *representation space* of instantiations of

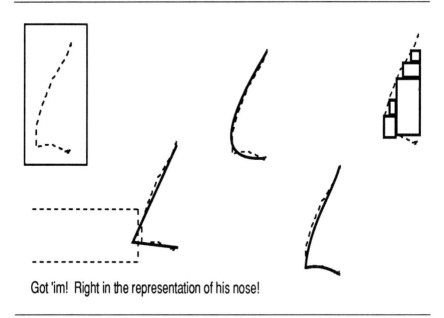

Got 'im! Right in the representation of his nose!

**EXHIBIT 12.4**
The nose that got away.

our model system. Each model instantiation thus represents an equivalence class of many different world states that have the same representation. Once we select the model system, we lose the ability to discriminate among the world states within each class.

We can summarize this by saying that the representation space is a subsampling of the world space, just as in the case of aliasing. But aliasing usually refers only to the sampling of continuous functions, so I prefer to call the general phenomenon by a new name: *model aliasing*. This name is meant as a reminder that whenever we choose a representational model scheme, we are at the same time defining a set of equivalence classes of world states for which we will use the same representation.

This way of thinking also provides a measure of the "power" of a representational scheme, namely, the merit of the configuration of those equivalence classes (e.g., how small they are). Exhibit 12.5 shows an example. Suppose I tell you that our victim's nose has the shape of a banana. You might say, no it doesn't. But, if my only choice were between a banana and a globe the size of Jupiter, then the banana model would be the right choice. The ridiculousness comes not from saying that the person has a nose like a banana, but from pro-

**EXHIBIT 12.5**
Banana nose! Banana nose!

viding so few choices of shape representation. Similarly, suppose I tell you a person's nose has the shape of a cube of size 4. If I can only represent cubes of sizes 4 and 99, then it has one significance; if I can represent cubes of any size, then it has more significance; and if I can represent any polyhedra with faces larger than .001 unit diameter, then the same "cube of size 4" has an altogether greater significance. A great deal of research in robotics has to do with developing new representations that provide finer granularity in the representation, e.g., representing uncertainty in sensing and control, and dealing with the resulting complexity of the system.

Statisticians have a useful terminology for these properties: for a given hypothesis that the world state corresponds to a particular model, "significance" refers to the number of different possible hypotheses and hence the importance of this hypothesis; while "confidence" refers to the number of world states represented by this hypothesis and hence the likelihood that the hypothesis is correct. Computer scientists don't have words for these properties, but we might adopt

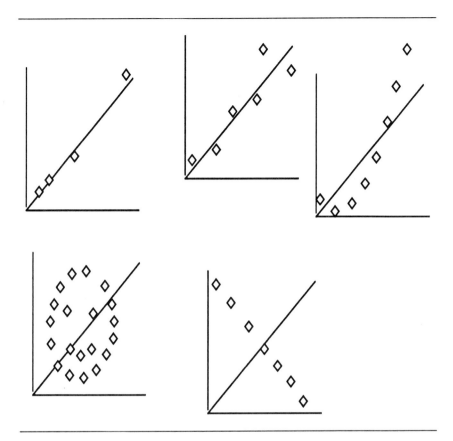

**EXHIBIT 12.6**
Amazingly, all observed data were linear!

terms along similar lines. I suggest *significance* or *discriminatory power* of a representation scheme as the number of states in the model space, each of which corresponds to an equivalence class of world states; and perhaps *convenience* or *simplicity* as the size of each of those equivalence classes. For example, Exhibit 12.6 illustrates the use of a model space with great convenience but little significance.

The upshot of this part of the discussion is that we need to represent continuous quantities by some kind of parameterization; but as soon as we choose the form of the parameterization, we lose the ability to distinguish among all world states. This problem I call *model aliasing*. Special cases of the problem are commonly discussed in various subareas of computer science, e.g., [3], and a brilliant example is presented in [2]. The consequence of model aliasing can

**EXHIBIT 12.7**
The person and the sandwich problem.

be an apparent nondeterminism in the relationship between the world and the model as described in [5]; this can even be a cue for machine learning [1].

## 12.4   Model Aliasing in Symbol Systems

So far the discussion has been limited to modeling continuous quantities, but similar things happen in any abstract representation. Exhibit 12.7 shows an example of this, less violent than the previous ones but nonetheless satisfying. It's the classical Person And The Sandwich Problem, in which we postulate someone in a room with a sandwich hanging from the ceiling; it's too high up for the person to reach by standing or jumping, but there's a handy stepstool nearby. Beginning artificial intelligence (AI) students are taught to wonder how it can be that the person might figure out that he can get the sandwich by moving the stool underneath the sandwich and stepping up onto the stool. The classic presentation proposes a set of objects such as Stool, Sandwich, and Person; a set of operators such as Goto X, Grab X, Let Go Of X, and Eat X; and a set of locations such as Where The Stool Is, Where The Top Of The Stool Is, Where The Sandwich Is, and Where The Person Is.

What I want to know is, how could the person *fail* to solve this problem? In this presentation, the set of operators and so on is so limited that the person could exhaustively enumerate all possible sequences of activities, perhaps by some diagonalization method, and dash about moving everything everywhere, reaching everywhere, and trying to eat everything, with no cleverness whatsoever, and probably still get that sandwich by lunchtime. This problem definition is so limited that the representation (and resulting solution) has great convenience but little significance. If you were in that room, you would find a much larger set of objects, such as Your Shoe, and likewise a much larger set of locations and actions such as Put X In Your Nose, Jump Up And Down, Shout, Jump Up And Down Harder, Call For The Experimenter To Come Get X For You, and Throw X At The String Holding The Sandwich. Now, *that's* the kind of problem we see in robotics.

For example, suppose you want your robot to pick up a wet bar of soap. There are many different strategies, depending on things like the shape of the soap, the shape of your hands, how long you're willing to play with it, how you want to be holding it when you're done, and where it might squish to if you don't hang onto it. Some of those strategies may be closed-form sequences of operations; some may be "reactive" and involve real-time decisions that depend on what happens as you are operating. Now, we might invent a vocabulary to describe the plan elements such as Move Hand To X, Open Fingers, Close Finger #2, etc. Even though the number of strategies might be finite, and even if it's a small number like 97, it's probably very difficult to find a vocabulary that can express all of them. So, the selection of this vocabulary itself constitutes a problem representation that induces model aliasing. More to the point, when we build robots or computer programs we are designing things, so we don't usually begin with the list of all 97 strategies. Instead, we begin with the vocabulary of all the things we think we can do, and then try to construct strategies using that vocabulary. So if we find that we have enumerated, say, 62 strategies, how do we know that's all there are? For a specific situation, maybe we need strategy #63, so we conclude that the robot can't do the task: it may be physically capable of it, but our chosen vocabulary couldn't express the necessary strategy. This is model aliasing in a symbolic domain, much the same way it occurred in the continuous domains discussed before.

In some sense, all abstractions (almost all, anyway) amount to representations that reduce the dimensionality and/or cardinality of the state space in question, thus increasing convenience at the expense of discriminatory power. This is a pervasive phenomenon in computer science, not just infecting robotics. One of my favorite examples of this concerns language-oriented editors, which in essence provide automatic enforcement of top-down programming style by instantiating program constructs during the editing process. I remember Joe Newcomer, a tremendous programmer, remarking once that his favorite programming style was not top-down, and not bottom-up, but "outside-in," working from the very top and very bottom levels of abstraction (both of which he could usually design easily) toward the murky middle level of code. I program the same way, and though I don't use language-oriented editors very often I hope that their designers would allow me the freedom to program MY way and not force me—by model aliasing—into a style I would rather avoid. I don't mean to pick on this particular segment of the computer science community, and anyway I assume they're smart enough to avoid the pitfall; the point is that model aliasing arises everywhere in computer science. By the act of selecting a model of a system, we commit our robots and computer programs henceforth to understand only those aspects of the system that are included in the model.

## 12.5  The Antidote: Coherence

I'd like to say that all computer scientists ought to get excited by this problem, but for some reason they don't. Roboticists, on the other hand, seem to care about this a whole lot. For example, if you write computer chess programs, you can represent the chessboard with pieces assigned to squares and be satisfied that all meaningful states are represented. Similarly, compiler writers transform programs into parse trees and know that all meaningful program elements are preserved. Why then is model aliasing so important in robotics?

To understand this, it's helpful to think of the dual property of model aliasing, which I call *model coherence*. As described above, model aliasing arises when the representation space is a subsampling of the world state space, so that the world states are partitioned into equivalence classes of states with the same representation. Model coherence is the opposite situation: the representation space is a supersampling, so that there are many representation elements that correspond to a single state or property instantiation of the world, i.e., many individually represented items have some common property in the world. That property can be thought of as an invariant over the set of elements. For example, program verification people can look at a loop in a program and summarize the whole thing by a "loop invariant" and some boundary conditions, which is a description that applies to the whole group of statements in the loop. Once the loop invariant and boundary conditions have been established, they never need to look back inside the loop, because this description applies to all those statements taken as a whole. The code in the loop can now be deleted from the verification process, and progress has been made. Once the coherence property is identified, it's no longer necessary to represent the individual elements of the original model. Computer graphics people and algorithm analysis people also explicitly use coherence, usually to make things run faster. In general, model coherence is the opposite of model aliasing: in model aliasing, your representation scheme isn't rich enough, so you miss important distinctions, whereas in model coherence, you realize that you have redundant information in the representation that you could squeeze out if you wanted to.

The problem with coherence is that you can always think of properties of things that differ, so how do you know if a set of things exhibit coherence? For example, in the case of loop invariants, each statement of source code may appear on a different line of the text, so in that property there's no coherence; but in terms of usefulness for program verification, there is coherence across the statements within the loop. So, coherence is not an intrinsic property of the representation space: rather, it also depends on the particular operations you intend to perform on the representation. Until you know the operations, you can't say whether there's any coherence to exploit.

However, if there is coherence, then this can be played off against model aliasing. In essence, if we alias the world states into equivalence classes, but the elements of each class have the coherence we need, then the aliasing hasn't cost anything. For example, when we sample a continuous function, we necessarily alias away the high frequencies. But if we only care about the low frequencies, then the representation is fine. I call a representation *safe* if the model aliasing it induces is balanced by coherence with respect to the intended computations. This explains why it's a forlorn hope for so many people in the computer aided design (CAD) and robotics communities to try to come up with the ideal general-purpose representation for geometry: as seen above, any particular geometric representation necessarily imposes severe problems of model aliasing, but if we don't know in advance what computations we want to perform, then we can't say for sure whether that aliasing is safe.

And now at last, we can begin to articulate why it is that we can't represent the physical world—or, better, why we can't *safely* represent the physical world. It's not just that model aliasing is endemic to representations of the physical world, as described above, but there's something more: the physical world is so complex that very many useful coherence properties that we can think of are violated somehow, and if we build a robot based on an assumed coherence property, it's only a matter of time until it goes astray. I recall the early months of the NAVLAB robot truck, making it drive down an asphalt path through Schenley Park. First, we built a vision program to discriminate the black path from the green grass. But one day the sun went behind a cloud, so we had to make the color analysis adapt to changing illumination. We drove into a shadow for the first time, and had to upgrade both the cameras and the software to deal with that. Then there was a drought and grass turned brown! In the fall, leaves fell from the trees and made a texture pattern on both the roadway and the grass. We got everything working again, just in time for the first snowfall of the season! No matter how hard we worked to build a robust system, nature always came up with some additional factor that made the problem more complex than our model. Even so, we had a fairly well-defined task to perform. If instead we had wanted to build a truly "general-purpose" road-perceiving system, one can imagine tasks for which we might have had to model such additional esoterica as the amount of thermal expansion of the asphalt, the presence of dirt and oil on the road, or perhaps the rate at which ice was melting and water evaporating at each point on the road surface. This is sometimes called a "medium number" behavior [5]: we can't afford to model every individual particle in the world, but if we just model them in aggregate properties we find that they deviate from any useful statistical model.

There simply is no such thing as a safe representation of the physical world for all tasks that we might want a robot to perform, and perhaps not even for individual tasks that we want to perform very reliably. It is suggested sometimes that therefore a general-purpose robot needs to be able to learn; the implication of this discussion is that in that case, the learning must take place not only within the existing model structure of the world state representation, but in fact the nature of those models itself, both descriptive and procedural, must be improved without limit. Otherwise, those limits induce model aliasing that will render any particular representation unsafe for some tasks. Likewise, when we dream sometimes about "verifiably correct robots," we have the same problem as software verifiers: the definition of "verifiability" is relative to the model space in which we represent the problem, and not in terms of the real world in which the system will act.

## 12.6 The Bottom Line

I have emphasized in this chapter the difficulties faced by robotcists attempting to model the physical world, but I didn't mean to exclude other computer scientists from these concerns. I suggest, in fact, that this set of representational issues is just as fundamental to computer science as the issues of what is called "the theory of computation." For some reason, computer science as a discipline has a tradition that emphasizes discrete math, formal languages, and computability theory, and calls these the theory of computer science. I suggest that there is another, equally important, body of knowledge that is concerned with continuous functions, sampling, the relationship between task definition and data representation, and perhaps even a kind of "theory of representation" that has yet to be articulated.

Here, in the Computer Science program at Carnegie Mellon, we teach the computatibility concepts but not the continuous math concepts or other representational concepts of the kind presented here. In fact, I believe we have even ceased to teach the elementary concepts of roundoff error and its propagation through numeric computations, and to my knowledge, we have never taught the rudiments of optimization theory and numerical analysis. One of our graduate students remarked recently, "We learned all about how to compute Fourier transforms, but we never learned what they're used for." Maybe there's a good reason for this orientation of our curriculum; I'm not sure. Still, I suggest that we take this occasion of our 25th anniversary to reflect on the situation and consider whether we could improve our program by adding to it a more advanced discussion of the concepts of representation in computing systems.

## 12.7  Acknowledgements

Thanks to Alan Christiansen and Danny Sleator for bringing related works to my attention.

## References

[1] M. T. Mason, A. D. Christiansen,and T.M. Mitchell. Learning reliable manipulation strategies without initial physical models. In *Intl. Conf. on Robotics and Automation*. New York: Institute of Electrical and Electronics Engineers (submitted for publication), 1990.

[2] L. Earnest. Can computers cope with human races? *Communications of the ACM*, 32(2):173-182, 1989.

[3] C. M. Hoffman. The problems of accuracy and robustness in geometric computation. *Computer*, 22(3):31-42, 1989.

[4] J. Hopcroft. Algorithmic problems in modeling and electronic prototyping. In A. T. Nozaki, Nishizeki, D. S., Johnson and H. S. Wilf, eds., *Discrete Algorithms and Complexity*, pp. 201-222. Cambridge, MA: Academic Press, 1987.

[5] G. Weinberg. *An Introduction to General Systems Thinking*. New York: John Wiley & Sons, 1975.

# 13

## Producing Behavior in a Searching Program

Hans J. Berliner

This chapter discusses issues that are encountered when behavior is being produced by a searching program. This usually requires the cooperation of both knowledge and search. There are issues that deal with the structure of knowledge, the structure of the search, and limitations that either can place on the other. We show how various levels of knowledge can coexist in a value surface. We demonstrate that the horizon effect is inevitable when using point-valued representations of a state. Using such facts, we reason toward a knowledge representation and a search for two-person games that can deal with all known idiosyncrasies. This representation provides a place for both discrete and continuous knowledge. It allows the represention of uncertainty and provides a method for reducing uncertainty. It can be used to drive the search and will effectively deal with such known problems as the horizon effect.

We show how constraint knowledge can reduce the branching factor of a search to the point where it is possible to penetrate so deeply (100 ply) into a problem that an expert cannot understand a computer solution until it is well past the half-way mark. Finally, we sum up contributions to search made at Carnegie Mellon University (CMU) during the last two decades.

## 13.1    Introduction

The subject of this chapter is the behavior of programs that search. Problems using search can be readily partitioned into three categories.

- □ Those for which any reasonable technique will produce an answer. This type of problem is usually the subject of studies to determine the *best* technique for a type of problem.

- □ Those that are generally intractable regardless of the technique used. In this class of problems, the search seldom penetrates to the point where a definitive solution exists. Thus the nature of the solution, or whether one even exists, is open to speculation. For problems such as this, the technique to be preferred is the one that results in visiting the largest number of states in the state space. Evolution is a brute force searcher, and species that use sexual reproduction will be more successful than those that do not because they produce a larger number of nodes in the space to be evaluated by survival.

- □ Those that are on the edge between the two above classes. Here a balance must be reached among tractability, solution rate, and solution quality. This is the most interesting and most difficult class.

In the latter category, two possibilities arise.

- □ It is necessary to evaluate leaf nodes that are not themselves terminal nodes, to approximate a satisficing solution. This solution is accepted as *a step in the right direction*, even though no path to the final goal has been found.

- □ It is possible to search all the way to a goal; however, there are too many possible paths to do this in any routine way. Therefore, knowledge is needed to guide the search, and even more difficultly, to decide whether a solution exists.

The behavior that such a program is able to evince is intimately tied to the type and quality of its knowledge. Knowledge can range from zero-specified knowledge, a mere enumeration of the rules of the domain, to fully-specified knowledge that specifies the correct action in every state of the domain. The degree of specification is dependent on the properties of the domain. High degrees of specification could only be accomplished if a domain had one of the following properties:

□ It were small enough so that it is possible to define a set of rules of order $10^3$ that will cover all potential states, or

□ It is compact[1] enough so that a small set of spanning functions exist.

There are many examples of the former in current rule-based systems. An example of the latter is the game of NIM, where a single function applied to all legal moves allows the selection of an optimal move.

Most problem solving systems thrive on what we call partially-specified knowledge. Heuristics make it possible to associate values with states, and thus to prefer one state over another. This in turn allows for the guiding of the search in what is hoped to be a fruitful direction.

It is interesting to note that the basic equation for the amount of effort that a search must perform is $E = B^D$, where B is the average branching factor of the problem, and D is the depth to which the search penetrates. The two basic methods for reducing the amount of work are given below. One can improve the heuristic specification (knowledge) at a node. This creates more subgoals and thus makes it possible to understand results earlier or solve subproblems that allow a divide and conquer approach. These techniques reduce "D" above. On the other hand, the introduction of constraints avoids searching certain subtrees and thus reduces "B."

□ *Heuristic specification.* Associating values with states attempts to produce an ordering such that an increase in value can be associated with progress toward a goal. The degree of specification can vary. As the degree of specification rises, local hills on the value surface appear. Consider "D," the average number of operators (or moves) that need be applied to go between any pair of local hills. We propose to define the degree of specification, $S = 1/D$. Clearly, the complexity of a solution is a function of the maximum distance between any adjacent pair of hills on the solution path, such that $V(hill_n) < V(hill_{n+i})$. The higher the degree of specification, the more likely it will be that the true merit of a state will be recognized, and that no "forward" step will be looked at as having no merit. As this situation is approached, less search will be required to solve the average problem, until with a fully-specified domain, $S = 1$, and no search is required. If the degree of specification is not sufficient for the power of the search, then not many problems in the domain will be solved. It will be impossible to form chains of states into a coher-

---

[1]By "compact" we mean that though the number of states may be large, they can be effectively partitioned so that the number of partitions is small and a function exists for each partition.

ent solution because certain states will not have a state of greater value within the searching radius of the problem solver. Therefore it would be impossible to discover a direction of progress from such a state, and any search that reaches this state is doomed to remain on top of its local hill. It should be noted that *as the search gets more powerful, the degree of specification can be allowed to diminish* thus putting fewer knowledge requirements on the most powerful searches. This was originally pointed out in [9].

□ *Specification by constraints and invariances.* Logical relations may exist that rule out the possibility that a solution exists in a certain subtree, and thus make it possible to avoid searching that subtree. Invoking such a relation has the effect of reducing the branching factor of the search. Further, if a certain action has been found to fail, it may be possible to posit an *invariance* that describes the conditions under which it will continue to fail. If enough constraints and invariances can be found, it is possible to radically reduce the branching factor of the search. In Section 13.10, we show an example of this from recent work.

The interaction between knowledge and the search is quite profound. The more knowledge that exists, the less searching need be done; however, the slower the process goes. The slower the process, the fewer the alternatives that can be investigated. This has led to a schism between animate and machine searchers: the former opting for the few nodes, deep understanding approach, and the latter for many nodes but shallow understanding.

Humans solve problems in a "knowledge-intensive" mode, applying small amounts of search when necessary. The human strategy is flexible and avoids the need to encode *all* knowledge. Many successful artificial intelligence systems mimic the human style, and rule-based systems offer the prime example. Competitive gaming systems typically employ the opposite scheme, relying primarily on search.

While each approach has its advantages, it is likely that an intermediate approach is optimal (humans are search limited by the nature of their wetware, while machines have problems acquiring sufficient amounts of accurate knowledge). Relying primarily on either approach eventually makes continued performance gains difficult. Exhibit 13.1 illustrates the tradeoff. For a given task, the constant-performance curves exhibit an approximately hyperbolic shape. A system positioned at point D can increase overall performance more easily by increasing knowledge than by increasing search.

In the development of this chapter, we will usually have recourse to games and puzzles, as among these can be found meaningful examples with the right degree of difficulty.

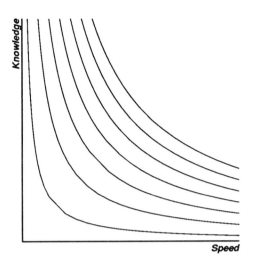

**EXHIBIT 13.1**
The knowledge/search performance tradeoff.

## 13.2    Facts and Heuristics

### 13.2.1    Some Problems with Heuristics

It should be self-evident that heuristics by themselves constitute a major kludge. Any large knowledge-based system that does not have automatic data acquisition is doomed to be a loser. By this we mean that the infusion of knowledge from expert to program is a very volatile process. As a domain expert, I can testify that given a set of 30 conditions to rank-order, I will not be able to do it identically 2 days in a row. There are just too many things to consider to be able to do this rigorously to the satisfaction of an oracle, should there be one.

If heuristic information is acquired automatically, it is well to acquire it in function form [7,11] as this assumes some smooth variation in the domain. In this way a single function can deal with some aspect of all states of the domain, and anoint the given state according to the degree of the aspect that it finds there. However, even excellent functions will have certain kinds of problems. For instance, in chess it is clear that a bishop is worth more than a pawn. Textbooks variously say that a bishop is worth from 3 to 3 1/3 pawns. This is true in the general case; however, at the very end of the game, an ending of King and Bishop versus King (KBK)[2] is a draw, whereas KPK may be a win. Thus our heuristic function can miscarry in the extremal cases. Another poignant case of this type is the ending KNNKP. It is known that a King and two Knights cannot win against a lone King. However, when the opponent has an extra pawn that can be forced to move at a critical moment, then it may be possible to win. A heuristic function would certainly recommend the capture of the last pawn, little realizing that this throws away the win.

### 13.2.2  Some Problems with Facts

In the domain of games, it is possible to assign a game theoretic value (GTV)[3] to each state of a particular game. If the game is vast enough, it may not be possible to assign such values to every state, but certainly states near the end of the game can usually be classified as won or drawn. However, this fact has rather limited utility. For instance, consider the ending KBK whose GTV = 0 (draw) and a particular ending KPK with a GTV = 0 in which only perfect defense will result in a draw. There is no question that it is better to have the KPK ending as there is *opportunity* to win if the opponent errs, whereas in the KBK ending there is none. In fact, there are some KPK draws that are difficult enough to warrant them being a problem in a book. How does one represent such knowledge? It is essential to represent it, as failure to do so can lead to serious errors.

There are many situations that have a GTV = 0, where one side must play extremely well in order to demonstrate this. If the initial position in the game of chess is a draw, as is popularly assumed, there must be a point where the GTV changes from 0 to +/-1 if the game is ultimately won by someone. Now every human chess player will be able to designate certain chess positions as having a GTV = +1. However, there may be a considerable disparity in what a world champion designates as won and what the average player is willing to so designate. And even a world champion may not be absolutely sure about the GTV of a position that is difficult and new to him. Yet players regardless of strength will usually agree on which side is better. This should make it clear that a complete set of GTVs may still not be good enough to equal the performance of good "judgement" when playing errorful opponents. Thus *the need for a continuous variable of goodness.*

From the above discussion, it should be clear that each player has a thresh-

---

[2]In this notation, the white pieces are enumerated first starting with the king, then the black pieces. Thus when the second "K" is encountered, this indicates the start of the black pieces.

[3]A game theoretic value is the value of the outcome of the game, if play from the current state were to proceed in an optimal manner

old with respect to what he or she believes is a sufficient advantage for winning. The fact that a winning threshold exists (for each class of player from duffer to oracle) implies a nonlinearity in the summing of advantages. Thus advantages above the win threshold have very little value, whereas those below are very valuable. In particular, the achieving of the actual threshold must be the most valuable increment of all.

## 13.3   Discrete and Continuous Representations

When we speak of discrete representations, we mean few-valued representations such as those encountered in various logics; and by continuous representations we mean many-valued essentially differentiable functions.

There are those that would argue that the issue of discreteness vs. continuousness in intelligent systems is a *nonissue*. According to this view, any continuous function can be represented to any desired degree of fidelity with a set of discrete rules. However, this reductionist view is just not sound.

First, there is the argument from the point of view of efficiency. Consider a simple sine wave. It takes only one function to represent it, whereas it would probably take thousands of rules to achieve reasonable fidelity over even a small interval. Clearly, a function serves best here. Conversely, consider a yes or no decision: Does white have a bishop in position it X? This question can presumably be answered to everyone's satisfaction. Thus it can serve as a predicate for a rule, and there is no need to equivocate about the presence of the bishop, or be able to associate its present location with future and past ones.

Now, consider the nature of the terrain made up from all the values. If one considers the values of states in a state-space, it may seem a matter of great indifference as to whether this value was assigned by a rule or by a function. However, *when search is involved in the problem solving, this is not true*. The values of states in a state-space form a *value surface*, and a searching program wishes to find its way along such a surface. Thus the values of states adjacent to the present state are extremely important. When a searching program considers departing from its present state, it makes a big difference whether the value surface in the immediate vicinity is smooth or if there are cliffs and precipices. Typically, a function can produce a smooth surface, while a surface constructed from many independent rules would very likely not have this property. We have discussed these issues in [1,7,11].

Finally, there is the fact, demonstrated below, that for large domains it appears to be inevitable that both types of representation appear. We turn now to issues of how discrete and continuous representations interface.

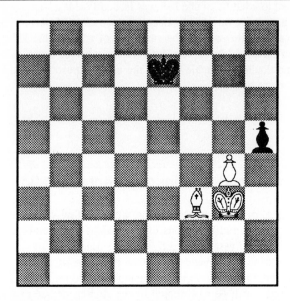

**EXHIBIT 13.2**
White wins with g5; other moves draw.

## 13.4   The Interaction of Discrete and Continuous Representations

There are situations in chess where one move wins while all others do not; see, e.g., Exhibit 13.2. Nor is this type of situation confined just to chess. It is a fact of life that in a state-space there will be adjacent states that have very different values because they are associated with very different outcomes. Thus the smooth surface, that we would like to see for our gradient-follower, will be configured with cliffs in certain parts of the space. These cliffs are caused by radical changes of value.

In a knowledgeable system that deals with a large domain it is inevitable that there be value cliffs. At certain locations in the state-space there will be divergences (such as when the last rook is captured, and knowledge pertaining to outcomes with rooks on the board will no longer be invoked). Actually, much larger value changes are possible, as for instance in situations where there is a move that leads to a win and all others lead to draws. All that is required is that the values associated with the new *state-class*[4] be significantly above or below the values of the old state-class.

Each state can be thought of as being describable by a set of features that are properties of the state. For instance, in chess the locations of the men are the major features of a state. As the magnitude of the values associated with features of a state increases, the gap caused by a sudden appearance or disappearance of a feature increases.

In chess one can identify at least three value categories, which from smallest to largest are

□ Values due to the location of the pieces, which all other things being equal are usually best placed near the center (except the king!) and near the opposing king. These are the so-called *positional* advantages. Bonuses for such favorable deployments range from about .01 pawn to .1 pawn per piece deployed.

□ Values associated with patterns such as that in Exhibit 13.3. These are what we have called second order knowledge [9], and require the detection of the interaction of two or more pieces. These are the so-called strategic advantages. Bonuses for this kind of advantage typically range from .1 pawn to 2.5 pawns or even higher in extreme cases.

□ Material values, which are well known and easily recognizable. They range in value from 1.0 pawns to 9.0 pawns (the value of a queen).

Now we can see that changes in the value surface occur in several grains. It is best that such changes be small; however, for the larger grains this is not possible, or else pawns would have to be captured in units of .01 pawn. However, since functions do the best job of keeping data smooth, they are to be preferred. It is true that, as the reductionist says, each function can be represented by a set of rules. However, this is a vacuous statement as the synthesis of the appropriate set of rules in near impossible without the function as model. Even then, the storage required for thousands of rules and functions is essentially impractical.

Now, we can see that *wherever there is a divergence in values due to the presence or absence (a discreteness) of some value-determining feature, there must be discontinuities. If this occurs at the lowest level value representation, these can be thought of as being quasi-continuous. However, when different value levels exist, higher level discontinuities are cliffs on the evaluation surface and require special attention.*

Having a rough value surface profoundly affects the behavior of searching programs, especially programs that employ a search algorithm that is depth-limited. This facet of the situation is discussed in the next section.

---

[4] A *state-class* is a class of states that have some common property.

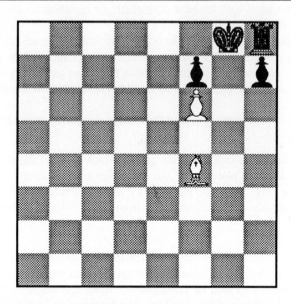

**EXHIBIT 13.3**
White traps Rook and King with Bh6.

## 13.5   Value Terrain and Search

Consider a value surface that is gently sloping in all directions. Such surfaces are ideal and have been well studied. It is known that a hill climber can perform within certain limitations on such terrains. The hill climber, or gradient-follower, will be able to find a local maximum on the surface by taking single steps. The main limitation of such a procedure is that the local maximum may not be the global maximum. This problem can be somewhat alleviated by not taking single steps and actually searching in units of many steps to find the largest value on the surface that is reachable in $n$ steps. This is a more powerful technique as it can produce paths that are more direct than the meander that a gradient-follower tends to produce. It may be able to avoid some local maxima since with its greater stride length it can find its way to a better maximum. The larger the search radius (the number of ply searched) and the greater the domain specification, $S$, the greater the chance of finding the global maximum.

This relation already has certain implications. It is important to not create functions that produce local maxima that cannot be escaped by the search.

Such maxima can then only be escaped by adding to the degree of domain specification. However, there are other fundamental phenomenon that are also very important. When a search does an $N$-ply search on a well behaved surface, it will find its way to the highest point reachable in $N$ ply, *regardless of the fact that this may be a hill-top from which any next step must be downward*. Thus the search is just blindly looking for maxima, without having the slightest idea of what is next. In our example, an $(N + 1)$-ply search in the same situation would do one of the following:

☐ Find a new path that strands it on the same hilltop in $N + 1$ ply, or

☐ Take a completely different path to a higher point on the value surface that could not be reached in $N$-ply from the original state.

☐ Find that it is in a pathological part of the space, and that it cannot reach as high a point in $N + 1$ ply as it was able to reach in $N$-ply.

It is not often that one encounters such behavior on a gently sloping terrain. However, the behavior described above is definitely due to the horizon effect [10]. A well-behaved surface has relatively few opportunities for a searching program to so radically change its mind in just one ply. However, when a value surface has irregularities and the search is depth limited, this can happen. Consider the position in Exhibit 13.3. Making the move Bh6 completes the "trapped rook" pattern. Trapping a valuable piece such as a rook must be worth some significant amount such as (say) 1.5 pawns. Now if the bishop can be attacked and driven away, the rook would still be encumbered but not *trapped*. The value would be considerably less. Further, with the additional black move h5, the rook will regain sufficient freedom to not even be considered encumbered. All these changes can happen very quickly and have considerable magnitude associated with them. Stopping at any one of the above states could lead a program to believe the world had one status, when that was about to change significantly. Thus given the standard point-value method of representing values, the horizon effect can occur at the level of *value of the location of pieces* (lowest grain), the level of *pattern values*, and as has been well known for some time, at the level of *material values*. Nor can we really get away from an irregular surface if we wish to represent all essential knowledge. So if the horizon effect is to be avoided, it appears one must look elsewhere (see Sections 13.6 and 13.7). But first let us look at some further issues of knowledge representation.

## 13.6   The Representation of Facts and Heuristic Knowledge

Facts must come from some oracle. In any game or puzzle, such facts tend to emerge over time as competent formalists rivet their attention on the puzzle. An example in recent time is the complete solution to Rubik's Cube, and before that was the rather astounding solution to the game of NIM. A more *ad hoc* method of achieving facts was a very interesting study performed on the game of Cubic (4 × 4 × 4 Tic-Tac-Toe) that developed a constructive proof that the game was a win for the first player [4].

Recently, such constructive proofs have been developed by a method we call *retrograde enumeration* [15,26]. This method creates a slot in a database for every possible position in a subdomain of a game, and establishes the value of each slot my first labeling all obvious wins and draws, and then making successive labeling passes at the database until no new slots are labeled. A slot is labeled as won if the on-move side has a move to a now-known winning position, and labeled as drawn if the on-move side has a drawing move but no winning move. A slot can also be labeled as lost if the on-move side has only losing moves.

This method has now been applied to all five piece endings in chess that do not have more than one pawn on each side. Several very interesting things that upset previous human "wisdom" have been discovered by Thompson. These results include the fact that the ending KQKR is much more difficult to win than was previously thought, that the ending KBBKN is a win in the general case (was thought to be drawn), and that the ending KQKBB is a win in the general case (was thought to be an easy draw).

Given that such oracular knowledge now exists, it seems incumbent on those that are building performance programs to figure out how to use this knowledge. This is not a trivial matter for two reasons

□ The four and five piece databases are very large, and would probably not be worth keeping in main storage.

□ Perfect information is not the most useful kind in certain situations.

  – When the program is losing and not sure if the opponent is fallible.

  – If the program has the better of a position with a GTV = 0, but the opponent may be fallible.

The first issue is one of developing functions that adequately partition the database. Recently Schaeffer [24] and Thompson have used an *exception list* to capture the essentials of databases being developed for the game of checkers. There is a certain *expectation* associated with every type of database. If the winning side has an advantage that is normally enough to win, then the expectation is "win." If not, then the expectation is draw. Their method records in encoded form those positions that are different than the expectation. When a position in the domain occurs during a search, the list is accessed by a binary search to discover if this is an exceptional or ordinary position. This method yields an excellent compromise between time to fetch the item required and space to store the information. It is a start in the right direction, with possible functions that look for piece patterns as a further refinement.

The second issue has important implications for the structure of the problem solver. The question is how to decide which of two positions with the same GTV offers better chances of achieving a result better than the GTV. The default method presently in use is to take the path that requires the longest solution, on the theory that this gives the largest opportunity for opponent error. This is fine as a first approximation; however, much more can be done.

If we are interested in making the move that is most likely to produce a good result against a possibly fallible opponent, then we could look for branching points where there is only one (or very few) good moves. This is rather naive, however, since if there is only one good move it is most likely to be a winning capture or checkmate, or some forced defensive move. Such moves tend not to be omitted by the opponent. A much more viable paradigm is to try to find the *intuitive appeal* (VI) of a move versus its *actual value* (VA). This rather imposing quantity could be approximated in the following way.

One can measure $VI_m$ by doing a three-ply search (with quiescence) starting with move $m$. A three-ply search will weed out certain obvious tactics and allow a reasonable approximation of the *intuitive* goodness of the move. A seven-ply (or more) search can then determine $VA_m$. When the absolute difference $VI_m - VA_m$ is large (say $>= 1$ pawn) then one of two situations exists.

☐ The intuitive appeal of the move is considerably better than its actual value, or

☐ The intuitive appeal of the move is considerable worse than its actual value.

The latter case (when $VI_m$ is the lower value) is the more interesting as this means that this move could be "overlooked." This occurs in a sacrifice or leaving a man to be taken. When $VI_m$ is the higher value, a different type of error is possible. Here we are speaking of moves that are appealing but not basically correct. "Appeal" could come from capturing a man, making a fork, or various other threats. That $VA_m$ is lower means that the appealing move did not work out. One could think of this as bait for a trap. In any case, what is required to select a move among equal GTVs in a drawn or losing position is that most refutations of the candidate move have one or the other property specified above. Clearly, "most" works best when *all* moves are in this category, and this is best when there is only one refuting move. The above process requires some mathematics to produce actual values for nodes. The process should be applied throughout the tree and values backed-up accordingly to reflect the likelihood of error by the opponent.

The standard *decision theoretic* model does well here. Each move is assigned a likelihood of being played that is a function of $VA_m$ and $VI_m$. The likelihood of a particular move being played is multiplied by the value of its subtree. This is determined by recursively applying the same procedure. Clearly, coefficients for the impact of certain types of move would have to be established to get the desired effect.

## 13.7    Point Values Versus Value Distributions

A representation that relies on a singular value to take all the foregoing into account would have to be impossibly clever. It is clear that positions that are irrevocable draws, even though one side may be materially ahead, should be assigned a value of zero. However, then KPKs with GTV = 0 should have a higher value for the superior side, since there is the possibility of opponent error. But what should this value be? For instance, some draws are quite difficult and some wins also. If we were to grade all KPK positions according to the ease of winning or drawing them, then we should have to know each of 180,000 positions, and assign one of (say) six values to them (easy win, moderately difficult win, difficult win, easy draw, moderately difficult draw, difficult draw). This poses certain methodological difficulties, especially when one considers somewhat larger domains such as KRPKR, of which there are 400 million positions. Even if it were possible to rank all positions in such databases, and establish a ranking, this would still not satisfy the situation where positions not in databases would have to be evaluated on the fly. It may be necessary for a side to choose between an "even" middle game position, or simplifying to a drawn ending in which the inferior side has a difficult draw. How can such a judgment be made? All the above assumes a fallible opponent, otherwise many issues are really nonissues. However, to make such decisions by comparing two integers seems ludicrous. Further, the situation gets even more involved in ordinary positions where one is trying to estimate the effect of opponent fallibility.

A range of values appears to be needed to capture the breadth of possible outcomes of a situation in a harmonious manner. The usefulness of a probability density function for representing the expected outcome of a state, as this relates to tree searching has already been demonstrated in [6,20,21]. The essence that a range, and even better a probability density distribution, can bring to evaluation is the ability to deal with uncertainty. A point value says there is no uncertainty. A probability density function can express the likelihood of outcomes along its entire range of values.

Since the evaluation function is known to be imperfect, there should be a way of expressing uncertainty. However, a value surface made up of point values has no way of expressing uncertainty. The horizon effect occurs on such a surface. The reason it occurs is that the value assigned to a node can misplace it in the partial ordering of node values. A searching program will seek out such situations, because they are in effect *a premature removal of uncertainty in a way that results in misrepresenting the true value of a node.*

## 13.8   Issues in Driving an Adversary Search

We now present our representation for state values in an adversary domain. There are basically three items of information that must be known to make optimal adversary searching decisions.

&#9633; *What is the value of node X.* This is a probability density function [21] with a center of mass at the expected value of the position. The tail of the distribution that expresses optimism is determined as given below. Only half the distribution need be generated as the other half comes from backed-up values from direct descendant nodes where the other side is to move. Probabilities are associated with values in the range based on

  – An *expected value* that is the value that would be assigned this node if values associated with states were singular.

  – *Threat-based optimism* is established under certain conditions by doing a null-move search that gives the side-on-move an extra move in order to determine the magnitude of threats.

  – *Optimism based on opponent error* as presented in Section 13.6. Since the search is being done for one side or the other, this kind of optimism is included only for the player's side; not the opponent's.

Typically, the expected value dominates, but the other factors are excellent tie-breakers. The major cause of large differences between the optimistic and expected values is the fact that there are threats around. As long as these threats make a difference, there will be pressure to resolve this issue. When there are plausible opponent errors the issue cannot be resolved by additional searching, and the tail of the distribution will make its presence felt in the process of selecting between comparable moves. Failure to take opponent error into account can lead to sterile play where neither side takes any chances.

&#9633; *What is the potential gain in expanding node X.* Comparison of backed-up probability density functions belonging to different nodes can be used to decide the degree of overlap that still needs to be resolved. As the overlap of the best alternatives at the root gets smaller, the utility of continuing to search likewise gets smaller. Recently, some work by McAllester [18] has shed some additional light on this subject by pointing out that values of nodes that depend heavily on a single (or small set of) supporting node(s) may be quite volatile. However, a cost-effective formalization of his notion of support remains to be realized.

☐ *What is the cost of expanding node X*. This is the least well understood of the issues. Some interesting contributions can be found in the work of Russell [23], which postulates cost and utility functions for selecting the next node to expand.

Search terminates when there is no longer any potential gain in expanding the node with the highest potential, or when, with limited resources, the cost of expanding the next node is exceeded by the benefit [23].

Recent results with the selective alpha-beta search method known as singular extensions [2] seem to indicate that this method, while providing devastating selective look-ahead at times, just barely pays for itself overall. The expense of doing the extra computation detracts minimally from the depth of search— just enough to balance the gains due to selectivity. Thus the issue of selective search is still wide open, and it appears more and more as if a true best-first search using techniques such as those pioneered in [21] could be a meaningful alternative.

The above considerations point to a certain style of search. It is interesting to note that other issues relating to evaluation point to a similar structure as we shall see below. Further, when a representation exists that

☐ allows *uncertainty* to be represented smoothly, and

☐ allows the *search* to be driven by this representation

then the horizon effect will almost certainly disappear as has already been shown by earlier research [21].

## 13.9  Resolving Value Uncertainty

Let us examine the following simple situation. As previously mentioned, the chess ending KBK is an irrevocable draw. Thus its value in the scheme of things, be it its GTV or some estimate of potential, given an errorful opponent is still 0, with a variability of 0! This creates certain problems for chess positions that are near a KBK position (in terms of the length of an operator sequence required to reach a KBK position). If the side with the bishop has only one pawn left, then the utility of the remaining pawn is enormous, and an opponent in an inferior position would be well advised to give up his or her last bishop, or last three pawns in order to exchange the last pawn of the side that might win. This causes great irregularities in the value space.

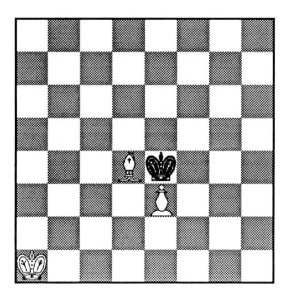

**EXHIBIT 13.4**
Safe win.

For instance, the ending KBPK, e.g., as shown in Exhibit 13.4, where the P is defended and anywhere except on the rook-file that has the opposite color queening square as the bishop, is a patently easy win. It is as sure and easy a win as an ending with KQQQK, although the latter may be over in a move or two, whereas in our ending a little straightforward work must be done. Let us set up a value system in which a pawn is worth 100 points. Then the original material complement for each side is worth about 3,000 points. It is also possible to have more material than this by promoting each pawn to a queen, and a mate is clearly worth more than this. Let us arbitrarily define a mate to be worth 100,000 points. Now there will be positions in which mate has not been achieved, but is considered child's play for even a player with no particular skill at chess. These positions should have values near the mate value. Failure to do so would result in a program that considers it better to go into a hopelessly lost ending rather than take a chance that the opponent will not find a complicated mating sequence.

As we have seen, the addition of one secure pawn can transform the value

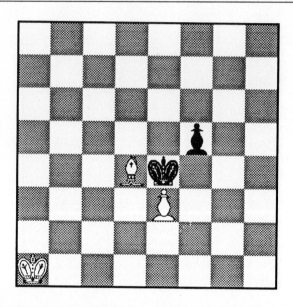

**EXHIBIT 13.5**
Not a win.

of the position from 0 to something near the mate value, in one small step.[5] The real question is how to deal with such gigantic changes in value brought about by very small changes in state. Consider, for instance, the position depicted in Exhibit 13.5. Here, regardless of whose move it is, the remaining white pawn will be exchanged when black plays f4. A searching program will see this coming already quite a long way off. The position may be a lot more complex with several pawns for the side that is trying to win, and the question may be (given that the search will not be able to resolve the question completely), which position that can be reached has the best chance of becoming a win; e.g., not having the last pawn exchanged off.

This involves assigning values from 0 to 90,000 to this set of positions; a rather awesome task, especially when one considers the set of positions where there is just one pawn left for the side trying to win, and it is not clear if it can be exchanged off. Ideally, it would be useful to follow every candidate branch for this set of values to the point where it is "clear" whether the GTV is 0 or 1.

---

[5]It is not a *legal* move to put a pawn on the board, but capturing one has the reverse effect, and that is what we are interested in.

**EXHIBIT 13.6**
Win no matter where Kings are.

In the example given, this can be done. However, there are more complicated examples where this would not be possible. In such situations, the search must terminate with a value that has uncertainty built into it. However, this value should be such that we could expect to *follow a gradient and most often be rewarded with the value toward which the gradient is trending.* What kind of structure can support this?

This problem has already been explored by myself and co-workers [6,21] in connection with the management of searches to avoid certain behaviors[6] that seem silly to human observers. It turns out that the probability density function is also excellent for representing the above problems. However, there must be a method for deciding what the value of a node is; it is not sufficient to leave it as a probability density distribution with range 0 to 90,000.

The key idea is the question of stability and we borrow here from the ideas of McAllester [18] to define a procedure for establishing stability. Consider the position in Exhibit 13.6. Here the two kings are not present, but it does not

---

[6]Such as doing a three-minute search to decide to recapture a queen when this is the only move that could possibly be good.

matter where they are. The position is a clear win for white. How can this be determined?

The basic question is whether the last white pawn can be captured. This generates two goals.

**1.** Capture the pawn.

**2.** Move a piece into position to capture the pawn.

Goal one cannot be accomplished with a king as the pawn is defended. Goal two could be accomplished by advancing the black pawn to f4. This represents a goal toward which progress should be made if the position is to be a draw.

The procedure is to search below this node to determine whether any progress is being made toward the goal. Progress constitutes moving the pawn closer to f4. If no progress is being made, then it is clear that there is sufficient support for the hypothesis that the position is a win.

If the black pawn were on f7 and could still advance two squares before it became blocked, then some progress would be possible. In this case, certain moves for black would constitute progress and their subtrees would be expanded. However, for each such move there will be many white responses that are sufficient to prevent the white pawn from being lost or exchanged. Even though black can make progress toward black's goal of advancing the pawn from f7 to f4, it puts very little stress on white, and once the pawn has reached f5, no further progress is possible. Thus the support for the hypothesis of *win* is very great, and the position should be assigned a value very near the absolute win score, say 85,000 to 90,000.

Now consider the position in Exhibit 13.7. Here the outcome depends very much on where the white king is, and possibly on who is on move. If the white king were on a1, then a very shallow search would establish that black can play Ke4 and f4 and the white pawn is exchanged. If the white king were on g3, we would again go through the procedure of trying to make progress for black and noting how much support there is to keep black from making progress. Thus if black were to play 1.-Ke4, then only the moves (Bc5, Bb6, and Ba7) would keep black from either capturing the white pawn or being able to play his or her pawn to f4 with impunity on the next move. Three out of 16 moves does not constitute great support, so it is justified to continue searching. However, already after 1.- Ke4; 2. Ba7,Ke5 there are no moves by white that allow black to draw (there is the trick 3. Kf2?,f4; 4. Bb8+ wins). Here, and if black had played 2.-Kd3 the number of moves that fail to win begins to decrease dramatically, and support for the win hypothesis is building rapidly. In this example it can be seen that if the issue can be clearly defined, the struggle about whether the goal is achievable is usually sharp and short, terminating with a considerably narrowed range.

How does one back up the distributions generated in this manner? This

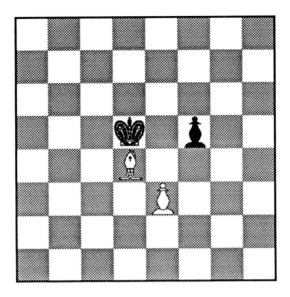

**EXHIBIT 13.7**
Win depends on location of white king.

question is answered in great technical detail in [21]. The answer basically consists of multiplying distributions during the backing up process. Each distribution is absorbed into its parent distribution, where point distributions and actual probability density distributions with large ranges can be absorbed in a uniform way to give a good representation of what is happening in the subtree below.

The effect of support for one extreme of the distribution or the other is to drive the values in the distribution in that direction. Even if there is no clear support for accepting or rejecting the hypothesis, the range will narrow as a function of the additional work.

The key idea of this section is that there are situations in which assigning a singular (point) value to a position is too unreliable. In general, it is necessary to assign a probability density function that ranges over values from optimistic to realistic. Such values can be backed up by precise methods. As long as a node has a large uncertainty associated with it, and as long the value of this node makes a difference in the top level decision of choosing a move, there will be great pressure on the search to resolve the value of the node. This can be done by deciding what actions it would take to arrive at either of the extremal values, and then doing more search below this node and monitoring whether progress is being made. The following possibilities exist.

- □ If one side is able to achieve an extremal goal, then this is the value of the node.

- □ If no progress can be made then the naive view (the expected value) of what is going on is correct.

- □ If progress is being made, but only in a situation where the other side has many equivalent moves, then it would seem that a stable value exists near the naive view.

- □ If progress is being made where the other side has little support, then the search should continue (if at all possible) until either the goal is reached or support is formed.

Ultimately, a more informed view of the value of the node will emerge. This is the fundamental structure of a true goal-oriented search.

## 13.10   Using Constraints and Invariances to Reduce the Branching Factor

Von Neumann [27] formalized the then not-so-clear relationship of singular node values to choosing a move in a perfect information zero-sum adversary game. This minimax algorithm was definitive, but considered too inefficient to be able to handle the exponential growth of possibilities in a search of chess. However, the discovery of the alpha-beta relationship [19] and the later discovery of iterative deepening with transposition and refutation tables [25] turned a search with a purported branching factor of 35 into one that in Hitech [9] had been reduced to the vicinity of 4.5. The status of computer chess would be quite different today without these advances. They were achieved by the use of *logic* within the search.

The alpha-beta relationship rules out having to find more than one *refutation* for any move. The refutation table remembers the move that served best the last time this position was encountered and thus makes the alpha-beta algorithm work very effectively by trying known refutations first. Finally, the transposition table turns a purported tree into a graph in which nodes can be accessed by differing paths. By remembering the values (or value bounds) of subtrees, it is thus possible to avoid re-searching a subtree whose value is already known. This whole experience is the best illustration of reducing branching factors by continually whittling away at not-too-obvious redundancies. Further, all the

| S3 | H2 | D2 | D4 | -  | D5 |  | D1 | D2 | D3 | D4 | D5 | - |
| -  | C4 | H3 | C5 | C1 | -  |  | H1 | H2 | H3 | H4 | H5 | - |
| D3 | S1 | D1 | S4 | S5 | -  |  | C1 | C2 | C3 | C4 | C5 | - |
| C2 | C3 | H4 | H1 | S2 | H5 |  | S1 | S2 | S3 | S4 | S5 | - |

Solution (names of moving cards only):

| D1 | C2 | S1 | D4 | D3 | D4 | C1 | C2 | C3 | S2 | H2 | S4 | C4 | D2 |
| S5 | C5 | H4 | S3 | D1 | H1 | S4 | D2 | H2 | S5 | D3 | D4 | D5 | H5 |

**EXHIBIT 13.8**
Start configuration—goal configuration.

improvements were domain-independent, which serves to endear them to a large group of users.

I have been investigating a solitaire card puzzle [14] that I modified from a standard solitaire game. The game is called SuperPuzz (Copyright Berliner, 1977) and it is the most difficult one-person game I know of. Briefly, the rules of $4 \times N$ SuperPuzz are as follows.

□ Take the first $N$ cards of each suit from a regular deck of playing cards.

□ Deal these out open-face in a raster four high and $N$ wide.

□ Remove the cards of denomination $N$ of each suit from the raster leaving four "holes."

□ A hole can be filled with the card directly following the one to the left of the hole. Thus the *only* card that can be placed into a hole with a spade 4 to the left of it is the spade 5. This in turn leaves a new hole where the spade 5 used to be. When an $N - 1$ denomination card is to the left of a hole, no card can be played there. This is also true if a hole is to the left of a hole. When a hole occurs on the left edge, any ace can be moved there, regardless of whether the ace is already on the left edge.

□ The game is won if the four suits can be organized sequentially, one in each row with the ace at the left. The game is lost when the above condition has not been fulfilled, and there are no more moves.

Exhibit 13.8 shows a starting and final configuration for the $4 \times 6$ game.

It turns out that a very high percentage of SuperPuzz deals can be won. Our data indicate that 82% of the $4 \times 6$ deals can be won and that this percentage is maintained through $4 \times 13$. It is interesting to note however, that expert humans are competitive only in the $4 \times 6$ puzzle and start to do worse as $N$ goes up.

The ideal width for a beginner is 4 × 6, and this can be increased as the player becomes more proficient.

We have been pursuing SuperPuzz with a variety of problem solvers for about 10 years now. In the 4 × 8 domain, solutions reach lengths of over 50 moves and include many that are so intricate and nonintuitive that they are difficult for a human to "understand." The branching factor of SuperPuzz is about 4.0. Each hole at the left raises the branching factor by four new moves. Near the end of the games the branching factor will be very near 1.0; however, during the critical parts of the solution process there are usually about four moves to choose from. The solutions in the 4 × 6 domain are usually less than 28 ply in depth, while 4 × 9 solutions are typically 60 to 80 moves long, and the 4 × 13 solutions range from 100 to 130 moves. Even if the branching factor were 2.0, this would be much too large a space to investigate without some very definitive approach. Typically, branching factors in the vicinity of 1.15 must be reached to get the solution effort to be tractable, although for the wider puzzles such as 4 × 13 this is still too large. Thus it is necessary to drastically reduce the branching factor to have any hope of finding solutions or asserting "no solution."

It should be noted that an original configuration of SuperPuzz may be winnable or not. However, it is possible to turn a winnable configuration into a nonwinnable one with one bad move. Typically, there are many ways to solve a problem, even if one discounts transposing moves that do not have to come in any exact sequence. However, there are many more thousands of ways to botch the solution. Thus the main effort in finding a solution is not to stray away from a winning path.

The original investigations were with the 4 × 6 puzzle where it offered a good vehicle for investigating various search paradigms [14]. Already with this puzzle width it was noticed by some students, who were given this as a problem solving task, that it was possible to detect that a given card was "deadlocked;" i.e., it could never move at any future time. Noticing this constraint allowed great search savings as the subtree of the deadlocked configuration need never be searched. As the wider varieties of SuperPuzz were investigated, it became clear that finding deadlocks was not enough. First, there were many positions that were not winnable that the deadlock algorithm could not reject. Second, as the puzzle got wider, the cost of doing the deadlock computation got greater, and the benefits did not increase commensurably.

We then turned our attention to other ways of reducing the branching factor. One way was already in place; this was a hash table that identified previously visited nodes. This saves having to repeat searches of positions reached by different paths; e.g., a move sequence such as A, B, C could easily lead to the same position as the sequence B, C, A. We estimate that this device, in itself, reduces the effective branching factor to the vicinity of 1.5. However, this is not nearly enough reduction as $1.5^{60} = 3.6*10^{12}$. Further, as the number

| S1 | C2 | C3 | C4 | C1 | - |
|----|----|----|----|----|----|
| H1 | H2 | H3 | D3 | D4 | D5 |
| D1 | D2 | - | - | H4 | H5 |
| - | S2 | S3 | S4 | S5 | C5 |

**EXHIBIT 13.9**
Moving C1 loses.

of potential entries into the hash table almost always exceeds the size of the hash table, some entry replacement algorithm must be applied. No matter how clever this may be, it turns out that many useful entires will be replaced and as the number of entries clambering to get into the hash table grows very large, the utility of the hash table starts to approximate that of a cache of recently used results—a considerable weakening of the whole process. Thus it is to the problem solver's advantage to tender as few nodes as possible to be entries in the hash table.

Now it is necessary to get more domain-specific. There are points in the solution process where knowing that a certain move does not lead to a solution allows important reductions. For instance, in Exhibit 13.9, if immediately moving C1 to the left fails, then we can be sure that if a solution can be attained from this position it can only be reached in the following two ways:

1. By moving one or more of the aces already on the left.

2. By maintaining the aces in their present positions, if the C2 were at some future point placed behind the C1 in its present position.

The reason for constraint 2 is that it has been determined that moving the C1 does not win. This includes all possible continuations *except* those that move the C2 into the space behind the present C1 location, which can no longer be done once the C1 has moved. Thus until the C2 has moved, there is no hope of a solution in this subtree. This observation can result in significant savings. Further, by always forcing an ace move into an unoccupied left-hand slot, such savings can be realized regularly. For instance, if the solution attempt now proceeds by moving one of the left-edge aces, the C1 should still be moved next to see if the new ace configuration has led to a solution. It happens, that in the above position moving C1 immediately loses, but both alternatives lead to wins.

A *constraint* results from applying a procedure at a certain node to determine that that node's subtree need not be searched. The procedure remains the same, requiring merely the appropriate set of parameters for each call.

Another useful device, if applicable, is the *invariance* [5]. An invariance is a rule that is produced when a certain *act* results in *failure*, and is cached for future use. An invariance is of the form (Until Cond:Do-not-do Act). This can result in multiple cached rules, any of which can be invoked when contemplating an action. Actually, constraint 2 above is an invariance that states that as long as no ace moves have taken place, there is no point in placing the C1 until the C2 has moved behind it. Invariances are more powerful than constraining procedures in that they avoid the need for recomputing whether the constraining relationship applies in the present instance. The invariance specifies under what conditions it does apply, and this is almost always easier to verify than it is to rerun the constraining procedure calculation.

During the SuperPuzz investigation a very powerful use of invariances was discovered by a co-worker [3]. It was noticed that, in general, once card X had been moved and the full-width search below that node had failed to produce a solution, then it was of no use to move card X in any further solution attempts in subtrees with alternate moves to X, unless the card located behind X or the destination to which X could go changed. This is called *freezing X*. It is a generalization of rule 2 above. It has a powerful effect in constraining the tree, as in many cases the cards that need be moved to invalidate the invariance cannot be moved or were already in place. This has the effect of bringing the search to a rapid conclusion once several freezing invariances have been posited.

Another excellent idea by [3] was the idea of an ace-wave. Earlier formulations allowed the shuffling of aces already on the left edge when there was a hole on the left edge. This meant that up to 24 different left-edge-ace configurations may have to be stored and investigated. By noticing that the location of an Ace was not permanently fixed until the 2 behind it was played while all other aces were in place, it was possible to associate unfixed aces in a *wave*, none of which would be bound to a particular row until ready. This reduced the storage and the search requirements considerably. The above give some idea of the clever devices that are available in almost any domain. Once discovered they may reduce the branching factor in a decisive manner so that intractable problems suddenly become tractable.

SuperPuzz has several highly attractive properties as a domain for investigating search:

☐ It is possible to measure performance in terms of solution rate across a set of randomly selected problems. This measure of success relates much better to real-world demands than solution path length, which is the standard measure for the current fare of single-agent testbeds such as the 15-puzzle.

☐ It comes in a variety of difficulties (widths).

☐ The solution rate of problems of a given width is not a function of that width, but the difficulty of solution is.

☐ Thus methods that are excellent at some width may not be so at wider problems.

The history of investigation of SuperPuzz is typical of what search can do for a problem. Initially, I was able to outperform my program at 4 × 6. That soon was no longer possible. After some time, performance of the program was so much better than mine at widths up to eight (all that was possible at the time) that I used it to learn new ideas and to track down simple knowledge that could help its performance further. The latest version solves 4 × 13 puzzles in an average time of 2 minutes using a C program running on a DEC-PMax. However, about 4% of the problems can run for 4 hours without producing an answer or a "no solution." This shows that there is room for additional ideas.

A human solves 4 × 6 problems in a series of up to six episodes, each relatively short (three to five moves) and accomplishing some purpose without creating too many additional problems. The question of boxing oneself in while trying to solve some subproblem is where expertise plays a part, and one can get better at anticipating the kinds of problems one can create in solving a subproblem. Already in the 4 × 8 puzzle the solution lengths are on the order of 45 moves, and it is extremely difficult to regularly synthesize solutions in the above manner. There are too many twists and turns in the more difficult solutions for even an expert human to make a correct decision every time without having recourse to some means of keeping track of places where it might be meaningful to investigate alternatives. This is, of course, where the computer has a tremendous advantage. When playing over a 4 × 13 solution, one almost always has no idea what subgoals are being accomplished until the solution process is about one-half complete. We feel this is typical of the mind-boggling results that search can and will produce for many well formed problems.

## 13.11   The Inter-mixing of Facts and Heuristics

As already stated, the research above was performed over a long period of time during which many ideas were introduced and retained or rejected according to their performance. Sometimes, the observation of some senseless pursuit by the search led to the formulation of an algorithm to prevent that behavior and thus reduce the branching factor. Such formulations were usually of the form: Under conditions (X, Y, Z) it is safe to not search the present subtree. Sometimes, after a number of such rules had been added, each producing a speed up in the solution process, it was noted that the addition of a new rule resulted in the failure to solve a problem with a known solution.

This was then found to be due to an error in the formulation of a rule that had been put in place earlier and had been serving well to speed things up and thus make more problems tractable and more solutions possible. However, the addition of the new rule took away enough additional options so that the very small set of solution paths disappeared completely. The logical flaw was then remedied and things continued apace.

What is interesting about this experience is that the supposedly "factual" rules were in reality not so. Thus they were really like *absolute heuristics* if I may coin a term. An absolute heuristic is something such as, "Never walk alone at night in Central Park." This would seem to be a good rule, but it should not be absolute, as it could be that by walking through Central Park on a particular night you might find a $10,000 bill. In practice, absolute heuristics tend to be quite useful, except for that once in a while situation. However, when tractability problems exist it seems to be clearly preferable to get more solutions even at the cost of sometimes missing a solution that could have been obtained if it were not for the flawed rule. That is the nature of heuristics.

However, no rule should be absolute unless it can be shown to be always true. Since this is unlikely to be possible for most rules, it means that we need some truth-likelihood measure for each rule that exists in a belief system. This will direct problem solving effort into those subtrees that are most likely to contain solutions, while preventing the arbitrary exclusion of even the most unlikely path.

The bottom line is that *there must be a continuum of likelihoods for all beliefs, ranging from facts to the merest of tenuous correlations*. In distinction to the previous observations about smooth value surfaces, we are now talking about the properties of problem solving operators. Apparently the likelihood of success of these operators should be a real-valued number. Thus it should be possible to move down the scale of likelihood of success in applying operators, ranging from facts to low-level heuristics. Further, in any kind of truth-maintenance system, such as a belief-system, it clearly should be possible to adjust the likelihoods of all nonfacts. My favorite example of a former nonfact that no one disbelieved is the four-color theorem, which by joining the realm of facts added almost nothing to its likelihood.

## 13.12   Structuring Knowledge to Get the Effect of Planning

Ideally, it should be possible to arrange a value space so that for every state it is possible to make a best move by merely following an upward gradient. This is theoretically possible for a game like chess, but not very likely to ever be achieved. When this amount of knowledge for any domain is available, the domain is *solved* and searches are no longer necessary. Our notion of a value space contains many surfaces that produce ordering of the elements that make up that surface. In chess, for instance, it is possible to arrive at an "optimal" location of one's pieces by following the lowest level gradient. As we have shown, there will be places where there are cliffs in the surface that must be dealt with. We now examine the interfacing of cliffs and plains.

Some chess programs, notably Belle, have made a point of having a heuristic value structure that precludes the sum of multiple *positional* advantages being equal to or greater than the value of the smallest *material* advantage, a pawn. This means that Belle would never sacrifice a pawn to get positional compensation. It might be forced to part with a pawn and would seek aid from heuristic knowledge in how to get the most for it, but it would never voluntarily do so. In contrast, programs such as Hitech do this occasionally. It is worth examining what the effect of such a schism between different types of advantages implies.

To stratify the value space as Belle does is to admit of two different kinds of moves.

1. Moves that affect the material balance.

2. Moves that deal with positional issues.

It is like prerelativity physics. Energy is energy, and mass is mass, and never the twain shall meet. However, in chess as in physics there are times when it is essential to metamorphose one form into the other. To deny the possibility of doing this, is to cut the program off from certain kinds of moves that are well recognized as being effective. This approach was taken in Belle to achieve certain efficiencies in the evaluation process (when one side is ahead in terms of material, that side *is* ahead). This appears to be wrong. However, there could be a point to having stratified value levels.

Certain advantages are generically more important than others. Usually, being a pawn ahead conveys a very meaningful, if not winning advantage on the side having this advantage. Players such as Bobby Fischer would take very large risks to have the advantage of a pawn (indicating that he thought this to be close to a winning advantage) while others such as Spassky would sacrifice a pawn to make his opponent sufficiently uncomfortable. Despite Fischer's successes, it is generally felt that he was wrong, and today's world champions lean more in the direction of Spassky.

In any case, it is clear that advantages come in different shapes and sizes. Further, it is necessary to be able to both

1. distinguish among several potential small advantages to choose from, and

2. be able to exchange several small advantages for a large advantage and vice versa.

The above is recursively true up the scale of advantages from slightly better placement of pieces to huge advantages in material (or a clear mating attack). To deal with this range of possibilities we have found it useful in Hitech [13] to have three ranges of values that can be associated with entities on the chessboard.

The following types of advantages can be discerned by Hitech, ranking from low to high.

- □ The position of the pieces, which in general should be encouraged to move to the center and to get into the vicinity of the opposing king.

- □ Groups of pieces that can form patterns of value. This includes king-safety patterns, pawn structure, detection of pawns that can be advanced to queen with no opposition, and changes in value of the pieces with changes in the pawn structure.

- □ The tried and true material count.

However, in Hitech it is possible to see advantages of all three types exchanged for one another, though exchanging between adjacent categories is most prevalent. By allowing three different levels of advantage, three different planes will occur on the evaluation surface. By making the height difference between adjacent planes the minimum possible, places are created on the value surface where exchanges of different types of value can occur. This means that a marble being propelled uphill on such a surface will have places where it can *change planes* with a minimal input of energy. The better this is done, the more such opportunities will exist. Each such opportunity provides the ability to implement a strategic, or planning, decision: *the ability to exchange one type of advantage for another*, something that is considered a very difficult subject in advanced texts on chess.

In playing chess one should not only try to place the pieces optimally. One should also be able to recognize patterns that may not optimize the location of the individual pieces at all. Patterns are hilltops on the value surface that are highly specified. The distance between such hilltops is of utmost importance. It is very much as with currency. If our currency only contained pennies, and one-thousand-dollar bills, it would be a difficult world in which to practice economics. However, the ability to exchange small units for somewhat larger ones makes economic transactions easy. Between large transactions, the focus is on the economics of small transactions. By making it possible to transit easily from one value surface to another, a program can attain the ability to execute what to humans appear to be strategies (the converting of one advantage to another).

## 13.13    Some CMU Firsts

In this section we recount some search related firsts that were achieved at CMU.

▢ The use of continuous evaluation functions together with *application co-efficients* to track changes in context was pioneered in the backgammon program BKG [7,11], which beat the world champion in 1979, and the importance of these issues to the structure of representations in general was described in [8].

▢ A history of excellence in game playing programs. CMU has pioneered computational Othello, and had the best program in the world during most of the 1980s [17,22]. Othello is the first game in which computers established a clear dominance over the best human players, although no visible contest with a world champion was ever arranged.

▢ Hitech, the first chess machine/program to be rated in the top 1% of all chess players, and Deep Thought, the first machine/program to defeat a grandmaster in tournament competition and establish a rating equivalent to grandmaster.

▢ The B* search algorithm, the first search using ranges as node values [6]. This was followed by the PB* algorithm [21], which was the first to use distributions to capture the value of a node. It is now widely held that this is the only correct way to proceed with the development of pure selective search algorithms.

▢ The singular extension algorithm for introducing massive amounts of selectivity into a brute force search at reasonable costs [2].

▢ The use of pattern recognition on a large scale in chess programs was pioneered by Hitech [9]. This achievement was made possible by parallel pattern recognition hardware and allowed the noticing of a set of advantages that had hitherto been ignored. It also made possible an additional layer of values on the value surface 13.4. One creative use of this pattern recognition capability was to recognize positions with a known GTV and thus bring the search in that subtree to a halt. This would be rather expensive to do in software, as it is expensive to maintain the higher-level primitives that our pattern recognition procedures use.

▢ TECH [16], the first chess program to demonstrate that the brute force approach to search could be made to work well.

▢ The first learning of nonlinear evaluation functions for Othello [22] was done with the aid of self-play. The first learning of linear coefficients for positional value functions was first done in Deep Thought, where 900 master games were used as exemplar for good piece locations. Learned evaluation functions appear to perform in a far superior manner to those that are hand-crafted.

▢ The use of a split (or double) hash table to remember nodes in a search was introduced by Hitech [13]. This method deals with the replacement strategy used in the hash table. Using a most-recently-used method to decide which entry to keep makes the hash table into a cache that is very useful for dealing with the current subtree. However, that allows important results near the root of the tree to be replaced, which can result in spending large amounts of time rediscovering these results. In Hitech a *privileged depth* was posited, and no node within that distance of the root could be replaced by a node further away. The privileged depth was chosen so that about 15% of the hash table was used for privileged nodes. In this manner the best of both worlds was achieved; important nodes were retained, and the hash table, which is always overburdened with new results, can keep those that would be most pertinent in the current subtree.

□ Excellent time control for chess programs. In Hitech [13] the decision as to whether to continue or abandon searches is made based on the degree to which the value of a move changes with successive iterations of search. When Hitech is sure it knows what it wants to do, search can be terminated quite early, while in situations where it is unsure or unhappy, searches can go on for quite some time.

□ The recapture extension heuristic for chess was pioneered in Patsoc [12] and brought to full fruition in Hitech [13]. This is a method of lengthening the analysis in tree branches that have recaptures in them. A capture-recapture pair constitute a highly forcing sequence. This in turn means that something important may be in the process of being accomplished (or avoided). Thus such branches should be extended.

## 13.14  Summary and Conclusions

We have presented a structure that captures those qualities of human searching that seem to be verifiable and useful in a knowledge structure. This structure encompasses the following facets.

□ It allows factual and heuristic knowledge to coexist.

□ It produces a value surface that is smooth when possible and yet allows different levels of understanding to be represented.

□ It allows the treatment of uncertainty due to

  – Lack of precise information.

  – Possibility of opponent error.

□ It makes it possible to have a search that is

  – Driven by context rather than prespecification.

– Free of the horizon effect.

Some aspects of this structure have already been adequately tested. It now remains to integrate those that have not, and to determine the performance of the vehicle.

There are now methods for reducing the effective depth of a search and for reducing the branching factor. Such methods have, in the case of chess, resulted in making a problem that was initially thought to be growing at too fast a rate, into a tractable problem. We consider SuperPuzz to be a considerably more interesting object of study then the 15-puzzle that seems to be today's standard. SuperPuzz provides the opportunity to study solution rates rather than the rather infertile path length, and also allows increasing the problem difficulty in moderate steps.

In the past, much effort has been expended in attempting to have machine searches duplicate the excellent behavior of humans. This type of effort is still appropriate. However, the state of the art in hardware and searching technology has now reached the point where searches can do things that humans would not dream of and can barely understand. This will allow many new problems to be attacked with impunity.

# References

[1] D. H. Ackley and H. J. Berliner. The qbkg system: Knowledge representation for producing and explaining judgements. Technical Report CMU-CS-83-116, Carnegie Mellon University, Pittsburgh, PA, 1983.

[2] M. Campbell, T. Anantharaman, and F. Hsu. Singular extensions: Adding selectivity to brute force searching. In *AAAI Spring Symposium on Computer Game Playing*, 1988.

[3] J. Barrera. Personal communication, 1990.

[4] E. R. Berlekamp, et al. *Winning Ways for your Mathematical Plays*. Academic Press, 1982.

[5] H. Berliner. The use of domain-dependent descriptions in tree searching. In A. K. Jones, ed., *Perspectives on Computer Science: From the 10th Anniversary Symposium of the Computer Science Department, Carnegie Mellon University*. Academic Press, 1977.

[6] H. Berliner. The b* tree search algorithm: A best-first proof procedure. *Artificial Intelligence*, 12(1), 1979.

[7] H. Berliner. On the construction of evaluation functions for large domains. In *Sixth International Joint Conference on Artificial Intelligence*, pp. 53-55. IJCAI, 1979.

[8] H. Berliner. Some observations on problem solving. In *Proceeding of the Third CSCSI Conference*. Canadian Society for Computational Studies of Intelligence, 1980.

[9] H. Berliner and C. Ebeling. Pattern knowledge and search: The suprem architecture. *Artificial Intelligence*, 38(2):161-198, 1989.

[10] H. J. Berliner. Some necessary conditions for a master chess program. In *Third International Joint Conference on Artificial Intelligence*, pp. 77-85. IJCAI, 1973.

[11] H. J. Berliner. Backgammon computer program beats world champion. *Artificial Intelligence*, 14(2):205-220, 1980.

[12] H. J. Berliner. Computer chess at Carnegie Mellon University. In D. Beal, ed., *Advances in Computer Chess—4*. Elmsford, NY: Pergamon Press, 1985.

[13] H. J. Berliner. Some innovations introduced by hitech. *Journal of the International Computer Chess Association*, 10(3), 1987.

[14] H. J. Berliner and G. J. Goetsch. A study of search methods and the effect of constraint satisfaction. Technical Report, Carnegie Mellon University Department of Computer Science, 1984.

[15] M. R. B. Clarke. A quantitative study of king and pawn against king. In M. R. B. Clarke, ed., *Advances in Computer Chess 1*, pp. 108-115, Edinburgh: Edinburgh University Press, 1977.

[16] J. J. Gillogly. The technology chess program. *Artificial Intelligence*, 3:145-163, 1972.

[17] S. Mahajan, K. F. Lee. A pattern classification approach to evaluation function learning. *Artificial Intelligence*, 36, 1988.

[18] D. A. McAllester. Conspiracy numbers for min-max search. *Artificial Intelligence*, 33(3):287-310, 1988.

[19] H. Simon, A. Newell, and C. Shaw. Chess playing programs and the problem of complexity. In E.A. Feigenbaum and J. Feldman, eds., *Computers and Thought*. McGraw-Hill, 1963.

[20] A. J. Palay. The b* tree search algorithm—new results. *Artificial Intelligence*, 19(2), 1982.

[21] A. J. Palay. *Searching with Probabilities*. Pitman Research Notes in Artificial Intelligence 1984.

[22] P. S. Rosenbloom. A world-championship-level othello program. Technical Report, Carnegie Mellon University Department of Computer Science, 1981.

[23] S. Russell and E. Wefald. Multi-level decision-theoretic search. In *AAAI Spring Symposium on Computer Game Playing*, pp. 3-7. IJCAI, 1988.

[24] J. Schaeffer. Personal communication, 1989.

[25] D. J. Slate and L. R. Atkin. Chess 4.5—the northwestern university chess program. In P. Frey, ed., *Chess Skill in Man and Machine*. Springer Verlag, 1977.

[26] K. Thompson. Retrograde analysis of certain endgames. *Journal of the International Computer Chess Association*, 9(3), 1988.

[27] J. Von Neumann and O. Morgenstern. *Theory of Games and Economic Behavior*. Princeton University Press, 1947.

# 14

---

# Computer Vision as a Physical Science

Takeo Kanade

---

## 14.1 Introduction

Vision is one of the most important perceptual capabilities that any autonomous intelligent system, either natural or artificial, can possess in order to operate in the real world. Computer vision encompasses the development of both the computational theories and the technological means to realize artificial vision systems with performance equal to or greater than that of humans.

The goal of computer vision turns out to be extremely difficult. Some of the difficulties are technological, such as the requirements for huge amounts of processing power, memory, and communication bandwidth. Other difficulties are more fundamental. A large number of factors, such as object shape, illumination, surface properties, sensor characteristics, and more, all contribute to determining the color and intensity of image pixels; the effects of any single factor are confounded by the effects of other factors. Consequently, many early vision problems of recovering scene properties (such as shape) from images are underconstrained, or ill posed, meaning that the images alone do not contain enough information to uniquely solve them. Therefore correctly interpreting images and constructing descriptions from them requires additional constraints and knowledge.

Yet, we humans seem to do very well at interpreting images. Given a two-dimensional (2D) image we easily determine the correct interpretation of the three-dimensional (3D) relationships among objects in the scene. We identify objects consistently over a wide range of viewpoints and lighting conditions. We determine surface properties such as roughness and reflectance from images. We effectively utilize vision to map the world around us, enabling us to move without collisions or to grasp objects accurately. Human vision is an existence proof of a most powerful vision machine, which can deal very robustly with many difficult vision problems, such as distortions by projection, motion, stereo, texture, shading, and color. In doing so, humans do not seem to use much knowledge about the physical processes underlying those problems. In fact, most people know very little about optics, geometry, and physics. Moreover, when given images from exotic sensors, such as synthetic aperture radars (SAR), scanning electron microscopes (SEM), and forward-looking infrared (FLIR) sensors, humans can often interpret them correctly without asking much about how the images were created.

Historically, the fact that human vision provides a most compelling reference model and yet does not seem to rely on the knowledge of physical aspects of vision led many vision researchers to rush out and attempt to invent vision "algorithms" or build vision "systems" without first determining the information that images actually contain. Attention naturally focused on phenomenological performance, since it appeared that the underlying physical phenomena were too complicated to model, that images were too noisy for reliable algorithmic feature extraction, and that humans seemed to resolve such difficulties by using empirical domain-specific knowledge. Consequently, this approach was inevitably heuristic, since the major source of ideas was introspection or analogy from mechanisms that natural systems might use. The results from this approach were hard to characterize and to generalize. Basic vision problems were neither identified nor addressed.

However, attention has recently turned to putting the geometrical, physical, and optical processes underlying vision into a quantitative, computational framework. Now the emphasis is on developing *physical* models for computer vision. Such modeling reveals the structure of visual information: the exact information that is contained in an image, the limits of processing algorithms, and the heuristic knowledge required to resolve any remaining ambiguity. Thus algorithms derived from physical modeling are far more powerful and quantitative, and their performance far more predictable and generalizable than previous ad hoc methods based solely on heuristics. In fact, one of the most exciting discoveries in recent computer vision research is that natural generic constraints are often sufficient to solve many fundamental vision problems, some of which had been thought impossible to solve without applying heuristics.

In the last 10 years, the vision group of Carnegie Mellon University (CMU) has been spearheading the development of a systematic theory for vision based on physical knowledge. This theory, which I refer to as physically based vision,

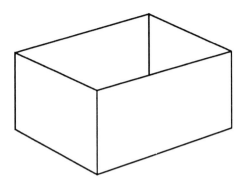

A "Box" line drawing

**EXHIBIT 14.1**
A "box" line drawing.

emphasizes the use of knowledge about geometry, physics, optics, and statistics to model and solve basic vision problems. It is appropriate on the occasion of the CMU Computer Science 25th Anniversary to highlight our contributions to this new approach to vision. This chapter will illustrate physically based vision by using examples that my colleagues and I have developed here at CMU. These examples are drawn from three areas in computer vision: the determination of 3D shape from images; the analysis of object color and surface reflection, and uncertainty in visual measurements. In each area, I will use a (seemingly) simple problem as the background, then present our solution, and then give a broader perspective in that area.

## 14.2   Geometry and Shape Constraints

### 14.2.1   A Problem: Interpreting Line Drawings

As the first example, consider the simple line drawing shown in Exhibit 14.1. What shape does this represent? Most people would be quick to say that this is a line drawing of a box with no lid. When asked about the reason for that interpretation, they would say, "I learned it over the years," or "That shape is the most familiar to me." Though not incorrect, these answers simply duck the questions about computational aspects of vision.

The line drawing is 2D, and the interpretation of it is a 3D shape. In general, many different shapes can give rise to the same line drawing. Therefore the process of interpretation must resolve ambiguity. To reach a single interpretation, some constraints about possible interpretations must have been used. Moreover, these constraints must be very strong: not only do people tend to agree on a single interpretation, but some people find the possibility of multiple interpretations difficult to accept. The line drawing does not have any shading or color, so the constraints must be geometrical in nature. The natural question to ask is, "How far does geometry constrain the interpretation of the line drawing?"

### 14.2.2   The Origami World

The study of computer interpretation of line drawings as three-dimensional scenes has captured interest in computer vision from the beginning. Guzman [1] wrote a program to segment line drawings into objects based on a collection of heuristic rules on the "strengths" of links between regions. Huffman [3] discovered a mathematical way to capture the geometrical constraints of a solid "trihedral" world by using labels that represent physical meanings of lines. Waltz [32] extended the idea to include shadows as well as devising an efficient procedure for labeling. However, the problem of multiplicity of interpretations was not addressed. Moreover, the Huffman-Waltz labeling could not handle the simple line drawing of Exhibit 14.1: it is classified as "impossible." I developed a theory of the Origami World [4] to begin to answer these questions.

Imagine a world that consists entirely of planar surfaces, which may be folded, cut, or glued together only along straight lines. This world is named the "Origami World." In the Origami World, we can develop a mathematical algorithm, which, given a line drawing like Exhibit 14.1, specifies all the shapes that can generate the given picture.

In the Origami World, Exhibit 14.1 could be any one of eight different shapes. Two of them are shown in Exhibit 14.2 by using special symbols to represent shapes. The interpretation on the left represents a "normal" box like the one we tend to consider. The interpretation on the right, however, represents another shape, which does not look like a "normal" box, but can actually generate the same picture. Moreover, the labelings shown in Exhibit 14.2 actually specify only the qualitative nature of the shape. For example, in the "normal" box interpretation, humans think of only a rectangular box where the front walls of the box meet at a right angle. However, any angle between 0° and 90° is in fact possible and the resultant shape projects onto the same line drawing, if other parts of the shape vary accordingly. Likewise, each interpretation in Exhibit 14.2 actually represents a continuous family of possible 3D shapes that

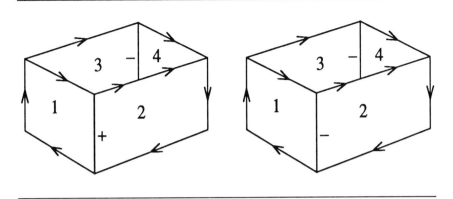

**EXHIBIT 14.2**
"Box" interpretations. Two are shown here by assigning Huffman's labels: +, −, and ↑ to each line. The labels signify the physical meaning of the lines. The labels + and − stand for a convex edge, that is, the two surfaces meet there and form convexity or concavity, respectively, when seen from the current viewing direction. The label ↑ stands for an occluding edge. That means that the region to its right, when standing in the direction of the arrow, occludes the region to its left. The interpretation on the left corresponds to a "normal" box, where surfaces 1 and 2 form convexity and occlude surfaces 3 and 4 which form concavity. The interpretation on the right, however, represents a "squashed" shape, since surfaces 1 and 2 also form a concavity.

can generate the same line drawing. Metaphorically speaking, there are 8 × ∞ interpretations of Exhibit 14.1 in the Origami World. It should be remembered that the real world is larger than the Origami World, and thus there are even more possibilities since the real world is not limited to planes and straight edges.

### 14.2.3  Principle of Nonaccidental Regularities

Why, then, do we tend to consider only a single interpretation, a so-called rectangular box shape? To say "the shape is *more* familiar" does not really answer the question, since most of us, in fact, *cannot* think of multiple interpretations. We do not select a particular interpretation after we think of all the possibilities. Rather we think of *only* the rectangular shape. Thus geometrically speaking, additional shape constraints must be used in a relatively early stage in order to reach the particular interpretation. One interesting class of constraints can be obtained from the principle of nonaccidental regularities [5], which states, "Regularities observable in the picture are not from accidental alignments, but are projections of real regularities." Examples of the principle include the following.

## Skew Symmetry

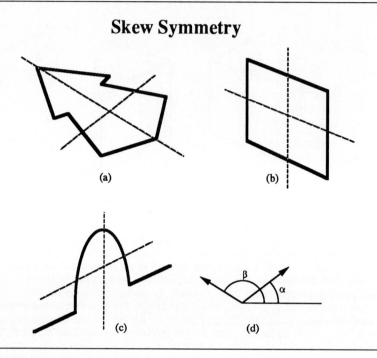

(a)        (b)

(c)        (d)

**EXHIBIT 14.3**
Skew symmetry.

□ *Parallelism*: parallel lines in an image are to be interpreted as parallel lines in 3D.

□ *Texture gradient*: a gradient in the spacing of textured elements is interpreted as regularly spaced elements in the 3D world with a surface slant relative to the viewer.

□ *Skew symmetry*: skew symmetry in an image is interpreted as real symmetry viewed from some unknown view direction.

Skew symmetry was a new concept that I introduced [5]. As illustrated in Exhibit 14.3, skew symmetry is an image feature in which a reflective property is observed with respect to skewed axes, rather than perpendicular axes. Relating a skew symmetry in an image to a real symmetry in space creates strong constraints on surface orientations.

An important point about nonaccidental regularities is that 3D regularities in the scene always result in corresponding 2D regularities in the image, but the inverse is not always true. For example, parallel lines in 2D could be the result of

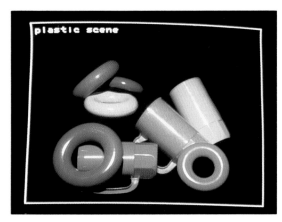

**COLOR PLATE 1**
A color photo of plastic objects.

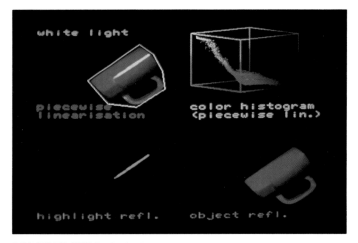

**COLOR PLATE 2** A single cup illuminated with white light source.

**COLOR PLATE 3**
Color histogram of the whole image of plastic objects.

**COLOR PLATE 4**
Segmentation of plastic objects by using dichromatic reflection model.

**COLOR PLATE 5**
(a) Body and (b) surface reflection images of plastic objects.

(a)

(b)

a particular alignment of nonparallel 3D lines. The probability of such an alignment is vanishingly small, however. The principle of nonaccidental regularities formalizes the fact that the preferred interpretation of 2D regularities is in terms of 3D regularities. Once we assert the principle of nonaccidental regularities, we can use a mathematical technique, such as the gradient space representation [6], to map the image properties into the constraints that the interpreted shape must satisfy. Those constraints can be used to narrow and screen the possible interpretations while creating partial interpretations. Coming back to the box example, we can actually prove that the so-called rectangular natural box is the only interpretation that can satisfy the nonaccidental regularities principle.

## 14.2.4  Perspective: Geometric Constraints

One of the contributions of the Origami World is that it demonstrated a simple fact in vision: there are a multiplicity of possible image interpretations, and *if* we want to reach a unique interpretation, we must use constraints or heuristics. Since humans usually think of only a single interpretation, many vision researchers accepted, probably too hastily, the requirement that a computer vision program *must* also generate only a single interpretation. Early researchers attempted to meet this requirement by incorporating heuristics, often implicitly, without understanding their effects, limitations, or implications. In contrast, in the Origami World, interpretation was constrained by the principle of nonaccidental regularities, which enumerated a collection of rules relating image and world features, and permitted an exact specification of the set of possible interpretations.

The individual rules of nonaccidental regularities may have been conceived from observations of human perception, and they are heuristic in the sense that they do not always hold. However, the principle of nonaccidental regularities was applied in ways that are purely geometrical and rigorous. The implications were clearly defined and therefore it was possible to predict the consequences when rules did not apply. In this sense they are not ad hoc. This is in direct contrast to the heuristic methods, ranging from Guzman's line-drawing interpretation method [1] of the early 1970s to the use of global minimization of a certain energy-related term to resolve ambiguities in matching, smoothing, or interpreting patterns. In these cases, the implications are neither clearly defined nor predictable in terms of physical reality.

A series of works appeared in the last decade which formalized many of the computational constraints which relate properties in the image domain to 3D shape constraints. The contributions of our CMU vision group include a theory for affine-transformable patterns by Kanade and Kender [6], Kender's theory of shape from texture [8], Shafer's theory for recovering shape from occluding contours of generalized cylinders [27], and, more recently, Krumm and Shafer's analysis of image spectrograms [12].

## 14.3    Color and Reflectance

### 14.3.1    A Problem: Highlights in Color Photographs

Examine the color image of Color Plate 1. In addition to cylindrical and toroidal shapes of objects, we can readily recognize that the object surfaces are plastic and glossy in appearance. Also, we can conclude that the bright white regions are due to highlights. Interestingly, we do not interpret them as white paint on the surfaces.

Shape, surface glossiness, and specularity are scene properties that we seem to be able to deduce from the color image, although there is no apparent direct one-to-one mapping between observable features in the image and those scene properties. From introspection we may develop a heuristic rule for the task of extracting highlights from the image, such as

*If*   intensity > 100,   *then*   highlight.

This rule may work most of the time. It is clear, however, that this rule does not capture the essence of highlights. Thus it will fail, but we don't know when or exactly why. Highlights in a color photograph must be a result of some physical process that involves shape, surface properties, and illumination. Isn't there a more systematic way, based on physical knowledge rather than phenomenological descriptions, to detect highlights, and even to recover some of the properties of the object and the illumination from the image?

### 14.3.2    Dichromatic Reflection Model

Shafer, Klinker, and myself have worked on this color understanding problem since 1984. Our approach was to call upon a physical model of color reflection. The model we used is called the dichromatic reflection model [28] for opaque dielectric materials, such as plastics. Exhibit 14.4 sketches the primary reflection processes. When light from the illumination source hits the surface, it strikes the interface with the transparent medium. Some of the light is reflected immediately according to Fresnel's laws. This light, which we call *surface reflection*, has a color that is typically about the same as the illuminant. Surface reflection accounts for the glossiness. Surface reflection is highly directional—if the surface is smooth, the surface reflection will be very specular, creating highlights; if the surface is rough, it will be somewhat diffused.

The light that is not reflected at the interface penetrates into the bulk of the material, and there it begins to scatter off the pigment or other colorant particles in the material. Eventually, some portion of it is reflected back across the interface into the air; we call this *body reflection*. Light from body reflection

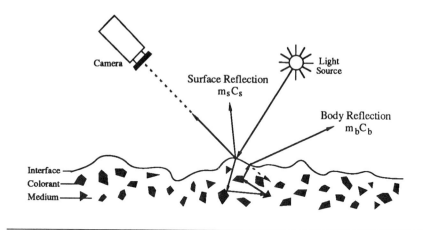

**EXHIBIT 14.4**
Dichromatic model of color reflection.

has a color that is determined by the object colorant as well as the illuminant. A typical and appropriate model for the strength of body reflection is the Lambertian model, which states that the amount of reflection is uniform in direction and is determined by the product of the reflectivity of the material and the cosine of the incident angle. Thus, surfaces facing more toward the light source show brighter color, while those facing more away from it show darker color. Body reflection is responsible for "object color," which is the characteristic color of a specific object, and its shading provides an important clue to the perception of the object shape.

In summary, the dichromatic reflection model states that the observed color at each point in the image consists of two colors, the surface reflection color and the body reflection color. Hence, the name "dichromatic reflection model." Under the same illumination, the two component colors themselves do not vary across surfaces with the same color, but the magnitudes (relative intensities) of these color components vary from point to point due to variation in the geometric relationships between the surface and the light source. Thus if we represent a color by the 3D color vector $\mathbf{C} = (R, G, B)$, the color at $(x, y)$ in an image is given by

$$\mathbf{C}(x, y) = m_s(x, y)\mathbf{C}_s + m_b(x, y)\mathbf{C}_b$$

where:

$\quad\quad \mathbf{C}_s = (R_s, G_s, B_s)$: color of surface reflection

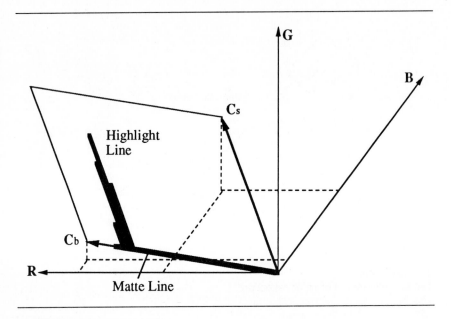

**EXHIBIT 14.5**
Color distribution is constrained on a dichromatic plane.

$\mathbf{C}_b = (R_b, G_b, B_b)$: color of body reflection
$m_s(x, y)$ and $m_b(x, y)$: scalar magnitudes of surface and body reflections, respectively.

An interesting interpretation of this model arises if we examine the histogram of image colors from the points belonging to a single surface. According to the model, the observed color vector $\mathbf{C}(x, y)$ at a pixel is a linear combination of two vectors $\mathbf{C}_s$ and $\mathbf{C}_b$. This means that even though the red plastic doughnut in Color Plate 1 includes various colors in it—bright red, dark red, and even white—they cannot be distributed arbitrarily in the color space. They must be on the plane, called the dichromatic plane, spanned by the two vectors as shown in Exhibit 14.5. Moreover, for most points, there is very little surface reflection; thus $m_s(x, y)$ is nearly zero and the color simply lies somewhere along the vector $\mathbf{C}_b$. We call this a *matte line*. All the points with significant amounts of highlight come from a small area on the object surface and thus have nearly the same amount of body reflection $m_b(x, y)$. Thus they form a sort of spike, called a *highlight line*, in the color space whose direction is parallel to the illuminant color $\mathbf{C}_s$.

This observation has been verified experimentally, both by ourselves [10] and other researchers [13,31]. In fact, Tominaga [31] has found that the model holds for a wide range of material surfaces. In the upper left image of Color Plate

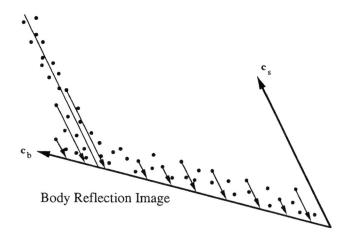

**EXHIBIT 14.6**
Body reflection image.

2, a plastic orange cup is illuminated by a white light. The upper right image of the plate shows the histogram of the color image. As expected, we see an L-shaped distribution in a color space. We observe a matte line in the direction of the body reflection, $C_b$, and a highlight line in the direction of the surface reflection, $C_s$. The bend at the end of the highlight line is due to saturation of the camera. The highlight is so intense that certain color components (in this case the red value) have reached their maximum value, and can no longer change, thus resulting in a bend, which we call the *saturation line*. By examining the distribution on the dichromatic plane, we can identify the matte line, the highlight line, and the saturation line.

### 14.3.3  Separation of Highlights and Image Segmentation

We can now write a program [10] that analyzes the color distribution of a given picture and identifies the matte and highlight lines, thereby calculating the vectors $C_s$ and $C_b$. Then, referring to Exhibit 14.6, imagine that we project all the colors in the dichromatic plane onto the matte line in the direction of the surface reflection, i.e., along the vector $C_s$. In other words, we force the value of $m_s$ to be zero and calculate the color consisting of only the body reflection. If we generate a picture from this projected distribution, we should see a picture of the scene with no surface reflection. Since the surface reflection accounts for glossiness and highlight, the resulting picture should lose all the glossiness and highlights and includes only shaded matte color. The lower right image in Color Plate 2 is such a result for the upper left image. It should be noticed that not only have we removed the highlight, but we have recovered the color behind it. This is the picture we would see if the object was not made of plastic, but of a material with a matte surface.

Similarly, if we project all of the colors on the dichromatic plane, along $C_b$, onto the vector $C_s$, then we force $m_b$ to be zero. This means that we have colors with only surface reflection and no body reflection. If we generate a picture from this distribution, it will show only highlights; this is shown in the lower left image in Color Plate 2. It should also be noted that highlights are not binary phenomena; they have gray scale.

The algorithm just presented cannot be applied directly to our original problem (see Color Plate 1), since the image includes multiple objects. The color histogram of the whole image is shown in Color Plate 3 and clearly shows that it consists of many L-shaped histograms, each of which must be treated individually. If we know that a particular region of the image comes from an object of a single color, the distribution of the color within that particular region will follow our constraints. However, since the image includes multiple colors, we have to find out which region corresponds to each color. In order to distinguish each region, we have to know its true color, since the apparent color in the image can vary significantly, even for the same object. This is exactly the same circular problem that computer vision researchers previously encountered in segmenting color images into objects, and without a systematic model they had to rely on the assumption of uniform color [24].

What we need to break the cycle is a way to group image points that accounts for the color variation accountable by the physical model. In fact, all we really need is a way to examine a small neighborhood of the image and make a good guess about the reflection color vectors. Once we make such a hypothesis about the model for each neighborhood, we can measure the extent of the neighborhoods whose color distribution can be explained by the model vectors, and then group together those neighborhoods. We have developed a method for color image segmentation by devising techniques for creating and testing such local hypotheses [9,11]. Color Plate 4 shows the result of segmenting Color Plate 1. Notice that the segmentation is not affected by highlights or shadings which have often fooled traditional image segmentation algorithms based on apparent colors.

Once we have segmentation, we can apply the previous analysis to each region and separate the body and surface reflections. In fact, since our segmentation method hypothesizes reflection color vectors, the projection into reflection components is a simple by-product of segmenting the image. Color Plate 5(a) shows the body reflection image of the whole scene, and conversely, Color Plate 5(b) shows the surface reflection image.

### 14.3.4  Perspective: Optical Constraints

Given the original input image, we have succeeded in automatically segmenting
highlights and in calculating the apparent, shaded color of the object. We did
not rely on any traditional heuristics based on clustering techniques or a phenomenological theory of color perception. The physical reflection model of color
provided constraints that we exploited for analysis. In the past, color segmentation and edge detection almost always been based on grouping of points with
uniform or nearly uniform color [24]; but these techniques utterly fail when presented with an image of an object that has a bright highlight of a color different
from the object color.

It should be noted that we did not assume any prior knowledge about the
real colors and shapes of objects nor the real color and direction of the light
source in separating body and surface reflections. Actually, once we have the
separation, there is a possibility for recovery of these four unknowns from the
given image. First, since the body reflection image admits a Lambertian model,
we can apply the shape-from-shading method for shape recovery. Second, once
the shape (and thus surface orientations) is known, the locations of the peaks of
surface reflection provide constraints on the direction of illumination due to the
mirror-like reflection geometry. Third, the color of surface reflection roughly
corresponds to that of the illumination. Finally, combining the knowledge of
illumination color and the body reflection image will enable us to recover the
real object color.

In the early 1970s, Horn of Massachusetts Institute of Technology pioneered
the use of a reflection model in computer vision in his work on image intensity
understanding [2]. Various methods, notably shape from shading and photometric
stereo, were developed thereafter. They have suffered, however, from the use
of models of reflection that were too idealized (such as a pure Lambertian
model) and the lack of appropriate models to account for interreflections. It has
been recognized that formulation of more sophisticated and realistic models of
reflection to deal with a broader class of surfaces and to cope with interreflection
is necessary to make the approach more realistic and powerful.

Nayar, Ikeuchi, and Kanade proposed a unified reflectance model composed of the diffuse lobe, the specular lobe, and the specular spike [21]. It
is capable of describing the reflection from surfaces that may vary from very
smooth to very rough. Another significant advancement deals with interreflection due to concave surfaces or concavities formed by multiple objects in the
scene. The interreflection causes almost all of the existing shape-from methods based on image intensity to produce erroneous results. Interreflection is a
very difficult problem for which very little research has been done [14]. Nayar, Ikeuchi, and Kanade developed a theory of shape from interreflections and
demonstrated recovery of the shape of an object even under interreflection with
unknown surface reflectances [20]. Also, Novak and Shafer have been develop-

ing a model for color interreflection as an extension of the dichromatic reflection model [26].

Appropriate physical modeling can result in practical, useful devices with robust capabilities. Based on the unified reflectance model, we have built a new device, called a photometric sampler, for surface inspection [19]. It uses extended light sources and can extract reliably both shape and reflectance properties of hybrid surfaces. Also, Nayar and Nakagawa developed a practical inspection device for such surfaces as a tungsten paste filling in a via-hole on a ceramic substrate that has a size of about 100 microns and includes specular reflection and 3D texture [22]. Based on an appropriate model of reflection of rough surfaces and focusing, the device can measure the shape with an accuracy of several microns.

Also, in developing physically based vision, we came to realize the need for a controlled environment where we can take images with accurate knowledge of ground truth and where we can control lighting and camera parameters. Such an environment is critical in order to accurately test and evaluate vision theories and methods. Traditionally, in the computer vision community, the test images were taken without much control, and therefore it was often unclear whether a theory being tested was incorrect or the data were inappropriate for testing the theory. We have built a unique facility called the Calibrated Imaging Laboratory (CIL) [25]. The CIL consists of many television cameras including a very high precision camera, controllable lighting, a high-precision 6-degrees-of-freedom computer-controllable jig to mount and move cameras, filters, test objects, and associated electronics. The CIL has made a significant impact on turning computer vision into a quantitative scientific discipline, and has introduced a new area of research in how to obtain high-quality images for computer vision by active control of the camera and lens [23].

## 14.4   Shape, Motion, and Uncertainty

### 14.4.1   A Problem: Baseline and Uncertainty in Stereo

Stereopsis is one of the fundamental ways to measure depth. Exhibit 14.7(a) illustrates the geometry for a binocular stereo system with the left camera $L$ and the right camera $R$ separated by a baseline $B$. If an image feature point, such as an edge, located at $x_L$ in the left image and an image point at $x_R$ in the right image are projections of the same physical point $\mathbf{P}$ in space, then by triangulation, we can measure the distance to $\mathbf{P}$. This is the principle of depth measurement by stereo vision.

In practice, the points $x_L$ and $x_R$ of features in the images can be located only within a certain accuracy. This is due to both image noise and limited sensor

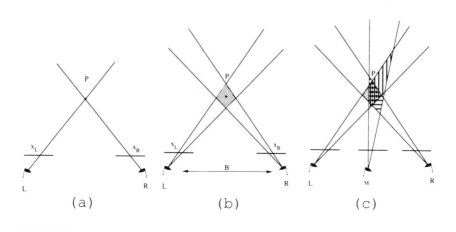

**EXHIBIT 14.7**
Stereo geometry.

resolution. Uncertainty in the image-position measurements leads to uncertainty in the final calculation of the scene point, as indicated by the diamond-shaped region in the Exhibit 14.7(b). The uncertainty in depth can be reduced by increasing the baseline (i.e., by spreading the cameras farther apart), since then the triangle becomes shallower, making the position of the vertex less sensitive to the orientation of the sides. This is exactly the constraint that civil engineers apply in surveying.

Finding pairs of corresponding points, $x_L$ and $x_R$, that come from the same physical point, usually called the correspondence problem, is actually the hardest part of the stereo problem. Making the baseline longer unfortunately makes the correspondence problem more difficult. The longer the baseline is, the more different the right and left images are from each other. The same point in space may appear differently due to a different viewpoint and foreshortening, or may even appear in only one image due to occlusion. Here we have a fundamental dilemma in stereo vision: as we make the baseline longer, the depth measurement becomes more accurate, but at the same time the matching becomes more difficult, and vice versa. How can we solve this dilemma?

## 14.4.2  Managing Uncertainty for Incremental Stereo

Matthies, Szeliski, and Kanade have analyzed the structure of uncertainty in stereo measurements [17]. Imagine that we place one more camera $M$ in the middle of the baseline as shown in Exhibit 14.7 (c). This creates two more stereo problems: one between cameras $L$ and $M$ and the other between cameras $M$ and $R$. With shorter baselines, the correspondence problems for the two intermediate stereos are less severe than the original stereo between $L$ and $R$, even though the depth measurements by them would not be as good. By solving the two new matching problems successfully, we have solved the original matching problem, because the middle point corresponds to both the left and right points. This idea is called trinocular stereo, and has been studied by several researchers to exploit the additional constraints that the middle camera provides.

However, an interesting question that had not been asked before concerns the uncertainty of measurements. Do the two new measurements due to the middle camera $M$ help reduce the uncertainty in the depth measurement of **P**? Matthies and Shafer [18] gave a way to relate the uncertainty of image measurements with the uncertainty of depth measurement and model it by a covariance. By using that formulation and the theory of optimal estimation, it was shown that the answer to the question is "yes" despite the fact that the two additional measurements are expected to be more uncertain than the original one. Though straightforward, this conclusion is very significant, since bringing in the third camera helps not only to simplify the matching problem but also reduce the uncertainty. We can add more camera positions between $L$, $M$, and $R$ for further improvement, and so on.

An analysis proves that if $N$ cameras are placed between $L$ and $R$, then the uncertainty of the depth measurement decreases at the rate of $N$ cubed. That is

$$\sigma^2(N) \sim \frac{1}{N^3}\sigma_e^2$$

where $\sigma^2(N)$ is the uncertainty of the final depth measurement with $N$ cameras, and $\sigma_e^2$ is the uncertainty of the image-position measurement. Experiments using real images demonstrated that the uncertainty decreases as expected, as shown in Exhibit 14.8 which plots $\sigma(N)$ versus the number of cameras.

The above derivation may have given the impression that the solution requires processing of all $N$ images at the same time. Rather, the solution can be implemented sequentially by using pairs of images from neighboring cameras at a time. Thus we can devise an incremental stereo system that produces and refines a depth map as a single camera is moved sideways. For this purpose we reformulated the system equations in terms of the current frame by using the feature position $x_i$ in the $i$-th image and the inverse of the depth $\frac{1}{z}$ to be the state variables of a dynamic system. This reformulation allowed us to view the incremental stereo as an instance of dynamic system estimation and to apply the Kalman-filtering technique.

The diagram of Exhibit 14.9 explains the method. A camera is moved from left to right by a small amount at each step. The sequence of images is processed

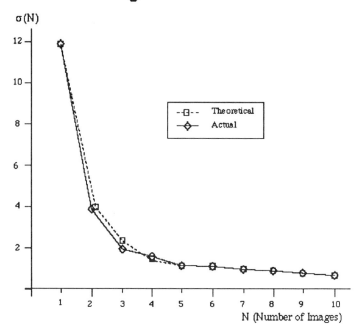

## Depth Uncertainty vs. Number of Images

**EXHIBIT 14.8**
Uncertainty versus number of images.

by the method shown in the diagram. The first pair of neighboring images are processed as a stereo pair. The resulting inverse-depth map, though very noisy, is stored. The next pair of images are then processed similarly to produce the second depth measurement. In the meantime, the stored depth map is transformed into the depth map in the coordinate system of the next camera position. The two depth maps are integrated by using the Kalman filtering technique, and stored. The process repeats until the camera reaches the end.

An actual experiment was done using a scale model of a city in the CIL. Ten images were taken in which consecutive images were taken only 0.05 in. (1.27 mm) apart. Thus the total baseline was only 0.5 in. (1.27 cm), while the distance to the scene was 20 to 40 in. (50 to 100 cm). Exhibit 14.10 shows the first image of the sequence. The final result was a depth map of the scene. Exhibit 14.11

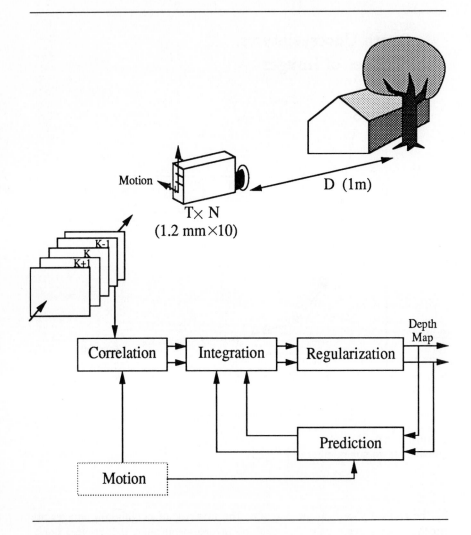

**EXHIBIT 14.9**
Depth map recovery by a Kalman filter method.

shows the depth map presented as a grey-level image, in which closer points are encoded brighter. A perspective view of the reconstructed scene, made by "painting" the original intensity image on the depth map is presented in Exhibit 14.12. We can see that the structure of the scene, including buildings, streets, cars, trees, and a distant bridge, is well recovered.

**EXHIBIT 14.10**
The first image of the sequence of ten images of a scale model of a city.

### 14.4.3 Perspective: Statistical Constraints

It should be noted that the above results were obtained for a stereo with an extremely narrow baseline: 1.27 mm for the neighboring pair and 1.27 cm for the farthest pair, and the triangle with a 1:100 ratio of baseline to scene depth. As a result, each pair of stereo images are so close that the matching or correspondence problem has become almost trivial. Therefore although many images must be processed, the total computation has not increased by much. In fact, there is a chance that it is reduced because the computation is now very local and uniform. This was made possible because we analyzed and modeled the structure of uncertainty in stereo, and developed the algorithm based on that model.

   In the past, literature on stereo exclusively dealt with correspondence problems. Our work on incremental stereo has shown that another important problem in stereo is management of measurement uncertainty. Uncertainty becomes particularly important when the stereo is used with a mobile robot for both re-

**EXHIBIT 14.11**
The computed depth map.

covering the depth map and locating itself in the environment; in this case, the uncertainty of depth measurements and the uncertainty of robot motion interact and create a cycle of uncertainty [16]. Matthies and Shafer demonstrated that appropriate modeling of depth uncertainty can greatly improve the accuracy in recovering the robot motion [18]. Matthies [15] developed dynamic stereo vision for using stereo vision both to estimate the 3D structure of the scene, and to estimate the motion of the robot as it travels through an unknown environment. The key idea is to monitor the uncertainty of the depth map and to use appropriate stereo systems, either narrow baseline or wide baseline, depending on the situation. Szeliski [29] developed a framework for Bayesian modeling of uncertainty in low-level vision. His framework allows us to define and compute a prior model of the scene, a sensor model and a posterior model.

A new stereo algorithm with an adaptive window developed by Kanade and Okutomi [7] relates the disparity uncertainty with the matching uncertainty. They showed that by modeling the disparity (inverse depth) variation within a matching window, the uncertainty of matching can be evaluated. Therefore it

**EXHIBIT 14.12**
Perspective views of the recovered depth map.

allows selection of the window size that results in the disparity estimation with the least uncertainty.

Tomasi and Kanade [30] showed that, in the problem of recovering motion and structure from a sequence of images taken from a long distance, it is far more advantageous to recover the relative shape of an object directly, rather than going through absolute depth. Their theory of shape-from-motion without depth captures the effect of noise as constraints on the approximate rank of a matrix. Based on the theory, they have demonstrated very accurate recovery of motion (less than 0.02% error) and shape (less than 0.5% error) from a sequence of images taken of an object of size 4 cm from a distance of approximately 3.5 meters.

## 14.5 Conclusion

The physically based theory of vision presented here has focused on determining the information that is contained in images and developing the constraints that are applicable to extract the information. We have emphasized the difference between heuristics that seem to work some of the time and constraints that are correct for a well-defined range of situations. These constraints can be derived from models of the geometry, physics, optics, and statistics of vision. Vision based on physical models results in the formulation of problems in such a way that extensions and modifications can be clearly stated and researched. Moreover, the limitations of such models can be deduced.

It may have been noticed that the presentation above included little or no discussion about "algorithms" that perform the task of extracting information or on "systems" or "computational mechanisms" that implement the algorithms. In physically based vision, the emphasis is on the formulation of the physical models and derivation of constraints; algorithms and implementations can be developed based on the models. This approach is almost parallel to Marr's three levels in understanding vision [14]: computational theory; representation and algorithms; and implementation. Our physically based theory is most akin to Marr's level of computational theory, in which the performance of the device is characterized as a mapping from one kind of information to another, the abstract properties of this mapping are defined precisely, and its appropriateness and adequacy for the task at hand are demonstrated. Our theory certainly deals with these issues rather than how to implement the theory efficiently on specific hardware.

A subtle, yet important, difference between our work and that of the Marr school is that our theory focuses on formulating the structure in which the physical processes involved in creating or acquiring images encode information, and in extracting the constraints that can be exploited in decoding images based on the physical models. Marr was largely motivated by human visual perception, so the "what," "why," and "how" of computer vision were often justified relative to human perception. We do not need to limit computer vision tasks to those for which human visual perception systems have counterparts. Currently, humans outperform machines by far in most tasks. Thus computer vision can learn much from human visual systems. However, this should not mean that copying or mimicking a human, in either defining goals (phenomenological performance), devising solutions (introspections), or implementing algorithms (neurons), is the best way to lead to the ultimate computer vision systems. In fact, machines may well exceed humans in the future (and in some cases do so already).

In the past, a vision problem was often stated as, "Given an image, devise an interpretation algorithm for . . . ." Vision researchers then rushed out to write a program for dealing with the given image. However, according to Marr [14], vision is the process of discovering from images (data) what is present in the (physical) world and where it is. If so, as with any physical science, a clear technical understanding of the physical nature of the data (i.e., images) is required for formulating a solution. The physical processes underlying vision take place before the interpretation of images starts. Hence, computer vision must be a physical science. At least half of it.

## 14.6  Acknowledgments

I would like to thank all the members of the CMU vision group for their contribution—not just those whose work I referred to in this chapter, but all the others that have contributed to transforming computer vision to a physical science. Steven Shafer, who is one of the strongest driving forces of the effort, provided critical comments on the chapter, and Keith Gremban spent long hours in reading and editing several versions of this chapter during its evolution. I thank them for their comments and inputs, which have greatly improved this chapter.

## References

[1] A. Guzman. Computer recognition of three dimensional objects in a visual scene. Technical Report MAC-TR-59, Massachusetts Institute of Technology, Cambridge, MA, 1968.

[2] B. K. P. Horn. Understanding image intensities. *Artificial Intelligence*, 8(2):201-231, 1977.

[3] D. A. Huffman. Impossible objects as nonsense sentences. In B. Meltzer and D. Michie, eds., *Machine Intelligence 6*, chapter 19, pp. 295-323. American Elsevier Publishing, New York, 1971.

[4] T. Kanade. A theory of origami world. *Artificial Intelligence*, 13:279-311, 1980.

[5] T. Kanade. Recovery of the 3D shape of an object from a single view. *Artificial Intelligence*, 17:409-460, 1981.

[6] T. Kanade and J. R. Kender. Mapping image properties into shape constraints: Skewed symmetry, affine-transformable patterns, and the shape-from-texture paradigm. In *Human and Machine Vision*. Academic Press, 1983.

[7] T. Kanade and M. Okutomi. A stereo matching algorithm with an adaptive window: Theory and experiment. Technical Report CMU-CS-90-120, Carnegie Mellon University School of Computer Science, 1990.

[8] J. R. Kender. *Shape from Texture*. PhD thesis, Department of Computer Science, Carnegie-Mellon University, 1980.

[9] G. J. Klinker. *A Physical Approach to Color Image Understanding*. PhD thesis, Carnegie Mellon University, Computer Science Department, 1988.

[10] G. J. Klinker, S. A. Shafer, and T. Kanade. The measurement of highlights in color images. *International Journal of Computer Vision*, 2(1):7-32, 1988.

[11] G.J. Klinker, S.A. Shafer, and T. Kanade. A physical approach to color image understanding. *International Journal of Computer Vision*, 4(1):7-38, 1990.

[12] J. Krumm and S. Shafer. Local spatial frequency analysis for computer vision. Technical Report CMU-RI-TR-90-11, Carnegie Mellon University The Robotics Institute, 1990.

[13] H. C. Lee. Method for computing the scene-illuminant chromaticity from specular highlights. *Journal of the Optical Society of America*, 3(10):1694-1699, 1986.

[14] D. Marr. *Vision*. Freeman, 1981.

[15] L. Matthies. Dynamic stereo vision. PhD thesis, Carnegie Mellon University, Computer Science Department, 1989.

[16] L. Matthies and T. Kanade. The cycle of uncertainty and constraints in robot perception. In B. Bolles and B. Roth, eds., *Robotics Research*, volume 4, pp. 327-336. Cambridge, MA: MIT Press, 1988.

[17] L. Matthies, T. Kanade, and R. Szeliski. Kalman filter-based algorithms for estimating depth from image sequences. *International Journal of Computer Vision*, 3:209-236, 1989.

[18] L. Matthies and S. Shafer. Error modeling in stereo navigation. *IEEE Journal Robotics and Automation*, pp. 239-248, December 1987.

[19] S. Nayar, K. Ikeuchi, and T. Kanade. Shape and reflectance from an image sequence generated using extended sources. In *Proceedings of 1989 IEEE International Conference on Roboticss and Automation*, pp. 28-35. New York: Institute of Electrical and Electronics Engineers, 1989.

[20] S. Nayar, K. Ikeuchi, and T. Kanade. Shape from interreflections. Technical Report CMU-RI-TR-90-14, Carnegie Mellon University, Robotics Institute, 1990.

[21] S. Nayar, K. Ikeuchi, and T. Kanade. Surface reflection: Physical and geometrical perspectives. In *Proceedings of Image Understanding Workshop*, Morgan Kaufman, 1990.

[22] S. Nayar and Y. Nakagawa. Shape from focus: An effective approach for rough surfaces. In *Proceedings of 1990 IEEE International Conference on Roboticss and Automation*. New York: Institute of Electrical and Electronics Engineers, 1990.

[23] C. Novak, S. Shafer, and R. Willson. Obtaining accurate color images for machine vision research. In *Proceedings SPIE Conference on Perceiving, Measuring, and Using Color*, Santa Clara, CA, 1990. SPIE.

[24] R. Ohlander, K. Price, and D. R. Reddy. Picture segmentation using a recursive region splitting method. *Computer Graphics and Image Processing*, 8:313-333, 1978.

[25] S. Shafer. The Calibrated Imaging Lab under construction at CMU. In *Proceedings DARPA Image Understanding Workshop*, p. 509. SAIC, 1985.

[26] S. Shafer, T. Kanade, G. Klinker, and C. Novak. Physics-based models for early vision by machine. In *Proceedings SPIE Conference on Perceiving, Measuring, adn Using Color*, Santa Clara, CA, 1990. SPIE.

[27] S. A. Shafer. *Shadow Geometry and Occluding Contours of Generalized Cylinders*. PhD thesis, Department of Computer Science, Carnegie-Mellon University, 1983.

[28] S.A. Shafer. Using color to separate reflection components. *Color Research and Application*, 10(4):210-218, 1985.

[29] R. Szeliski. *Bayesian Modeling of Uncertainty in Low-Level Vision*. PhD thesis, Carnegie Mellon University, Computer Science Department, 1988.

[30] C. Tomasi and T. Kanade. Shape and motion from image streams: a factorization method. Technical Reports CMU-CS-90-166 and CMU-CS-91-105, Carnegie Mellon University, School of Computer Science, 1990, 1991.

[31] S. Tominaga and B.A. Wandell. Standard surface reflectance model and illuminant estimation. *Journal of the Optical Society of America*, 6(4):576-584, 1989.

[32] D. Waltz. Generating semantic descriptions from drawings of scenes with shadows. In P. H. Winston, ed., *The Psychology of Computer Vision*, pp. 19-92. McGraw-Hill, New York, 1975.

# 15

## Running Experiments
## with a Planar Biped

Jessica Hodgins, Jeff Koechling, and Marc H. Raibert

Bipeds typically run with an alternating gait, using only one leg for support at a time. This characteristic of bipedal running suggests that a biped could be controlled by algorithms designed for one-legged hopping. With this approach, the leg providing support is considered to be active, while the other leg is considered idle. The one-legged algorithms control the position, thrust, and hip torque of the active leg, while they keep the idle leg short and out of the way. Laboratory experiments with a planar biped running machine were used to verify the approach. The machine maintains its balance while it runs in place, travels at specified speeds, and alternates between running and hopping gaits. The approach has also been used to study high-speed running, travel over rough terrain, and simple gymnastic maneuvers.

## 15.1  Introduction

Bipedal locomotion is a behavior that humans and animals perform with agility, grace, and speed, but robots have not yet mastered. In this chapter we examine bipedal locomotion by exploring the control and coordination of a two-legged laboratory robot. Our approach takes advantage of the fact that a biped frequently runs with a gait that uses one leg for support at a time. For such a gait, the support leg can be controlled as though it were the only leg in the system, while the other leg is kept immobile so that it acts like part of the body. This approach allows algorithms developed to control one-legged hopping to be extended for two-legged running.

The algorithms for hopping on one leg consist of separate control laws that regulate hopping height, body attitude, and running speed. These algorithms are adequate to provide dynamic balance for planar and three-dimensional one-legged hopping machines [15,16]. To extend the one-legged hopping algorithms for bipedal running, we added a bookkeeping mechanism so that the legs take turns providing support, and a controller for the idle leg to ensure that it does not collide with the ground.

We built a planar bipedal robot to test our approach to bipedal running. We simplified the problem by constraining the biped to move in a plane, and by using an off-board computer and power supply. The machine runs in place, travels at specified speeds, maintains balance when disturbed, and changes gaits between running and one-legged hopping. The one-legged hopping algorithms are adequate to control biped running, but we found that performance is improved when the idle leg mirrors the the active leg by making the same motions 180 degrees out of phase. This tail-like use of the idle leg reduces the pitching motions of the body.

After a brief review of previous work on biped locomotion, we review the algorithms used to control one-legged hopping machines and describe the modifications needed for bipedal running. Then we describe the biped apparatus used for laboratory experiments and present data that characterize the machine's operation. We close with a discussion of how the biped running algorithms have been extended to allow more advanced bipedal behavior, including fast running, running on rough terrain, and simple gymnastic maneuvers.

## 15.2  Background

Kato and his colleagues built an early computer controlled biped [13]. Their biped had ten hydraulically powered degrees of freedom that moved two large feet. The first version of their machine was statically stable, moving along a preplanned trajectory that kept the center of mass of the body located over the base of support provided by the grounded foot. Each step took several seconds.

A later version of Kato's machine transferred support from one foot to the other during a dynamic tipping phase [7]. This machine was statically stable most of the time. Once during each step, however, the machine slowly leaned forward until the center of mass moved forward past the front edge of the supporting foot. The machine then tipped forward onto the other foot, which was positioned so that it would catch the machine and passively return the system to static equilibrium. An inverted pendulum model of the system was used to determine where to place the catching foot.

This approach was an interesting way to achieve dynamic behavior. The system was not dynamic in the sense of reacting at run-time to the progress of the motion. Instead, an off-line analysis of the dynamics of the system specified how to position the catching foot statically to get run-time dynamic behavior. Knowledge of dynamics of the system were *compiled*, if you will, into a simple run-time strategy.

Miura and Shimoyama [12] built the first walking machine that balanced actively. It adjusted its motions in response to changes in the dynamic state of the system. Their stilt biped, Biper 3, was patterned after a human walking on stilts, with each foot providing only a point of support. The machine had three actuators. One actuator moved one of the legs sideways, one actuator moved the other leg sideways, and a third actuator separated the legs fore and aft. Sensors in each foot detected ground contact and measured the angle of the leg with respect to the ground.

The control for Biper 3 was also derived from the inverted pendulum model of tipping during single support. Unlike the Kato machine, this biped adjusted the placement of each foot in response to the ongoing behavior of the system as measured by the sensors. Separate mechanisms controlled tipping in the forward and sideways directions. In each direction, placement of the foot was adjusted in response to the actual and desired tipping motion. Since the legs could not shorten, the machine lifted each leg by rocking onto the other leg. The machine rocked from one foot to the other, while the airborne foot was repositioned according to the algorithm. Because of the stiff legs, the machine looked like Charlie Chaplin when it walked.

There are many theoretical studies of biped locomotion. These studies can be characterized by the techniques used to reduce the order of the model and to make the problem tractable. For example, Gubina, Hemami, and McGhee [3] assumed a massless leg. Vukobratovic and Stepanenko [18] added extra constraints to the motion of their biped model to resolve the indeterminacies that occur when both feet are on the ground. Furusho and Masubuchi [1] assumed that the ankle joint of the support leg was passive. A recent survey of biped robot research in Japan is given by Furusho and Sano [2].

Matsuoka [10,11] was the first to build a machine that ran with periods of ballistic flight. He formulated a model consisting of a body and one massless leg and derived a time-optimal state feedback controller that provided stability for hopping in place and for hopping with translation. To test this controller, Matsuoka built a planar one-legged hopping machine that operated in low gravity by lying on a table inclined 10° from the horizontal. The machine hopped about once per second and balanced as it traveled back and forth on the table.

## 15.3 Review of Hopping on One Leg

Raibert and his colleagues built planar and three-dimensional one-legged hopping machines that hopped in place, traveled along simple paths, jumped over obstacles, and maintained balance when disturbed mechanically [15,16]. These machines used a simple control system that had independent controllers for hopping height, forward speed, and body attitude. The purpose of their experiments was to explore the role of balance in legged locomotion, while avoiding the issues of gait and interleg coordination. In this section we give a brief description of the one-legged hopping algorithms because they provide the basis for our approach to biped locomotion.

Each one-legged hopping machine had a rigid body and a springy telescoping leg that pivoted with respect to the body at a hinge-type hip joint. One actuator exerted torque between the leg and the body and a second actuator acted along the axis of the leg, in series with a spring in the leg.

The task of controlling the hopping machines is decomposed into three parts. One part sustains the machine's bouncing motion, the second part regulates the angle of the body, and the third part stabilizes the forward running speed. A summary of the control as follows.

- □ *Hopping height*—Hopping is a resonant bouncing motion of the spring-mass system formed by the springy leg and the mass of the body. A leg actuator excites the motion by thrusting during stance. The hopping converges to a height for which the mechanical losses occurring throughout the hopping cycle balance the energy added during thrust.

- □ *Body attitude*—The control system regulates the angle of the body by applying torques to the body during stance. Vertical loading on the foot keeps it from slipping when the hip actuators apply torque. A linear servo moves the body toward its nominal angle whenever the foot is on the ground:

$$\tau = -k_p(\phi - \phi_d) - k_v(\dot{\phi}) \qquad (15.1)$$

where $\tau$ is the hip torque, $\phi$ is the angle of the body, $\phi_d$ is the desired angle of the body, $\dot{\phi}$ is the angular rate of the body, and $k_p$, $k_v$ are gains.

- □ *Forward running speed*—During each flight phase, the control system positions the foot to control the acceleration of the body during the next stance phase. When the control system places the foot in the center of the distance the body travels during stance, the forward speed is the same at liftoff as it is at touchdown. We call this position of the foot the *neutral point*. When the control system displaces the foot from the neutral point, the body accelerates, with the magnitude and direction of acceleration pro-

neutral point

**EXHIBIT 15.1**
Displacement of the foot from the neutral point accelerates the body by
skewing the symmetry of the body's trajectory. When the foot is placed closer
to the hip than the neutral point, the body accelerates forward during stance
and the forward speed at liftoff is higher than the forward speed at
touchdown (left). When the foot is placed further from the hip than the neutral
point, the body accelerates backward during stance and the forward speed at
liftoff is slower than the forward speed at touchdown (right). Horizontal lines
under each figure indicate the distance the body travels during stance, and
the curved lines indicate the path of the body.

portional to the magnitude and direction of the displacement, as shown
in Exhibit 15.1. The control system displaces the foot from the neutral
point by a distance proportional to the difference between the actual speed
and the desired speed. The algorithm for the control system computes the
desired foot position as

$$x_{fh,d} = \frac{\dot{x}T_s}{2} + k_{\dot{x}}(\dot{x} - \dot{x}_d) \tag{15.2}$$

where $x_{fh,d}$ is the forward displacement of the foot from the projection
of the center of gravity, $\dot{x}$ is the forward speed, $\dot{x}_d$ is the desired forward
speed, $T_s$ is the predicted duration of the next support period, and $k_{\dot{x}}$
is a gain. The first term of Eq. 15.2 is an estimate of the neutral point
and the second term is a correction for the error in forward speed. The
duration of the next support period is predicted to be the same as the
measured duration of the previous support period. Once the control system
finds $x_{fh,d}$, a kinematic transformation determines the hip angle that will

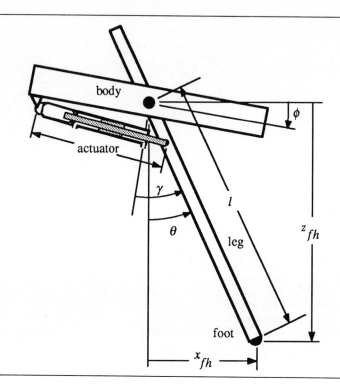

**EXHIBIT 15.2**
Kinematics of planar two-legged running machine. The length of the leg is $\ell$, the angle between the leg and vertical is $\theta$ and the pitch angle of the body is $\phi$. The control system has computed $x_{fh,d}$ according to Eq. 15.2. The required leg angle is $\theta_d = \arcsin(\ell/x_{fh,d})$, and the desired hip angle is $\gamma_d = \theta_d - \phi$. The hip linkage of our biped uses a linear hydraulic actuator, the desired position of which is $w_d = \sqrt{c^2 + d^2 - 2cd\cos(\gamma_d - \alpha - \beta + \pi/2)} - w_0$. The parameters are: $a = 0.3194\,\text{m}$, $b = 0.0032\,\text{m}$, $e = 0.0439\,\text{m}$, $f = 0.0062\,\text{m}$, and $w_0 = 0.316\,\text{m}$. The hip actuator servo law is $\tau = k_w(w_d - w) + k_{\dot{w}}\dot{w}$.

position the foot as specified, and a linear servo drives the hip actuator. Exhibit 15.2 describes the kinematic transformation for the planar biped.

The control system uses a cyclic state machine (see Exhibit 15.3) to keep track of the behavior of the mechanism as it hops. The state machine specifies which of the three controllers operates during each phase of the hopping cycle. These algorithms stabilized the hopping of both a two-dimensional one-legged machine that was mechanically constrained to operate in a plane, and a three-dimensional one-legged machine that traveled freely about the laboratory. More

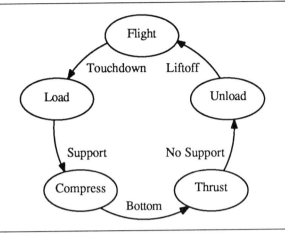

**EXHIBIT 15.3**
State machine for planar one-legged hopping machine. The five states are
shown along with the events that trigger the state transitions.

detailed accounts of the control algorithms used for the one-legged machines
and of the experimental results can be found [14,17].

## 15.4   Bipedal Running Is Like Hopping

Running bipeds typically use only one leg for support at a time. During running,
there is a strict alternation between support phases, during which one or the other
leg supports the body by pushing downward on the ground, and flight phases,
during which no legs touch the ground. During stance, we call the leg providing
support the *active leg,* and the other leg the *idle leg.* During flight, we call the
leg that will next provide support the active leg, and the leg that just left the
ground the idle leg. The two legs exchange roles at liftoff.

We argue that the active leg can be controlled using the algorithms developed for the one-legged machines. If the idle leg is kept immobile with respect
to the body, then the dynamics of bipedal running are the same as the dynamics of one-legged hopping. Because the biped uses just one leg for support at
a time, the vertical thrust delivered by the active leg can be calculated using
the algorithm that the one-legged system used. The torque exerted between the
active leg and the body to keep the body level can also be calculated using the
one-legged algorithm. Finally, because just one of the biped's legs is placed on

the ground at a time, the algorithm for calculating the placement of the active leg can be the same as that used by one-legged systems. Thus the control system for a biped can use the same three algorithms for controlling hopping height, body attitude, and forward running speed as were used by the control system for a one-legged hopping machine.

Despite these similarities, there are several differences in the control of one- and two-legged running. One difference is that a two-legged system needs the ability to shorten and lengthen its legs substantially. The idle leg must shorten so that it does not strike the ground while the active leg is compressed during stance, and it must lengthen again in preparation for providing support, soon after it becomes the active leg. The mechanical design of the leg must allow these motions.

Another difference is in the sequence of states that occur during running. The state machine for a biped must keep track of which leg is active and which is idle, and switch between them at appropriate times. The composite state machine shown in Exhibit 15.4 performs this function. It is essentially two copies of the state machine used for the one-legged systems, joined together so that the legs take turns providing support. At liftoff, the legs switch roles with the idle leg becoming active and the active leg becoming idle. These two changes extend the one-legged control algorithms for bipedal running.

A third modification of the algorithms, called mirroring, improves stability and reduces pitching of the body. Mirroring causes the hip motion of the idle leg to follow the hip motion of the active leg, but with opposite sign. This control strategy allows the net angular momentum of the system to remain small when the legs sweep back and forth, and reduces the disturbance to body attitude.

## 15.5  Planar Biped Experiments

We built a planar two-legged running machine to test the control of bipedal running using the one-legged algorithms. The machine, shown in Exhibit 15.5, has two telescoping legs connected to the body by pivot joints at the hips. A hydraulic actuator exerts a torque about each hip, between the leg and the body. A hydraulic actuator within each leg works in series with a pneumatic spring. Together, they change the length of the leg and make the leg compliant along its long axis.

A tether boom mechanically constrains the machine to move on the surface of a large sphere. Locally, the machine can move fore and aft, up and down, and pitch nose up or nose down. Exhibits 15.6 and 15.7 show the details of the planar biped machine, and Exhibit 15.8 indicates the motion permitted by the

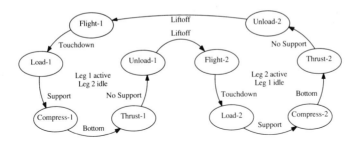

| State | Trigger Event | Actions |
|---|---|---|
| FLIGHT | Active leg leaves ground (liftoff) | Interchange active and idle leg |
| | | Lengthen active leg for landing |
| | | Position active leg for landing |
| | | Shorten idle leg |
| | | Mirror angle of active hip with idle hip |
| LOADING | Active leg touches ground (touchdown) | Zero active hip torque |
| | | Keep idle leg short |
| | | Mirror angle of active hip with idle hip |
| COMPRESSION | Active leg air spring shortens (support) | Servo pitch with active hip |
| | | Keep idle leg short |
| | | Mirror angle of active hip with idle hip |
| THRUST | Active leg air spring lengthens (bottom) | Extend active leg |
| | | Servo pitch with active hip |
| | | Keep idle leg short |
| | | Mirror angle of active hip with idle hip |
| UNLOADING | Active leg air spring approaches full length (no support) | Shorten active leg |
| | | Zero hip torques active leg |
| | | Keep idle leg short |
| | | Mirror angle of active hip with idle hip |

**EXHIBIT 15.4**
Finite state machine that coordinates two-legged running. The state shown in
the left column is entered when the event listed in the center column occurs.
The controller advances through the states in the sequence indicated by the
arrows. The LOADING and UNLOADING states occur when the foot is on
the ground, but the leg spring is not compressed. To avoid skidding the foot
along the ground, no hip torque is applied in these states.

**EXHIBIT 15.5**
Photograph of the planar biped. Light sources were attached to the feet and
the center of the body. The dashed line is a flashing light source on leg 1,
which is the leg farther from the camera. The biped ran from left to right in
the darkened laboratory. The control computer triggered the flash when the
machine was directly in front of the camera. The trajectory of the light
sources illustrates the bouncing motion of the machine.

tether boom. The machine has a total of nine degrees of freedom, described in
Exhibit 15.9. The appendix gives the physical parameters of the machine.
    Constrained by its tether boom, the biped runs in a circle in the laboratory.
It steps alternately on each foot as it bounces rhythmically up and down. Exhibit 15.5 shows the paths of the feet and the vertical bouncing motion of the
body. The top graph of Exhibit 15.10 shows the vertical motion of the biped as it
ran with an alternating gait. The two legs operated 180° out of phase, as shown
by the middle graph. During each support phase the leg spring first compressed
and then extended, as shown in the bottom graph.

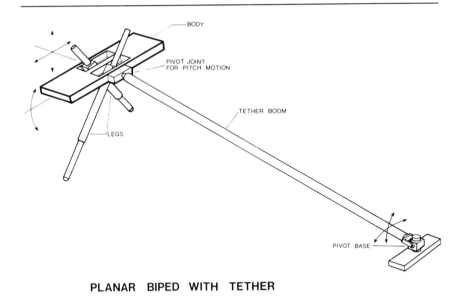

**PLANAR  BIPED  WITH  TETHER**

**EXHIBIT 15.6**
Planar biped running machine used for experiments. The body is an
aluminum frame, on which are mounted hip actuators and computer interface
electronics. Each hip has a low-friction hydraulic actuator that positions the
leg fore and aft. An actuator within each leg changes its length, while an air
spring makes the leg springy in the axial direction. Sensors measure the
lengths of the legs, the positions and velocities of the hip actuators,
pressures in the leg air springs, contact between the feet and the floor, and
the pitch angle of the body. An umbilical cable connects the machine to
hydraulic, pneumatic, and electrical power supplies, and to the control
computer, all of which are located nearby in the laboratory. The arrangement
of body, legs, hips, and actuators provides a means to control the position of
the feet with respect to the body, to generate an axial thrust with each leg,
and to provide hip torques during running. The tether boom constrains the
machine to motion in two dimensions, fore and aft, up and down and rotation
in the plane, and it provides a means of sensing body pitch angle and vertical
and horizontal position in the room.

A bipedal running machine has more opportunities to regulate the angular
momentum of the body than does a machine with only one leg. During flight,
a machine hopping on one leg must swing its leg forward to position it for
the next support phase. The hip torques that swing the leg forward also pitch
the body forward, so the body accumulates a pitch error that must be corrected
during the stance phase.

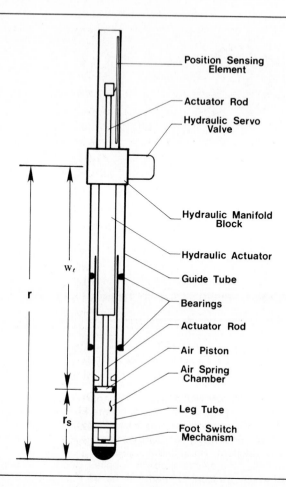

**EXHIBIT 15.7**

Diagram of leg used in running machine. A hydraulic actuator acts in series with an air spring. The hydraulic actuator is used to drive resonant bouncing motion of the machine and to retract the leg during flight. It also acts in conjunction with the air spring to determine the axial force the leg exerts on the ground. Sensors measure hydraulic actuator length, overall leg length, air pressure in the spring, and loading on the foot.

A machine with two legs can both swing its legs and keep its body level while conserving angular momentum. It does so by moving the two legs with equal and opposite motions, so that the hip torques exerted on the body to move one leg cancel the hip torques exerted on the body to move the other leg. We call this action *mirroring*, because the motion of the idle leg mirrors the motion

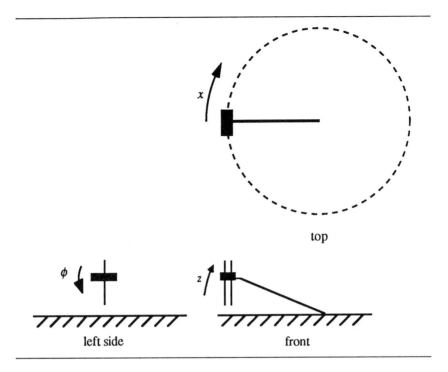

top

left side                          front

**EXHIBIT 15.8**
The boom constrains the biped's motion to the surface of a sphere. The
boom pivots at the base, allowing the machine to run around the circle and to
jump up and down. There is also a pivot joint at the machine end of the
boom, which allows the machine to rotate about its pitch axis. These three
degrees of freedom allow the machine to move fore and aft, up and down,
and to rotate in the plane.

of the active leg. Mirroring is reminiscent of the way that a kangaroo reduces
the rotation of its body by moving its tail in the opposite direction from the
motion of its legs. Mirroring does not totally eliminate disturbances to the body,
because the two legs do not have the same length all the time, so their moments
of inertia are not always equal.

The effect of mirroring the legs is illustrated in Exhibit 15.11. For this
experiment, the planar biped hopped on one leg, with the idle leg servoed to
a fixed angle with respect to the body. After the time indicated by the vertical
dashed line, the hip angle of the idle leg was servoed to the negative of the hip
angle of the active leg. This mirroring of the legs reduced the maximum pitch
oscillations of the body by about a factor of 2.

The planar biped can run with the alternating gait described above, it can

| *Planar Biped Degrees of Freedom* | |
| --- | --- |
| *degree of freedom* | *range of motion* |
| horizontal position, $x$ | 0–16 m |
| vertical position, $z$ | 0.4–1.4 m |
| pitch, $\phi$ | $\pm 180°$ |
| leg lengths, $\ell_1, \ell_2$ | 0.44–0.67 m |
| leg actuator positions, $h_1, h_2$ | 0.00–0.23 m |
| hip actuator positions, $w_1, w_2$ | $\pm 0.025$ m |

**EXHIBIT 15.9**
The planar biped has nine degrees of freedom. A potentiometer senses the
position along each degree of freedom. The length of each leg spring is
determined by the difference between the total leg length and the position of
the leg actuator: $s = \ell - h - 0.338\,\text{m}$.

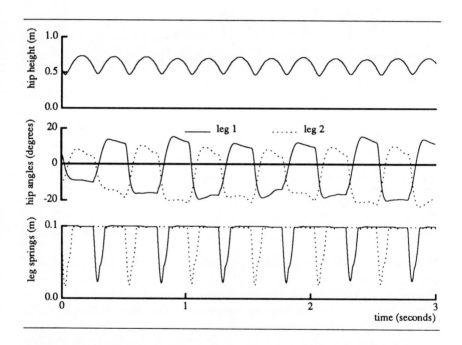

**EXHIBIT 15.10**
Running data for the planar biped. The top curve shows the height of the hip
above the floor. The middle curve shows the angles of the two legs with
respect to the body in the fore-aft plane. The legs oscillate 180° out of phase
and at half the frequency of the bouncing motion. The bottom curve shows
compression of the air springs as the legs are used for support in alternation.

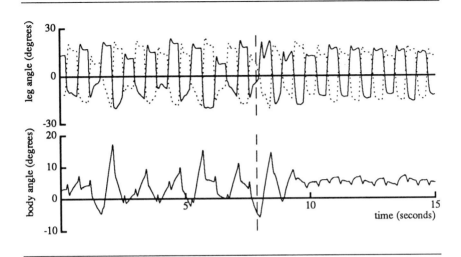

**EXHIBIT 15.11**
A control algorithm that kept the leg angles equal and opposite reduced the
the amplitude of the oscillations in body attitude. The top graph shows the
angle of each leg with respect to the axis of symmetry of the body. The
vertical line marks a switch from an algorithm that moved the legs
independently to one that ensured that the leg angles were mirror images.
The axis of symmetry was a line passing through the hip joint perpendicular
to the body. The bottom graph shows that mirroring reduced the oscillations
in body angle from about 20° peak-to-peak to about 6° peak-to-peak. In this
experiment the planar biped was running about 2.5 m/s.

run by hopping on one leg, and it can switch between the two gaits. It runs
with a hopping gait by making one leg active all the time, and the other idle.
The bouncing motion of the machine is unchanged when running on one leg
and, if mirroring is turned on, the idle leg acts like a tail. It is easy to do a
transition from one gait to the other by switching between state machines at
the beginning of a flight phase. Exhibit 15.12 shows data recorded as the biped
switched from two-legged running to one-legged hopping and back again, as it
traveled forward at 2.8 m/s.

## 15.6    Fast Running, Rough Terrain, and Gymnastics

We have used the bipedal locomotion algorithms just described as the basis for
other legged behaviors. We have done experiments in which the planar biped ran

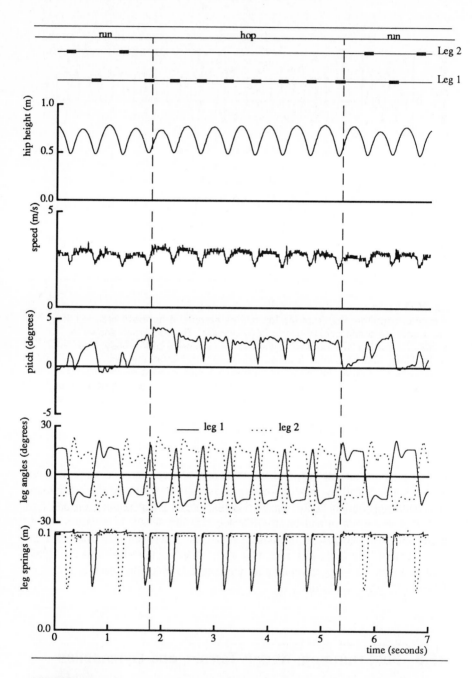

**EXHIBIT 15.12**
Gait transitions. The top plot shows the pattern of footfalls as the planar
biped switched from two-legged running to one-legged hopping and back to
two-legged running. The vertical dashed lines mark the transitions, which did
not affect the forward speed or vertical bouncing. The biped had a slightly
greater pitch angle during hopping than during running.

at high speed, traveled over simple forms of rough terrain, and did gymnastic maneuvers. In each case we started with the algorithms described earlier, and either modified them or used them as a substrate on which to build additional layers of control.

In the course of studying the limits of running speed in legged locomotion, Koechling made the planar biped run fast [8,9]. In the fastest experiment, the machine traveled at 5.9 m/s (13.1 mph) for over 40 m. To achieve top speed, the legs of the planar biped were lengthened by 0.18 m, the control algorithms for body attitude were modified to compensate for the pressure/flow characteristics of the hip actuators, and the leg springs were made about twice their normal stiffness. Aside from these changes, the control algorithms for high-speed running were same as the algorithms described earlier.

Hodgins [4,5] studied how an actively balanced legged system could adjust the length of each of its steps without losing balance. The ability to adjust step length is an important component of traveling on rough terrain. Hodgins found that the control system could adjust the length of each step by manipulating the duration of the stance phase, the duration of the flight phase, or the forward running speed. In the course of these experiments, Hodgins programmed the planar biped to step on particular spots, to jump over obstacles, and to run up and down a short flight of stairs. Exhibit 15.13 shows the climb and descent of the stairway.

To study the production of discrete maneuvers and to have some extra fun, we made the planar biped do a forward flip [6], shown by Exhibit 15.14. To perform a flip the biped machine runs forward, brings the legs together and thrusts with both legs to jump high, exerts a large hip torque to pitch the body forward, shortens the legs to tuck once airborne, untucks in time to land on the feet, and then continues running. To develop this behavior, we modified the algorithms that operate during three steps of otherwise normal running.

## 15.7 Summary

There is a class of gaits for which only one foot touches the ground at a time and each stance phase is followed by a flight phase. A biped executing such a gait can be controlled with algorithms developed for one-legged hopping machines. One of the two legs is designated the active leg, which is used to adjust hopping height, body attitude, and forward speed. The other leg is designated the idle leg, which is kept short to clear the ground and made to mirror the sweeping motions of the active leg. A state machine synchronizes the actions of the control computer to the behavior of the running machine, and selects which leg will be active on each step.

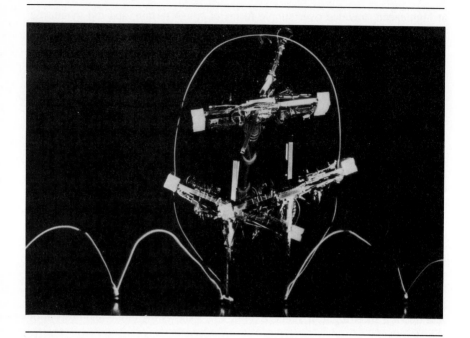

**EXHIBIT 15.13**
Photograph of the planar biped running up and down a short flight of stairs.
The machine is running from left to right, with the lights showing the paths of
the feet. The flash caught the machine on the last step going down the stairs.

We have demonstrated the feasibility of this approach with a planar two-
legged running machine that operates in the laboratory. It runs with an alternating
gait, a one-legged hopping gait, and it can switch between gaits. The planar
biped and the basic control algorithms have also been used to investigate the
limitations of fast running, the control of step length for rough terrain, and
simple robot gymnastics.

## 15.8   Acknowledgments

We thank Ben Brown, Mike Chepponis, Jeff Miller, David Barrett, and Kevin
Brennan for their roles in designing, assembling, photographing, and repair-
ing the machine. Much of the work reported in this chapter was done when
the authors where members of the Carnegie Mellon University Computer Sci-

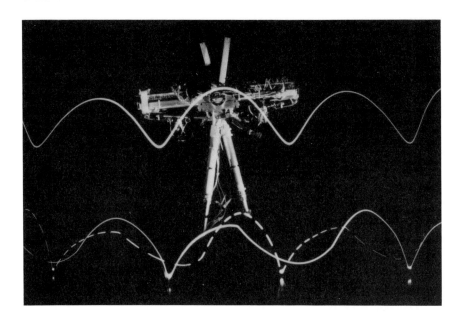

**EXHIBIT 15.14**
Photograph of planar biped doing a flip. Three flashes were synchronized
with liftoff, the top of flight, and touchdown. The machine was running from
right to left, with a light indicating the path of the near foot. The tether boom
is hidden behind the body.

ence Department and the Robotics Institute. This research was supported by
the Defense Advanced Research Projects Agency and the System Development
Foundation.

## 15.9  Appendix: Physical Parameters of Planar Biped Running Machine

*Body*

| | | |
|---|---|---|
| Length | 0.75 m | 30 in. |
| Width | 0.23 m | 9 in. |
| Mass | 11.5 kg | 25 $\text{lb}_m$ |
| Moment of inertia | 0.4 kg-m$^2$ | 1,370 $\text{lb}_m$-in.$^2$ |

*Leg*

| | | |
|---|---|---|
| Total mass | 1.66 kg | 3.66 lb$_m$ |
| Unsprung mass | 0.29 kg | 0.64 lb$_m$ |
| Moment of inertia | 0.13 kg-m$^2$ | 444 lb$_m$-in.$^2$ |

*Hip actuator*

| | | |
|---|---|---|
| Bore | 0.01613 m | 0.625 in. |
| Rod diameter | 0.00953 m | 0.375 in. |
| Area | 1.27×10$^{-4}$ m$^2$ | 0.197 in.$^2$ |
| Stroke | 0.051 m | 2.0 in. |
| Hip sweep | ±0.52 radian | ±30° |
| Maximum velocity | 0.500 m/s | 19.7 in./s |
| Maximum force | 2,630 N | 591 lbf |
| Moment arm | 0.0444 m | 1.75 in. |
| Maximum torque | 117 N-m | 1,030 in.-lb$_f$ |

*Leg actuator*

| | | |
|---|---|---|
| Bore | 0.0127 m | 0.500 in. |
| Rod diameter | 0.00953 m | 0.375 in. |
| Area | 5.54×10$^{-5}$ m$^2$ | 0.0859 in.$^2$ |
| Stroke | 0.23 m | 9.0 in. |
| Maximum velocity | 3.42 m/s | 11.21 ft/s |
| Maximum force | 1,146 N | 258 lb |
| Maximum leg length | 0.67 m | 26.4 in. |
| Minimum leg length | 0.44 m | 17.3 in. |

*Air spring*

| | | |
|---|---|---|
| Bore | 0.0286 cm | 1.125 in. |
| Area | 6.42×10$^{-4}$ m$^2$ | 0.994 in.$^2$ |
| Length | 0.10 m | 4.0 in. |
| Hip spacing | 0.090 m | 3.54 in. |
| Boom radius | 2.54 m | 100 in. |
| Circle circumference | 15.96 m | 628 in. |
| Computer | VAX 11/785 | |

# References

[1] J. Furusho and M. Masubuchi. Control of a dynamical biped locomotion system for steady walking. In H. Miura, I. Shimoyama (eds.), *Study on Mechanisms and Control of Bipeds*, Tokyo: University of Tokyo, 116-127, 1987.

[2] J. Furusho and A. Sano. Sensor-based control of a nine-link biped. *International Journal of Robotics Research*, 9:83-98, 1990.

[3] F. Gubina, H. Hemami and R. B. McGhee. On the dynamic stability of biped locomotion. *IEEE Trans. Biomedical Engineering* BME-21:102-108, 1974.

[4] J. Hodgins. Legged robots on rough terrain: Experiments in adjusting step length. In *Proceedings of the IEEE International Conference on Robotics and Automation*, Philadelphia, 1988.

[5] J. Hodgins. *Legged Robots on Rough Terrain: Experiments in Adjusting Step Length.* Ph.D. thesis, School of Computer Science, Carnegie Mellon University, Pittsburgh, PA, 1989.

[6] J. Hodgins and M. H. Raibert. Biped gymnastics. *International Journal of Robotics Research,* 9:115-132, 1990.

[7] T. Kato, A. Takanishi, H. Jishikawa and I. Kato. The realization of the quasi-dynamic walking by the biped walking machine. In A. Morecki, G. Bianchi, K. Kedzior (eds.), *Theory and Practice of Robots and Manipulators, Proceedings of RoManSy'81,* Warsaw: Polish Scientific Publishers, 341-351, 1983.

[8] J. Koechling. *The Limits of Running Speed: Experiments with a Legged Robot.* Ph.D. thesis, Mechanical Engineering Department, Carnegie Mellon University, Pittsburgh, PA, 1989.

[9] J. Koechling and M. Raibert. How fast can a legged robot run? In K. Youcef-Toumi and H. Kazerooni, (eds.), *Symposium in Robotics, DSC-Vol. 11.* American Society of Mechanical Engineers, 1988.

[10] K. Matsuoka. A model of repetitive hopping movements in man. In *Proceedings of Fifth World Congress on Theory of Machines and Mechanisms,* International Federation for Information Processing, 1979.

[11] K. Matsuoka. A mechanical model of repetitive hopping movements. *Biomechanisms* 5:251-258, 1980.

[12] H. Miura and I. Shimoyama. Dynamic walk of a biped. *International Journal of Robotics Research,* 3(2):60-74, 1984.

[13] K. Ogo, A. Ganse and I. Kato. Dynamic walking of biped walking machine aiming at completion of steady walking. In A. Morecki, G. Bianchi, K. Kedzior (eds.). *Third Symposium on Theory and Practice of Robots and Manipulators,* Amsterdam: Elsevier Scientific Publishing, 1980.

[14] M. H. Raibert. Dynamic stability and resonance in a one-legged hopping machine. In A. Morecki, G. Bianchi, K. Kedzior (eds.), *Fourth Symposium on Theory and Practice of Robots and Manipulators,* Warsaw: Polish Scientific Publishers, pp. 352-367, 1983.

[15] M. H. Raibert and H. B. Brown, Jr. Experiments in balance with a 2D one-legged hopping machine. *ASME Journal of Dynamic Systems, Measurement, and Control,* 106:1, 75-81, 1984.

[16] M. H. Raibert, H. B. Brown, Jr. and M. Chepponis. Experiments in balance with a 3D one-legged hopping machine. *International Journal of Robotics Research,* 3:2, 75-92, 1984.

[17] M. H. Raibert. *Legged Robots That Balance.* Cambridge, MA: MIT Press, 1986.

[18] M. Vukobratovic and Y. Stepaneko. Mathematical models of general anthropomorphic systems. *Mathematical Biosciences,* 17:191-242, 1973.

# Technology Transfer

# 16

## Technology Transfer: A Time for Reassessment

Samuel H. Fuller

Technology transfer is essential if today's inventions are to inspire tomorrow's innovative products. The computer industry is one of the principal engines of change moving our society toward an increasingly competitive and interdependent world economy. Given the rapid pace of technological change and the increasing internationalization of research, development, and production, it is imperative that we reexamine the technology transfer mechanisms we use. Universities, government, corporations, individual researchers, engineers, and the end-users of new knowledge must recognize, strengthen, and redefine their own interdependence in order to make critical adjustments toward more effective technology transfer.

## 16.1  Introduction

In an increasingly competitive world, technology alone will not determine economic leadership. Those who manage the difficult task of transferring technology out of the laboratories and into new products quickly and effectively will set the competitive agenda for the future. This is especially true in the field of computing. Computer science provides the essential enabling tools for scientific research, commerce, communication, and education throughout the world.

Twenty-five years ago, when the Carnegie Institute of Technology created its Department of Computer Science, technology transfer was not as big an issue as it has become today. Researchers, to borrow a term from economics, subscribed to the "trickle down" theory. Everybody assumed that great research results would eventually show up in commercial products.

But the fact is that product development cycles are getting shorter. We cannot afford to sit back and hope the new technology required to maintain the U.S. computer industry's leadership will trickle down fast enough.

Technology transfer doesn't just happen; it has to be accomplished, consciously and purposefully. Innovations occur when a researcher with a new idea is motivated to understand a customer problem. By *customer*, I mean the consumer of the new technology—an engineering group that will implement the technology in a product or the end-user of the product that employs the new technology. Innovations also occur when a developer with an understanding of the customer's problems is motivated to look at new ideas. There is technology *push* from the research side; there is also technology *pull* from the development side.

Technology transfer works best, however, when the researcher with the new idea is motivated to become a developer who will carry new technology through all the stages of product realization to the consumer. Scientist/entrepreneurs like Thomas Edison and Dr. Edwin Land come to mind.

It's fine to cite examples, but as we all know from daily experience, there are formidable obstacles between knowledge and a successful product or service. Many of these obstacles are rooted in business-as-usual practices, entrenched policies, and organizational structures that separate the research and development functions. People cherish preconceived notions about how science and engineering should be conducted. These attitudes get in the way of improving the process of technology transfer.

I think we need to take another look at the traditional mechanisms for technology transfer and at some of the new ones that are emerging.

## 16.2   The Unique Innovation Engine

The Computer Science and Technology Board of the National Academy of Science says America's "Unique Innovation Engine" is breaking down and, if it is not fixed, we are going to be left behind in the competition for global markets [3].

This Unique Innovation Engine (see Exhibit 16.1) starts at CMU and at

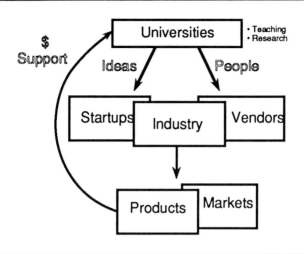

**EXHIBIT 16.1**
The Unique Innovation Engine.

the other research universities. Innovative new companies spin off from that work. They create new products, new markets, new jobs. Some grow up to be big companies who bring people—and their fresh new ideas—in from the laboratories where they were only recently graduate students. That results in more products and more jobs. Economic growth stimulates the demand for more innovations.

In contrast, European universities tend to separate research from the classroom and the marketplace. The Japanese have, until recently, focused on emulation and incremental improvements on existing technology. That's changing, however, and represents a serious challenge.

Federal, primarily defense, funding has been behind many of the new research projects in academic and private research laboratories since then (Exhibit 16.2). The National Science Foundation has funded work that has made major contributions to theoretical computer science. The three major branches of the military, the National Aeronautics and Space Administration (NASA), the National Institutes of Health, and the Department of Energy (DOE) have also funded basic research to the pool of technology. Industrial innovations include modern semiconductor technology, the microprocessor chip, personal computers, and breakthroughs in packaging, materials, and manufacturing processes.

But the biggest funder of technology has been the Defense Advanced Research Projects Agency (DARPA). DARPA funding produced timesharing, artificial intelligence and expert systems, packet-switched networks, very large-scale

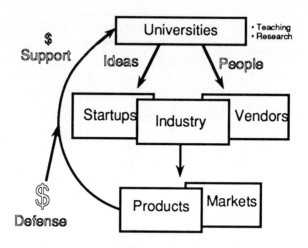

**EXHIBIT 16.2**
The Unique Innovation Engine.

integration (VLSI) design tools, computer-aided design (CAD), and new architectures for multiprocessors and distributed systems.

It is now a federal directive that technology developed or sponsored by the government must be disseminated to the commercial sector. What happens when the system of investment in the innovation engine that worked so well for 50 years is throttled back along with the defense budget?

## 16.3    The Technology Transfer Model

It is useful to examine a model of how technology transfer works. This model is based on Digital Equipment Corporation, but it's a reasonable representation of much of the computer industry. Technology transfer isn't a linear flow from research to development to customer. It's a complex, iterative process with a lot of contributing elements and interrelationships.

In Exhibit 16.3, we see that the primary flow of information in the corporation is between the product and process development organization and customers. The engineers transfer technology effectively by delivering innovative products to the customer. Customers provide feedback on what they find most and least useful.

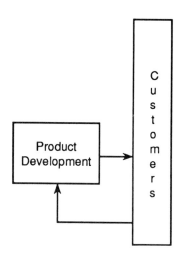

**EXHIBIT 16.3**
Technology transfer.

Companies like Digital have been fortunate in that many of their customers have been and are the people doing the basic research. This provides a powerful and direct way to ensure that product developers will have access to new ideas. Digital learned about packet-switching because most of the nodes on the early ARPAnet were Digital computers. Digital, IBM, and SDS learned about time-sharing because technically sophisticated customers asked for modified machines to support timeshared operations. Scientists in laboratories who had the technical skills to jury-rig computers and instruments together for data collection and analysis spawned a whole segment of our industry—real-time systems and applications for everything from factory automation to image processing and command and control systems.

In small and startup companies, this producer/customer feedback loop may be the only technology transfer mechanism in play. It has one big advantage—the next product developed will be responsive to customer requirements.

But customers are inherently conservative. New technology involves risk and disruption. Over time, if the product development group is only getting stimulus for new ideas from contact with existing customers, the company gets trapped into making incremental refinements and loses out in the subsequent race based on breakthrough innovations.

In Exhibit 16.4, the primary customer/developer feedback process has been

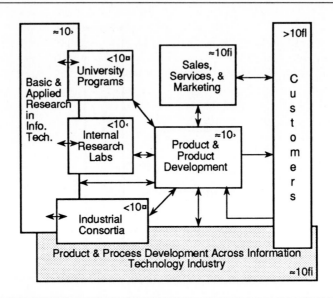

**EXHIBIT 16.4**
Technology transfer.

enlarged to include the research community and three conduits for getting innovations from research to the development. In the center are the company's internal laboratories. In order to be effective, internal research laboratories have to be fully integrated and productive members of the commercial organization. The effectiveness of research and development (R&D) is measured in the successful marketing of competitive products. And, of course, they have to keep a competitive eye on the product and process development that's going on generally in the industry.

But aren't targeted research projects based on business objectives as limiting as customer-driven ones? Product development and planning groups in larger companies can suffer from an inherent conservatism more intense than their customers' because there are enormous risks in bringing new technology to the marketplace.

Therefore in addition to their direct involvement with achieving the business goals of their companies, internal research laboratories also have to be productive members of the open research community. On the order of 3,000 engineers and scientists and $5 billion are invested in computing research in the world today [5]. This is a tremendous resource. Ideas have to flow back and forth between the universities, government-funded research laboratories, and researchers in industry. Policies and practices that bias the internal laboratories too strongly toward one side and away from the other will limit their effectiveness.

Furthermore, to heighten the chances of transferring knowledge, there have to be direct links between interested people within the development groups and these outside sources of technology, not just links between external and internal research laboratories. Much of the basic research in information technology is done at universities. Companies create a direct conduit to the universities by providing research grants, equipment, and personnel. The extensive university program at Digital currently supports more than 300 university-based research projects.

The third link between the research community and product development is a new trend in technology development transfer, industrial consortia. Sematech, MCC, and Esprit are examples. Consortia and the changing role of federally funded research programs are the two major new technology transfer mechanisms to emerge recently and they deserve special attention. First, however, it's useful to list the existing mechanisms for technology transfer. We need them all!

## 16.4  Mechanisms of Technology Transfer

Obvious technology transfer mechanisms include technical seminars, reports, and research reviews. More effective mechanisms include prototypes, the movement of people between research and development environments, consulting, and joint projects. The unfortunate fact of life with respect to technology transfer is that no one, two, or three mechanisms are sufficient. A healthy R&D organization uses any and all of these mechanisms from time to time. The truly competitive firm goes on to invent yet more new mechanisms as the need arises.

Technical seminars led by researchers inform development groups, identify development personnel who have an interest in specific topics, and often lead to opportunities for researchers to consult on product development projects within the company.

Company research organizations develop a number of different types of reports for different purposes. Management reports chart progress across a wide range of activities. Research reports convey and document results. The research report series of a laboratory is probably its most accurate record of its research contributions. Such report series often make difficult reading, but in the final analysis they usually are the definitive reference.

*Research reviews* are a sanity check. Their intent is to inform the development groups of the progress of research projects and to elicit feedback.

These sources of information are important, but they are indirect. I said above that the best technology transfer takes place when the researcher becomes part of the implementation team and through direct people-contact.

*Prototypes* provide a powerful mechanism to demonstrate the value and applicability of research results to developers.

The *movement of people* back and forth between research and development environments is the most effective way to transfer knowledge. At Digital we consider a wide range of assignment arrangements in research and product business units, from temporary rotational assignments of short duration to long-term career moves between research and development groups.

*Consulting* on product development takes about 20% of our principal researchers' time at Digital. They work with development teams who may be having problems in their particular areas of expertise. These consulting arrangements provide an excellent opportunity for the researchers to apply their results and to learn first-hand of the issues and concerns of the development group.

*Joint projects* is an exceptionally good mechanism for technology transfer. Researchers and development people are teamed on specific projects. The team sets the goals and works together to achieve them.

The joint project mechanism is used by many effective research organizations, including General Electric and IBM. Ralph Gomory, formerly Senior Vice-President for Science and Technology at IBM, points out that prior to adopting the joint projects method, he realized that, "Technology transfer takes work and that someone has to do that work. And it was also clear to us that Research would have to do that work. We could see that sitting back and waiting for others to pick up our results wasn't good enough, and neither was meeting our development counterparts halfway. Somehow, by hook or by crook, we had to find a pathway for our efforts that would get the results into the company's product plan" ([4], p. 28).

Temporary liaisons, or gatekeepers, didn't work well because the researchers involved weren't committed to product development and the product developers weren't committed to the technology. The 10-year technological lead research had over the product developers was perceived, according to Gomory, as "a perpetual void between us."

In the 1960s, a joint project helped transfer early work on field effect transistors. Later, the same mechanism worked well in transferring technology for thin-film head magnetic disks. In the 1970s, under Gomory's leadership, research actively accepted the responsibility for technology transfer. It became a "guiding principle" at IBM. Today IBM joint programs have grown from 1 to 19 or 20.

In the early days of computing, companies supported big centralized research facilities that did research that was eventually commercialized by many companies. UNIX came from Bell Laboratories, icons and mouse interfaces came from work done by Xerox's Palo Alto Research Center (PARC). Later as newer companies like Digital and Hewlett-Packard built research programs, they were motivated to more closely integrate research into their business organizations. They discovered that putting people together in teams speeded up the process of product realization and made research more effective.

## 16.5   X Window System—An Iterative Process

When direct involvement in R&D teams also includes companies and universities, the technology transfer can take place with excellent results. I'd like to cite two examples—one in an open research environment and the second in an internal, company environment. The first is the development of the X Window System as a part of the Massachusetts Institute of Technology's (MIT's) Project Athena. The second is the development of Digital's XCON and related expert systems.

MIT's Project Athena was established in 1983 to explore innovative uses of computing in the MIT curriculum.

The technical objectives for Athena's proposed distributed network of systems and workstations were (1) heterogeneous hardware, (2) a hardware-independent user interface, (3) a software development environment independent of hardware, and (4) maximum portability of software.

MIT went outside for help with funding, research, and development. The Project Athena proposal came at the right time for Digital: we needed a suitable partner to explore the future of workstations, how they would be used, and what technologies would be needed.

IBM and Digital became the two major corporate sponsors of Project Athena, providing equipment, money, and permanently assigned personnel. In fact, over the course of 8 years, MIT's proposal raised more than $100 million from corporate sources and the scope of the project was expanded from the engineering department to campus-wide computing. The Project Athena academic/industrial partnership was unique. And what was best about it was that the research would be carried out in an open academic environment. The results would be the intellectual property of MIT with the intent—from the beginning—to make new technology available to all interested parties.

The X Window System is a good example of technology transfer working well in an iterative process (Exhibit 16.5). Stanford had developed a window system for the experimental V operating system in 1980. It was subsequently ported to a VAXstation 100, as the W window System, by researchers in Digital's Western Research Laboratory. There, its functions and performance were extended.

Some of the ideas that came from Stanford and the further developments by the Digital lab went to Project Athena. In early 1984, work on what would become the X Window System started as a joint project between Robert Schiefler

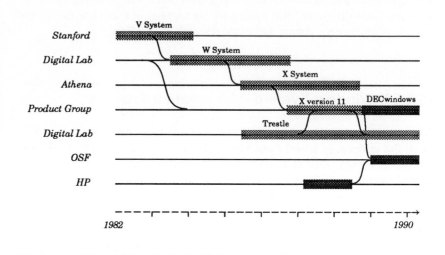

**EXHIBIT 16.5**
X Windows system chronology. *Abbreviations*: HP, Hewlett-Packard; OSF, Open Software Foundation.

of MIT's Laboratory of Computer Science, who needed a user interface for the Argus project, and Jim Gettys, a Digital software engineer working on Athena.

The X Window System Version 9 went into production in September 1985. Version 10 came a year later. The X Window System Version 10 satisfied the needs of Project Athena, but lacked the documentation and robust design needed if it was to be distributed across the industry as a standard. Consequently, Version 11 of the X Window System was developed back in Digital in the product development group that had earlier spun out of a research lab. Version 11 was produced early in 1987.

The technology for the first X window based commercial product, DECwindows, didn't come down in a straight line, as you can see. There was all this creative give-and-take involving Stanford, internal laboratories, MIT, product development engineers, and graduate students. According to George Champine, Digital's Athena director, "The use of students proved to be very effective. The quality and quantity of work done by them exceeded expectations, even though they worked strange hours and broke most of the conventional wisdom management rules" ([2], p.28).

In 1988, the Open Software Foundation, a vendor-independent industry consortium, got the X Window System Version 11 from Digital and other technology from Hewlett-Packard. These technologies went into the OSF/Motif toolkit. The

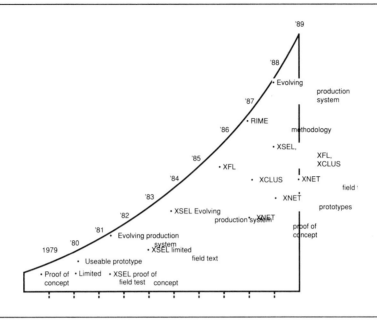

**EXHIBIT 16.6**
XCON Expert Systems Prototype.

synergy between the goals of OSF and Athena led OSF to provide MIT with a grant to test and extend Motif in 1989.

The X Window System is the de facto standard for graphical user interfaces today.

## 16.6   XCON Technologist and Advocate

The second example is XCON [1]. Digital initiated a project to develop an automated configuration system for internal use over ten years ago (Exhibit 16.6). XCON is one of half a dozen expert systems Digital has since put into production. The XCON project is an interesting example of effective technology transfer for two reasons. First, it is a demonstration of the value of prototyping new technology. And, second and more significantly, it demonstrates the tremendous impact made when the originator of the idea follows though on its implementation—when the enthusiasm and commitment are exported from the research lab along with the knowledge.

General Electric (GE) has one of the most successful R&D organizations in the world based on their ability to bring products to market based on work done in their research laboratories. In contrasting GE's approach with Bell Laboratories', Roland W. Schmitt, GE's head of R&D, asserts that industry needs both basic and targeted research. He argues that GE's success has come from close linkages between research and the plans, programs and strategies of the company's individual businesses ([6], p. 124).

He further contends that the choice of basic or targeted research methods depends on what you're working on. With fundamental technologies such as submicron integrated circuits, targeted programs are too limiting and expensive. About expert systems and artificial intelligence, however, Schmitt says, "Here there is considerable scope for new knowledge about inference mechanisms, knowledge structures, and the best languages in which to express them" ([6], p. 125). He says a lab can explore these best in the context of actual applications and cites XCON, Schlumberger's oil exploration analysis systems and GE's own locomotive maintenance expert system.

That's exactly what happened in the XCON project. R&D proceeded iteratively. Rule-based systems were not a mature technology. The application development effort pushed existing technology to its limits and contributed to new discoveries. We started out focused on the accuracy of the knowledge base and grew to devise various ways to do database access, the user interface, and interfaces to other applications. We had to develop a toolkit, RIME, to accomplish our goals and we had to improve the technology in the VAX OPS5 language.

We learned techniques for managing complexity that carry over into major areas of business for us. Expert systems will be critical in the future, for example, in managing huge, worldwide distributed networks. XCON has saved the company tens of millions of dollars and helped us come up the expert systems learning curve.

There was a time, however, when it looked like XCON might not ever get off the ground. That it did can be, in large part, attributed to the efforts of John McDermott. John wrote most of the original code for XCON and was, until he joined Digital in 1988, a researcher at Carnegie Mellon.

The spark of enthusiasm has to come from the initiator of the technology. The close, ongoing teamwork between McDermott and Digital developers and implementers was a major factor in the successful technology transfer. But first, managers, manufacturing people and engineers had to be "sold" on taking the risk. John McDermott himself said, "I had to decide whether or not I saw myself exclusively as a technologist or as an advocate." He accepted responsibility for both. He went on to say, "The successful scientist has to have a strong engineering desire to see the idea become something with practical meaning."

CMU seeded several expert systems projects at different companies around the country. The seeds germinated only where the university researcher actively accepted the role of technology advocate.

## 16.7 Two New Mechanisms—Federal Laboratories and Consortia

Two significant new mechanisms for technology transfer we will have to consider for the future are the changing role of federally funded laboratories and consortia.

As the focus in federal R&D funding shifts its focus from defense to commercial needs, and as international competition becomes more intense, new approaches to R&D funding are being proposed.

In 1988, Congress mandated that federally funded laboratories must find ways to make their skills available to the commercial sector. There is a wealth of technical talent at federal laboratories such as Los Alamos and Lawrence Livermore. However, until now, these laboratories have had a single customer—Department of Energy. If technology transfer is to work to the benefit of the society and the economy at large, simply relying on the usual mechanisms—papers, conferences, and liaison offices—isn't going to be enough. We will have to establish some aggressive, direct new ways to ensure that the research continues and to ensure technology transfer.

Three major suggestions are surfacing.

First, the president's science advisor has called for a program under the Department of Commerce that has been characterized as a "civilian DARPA." This could be a good idea. We need to examine the history of DARPA from the 50s to the present to see what made it effective and see what can be done to maximize the chances of repeating its successes. It will not be easy.

Second, federal R&D programs should first undertake commercial projects where there are at least matching funds from corporations. With commitment of their own R&D funds, companies will be motivated to pull in results. Companies should also be required to assign several engineers on site at the federal laboratories so they really learn the technology first-hand.

Third, we need to make it easier for companies to hire people out of the federal laboratories. The most enthusiastic implementors of new technology are the people who helped create it. An objective could be set to have as many as 10% of the lab personnel move from the federal laboratories to commercial companies annually. This would also open slots in the federal laboratories for young scientists and engineers fresh from research projects at the universities.

Consortia are another new approach to technology transfer. Consortia began to emerge in the early 80s in the face of international competition. They were started with commercial rather than defense needs in mind. Like the federally funded laboratories, however, they are independent of the firms that will ultimately take their technology to the marketplace.

It was hoped that the consortia would allow companies to pool funds and scientific talent to do research on a wide front. The advantages are the economy of scale and because the consortia get feedback from many companies, they have a broader perspective and a larger set of potential implementors of their results.

The consortia have structures designed to ensure equitable access to technology by all corporate supporters. These structures as clearly require. The effect of these structures governing technology transfer, however, is to throw up barriers to communication and interaction.

Perhaps the best and certainly the largest industrial R&D consortium today is BellCore. It has an annual budget of more than $1 billion and does R&D in support of the seven regional Bell operating companies. Compared to the other major computer industry consortia such as Sematech and MCC, BellCore has several major advantages.

First, the supporting companies have similar corporate missions, a common corporate heritage in AT&T, and yet they do not compete with each other in their core business—telephony. Second, BellCore does development work as well as research. That means that much of the technology transfer can take place within the walls of BellCore itself.

BellCore's heritage is unique. However, the movement of people between the federal laboratories, universities, consortia and companies and the use of more integrated R&D teams could, to some degree, emulate the second BellCore advantage.

The success of cooperative research efforts was recently demonstrated by Mark Manasse, at Digital's Systems Research Center, and Arjen Lenstra from BellCore. In the best tradition of open scientific inquiry, Manasse and Lenstra "borrowed" time on a volunteer network of more than 1,000 computers and workstations across the country. Using this ad hoc distributed system, they factored the 155-digit number—the ninth Fermat. On one level, their achievement was in pure mathematics. On another, it yielded information critical to the advanced encryption techniques that will be needed for tomorrow's vastly expanded communications environment. They also established prototypes and tested the power of distributed computing in a very dramatic way.

## 16.8   Transferring Conviction as Well as Knowledge

Technology transfer is as important a responsibility for the researcher as is the basic research work itself. Ideas are driven by people who are committed to doing whatever it takes to interest, educate, and secure the commitment of others to the successful implementation of that technology in a useful way.

Transferring technology is an intrinsically difficult set of tasks. No amount of analysis or study will make it easy. But we can start by recognizing that it is not a neat, linear chart like the one shown in Exhibit 16.7.

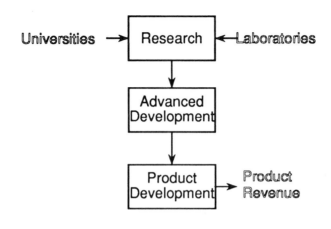

**EXHIBIT 16.7**
Technology transfer instrinsically difficult: the model.

We did a case study at Digital that revealed the reality of the situation (Exhibit 16.8) for a recently introduced product. Technology transfer is often chaotic. It's iterative. There are lots of feedback loops and interdependencies. Here are some of the major conclusions we reached as a result of that study.

Effective technology transfer requires (1) direct communications between researchers and developers; (2) high technical risk requires a stable, open environment with long-range goals; and (3) effective applied research requires a thorough understanding of the customers' needs. Insulating research groups from operating divisions eliminates their impact. By the same token, university researchers need the feedback of the marketplace that they get from working closely with companies and end users.

The major pitfalls in the path to effective technology transfer are: (1) success in today's market encourages engineers to stick with what's been proven rather than to risk new technologies; and (2) U.S. corporations and academic institutions reward outstanding individual achievement to a degree that discourages involvement in integrated project teams. I suspect this is why many of the most successful examples of technologies coming to market are the work of scientist/entrepreneurs.

In large companies with the financial resources to have separate research, engineering, manufacturing, and support groups, management is well advised to make it easy for committed people to move—with their ideas—across these

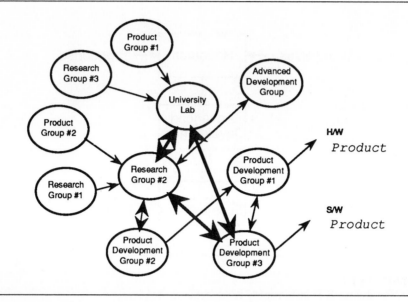

**EXHIBIT 16.8**
Technology transfer instrinsically difficult: the reality.

functions. We have to figure out how to transfer the idea or it dies. The conviction must move with the knowledge.

If we are going to keep the innovation engine going in the critical field of computer science, we have to value research and technology transfer equally. And we have to work at them both.

## References

[1] V. E. Barker and D. E. O'Connor. Expert Systems for Configuration at Digital: XCON and Beyond. *Communications of the ACM*, pp. 298-310, March 1989.

[2] G. A. Champine. MIT Project Athena: An Experiment in Educational Computing. Unpublished manuscript, June, 1990.

[3] Computer Science and Technology Board. *The National Challenge in Computer Science and Technology.* Washington, DC: The National Academy Press, 1988.

[4] R. E. Gomory. Moving IBM's Technology from Research to Development. *Research-Technology Management.* pp. 27-32, Nov/Dec 1989.

[5] National Science Board. *Science and Engineering Indicators—1989.* Washington, DC: U.S. Government Printing Office, 1989.

[6] R. W. Schmitt. Successful Corporate R&D. *Harvard Business Review.* pp. 124-128, May/June 1985

# 17

# Mach: A Case Study in Technology Transfer

Richard F. Rashid

A research organization cannot be successful if it fails to transfer the technologies it develops to others. The transition from idea to prototype to product can, however, be difficult in areas where the existence of entrenched products can cause potentially significant startup costs. One such area is the that of operating system software. This chapter describes history of the Mach operating system research project and its efforts to transfer the ideas imbedded in that system from the research laboratory to industry.

## 17.1  Introduction

In October 1984 I and a number of graduate students and research staff personel began a research project on the design and implementation of multiprocessor operating systems. Within a year and a half that project had adopted the name *Mach* and the first implementation of the Mach operating system was running on a four-processor VAX 11/784.

In November 1989 the Open Software Foundation (OSF)—a corporation formed by a consortium of major computer vendors—announced plans to base its first operating system offering on Release 2.5 of the Mach operating system.

411

In March 1990, a number of OSF member announced plans to bring products to market in 1991 based on this operating system. These announcements followed the September 1988 announcement by NeXT, Incorporated that it would base its new workstation software environment on a version of the Mach operating system. At the time of this writing, thousands of Mach-based systems— uniprocessors and multiprocessors—had been sold worldwide and Mach was in use in a large number of research and development projects in a variety of universities and companies.

I believe a number of factors were responsible for this rapid transition from university research project to industry product.

1. *We began our work from a solid base of previous research experience.*

   At the time the Mach project began, I and other members of the project already had as much as 10 years of experience in the design and implementation of network operating systems. This experience led to simpler interfaces and more rapid and effective implementation.

2. *We had as an explicit goal of the project the transfer of technology to other research groups and industry.*

   This was due in part because the project began as a collaboration with government and industry and in part because our earlier experiences with operating systems had led us to believe that we could only successfully validate our research ideas through extensive use by application programmers.

3. *We met important needs at a time when more traditional system software platforms did not.*

   By stressing hardware independence in the design and engineering of the system and by implementing Mach on many hardware platforms we were able to satisfy the needs of many groups outside and inside Carnegie Mellon University (CMU) who need a single software platform for multiple machine types. By providing support for a variety of multiprocessor systems we were able to provide groups with a UNIX-style multiprocessor operating system environment not readily available in the commercial marketplace.

4. *We recognized the need to provide binary compatibility with earlier systems.*

   By reducing the cost of technology transfer to zero through binary compatibility with existing UNIX systems, we could easily entice application builders to use Mach and experiment with its new features and facilities.

5. *We did not set out to build a prototype.*

   We intended from the beginning that the system we built from our ideas would be robust enough for use by ourselves and our peers. We used

Mach ourselves from the earliest days of the project and we worked with the facilities organization within the School of Computer Science to make Mach available as the primary computing environment for the school.

6. *We did not forget about performance.*

Experience had shown us that the best laid plans for technology transfer can be led astray by poor performance of a new technology. We were determined from the beginning to equal or exceed the performance of existing systems.

7. *We actively pursued external distribution of our software.*

We developed tools and procedures to make Mach readily available to outside organizations.

## 17.2  The Genesis of the Mach Project

From the earliest days of the Mach project, it was envisioned to have an impact on the industrial and research development of operating systems for parallel architectures. In fact, the project owed its origins to a planned collaboration between Digital Equipment Corporation (DEC) and CMU and to an innovative Defense Advanced Research Projects (DARPA) program in high performance computing.

In the fall of 1983, DEC approached CMU with a proposal to do joint research on a 32-processor VAX multiprocessor system. Digital's efforts were to be concentrated in the area of multiprocessor hardware design and multiprocessor versions of its commercial operating systems. CMU's contributions to this project were expected to be in the area of operating systems, measurement and performance evaluation—all areas in which CMU had considerable experience owing to its past work on the research multiprocessors C.MMP and CM*.

At the same time, DARPA was beginning to fund a major initiative in high-performance parallel processing—the Strategic Computing Program. This project was envisioned to support innovative high performance parallel computers and new applications for such systems. This goal could not be reached, however, without a common software base that could be used on a wide range of new architectures and provide a single system software environment for application designers. Mach was thus designed both as a basis for research into parallel operating systems software and as a support environment for parallel programming on a wide collection of hardware platforms.

Initial implementation of Mach began during the summer of 1985. By February 1986 the first multiprocessor version was running on a four-processor VAX 11/784. The fact that the Mach project was able to produce an initial

version of the system in less than 1 year was due in large part to the fact that
many of the key ideas and much of the implementation strategy used in Mach
derived from 10 years of experience with earlier systems—specifically CMU's
Accent [4] and the University of Rochester RIG system [1,3]. The knowledge
of virtual memory implementation techniques gained in the development of
Accent, in particular, was critical to our ability to build Mach quickly and with
good performance. Nearly half a dozen different virtual memory algorithms and
implementation strategies had been tried in Accent and a considerable emphasis
had been placed on extensive performance evaluation and testing [2].

## 17.3   Addressing Hardware and Software Diversity

In addition to technical experience, RIG and Accent yielded important lessons in
technology transfer. Both RIG and Accent were implemented for specific hardware engines (the Data General Eclipse and Perq Systems PERQ, respectively)
and both provided unique programming environments. Neither succeeded in developing enough of a user community to sustain them and both died with the
decline of the hardware platforms for which they were built. It was clear from
the experiences of Accent and RIG that the success of Mach would depend on
its ability to allow new hardware and software technologies to develop without
invalidating investments already made in existing systems.

The problems RIG and Accent had faced were in fact symptomatic of problems faced by manufacturers and researchers in the mid-1980s as they strained
to accommodate old and new hardware and software systems:

- □ Old and new central processing unit (CPU) architectures (e.g., complex
  instruction set computers (CISC) and reduced instruction set computers
  (RISC))

- □ Old and new memory architectures (e.g., uniprocessor and multiprocessor)

- □ Old and new input/output (i/o) organizations (e.g., buses and networks)

- □ Proprietary operating system environments developed during the 1960s
  and 1970s in addition to new operating system environments demanded
  by customers (e.g., OS/2 and UNIX)

Mach was designed to operate on both uniprocessors and multiprocessors
and to provide a small set of basic facilities that would permit a wide variety of
operating system environments to be efficiently implemented. The key features
of the Mach in its role as a system software kernel were

- □ Support for multiple threads of control within a single address space

- □ An extensible and secure interprocess communication facility (IPC) [6];

□ Architecture independent virtual memory (VM) management [5]

□ Integrated IPC/VM support, including: copy-on-write message passing, copy-on-reference network communication, and extensible memory objects

□ Transparent shared libraries to supply binary compatibility

□ An object programming facility integrated with transparent network communication

The Mach design provides for an unusually flexible execution environment for both system and user applications. It exposes the management of CPU, communication, VM, and secondary storage resources in a way that allows system applications such as database management facilities to use those resources efficiently. In effect, the Mach kernel provides software equivalents of the key elements of uniprocessor and multiprocessor architectures. The Mach thread mechanism, for example, is a kind of software processor. By allowing multiple threads to run within the same program, Mach permits a system or application programmer to directly manage multiple CPUs in a multiprocessor. Mach's IPC provides the kind of i/o channel between threads that may exist in a multiprocessor with a message-passing bus or between workstations on a network.

Interprocess communication and memory management in Mach are tightly integrated. Memory management techniques (such as the use of memory remapping to avoid data copying) are employed whenever large amounts of data are sent in a message from one program to another. This allows the transmission of megabytes of data at very low cost.

One of the most unusual and important facilities Mach provides is the notion of a memory object that an application program may create and manage. The memory object is like a file or data container that can be mapped into the address space of a program. Unlike traditional systems in which the operating system has complete control of "paging" data to and from such a data object, Mach allows the application that creates the memory object to act as though it were the disk storage or "pager" for that object. Mach VM objects are represented as communication channels. On a page fault the kernel sends a message to the backing storage communication channel of a memory object to get the data contained in the faulted page. This provides the flexibility necessary to implement efficiently such system applications as file systems, databases, dynamic encryption, or compression of data on access or even network shared memory.

## 17.4  The Role of Mach in Industry

The transfer of Mach technology to industry was greatly aided by fundamental changes in the operating system marketplace. During the late 1980s operating systems became a hotly contested battleground for "open system standards." This was due in large part to the success of workstation companies such as Sun Microsystems, which relied on UNIX as their operating system environment. Various national, international, and industry groups attempted to define, implement, and ultimately convince users to buy new "open" computing environments. Most of these efforts centered around versions of the UNIX operating system, but there was no consensus among industrial groups as to which "version" of UNIX was ultimately the correct basis for an open system standard. Two major industrial organizations, the OSF and UNIX International, were formed to endorse two rather different UNIX implementations: OSF/1 and AT&T's System V.4. Non-UNIX systems such as the Macintosh OS, MS-DOS, and OS/2 were also seen as "standards" by various hardware and software developers.

This divergence of systems and standards raised fundamental issues within industry about the strategy that should be employed in the development of open operating systems. It became increasingly important to provide support within a single computing environment for "multiple standards," i.e., multiple operating system environments that could be tailored to different vendor or user needs. Moreover, manufacturers frequently needed to provide customers with continuing access to proprietary operating systems developed during the 1960s and 1970s (e.g., VMS, MVS, and MS-DOS).

All of this activity opened the door for Mach and other kernel-style operating systems. Traditional systems such as UNIX or VMS had historically been implemented "all in one piece" with knowledge about the basic system structure spread throughout. This makes them poorly suited to the compatible support of multiple operating system environments. As a result, the large computer manufacturers that use them are commonly forced to support several completely distinct groups of operating system engineers: one for OS/2, one for UNIX, and one or more for proprietary systems—each at considerable expense. The resulting software development costs translate directly into increased cost for the user and delays in the introduction of new features and new applications.

Because of its modular design, Mach offered an alternative approach that allowed systems builders to separate those parts of the operating system that control the basic hardware resources—often called the operating system "kernel"—from those parts of the operating system that determine the unique characteristics of an operating system environment, e.g., a particular file system interface. The advantage of this scheme is that it can allow more than one operating system environment to be implemented on the same hardware/software base so that machine-dependent software need be written only once for each new architecture. It also allows, at least potentially, for more than one operating system environment to be supported in "native mode" simultaneously on the same hardware.

There are two distinct ways in which a kernel system such as Mach can be used to aid the development of open operating systems.

First, the Mach kernel can be used as the lower layer of a two-tier operating system implementation. In such a scheme the Mach kernel provides support for key functions such as VM, scheduling, interprocess communication, and device access. The target operating system can then be implemented using these functions. In this approach the entire system, kernel and operating system environment, would be packaged as a unit and run in a priviledged state just as in a traditional operating system design. In many respects it would continue to resemble the more traditional operating systems it replaces. One advantage to this approach, however, is that more than one operating system environment can be implemented using the same kernel interface—reducing the software effort required to bring a new architecture to market with several supported operating systems. Another advantage is that the basic kernel could be made freely available to all without compromising the proprietary added value of the particular operating system environment layered above it. This approach would allow companies to share the costs of porting the kernel to a new architecture.

A second approach to building a layered operating system environment has even greater potential for open system development. The kernel can be packaged by itself as a "pure" kernel with no operating system environment. In this approach, only the kernel would run in privileged state. The rest of the operating system environment would, in effect, run as one or more programs (or, more precisely, one or more server processes) on top of the kernel. User applications would run as before, but instead of making direct calls on the operating system via system calls traps, the kernel's communication and memory management facilities would be employed to communicate information between the application and operating system processes. The reason implementation strategy is so attractive for open systems, is that it can allow more than one operating system environment to be supported on the same machine, on the same kernel, at the same time. Systems such as UNIX or OS/2 could potentially coexist in their native form. The kernel becomes a kind of universal "socket" into which more than one operating system environment can be plugged, insulating that software from the hardware itself. Exhibit 17.1 shows how this software strategy could be applied to a variety of system software environments.

We pursued both of these approaches with Mach. The initial target operating system environment for Mach was Berkeley's 4.3 BSD version of UNIX. As a result the commercial versions of Mach available today are, in fact, examples of 4.3 BSD UNIX layered above Mach kernel primitives. UNIX system calls are still handled in supervisor mode but their actual implementation has been substantially altered to take advantage of Mach mechanisms.

Later in the Mach project we began development of a 4.3BSD environment that would run purely as a Mach application program with no UNIX-specific code residing in supervisor state. Today that implementation is running on the pure Mach kernel with performance comparable to traditional UNIX implementations [7]. Exhibit 17.2 illustrates the implementation of the UNIX read system call on the Mach kernel.

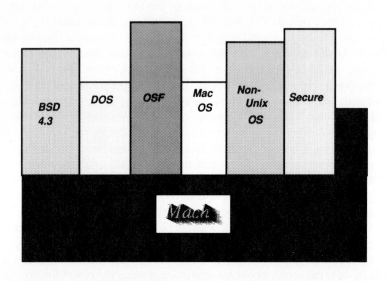

**EXHIBIT 17.1**
Mach as a system software platform.

## 17.5    Reducing the Cost of Technology Transfer

### 17.5.1    Zero Effort Upgrades

Although it was costly in terms of time and manpower, we have adopted during the project the principle of providing binary compatibility for any operating system environment we implement. This has been of major importance to the success of the project. It means no user has to be inconvenienced by switching from UNIX to Mach and yet these same users can take advantage of new Mach applications and programming interfaces.

### 17.5.2    Positive Performance Impact

Although one might assume that Mach's layered approach to UNIX implementation would be a performance disadvantage, measurements of Mach versus traditional UNIX implementations indicate otherwise. Simple compilation benchmarks on SUN 3/60 workstations, for example, run nearly 40% faster under Mach than they do under Sun Microsystems own SunOS version of UNIX.

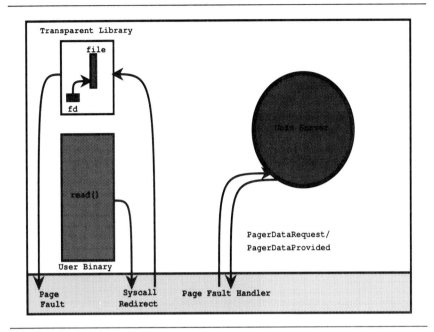

**EXHIBIT 17.2**
Binary emulation of UNIX read system call on Mach. The read system call
trap is redirected to a transparent shared library that implements the UNIX
read system call using a Mach memory object. The file information is copied
by the transparent library from a window on the memory object to the
application buffer. If the data have not been previously referenced page faults
are taken that are handled by a system server which translates faults on
memory object pages into UNIX file read operations.

Times for UNIX "fork" and "exec" operations are also nearly a factor of two
faster under Mach than SunOS.

## 17.5.3  No Cost Licensing

From the standpoint of technology transfer, the single most important decision
that was made in the early days of the project was that all of the software
developed by the Mach project would be provided free of distribution fees or
royalties to any university, company, or other organization. A simple license
form was generated that allowed CMU-created software to be used subject only
to the requirement that changes and modifications to that software must be
returned to CMU.

### 17.5.4  Aggressive Distribution

Not only was it decided to make the software created by the project free, but an agressive distribution policy was followed. Beginning in January 1987, the first Release 0 tapes of Mach were distributed to groups outside CMU. By April 1987 a second Release 1 tape was made for the VAX, Sun 3, and IBM RT PC. By the time Release 2 of Mach began distribution in May 1988 there were over 100 sites outside CMU with Mach tapes from CMU.

One important aspect of Mach distribution has been our ability to electronically update external sites with modification and changes. A network software update program called SUP was implemented at CMU in the early 1980s by Steve Shafer and became over time the primary tool used by the Computer Science Department's Facilities organization for upgrading and maintaining workstations on our local network. The Mach project adapted SUP for use as an ARPANET wide electronic software distribution facility. This enabled us to reduce our costs for maintaining software releases at industrial sites that depended on new Mach versions. It also provided us with a convenient tool for engaging in joint software development with such groups.

## 17.6   Conclusions

I have identified a number of factors that I believe were responsible for the relatively rapid transition of Mach from idea to product. Not all these factors are applicable to other research projects, but I believe there are several bits of general wisdom for other researchers that can be derived from our experiences:

□ *Don't build prototypes.*

Software prototypes are generally poor vehicles for technology transfer. Code that both embodies new ideas and that works and works well is the best form of publication and most convenient vehicle for technology transfer.

□ *Preserve compatibility with the past if possible.*

The less effort required by others to use a new piece of technology the more likely it will be that the technology will be used by them. Binary compatibility with older systems, tools, or applications is often difficult but the effort required to provide it is usually paid back in greater use by others.

□ *Be aggressive in marketing new ideas and systems.*

Technology transfer can happen by accident, but is more reliable when done by design.

## 17.7   Acknowledgments

The original implementors and designers of Mach were (in alphabetical order):
Mike Accetta, Bob Baron, Bob Beck (Sequent), David Black, Bill Bolosky,
Jonathan Chew, David Golub, Glenn Marcy, Fred Olivera (Encore), Rick Rashid,
Avie Tevanian, Jim Van Schiver (Encore), and Mike Young. Too many people
have since contributed to the project and it is now impossible for me to provide
an exhaustive list. I would like to credit later members of the Mach project for
their efforts: Joe Barrera, Randy Dean, Richard Draves, Alessandro Forin, Lori
Iannamico, Mike Jones, Dan Julin, Mark Stephenson, and Mary Thompson.

## References

[1] J. E. Ball, J. A. Feldman, J. R. Low, R. F. Rashid, and P. D. Rovner. Rig, rochester's
intelligent gateway: System overview. *IEEE Transactions on Software Engineering*,
2(4):321-328, 1976.

[2] R. Fitzgerald and R. F. Rashid. The integration of virtual memory management and
interprocess communication in accent. *ACM Transactions on Computer Systems*,
4(2), 1986.

[3] K. A. Lantz, K. D. Gradischnig, J. A. Feldman, and R. F. Rashid. Rochester's
intelligent gateway. *Computer*, 15(10):54-68, 1982.

[4] R.F. Rashid and G. Robertson. Accent: A communication oriented network operating
system kernel. In *Proc. 8th Symposium on Operating Systems Principles*, pp. 64-75.
ACM, 1981.

[5] R. F. Rashid, A. Tevanian, M. W. Young, D. B. Golub, R. V. Baron, D. L. Black,
W. Bolosky, and J. J. Chew. Machine-independent virtual memory management
for paged uniprocessor and multiprocessor architectures. In *Proceedings of the 2nd
Symposium on Architectural Support for Programming Languages and Operating
Systems*. ACM, 1987.

[6] R. D. Sansom, D. P. Julin, and R. F. Rashid. Extending a capability based system
into a network environment. Technical report, Department of Computer Science,
Carnegie Mellon University, Pittsburgh, PA, 1986.

[7] D. Golub et al. UNIX as an Application Program. In *Proceedings of the Summer
1990 USENIX Conference*, 1990.

PART SIX

Reflections

# 18

---

# Technology and Courage

Ivan Sutherland

---

## 18.1  Introduction

Sutherland is a Scottish name. My ancestors came from the northernmost county in Scotland, called Sutherlandshire, a land where cows grow long hair against the cold, trees mostly refuse to grow at all, and the farmers cut peat to heat their homes. I enjoyed the sunrise at 3 am there one summer morning, it having set about 11 pm the previous evening. Because the bonus of summer sunshine is merely borrowed from winter, winter must be bleak indeed. A British friend who was with me in Sutherlandshire remarked that Sutherlands there are "two for a penny;" I had thought of them as "a dime a dozen," but considering the pound to dollar exchange rate, it's about the same value.

I often wear a tie bearing my family colors, the Sutherland tartan. Depending on the listener, I claim to wear it either (1) because I own only one tie, which is not true; or (2) as a default to avoid having to choose a tie, which is true but unimportant; or (3) in honor of my late father who also generally wore such a tie, which is also true and is my real reason: like my father before me, I am proud of my lineage, and I draw courage from identifying with my ancestors.

Nearly all of the talks I have ever given were technical. Because I am a professor at heart, you can wind me up and I will easily go on for exactly 50 minutes on any of my several technical interests. I go on easily because I know my subjects well, I know what is interesting about them, I know that I can talk clearly about them, and I have had favorable responses from previous audiences.

Today, however, I want to do something very much harder for me. I want to depart from my familiar technical fields to address a different subject: *courage*. I direct my remarks to young people who may soon discover for the first time that to do technology requires courage and to my older colleagues who, like me, have languishing technical projects and reports that seem less important than today's urgent tasks. I am going to talk about the courage required to do creative technical work, and because I have mainly my own experience to draw on, this will be an intensely personal talk, revealing of my own failures of courage. I ask you to apply to yourselves any lessons you may learn.

### 18.1.1   What is Courage?

Many activities require courage, a human trait we find admirable. We admire the courage required to explore a wilderness and so great explorers become famous: Lewis and Clark, Admiral Byrd, Amelia Earhart, and John Glenn, for example. We also admire political courage, as exhibited by Abraham Lincoln or Winston Churchill, or more recently by Mikhail Gorbachev. Taking financial risks in business also requires courage, as exhibited by Lee Iacocca, although less so when someone else's money is at risk. Changing to a new job or a new school requires personal courage, especially so when making a home in a new city.

What is courage? *Courage* is what it takes to overcome *fear*. *Fear* is an emotion appropriate to *perceived risk*. Thus to exhibit courage one must both perceive a risk and proceed in spite of it. Suppose a child has fallen through the ice on a lake and could be saved if reached. A person who walks out on the ice believing it to be very thick requires no courage because he or she perceives no risk even though others may think him or her courageous. A person who correctly perceives that the ice is thin and stays off it likewise exhibits no courage; rather we call his or her action prudent or cowardly, depending on whether or not the ice is, in fact, too thin for safety. Courage is required only of a person who proceeds to rescue the child in full knowledge that the ice is thin.

### 18.1.2   Courage in Technology

Exploring the horizons of technology requires courage because research carries risks, even if we cannot always articulate them in advance. Generally they are not physical risks, although physical risks exist in some fields of science. Often they are not immediate personal financial risks, because these may be borne by the university, an industrial employer, or the government sponsor of the work. Usually the risks are more subtle but no less strong: they are social and emotional risks, risks to reputation and to pride; they are risks that are felt but difficult to identify and describe.

In addition to the risk to reputation and to pride, the very nature of research poses its own special risk. In research we daily face the uncertainty of whether our chosen approach will succeed or fail. We steep ourselves in elusive, mysterious, and unnamed phenomena, and we struggle to unravel very complex puzzles, often making no visible progress for weeks or months, sometimes for years. We strive for simplicity and clarity in a cloudy and often baffling world. The special risk of research starts with the high probability that any particular attempt will fail and follows from the resulting experience of repeated failure. Research carries a special risk of discouragement.

### 18.1.3  Failures of Courage

When you have inadequate courage for a task, you can work up your courage, reduce the real risk, reduce your perception of the risk, or leave the task undone. I use all four methods. All too often, however, I leave tasks undone because I don't recognize that my courage is inadequate to the risks I feel but don't verbalize. Our universities provide mechanisms, both formal and informal, for reducing the risks of research and for building up the courage of researchers. Our free enterprise system also provides mechanisms to encourage entrepreneurs to undertake new challenges. Each of us also has ways to conserve and bolster our own courage. The body of this chapter is my list of some of these mechanisms. I suggest that you can draw on them as well as invent some of your own, and that by doing so you may be better able to face the difficult challenges technology offers.

## 18.2  External Encouragement

Because individuals are often unable to get things done without encouragement, society has devised many forms of encouragement. There are rewards of money, fame, acclaim, recognition, status, or love. Prizes, statues, certificates, medals, and honorary titles are some of the adult equivalents of the gold stars we got as children for good work. Large offices, with carpets, maybe with windows, and with or without a flag or fancy plants in them are also symbols of status. There are also punishments for inaction. Often we formalize such rewards and punishments in the form of written or unwritten contracts.

Contracts often contain deadlines. Deadlines help inspire us to extra effort because the task must be done on time. In some research, deadlines are absolute:

a space mission to study Halley's Comet must be launched on time, but softer, self-imposed deadlines are also useful for raising the urgency of tasks. An architect friend of mine taught me the word "charette," meaning the feverish activity immediately preceding a deadline. The term comes from the French name for the horse-drawn carts in Paris that carried architectural students with their architectural models from their workshops to their examinations, still feverishly finishing the models "en charette." In the vernacular English we can speak of "having a charette," and, of course, there is a verb form: "charetting it up." Without a deadline there could be no charette. A designer friend of mine is completely unable to function without a deadline to work against. Several times I have asked him to do simple tasks for me: designing a letterhead, for example, "when he had time." Until I figured out that he works only against a deadline, I got no result at all. Now I ask him for something by a particular date and he usually delivers on time. Evidently he can work only "en charette."

The fellowship of people in groups offers encouragement. Groups of people will even do things that single individuals wouldn't do; lynchings and riots are an extreme form of this. Group activities seem easier. Boards and committees share not only knowledge but also responsibility and thus increase their participants' willingness to undertake risk. Moreover, the fellowship of such groups makes working more fun. Is this because man is a social animal, or is this why we call man a social animal?

I always thought that working with a partner or with a few colleagues was better than working alone, in part because I can rarely think about difficult subjects without verbalizing them to someone else. I like to collaborate with someone to whom I can express my ideas, even poorly formed ones, and from whom I can draw a fresh look at them. The names of my companies bear witness to my need to collaborate: the Evans and Sutherland Computer Company and my present employer, Sutherland, Sproull, and Associates, Inc. I owe much to my partners in these enterprises.

### 18.2.1  Encouragement in Academia

One of the beauties of a university such as Carnegie Mellon University (CMU) is that it abounds with mechanisms to encourage people to do research. Some of these, like formal classes, reduce the risk of learning new things. Some of them, like observing other people at work on other research tasks, can bolster a graduate student's courage to do likewise. Others, like the traditional academic tolerance of nonconformity, reduce the social risk of entertaining new ideas.

The university provides mentors. My former student, Dan Cohen, called me for advice nearly 15 years after getting his Ph.D., asserting that he wanted counsel from his "faculty advisor." I demurred, claiming that I had stopped being his advisor more than a dozen years ago. Not so, he said, "It's a tenured position." Because attachments between students and faculty become strong, contact with the mentors provided by the university is valuable indeed, almost as valuable as contact with students. I have learned far more from my students and gained more pleasure from them than I can ever have offered in return.

Formal Mechanisms.    Among university classes, I find the study seminar most interesting for several reasons. Such a seminar gathers together a group with similar interests who read up on a subject and pool their knowledge at regular meetings. By providing a series of regular meetings and homework assignments, the study seminar provides deadlines for its participants. Working together with colleagues reduces the labor required from each participant and makes the learning experience more pleasurable. Finally, working in a group reduces the perceived risk inherent in the new material.

The immigration course in computer science at CMU is one of the best examples of a formal way to help new graduate students get started. It forces them to learn about what facilities are available, it gives them the opportunity to meet and get to know the people they may work with, and it introduces them to the existing research projects. By providing a broad range of background knowledge and forcing the students to do a small warm-up project, it not only reduces the risk of learning what equipment is available and how to use it but also builds confidence. I applaud the makers of the immigration course for finding such an effective way to launch would-be researchers.

The university also offers formal mechanisms to encourage graduate students to keep going when the going gets tough. One of these in Computer Science at CMU is called Black Friday. As I understand it, Black Friday is a knock-down, drag-out meeting of the faculty at which each and every graduate student is individually discussed to detect those making inadequate progress. The laggards are then given formal notice to move forward or leave. By increasing the risk of inaction, the threat of Black Friday forces students to bolster their courage and get on with their work.

My advice for a new graduate student seeking to get started in research is to join an ongoing research group. Of course there is an opportunity cost to joining up with a particular group: you can't then join others. But it matters far less what a new student does than *that he or she do something*. If the first two or three things don't work out, you can always switch to another group or another project. The key thing is to get involved in something, get some basic knowledge, and get started.

Talking and Writing.    A thesis proposal can provide a starting mechanism for a thesis project: it can serve as a guide to the proposed research. It indicates that some thought has gone into what to do, even though the real work may not yet have started. Most important, the thesis proposal can serve as a point of discussion between the proposer and his advisors, both formal faculty advisors and student colleagues. Accepting the thesis proposal is in and of itself a way for the faculty to encourage a student to get on with the work. All too often thesis proposals are an afterthought to research already done, becoming at best an outline of the thesis document. I far prefer them earlier as a guide to the research itself.

Academia provides mechanisms to encourage publication of which the strongest one is known as "publish or perish." A new untenured faculty member must obtain tenure or leave the university after a fixed period of time, but to obtain tenure he or she must publish. A journal editor I know once remarked that she sits on the tenure committee of every university in the country.

Tenure itself can be encouraging. A young and talented friend of mine, a computer scientist by training and a tenured professor of computer science at a major institution, has recently become interested in combustion. He commented to me recently that he feels guilty for pursuing studies so far outside his departmental boundary. I hope you share my feeling that he should follow his interests exactly where they lead; that, after all, is precisely what tenure should encourage him to do.

Universities also provide a host of places where talking about research is easy. Seminars provide a knowledgeable and usually friendly audience for new ideas. By providing peer pressure to participate and share results, seminars can encourage students to practice talking about their work. Even in an informal seminar, the first few presentations take an extra batch of courage, but with practice comes familiarity and skill, a better assessment of the minimal risk, and increasing comfort. I have often seen student speakers literally shake before and during their talks.

Practice in teaching is a good way to learn how to present ideas to groups. Graduate student teachers not only staff undergraduate classes, but also learn to speak in public. One hopes that they do not damage the undergraduate students too badly. Practice in writing is also valuable, starting in high school or undergraduate English classes. All too often technical writing has to be a part of graduate education.

Informal Interactions.   One of the difficult lessons of graduate school is the lesson of autonomy from the faculty. At first a graduate student may feel unable to question his or her mentors, but by the end of graduate training, that same student will be able to take a place as a researcher in their ranks. Graduate school is the place where the distinction between mentor and student begins to blur and faculty and graduate students become colleagues.

Informal interaction between students and faculty helps students join the ranks of full fledged researchers. I recall playing with blocks at Claude Shannon's house when he was my thesis supervisor. Although at the time I thought of it as recreation, and he may also have, it provided me with courage because

I saw his less daunting facets, his human side. He became my friend as well as supervisor, and this made him more approachable and raised my confidence.

Universities encourage informal social interactions. Although some social functions may seem to be just for play, e.g., thank God it's Friday parties (TGIF), or the Nth annual "pretty good race" at CMU, such social interactions help us get to know each other, and by knowing each other we become better able to share our burdens of discouragement; we provide each other with courage. Within the fellowship provided by such social functions we can gain insight into the habits of our mentors and friends, and can discuss ill-formed ideas that would be too risky to reveal in a more formal context.

In Academia It's Hard to Stop.    Some academics go on and on doing the same research year after year, often as a continuation of their thesis work. Academia seems to me deficient in mechanisms to help people stop old and stale projects. Advice from faculty and peers offers one means, and lack of financial support offers another; the sponsors of research do sometimes stop supporting it. Academics usually stop working on old things only to turn to newer and more interesting projects.

### 18.2.2   Encouragement in Business

A person with the courage to start a new business is called an entrepreneur. When I was a child, my parents offered high praise for he who was "enterprising." By starting several companies myself, and through my work in venture capital, I have observed many ways that entrepreneurs work up their courage to the point where they are ready to start a business. The most important formal mechanism, nominally intended to present the prospects of the business to the financial community, is called the business plan. A business plan is very much like a thesis proposal. It says what its proponents intend to do, what they plan to spend, what competition they expect, and what return they anticipate. Its preparation requires that the entrepreneurs do the basic work that is needed to assess the business risks. Its approval encourages the entrepreneurs to begin by providing not only the capital required, but also the moral encouragement of the supporting investors. In effect, the business plan records the entrepreneurs' estimate of the thickness of the ice.

The financial backers of an enterprise back it only after examining its prospects with "due diligence." Sometimes it seems to me that a plan is so obviously timely and the entrepreneurs' ability so obviously great that little further diligence is due. My venture capital friends, however, often forget what "due" means, and treat "due diligence" as if it were a single noun denoting the collection of paper that justifies investment in the business. They may say, "let us gather some due diligence," and they have files of due diligence. It seems to take due diligence about 1 inch thick per million dollars invested. Ultimately, the financial backers of a new business must express their faith in the entrepreneurs and have the courage to invest. They should exercise due diligence in making their own estimate of the thickness of the ice.

Although business plans are rarely followed in any great detail, they are nevertheless very useful. They build courage in the entrepreneurs by letting them plan a real business and see its potential profit. They provide a way for financial backers to understand the proposed business, milestones for measurement of progress, a common ground for discussing changes in plan, and a common target for both entrepreneurs and backers to seek. The plan's real function is to endow everyone with the courage to proceed.

It turns out that a large fraction of new businesses fail, just as a large fraction of research ideas fail. Fortunately for our society we, collectively, have more than enough courage to keep trying, even trying things that prove imprudent. Were we a more cautious lot, a much slower pace of scientific and industrial progress would prevail. If you don't fail regularly, you are not trying hard enough things. The trouble, of course, is that it is emotionally much harder to restart after a failure because the risks seem clearer. This may be why the energy and enthusiasm of youth are so important in research and in new businesses.

Business Incentives.   Our system of capitalistic free enterprise provides equity incentives. It is amazing to me how effectively stock ownership motivates hard work, and more important, how common ownership of identical stock makes people pull together. If you and I both own the same type of stock, I can make a return *if* and *only if* you do, and thus my objective becomes to make you rich. This is the power of the capitalistic system that once raised our standard of living to the highest in the world.

In addition to stock ownership, income and bonus incentives to business people often help keep their minds focused on their essential tasks. Commissions for salespeople are very common, probably because selling takes so much courage to face the high risk of rejection by the potential customer. There is almost nothing I like less than selling, particularly against competition that undoes my sales pitch as soon as I turn my back. Amazingly to me, a salesperson with a commission program will keep at this difficult task; I can only conclude that the salesperson draws courage from the commission. Presidents of companies often have bonus programs tied to the profitability of the company. Such plans let the president do well *if* and *only if* the shareholders do well, and thus encourages the president to keep the shareholders' interests at heart.

Contracts are an essential ingredient of modern business. Contract milestones often include partial payments, and thus powerful encouragement to getting on with the job. Contract deadlines can include penalty clauses. For example, the repaving contract for the Golden Gate Bridge included penalty clauses of tens of thousands of dollars per hour for delay in reopening the bridge to traffic each day.

Social incentives also work in business. I spend much of my time as a consultant and have discovered that one of my tasks is to provide deadlines to my client's employees. My visits provide the deadlines for "charetting it up," for getting all of the reports done, for getting the presentations ready, and for getting on with the work. I can and do provide praise for good work. I like to think I have something technical to contribute also, but even if I did not, the deadline and appraisal value of my visits may easily make them worthwhile to my clients.

It is not accidental that the word "company" as applied to a business enterprise is the same word that we apply to social occasions, as in "having company," or "keeping company," or "being company." Indeed, the Hudson's Bay Company, chartered in May 1670, was literally called "The Governor and *Company* of Adventurers of England Trading into Hudson's Bay."

The corporate form of business as we practice it has a board of directors to provide policy guidance. The board is elected by the owners of the company, the shareholders, and in turn, the board elects the officers of the company who manage its day to day affairs. In a very real sense such boards along with the corporate officers are the Company of Adventurers who do our business. The board meets quarterly or monthly, or more often as required. My experience suggests that the most effective boards have a measure of fellowship that helps them seek wise decisions together. When business prospects seem good, there is often humor at board meetings. It may be that the number of jokes told at board meetings is an important, albeit unreported, leading indicator of the business climate.

Stopping a Business.    Unlike academia, the capitalist system of free enterprise provides a very clear mechanism to detect when to stop, namely, lack of profits. Businesses fail when customers refuse to purchase their products: as one of my venture capital partners says, when "the dogs just don't like the dog food." In fact, most businesses fail; few succeed.

But even in business it can take courage to stop. Investor courage is required to withdraw support from a failing business and its employees, but support must be withdrawn if the prospects do not warrant further investment. An investor friend of mine said he got into a multimillion dollar unsuccessful investment "one nickel at a time." He couldn't stop.

Personal courage is required to admit that one's skills do not match the business needs. I have admired two chief executives who gracefully turned over control of their businesses to others after realizing their own inadequacy; more often the incompetent hang on far too long. When a business fails there are legal details to tidy up as well as odds and ends of value to be sold. Individuals who do this well can extract value for the owners of the business that might otherwise be lost, but it is hard to do a good job while carrying the sense of defeat and loss of a failed business.

I think that the most subtle form of the courage to stop is to know when to sell a security. My portfolio of investments is dear to me; they are like old friends, the family dog, or my ancient automobile. I shudder to part with one. Nevertheless, prudent management requires that I sell those that are not destined to be winners and use the funds instead to buy better equities. The hard part, of course, is deciding which are not to be winners. It takes courage to sell stocks, far more than it takes to buy them.

Investment Courage.    I believe that investment courage is in short supply in the United States today, individually, institutionally, and nationally. Our collective failures of courage are, I believe, the cause of our decreasing economic success vis-à-vis our international competition. Long-term projects take more courage than short-term ones because the greater uncertainty of the distant future seems riskier, whether or not it really is. Our industrial and governmental institutions are not, I believe, making the courageous long-term investments in education, training, research, development, equipment, and infrastructure required for long-term economic strength, and as a direct result we are losing a global economic war.

One reason for the shortsightedness of business in the United States today is that the profit sharing plans of executives consider only immediate profit and not long-term growth. Another reason for business shortsightedness is that the judgment of shareholders about winners and losers is based on quarterly results instead of long-term gains. Are you aware, for example, that although the trading rate on the New York Stock Exchange is slow enough to turn over all of the securities represented in about 2 years,[1] many companies trade rapidly enough to turn over in 6 months or less? I am particularly offended that pension fund holdings turn over quite quickly even though pension funds, above all, should take a long-term view.

We seem unable to make the long-term investments required for economic strength. Is this because, as some say, our cost of capital is too high? John Maynard Keynes showed that investment decisions are largely independent of the cost of capital, but depend only on expectations of future return. Is our inability to face long-term investment related to our uncertainty about the future of a world harboring nuclear weapons? It can't be, for other nations make long-term investments. Is our inability to face long-term investment related to our ethnic diversity, our view of an end to our abundant supply of raw materials, or is it a symptom of a general breakdown in family values? I don't know the reasons,

---

[1] There are 83,605,000,000 shares represented on the exchange with a total capital value of about $2,814,429,000,000. About 150,000,000 shares trade each day with a value of about $5,000,000,000.

but the facts seem plain: we lack courage, and nations with more courage are eating our lunch. We desperately need ways to encourage investors to hold on to securities for long-term gains, and by so doing encourage them to take an interest in, indeed demand, that their companies invest for long-term growth. We desperately need governmental investment in the intellectual infrastructure of an educated populace confident of the long-term future. We have become a "now" nation to the extent of jeopardizing our future.

## 18.3  Self-Encouragement

So much for the institutional mechanisms for helping courage surmount risk. Now let me turn to some more personal ones. Along with several of my own, I offer the confession that I feel both inadequately equipped with mechanisms and all too often unable to apply those I have.

What I find interesting about the need for personal courage in advanced technology is its elusive nature. When my courage has been strong, going forward seemed easy: courage seemed unnecessary, perhaps even irrelevant. When my courage has failed me, however, something else seemed to be wrong; I could always generate many valid reasons for not moving forward. Courage and cowardice in technology have seemed to me attributes of other people; I have been able to recognize them in myself only in hindsight and only by careful introspection.

By describing how my own failures of courage feel to me, I hope to help you recognize such failures in yourselves; I seek to *encourage* you. I take that literally; I seek to extend your courage by making you aware of your need for it and by describing some symptoms of its failure. I will offer some ways to reduce your need for courage, to marshal what courage you can muster, and to husband your store of it.

### 18.3.1  Courage to Start

It's often hard to get started. I always find it hard to start a lecture, and so I cover my difficulty by telling a story. I select a story in advance, choosing one that is relevant to my topic, is familiar enough to me so that I won't muff it, can establish common ground with my audience, and will make them laugh. If it works, my story builds rapport with my audience, but more important, their response encourages me, or literally gives me the courage, to get on with my topic.

How often have you found it hard to get started on something? Have you ever thought of that difficulty as a failure of courage? Recognizing that there are risks in starting anything new helps reveal the difficulty of getting started as a reluctance to overcome those risks. Recognizing that it takes courage to get started may help in identifying the excuses you have as excuses and not reasons.

What It Feels Like to Me.   I feel many different risks in getting started. One common one is that, being ignorant in the new field, I will make a fool of myself. Many years ago when I was a ham radio operator, poor operators were called "lids" and were viewed with some contempt. Faced with such contempt, how was I to learn? Well, for a while I was a lid. Poor computer programmers are likewise looked on with some contempt; I have heard their programs described as "wedged." Whenever we start something new we must risk being "lids" or writing "wedged" programs. The risk is real and has kept many people from setting out in new directions. We prefer to continue with familiar things because they are, on the whole, less risky than new ones.

But my failures of courage to start have never felt to me like cowardice. Rather, I have been able to invent a host of reasons for not starting, all perfectly rational, and all quite valid if irrelevant. There are never enough funds to start the project, and the equipment available is never quite right. Often the programming languages available do not suit the need, especially if the procrastinator happens to be expert at making programming languages and can fix the problem by doing something familiar rather than getting on with the main task. Are you merely building tools or are you doing something directly productive?

Everything we do has an opportunity cost of other things not done. I often use that cost as a reason for procrastination, thinking that I am too busy, or that the investment of my time to learn something new is too great. It took me a long time to work up the courage to face a drawing program on my personal computer because I was just too busy to "take the time." While I was learning the drawing program I would not be meeting any of the hundred other demands on my time. In retrospect, I wish I had learned the drawing program earlier, for not only has it given me great pleasure, but also it has permitted me to explore some geometric ideas I would not otherwise have been able to consider. It is all too easy to overemphasize opportunity cost as a cover for fear; the truth is that I avoided learning to use the drawing program simply because it was unfamiliar and I risked frustration and failure. I may have been more sensitive to this risk than some of you might be, because I achieved some fame from writing an early drawing program [7]. It would be especially embarrassing for me if I should ask dumb questions about a drawing program.

My unwillingness to learn new things, risking frustration or failure, is related to another familiar phenomenon. People love their home towns, the model of car that they drive, the type of computer they already own, and are especially fond of the text editor most familiar to them, especially EMACS. We base these loyalties not on comparative analysis, but on our hidden fears of the unknown. Make no mistake, it takes courage to learn a new computer program; you face the risk of frustration at least, and seeming stupidity if you ask dumb questions. By the way, for some time now I have been far too busy to learn "Excel."

Overcoming Risks.   One start-up aid I have often used is ignorance; to use this approach I avoid ever measuring the thickness of the ice. I have often been told that it was a very courageous act to start the Evans and Sutherland company. Had the company failed, it might have been called foolish rather than courageous, but it certainly didn't feel courageous to me at the time. I simply had no idea of the risk I was undertaking. I believe that before people have children they have little idea of the risks or they might never start. Raising a family is a courageous act, but only for those who know how hard it is. One of the wonders of graduate students is that they haven't yet learned all of the things that can't be done, and so they are willing and able to do some of them.

A warm-up project is very helpful in getting any new research going. Do something fairly easy and carry it all the way through from beginning to end. When I was a new graduate student at the Massachusetts Institute of Technology (MIT) in 1961, I did a project on solving arbitrary wall mazes by computer. It involved a few thousand lines of computer program and some simple equipment. Later on my warm-up project saved me time in my thesis work by helping me avoid problems that I had solved before.

More important, my warm-up project gave me valuable experience and the courage that comes with experience. After finishing it, I knew that I could write a complex computer program and make it work. My warm-up project encouraged me to go on to the larger programming task involved in thesis work [7] and it encouraged my sponsors to support the more complex project. My point is that a warm-up project not only teaches, but also encourages. Some universities, including MIT, even require a master's thesis, a formal warm-up project, before the student embarks on a Ph.D. Remember, "programs are like pancakes; throw the first one away."

Procedures.   I used to hate washing dishes. I would delay as long as possible. Eyeing the daunting pile of dishes, I would say to myself, "I'll be here forever at this dumb task." The enormity of the task deterred me from starting. I still dislike washing dishes, but I now get the dishes done promptly because I learned a simple procedure for doing the job from my wife's uncle. The procedure starts out "Wash first dish . . . " I have a similar procedure for starting travel vouchers, it goes "Record first expense . . . "

Each of my little procedures embodies two different aids to getting started. By invoking a familiar procedure I reduce my need for courage. By breaking the task into smaller tasks through emphasizing that only the first dish need be washed or the first expense need be recorded, I reduce my estimate of risk. Both mechanisms work. These sources of courage are sometimes called "discipline," especially when being taught to the young. Discipline relies on a practiced use of routine subgoals to avoid defeat by fear. Its highest form comes when the lieutenant, charging up a heavily defended hill, says, "Follow me men!"—and they do.

### 18.3.2  Courage to Go On

"When the going gets tough, the tough go shopping" is the caption to a cartoon mocking all inveterate shoppers. Its humor comes from our certainty that when the going gets tough, it takes courage to go on rather than to go shopping.

What It Feels Like to Me.   When I get bogged down in a project, the failure of my courage to go on never feels to me like a failure of courage, but always feels like something entirely different. One such feeling is that my research isn't going anywhere anyhow, it isn't that important. Another feeling involves the urgency of something else. I have come to recognize these feelings as "who cares" and "the urgent drives out the important."

For me the urgent often takes the form of a crowded desk that must be cleared. All those letters to write, a timesheet to bring up to date, bills to pay, checkbook to balance, personal computer disk to back up, and a host of other easy little routine tasks are available to help me avoid the difficult big task at hand. Another sense I have is of the abundance of time remaining to think about the major research task; after all, the due date for my report is a year or more away. The other tasks with closer time horizons seem more urgent and thus should get more attention. I cower behind my routine little tasks to avoid the risks of failure associated with working on my main projects.

If your research feels less important than other tasks, examine your courage. Your research may indeed be unimportant, and it's OK to abandon projects as unsuccessful. In fact, I believe it takes courage to abandon projects. To remain in research, however, you must substitute some other research task for the abandoned one and not simply get involved in trivia, however urgent. When examined critically, the urgency of the little tasks is never so great as I suppose, nor is the risk of the big tasks so overwhelming. Many successful researchers recognize that and refuse to let the urgent drive out the important: Alan Newell of CMU and Fred Brooks of the University of North Carolina come to my mind as examples; they share an admirable ability to decline trivia.

Overcoming Risks.   Research has its special risk of continued inability to get a new idea. I have found that a change of scene helps my thoughts on a subject to gel. I escape from the local pressures by going far away in an airplane, or not so far to a quiet library, or even closer to the seclusion of my study, particularly early in the morning. The important thing about all these retreats for me is that

I can cast aside the urgent problems; the phone won't ring, the checkbook can't be balanced, and I can focus on my larger tasks with a fresh mind. After each of two extended "vacations" in Australia, I returned with patentable ideas [8,9], and on a third such trip developed a new algorithm for building vector quantization code books, as yet unpublished. I sometimes jokingly start out describing these ideas by saying, "When I was lying on the beach ..." The combination of a change of location, rest, and lack of distraction seems to be effective for me. Some universities formalize such changes as sabbatical leave.

This kind of change of scene works locally too. Enjoy letting off steam with your family or your drinking buddies; perhaps it will give you a fresh viewpoint on your technical problems, or at least more courage to face them. I have often "helped" friends debug their computer programs merely by asking for an explanation of how the program works. Midway through the explanation my friend will strike his head and say, "Oh, that's the bug." I did nothing but provide the encouragement for one more look at how the program was supposed to work.

Pride offers personal encouragement. We all have pride in a "job well done." I often feel like the child learning to tie his own shoes determined to do it himself. I think, "I'll show them that I can do it," so strongly that I must work hard at my task to satisfy my own pride. Take pride in your work.

When the going gets tough, discipline is another good mechanism for going on. My algorithm for washing dishes continues with the sequence "...WHILE dishes remain, DO wash next dish; ..." Notice again the two aids offered by this procedure. First, it makes the task routine; I have a known procedure to apply. Second, it limits the task to considering only the next dish, thus reducing my perception of the risk.

Effective novelists write for several hours every day, successful musicians practice several hours every day, and successful athletes train several hours every day. Should not a successful researcher discipline himself to research for several hours every day? The novelist writes a chapter a day, the musician does her scales and her selections each day, and the athlete does his setting up exercises and his main event. Each uses routine subtasks. I believe that which particular routine subtasks you choose are far less important than that you discipline yourself to do them regularly. My technology heroes have the courage to devote a period each day to the important tasks, leaving the merely urgent ones to fester if necessary.

You can set your own personal deadlines and provide yourself rewards for meeting them. This mechanism works less well for me, but I do sometimes use it, often in the most childish way. If I work hard today, I'll permit myself a drink before dinner or dessert afterwards. In fact, I find that when I am really engaged in interesting work I forget to eat, but when my work is overly stressful I gain weight.

Do not overlook family and friends as an explicit source of encouragement. Affection from family and friends can provide confidence to face the world outside. A great man once said to me, "Get your priorities right: family, friends, business, in that order." Another great man told me, "If things aren't right at home, nothing is right." I find that I am best able to do creative work when I feel cared for and happy; it is as if I can devote my finite store of courage either to solving technical problems or personal ones but not both at once.

### 18.3.3  Courage to Talk or Write

Perhaps the hardest part of research is talking about it, writing about it, and publishing it. Here we really get down to the big risks. When all is said and done, will my reputation outlast my publishing this very chapter? Suppose someone thinks that my ideas about courage are bad. Suppose I am criticized for them. Suppose my writing is inadequate or unacceptable. In truth it's often easier to start a project or get on with it than it is to present the results. Robert Heinlein, author of *Stranger In a Strange Land*, said in an editorial on professional authorship that you have to send stories, articles, and novels to editor after editor and risk rejection slips or you'll never get published. I know several unpublished authors of incomplete novels. There is less risk in "writing the great American novel" than in sending it to a publisher and waiting for it to be rejected.

What It Feels Like to Me.   My own failures of courage to talk or write do not, to me, seem like failures of courage at all. Rather, it seems to me that my ideas are unworthy, that no one would be interested, or that they are not yet well enough expressed. Recall the maze solving work I did in 1960 as a warm-up project. I was so sure no one would care about it that I never "bothered" to publish it until 1969 [5]. It turned out that my 1960 work drew questions even many years after publication, so someone must have cared.

This very chapter is another example for me. I first began to think about these ideas in the mid-1970s, but it took me until 1982 to first express them publicly. I wouldn't have done that except that my good friend, Marc Raibert, invited me to give "an informal talk" to some new graduate students. That being a low risk event, I agreed. Next thing I knew the informal talk had turned into a "distinguished lecture" complete with television camera and an auditorium full of people, but I was committed, and I talked. Six years later I finally worked up the courage to get the video tape transcribed. I was, and still am, literally too afraid to look at it myself. Now, two more years later, I am writing the ideas down more formally.

My pride demands that this written form of my ideas be perfect. I sought long and hard for an Anglo-Saxon word combining the ideas of disclose, publish, report, and talk about. I have finally chosen the compound "talk or write" to mean all of them, focusing most on public oral presentation, for it seems to take the most courage. I fear criticism of my choice, and in addition I fear that you will think my ideas irrelevant, stupid, or even wrong. I fear coming to an end of this work; at some point I shall have to release this chapter to the publisher and I will have lost a good friend.

But in both of these failures of my courage, during my procrastinating period I did not feel afraid. Rather, I believed simply that no one would be interested; my ideas seemed unimportant, irrelevant, and immaterial. No one would care, I thought. I'm still reasonably sure no one will care about my ideas on courage, but my deadline approaches.

Who among my audience has unpublished work that "no one will care about?" Who among my audience has a paper partly written but not yet quite right? Who the hell are you to judge? The rule for research is that you get credit only for ideas you have disclosed, not for ideas kept secret. It is absolutely true that the paper never submitted is never rejected, but of course, it is never published, either. I believe that it is better to be the published author of a slightly flawed document than the unpublished author of a perfect one.

Because I spell in original ways and my handwriting is illegible, writing has always been a great embarrassment to me. When I got a typewriter half of the problem went away; long ago I learned to type faster than I can write by hand. With a computer spelling checker that will make suggestions I am even better off, but not yet free of risk. I remember well when Claude Shannon, my thesis supervisor, chastised me for spelling the top to bottom measurement of an electrical wave form "peek to peek" rather than "peak to peak." I had put, as my Victorian aunt used to say, "a blot in my copybook." Even today I'm not sure which spelling is which and had to look them up in a dictionary because my spelling checker cannot distinguish cognates. I also once spelled naval incorrectly in a letter to my brother who was then in the Naval Reserve. Unfortunately, I put that blot on the outside of the envelope.

**Overcoming Risks.**   It may be that everyone is embarrassed by his own writing, especially at the start. The courage to get a paper done is made up of a sub-courage to start, and a subcourage to go on, and a subcourage to stop perfecting it. The hardest part of writing seems to be getting the first rough draft. Of course it won't be perfect. Of course it won't be complete. But at least a first draft, even a rough one, gives you something to work with and can encourage you to go on. Apply everything you have learned here to the task of getting that first draft.

I have learned three tricks that make talking and writing easier. First, J. C. R. Licklider taught me to treat an unfamiliar topic by making lists of things to say. I call this kind of presentation the "enumeration special." For example, in this chapter I describe four kinds of courage: *to start, to go on, to talk or write*, and *to stop*. The enumeration special is effective if trite. Second, my late mother offered advice on the choice of words in English, pointing out that Anglo-Saxon words have more punch than Roman ones. Just try to think of a Roman swear word. Unfortunately, technologists seem to think that polysyllabic pseudonyms are better than short words. Pick Anglo-Saxon names for things and they will last. Third, because English was spoken long before it was written, good English writing is always easy to read out loud. I am always suspicious of single words or phrases placed in parentheses because they have no spoken equivalent. Examine each use of the symbols "(" and ")" in your papers. Do they destroy your ability to read the writing out loud? Could you rephrase what you have to say in plain English, for example by using a phrase instead of a single word in parentheses? I suspect that parentheses creep into English writing when authors are either too lazy or too muddled to write down exactly what they mean.

There are a variety of media available to expose ideas in writing. Every technical organization has an internal report series, and for greater exposure technical papers appear in conference proceedings and journal articles, or in books. However, I have found greatest value from the least formal type of publication possible, informal memos. My group at Harvard in 1966 named its series of internal memos the "display file," a pun not only on the name of the part of computer memory that stores the output picture but also on the open file cabinet in which we kept these memos for easy access by any member of our group. My associates and I have used display file memos ever since to record new ideas, new mathematical formulations, new circuits, and anything else that strikes our fancy, including local procedures for ordering lunch. Our series of display file memos has become my archive of familiar things from the past, an archive to which I turn from time to time for reminders. Some of them have later become patents, some full fledged papers, and some portions of books. Initially, however, each was just my record of some little idea not always well expressed.

Learning from Others.   Although it obviously takes courage to expose your ideas to criticism, it takes even more courage to learn from the criticism. The not-invented-here (NIH) syndrome is rampant in technology. People cling to their own ideas. Naturally, you and I don't do that, it's just that our ideas, like our favorite text editor, are better than others.

A good way to learn clearly from what others say to you is to play back their words immediately to them. I used this mechanism with the industrial sponsors of the Silicon Structures Project at Caltech. Twice a year we presented our results at a 2-day sponsor's meeting. We used the last half day as a feedback session where each sponsor's representative made comments about our work. I took careful notes. After each sponsor had spoken, I played back what I thought he had said. The sponsors liked the immediate feedback because they knew that I had heard their comments and because they got a chance to correct my notes. I learned this trick in a class on domestic relations, but it goes well in nearly any context.

### 18.3.4  Courage to Stop

The risk of stopping work on a project is also large. First, there's the loss of the goal you will never reach. Second, there's a loss of face in giving up a task in which you have believed. Third, there's the waste of the time you have already invested in the project and the knowledge about it you have gained. Fourth, there is the criticism you may face for having wasted the investment. Finally, there is the risk of having to find something new to do.

What It Feels Like to Me.   Failures to stop don't feel like failures of courage to me. Rather they feel like I'm still "doing my thing." I'm involved with the people and they have become meaningful to me. I know the vocabulary. Success, it seems, is always just a month or two away. I know that with just a little more effort we can make something really good. The incremental reward always seems to outweigh the incremental effort.

Overcoming Risks.   Ted Meyer and I once noticed that every architecture for a computer display system can be improved for just a little more money [6]. This kind of observation offers a reason to stop a research program because it has proven to be recursive. Another example of a good reason to stop is that you are proven wrong. Martin Newell and I once spent days trying to prove a geometry theorem until we discovered a counter example. No wonder it was so hard to prove.

I stopped doing graphics research just after Bob Sproull, Bob Schumacker, and I wrote "A Characterization of Ten Hidden Surface Algorithms" [3]. We discovered that the task of computing which surfaces of a solid object are hidden and which are visible is a sorting problem. Moreover, we were able to build a taxonomy for hidden surface algorithms on the basis of the types of sorting used and the order of variables sorted. Realizing that new hidden surface algorithms would merely be elaborations on sorting killed my interest in the problem. Since then, of course, younger and more courageous people have made ever more beautiful pictures at a pace I cannot hope to match. Maybe the truth is that I stopped for lack of courage to compete; I don't think so, but I'll never know.

## 18.4   Rewards

### 18.4.1   The Emotional Side of Research

One of the greatest thrills for me is when a new idea emerges. In 1986 at Imperial College in London, I was working with complementary metal oxide semiconductor (CMOS) integrated circuits. I was attempting to design circuits that would operate very fast, but I had inadequate computer support for simulating them. Because I couldn't simulate the circuits I had to think about the problem instead. Fortunately for me, the circuits I was working on used a lot of Muller C elements and XOR gates, both of which are symmetric with respect to ones and zeros at input and output. Because of this symmetry I began to notice that my logic gates behaved as amplifiers, and that the more complex a logic gate was, the less good it was at amplification. The simplest inverter makes the best amplifier. It seemed as though each gate had only so much ability to exert "effort" and could put that effort either into amplification or into doing logic but not both.

Once I understood the idea, I gave it the obvious name: "logical effort." Using the idea of logical effort, and without going to the trouble of optimizing them, I can predict quite accurately the least possible delay for most CMOS logic circuits, literally on the back of an envelope. If the optimum circuit is required, I can easily compute the transistor sizes required for least delay. More important, I can decide how to change the topology of the circuit to reduce overall delay.

I want to describe what it felt like to make this discovery. I had worked on the problem for some months, designing many circuits. About a week before I finally understood and was able to name logical effort, I began to sense a distinct and strong feeling that there was an important idea to be found. I can only describe the feeling as *smelling* the idea inside the complexity. Much as a dog is sure a bone is buried beneath the earth, I was sure there was something simple and beautiful beneath the complexity of my task; I had but to dig it out.

But the idea wasn't captured until I wrote a very crude paper about the idea for my friend and colleague, Bob Sproull. Bob, I was sure, would be able both to understand the still slightly vague idea, and to help enunciate it. Moreover, I was sure that he would not dump criticism on me. From then on it was all much easier. The very name, logical effort, captured the essential feature of the idea. Bob and I formulated the idea, that is, expressed it as a formula, as the ratio of the electrical capacitance at the input of the logic gate to the current at its output normalized to the corresponding ability of an inverter. This ratio turns out also to express how much slower than an inverter each type of gate will be if driving a gate identical to itself. More complex logic gates turn out to have higher logical effort; the theory quantifies how much higher. My second paper on the subject was more understandable, and with subsequent exposure to a number of students, Bob and I have made the idea of logical effort very easy to teach. We are now trying to work up the courage to finish our book on the subject. Naturally it feels as though we do not have the time.

Those of us who come after and have the advantage of previous discovery often forget just how hard those discoveries were. When Steinmetz first used imaginary numbers to describe alternating current, only a very few people understood the required math. Now every undergraduate electrical engineer becomes familiar with the square root of minus one, although they spell it, j, rather than, i, as mathematicians do. Many of my young friends at Apple Computer know the Gouraud shading [10] and Phong shading [11] algorithms. When I asked them who Gouraud and Phong were, none knew that both were graduate students at the time of their discoveries nor even thought of them as real people. Certainly they don't remember, as I do, how hard we thought it would be to make beautiful pictures by computer before Gouraud and Phong. It's always much easier in hindsight. Indeed, I think of scientific progress as the reduction of subjects from complete mystery to teachable form.

The best personal sources of courage are self-confidence and comfort with yourself and your peers. In some people these develop early. In others they never appear. If you can find things that bolster your own self-confidence, you can use them to good effect. I find that I have only so much room for taking risks. When I can reduce the risk in some places in my life, I can more easily face risk in other areas. I provide myself the courage to do some things by reducing my need for courage in other areas. In effect I husband my courage.

## 18.4.2  Technology as Play

The basic personal start-up mechanism for research has to be curiosity. I find myself curious about how something works, or I observe something strange and begin to explore it. Since I am fond of symmetry I observe some simple symmetry and am almost inexorably drawn into exploring it. For example, one day Don Oestreicher, who was then a graduate student, and I noticed that the number of random wires expected to cross the midsection of an N terminal printed circuit board is N/4 independent of whether the wires connect two or three terminals on the board. This comes about because although the probability of crossing is higher for wires connecting three terminals, 3/4 rather than 1/2, the number of wires is correspondingly reduced from N/2 to N/3. This simple observation led us to explore other wiring patterns, gather some data from real printed circuit boards, and eventually to publish a paper [4] called "How Big Should a Printed Circuit Board Be?" Follow your curiosity.

Beauty provides another form of personal encouragement for me. Some of the products of research are just pretty, although mathematicians prefer to use the word "elegant." The simplicity of $E = mc^2$, the elegance of information theory, and the power of an undecidability proof are examples. I got interested in asynchronous circuits by discovering a very simple form of first-in, first-out (FIFO) storage that has rather complete symmetry [1,8]. It simply amazes me that my simple and symmetric circuit can "know" which way to pass data forward. The beauty itself piques my curiosity and flatters my pride.

Simplicity is to be valued in research results. Many students ask, "How long should my thesis be?" It would be better for them to ask, "How short can it be?" The best work is always simply expressed. If you find something simple to explore, do not turn it aside as trivial, especially if it appears to be new. In a very real sense, research is a form of play in which ideas are our toys and our objective is the creation of new castles from the old building block set. The courage to do research comes in part from our attraction to the simplicity and beauty of our creations.

I, for one, am and will always remain a practicing technologist. When denied my minimum daily adult dose of technology, I get grouchy. I believe that technology is fun, especially when computers are involved, a sort of grand game or puzzle with ever so neat parts to fit together. I have turned down several lucrative administrative jobs because they would deny me that fun. If the technology you do isn't fun for you, you may wish to seek other employment. Without the fun, none of us would go on.

I tried to capture the spirit of research as a game in my paper about our walking robot [2]. Unfortunately, the editors removed from my paper all of the personal comments, the little poem about the robot by Claude Shannon, the pranks and jokes, and in short the fun. The only fun they left was the title: "Footprints in the Asphalt." All too often technical reports are dull third person descriptions of something far away and impersonal. Technology is not far away and impersonal. It's here, it's intensely personal, and it's great fun.

## 18.5   Acknowledgments

This is where I get to recognize my friends, my sponsors, and my sources of encouragement. Thanks to Sara Kiesler whose critical reading was key in making this chapter presentable. Thanks to my partners in business, Dave Evans and Bob Sproull, for a lifetime of intellectual stimulation and friendship. Special thanks to my brother, Bert Sutherland, who has both taught and encouraged me since we were boys. I thank also my children, Juliet and Dean, and the few other close friends without whose encouragement I would not have been willing to talk or write about these ideas. The work reported here was supported by Sutherland, Sproull, and Associates, Inc., independent consultants in computer hardware and software, and by Advanced Technology Ventures, private investors in high-technology start-up companies.

## References

[1] I. E. Sutherland. Micropipelines. *Communications of the ACM*, June 1989.

[2] I. E. Sutherland and M. K. Ullner. Footprints in the Asphalt. *The International Journal of Robotics Research*, 3(2), 1984.

[3] I. E. Sutherland, R. F. Sproull and R. A. Schumacker. Characterization of Ten Hidden-Surface Algorithms. *Computing Surveys: Journal of the ACM*, March 1974. Summarized in *Research Reviews*, pp. 21–23, June, 1975.

[4] I. E. Sutherland and D. Oestreicher. How Big Should a Printed Circuit Board Be? *IEEE Transactions of Computers*, C-22(5), pp. 537–542, 1983.

[5] I. E. Sutherland. A Method of Solving Arbitrary Wall Mazes by Computers. *IEEE Transactions on Computers*, C-18(12), pp. 1092–1097, 1969.

[6] T. H. Meyer and I. E. Sutherland. On the Design of Display Processors. *Communications of the ACM*, 11(6), pp. 410–414, 1968.

[7] I. E. Sutherland. Sketchpad—A Man-Machine Graphical Communication System. *Proceedings of the Spring Joint Computer Conference*, Detroit, Michigan, 1963, and MIT Lincoln Laboratory Technical Report No. 296, 1963.

[8] I. E. Sutherland. Asynchronous First-In-First-Out Register Structure. United States Patent 4,837,740, June 6, 1989.

[9] I. E. Sutherland. Reaction Control Valve. United States Patent 4,622,992, November 18, 1986.

[10] H. Gouraud. Computer Display of Curved Surfaces. University of Utah, UTEC-CSc-71-113, June 1971, and in *IEEE Transactions* C-20, 623, June 1971.

[11] B. T. Phong. Illumination for Computer-generated Image. University of Utah, UTEC-CSc-73-129, July 1973, and in *CACM*, 18(6) pp. 311–317, 1975.

[12] R. May. *The Courage to Create*. Bantam Books, New York, 1975.

# 19

---

# Problem Representation

Herbert A. Simon

---

## 19.1 Introduction

From its origins in the 1950s, programming in most domains of artificial intelligence (AI) has employed list processing languages that incorporate description lists (a.k.a. property lists), and consequently represent information in schemas (a.k.a. scripts, frames, objects). The principal exceptions to this practice are programs for visual and auditory pattern recognition, which present special problems of representation, and "neural network" or "connectionist" representations, none of which will be discussed in this chapter.

In the middle 1960s, list processing was combined with production system formalisms in such languages as OPS5. Still more recently, languages like PROLOG were invented that represent declarative information as sentences in the predicate calculus and employ resolution as a principal means for generating new sentences from old. Currently, so-called object-oriented programming elaborates these representations by linking subsets of productions closely with subsets of schemas.

It is the purpose of this chapter to discuss issues of representation of information and processes within the domain just outlined. In writing AI programs, why does it matter how they are represented? And under what circumstances do particular representations have advantages over others?

## 19.2    What is a Representation?

A representation is defined by the form in which information is stored in memory and by the elementary operations that are available for modifying the information. Both the structure of the information and the processes for operating on it are essential parts of the specification of a representation. Neither suffices to define it without the other.

For example, in one of the early list processing languages, IPL-V, each symbol was stored in a computer word, together with the address of the *next* symbol on the list.[1] One elementary operation in the language stored new symbols in words not currently in use (unused words were held in a list called the "available space list.") Another elementary operation, given the address of a symbol as input, found the address of the next symbol on the list. And so on [12].

The IPL-V representation consists of information stored in lists (and description lists), together with elementary processes for performing such operations as creating a new symbol, finding the next symbol on a list, finding the value of an attribute on the description list of a symbol, assigning a value to an attribute of a symbol, etcetera. Of course this representation can be implemented in many ways other than the one sketched in the previous paragraph. (For example, a symbol and its address might occupy two successive computer addresses instead of two halves of a single address.) The language, like all higher level languages, is defined at the symbolic level and not at the level of machine implementation.

## 19.3    Equivalence of Representations and Programs

The Turing Machine has taught us many things, among them that almost any real computer has the power of a Universal Turing Machine (or is readily extendable to one). Since all such Turing Machines are equivalent, i.e., can compute partial recursive functions and only such functions, it might seem that representation is unimportant. Clearly it is not, but to see why, we must elaborate on the notion of *equivalence* of representations and machines. We will see that there are many different notions of equivalence.

*T-Equivalence.* Starting with the original notion, two machines may be regarded as equivalent if they compute the same class of functions [7]. We

---

[1] IPL-5 is nearly, but not quite, a dead language. A gloriously living version of it, implemented by Howard Richman, lives on in a personal computer.

will call this T-equivalence. The equivalent machines need not be Universal Turing Machines. For example, we might have two T-equivalent machines each of which is capable of evaluating only the function $+(x,y)$ for natural numbers, $x$ and $y$.

*K-Equivalence*. Closely akin to T-equivalence is Knowledge equivalence (K-equivalence). Two machines are K-equivalent if any knowledge obtainable from the one is obtainable from the other, and vice versa. I will not undertake a formal definition of "knowledge," but simply illustrate how it extends beyond evaluations of computable functions.

Consider a program that undertakes to solve the word problem for semigroups by heuristic search. It is well known that, in general, the word problem for semigroups is undecidable. This does not prevent an appropriate program from sometimes demonstrating the equivalence of two words from the dictionary of a word problem. The undecidability simply means that the program may sometimes fail to find a path demonstrating equivalence and also fail to halt with a demonstration that there is no such path.

The term "computability" in the Church-Turing thesis means decidability for *all* values of the independent variables in the domain of the function [7]. Within this domain, the program must either find the value or halt with a determination that it is undefined. The thesis says nothing about what a Turing Machine will do when confronted with values of the independent variables that lie outside the domain of the function it computes.

Conversely, given a function (computable or not) it may be quite easy to write a program for a Universal Turing Machine that computes the function in some subpart of its domain without any guarantee that it will compute it or even halt in other parts of the domain, and without our necessarily knowing the exact boundaries of this restricted subpart. The restricted function is computable, the original unrestricted function is not. Let F be the noncomputable function, $F_*$ a computable subfunction, and P a program that computes $F_*$. We will call P an algorithm for $F_*$ and a heuristic program for F.

We see that a Turing Machine may be a heuristic program for a function that is not computable. The usual supposition that, by virtue of the Church-Turing hypothesis, Turing Machines can be used only to find values of computable functions is wrong. Providing we do not require the guarantee that the procedure will always succeed, we may use Turing Machines as problem solvers in noncomputable domains.

Most programs in "real life" are heuristics, not algorithms, for the functions that we evaluate with them. Some people regard this as deplorable, but it would be even more deplorable if we limited ourselves to computing only those functions that are (universally) computable, and denied ourselves heuristic programs that often succeed with only acceptable numbers of operations (but are not guaranteed to be successful throughout the domain of interest).

Even when dealing with computable functions, we may find it advantageous to use heuristics rather than algorithms for evaluating them, as will appear evident in a moment. To ensure that our heuristic programs will always terminate, with or without a value, we may incorporate in them an upper limit on the number of operations they will perform before halting. We may wish to add such a stop rule even to our algorithms, since computability "in principle" says nothing about whether we can expect a computation to be completed in a human lifetime, or a reasonable fraction thereof.

*C-Equivalence.* Two machines are Computationally Equivalent (C-equivalent) if the functions that the one evaluates easily are easily evaluated by the other [16]. "Easily" is, of course, a vague term. One may regard a function as easily evaluated if the evaluation requires only a moderate number of executions of the elementary operations. A similar (and equally vague) concept may be applied to programs.

There is some (negative) connection between the idea of easy evaluation and the idea of computational complexity, but not a close one. First, most theories of computational complexity are concerned with worst-case analysis. But in the worst case, a heuristic program does not find an answer at all. Second, computational complexity is usually concerned with the rate at which the required amount of calculation increases with increase in some parameter that measures problem size. But a program for solving a problem that is NP-complete or exponential may solve some (or many) problems in the domain in quite reasonable times.

If we measure easiness of domains by the fractions of their problems that can be solved in an hour, say, on a specified computer, we may find many problems in NP-complete or exponential domains that are "easier," for moderate values of the parameter, than problems in polynomial domains. The theorems of complexity too often provide precise answers to uninteresting questions: questions of what can be computed "in principle" rather than questions of what can be computed in fact (i.e., using real computers for acceptable periods of time).

In practice, the easiness of problems is measured empirically, by using various programs to try to solve them. In a number of fields, a battery of standard test problems has emerged against which new algorithms and heuristics are evaluated. In the absence of mathematical theorems about the relative power of different programs, performance on test problems provides empirical guidance to the improvement of programs.

This research may, in turn, lead not only to concrete empirical findings but also to empirical generalizations. For example, we might compare breadth-first, depth-first, and best-first programs and find that, when reasonable evaluation functions are available, the latter are usually more efficient in avoiding the compulsive completeness of the first and the endless searches down wrong alleys of the second. We might also find the computational efficiency lower for programs that seek optima than for programs that satisfice (halt when they find satisfactory solutions).

Neither the exact scope of such findings nor their validity within that scope can be established with certainty by empirical procedures, but that does not distinguish programming design from other areas of engineering design, nor programs from race horses. The history of computer chess provides a good example of research on program efficiency in which programs are evaluated empirically, and with considerable precision, by their success in play against other programs or human players.

C-equivalence is what it's all about. In both cognitive science and artificial intelligence we are interested in what can be computed easily, using the computing resources that people and computers have available and can afford to devote to a particular task. We are interested in the relative advantage, measured by computational efficiency in some average sense, of using one representation rather than another, or of using a particular strategy that requires a certain representation for its implementation. The remainder of this chapter is concerned with problem representation from the standpoint of C-equivalence and computational efficiency (C-efficiency). From what has been said already, the analysis must rest mainly on empirical evidence rather than mathematical theorems.

## 19.4  Some Species of Representations

A comprehensive taxonomy of representations does not exist. In lieu of such a taxonomy, I will limit my discussion to some species that have already had wide use in AI.

The species I will consider fall into two main genera: propositional representations and diagrammatic or pictorial representations. Propositional representations may use natural language or formal languages, including among the latter, formal logics and formal mathematics. Pictorial and diagrammatic representations may convey information in an array (raster) of pixels, similar to a television screen. Alternatively they may use schemas, i.e., node-link structures (list structures and description lists).

### 19.4.1  Propositional Representations

Communication between human beings takes place almost entirely in natural language, spoken and written. The memory of a society, apart from what is stored in brains, is recorded in books and documents, most of which are written in natural language. It is less clear what role natural language plays in representing information inside the human head. Most likely it plays a very small role: natural language inputs are recoded into another representation in the process of listening or reading and before they are stored in memory [6].

Of course, a person may memorize a poem or other linguistic string, and reproduce the exact linear sequence upon demand. In preliterate cultures rote memory of this kind is an important component of social memory. But most of the information stored in our heads is not stored as sentences that can be recalled literally. If there were any doubts on that point, those doubts were settled some years ago by the studies of Bransford and Franks [1], who showed that people ordinarily store the *meanings* of what they hear or read, and are unable to report reliably which of several syntactically distinct but synonymous statements supplied the information that they stored.

Although natural language is communicated in one-dimensional strings, the presence of punctuation (as well as syntactical analysis) shows that its underlying structure is more nearly treelike. Most theories of natural language processing assume that the first step in extracting information from natural language strings is to parse them, i.e., to convert them to tree structures corresponding to sentences, clauses within sentences, and phrases within clauses. One possibility is that it is these tree structures that are stored.

The reality is almost certainly more complex. Consider the following paragraph.

"John is a computer science student at Carnegie Mellon University. He earned his bachelor's degree at Rutgers. He is 5-11 in height, weighs 160 pounds, and is married, but has no children. He hopes to write his dissertation in the field of artificial intelligence. As an undergraduate, he took a fascinating course on that subject with Saul Amarel ... "

This information could be stored as a tree, consisting of four main branches, one for each sentence. Each of these branches, in turn, could be a subtree consisting of the parsing of the sentence. An alternative might be a node-link structure of the kind usual called a schema. It would describe a person whose NAME is John, whose CURRENT UNIVERSITY is CMU, whose UNDERGRADUATE UNIVERSITY is Rutgers, etc. Probably, we would want the structure to be a little more sophisticated, with principal subtrees having such labels as PERSONAL CHARACTERISTICS, EDUCATION, and the specific information arranged in structures under these.

Notice that the schema representation, although quite different from the one-dimensional structure of natural language, is still propositional. In their simplest form, schemas recode natural language statements as assertions that particular attributes of specific objects have particular values: the HEIGHT of JOHN is 5-11, or HEIGHT(JOHN, 5-11). With this translation we have transformed the natural language into the formulas of a formal logic, built from predicates, relations, and arguments. To achieve a full-fledged logic, a few additions are needed, notably, some way of expressing quantifiers.

At the next level of implementation systems of schemas are very naturally represented by list structures, which, in turn, can readily be represented in higher-level languages for ordinary digital computers. In today's AI technology, this is by far the predominant way in which natural language information is recoded, stored and processed.

A widely accepted general hypothesis about the processing of natural language inputs is that they are first parsed (recoded by the rules of syntax into tree structures), and that the information is then stored in schemas. The parsings and the schemas are represented as list structures (including description lists). In our discussion, we will take this as the canonical class of representations for information extracted from natural language.

## 19.4.2 Recognition Processes

Equally important with the use of natural language to provide new information that can be stored in memory schemas is its use to evoke schemas that are already stored, and thereby to make available the information they contain. This evocation depends on *recognition* of symbols or strings in the incoming language stream [3]. When someone shouts "Fire!," information is communicated. At the same time, recognition of the word, "fire," gives access to the information about fire that is already stored in memory, including information about what to do when a fire breaks out (means of escape, sources of water, location of fire extinguishers, how to call the fire department, etc.).

In fact, even when the primary intent of the incoming stream is informational, understanding the stream, i.e., being able to store and use it appropriately, depends wholly on the presence in memory of schemas that, by recognition and evocation, can serve to extract meaning from the incoming symbols. Language understanding is a continual interaction between new incoming information and the information already available in the store.

The bottleneck of human short-term memory is central to the architecture of this scheme. Only a tiny fraction of the information stored in long-term memory can be present in attention and available to active processes at any one time. (Human beings are notoriously inept at driving a car while carrying on a profound conversation.)

Attention to information, and thereby the course of thought, are controlled by successive acts of recognition of external stimuli or of cues in symbols previously evoked. Context (i.e., the sum of information evoked at any given time and therefore available for processing) is limited and changes constantly. And this limited and changing context determines how new information will be interpreted. In a sports context, "ball" will designate a round object; in an entertainment context, it will mean a formal dance.

### 19.4.3 Diagrammatic Representations

The initial recoding of visual information may well be rasterlike. Certain areas of the visual cortex hold images that are mapped topologically from the retina [8]. How metric information (e.g., information about symmetries) is recorded in this representation is not clear.

Certain information can be extracted easily from raster-like stores that would be hard to compute from other representations. For example, if we draw two nonparallel straight lines on a sheet of paper, it is immediately "obvious" whether they intersect or not. Constructing a formal proof of their intersection or nonintersection on the paper would be a formidable task, at which most of us would not succeed.

Of course, if we used analytic geometry to translate the lines into equations, and solved the equations simultaneously, we could also answer the question of intersection. However they do it, people can with great facility extract, from external diagrams or from images of them (the mind's eye), information about intersections, symmetry, approximate parallelism, etc. For these kinds of tasks, the raster representation has great computational efficiency.

Very often, however, the principal information we wish to convey with diagrams is what objects are connected to what other objects, and in what way. For such information, the same list processing languages that we discussed for representing natural language can often be employed to good effect [9]. In this case, however, we use the list structures to represent diagrammatic connections instead of propositions. Consider the following example.

"A weight of 1 kg hangs from a string that runs over a pulley wheel. The other end of the string is attached to a second weight. The pulley is supported by another string that runs over a second pulley, under a third pulley, and the end of which is attached to the ceiling. The second pulley is also suspended from a string that is attached to the ceiling. The third pulley is attached by a string to the second weight, helping to support it. The entire system is in stable equilibrium, and all strings are vertical. How many kilograms is the second weight?"

This statement in natural language is very easily formalized: $W(W1,1)$, $HL(S1,W1)$, $RO(P1,S1)$, $HL(S2,P1)$, $RO(P2,S2)$, $H(P2,S3)$, $RU(P3,S2)$, $A(C,S3)$, $A(C,S2)$, $H(P3,S4)$, $HR(S1,W2)$, $H(S4,W2)$, $W(W2,?)$; where $W$ means "weight," $HL$ means "hangs on the left end of," $RO$ means "runs over," etc. This formal representation would be a very natural one for a logic language like PROLOG. The salient characteristic of this notation is that objects are given names that serve as the names of arguments in the relations in which these objects participate.

In an example like this one, it is not very difficult to recode the formal representation into an algebraic one, where each formal relation now becomes an equation (or a component of an equation) whose arguments are the forces exerted on or by the corresponding objects. Thus, the first relation listed above, W(W1,1), becomes the equation, W1 = 1, where W1 now stands for the weight of the object W1. Similarly, the second relation becomes, S1 = W1, where S1 is now the force exerted by the first string. RO(P1,S1), combined with HL(S2,P1), becomes S2 = 2S1, the force on the string holding up P1 being twice the force on each side of the pulley. The combination of HR(S1,W2) with H(S4,W2) gives W2 = S1+S4, the weight of W2 in equilibrium being the sum of the forces exerted on it by S1 and S4.

Notice, however, that the recoding depends on knowledge of the laws of physics; not all of the information required for it was contained in the symbolic formalization. We have to know, e.g., that the force on a pulley (hence, the force needed to suspend it) is the sum of the forces on its left and right sides (which are equal if the rope running over it is in equilibrium). If we wished to carry out the translation automatically, we would need to build some productions to do it that would embody these physical laws. Moreover, to apply these laws correctly, the formalization must be searched to find multiple appearances of each argument [9].

By a slight, but significant, change in representation we can transform the propositional formulation of the pulley problem into a diagrammatic formulation. Instead of assigning a symbolic name to each weight, string, and pulley, we assign to it the location of a node in memory. All relations in which that object participates become elements of the description list of its node, the values of the attributes being the names of the other nodes that are the arguments of the relations corresponding to those attributes.

Thus a node, say 001, would be assigned to W1, and another, 002, to S1. 002 would then be the value of the attribute H on the description of 001. The value of attribute W of 001 would be 1, etc. Essentially, all we have done is to identify objects with memory nodes instead of with symbols. Each object is represented once in memory, instead of being mentioned by name in a number of memory locations. But a consequence of representing it in this way is that we can now find all of the relations in which a given object is involved by examining the description list of its node, without any additional search.

In list processing languages there are elementary operations for finding the value of an attribute of an object. Three productions representing the relevant laws of physics can now use this representation to solve the pulley problem without search. The first production assigns as the weight of an object the sum of the forces holding it up. The second assigns, as the force on a string, the force exerted on it at one of its ends, the third assigns, as the force on a pulley, twice the force on the string on its left or right side. Each production is executed whenever the forces mentioned in its conditions are known.

In the example, this production system would assign a force of 1 to S1 (because it holds up W1, whose weight is 1). Examining the relations associated with S1, it would assign a force of 2 to P1, which would lead to a force of 2 for

S2, and then of 4 for P2 and S3. From S2=2, it would be found that P3=S4=4, and then that S1+S4=W2=5. The algebra is the same as in the propositional representation. What is different is that no search is required to find the equations in the diagrammatic representation.

### 19.4.4  Human and Computer Use of Diagramatic Representations

There is much evidence that people make extensive use of diagrammatic representations in solving problems in algebra, physics, and other domains [15]. In some cases (e.g., geometry) extracting the information from diagrams appears to call for a rasterlike representation, or some computational equivalent. In other cases (e.g., pulley problems, circuit problems, and many other kinds of physics problems), a list-structure representation of the kind we have just been considering would be most plausible. It is not unlikely that people have representations of both kinds available, and use one or the other when appropriate.

Whatever the exact nature of the representations, there is also strong evidence that many people do not ordinarily transform natural language descriptions of physics or algebra problems directly into equations in order to solve them. Instead, they translate first from natural language into a diagrammatic representation, and from the diagram into the mathematical formalism. This is an efficient thing to do because it takes advantage of the capabilities of diagrams to organize information into schemas.

If we examine Gordon Novak's ISAAC program, which solves physics problems stated in natural language, we see that it uses schemas (diagrams) already stored in memory to interpret terms in the language of the problem [14]. A lever schema allows interpretation of information about a lever in the problem, and allows an instantiated lever to be constructed from the general schema and combined with other objects mentioned in the problem to form an instantiated problem schema. The problem schema contains the information that is used to write the equations.

The same process has been observed in students solving algebra problems. They convert the problem language into a diagram that is instantiated with information from the problem statement and converted into equations, which are then solved [15].

Turning from physics and algebra to puzzles, we see similar phenomena. Subjects solving the Missionaries and Cannibals problem, or the Tower of Hanoi, identify the objects mentioned in the problem and the kinds of relations among the objects that are postulated. They identify also the operations that can be performed on the objects (legal moves). Then, they form an internal representation of the situation that can easily be programmed as a diagram of list structures [4]. Two nodes correspond to the two sides of the river, the values of attributes of those nodes represent the numbers of missionaries, cannibals, and boats on each side. A move consists in decreasing the numbers on one side and increasing them correspondingly on the other. In the psychological literature, diagrammatic representations of this kind are often called *mental models* [5].

In our work on problem solving, Newell and I [11] called these forms of representation problem spaces, and called the problem solving activity heuristic search in a problem space. Whatever we call them, these representations certainly fall in the genus of diagrammatic or pictorial representations. As we have already seen, they are *not* computationally equivalent to propositional representations, although they can often, perhaps usually, be recoded rather easily into propositional form. The ease of recoding should not blind us to the significance of the C-*in*equivalence.

To look at these issues of C-equivalence and inequivalence a little more generally, it is useful to consider the points of view (I will call them metaphors) that motivate the propositional and diagrammatic representations, respectively.

## 19.5 Contrast of the Logic and Search Metaphors

Two metaphors have dominated research in AI. The first of these compares problem solving with the proving of theorems. A problem solution is a proof, and since proofs lie in the domain of formal logic, artificial intelligence should borrow from logic for its representations and for its problem-solving algorithms.

Nilsson is employing the logic metaphor when he argues that the first-order predicate calculus should be the language of AI [13]. The PROLOG language employs this metaphor in encoding information in propositional form and processing it by resolution of Horn clauses [2]. John McCarthy employs this metaphor in seeking to carry out common sense reasoning by means of proofs in appropriate modal logics [10].

The second metaphor compares problem solving with search through a problem space for an object that meets the specifications of a goal. Al Newell and I have employed this metaphor from the beginnings of our research in AI Although the task of our first program, the Logic Theorist, was to discover proofs for theorems, we made a sharp distinction between *discovering* proofs and *verifying* them. Proof verification falls in the domain of formal logic; proof discovery involves search that might rely on heuristics as well as algorithms for guidance.

In the General Problem Solver and later work, the problem space was more often than not represented by diagrammatic schemas instead of propositions, thus embracing the "mental models" metaphor as well. Problem solving involves search that brings about a repeated change of state, i.e., a repeated modification of the mental model of the situation.

### 19.5.1   Problems in Using the Proof Metaphor

What does it matter whether we use the logic metaphor or the .heuristic search metaphor? PROLOG and LISP can both be regarded as T-equivalent and even K-equivalent. Anything that can be done with the one can be done with the other.

But of course this says nothing about the C-equivalence of these languages or of the problem representations that are natural for them. It may make an enormous difference in computational efficiency whether we follow the logic metaphor in constructing our AI programs, or the search metaphor. Different metaphors may lead us to select different programming languages and may lead us to use these languages in quite different ways.

The consequences of adopting a particular computational metaphor are clearly visible in the history of automatic theorem proving, which has been dominated by the logic metaphor and the norms of formal logic. Historically, formal logics developed as a means of guaranteeing rigor in reasoning by making it easy to check the validity of proofs. They express all information as propositions, and eschew diagrams as potential sources of error.[2] New propositions are obtained from axioms and previously proved theorems by applying a small and fixed number of inference rules, designed to make it easy to check whether a rule has been applied correctly. The inference rules are tautological: universally valid and not dependent on what is empirically true. As a consequence, they are also independent of the domain to which they are applied.

The bias in this metaphor toward limiting inference rules to a very small number of tautologies, axiomatizing all other assumptions in propositional form, was carried so far in the early years of computer theorem proving that even transitivity, associativity, and commutivity were axiomatized instead of being incorporated in inference rules. Whenever it was necessary to go from one expression to another that was equivalent to it under transitivity, the equivalence had to be proved from these axioms, and similarly for associativity and commutivity. As a consequence, the proofs proceeded by tiny steps, an enormous number of which were needed to trace out any significant proof path. The result was that nothing interesting could be proved with a tolerable amount of computing.

In subsequent years, programs for automatic discovery of proofs have generally retreated from this extreme position, and some investigators (e.g., W. W. Bledsoe) never succumbed to the spell of the logic metaphor in this strict form. Nevertheless, the norms that prevail in formal logic (especially the insistence on completeness of algorithms) strongly influenced theorem prov-

[2]We are all familiar with the fallacious geometric "proofs" we can construct from diagrams that contain subtle inconsistencies.

ing research, to the detriment of its C-efficiency. If it is still hard, after more than 30 years of research, to find examples of significant theorems discovered and proved by machine, the logic metaphor must bear a large share of the blame.

In reply, it may be argued that nothing about the task of theorem proving, or the metaphor for that matter, *required* a parsimonious attitude toward inference rules or a preference for axioms. The objection is quite valid. Metaphors do not require anything; they persuade. Under the influence of a particular metaphor, the task is viewed in a certain way. Certain procedures seem "natural," others "unnatural."

Thus when one programs in LISP it is "natural" to make generous use of recursion. But many algorithms based on recursion are extremely inefficient from a computational standpoint. In the same way, when operating within the logic metaphor with PROLOG, it is "natural" to try to preserve resolution as the only inference rule. But in practical applications, it soon enough becomes obvious that expressions must be operated on in other ways as well, and that procedural control must be exercised over the search.

All of these modifications can be introduced into an appropriately extended PROLOG; doing so simply runs counter to the metaphor, hence is a method of last resort. The metaphor, if it is the wrong metaphor for the task, makes us reluctant to search out and apply efficient representations and processes. The right metaphor works with us, not against us.

## 19.5.2 Characteristics of the Search Metaphor

Let me now turn to the search metaphor. The metaphor does not dictate that information should be represented in propositional form, but is quite open to both propositional and diagrammatic representations. If it biases the selection of a representation, it is toward a "mental model" of situations in the problem space. Then search can be carried out by applying move operators to a current situation to produce a new situation. Such move operators are not rules of logic; they are not tautological. Instead, they are task dependent, incorporating knowledge of what kinds of changes can and cannot be made. The move operator in a representation of the Missionaries and Cannibals problem, guided by the search metaphor, would likely change the number of missionaries, cannibals, and boats on each side of the river, conserving objects and respecting the limits on the capacity of the boat.

Similarly, in the description, above, of the diagrammatic representation of the pulley problem, the inference rules take the form of laws of Newtonian mechanics that compute the forces on members as a function of the known forces on the others connected with them. Each step toward the solution is a giant stride because it already incorporates knowledge about the laws of the situation. It is difficult to imagine what an immense computation would be required if these laws were axiomatized and could only act through the mediation of logical tautologies.

Again, there is nothing in the search metaphor that requires us to construct the kind of representation and processes for this problem that we did. The metaphor does not impose requirements; it persuades.

### 19.5.3  Conclusion: Which Metaphor?

Nothing that I have said shows that the search metaphor is to be preferred to the logic metaphor in all AI applications. If I were constructing a proof checker (instead of a proof finder), I would very likely use the latter rather than the former. However, experience in AI demonstrates that it is unwise to allow a metaphor to control one's strategy without carefully considering the nature of the problems to which it will be applied.

In each application, we should ask whether a propositional representation, a diagrammatic representation, or some other, will be most efficient from a computational standpoint. Then we should ask whether there is any reason to restrict our operators to a small number, or to limit them to tautologies. Unless there is such a reason, and a very compelling one, we will probably be well advised to admit numerous operators, and to incorporate a good deal of the domain knowledge in them, thereby greatly reducing the sizes of the spaces we have to search.

We should ask also whether it is essential that our method be an algorithm, guaranteed in each case (and with what expenditure of time?) to terminate with an answer. If it is not essential, we are likely to be much better off with a heuristic program that often, but not always, finds problem solutions with a modest amount of computation.

We are still far from having an adequate taxonomy of representations. We are even farther from a full understanding of the computational properties of representations, and how to determine them in particular domains of application. We have had more than enough experience, however, to convince us that we cannot afford to be guided by unanalysed slogans which persuade us to propositionalize everything (or proceduralize everything), or to segregate rules of logic from subject-matter knowledge, or to insist on optimizing, at great computational expense, when we only need to satisfice.

These are issues that cannot be settled by slogans. They can only be settled by painstaking analysis of their computational consequences. And in most cases, these consequences will have to be explored empirically, although guided (heuristically) by mathematical generalizations whose validity we can prove for simple cases.

# References

[1] J. D. Bransford, and J. J. Franks. The abstraction of linguistic ideas. *Cognitive Psychology*, 2:331-350, 1971.

[2] W. F. Clocksin and C. S. Mellish. *Programming in PROLOG*. Berlin: Springer Verlag, 1981.

[3] E. A. Feigenbaum and H. A. Simon. EPAM-like models of recognition and learning. *Cognitive Science*, 8:305-336, 1984.

[4] J. R. Hayes and H. A. Simon. Psychological differences among problem isomorphs. In N. J. Castellan, D. B. Pisoni, and G. R. Potts (eds), *Cognitive Theory*, 2:21-41, Hillsdale, NJ: Erlbaum, 1977.

[5] P. N. Johnson-Laird. *Mental models*. Cambridge, MA: Harvard University Press, 1983.

[6] M. A. Just and P. A. Carpenter. *The psychology of reading and language comprehension*. Newton, MA: Allyn & Bacon, 1987.

[7] S. C. Kleene. *Introduction to metamathematics*. Princeton, NJ: Van Nostrand, 1952.

[8] S. M. Kosslyn. *Image and mind*. Cambridge, MA: Harvard University Press, 1980.

[9] J. H. Larkin and H. A. Simon. Why a diagram is (sometimes) worth 10,000 words. *Cognitive Science*, 11:65-99, 1987.

[10] J. McCarthy. Circumscription: a form of nonmonotonic reasoning. *Artificial Intelligence*, 13:27-39, 1980.

[11] A. Newell and H. A. Simon. *Human problem solving*. Englewood Cliffs, NJ: Prentice-Hall, 1972.

[12] A. Newell and F. M. Tonge. An introduction to information processing language IPL-V. In *Communications of the Association for Computing Machinery*, 3:205-211, 1960.

[13] N. J. Nilsson. *Principles of artificial intelligence*, Palo Alto, CA: Tioga Press, 1980.

[14] G. S. Novak. Representation of knowledge in a program for solving physics problems. In *Proceedings of the Fifth International Joint Conference on Artificial Intelligence*, 1003-1007, 1977.

[15] J. M. Paige and H. A. Simon. Cognitive processes in solving algebra word problems. In B. Kleinmuntz (ed.), *Problem Solving*, NY: Wiley, 1966.

[16] H. A. Simon. On the forms of mental imagery. In C. Wade Savage (ed.), *Perception and Cognition: Issues in the Foundation of Psychology*, Minneapolis, MN: University of Minnesota Press, pp. 3-18, 1978.

# 20

---

# Will 3G Supercomputers
# Also Gather Dust?

Raj Reddy

This chapter explores what one might do given access to a supercomputer on a desktop. Unless widespread use of such systems leads to improved productivity in every walk of life, they will also gather dust like many personal computers (PCs) do at home. The 3G supercomputer on a desktop will have the potential to use voice and vision for communication, tolerate error and ambiguity in human/computer interaction, provide rapid access to information and knowledge, and facilitate communication and coordination within a group of coworkers. We present several examples that exploit these possibilities and offer the potential for widespread use of low cost supercomputer workstations.

---

## 20.1   Introduction

One class of supercomputer workstations, what we call 3G workstations, is a system with at least a billion instructions per second processing power (a "giga ips"), a gigabyte of primary memory, and processor-memory bus bandwidth of at least a gigabyte. It now appears possible that we could soon have a 3G supercomputer on every desktop. However, it is not clear how this power can be used to make these systems truly useful and necessary to a wide spectrum of

465

the population. The new computational power could be used to make computers easy to use and/or to create new markets. In this chapter we will explore both alternatives. A 3G supercomputer would make it possible to use speech and image processing techniques for human/computer communication and to use language and knowledge processing tools to tolerate the error and ambiguity inherent in human/human interactions. Taken together, these technologies hold the promise of expanding the scope and uses of information systems given low cost 3G supercomputers. In this chapter we will present several examples of interest to a broad cross-section of the population.

Over the past 20 years, we have observed an increase in computation power of over three orders of magnitude, or over 3% compound growth every month. Recently, this rate has been observed to be around 6% to 7% compound growth every month. It is not clear how long such a growth rate can be sustained. Even if we go back to the old rate soon, it is clear that we can expect to have a 3G supercomputer for under $10,000 before the turn of the century. Optimistically speaking, we could cross this $10 per million instrucitons per second (MIPS) barrier as early as 1995.

Each new epoch in advances in computer technology witnessed the creation of brand new applications and opened up new markets. Minicomputers made it possible to use computers in laboratories and instrumentation. Personal computers led to word processing and spread sheets. Workstations made computer-aided design (CAD), computer-aided manufacturing (CAM), and computer-aided engineering (CAE) possible. What will 3G supercomputers bring? To understand the space of alternatives, we should look back to the failure of the home computer market.

In the late 1970s, there were great expectations for the future use of home computers. There was euphoria over the potential for personal computers to help us overcome illiteracy. There was also hope that these computers might be used routinely in education and entertainment. Indeed, they are used routinely, but not in the form predicted. It is not uncommon to find several microprocessors in every home, but usually as embedded special purpose dedicated systems rather than as general purpose assistants. PCs that were bought by the millions in the 1980s were soon gathering dust. What happened? We discovered that creating a "plug and play" home computer system requiring little or no additional training by family members required a degree of sophistication in software and user interface technology that did not exist. The graphics were inadequate, the computational power was inadequate, the sound quality was inadequate, and the applications were nonexistent. The situation is not much different today. However, we now have a better understanding of the necessary conditions that must exist before a widely used home computer can be successfully launched.

To be successful, a 3G workstation in the office and home must in some visible way *improve productivity and reduce cost* to make the investment worthwhile. If in addition the system can be used for education and entertainment, so much the better. Much like the automobile, the desktop supercomputer must provide a new capability and convenience to the owners that is highly valued. The three necessary conditions for success are: the availability of a low cost 3G supercomputer, an easy-to-use human/computer interface, and the creation of new applications that improve the productivity of almost all knowledge workers.

The cost will follow the inexorable exponential improvement of silicon chips and computer systems. In Sections 20.2 and 20.3, we discuss options for creating an easy-to-use multimedia interface that tolerates error and uncertainty in human/computer interaction. In Sections 20.4 and 20.5, we discuss the need to create an information infrastructure for rapid access to global information and several new uses of computers that only become feasible using a 3G workstation.

## 20.2  Human/Computer Communication

For over three decades, researchers have pursued methods of human/machine communication that extend the conventional "teletype" model. Sutherland's work on SketchPad pioneered interactive computer graphics and pointed the way for subsequent work. Engelhart's work at Stanford Research Institute in the 1960s and 1970s led to Xerox Palo Alto Research Center's research on personal workstations. One influential result was the Alto workstation, a self-contained PC that boasted a bit-mapped display, a mouse, and an Ethernet connection. The Alto offered all the features fundamental to modern-day workstations, including high-quality interactive graphics, display of formatted documents, WYSIWYG (what you see is what you get) editing, and high-bandwidth communication. Xerox made Altos available to several university research centers, and thus significantly influenced later research.

We now have the opportunity to influence the way computing will be perceived in the 1990s. This opportunity comes from remarkable hardware advances that combine high-quality graphics, sound, video, and very large storage in workstation-sized machines. What is needed is a software environment that can fully utilize this combination of capabilities and bring multimedia capabilities to all workstation users.

Research in speech, image, and language processing techniques date back to the 1960s. For the past 30 years, this research has been primarily of academic interest because of the high data rates and large amount of data involved. However, given voice and image input facilities within a 3G workstation, judicious use of SILK (speech, image, language, and knowledge) technologies can significantly enhance human/computer communication.

### 20.2.1   Speech Processing

The availability of voice as a medium of communication significantly increases the user population that could benefit by using multimedia workstations. It also provides a new capability and convenience previously unavailable in paper-based environments.

Using a microphone and an analog-to-digital converter, one can acquire, manipulate, store, and retrieve a sound object much as one can create a text object using a keyboard. In the past, when memory capacities and bus bandwidths were limited, recording speech at 8-32 Kbps per second, not knowing when the speaker might begin or end the utterance, meant using ad hoc solutions to record, detect beginning and end of the utterance, and store the data. High data rates, large amounts of data, and real-time processing requirements have limited the scope of speech-based applications so far. Much of the research was focused on recognition and synthesis as a means of coping with the data glut where digitized speech was viewed as purely a transient representation. With the availability of 3G workstations, we can seriously consider that sound objects, in spite of their higher storage requirements, can also be part of a persistent database.

Just as text objects can be viewed and manipulated at different levels of abstraction (bits, characters, words and symbols, paragraphs and programs), 3G machines permit us to view sound objects in a similar manner. To record and store *an hour of speech* would require anywhere from 28 Mbytes for telephone quality speech to 635 Mbytes for a stereophonic compact disk (CD) quality recording. Given the limitations of primary and secondary memories of the 1970s, any thought of online access of significant number of sound objects would have been impractical. However, in a 3G machine environment, routine use of speech objects will not only be practical but can become the preferred mode of communication. From a programming point of view it is simply another data type in a multimedia environment. Editing operations such as *cut, paste,* and *delete* can be defined for this data type as well.

Why do we need sound objects? Isn't it enough to transcribe (either manually or automatically) the content of a message? At present manual transcription of a dictation is expensive and time consuming, whereas automatic transcription (using a speech recognition system) is error prone. Further, given the nongrammatical nature of spontaneous spoken language, a transcription may be difficult to understand even though the original speech was clearly meaningful. Some simple uses of sound objects follow.

□ *Voice Mail.* Exhibit 20.1 illustrates the use of speech within an e-mail application. The lip-symbol icon near the bottom represents an attached message. To hear the message, one can point and click on the icon. To create a voice message in response, one uses the "lip-service" icon to record and insert a sound object at an appropriate point in the "send-window."

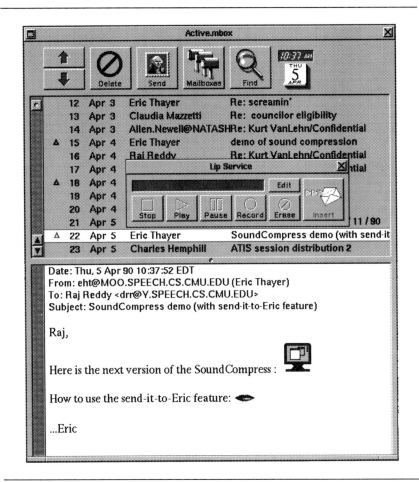

**EXHIBIT 20.1**
Example of the use of voice mail.

□ *Voice Annotations.* Comments on or responses to a letter or a document can be attached using "electronic Post-It notes" (EPNs). In a multimedia environment, the EPNs may contain text, speech, or handwritten response. Furthermore, a photo-icon of the respondent can be attached to the EPN, which can identify the author of the comment. Exhibit 20.2 illustrates this concept. The original letter (if not electronic) can be scanned and stored in an "electronic in-basket" for comments. The return response is attached at appropriate locations in the margin.

Deutsches
Forschungszentrum
für Künstliche
Intelligenz GmbH

Erwin-Schrödinger-Straße
Postfach 2080
6750 Kaiserslautern
Telefon (0631) 205-3211/13
Telefax (0631) 205-3210

Vorsitzender des
Aufsichtsrates:
Prof. Dr. Heinz Schwärtzel
Technisch-wissenschaftlicher
Geschäftsführer:
Prof. Dr. Gerhard Barth
Kaufmännischer
Geschäftsführer:
Friedrich J. Wendl

Amtsgericht Kaiserslautern
HRB 2313

Professor Dr. Raj Reddy
Carnegie-Mellon-University
Robotic Institute
Forbes Ave. 5241

USA-Pittsburgh, PA 15213

July 20,1989
gb-sh

Dear Professor Reddy:

You might have already learned that last year the German Research Centre for Artificial Intelligence was founded. It is mainly supported by the Federal Department of Science and Technology. Furthermore, 9 industrial companies (among them SIEMENS, IBM, NIXDORF, PHILIPS, AEG) as well as the Gesellschaft für Mathematik und Datenverarbeitung (GMD) and Fraunhofer-Gesellschaft will fund the research projects conducted at the DFKI.

Professor Schwärtzel is the Chairman of the Board of Directors, whom as I understand you know very well. I am the executive officer of the DFKI.

For October 12, we have scheduled a one-day conference in Kaiserslautern. There, we would like to demonstrate what we have established so far to a wide audience. Additionally, we are keen to present future research projects to our guests. The highlight of the event shall be a talk by a distinguished and well known person of the international AI community.

I invite you to be this speaker.

**EXHIBIT 20.2**
Voice annotations in the form of an electronic Post-It note (courtesy of Bob Thibadeau).

Speech Compression.   3G processors make it possible to explore expensive compression and decompression techniques that preserve the quality of speech sound objects. Past research in speech compression emphasized preserving intelligibility but not quality. It has now become possible to explore quality-preserving transformations that provide compression of both time and space. By "time compression" we mean a technique that permits us to listen to a 3-minute message say in 2 minutes. Exhibit 20.3 provides a simple time compression example. By detecting and eliminating the "thinking time" represented by pauses within a message without otherwise altering the sound structure, one can often

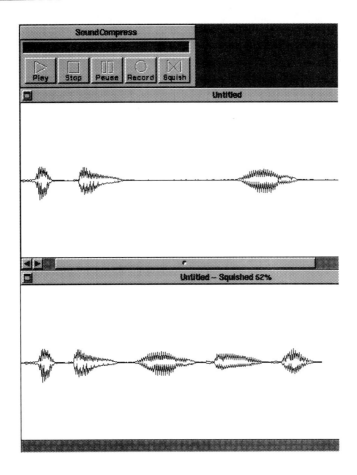

**EXHIBIT 20.3**
Example of time compression (courtesy of Eric Thayer).

achieve 20% to 30% time (and bandwidth) reduction. Systems that can actually recognize and understand sound units can achieve further time compression by detecting and removing "ums," "ahs," and repetitions within a message.

Time compression techniques, in conjunction with conventional waveform coding techniques that preserve quality, can lead to a factor of 5-10 reduction in the storage requirements for sound objects. For example, 64 Kbps of telephone-quality PCM speech can be compressed to 16 Kbps using classical ADPCM technique without loss of quality. Subsequent use of time compression techniques on a spontaneous speech message could lead to compression rates of 8-12 Kbps of speech. Thus an hour of speech would require about 4-5 Mbytes instead of 28 for the uncompressed speech. Similarly, compressed CD quality stereo sound would require around 100 Mbytes of storage per hour instead of 635 Mbytes per hour for uncompressed speech, without any noticeable loss of quality.

**Speech Recognition.**  Speech recognition has a long history of being one of the difficult problems in artificial intelligence (AI) and computer science. As one goes from problem solving tasks in AI to perceptual tasks, the problem characteristics change dramatically: knowledge poor to knowledge rich; low data rates to high data rates; slow response time (minutes to hours) to instantaneous response time. These characteristics taken together increase the computational complexity by several orders of magnitude relative to non-perceptual AI tasks.

Sphinx, the recent speaker-independent speech recognition system developed by Kai-Fu Lee at Carnegie Mellon University, best illustrates the current state of the art. This system is capable of recognizing continuous speech without training the system for each speaker. The system operates at about twice real time using a 1,000 word resource management vocabulary on a 20 MIPS processor. The system achieves 94% word accuracy in speaker independent mode on a task with a grammar perplexity of 60. The system derives its high performance by careful modeling of speech knowledge, by using an automatic unsupervised learning algorithm, and by fully utilizing a large amount of training data. These improvements permit Sphinx to overcome the many limitations of speaker-dependent systems resulting in a high performance system.

Exhibit 20.4 provides an example of the output of the Sphinx system. The system runs at about 10-20 times real time on a 68030-based 4 MIPS processor. As we go toward unlimited vocabulary dictation with higher accuracies, computational load for near real-time performance is expected to require the full capabilities of a 3G supercomputer workstation. Even with a 3G system, large vocabulary speech recognition systems will continue to have at least a 1%-2% error rate.

How can we expect to use recognition capabilities that will never be perfect? One hundred percent accuracy may be an unreasonable requirement. We do not expect typing to be perfect either. We tolerate an occasional error and provide editing capabilities that provide for error correction.

Speech recognition systems have been used in several applications:

❑ *Voice Retrieval.* Recognition capability can be used in its simplest form for database retrieval. Who needs it every day? In an office environment, daily use might consist of using a database of addresses and telephone numbers in conjunction with an autodialing system.

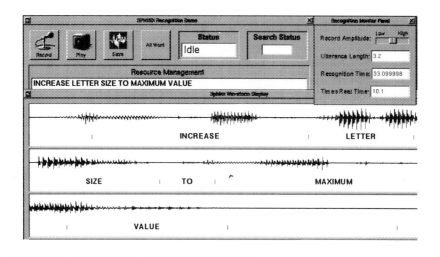

**EXHIBIT 20.4**
Example of the output of the Sphinx Speech Recognition System (courtesy of Kai-fu Lee).

□ *Voice Data Entry.* Recognition capability can also be used for data entry. Most of us don't need or use conventional data entry capability every day. However, tasks such as entering names and net addresses for e-mail systems can benefit from such a capability. Special applications such as medical data entry are already in routine use at present.

□ *Transcription, Summarization, and Indexing.* Perhaps the most exciting opportunity that does not require error-free recognition is automatic indexing of verbal messages. Given the capability of dictation transcription (which will be facilitated by the availability of 3G workstations), it will become possible to select and listen to a portion of a message using transcription as a pointing aid. Exhibit 20.5 shows an actual example of dictation transcription. The accuracy of the current system is about 60%-65%. At this level of accuracy, the transcription is not very useful. However, as we approach error rates of 5% (1 in 20) or less, the transcriptions might begin to be useful. When the text is not clear, one can always listen to that portion of the original speech. In the column labeled "Original," white spaces are errors. Out of vocabulary items are boxed. Note that only three words are incorrect in the second paragraph, making the transcription column almost readable.

## Dictation Transcription

| Original | Transcription |
|---|---|
| I would like to request your participation in the next Computer Science Research Review 1989-90. The publication will feature five or six technical articles from our research staff and provide updated listings of our faculty, staff, graduate students, Ph.D. recipients, publications/technical reports, colloquia, and sponsors. | I would like to request your participation of the index computers that's this effort in 1989-90. The public mission will feature five four six technical articles from research of provide up in the listings or thought it will staff club will graduate students, teach you should be school publication/technical reports, called the col and sponsored which. |
| I hope you will view this publication as an opportunity to report on the technical progress of your project. Your submission should describe recent project accomplishments and the current focus of your research. | I hope you will do this publication as opportunity to report on the technical progress of your project. Your submission should describe recent project accomplished of the current focus the research. |

**EXHIBIT 20.5**
Example of the current status of Unlimited Vocabulary Speaker Independent Dictation. The original speech is shown in the left column. Words correctly recognized are shown in the "gray" highlight. Words in white were incorrect or missed. A box around a word indicates that the system does not yet have a model for this word. Thus unknown words automatically result in an error in transcription. The column on the right shows actual transcription. Note that unless we get to better than 95% word accuracy, the transcription may be unusable. If part of the transcription at a given location (highlighted in the right column) is not clear, one can always listen to it by selecting the relevant portion of the original sound object which is preserved as part of the persistent object database (courtesy of Fil Alleva).

Speech Synthesis.    Another area that will benefit from the availability of 3G workstations is *high quality* speech synthesis. Current monotonal robot speech with nasal congestion can be replaced by more sophisticated models of stress and intonation representing characteristics of speaker, emotional state, and naturalness. If successful, it should be impossible to tell whether we are listening to human speech or synthesized speech.

## 20.2.2  Image Processing

Image input to computers is usually accomplished by two means: scanners and videocameras. Scanners permit high precision recording (300-2,000 pixels per inch). Color scanners often require multiple scans to achieve RGB (red, green, blue) decomposition. Time per scan varies from several seconds to several minutes per page. Videocameras, on the other hand, use a light sensitive CCD (charge-coupled device) silicon target for higher speed recording at about 30 frames a second. Recently, spurred by the large consumer markets for FAX machines and camcorders, the cost of page scanners and videocameras attachable to workstations have come down to a few hundred dollars per unit. Low cost widespread availability of image input devices integrated within a 3G workstation will spawn a wide range of new applications.

Images tend to create 100-1,000 times more data than speech, for example, high-quality speech versus HDTV (high-definition television) video, and are usually computationally intractable for all but a limited number of simple images. There are several classes of image data of interest: black-and-white image data from page scanning, gray scale and color image data from photographs, satellite and x-ray images, and video data of 30 (or more) images per second. Applications for home use are likely to involve all the image types: black-and-white images as an electronic paper substitute, photographic images as a camera substitute (black-and-white, color, and high resolution), and video for education, entertainment, and security applications. All of these alternatives represent new capabilities previously unavailable.

Image objects are data intensive. An 8 1/2 in. × 11 in. page of textual material scanned as a black-and-white (1 bit per pixel) image can result in 1-12 Mbytes of data depending on the resolution of either 300 or 1,000 dots per inch. Thus a book of 500 pages would require 500 Mbytes of storage using up half the memory of a 3G workstation. The same book stored as ASCII (American Standard Code for Information Interchange) text would only require 1 Mbyte of memory. Fortunately, the image compression technology can reduce the storage requirement by 15-50 if one uses the industry standard CCITT (International Telephone and Telegraph Consultative Committee) group 3 or group 4 compression techniques resulting in 10-30 Mbytes per book in compressed image representation.

Storage requirements increase dramatically as one goes from black-and-white to grayscale and color. The data increase by a factor of 8 for grayscale images and 24 for color (assuming 8 bits of resolution per primary color). Thus an 8 1/2 in. × 11 in. color photograph scanned at 1,000 pixels per inch resolution would require 280 Mbytes of storage. Quality-preserving compression techniques (yet to be developed) are likely to reduce this storage requirement by 100. Near real-time compression and decompression will be computationally intensive, requiring the full power of a 3G workstation.

Video data adds an additional dimension of complexity. The time synchronous nature of the input, say 30 frames per second, results in high data rates and large amounts of data. A 480 × 640 NTSC black-and-white image would generate 9.2 Mbytes of data per second and a 1,200 × 2,000 HDTV color image would generate 216 Mbytes of data per second. Thus even 3G machines will run out of memory in less than 2 minutes for NTSC and 5 seconds for HDTV. The only solution is to compress and decompress the images at video rates. This will stress even a 3G machine to the limit. With compression, a factor of 100 reduction can be achieved without loss of quality. A CD-ROM disk (compact disk, read-only memory), which would only hold 69 seconds of NTSC-quality digital video, would hold almost 2 hours with a factor of 100 compression. This is the basis of the current laser video consumer product attempts. A HDTV recording of 2 hours is expected to take 5-6 CD-ROM disks. A more elaborate digital representation would permit us to watch high-quality animation mixed with real life imagery (e.g., *Who Framed Roger Rabbit?*) of 1-2 hr duration on a 3G workstation.

Given a low cost 3G multimedia workstation with scanning and video capabilities, a number of new applications of computers become possible. The following is a sampling of applications of broad general interest.

□ *Talking Paper.* An image object (electronic page) can be cut, pasted, analyzed, and manipulated just as a text or a sound object. Further, verbal comments can be attached to the electronic page, creating a new capability not available in plain paper-based communication. Exhibit 20.2 illustrates the use of verbal and textual EPNs attached to a scanned document.

□ *Electronic File Cabinets.* With the availability of scanners on a 3G machine, one can scan and store on electronic media letters, papers, and documents that would be normally kept in conventional file cabinets. Retrieval of documents would then be facilitated by a hypertext type of indexing, which is not practical in physical file cabinets.

□ *Personal Digital Library.* With the increasing availability of electronic books, journals, and newspapers, one can envision replacing a physical personal library by a digital library. Such a system will provide instantaneous access to the desired material while saving physical space. A 3G machine on a desktop can hold around 3,000 volumes in primary memory and an unlimited number in secondary storage. The 3,000-volume estimate assumes we can achieve a factor of 3 compression by linguistic coding. If the books or magazines have figures or color images then the number would be smaller.

□ *Digital Camera.* A camcorder equipped with a high-speed special purpose image processor can compress and store, on a digital audio tape (DAT), high-quality video, which can then be transferred, stored, retrieved, and played back on the 3G machine's HDTV monitor. Hard copy scanning and printing can be shared services or provided on a fee-for-service basis.

☐ *Digital Movies.* When an entire 2-hour movie can be transmitted to homes on demand in less than 60 seconds in HDTV format, it will transform the entertainment industry. Quality will be superb and trips to the video store will be a thing of the past. New organizational players like AT&T will become the dominant distributor of the media, and creation of films would move substantially from celluloid to the electronic medium. More importantly, electronic manipulation of image and voice data can significantly reduce the number of takes and other routine chores, providing more time for creative pursuits. In such a situation, a 3G workstation can probably play a more central role than decompression of the bits. It can take a high level script and literally create movie scenes on the fly!

Image Interpretation.    Image objects by themselves are devoid of meaning and can be manipulated like any other object. However, through the use of OCR (optical character recognition) and other image interpretation techniques, the content of the image objects can be related to other meaningful units such as text. This capability would permit content-based indexing of large image databases, which is currently impractical.

Exhibit 20.6 illustrates the use of OCR technology to identify words from a scanned image. The window shows OCR transcription of the top left paragraph. Note that given a low quality image, a current OCR system will occasionally make mistakes. This technology, which is already over 99% correct, will further improve in a 3G machine environment.

## 20.2.3  Language and Knowledge Processing

One of the important uses of 3G workstations will be to cope with the avalanche of data and information. The situation is already bad, and it will continue to get much worse. The problem will be how to convert data into information, information into insight, and insight into decision. This is where the tools of language and knowledge processing become important. Much of the data is natural language text. To date, language processing research and computational linguistics have primarily concentrated on the problems of parsing and understanding of text in narrow-structured domains. Recently there has been increasing interest in the use of language tools for reading, writing, and translation aids for helping human users to improve their productivity.

☐ *Reading Assistant.* A reading assistant program developed at Carnegie Mellon University (CMU) can read a letter and highlight the "operative" sentences much as a secretary might do. Such highlighting does not have to

90apr18.09am.1226.pst - /usr0/reddy/Scans/Unfiled  Page: 0001 of 0001

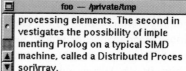

processing elements. The second in vestigates the possibility of imple menting Prolog on a typical SIMD machine, called a Distributed Proces sor\rrav.

processing elements. The second investigates the possibility of implementing Prolog on a typical SIMD machine, called a Distributed Processor Array.

The author's objectives are to define a parallel computational paradigm (the Extended Cellular-Dataflow Model) that can be used to create a Parallel Prolog Abstract Machine as a general starting point for implementing logic programming languages on parallel computers, to exploit the different types of parallelism of these programs, to define an efficient parallel logic machine, to explore the possibilities of implementing logic programming languages on array processors (such as the DAP), to invent parallel implementation techniques for effectively executing Prolog on the DAP, and to define a parallel exten-

$40

Object-oriented concurrent programming is a new programming paradigm that exploits the benefits of object orientation, concurrency and distributed systems. This book provides an overview of the new paradigm through the programming language ABCL. It presents a complete description of the theory, programming, implementation, and application of the

current systems. ...zawa and ...arlier in ...Program... ).

...tutorials ...computa... ...languages, ...language ...processor

architectures, programming environments, applications in distributed event simulation and construction of an operating system, parallel algorithms for natural language on-line parsing, and such new theoretical issues as reflective computation. The book also includes a user's guide to ABCL.

*Akinori Yonezawa is Professor, Dept. of Information Science, at the University of Tokyo.*

# Orders for robots set record in 1989

US-based robot manufacturers posted a record year in 1989, with net new orders totalling $513.6 million, a 55% increase over 1988 and $29 million higher than the previous record set in 1984. According to Robotic Industries Association (RIA) (Ann Arbor, MI), the majority of the upswing resulted from increased purchases by the automotive industry, both in the US and overseas.

Shipments increased by 42% in 1989, totalling $437.4 million, approximating the industry's high set in 1985. The year-end backlog of unfilled orders totalled 2,934 units valued at $233.7 million, the industry's strongest in four years.

"Clearly, 1989 was an outstanding year, one of the best ever for the US robotics industry," said Donald A. Vincent, executive vice president of the RIA, the industry's trade group. "However, because automotive buying tends to be cyclical, we're uncertain that this strong order rate can be maintained in 1990. Our industry still needs to make greater inroads into non-automotive markets. We must find ways to improve the participation of aero-

ceutical, and other non-automotive customers in the utilization of robotics and advanced automation. It's interesting to note that in Japan, which is the world's largest user of industrial

robots, sales for the past few years in non-automotive markets have surpassed automotive sales by a wide margin. That's a good goal for US-based robotics firms to shoot at," Vincent explained.

RIA estimates that some 37,000 industrial robots are now being used in

100,000 in Japan. In 1989, leading applications for robots sold by US-based firms were painting/coating, welding, material handling, and assembly.

While Vincent expects 1990 to be flat, or perhaps down from the records posted in 1989, he remains highly optimistic about the long-term outlook for the US robotics industry. "We fully expect the 1990s to be the decade for flexible automation, as companies in virtually every industry realize that robots, machine vision and related factory automation systems are essential elements in remaining competitive in the global marketplace," he said.

"US manufacturing companies should not be lulled into thinking that better management practices alone account for the success of their foreign competitors in the last decade. The combination of a strong commitment to automation and improved manufacturing management is how major gains are being achieved today. I firmly believe that overseas manufacturing firms are making a greater commitment than ever to automation as a strategic com-

**EXHIBIT 20.6**
Example of the use of OCR and annotations given a scanned image in a database.

be perfect because the reader has the entire letter on the screen anyway. If the letter is on paper, then it would have to be scanned, converted to a text object using OCR and passed to the reading assistant for analysis and display.

□ *Writing Assistant.* Several commercial systems already provide assistance for spelling correction, grammar correction, and style correction. A more exciting possibility is a parameterized letter-writing system, which takes hints about the gist of a letter and produces a personalized letter in an arbitrary language. Similar systems for creation of proposals, funding agency announcements such as requests for proposals, and product specifications are possible with today's technologies.

□ *Translation Assistant.* Exhibit 20.7 gives an example of a translation assistant. Suppose you have a letter or a document to read, say in Italian, and you are not fluent in Italian. The letter is scanned and transcribed using OCR. The resulting text object appears in the left window. Given an unknown word or phrase, the system does a contextual analysis and provides the most appropriate entries from a digital dictionary instantaneously. It saves several minutes of time that it usually takes to locate the entry in a paper dictionary and additional time it usually takes to infer the correct meaning from a large number of alternatives. For English, the average number of alternative meanings per word is 17.

□ *Filing Assistant.* One of the promising uses of language processing is to provide a solution for the information glut in the form of an intelligent indexing and filing system for electronic file cabinets. A number of content-based indexing techniques have been proposed, but they tend to be inadequate when compared to human abilities. As our ability to disambiguate and understand language improves, we can expect to have more robust intelligent filing subsystems.

□ *Monitoring Assistant.* "Daemons" that monitor all sources of information of interest can substantially reduce the information glut. Information of interest for an average household might include: the status of your bank account, energy consumption in the home, outrageous telephone charges, news stories about investments, news stories about your company, buying or selling opportunities by monitoring advertisements, and other items of individual personal interest. A knowledge-based "monitoring assistant" can sufficiently improve productivity so as to achieve annual savings exceeding the annual base cost of a 3G workstation by an average "knowledge worker of the future."

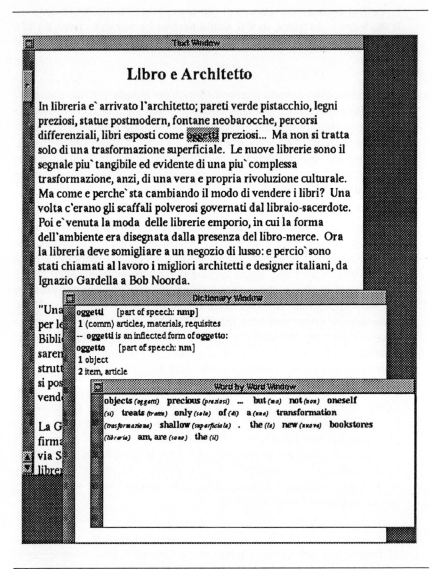

**EXHIBIT 20.7**
Example of a translation assistant. Exhibit shows an Italian document in which selecting a word would cause the meaning to show up in a "Dictionary Window," and word-by-word translation in another window. As the translation system gets more sophisticated, this window can be replaced by phrase-level and sentence-level translations (courtesy of Dario Giuse).

## 20.3   Tolerating Error and Ambiguity in Interaction

Nonexperts wonder why computers use constrained languages such as Fortran and Lisp. The reason is that natural languages are inherently ambiguous, and techniques for ambiguity resolutions were either unknown or require computational resources that would have been impractical in the first 25 years of the information revolution. The situation is changing. We are beginning to see systems with natural language interfaces in a few restricted task situations. Let us examine some of the sources of confusion in natural language by considering the sentence "Take a bus to the bank." This sentence illustrates the ambiguity resulting from different meanings a word can take. In this example, words such as "take" can have different meanings (take a shower, take a book, take a meaning, take off). One can take a book and carry it, but it would be impossible to carry a bus, unless you happen to be King Kong. "Bus" and "bank" can also have many different meanings (bus is full of people, bus bandwidth; river bank, bank robbery, bank a plane). In modern natural language systems, these different interpretations are stored as semantic networks. The intersection of different networks usually leads to unique interpretation.

We have a similar problem at the grammar level where sentences such as "I saw John on the hill with a telescope" could have many different meanings. It could mean, "one uses the telescope to see John" or it could mean, "John was carrying the telescope." Again, the context of the situation helps to resolve ambiguity.

Anaphoric references such as *he*, *she*, and *it* can also lead to multiple interpretations. For example, in the sentence, "John took the cookie from the table and ate it," one can eat a cookie, but not a table. Ellipsis, where a shortened phrase is only meaningful in the context of a dialogue, is another example when the uncertainty is only resolved by the use of context.

In the English language, on the average, words have 17 different meanings, and a sentence has three different parses and three alternative interpretations as a result of anaphora and ellipsis. This produces substantial ambiguity in interpretation of English sentences.

Availability of the 3G workstation will dramatically alter the preferred modes of communication. Spontaneous speech with the "ums" and "ahs," non-grammatical constructs, and ambiguity inherent in the language can be interpreted in less than real time on a 3G machine. Any remaining errors can be handled by an "error-correcting" editor, which can also "undo" the changes in state resulting from the execution of an erroneous command.

Exhibit 20.8 illustrates the operation of an error-correcting flexible semantic parser for spoken language. The Phoenix system is able to accept spoken commands such as "Ah, how about LaGuardia" and convert it to case frame rep-

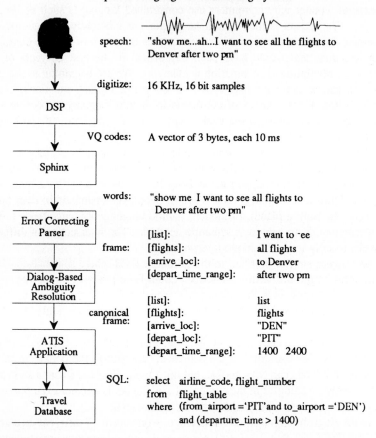

## Structure of Phoenix
### A Spoken Language Understanding System

speech:   "show me...ah...I want to see all the flights to Denver after two pm"

DSP

digitize:    16 KHz, 16 bit samples

VQ codes:    A vector of 3 bytes, each 10 ms

Sphinx

words:    "show me  I want to see all flights to Denver after two pm"

Error Correcting Parser

frame:
| [list]: | I want to see |
|---------|---------------|
| [flights]: | all flights |
| [arrive_loc]: | to Denver |
| [depart_time_range]: | after two pm |

Dialog-Based Ambiguity Resolution

canonical frame:
| [list]: | list |
|---------|------|
| [flights]: | flights |
| [arrive_loc]: | "DEN" |
| [depart_loc]: | "PIT" |
| [depart_time_range]: | 1400  2400 |

ATIS Application

SQL:
```
select   airline_code, flight_number
from     flight_table
where    (from_airport ='PIT'and to_airport ='DEN')
         and (departure_time > 1400)
```

Travel Database

---

**EXHIBIT 20.8**
Error-correcting flexible semantic parsing system for spoken language (courtesy of Wayne Ward).

resentation in which nonverbal sounds and errors in recognition do not confuse the error-correcting flexible parser. The system is also able to use knowledge of dialog and context to resolve ambiguity resulting from anaphora and ellipsis. If the preceding sentence was "List flights from Pittsburgh to JFK," ellipsis resolution would fill in the depart location as Pittsburgh in the course of interpreting the above example.

This is just one example of the type of software we must develop with several levels of "information filters," which will lead to a robust, easy-to-use interface that will detect and handle errors and noise in the system without getting flustered by unanticipated events.

## 20.4  Rapid Access to Information and Knowledge

Do we need high powered 3G workstations for accessing information and knowledge? At first glance, access to databases does not seem to require the full power of a 3G machine—or does it? Spoken language access to databases, content-based indexing and search, HDTV quality high resolution color graphics for electronic magazines, information filters that can access large amounts of information and ignore all but most relevant information will all need the availability of a 3G workstation. Indeed, Dow Jones uses a connection machine at present to do rapid search of large textual databases.

Creation of databases and knowledge bases containing the sum total of human knowledge is an enormous undertaking, which is yet to begin. Dertouzos, Kahn, and others have been advocating the creation of a national information infrastructure including a gigabit network and a national digital Library of Congress.

Rapid access to information requires solving a number of problems. First, paper-based information in books, documents, and newspapers must be transferred to an electronic medium. Second, image-based representations must be converted to text-based representations. Third, an intelligent index must be created that can be easily used by human users.

Rapid access to knowledge requires the creation of knowledge bases. Knowledge is active information codified in a form that can be easily used by expert systems and knowledge-based systems.

At present, there are a large number of commercially available databases that operate on a fee-for-service basis, which can be accessed through Western Union Infomaster, Source, Compuserve, and other information wholesalers. At last count there were over 5,000 such databases available, covering finance, patents, and journal and trade publications such as *Art Index, Books in Print, Electronic Yellow Pages, Marquis Who's Who, Agrochemical Databank, and Foundation Directory.*

To broaden the scope and use, we need to lower the cost of access to these databases. This in turn implies the cost of creation and communication of this information and knowledge bases has to be subsidized in the formative stages by creating a trust fund for creation of a national information infrastructure along the lines of the interstate highway system. A national information infrastructure would include or provide access to the following:

- □ *National Digital Library.* If we can provide online access to 20 million volumes in the Library of Congress, it would spawn wide use of workstations. A feasibility study undertaken by Cerf and Kahn at the National Research Institute (NRI) points out a number of technical, legal, and financial obstacles that must be resolved before a digital library can be a reality.

- □ *Electronic Magazines.* Magazines and newspapers can be made available electronically at present if the necessary standards can be agreed upon. What is needed is the browsing software and HDTV quality display, and multimedia communication standards.

- □ *Electronic Shopping.* A number of videotext services such as Prodigy (created by IBM and Sears) already provide this option. However the range of services, quality, and ease-of-use can be significantly improved given a 3G multimedia workstation.

## 20.5   Collaboration and Presentation

An area of broad interest that would be facilitated by a 3G machine is the area of group interaction. We will consider two types of interactions: collaboration technologies (many-to-many) and presentation technologies (one-to-many). In collaboration, the availability of speech, image, and language processing facilities on a 3G machine open new possibilities.

- □ *Collaborative Writing.* Current methods that allow a group of scientists to collaborate in creating a document tend to be time consuming and hard to use. Typically, even with computer-based tools, two people cannot simultaneously edit one document. In addition, the marginal notes and scribbled figures common to hardcopy documents remain confined to that medium. A 3G workstation can add dramatic improvement to collaborative writing by allowing group members to create text and annotations using spoken comments, handwritten and graphical notes, and typed text. Annotations can be permanently linked to specific portions of the document, and users will be able to conduct an editorial "conversation" that focuses on a particular issue or a piece of text. Figures 20.2 and 20.5 hint at this possibility.

- □ *Collaborative Design.* Exhibit 20.9 shows an example of collaborative design. A sketch or drawing is scanned and incorporated within an e-mail message as an image object and distributed to the design team for

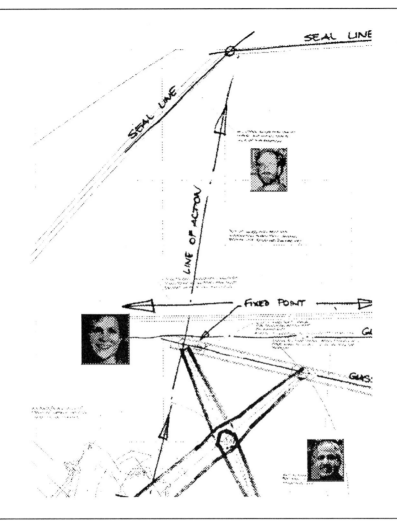

**EXHIBIT 20.9**
Collaborative design: instead of assembling in the same room at the same
time, a group of designers can interact using multimedia annotations within
an advanced e-mail system (courtesy of Bob Thibadeau).

comments. Recipients can provide comments in the form of an overlay
of electronic multimedia EPNs. The overlay object is mailed back to the
designer where the system displays multiple overlays with photo-icons
of the respondents. Users will be able to conduct asynchronous "editorial"

conversations back and forth, with all the relevant communication grouped together in a tree-structured hypermedia representation.

□ *Collaborative Planning.* Complex planning problems require multi-agent distributed problem solving involving scheduling of tasks, resources, and time slots satisfying dynamically changing constraints. Current paper-based and phone-based systems involve access to large numbers of incompatible databases and multiple levels of approval, often leading to suboptimal solutions. A multimedia collaborative planning system, analogous to the collaborative writing and design systems described above, would permit collaborative planning with people and expert systems acting within an integrated environment.

Many of us have to travel long distances just to attend or give presentations of the latest new ideas. Over 10% of a research professional's time may be spent in either creating, presenting, or listening to talks. A 3G workstation for the first time makes it possible for a listener to be in control of a presentation.

□ *Presentation Expediter* is a system that permits a listener to hear a talk in less time than it took the speaker to give it. This is accomplished by using time compression of speech (see Section 20.1.2), synchronizing audio and video, and providing for listener control of presentation dynamics. User control includes *fast-forward*, *slow*, *halt*, and *backup* buttons that maximize the information communication based on the viewer's level of interest.

## 20.6  Conclusions

We started with a question about 3G supercomputers gathering dust. There will be no machines gathering dust if the cost is high enough that only professionals can afford to buy them—for them functionality rather than cost will be the determining factor. However, every white collar worker could be a candidate for using one of these systems if the cost goes below $10,000. Depending on how one counts, there are 40-80 million white collar workers (including clerks and secretaries) in the United States. If their productivity could be improved at least 10% at an annual cost per seat of $1,000-$2,000, then we might see a widespread use of 3G workstations. For such workstations not to gather dust, it is *essential that new applications be created* that are universal in that they satisfy an existing daily need. Word processing may have been one such application. In this chapter, we propose two broad areas that offer the prospect of universal use: *rapid access to information* and *coordination and communication*. We also state that universal applications will not be universal unless computers become easier to use by offering speech, image, and language processing capabilities, and tolerate error and ambiguity in interaction. Only a 3G workstation can provide adequate power to accept voice and vision input, tolerate error and ambiguity, provide rapid intelligent access to large databases, and permit coordination and communication within a group.

# 21

# What Is Scientifically Knowable?

J. F. Traub

> **Postmodern science**—*by concerning itself with such things as un-decidables, the limits of precise control, conflicts characterized by incomplete information, "fracta", catastrophes, and pragmatic para-doxes—is theorizing its own evolution as discontinuous, catastrophic, nonrectifiable, and paradoxical. It is changing the meaning of the word* **knowledge**, *while expressing how such a change can take place. It is producing not the known, but the unknown.* (Jean-Francois Lyotard, *The Postmodern Condition: A Report on Knowledge.* University of Minnesota Press, 1984, p. 60.)

## 21.1   Introduction

This is a highly speculative chapter on what is scientifically knowable, the goal of which is more to suggest directions for thought and to pose questions than to answer them. I plan to pursue the themes enunciated here in future works.

A number of authors including Feynman [5], Geroch and Hartle [8], Landauer [10], Wheeler [20], and White [21] have written about the relation of science and computation. That relation motivates this chapter. What are the intrinsic impediments to the computational solution of scientific problems?

Here is the path I will follow. I first briefly discuss the kind of scientific problems we have in mind and the connection between science and computation. Then I list some intrinsic impediments to computation and choose one of them to explore further in this chapter, intractability in the sense of computational complexity.

Next, I give a summary of what is conjectured or known about intractability. In discrete computational complexity a basic conjecture is that $P \neq NP$. If this conjecture is true then the complexity of many problems grows exponentially with the number of objects. In continuous computational complexity, it has been established that the complexity of many problems grows exponentially with the number of variables, i.e., with dimension. If a problem exhibits such exponential growth we say it is intractable.

The above conjecture and results are for a deterministic worst-case setting. Can we circumvent them by settling for a weaker assurance that we have solved the problem? One attack is by randomization (Monte Carlo is one important example of randomization), and I will indicate what is known about the power and limitations of randomization. A second attack is to settle for an assurance on the average.

Research to date has been on intractability in various settings such a worst case, randomized, and average. It seems desirable, however, to have a notion of intractability independent of the setting, and so I introduce the concept of strong intractability. A problem is *strongly intractable* if it remains intractable no matter how we weaken the assurance regarding its solution. I believe that strongly intractable problems exist.

I speculate next on what these results from theoretical computer science might imply for science. They might indicate intractability of many supercomputing problems, and for the foundations of physics. For example, computational chemistry, computational design of pharmaceuticals, and computational metallurgy involve computation with huge numbers of particles and therefore high dimensionality. As another example, path integrals are infinite dimensional, and therefore invite high dimensional approximations.

But do intractability results really limit what is scientifically knowable? They might not, and I offer reasons why. Perhaps the most important of these is that intractability results are for a particular mathematical formulation. But a scientific problem need not have a unique mathematical formulation, or indeed, any mathematical formulation at all. Mathematical formulations should meet twin desiderata.

1. They should capture the essence of the science.

2. They should be computationally tractable.

This suggests the need for a theory of computational complexity of scientific problems. A central question in such a theory would be the following.

*Do there exist scientific problems such that every mathematical formulation is strongly intractable?*

I believe that there are such scientific problems and that they are unknowable.

## 21.2   Science and Computation

A number of researchers have commented on the relation between science and computation. Although the following quotations are primarily about the foundations of physics, the same relation holds for other sciences.

Pagels [13] put it succinctly "To know a mathematical proof you must be able to compute it."

White [21] writes "Foundational Physics seeks predictive theories, and that predictive process must be a computational algorithm executed on a real physically limited computer, a relationship termed the Wheeler cycle."

Feinberg [4] states, "I am not saying that theoretical physicists who work on fundamental questions, such as the behavior of subatomic particles, do not perform calculations. Doing calculations is what makes them theoretical physicists."

Geroch and Hartle [8] require that a physical "theory be such that its predictions can be extracted not merely in principle, possibly by ever higher levels of skill and sophistication, but also in practice, mechanically."

Rolf Landauer [10] summarizes the issue eloquently.

> What computers can do will define the ultimate nature of the laws of physics. After all, the laws of physics are algorithms for the processing of information, and will be futile, unless these algorithms are implementable in our universe, with its laws and resources. "What computers can do" refers not to the forseeable technological future, but rather to that which can be done in principle with the resources available in our actual physical universe.

What intrinsic impediments are there to "what computers can do?" We mention three of them here.

□ *Chaos.* Chaos is extreme sensitivity to initial conditions. Since the precise initial conditions are either not known or, even if known, cannot be exactly entered into a digital computer, the behavior of a chaotic system cannot be predicted.

□ *Physical Limits*. There is an extensive literature on physical limits to computation. See, for example, Landauer [9] and Bremmerman [3].

□ *Intractablity*. A problem is said to be *intractable* if there can never be sufficient computer resources for its solution. Of the various impediments to computation, I will confine myself in this chapter to intractablity.

---

## 21.3   Intractability of Discrete Problems

Here is a famous problem that we believe to be intractable, although we do not know for sure. Given a set of cities and the distances between them, determine the order in which the cities should be visited so that each city is visited exactly once, the tour ends in the starting city, and the distance traveled is as small as possible. This "Traveling Salesman Problem" is an abstraction of many scheduling and layout problems that are common in real life.

Say the number of cities is six. Then the problem could be solved at sight or with a little pencil and paper work. But what if the number of cities is 50 or 100 rather than 6? Then how long will it take to find the shortest tour?

Many people have puzzled over this for decades. No matter what methods they devised for finding the shortest tour, and no matter how clever they were, they discovered that the time required to solve the problem, for even a moderate number of cities, would take hundreds of years on the fastest computers. Since computers were only invented some 40 years ago, no one has computed for hundreds of years: analysis reveals that if the methods were implemented, that is how long they would take.

If people keep devising methods to solve the traveling salesman problem and any of these would require centuries to run, a natural question arises—*can* there be any method for solving the problem faster?

To answer this question we must know the *least* computational effort to solve the traveling salesman problem by any method that has been invented or ever may be invented. The least computational effort to solve a problem is called its computational complexity, or, for brevity, its complexity. The complexity of a problem measures its intrinsic difficulty.

What is the complexity of the traveling salesman problem? As of today, no one on earth knows.

In particular, we do not know if the traveling salesman problem is tractable or intractable. I remind you that a problem is intractable if computer resources can never be sufficient to obtain a solution. Mathematically speaking, the traveling salesman problem is intractable if it is exponential in the number of cities. That is, adding just one city doubles the complexity. Fifty cities means 50 doublings.

The complexity of the traveling salesman problem is unknown but computer scientists have made a remarkable discovery. There exist numerous problems, hundreds of problems, some of them very important, that all have essentially the same complexity. They are *all* intractable or all tractable and the common belief among experts is that they are all intractable. For technical reasons these problems are said to be NP-complete; see Garey and Johnson [7]. One of the great open questions in computer science is if $P \neq NP$ or equivalently, whether the NP-complete problems are indeed intractable.

Intractability means the problem does not scale. That is, the problem can be easily solved for a small number of objects (cities in the traveling salesman problem, vertices and edges in the graph isomorphism problem) but cannot be solved for a large number of objects.

Discrete problems can be solved exactly. If we are prepared to live with an approximate solution does that lower the complexity? Will an approximate solution make an intractable problem tractable?

It turns out to depend on the particular discrete problem; at least so far, there is no general theory. The interested reader is referred to Garey and Johnson [7].

## 21.4  Intractability of Continuous Problems

Many problems of the physical, biological, engineering, and social sciences have continuous mathematical formulations. A typical example is an initial value problem where a condition is specified at a certain time and we watch as the system evolves.

The initial condition is given by a "continuous" function. This is an infinite dimensional object. Since digital computers can only store and manipulate finite sets of numbers the function must be replaced by a finite set of numbers. Hence the information is *partial*.

The scientist or engineer would like to solve the original continuous problem. Since the information in the computer is partial the investigator *must* settle for an approximate solution. (This should be contrasted with discrete problems where one can *choose* to solve the problem approximately.)

Typical continuous problems where the information is partial are weather prediction and geophysical exploration. In weather prediction one must solve the hydrodynamic equations: initial conditions are provided by data at a finite number of points from a variety of sensors. In geophysical exploration the location of mineral deposits or oil reservoirs is estimated by measurements taken at the earth's surface. The cost of these measurements can be stupendous.

Finally, information obtained by measurement or calculation is usually *contaminated* by error.

The discipline that studies how to solve problems where the information is partial, contaminated, and priced is called *information-based complexity*.

The research monograph by Traub, Wasilkowski, and Woźniakowski [17] provides a comprehensive treatment of information-based complexity. Expository accounts may be found in Packel and Traub [11], Packel and Woźniakowski [12], and Traub and Woźniakowski [18].

If the information is insufficient there must be *intrinsic* uncertainty in the solution. Even with uncertainty the computation of a solution may still be noncomputable or intractable. A number of notions of noncomputability have been utilized over the past 50 years; these notions are grounded in logic. In information-based complexity we use a rather pragmatic notion. A problem is noncomputable if its complexity is infinite, even if one is willing to live with a great deal of uncertainty. As before, it is intractable if the complexity is very large, so large that no computer or set of computers now or in the future, will ever solve it.

In information-based complexity many problems have been proven noncomputable or intractable. Here is the computation of a multivariate integral as an example.

Let the dimensionality be $d$ and let the smoothness of the integrand be $r$. Assume we want to guarantee an error of at most $\varepsilon$.

Many problems have complexity given by

$$\text{comp}(\varepsilon) = \Theta\left( \left(\frac{1}{\varepsilon}\right)^{d/r} \right).$$

Examples include nonlinear optimization, integration, and systems of integral equations; see Traub, Wasilkowski, and Woźniakowski [17].

Here, note the big $\Theta$ notation, which means that there exist positive constants $c_1, c_2$, and $c_3$ such that $c_1 e^{-d/r} \leq \text{comp}(\varepsilon) \leq c_2 e^{-d/r}$ for $\varepsilon \in [0, c_3]$.

One reason that problems are noncomputable is because they have too little smoothness. In the multivariate integration example, if the integrand is only continous ($r = 0$), then the problem is noncomputable. A second reason is that the problem is ill posed. Let a problem be specified by a linear solution operator. A problem is ill posed if the operator is unbounded. Werschulz [19] shows the solution is then noncomputable and applies his general results to Fredholm problems of the first kind.

High dimensionality often causes intractability. In the multivariate integration example, let $r$ be positve. For simplicity, assume $r = 1$. The complexity then grows as $(1/\varepsilon)^d$. Thus when we raise the dimension by unity, the complexity is multiplied by a factor equal to the reciprocal of the error. If we want an eight-decimal answer then when we increase the dimension by unity the complexity is multiplied by 100,000,000.

Small $\varepsilon$ occur in practice. Berni Alder [1] has pointed out that for certain problems in computational chemistry $\varepsilon = 10^{-8}$ or $10^{-9}$.

The dimension does not have to be large for the complexity to be prohibitive. Let $d = 3, r = 1, \varepsilon = 10^{-8}$. Then $(1/\varepsilon)^{d/r} = 10^{24}$. In the integration example this is how often the integrand must be evaluated. Assume $10^{10}$ evaluations can be performed per second. This is patently an overestimate since even $10^{10}$ floating point operatons per second would challenge any contemporary machine. Even with this overestimate, it would take $10^{14}$ seconds to perform the integrand evaluations. Parallel processing would not eliminate the difficulty. Even with a million processor computer and assuming linear speed-up, the compuation would still take $10^8$ seconds. And this is for a three dimensional example!

## 21.5  Randomized and Average Case Settings

The intractability and noncomputability results reported so far, of both discrete and continuous complexity, are deterministic worst-case results. *Deterministic* means we do not toss coins during the calculations. *Worst-case* means we guarantee to solve every problem instance. Will it help significantly to relax either of these assumptions? Can we make intractable problems tractable and noncomputable problems computable?

Consider first the use of randomization. Physicists have long known about the power of randomization. For example, classic Monte Carlo methods may be regarded as using randomized information to make the number of integrand evaluations needed to compute an approximation to a multivariate integral independent of dimension. More recently, computer scientists have used randomized algorithms to solve problems such as primality testing; see, for example, Rabin [14].

When randomization is introduced it weakens the assurance we can offer regarding the computed solution. Even if we are willing to live with this weaker assurance, will randomization decrease complexity? It turns out that randomization may help a great deal—or not at all.

A problem where randomization helps greatly is multivariate integration. Let the dimension be $d$ and the smoothness of the class of integrands be $r$. Recall that in the worst-case deterministic setting,

$$\text{comp}(\varepsilon) = \Theta\left(\left(\frac{1}{\varepsilon}\right)^{d/r}\right).$$

Therefore, if $r = 0$ multivariate integration is noncomputable and for $r > 0$ it is intractable.

For $r = 0$, the cost of Monte Carlo is proportional to $1/\varepsilon^2$, independent of dimension. It can be shown this is also the complexity. Thus the problem is now computable and tractable. It can be shown that for $r > 0$, the complexity is less than $1/\varepsilon^2$.

On the other hand, there are problems for which it has been shown that randomization does not help.

To date, we only have examples where randomization does or does not break intractability and noncomputability. There is no theory that characterizes those problems for which randomization helps.

Traub and Woźniakowski [18] pose the following question: Characterize those problems for which randomization helps significantly. In particular, for which problems does randomization break intractability or noncomputability?

Next consider next replacing a worst-case assurance by an average case assurance. That is, we minimize the *expected* resources required to solve the problem. It turns out that an average assurance may help a great deal—or not at all.

The average case setting requires a measure on the problem elements. For discrete problems, an equiprobable distribution is often used. No such measure exists for continuous problems and often Gaussian measures and, in particular, Wiener measures are used.

Recently, Woźniakowski [22] solved a long-standing open problem by giving optimal deterministic sampling and an optimal algorithm for approximating a multivariate integral on the average. Woźniakowski assumed a Wiener measure and $r = 0$. Multivariate integration is computable and tractable on the average even if $r = 0$.

I mentioned in Section 21.4 that if a problem is specified by a linear unbounded operator, that is, if it is ill posed, then the solution is noncomputable. Werschulz [19] has shown that if an unbounded operator is *bounded on the average* then the solution is computable.

These are two examples where a problem that is noncomputable for the worst case becomes computable in the average case setting. On the other hand, there are problems for which it has been shown that an average case assurance does not help.

As with randomization, we only have examples where the average case setting does or does not break intractability and noncomputability. There is no theory that charaterizes those problems for which the average-case setting helps.

Traub and Woźniakowski pose the further question: Characterize those problems and measures for which the average case setting helps significantly. In particular, for which problems and measures does the average case setting break noncomputability or intractability?

We have discussed weakening the worst case deterministic assurance by a randomized or average case assurance. A third way to weaken the assurance is the probabilistic setting. Here we guarantee a solution with small error except on sets of small measure; see Traub, Wasilkowski, and Woźniakowski [17]. A question, analogous to those posed above, can be posed for this setting.

In summary, the only way to circumvent intractability or noncomputability results in the worst case deterministic setting is by settling for a weaker assurance. Settling for such an assurance may not mitigate the negative conclusions.

## 21.6   Strongly Intractable Problems

To date, research in computational complexity has been for particular settings such as worst case, randomized, average, probabilistic, and asymptotic. It seems desirable to have a notion of intractability that is independent of the setting.

I will introduce the concepts of *strong noncomputability and strong intractability*. The description of these concepts will be rather vague; how they might be made precise will be discussed elsewhere. I will describe strong intractability; the description of strong noncomputability is analogous.

Consider a problem that is intractable in the worst case deterministic setting. Assume that as we back off from the deterministic worst case assurance to randomized, average, or probabilistic assurances the problem remains intractable. Furthermore, this is to hold for every "fair" measure. (By a fair measure we mean one that rules out measures that make the problem trivial.)

Such a problem is *strongly intractable*. If a problem is strongly intractable the computer resources will never be found to solve the problem, even for weakened assurances.

Do strongly intractable problems exist? The concept of strong intractability is new and this question has not been previously posed. Although no problem has been proven to be strongly intractable, I believe strongly intractable problems exist. What this implies for what is knowable will be explored in the concluding section.

## 21.7   Why We Might Expect Difficulties with Supercomputing and with the Foundations of Physics

Now that I have discussed the known or conjectured results regarding intractability from theoretical computer science let me very briefly summarize why intractability might be an impediment to what is knowable in science.

To repeat, in the worst case deterministic setting, the complexity of many discrete problems is conjectured to grow exponentially with the number of objects while the complexity of many continuous problems is known to grow exponentially with dimension. Furthermore, although some problems are tractable in the randomized or average settings, there are others that remain intractable. Indeed, I believe there are problems that are strongly intractable, i.e., intractable in all settings.

In scientific applications, many supercomputing problems involve large numbers of objects or high dimensions. See Raveché, Lawrie, and Despain [15] for a selection of such problems. In the foundations of physics, path integrals are infinite dimensional and therefore invite high dimensional approximations.

## 21.8    Do Intractability Results Really Limit What is Knowable?

We have reviewed what is known about intractability for both discrete and continuous problems and introduced the concept of strong intractability. The intractability results and conjectures are certainly daunting. They suggest that many problems involving a large number of objects or high dimensionality might be impossible to solve.

Nevertheless, in this section we advance some reasons why the intractability results might not prevent us from solving scientific problems.

1. *A Scientific Problem May Have Many Mathematical Formulations.* Intractability results are for a particular mathematical formulation. However, a scientific problem need not have a unique formulation. Although a particular formulation may be intractable, it may be possible to find another one that is tractable. I believe this issue is so fundamental that I shall devote the concluding section to its exploration.

2. *The Problem Instance May Be Easy.* Complexity theory tells us about the computational complexity of a class of problem instances. It does not tell us anything about a particular problem instance. Two examples will illustrate this observation. The Traveling Salesman Problem is NP-complete and therefore probably intractable. However, that does not imply that a particular instance of this problem is difficult. As a second example, consider integrating a function of $d$ variables of smoothness $r$. For $r$ fixed, the complexity grows exponentially with $d$. This tells us nothing about the difficulty of integrating a particular integrand. In the probabilistic setting of information-based complexity we wish to be assured of a small error at most $\varepsilon$ except on sets of small measure. That is, we wished to be assured of a small error on "most" problems. Even in the probabilistic setting, the fact that a problem is intractable does not mean that a particular problem is difficult. Even if a problem is strongly intractable, we cannot draw an

inference about a particular problem instance. To what extent does nature give us easy problem instances?

3. *The Gödel Effect.* Gödel's theorem states that in a sufficiently rich mathematical system there are theorems that cannot be proven. Although the theorem has had the most profound effects on logic and the foundations of mathematics, it has had little or no impact on the work of mathematicians. Since a thorough discussion would take us too far afield, I will only indicate a couple of the possible reasons for the lack of impact Mathematicians do not prove arbitrary theorems. They prove theorems that arise from areas of interest to mathematicians and in a historical context. It has been observed that mathematicians prove theorems they can prove. Note an analogy between Gödel's theory and computational complexity. Gödel's result does not permit us to infer that a particular theorem is undecideable, just as computational complexity does not permit us to conclude that a particular problem instance is hard. This raises a series of questions. Will computational complexity have as little impact on science as Gödel's theorem has had on mathematicians? Will it turn out that noncomputability and intractability will have the same relation to science that Gödel's theorem has had with mathematicians? That is, are the results profound but insignificant to the practice of science? Of course, mathematicians have broad latitude in their choice of problems. How much latitude do scientists have in their choice of scientific problems and mathematical formulations? I return to this question in Section 21.9.

4. *Other Modes of Computation.* Complexity results hold for certain models of computation. These models, such as the Turing machine model and the real number model, are abstractions of contemporary digital computers. (A discussion of these models may be found in Traub and Woźniakowski [18].) There is great current interest in other modes of computation. Some, such as reversible computation, are futuristic while others, such as cellular automata, have a venerable history but have seen only limited use to date. Will some of these other modes of computation enable us to circumvent the existing intractability results? Few of these computational modes have complexity results. Indeed, models of computation have not yet been formulated for most of them. In this subsection I will briefly discuss some of these other modes of computation

a. *Neural Networks.* Although there is enormous interest in the potential for neural networks, the complexity theory of neural networks is in its infancy. It is an interesting open question for what problems the promising experimental results obtained so far will scale.

b. *Special Purpose Machines.* Special purpose machines, such as the one constructed in the Physics Department at Columbia University by Norman Christ and his colleagues, can be used to attack especially important problems. Although such special-purpose machines cannot make an intractable problem tractable they can make it possible to perform an extremely long calculation in a feasible amount of time.

c. *Massively Parallel Computers.* It is clear that massively parallel machines are an important mode of computaton with a number of such computers currently available and others planned. A model of computation and complexity theory have been developed. A parallel computer with a polynomial number of processors cannot make an intractable problem tractable. However, just as with a special-purpose computer, a parallel computer can make a large calculation feasible. A cogent example is the human vision system, which uses massive parallelism.

d. *Analog Computers.* Analog computers may be useful as special-purpose machines, particularly for fairly low accuracy answers.

e. *Cellular Automata.* Although cellular automata date back to von Neumann, Ulam, and Zuse they have seen only limited use to date. There is considerable current interest. One goal is a computer "whose hardware will directly reflect the character of physical law, and which will only wait to be given specific initial conditions to merrily go reproducing the details of a complex physical experiment, without having to follow a long script for every operation"(Toffoli [16]).

f. *Reversible Computation.* In Section 21.2, I pointed out that the physical limits of computers have been studied. To circumvent some of these limits, reversible computation has been considered. Also, since the laws of quantum mechanics are reversible in time, the theoretical possibility of quantum computers have been studied. See, for example, Bennett [2], Feynman [5], Fredkin and Toffoli [6], and Zurek [23].

g. *It from Bit.* John Wheeler [20] argues eloquently that "every physical quantity, every it, derives its ultimate significance from bits, binary yes-or-no indications, a conclusion which we epitomize in the phrase, *it for bit.*" On the other hand, he asks, "Can we formulate the laws of physics without recourse to the continuum? We do not know how" [20]. If physics could indeed be reformulated according to Wheeler's dictum, the computational requirements are not clear.

## 21.9 Complexity of Scientific Problems

Computational complexity studies the complexity of a particular mathematical problem. Sometimes, as with NP-complete problems, a class of mathematical problems are studied, all of which have the same complexity.

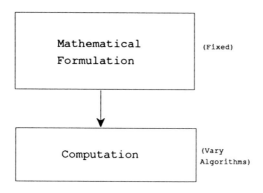

**EXHIBIT 21.1**
Compuational complexity.

A scientific problem need not have a unique mathematical formulation. Indeed, one may attack a scientific problem without creating a mathematical formulation at all. However, if we assume there are mathematical formulations corresponding to our scientific problem, they should meet twin desiderata.

1. They should capture the essence of the science.

2. They should be computationally tractable.

This suggests the need for a theory of computatonal complexity of scientific problems. We contrast such a theory with computational complexity. In computational complexity the mathematical formulation is given and we vary algorithms for its solution. The resources required by the optimal algorithm is the complexity. This situation is diagrammed in Exhibit 21.1.

In the proposed theory of the computational complexity of scientific problems a scientific problem is given. Mathematical formulations are then varied to see if any meet the twin desiderata above. For each mathematical formulation the complexity is obtained to check tractability. This situation is diagrammed in Exhibit 21.2.

A central question in such a theory would be

*Do there exist scientific problems such that every mathematical formulation is strongly intractable?*

I believe that there are such scientific problems and that they are unknowable.

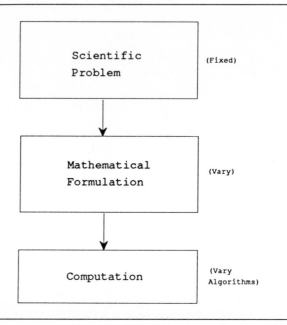

**EXHIBIT 21.2**
Computational complexity of scientific problems.

## 21.10   Acknowledgments

Earlier versions of these ideas were presented at a panel on *The Dreams of Reason: The Computer and the Rise of the Sciences of Complexity*, in Memory of Heinz Pagels, February 1, 1989, New York City and as the Second Charles Babbage Foundation Lecture, October 16, 1989, University of Minnesota.

I benefited greatly from discussions with Berni Alder, Bruce Berne, Terry Boult, James Crutchfield, Freeman Dyson, Gerald Feinberg, Mike Fischer, Zvi Galil, Tad Hogg, Rolf Landauer, Martin Schultz, and John Wheeler. This work was supported in part by the National Science Foundation.

## References

[1] B. Alder. Private communication, 1990.

[2] C. H. Bennett. Notes on the History of Reversible Computation. *IBM J. Res. Devel.*, 32 , pp. 16-23, 1988.

[3] H. J. Bremmerman. Complexity and Transcomputability. In *The Encyclopedia of Ignorance*. R. Duncan and M. Weston-Smith, eds., Oxford: Pergammon, 1977.

[4] G. Feinberg. On the Method of Theoretical Physics (Redux). Unpublished manuscript of lecture presented at *Conference on Method in Science and Philosophy*, Columbia University, New York, December, 1988.

[5] R. P. Feynman. Quantum Mechanical Computers. *Foundations Phys.*, 16 , pp. 507-531, 1988.

[6] E. Fredkin and T. Toffoli. Conservative Logic. *International Journal of Theoretical Physics*, 21, pp. 219-253, 1982.

[7] M. R. Garey and D. S. Johnson. *Computers and Intractability: A Guide to the Theory of NP-Completeness*. New York: W.H. Freeman, 1979.

[8] R. Geroch and J. B. Hartle. Computability and Physical Theories. *Foundations Phys.*, 16, pp. 533-550, 1986.

[9] R. W. Landauer. Wanted: A Physically Possible Theory of Physics. *IEEE Spectrum*, 4, pp. 105-109, 1967.

[10] R. W. Landauer. Computation and Physics: Wheeler's Meaning Circuit?, *Foundations Phys.*, 16, p. 551, 1986.

[11] E. W. Packel and J. F. Traub. Information-Based Complexity. *Nature*, 327, pp. 29-33, 1987.

[12] E. W. Packel and H. Woźniakowski. Recent Developments in Information-Based Complexity. *Bull. Amer. Math. Soc.*, 17, pp. 9-36, 1987.

[13] H. R. Pagels. *The Dreams of Reason: The Computer and the Rise of the Sciences of Complexity*. New York: Simon and Schuster, 1988, p. 44.

[14] M. O. Rabin. Probabilistic Algorithms. In *Algorithms and Complexity: New Directions and Recent Results*. J. F. Traub, ed., New York: Academic Press, 1976, pp. 21-39.

[15] H. J. Raveché, D. H. Lawrie and A. M. Despain. A National Computing Initiative. *SIAM*, 1987.

[16] T. Toffoli. Cellular Automata Machines as Physics Emulators. In *Proc. Impact of Digital Microelectronics and Microprocessors on Partical Physics*, International Center for Theoretical Physics, Trieste, Italy, 1988.

[17] J. F. Traub, G. W. Wasilkowski, and H. Woźniakowski. *Information Based-Complexity*. Boston: Academic Press, 1988.

[18] J. F. Traub and H. Woźniakowski. Information-Based Complexity: New Questions for Mathematicians. *Mathematical Intelligencer*, (in press).

[19] A. G. Werschulz. What is the Complexity of Ill-Posed Problems? *Numerical Functional Analysis and Optimization*, 9 , pp. 945-967, 1987.

[20] J. A. Wheeler. How Come the Quantum. In D. M. Greenberger, ed., *New Techniques and Ideas in Quantum Measurement Theory*, Ann. New York Acad. Sci., 480, pp. 304-316, 1987.

[21] I. White. The Limits and Capabilities of Machines—A Review. *IEEE Trans. Systems, Man and Cybernetics*, 18, pp. 917-938, 1988.

[22] H. Woźniakowski. Average Case Complexity of Multivariate Integration. Bulletin AMS, 24, pp. 185-194, 1991.

[23] W. H. Zurek. Reversibility and Stability of Information Processsing Systems. *Phys. Rev. Lett.*, 53, pp. 391-394, 1984.

# 22

# Exploration with Mathematica

Dana S. Scott

## 22.1  Introduction

During the fall semester of 1989 I presented a junior/senior mathematics course on *projective geometry* (with a syllabus organized along fairly traditional lines) using a Macintosh II computer and the *Mathematica* symbolic computation program, a product of Wolfram Research, Inc. The lectures were delivered primarily from the console, using a screen attached to the computer and projected by an overhead projector. The students were expected to do their homework on a computer, and the final examination was a project on a topic selected individually by each student, again, to be done on the computer.

This was an experimental course pretty much outside the current mathematics program, and the enrollment was very small. In fact, there were only three registered students by the end of the semester, but several auditors came faithfully to the lectures. For a number of reasons it seems quite unlikely that exactly the same course will be soon offered again at Carnegie Mellon University (CMU), but it has been a worthwhile project nevertheless. In the first place, the effort of giving a systematic course over a whole semester on a day-to-day basis helped make a number of issues about computer-based teaching clear to me, and the need to put together a comprehensive body of information forced me to do a lot of thinking about the subject matter itself. I have been pleased that presentations at other institutions, at a *Mathematica* conference in California in January, and at the June *Computational Geometry* conference at Berkeley have been most enthusiastically received. Several people have asked for the computer files, and a number of invitations to speak about the experience and the approach at other meetings have been received.

The planning of the course was substantially aided by the work of three CMU graduate assistants (Jean-Philippe Vidal, Marko Petkovšek, and J. Todd Wilson) and one postdoctoral visitor (Dr. Christine Luksch) conducted over several months. Their help has been much appreciated. Professor John W. Gray of the University of Illinois Mathematics Department was at CMU on sabbatical during the fall semester, and he offered invaluable advice on using *Mathematica*. It was also he who a year before introduced me to *Mathematica* in the first place and to many people at Wolfram Research, Inc. I am grateful particularly to Stephen Wolfram for the free use of his software in conducting these developments and experiments. Special thanks are due to the School of Computer Science, the Mathematics Department, and the Mellon College of Science Dean's Office for grants to help pay the course advisors in part during 1989. The equipment used was supplied through Computer Science. Preparation of this chapter was carried out while visiting the International Computer Science Institute, Berkeley, California, to which the author is indebted for the generous hospitality. Both the preliminary and final versions of the present chapter were prepared as a Notebook entirely by using *Mathematica* on the Mac II.

In this brief presentation, it will not be possible to describe the contents of the geometry course, because the material is too technical and it takes too many definitions to get to the examples showing the main advantages of the use of symbolic computation for such work. Reports and software are available from the author for those who are interested in the full details. Instead, we will discuss here some general pedagogical issues about the use of computers in teaching and look at some simpler examples of the use of *Mathematica*.

## 22.2    Evaluating the Teaching Experience

In doing the projective geometry course, I found that it took roughly 2 *very full days of work per week* to prepare sufficient lecturing material for the required 3 class hours. The two graduate assistants (Petkovšek and Wilson) offered much help during the semester, and the preparatory work over the previous six months was very valuable; but the final choice of the organization of the topics for the lectures and the systematic working out of the implementation in *Mathematica* had to be done by me as the course unfolded. Obviously it would not take as much effort to rerun the course, as it is very fully documented in a series of

*Mathematica* notebooks, which I revised at the end of the semester. Thus the next instructor could devote most of his or her time to improving the examples (especially with respect to graphics) and finding better homework problems.

From a broader point of view, there are, I think, six main questions to be asked in evaluating the experience and the approach.

1. Is it worth the time and trouble trying to use a computer systematically in teaching?

2. Is *Mathematica* suitable as educational software?

3. Did symbolic computation enhance the presentation and understanding of the material?

4. What other courses would benefit from such a presentation?

5. Can the implementation of mathematical ideas on a personal computer help research?

6. Can we implement an interesting part of mathematics **as is**?

I cannot pretend to have completely definitive answers to these questions, but I personally found the overall experience to be positive. Let me go into a more detail and say why.

*Question 1.* Though the work was heavy, the advantages of having it captured in the computer were many. First, one can *replay* the ideas in a dynamic fashion while talking about them. Therefore I could explain things many times over using the same files to which additional examples could be added very quickly. The retentiveness and flexibility of the computer (and of *Mathematica*) made many class discussions much more definite and detailed than would have been possible otherwise. The files could also be replayed by the students themselves on their own time. These advantages were obtained *during* the course, and advantages for *future* courses are expected. Second, the ability of being able to do *both* symbolic algebra *and* graphics made it possible to illustrate notions and solutions in a way that I claim cannot be done without a computer. This power has a very special value, but I could not have taken advantage of it if I had not worked on a systematic development of the course in advance.

*Question 2.* Yes, *Mathematica* is suitable and useful as educational software. I think I proved that it works well—both for lectures and for doing review and homework. In particular, the *Mathematica* programs as implementations of the basic ideas are transparent and easy to explain. Since I do not have experience in using other programs for presenting a complete course, I cannot make a comparison with other software at this point. There are improvements in *Mathematica* that I could suggest, however, that would make it even more useful.

*Question 3.* The proofs of many theorems showed me that it is possible to see and manipulate complex formulae that could not be obtained easily by hand.

I claim that until you actually see such answers, you cannot easily know what to do next. *Mathematica* was fast enough to come up with answers so that thinking could progress at a solid pace. Being able to link algebraic formulae directly to geometric pictures is also a substantial aid to comprehension—a feature I was not able to exploit as fully as I had hoped during this first time through the course.

*Question 4.* Here are some preliminary suggestions about other course work in mathematics that I think would benefit from using *Mathematica*. (I will not discuss here the staple courses with very large enrollments, because the twin problems of getting students enough machines to use and of lecturing to large audiences on a computer are hard to solve. We need more experience in smaller courses first, in my judgment.)

1. *Linear algebra* (including work in tensors and exterior algebra).
2. *Commutative algebra* (including details of finite fields).
3. *Non-commutative algebra* (including an exploration of representation theory for groups and further connections with geometry).
4. *Preparation for the study of functions of a complex variable* (including extensive graphing of aspects of complex functions).
5. *Combinatorics and discrete mathematics.*

For the author's own taste, this suggestion (4) seems to be the most exciting proposal. Complex analysis is needed in many areas of science generally, and most mathematics texts are quite tough for non-majors. Materials that would make ideas easier to grasp could have lasting value. Much work on (5) has already been done by others.

*Questions 5 and 6.* I will take these together. Mathematically, for me the most interesting outcome of the experiment of teaching the projective geometry course was to find how easy it is to use the ideas of *linear space theory*, *exterior products*, and *partial differential operators* in presenting geometry, both in *computations* and in *proofs* aided by the powers of symbolic computation in *Mathematica*. The implementations of these ideas were done in a natural way ("as is" as it were), and the programming did not detract from the mathematics. I did not expect the development to go so smoothly. From the research perspective, I felt I was able to think about many questions of geometry that I could never come to grips with before. This is a preliminary indication that a reasonable investment of time in learning about computers can bring all of us to a level of computer literacy where our research can be very positively affected.

Let me include some other points in favor of the approach I think are especially relevant to teaching.

□ *Mathematica* implements the *algebra*; the instructor, the *concepts*.

□ *Examples* may be multiplied at will.

□ *Formulae* for answers can be worked out exactly.

□ *Symbolic* and *numerical* computation can be mixed.

□ All this can be done *on the fly* in the classroom.

□ *Experimentation* is encouraged; *discovery* is enabled.

□ *Graphics* can be generated as needed.

□ *Course notes* and *personal work* can be preserved.

□ *Sharing* with others is made more immediate.

More generally, a continuing difficulty for students I see in undergraduate education (and not just at this university) is in their being able to gain sufficient perspective in a subject for them to be able to know *for themselves* what they really should be interested in. There are many reasons for this difficulty: Time is always very short in the curriculum. There are too many required courses. Elective courses are not always available at convenient times. Mathematical talent is often not uncovered at the right moment to take advantage of the offerings that do exist. Students, in any case, are always changing their minds about their programs and future strategies. The computer can help with all these difficulties.

## 22.3  Pushing the Button

Many years ago when we were living in England I gave my daughter, Monica, a hand-held scientific calculator. She did well in mathematics in school (despite the boring, old-fashioned mathematics textbooks they used), but she hated to look up functions in tables, and she particularly hated interpolation (just as I did!). Thus a calculator with the exponential, logarithmic, and trigonometric functions was a welcome gift.

She played with the calculator quite a lot at first, and then one day she brought it to me looking very sad. "It's broken!" she exclaimed. "When I push the button, nothing happens!" She was right. Nothing happened when one particular button was pushed. The calculator was quite OK, however.

The apparent problem was with the **cosine** button. Monica would enter any angle (in radians, say) and then see what the trig functions had to say about it. But the *result* of the previous calculation could also be the *input* for the next operation. Thus it was easy to go on pushing the cosine button time after time having given only one initial input. The procedure converges rather quickly to the (unique) fixed point $x == Cos[x]$ of the cosine function. I had to draw her a picture of the curve—which she knew but had never reasoned about—to show her why this number exists and why the convergence happens. Here is a picture showing the existence of the fixed point.

**pict = Plot[{xx, Cos[xx]}, {xx, #1, #2}, AspectRatio –> 1, Ticks –> {Range[#1, #2, 0.2], Range[#1, #2, 0.2]}]& [0,1];**

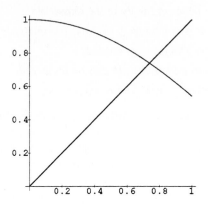

In *Mathematica* we can trivially program the successive hitting of the keys by using the **NestList** construction for the iteration. Let us do it first symbolically, so you can see what is happening, and then we will do it numerically. The notation (...#...)& is a *Mathematica* shorthand for the function to be iterated by **NestList**. The notation % means take the previous result. N[...] means take the numerical result—if appropriate.

**NestList[F, x, 5]**

```
{x, F[x], F[F[x]], F[F[F[x]]], F[F[F[F[x]]]], F[F[F[F[F[x]]]]]}
```

**NestList[Cos[#]&, 1, 5]**

```
{1, Cos[1], Cos[Cos[1]], Cos[Cos[Cos[1]]],
  Cos[Cos[Cos[Cos[1]]]], Cos[Cos[Cos[Cos[Cos[1]]]]]}
```

**N[%]**

```
{1., 0.540302, 0.857553, 0.65429, 0.79348, 0.701369}
```

And we see that hitting the button five times is not enough; so here is a longer run:

**NestList[N[Cos[#]]&, 1, 20]**

```
{1, 0.540302, 0.857553, 0.65429,
  0.79348, 0.701369, 0.76396, 0.722102,
  0.750418, 0.731404, 0.744237, 0.735605,
  0.741425, 0.737507, 0.740147, 0.738369,
  0.739567, 0.73876, 0.739304, 0.738938, 0.739184}
```

Still not enough.

**seq = NestList[N[Cos[#]]&, 1, 36]**

```
{1, 0.540302, 0.857553, 0.65429,
   0.79348, 0.701369, 0.76396, 0.722102,
   0.750418, 0.731404, 0.744237, 0.735605,
   0.741425, 0.737507, 0.740147, 0.738369,
   0.739567, 0.73876, 0.739304, 0.738938,
   0.739184, 0.739018, 0.73913, 0.739055,
   0.739106, 0.739071, 0.739094, 0.739079,
   0.739089, 0.739082, 0.739087, 0.739084,
   0.739086, 0.739085, 0.739086, 0.739085,
   0.739085}
```

Good. The calculator is now firmly broken. Rather more precisely put, we see that convergence has taken place (to a certain degree of accuracy).

We can see *why* convergence is happening if we graph the successive steps we have just computed. To do so we need to place points both on the cosine curve and on the diagonal line. We can program this in *Mathematica* by setting up some list structures. First we double the occurrences of all the numbers in the list just calculated.

**seq = Flatten[Map[{#, #}&, seq]];**

We then get coordinates of points by forming successive pairs out of this list.

**points = Partition[seq, 2, 1];**

The broken line joining all these points can be superimposed on the original graph showing the fixed point.

**Show[{pict, Graphics[Line[points]]}];**

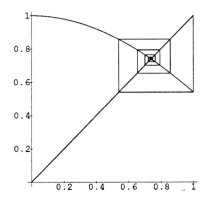

Clearly this very simple example—even done on a pocket calculator—
qualifies for consideration as a first attempt at non-trivial experimental mathematics. Of course in itself this calculation is not especially interesting, but it is
an *instance* of a phenomenon. If you can explain to yourself why it turns out
the way it does, then you have learned something. I think we did so in this case.

The difference between *Mathematica* and a hand-held calculator is that
the calculator has a rather limited number of operations and a limited capacity
for programming—though there are some remarkably powerful calculators out
there—while *Mathematica* provides a full programming language *and* symbolic
computation (and has a great Macintosh interface).

I will try to show the interesting interplay between numbers and symbols in
other examples. Before we leave the cosine illustration, however, let us remark
that *Mathematica* has a built-in numerical root solver called **FindRoot** which,
in being called by

$$\text{FindRoot[lhs == rhs, x, x0]}$$

searches for a numerical solution to the equation **lhs==rhs**, starting with **x=x0**.
In calling this powerful program, you can adjust many options: **AccuracyGoal**,
**WorkingPrecision**, **MaxIterations**, **Jacobian**, and **DampingFactor**. For exam-
ple, here is a much more precise answer to the cosine fixed-point problem:

**x = xx /. FindRoot[ xx == Cos[xx], {xx, 1},**
**AccuracyGoal –> 25, WorkingPrecision –> 35, MaxIterations –> 55];**
**N[x, Cos[x], x == Cos[x], 32]**

```
{0.73908513321516064165531208767387,
 0.73908513321516064165531208767387,
 True}
```

The only trouble with calling such a built-in routine is that you do not
really know exactly how it works. But if you use it enough, a certain confidence
will be gained—and you can always ask to check the answers as we have just
done. By the way, this interesting number that is the fixed point of the cosine
function can be proved to be transcendental by using the well known classical
results.

## 22.4  Exchanging Exponentials

Consider two of the best known transcendental numbers in mathematics, **E** and
**Pi**. There are fairly close together; indeed, they lie within half a unit of each
other:

**N[Pi - E, 10]**

```
0.4233108251
```

The question to be considered is, which is bigger, **Pi^E** or **E^Pi**? (For typing, *Mathematica* uses ^ to indicate exponentiation.) The reason that the answer is not quite so obvious, is that within this range we cannot be instantly sure whether it is the base or the exponent that is the more dominant member. A quick, rough calculation, however, answers the following queston.

**N[{Pi^E, E^Pi}]**

```
{22.4592, 23.1407}
```

Is it always the case that x^y and y^x are *different*, say, for x and y positive reals? Well, clearly *not*, since **x == y** is possible. And, we all know the case where **2^4 == 4^2 == 16**. What else is possible? In particular, if we kept **Pi** fixed and varied **E**—if you know what I mean—can we find a solution of the equation? Let us try the black box method.

**x = Pi; y = yy /. FindRoot[x^yy == yy^x, {yy, 2}, MaxIterations -> 50];**

**N[{x, y, x^y, y^x}]**

```
{3.14159, 2.38218, 15.2862, 15.2862}
```

So, the desired number has to be just a little less than **E** to get an equality. What about other examples?

**x = E; y = yy /. FindRoot[x^yy == yy^x, {yy, 2}, MaxIterations -> 50];**
**N[{x, y, x^y, y^x}]**

```
{2.71828, 2.71828, 15.1543, 15.1543}
```

**x = 5; y = yy /. FindRoot[x^yy == yy^x, {yy, 2}, MaxIterations -> 50];**
**N[{x, y, x^y, y^x}]**

```
{5., 1.76492, 17.1249, 17.1249}
```

**x = 20; y = yy /. FindRoot[x^yy == yy^x, {yy, 2}, MaxIterations -> 50];**

**N[{x, y, x^y, y^x}]**

```
{20., 1.19624, 36.003, 36.003}
```

The **FindRoot** procedure is a version of Newton's Method, and it is quite sensitive to the choice of the starting guess in doing the iteration.

**x = 5; y = yy /. FindRoot[x^yy == yy^x, {yy, 1.3}, MaxIterations -> 50];**

**N[{x, y, x^y, y^x}]**

```
{5., 5., 3125., 3125.}
```

**x = 5; y = yy /. FindRoot[x^yy == yy^x, {yy, 1.4}, MaxIterations ->**
**50];**
**N[{x, y, x^y, y^x}]**

```
{5., 1.76492, 17.1249, 17.1249}
```

And, here is a little surprise I found, just through idle button pushing:

**x = 20; y = yy/ . FindRoot[x^yy == yy^x, {yy, 1}, MaxIterations ->**
**50];**
**N[{x, y, x^y, y^x}]**

```
{20., -0.876911, 0.0722957, 0.0722957}
```

Ha! Apparently, there are solutions to the equation x^y y^x == 1 as well. But that is quite another matter (involving complex numbers). The question of discussing solutions to the equation x^y == y^x goes back at least to Euler (*see* L. E. Dickson, *History of the Theory of Numbers*, vol. II, p. 687), and a rather complete review of real solutions can be found in E. J. Moulton, "The real function defined by x^y == y^x," *American Mathematical Monthly*, vol. 23 (1916), pp. 233-237. (Thanks go to Marko Petkovšek for uncovering these and other references.) For today, let us try to understand what is going on just with the positive values of x and y by using the computer to explore. To help us do so, we can plot in *Mathematica* the relationship x^y >= y^x using **DensityPlot**. In the picture below **black** (= no color) means **0** or **False** and **white** means **1** or **True**.

**DensityPlot[If[xx^yy >= yy^xx, 1, 0], {xx, 1, 6}, {yy, 1, 6}, PlotPoints**
**-> 50];**

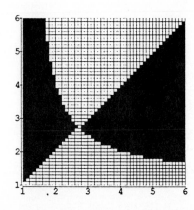

Of course the diagonal line **x == y** is a critical line, but there is another lovely curve that represents another line of equality. We can see that the points {**2,4**} and {**4,2**} lie on the curve. And, if a quick inductive interpolation to infinity is valid, we can assert that there are *no other* integer points on the curve. We can also guess that the lines **x == 1** and **y == 1** are asymptotes.

What is the crossing point? Well, it looks like **E** to me! It also looks as though it may be a way to characterize **E** uniquely. Here is graphical proof about the crossing point, where with the x-value fixed at **E**, we see that the **E^y** values *always dominate* (except at one tangent point). This shows that this is the point where the vertical line has white on both sides of the diagonal.

**Plot[{E^yy, yy^E}, {yy, 1, 4}];**

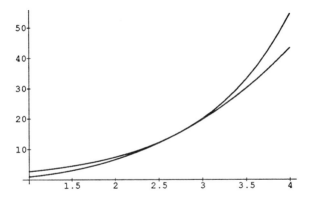

I claim **E** is the only number that will result in a pair of pictures like that. When we put **x** equal to **4** there are *two* crossing points of the curves:

**Plot[{4^yy, yy^4}, {yy, 1, 5}];**

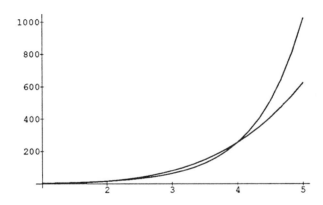

**Plot[{4^yy, yy^4}, {yy, 1, 3}];**

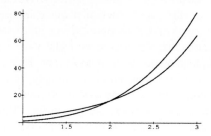

By some manipulation of the equation, we can make the results we have intuitively arrived at by pictures more precise. The trick is to take logarithms:

$$x^y == y^x$$
$$y \, Log[x] == x \, Log[y]$$
$$Log[x]/x == Log[y]/y$$

In other words, consider the curve given by the function **Log[x]/x** and see where horizontal lines above the x-axis intersect it. (A horizontal line has a fixed function value.)

**Plot[{Log[xx]/xx, 0.25}, {xx, 1, 50}];**

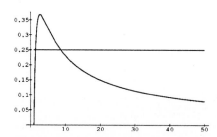

The x-axis is an asymptote, as *Mathematica* helps us verify:

**Limit[Log[xx]/xx, xx->Infinity]**

0

And, to find the turning point, we differentiate:

**D[Log[xx]/xx, xx]**

```
xx^(-2) - Long[xx]/xx^2
```

And clearly, the only positive value of the variable that makes this expression vanish is **E**. So, for any horizontal line strictly above the x-axis and below the value **E**, there are exactly two intersection points—the coordinates of which give us the solutions to the original equation. And the same is true for any curve **Log[x]/x** no matter what base we take for the logarithms.

This discussion, heavily based on pictures, could be turned into a real proof that the curve in the black-and-white **DensityPlot** shown above is an analytic function with the required asymptotic properties. Unfortunately, nothing we have done here suggests a *formula* for the curve, and it may indeed be a non-elementary function. From preliminary investigation, it looks to be a hard problem to actually identify this curve as something familiar. And then there is the question of negative and complex values—but enough.

## 22.5  Conclusions

In his keynote address at the *Second Annual Conference on Technology in Collegiate Mathematics* November 1989 at The Ohio State University (see the newsletter UME TRENDS, for January 1990), Professor Lynn Steen effectively spoke for parents and students, scientists and engineers, colleagues and administrators by raising the following *20 questions for calculus reformers*. Steen suggested that responding to these questions could form an agenda for the current work of people exploring the use of computers in curricular reform. Let us look at the questions, remembering that they are addressed to mathematics departments.

 □ *Learning*
   1. Can computers help students understand mathematics?
   2. Can students develop mathematical intuition without performing extensive mathematical manipulations?
   3. Do the mechanics of computing obscure mathematical insight?
   4. Will using computers reduce students' facility to compute by hand?

 □ *Curriculum*
   1. How does computing change what students should know about mathematics?
   2. How does computing change what students can learn about mathematics?
   3. Where in the curriculum is computing most appropriate?
   4. Will use of computers reduce the need for remediation?

□ *Resources*

1. Can colleges afford computers for all mathematics students?

2. How much time and distraction is computing worth?

3. When will there be good software and compatible hardware?

4. Can textbooks ever reflect contemporary computer examples?


□ *Teaching*

1. How much programming should be taught in mathematics courses?

2. Can pure mathematicians convey an appropriate computational perspective?

3. Will use of computers improve teaching of mathematics?


□ *Dilemmas*

1. Won't computer packages for calculus lead, as they have in statistics, to much meaningless calculation?

2. If computers handle routine calculations, what will students do instead?

3. What are appropriate prerequisites for computer-based calculus courses?

4. Should mathematics be a laboratory science?

I have many answers to and opinions on these questions. The bottom line is that, yes, I personally believe that math *is* a laboratory science—the problem in the past has been that we have not had sufficiently powerful tools sufficiently available to do the necessary experimentation. I hope I have illustrated to some extent by way of examples that programs like *Mathematica* can be both a telescope and a microscope—the sense of being an aid for seeing both the bigger picture and the smaller picture in a better "perspective" and at a better "resolution" than is possible with paper and pencil. Of course the machine does not replace imagination—and neither does the laboratory in any other science.

The biggest problem colleges (and schools) face is one of resources. Educational institutions generally do not have the money to get sufficient equipment— and even if they do, they cannot give teachers enough extra time to develop the necessary course materials. We need many orders of magnitude more of information to be put into machine-readable form—the mathematical specimens collected and cataloged, if you will—before the math laboratory will come into its own in teaching and research. We need much longer development of mathematical software as well to manipulate the specimens. All this time and effort (and thinking!) costs money.

One possible suggestion about how we might better make use of the power of computers is this. *Mathematica* as it stands is an interactive computer-held *handbook*. Indeed, it is comparable to classical, well known published handbooks. Of course it is much, much more than that, but to students it may be too much of a *blank page* when they face it for the first time. Thus it could be helpful and interesting to make up smaller files of *resource materials* that explain a few key ideas, outline possibilities, ask questions, suggest projects, and point the way to things that students can do for themselves with *Mathematica*. Students need good examples to see how to take advantage of the interactive character of such computing systems. I believe that my course in projective geometry was a good start along such lines, for example; and the recently published book of Steven Skiena, *Implementing Discrete Mathematics: Combinatorics and Graph Theory with Mathematica*, Addison Wesley Publishing Co., is another. But full, detailed, *semester-long* courses need not be the only form of materials to have available. It is easy to construct smaller units in *Mathematica*. And then—provided a good way could be found to index files—it would be possible to have a large growing body of enrichment materials that could awaken interest in students in attempting exploration and discovery on their own. The recently launched *Mathematica Journal* will be a help in starting up communication, but we need to have lots and lots of examples in machine-readable form readily available. Many practical and technical problems will have to be solved before teachers can really get the best out of the potential of the electronic medium.

Come on! Let's work at it!